SHREVEPORT
LIBRARY

Presented by

Dr. James W. Bennett
Dr. LaVerne R. Bennett

STUDYING PERSONALITY CROSS-CULTURALLY

STUDYING PERSONALITY

CROSS-CULTURALLY

Editor

BERT KAPLAN
University of Kansas

HARPER & ROW, PUBLISHERS

New York, Evanston, and London

To the Memory of Clyde Kluckhohn

TABLE OF CONTENTS

viii *Contents*

PART III: METHODOLOGICAL ISSUES IN THE CROSS-CULTURAL STUDY OF PERSONALITY

PART IV: PROBLEMS OF CROSS-CULTURAL RESEARCH

PART V: APPROACHES TO CROSS-CULTURAL PERSONALITY STUDY

EDITOR'S INTRODUCTION

This volume is presented in the belief that progress in the social sciences depends to a considerable degree upon the continued development of the culture and personality field which stands at the crossroads of many of the most important problems of both individual and societal functioning. One of the major roadblocks to this development is the difficulty of collecting and interpreting adequate empirical materials descriptive of personality processes in the world's cultures.

Although the culture and personality field is relatively new it has already passed through two main phases. The first, a period of tremendous enthusiasm, began in the 1940's. Large numbers of workers eagerly embarked on cross-cultural personality studies and the swiftly mobilized interest almost had the proportions of a fad. In part, this work was stimulated by the availability of a ready-made methodology and a set of methods—mainly utilizing projective techniques—which promised definitive results with a relatively small commitment of time and energy. This promise proved to be an illusion. The materials were easy enough to collect but were difficult or impossible to interpret and to integrate, with any reasonable claim to validity, into ongoing anthropological studies.

The consequent disillusionment led to the second period, one characterized by a sharp decrease in culture and personality research, although interest in its positive accomplishments probably remains as high or higher than ever. What has now come to be generally realized is that in the culture and personality field there are few easy answers and the most fundamental and elementary issues still need considerable clarification and research.

This volume is an introduction to the culture and personality field viewed from the vantage point of workers in it who are struggling to clarify a variety of theoretical and methodological issues and to develop adequate methods for collecting and interpreting empirical personality

1

materials. It is not a manual describing how to go about doing cross-cultural personality studies because, at this primitive stage, we do not know how; a simple concentration on methods might give the impression that we did. Rather, the book seeks to grapple with the issues preliminary to actual empirical study. These problems involve so much more than personality study itself that they lead into almost every important realm of social science and reveal the complex network of psychological and social issues, at the nexus of which the culture and personality field stands.

The volume thus comprehends a broad area of theory and research but organizes materials in such a way that they become relevant to the special problems of personality study. Through its various contributions it presents successively, an extended historical account of the major issues in the culture and personality field, a series of theoretical papers analyzing the role of personality and motivational processes in societal functioning, a discussion of the development of personality as it involves socialization and preparation for social participation, a series of methodological papers that clarify problems of doing cross-cultural research, a survey of relations between linguistics and cross-cultural personality study, an attempt to develop a framework for seeing the influence of cultural factors in personality study, discussions of projective techniques, dreams, and psychiatric interviewing, a discussion of the problem of interpreting psychic symbolism across cultures, an analysis of the role of myth and artistic productions and finally a discussion of methodological issues in the cross-cultural study of mental illness.

An integral part of the present volume is a series of case studies presented in appropriate places throughout the book. These cases serve as concrete illustrations of some of the issues discussed in the more theoretical chapters and show how the latter can be transformed into empirical research or analysis. Many of the cases, moreover, are themselves major contributions to theory and methodology, although their analysis is presented in the context of a particular set of empirical data.

The book does not attempt to offer complete and comprehensive coverage of the culture and personality field. Students should be directed to use it in conjunction with three or four other works with which most workers will be familiar. Salient among these are Inkeles and Levinson's paper, "National Character: The Study of Modal Personality and Sociocultural Systems" which ably clarifies the present course of the culture and personality field, Honigmann's textbook, *Culture and Personality* which provides an admirable and comprehensive account of the field, and Mead and Metraux's provocative collection of essays on *The Study of Culture at a Distance* which embodies a wide variety of imaginative approaches to the problem of personality study. It also should be supplemented by discussions of particular methods like Hallowell's fine paper, "The Rorschach Technique in Personality and Culture Studies."

Although the great bulk of the work in the culture and personality field has been done by anthropologists, the authors of these chapters come from a half dozen different disciplines: anthropology, psychology, psychiatry, sociology, psychoanalysis and history. This reflects the nature of the problem of cross-cultural personality study, which so urgently requires interdisciplinary collaboration. The field as a whole is one of the great meeting grounds of the social sciences, a situation that virtually insures its continuing to be exciting, important, and reactive to crosscurrents of ideas coming from many different directions. Unfortunately, there are disadvantages as well; the most obvious is the difficulty in communication among workers who have different backgrounds and the differences in professional values which lead workers to approach the same problem with a variety of conceptions of what is important. It is well to recognize that culture and personality research in general and cross-cultural personality study in particular can occur in quite different frameworks. The sociologist and anthropologist for example, preoccupied with the problems of societal cohesion and functioning, of understanding the bases of social order and of social change, utilize the data of personality studies in a way that undoubtedly seems strange and alien to the psychologist and psychiatrist, concerned with the understanding of personality development and functioning and only interested in those aspects of socio-cultural systems that have to do with these problems. The need for interdisciplinary collaboration does not eliminate the basic difference in the problems that concern the social and the psychological sciences. In the midst of this collaboration a chasm exists, which can be ignored only at the risk of confusion and frustration.

From the sociologist's perspective the main question is whether the kind of personality processes that exist in a group make a difference in the way that societies function. The hypothesis which has most dominated the culture and personality field derives from the work of such thinkers as Max Weber, Abram Kardiner, Erich Fromm, Talcott Parsons and David Riesman. It holds that efficient societal functioning depends upon the existence in its members of congruent personality or motivational structures, sometimes referred to as social character. This congruence is thought to be produced by the shaping of personality by society's socialization institutions. While the correctness of this theory is generally taken for granted, there are enough doubts that its testing and evaluation are one of the main tasks of empirical cross-cultural research. Inkeles, for example asks, "Is there a significant difference between various national and sub-national populations in the distribution of discrete traits or personality types, and if so how does this affect the functioning of the social system? Can we assume that a given social structure will operate in much the same way regardless of the set of personalities placed in that context?" He asserts, "No one has ever tested a national population or even a main sub-population rising either on adequate sample or adequate psychological instruments. All assertions or details of national, sub-national, regional or class differences of major magnitudes therefore remain mere statements of faith. And until we have accumulated the basic facts, the other questions of course must be held in abeyance." *

The culture and personality field is no less important for an understanding of personality functioning than it is for social functioning. The question that is most generally posed by psychologists and psychiatrists concerns the nature of the influence of the social environment in which the person develops, and its effect on the course of his development. Almost all of our present theories hold that this social influence is a profound one. There is much room, however, for more differentiated theories to tell us what sorts of environmental conditions will produce what kinds of effects. Cross-cultural personality studies have a vitally important role in providing the necessary data. The problem of influence itself is an interesting one. Work in the field of communication has been especially concerned with what actually goes on when one person influences another. One might ask as well, what happens when a person is influenced by a culture pattern.

While the volume provides a general introduction to the culture and personality field its main focus is the problem of cross-cultural personality study. A number of workers have given this problem attention, notably Margaret Mead and her colleagues and A. I. Hallowell. But there has in general not been the realization that, until much greater progress is made, the data collected in empirical studies of personality may be actually incorrect and misleading. The tendency during the past fifteen years has been to apply techniques developed in our own society. This is done reluctantly because it is not clear how valid they are in other cultures. Still, in the absence of a real science of cross-cultural study, there is no good alternative. It is the purpose of this book to contribute to the development of this science. Its contribution consists principally in calling attention to the importance, and interest of cross-cultural studies and pointing to some directions from which they may be approached. The science itself is undoubtedly a great many years from fruition and is dependent in part on the development by psychologists and psychiatrists of more sophisticated and more valid ways of studying personality in our own society. It depends also, however, on the an-

* "Personality and Social Structure," in Merton, R. K., Broom, L., and Cottrell, L. S., *Sociology Today*, Basic Books Inc., New York, 1959.

thropologist's ability to comprehend and apply what goes on in the personality study situation, and on the ability of social scientists to fathom the difficulties of communication and understanding between people who are different from each other. When these problems are even partially solved the benefits will extend far beyond the confines of the culture and personality field and become relevant to the general problem of intercultural understanding.

ACKNOWLEDGMENTS

In the conception of this volume and in its editing, I have been helped by a great many friends and colleagues. I would like especially to express my gratitude to Dorothy Eggan, Rollin Posey, Melford Spiro, Jay Jackson, Louise and George Spindler, A. Irving Hallowell and Milton Singer. Although they had no direct connection with the book I am most keenly aware of the great influence of Clyde Kluckhohn, Talcott Parsons, Gardner Murphy, David Riesman, Robert W. White, Henry A. Murray and Alex Inkeles. My appreciation is deepest to my wife Hermia.

I

CULTURE AND PERSONALITY THEORY AND RESEARCH

About the Chapter

Dr. SINGER's survey of the culture and personality field sets the stage for our consideration of the more specific questions of cross-cultural personality study. He delineates the main theoretical and empirical issues in the field and places them in historical perspective. Major empirical studies and theoretical works are reviewed critically. The relationship of the study of the personality characteristics of individuals to such concepts as cultural character, social character, basic personality structure, and modal personality is clarified. The chapter also explores the field of national character and relates it to culture and personality study.

About the Author

Milton Singer is Paul Klapper Professor of the Social Sciences in the Department of Anthropology and in the College, University of Chicago. He received his Ph.D. from the University of Chicago in 1940. During 1954–55, he travelled in India and Asia. He is co-author, with Gerhart Piers, of *Shame and Guilt, A Psychoanalytic and a Cultural Study*. With Robert Redfield he wrote "The Cultural Role of Cities," for *Economic Development and Culture Change*, and for *Man in India*. Dr. Singer was co-editor with Robert Redfield of the series *Comparative Studies of Cultures and Civilizations;* editor of *Introducing India in Liberal Education, Proceedings of a Conference;* and editor and co-author of *Traditional India: Structure and Change*. His special interests are the comparative study of civilizations and particularly India, the relations of cultural anthropology to psychology, and philosophy of the social sciences. He is a Fellow of the American Anthropological Association and, for 1957–58, was a Fellow at the Center for the Advanced Study in the Behavioral Sciences.

Acknowledgments

This article is based on material developed by the author over a period of years in classes and seminars at the University of Chicago. Colleagues and students there provided a unique interdisciplinary forum for the free exchange of ideas. To the late Robert Redfield especially and the program of Comparative Studies of Cultures and Civilizations under his direction, and supported by the Ford Foundation, the author owes much in intellectual stimulation and professional support. While a Fellow at the Center for Advanced Studies in the Behavioral Sciences during 1957–58, discussions with John Tukey and Edgar Anderson elucidated some of the statistical issues in personality and culture research. Helen Singer, Dorothy and Fred Eggan, Bert Kaplan, Alfred Kroeber, Clyde Kluckhohn, and Melford Spiro were kind enough to read the manuscript and to make helpful suggestions for its improvement. The author is indebted to Margit Gerow and Barbara Dwyer for help in preparing the manuscript for press.

1

A Survey of Culture and Personality Theory and Research

MILTON SINGER

University of Chicago

EMERGENCE OF THE FIELD

Until a few years ago the field of culture and personality theory and research was considered an American heresy in anthropology. Today it is no longer a heresy, and in a few more years it will no longer be distinctively American.

Before 1920, anthropology in the United States was predominantly non-psychological if not anti-psychological, and the culture and personality approach was unknown (Kluckhohn, 1944b). Within the next fifteen years, say from 1920 to 1935, not only were the ideas inherent in such an approach actively discussed, but field research was undertaken and collaboration between anthropologists and psychiatrists was begun. This was the period of Margaret Mead's South Sea studies, Ruth Benedict's articles and book on patterns of culture, and Edward Sapir's influential articles on the relations of anthropology and psychiatry.

In 1931, after Sapir left Chicago for Yale, he collaborated with John Dollard on a special seminar on culture and personality at the suggestion of Lawrence Frank, then of the Rockefeller Foundation. During this same period the Social Science Research Council recognized the

9

new interdisciplinary field by sponsoring symposia and by having William I. Thomas prepare a special report on the possibilities and problems of research on culture and personality (Volkart, 1951).

The most important stimulus during this formative period was psychoanalytic psychology. It was in fact the encounter of anthropology, and to a lesser extent sociology and political science, with psychoanalysis, that gave rise to culture and personality studies. One of the first public records of this encounter is A. L. Kroeber's review of Freud's *Totem and Taboo,* which appeared in the *American Anthropologist* in 1920. Although he found the book "an important and valuable contribution" to the psychology underlying cultural anthropology, which "every ethnologist must sooner or later take into consideration," and expressed interest in extending Freud's point of view, Kroeber devoted most of the review to demolishing Freud's principal thesis that the origins of culture and society meet in the Oedipus complex. The general tone of the review is highly critical: "This book is keen without orderliness, intricately rather than closely reasoned, and endowed with an unsubstantiated convincingness." Psychoanalysts who wish to establish serious contacts with historical ethnology are told that they "must first learn to know that such an ethnology exists."

Twenty years later, in 1939, Kroeber wrote another review of *Totem and Taboo,* in which he said he saw "no reason to waver" over his earlier critical analysis. Nevertheless, as an *amende honorable,* he took a kindlier view of psychoanalysis. He now thinks Freud's explanation of culture would deserve at least "serious consideration as a scientific hypothesis," if it were restated as a proposition about the constant operation of certain psychic processes—for example, the incest drive, incest repression, and filial ambivalence—in widespread human institutions. He still finds that psychoanalysis refuses to undertake such a restatement, because of its indifference to history and to accepted scientific attitudes, and its dogmatic all-or-none attitude which resists influences from without. Kroeber cites as examples of this last trait Ernest Jones's resistance to Malinowski's discovery of a matrilineal form of the Oedipus complex among the Trobriand Islanders and Róheim's *Psychoanalysis of Primitive Culture Types* of 1932.

In this later review, nevertheless, Kroeber lists Freud's concepts of repression, regression, infantile persistences, dream symbolism, overdetermination, guilt sense, and the affects toward members of the family, as ideas which have "gradually seeped into general science and become an integral and important part of it." On the other hand, the concepts of the censor, the superego, and the castration complex, and the explanations of specific cultural phenomena have not, he says, found their way into science. The conclusion of the review is a tribute to Freud:

We . . . if I may speak for ethnologists, though remaining unconverted, have met Freud, recognize the encounter as memorable, and herewith re-salute him.

Anthropology's encounter with psychoanalysis was not restricted to the United States. In 1924 the British anthropologist, C. G. Seligman, then president of the Royal Anthropological Institute of Great Britain and Ireland, took for his presidential address the subject "Anthropology and Psychology: A Study of Some Points of Contact." In this address, Seligman suggests several possible developments in the "little known borderland where social anthropology, psychology, and genetics meet in common biological kinship." He discusses Jung's introvert and extrovert "types" in relation to racial genetics, as exhibited in art, and as charac-teristic of some races. Seligman's classifications are a bit casual: "sav-ages" belong to the extrovert type, although chiefs and medicine men may be introverts; Europeans are predominantly extrovert, and Hindus are introvert. The same address also suggests "the beginning of a pur-posive investigation of the unconscious among non-European races" through the study of their dreams. Referring to dreams collected for him by officials and missionaries in the Sudan as well as to those he himself collected among Sudanese Arabs, Nile Negroids, Papuo-Melanesians, and Veddas, Seligman concludes that the dream-mechanisms of non-Europeans "appear to be the same as in ourselves" and include dreams with the same manifest content, to which identical unconscious meanings attach.

In a later paper of 1932, "Anthropological Perspective and Psycho-logical Theory," Seligman appeals to anthropologists "to study more deeply than has hitherto been the common practice the ideas, seldom, I think, verbally expressed, that lie behind the beliefs and customs which we, as anthropologists, are accustomed to describe." In this paper he ap-plies a Freudian theory to a group of observances which dramatize the desire or fear of an individual. He also suggests that the works of Freud and Jung are important for anthropology because the psychological prob-lems arising in anthropology "lie for the most part not in the sphere of cognition—to which most attention has been paid in the psychology of consciousness—but in the sphere of motive and emotion." This too is the reason Seligman gives for the failure of the psychological research of the Torres Straits expedition to raise fresh questions: ". . . it was almost entirely limited to the experimental psychology of the sense or-gans and to reaction time."

Perhaps better known and more directly influential than Seligman's efforts to bring anthropology and psychoanalysis together were the stud-ies of Malinowski in the Trobriand Islands, particularly his *Sex and Re-pression in Savage Society* (1927) and *The Sexual Life of Savages*

(1929). The first of these was in part the outcome of a debate in writing with the British analyst, Ernest Jones. Malinowski acknowledges, however, the stimulus of Seligman in the preface to the 1927 edition of *Sex and Represssion:*

> The instructions sent to me by my friend Prof. C. G. Seligman, and some literature with which he kindly supplied me, stimulated me to reflect on the manner in which the Oedipus complex and other manifestations of the "unconscious" might appear in a community founded on mother right. The actual observations on the matrilineal complex among Melanesians are to my knowledge the first application of psychoanalytic theory to the study of savage life . . .

What these instructions were Malinowski does not say, but they probably were not too different from the list of questions which Seligman discusses in his 1932 paper and which he says were proposed by Evans-Pritchard:

> (1) Can the anthropologist collect data full enough and of sufficient relevance to throw light on psychoanalytic theory?
> (2) Are the phases called by the psychoanalyst "oral", "anal", "genital", and "latent" in the life-history of the individual, common to all races and cultures?
> (3) If so, are these stages universally determined by biological factors, or by social conditions?
> (4) Are the same symbols used by different races in similar circumstances or identical situations?
> (5) Do the symptom-formations of members of our Western civilization differ from those of other communities? (p. 209)

In addition to these anthropologists who saw the relevance of psychoanalysis for their work, there were also psychoanalysts who ventured into anthropological applications. Freud's *Totem and Taboo* may have been an irritant, but it was also a stimulant. His *Civilization and Its Discontents* (1930) and *Group Psychology and the Analysis of the Ego* (1922) were more direct applications of psychoanalysis to culture and society. Rank, Jones, and Sachs also wrote in these fields. It was, however, Géza Róheim, a psychoanalytically trained ethnologist, whose fieldwork and point of view came closest to what was to become the culture and personality approach. Róheim did some psychoanalytic field studies in 1928–31 in Central Australia, Somaliland, and the Normanby Islands, with the support of Marie Bonaparte. The first report on these studies was published in a special number of *The International Journal of Psychoanalysis* for 1932 under the title "The Psychoanalysis of Primitive Culture Types." Róheim says that much of this report was written as preparation for lectures which he gave during his return journey at the University of Chicago, Columbia University, the New York Psychoanalytical Society, the Paris Psychoanalytical Society, the Berlin

Psychoanalytical Institute, and the Budapest Psychoanalytical Society and Ethnographical Society.

While Róheim eventually came to influence many anthropologists, this early report and the lectures were too strong a brew for most of them to swallow. Róheim on his part was, like many of his fellow analysts, pretty haughty toward anthropologists. Here is his comment on Malinowski:

> Some of you may be under the impression that psycho-analysis has already been applied in anthropological field-work by Professor Malinowski. Although he does not claim to be a psycho-analyst himself, some of his statements are rather misleading. Thus, for instance, he mentions that when he was in the Trobriands and Professor Seligman sent him some of Freud's books to read he set out to *test* the validity of Freud's dream-theory on the Trobrianders. Fancy! Somebody who admits that he has never analysed a dream himself—for the obvious reason that he does not know how to do it—is *testing* Freud's theory! (1932, p. 7)

On the side of method, Róheim stressed that the aim of anthropology should be "to find the latent wish-fulfilment in each specific type of social organization just as we can reduce a dream or a neurosis to such a latent formula." In order to do this, he proposed that anthropologists collect and interpret data which would open the door to the unconscious —information on dreams, life histories, sexual life, rearing of children, myths, ceremonies, customs interpreted with the help of a personal knowledge of the informant, jokes, casual remarks, slips of the tongue, etc. This "new anthropology" would not be able to do what the clinical analyst can do, but it could do "all that the old style anthropology could do and much more besides." On the basis of investigations similar to his, he believed that it would be possible to set up a psychological classification of mankind.

Despite these early and serious interests of Seligman, Malinowski, and Róheim in bringing anthropology and psychoanalytic psychology closer together, their example was not immediately followed in Europe by a significant number of anthropologists and did not result in the recognition of a new field (Evans-Pritchard, 1929; Richards, 1932; Fortes, 1957). In the United States, the pioneer writings of Margaret Mead, Sapir, and Benedict were quickly followed after 1935 by a rapid increase of research, teaching, and publication in personality and culture. A growing number of anthropologists were psychoanalyzed, and some leading psychoanalysts and psychiatrists collaborated with anthropologists or were influenced by anthropology. One of the most notable instances of such collaboration was a series of seminars organized by Dr. Abram Kardiner, a psychiatrist, at the New York Psychoanalytic Institute from about 1936 to 1940. Among the anthropologists who participated in these seminars were Cora DuBois, Ruth Benedict, Ruth Bun-zel, and Ralph Linton. Several important publications resulted directly or indirectly from these seminars. (See the sections on "Basic Personality Structure" and "Modal Personality" in this chapter.)

A larger scale example of collaboration at the research level was the Indian Education Research Project organized by the United States Bureau of Indian Affairs in 1941 in cooperation with the Committee on Human Development at the University of Chicago. This project studied personality development among the Hopi, Navaho, Papago, Sioux, and Zuni. Monographs on the first four tribes have already appeared. (Thompson and Joseph, 1944; Kluckhohn and Leighton, 1946; Mac-Gregor, 1946; Joseph, Spicer, and Chesky, 1949.) In addition to anthropologists, psychologists and psychiatrists participated. The influence of psychoanalysis was more indirect here than in Kardiner's seminars, but psychological tests were systematically used.

After the Second World War, another large-scale research project was organized in New York City to apply the personality and culture approach to the study of modern nations. This research was directed first by Ruth Benedict at Columbia University and later by Margaret Mead at the American Museum of Natural History. This series of projects, which ended in 1953, involved a group of more than 120 researchers, representing fourteen disciplines and sixteen nationalities. Many publications have resulted from it, and others are still to appear.

The interest stimulated by psychoanalysis in the individual life history and in personal documents affected not only anthropology but sociology, political science, and other social sciences. This interest seems in fact to have had sources partly independent of psychoanalytic theory and technique. In sociology one of the influential sources was *The Polish Peasant* (1917–18) by W. I. Thomas and F. Znaniecki, a work that made extensive use of personal documents and included a lengthy methodological note on their use (Hinkle, 1952; Volkart, 1953). From the Social Science Research Council's selection of this work for appraisal (Blumer, 1939) grew a special series of studies on personal documents in psychology (Allport, 1942), in history (Gottschalk, 1945), in anthropology (Kluckhohn, 1945), and in sociology (Angell, 1945).

The pioneer life histories in anthropology (e.g. Radin 1913, 1926) were not psychoanalytically or even psychologically oriented. Only in the late thirties and early forties do the full-length life histories begin to appear (Dyk, 1938, 1947; Ford, 1941; Simmons, 1942). In addition to Seligman's early efforts, an important collection of primitive dreams, culturally as well as psychoanalytically interpreted, was published in 1935 by Lincoln.

In political science, Lasswell was one of the first to introduce personal documents and psychoanalytic orientations, and to see their implications for personality and culture theory (Lasswell, 1930, 1937, 1939, 1948). John Dollard's *Criteria for the Life History,* 1935, was a major formulation by a psychologist which both reflected and influenced the social scientist's growing preoccupation with the individual personality.

One may measure the present status of personality and culture as a field in anthropology by noting that the first comprehensive collection of readings from periodical literature was published in 1948 by Kluckhohn and Murray. For their selections, the editors say they examined over a thousand relevant articles. A second and revised edition appeared in 1953. Other collections of readings by Haring (1949, 1956), and by Sargent and Smith (1949), also appeared about the same time. The second edition of Kroeber's general survey of anthropology appeared in 1948 and contains a substantial discussion of "cultural psychology," whereas the first edition of 1923, which I used as an undergraduate in the 1930's, contained nothing on this subject. The first general textbook on culture and personality was published in 1954 by John Honigmann. Courses in the field are now an accepted part of the anthropology curriculum, and papers on it are regularly presented at professional meetings and appear in the professional journals.

MAJOR PROBLEM AREAS

The relationship of personality and culture theory to research has always been a close one. Very little theory has been developed without immediate reference to ongoing research, and the research has usually been designed to answer questions raised by theory. This fruitful interaction of theory and research has tended to cluster about problem areas which constitute the dominant themes in the development of the field. I discern three such major problem areas: the relation of culture to human nature; the relation of culture to typical personality; and the relation of culture to individual personality. There are additional important problem areas, among them the relation of culture change to personality change and the relation of culture to abnormal personality. But these grow out of and are subsidiary to the dominant three problems which have been the persistent preoccupations of the field. The prominence of just these three groups of problems is not surprising, for they reflect the efforts of anthropologists to relate culture to the three elementary logical possibilities which Kluckhohn and Murray (1948, 1953) have so clearly stated and explained, namely, that every man is in certain respects like all other men, like some other men, and like no other man. If we ask how far a man's resemblance to all other men is a matter of culture, we raise the question of culture and human nature; if we ask how far his resemblances to some other men derive from the fact that those others are members of his tribe, his nation, his class, his occupation, and the like, we raise the question of culture and typical personality; and finally, if we ask how far an individual's uniqueness is a matter of culture, we raise the question of how the individual personality is related to culture.

All these problem areas have received some attention, but there have been significant relative shifts in the attention given to each group of problems. In the formative period, i.e., about 1920–1935, the relation of culture to human nature was the chief preoccupation of theory and research; then this problem receded and has only recently been returning to the forefront of interest. The relation of culture to typical personality has probably been the most persistent and popular problem; it was taken up immediately after the formative period and has continued to the present. Although the relation of individual personality to culture is in a sense the heart of the culture and personality field, this problem area has been somewhat underdeveloped in both theory and research as compared with the other two. There are evidences of increasing attention in some recent publications. I shall now describe in greater detail some of the most significant contributions to each of these problem areas.

CULTURE AND HUMAN NATURE

In the preface to the 1939 reissue of her South Sea studies, Margaret Mead graphically describes the climate of opinion in the 1920's which stimulated her and other anthropologists to concern themselves with the relation of culture to human nature:

> It was a simple—a very simple—point to which our materials were organized in the 1920's, merely the documentation over and over of the fact that human nature is not rigid and unyielding, not an unadaptable plant which insists on flowering or becoming stunted after its own fashion, responding only quantitatively to the social environment, but that it is extraordinarily adaptable, that cultural rhythms are stronger and more compelling than the physiological rhythms which they overlay and distort, that the failure to satisfy an artificial, culturally stimulated need—for outdistancing one's neighbours in our society, for instance, or for wearing the requisite number of dog's teeth among the Manus—may produce more unhappiness and frustration in the human breast than the most rigorous cultural curtailment of the physiological demands of sex or hunger. We had to present evidence that human character is built upon a biological base which is capable of enormous diversification in terms of social standards. (p. x)

Educated opinion in the 1920's and 1930's quickly accepted the anthropologists' evidence of human nature's plasticity. Theories of original human nature were put on the defensive and became unfashionable. Although psychoanalysis was becoming popular with this same group, psychoanalytic theories about the universal Oedipus, the ubiquity of dream symbolism, the stages of personality development, and the differences between male and female psychology, were generally regarded as over-generalizations from a single culture and in need of qualification by such cross-cultural studies as Margaret Mead's and Malinowski's. The general stance was critical and disposed to reiterate the formula: "It's not human nature, but only our culture."

This formula was first stated and developed in this period not by anthropologists but by a social philosopher. It will be found very persuasively presented in John Dewey's *Human Nature and Conduct,* published in 1922 on the eve of the field studies that were to document it. References to this work of Dewey's as a standard text recur in Malinowski, Mead, Benedict and other anthropologists. Malinowski quotes several apt paragraphs from it as the motto for his *Sex and Repression in Savage Society,* among them the following:

We need to know about the social conditions which have educated original activities into definite and significant dispositions before we can discuss the psychological element in society. This is the true meaning of social psychology . . . Native human nature supplies the raw materials but custom furnishes the machinery and the designs . . . Man is a creature of habit, not of reason nor yet of instinct. (p. xv)

In the same 1939 preface, Margaret Mead sums up the general result of this "battle" against human nature:

The battle which we once had to fight with the whole battery at our command, with the most fantastic and startling examples that we could muster, is now won. As the devout in the Middle Ages would murmur a precautionary "God willing" before stating a plan or a wish, those who write about the problems of man and society have learned to insert a precautionary "in our culture" into statements which would have read, fifteen years ago, merely as "Adolescence is always a time of stress and strain," "Children are more imaginative than adults," "All artists are neurotics," "Women are more passive than men," etc., with no such precautionary phrase. (pp. x–xi)

From our present vantage point, the issues appear more complex, the victory less decisive. A good deal of psychoanalytic theory, for example, was incorporated in the very process of resistance to it, and the problem of integrating this theory of individual psychology with cultural theory itself became and continues to be a major issue. The work of Lorenz, Tinbergen, and other "ethologists" has again made "instinct" a respectable word. Since the second world war, also, "human nature" and the "psychic unity of mankind," or at least the problem of their relation to culture, has reasserted itself among anthropologists. Kroeber, recognizing that the "psychic unity of man" cannot be considered to be either a proved fact or an axiomatic principle, thinks it is

. . . so overwhelmingly borne out by the run of total experience that the anthropologist or the sociologist feels warranted in assuming the principle of essential psychic unity as at least a sufficient approximation to the truth, and to employ it as a working hypothesis, or at any rate as a convenient symbol. (1948, pp. 527–73)

The facts of cultural transmission from generation to generation and from one population to another would not, according to Kroeber, be what they are if we did not have a uniform human nature. Basing himself on a somewhat different order of facts, Róheim feels that

the psychic unity of mankind is more than a working hypothesis, it is so obvious that it hardly needs proof. Even if mankind should prove to be derived from a variety of semi-anthropoid ancestors, it is evident that some sort of common process is involved in becoming human and that we have more in common even with a South African Bushman than with an ape or monkey. (1950, p. 435)

But what is so obvious for Róheim—that this common process is the unconscious and its mechanisms—is not so obvious for others. For Róheim, the basic oedipal tendencies are the same in all, although the "customary traumata" involved in different child-rearing practices may introduce *quantitative* variations and, in primitive cultures at least, different basic personalities.

Róheim's polemic against Kardiner and the cultural anthropologists is the recent counterpart of Ernest Jones' polemic against Malinowski. But the present argument has profited from the earlier, and from what has happened since. The antagonists are now closer together than they were in the 1920's. Both sides have scaled down Freud's "archaic heritage" to some inherited dispositions and capacities, a limited number of unconscious mechanisms, and possibly a bit of universal symbolism. The recapitulation theory has been abandoned, as has the theory that the Oedipus complex was at the origin of prehistoric cultures. The points of disagreement are some details in the assumptions about human nature and the degree to which specific institutions can modify the "common process" involved in becoming human.

This more complex and sophisticated position has been stated on the side of the psychoanalysts by Hartman, Kris, and Loewenstein in their comments on personality and culture (1951). These analysts "assume readily" that "cultural conditions produce variations of behavior during the [oedipal] conflict situation." They are inclined to believe in the wide range of these variations, many of which they have observed in clinical situations. They also do not find it necessary "to stress as much as he [Freud] the hereditary elements in the formation of the oedipus complex." Yet they are not prepared to accept reports concerning the absence of the Oedipus complex under given social situations. Such statements seem to them "frequently due to the fact that observers have too simple or too narrow a view of what is meant by oedipal conflict." Alleged variations of oedipal phantasies, e.g. the phantasy of adoption among American children, can be meaningfully related to American family size, frequency of adoption, etc., "if seen against the background of the universal patterns." Anthropologists, they believe, are still tempted "to draw conclusions from observed behavior to underlying motivations and neglect frequently, paradoxically enough, to take into account that in different environments similar impulses may find different expressions." They do this when they emphasize institutional factors in personality formation, overlooking the fact that "institutions affect different individuals in different degrees and in different directions," and when they rely on external observations of mother-child relationships without reference to the psychoanalyst's reconstructive studies of life histories.

The anthropologist's position too has been moving closer to the universalism of psychoanalytic theory and away from an exclusive preoccupation with differences. A very interesting "confession" of Kluckhohn's published in 1951 sets forth this shift:

> When I began serious field work among the Navaho and Pueblo Indians, my position on psychoanalysis was a mixed one. I had been analyzed and was thoroughly convinced that Freudian psychology was the only dynamic depth psychology of much importance. I had also been influenced by the writings of psychoanalysts on anthropological matters, notably Róheim. On the other hand, I tended to believe that psychoanalysis was strongly culture-bound. I was persuaded, for example, that Malinowski's interpretation of the oedipal situation in the Trobriands was substantially correct.
>
> Over the years, at least in certain crucially important respects, my position has steadily drawn closer to that of Róheim. I still believe that some of the cautions uttered by Boas and others on the possible extravagances of interpretations in terms of universal symbolism, completely or largely divorced from minute examination of cultural context, are sound. But the facts uncovered in my own field work and that of my collaborators have forced me to the conclusion that Freud and other psychoanalysts have depicted with astonishing correctness many central themes in motivational life which are universal. The styles of expression of these themes and much of the manifest content are culturally determined, but the underlying psychologic drama transcends cultural difference.
>
> This should not be too surprising—except to an anthropologist overindoctrinated with the theory of cultural relativism—for many of the inescapable givens of human life are also universal. Human anatomy and human physiology are, in the large, about the same the world over. There are two sexes with palpably visible differences in external genitalia and secondary sexual characteristics. All human infants, regardless of culture, know the psychological experience of helplessness and dependency. Situations making for

competition for the affection of one or both parents, for sibling rivalry, can be to some extent channeled this way or that way by a culture but they cannot be eliminated, given the universality of family life. The trouble has been —because of a series of accidents of intellectual and political history—that the anthropologist for two generations has been obsessed with the differences between peoples, neglecting the equally real similarities—upon which the "universal culture pattern" as well as the psychological uniformities are clearly built. (Kluckhohn and Morgan, 1951)

In several other papers (1946, 1953, 1956) Kluckhohn qualifies this thesis and presents longer lists of the "universals." The Oedipus complex is included in all these lists. Hallowell (1950), Spiro (1954), Howells (1955), Kroeber (1955), Redfield (1957), and others have also returned to this earlier problem in later papers, and in several publications Mead acknowledges the importance of "human nature" for comparative studies of personality and culture (Mead and McGregor, 1951; Mead 1954b; Mead and Wolfenstein, 1955).

In the study of personality and culture we start with the recognition of the biologically given, of what all human beings have in common. . . . Because of these recurrent biological similarities—of growth, of parent-child relationships, of needs and fears, and reassurances—it is possible to compare childhood in one society with childhood in another. (Mead and Wolfenstein, 1955, pp. 6–7)

And this common human nature includes the capacity to accumulate and to participate in culture.

Humanity as we know it is not merely a matter of human physique, of our prehensile thumbs, upright posture, and highly developed brains, but of our capacity to accumulate and build upon the inventions and experiences of previous generations. A child who does not participate in this great body of tradition, whether because of defect, neglect, injury, a disease, never becomes fully human. (*ibid.,* pp. 6–7)

I do not, however, wish to give a misleading impression of a simple pendulum swing in the intellectual climate of opinion. There has been an important swing, but the present position is not a return to the *status quo ante.* It has benefited from the earlier work and suggests new directions of inquiry.

The earlier position on "human nature" was not, as is usually supposed, a *tabula rasa* position. It was assumed, on the contrary, that there is a core of original human nature which is universal, but that this core is very small in comparison to what is culture-made, and that its nature can be disclosed only through a wide range of cross-cultural studies (Mead 1942b, Benedict, 1934b).

In essentials, this position is probably still accepted at the present time, but there is now a stronger and more direct interest in stating the content of the core and in developing new methods for research. Kroeber, for example, noting that attempts to inventory common denominators of culture and universal human needs have not proved very fruitful in research, proposes two methods for finding out more about original human nature; one is to study the extremes to which particular cultures have pushed particular facets of human nature, and the other is to undertake a systematic comparison of human and non-human traits. There are now sufficient data, he believes, for these studies. These data, we may note in passing, have been in the main products of cross-cultural research.

In the recent revival of interest in "human nature," there is also evident a desire to develop a concept of "human nature" that goes beyond the phylogenetic core to include a "developed human nature" which is found in all human societies. Redfield, who shortly before his death brought forward this concept, argued the need for it because it is true of men that "in whatever established group they develop, certain outcomes of the development are always the same" and these similarities cannot be explained entirely on the basis of the "modal inborn potentialities" in *Homo sapiens*. He believes that this "universally or frequently developed human nature" is a reality, but "it is not a reality that is easily amenable to investigation by precise method and subject to dependable proof. The intuitions as to this reality are stronger than the demonstration of its content." There are, he suggests, two contrasting ways in which this "developed human nature" may be conceived and described: culturally as a universal culture pattern, and psychologically in terms of the modal personality of mankind. He finds some suggestions about the latter method in certain sociologists, social psychologists, and philosophers (Cooley; Park and Burgess; Faris; Riezler). Examples of such universal statements are the following: "All people feel shame or guilt or some combination of these; all take satisfaction in or feel dissatisfaction with regard to the enterprises and productions."

To these, attributed to Cooley, Redfield adds others: "All men are aware of self, distinguish an I and a Me. All men look out upon a not-self, a universe in which people are distinguished, one from another, as persons. All are disposed to feel and think more intimately and kindly toward the members of their own immediate group than they feel and think about people in more remote groups in situations where a choice of loyalties is required. All recognize and adjust themselves to the alternation of day and night; all know the passage of time; all anticipate death and have thoughts and feelings about death that are serious and important, not just trivial" and so on (1957, p. 159).

Redfield's concluding comment on a remark of Park's expresses the mood of the 1950's toward human nature:

Robert E. Park admired Sumner's *Folkways* and used to quote Sumner's dictum, "The mores can make anything right." Then Park would add: "But they have a harder time making some things right than others." I think now that this was a profound remark. I am sure that the mores have an easier time making it right for mothers to cherish their children or somebody's children, than they have to make it right for a mother to cherish her child and then eat it. The insight we have in condemning as "inhuman" certain extremes of conduct such as the cold cruelty of the Nazis, or cannibalism within the in-group, is an insight into a truth that might perhaps some day be expressed in scientific form: that the rules of conduct, in the societies the world has known so far, have their modality, their tendency toward a very general similar content. (Redfield, 1957, pp. 159–60)

CULTURE AND TYPICAL PERSONALITY

From the time when the first battle against human nature was won until the question was reopened, say from about 1935 to 1950, personality and culture theory and research concentrated heavily on the problem of the relation of culture to typical personality. The theories of configurational personality, of basic personality structure, of national and cultural character, and of modal personality were all developed and served as guides to field research during this period. It has become usual to consider these theories as more or less equivalent, and the differences among them as primarily semantic. This is a mistake. Such a view overlooks significant differences in concepts, methods, data, and fields of application. These theories have obviously influenced one another and have some features in common, but there is more to be said about them.

They all agree that every culture has a typical personality which is characteristic and distinctive of that culture and which is produced or conditioned by some aspect of the culture. This much of the theory is not very far from older theories of national character and "genius" of peoples, except that the units are now cultures rather than "races" or "peoples," and the typical personalities are conceived as products of learning rather than of genetics. Beyond this shared core, however, the contemporary theories differ in many significant respects: the particular psychological types employed, the number of personality types attributed to a given culture, the number of individuals who are supposed to bear a given type within a culture, how a particular type is learned, whether it is derived from cultural or psychological data, whether it is attributed to the culture as a whole as well as to individuals, by what causal theory it is related to the culture at a given time and historically, whether it applies only to primitive cultures or to modern nations as well. I shall now analyze briefly some of the major theories with respect to these criteria of differentiation and shall indicate the relevant research studies.

CONFIGURATIONAL PERSONALITY

"Cultures . . . are individual psychology thrown large upon the screen, given gigantic proportions and a long time span." (Benedict, 1932, p. 24)

Ruth Benedict is generally and properly credited with the theory of culture configurations. There are some anticipations of the theory in several of Sapir's early papers (1924, 1927) and some parallels to aspects of it in the applications of Jungian and Freudian typologies to cultures by Seligman (1924) and Róheim (1932). But it was *Patterns of Culture* (1934b) with its highly readable formulation of the theory, together with a detailed application to three primitive cultures, the Zuni, the Dobu and the Kwakiutl, which brought the theory of configurations to the attention of a wide professional and lay public.

In two earlier papers (1928, 1932), Benedict sketched the essentials of the theory and acknowledged Dilthey, Spengler, Nietzsche, and *Gestalt* psychology as intellectual sources. In another paper, published simultaneously with *Patterns of Culture* in 1934, she elaborated the implications for a comparative psychiatry.

The earlier papers are significant because they show that the problem with which Benedict starts is not psychological but cultural. She wanted to know how and why the culture of the Southwest Pueblos differed so strikingly from its neighboring cultures. She did not think that explanations in terms of the presence or absence of certain traits, such as ritualism, and their diffusion, could account for the difference, and suggested instead that the dissimilarity was due to variations in the "psychological type" or "psychological set" of the various cultures:

The ritual of the sun dance, the peace pipe ceremonies, the cult groups, and age-societies of the Plains, or the winter ceremonial of the Northwest Coast bulk perhaps slightly less prominently in the total life of these people than the calendric dances and retreats of the Southwest, but it is not by any such matter of gradation that the Southwest is set off from other American Indian cultures. There is in their cultural attitudes and choices a difference in psychological type fundamentally to be distinguished from that of surrounding regions. It goes deeper than the presence or the absence of ritualism; ritualism itself is of a fundamentally different character within this area, and without the understanding of this fundamental psychological set among the Pueblo peoples we must be baffled in our attempts to understand the cultural history of this region. (Benedict, 1928, p. 572)

This is not necessarily an attempt to explain cultural facts in terms of individual psychology, for Benedict's "psychological types" were at first the Apollonian and Dionysian types Nietzsche described in his studies of Greek tragedy, a classification essentially of "confidence in two diametrically different ways of arriving at the values of existence" (1932). Such psychological "types" or "sets" derive from an analysis of cultural data and describe the *ethos* of cultures; they need not be applied to individuals at all. Their primary use might be to describe the differences among cultures, and the processes of culture change. This certainly seems to have been Benedict's first approach to the problem:

> The cultural situation in the Southwest is in many ways hard to explain. With no natural barriers to isolate it from surrounding peoples, it presents probably the most abrupt cultural break that we know in America. All our efforts to trace out the influences from other areas are impressive for the fragmentariness of the detail; we find bits of the weft or woof of the culture, we do not find any very significant clues to its pattern. From the point of view of the present paper this clue is to be found in a fundamental psychological set which has undoubtedly been established for centuries in the culture of this region, and which has bent to its own uses any details it imitated from surrounding peoples and has created an intricate cultural pattern to express its own preferences. It is not only that the understanding of this psychological set is necessary for a descriptive statement of this culture; without it the cultural dynamics of this region are unintelligible. For the typical choices of the Apollonian have been creative in the formation of this culture, they have excluded what was displeasing, revamped what they took, and brought into being endless demonstrations of the Apollonian delight in formality, in the intricacies and elaborations of organization. (Benedict, 1928, pp. 74–5)

But by the time Benedict wrote *Patterns of Culture* and "Anthropology and the Abnormal," the analogy between a culture and an individual personality had been enlarged. Not only was a culture, as was an individual personality, an organized whole which develops through a series of basic choices that select a "character" from among a wide range of possibilities, but the "psychological types" of character attributed to cultures now also drew upon the classifications psychiatrists used for individuals. The dominant cultural *ethos* is characterized in psychiatric terms. In *Patterns of Culture* both kinds of typologies are employed: the Zuni are described as Apollonian and the Plains Indians as Dionysian, as they were in the earlier papers, but the Dobu are characterized as "paranoid" and the Kwakiutl as "megalomaniac paranoid." Margaret Mead (1959) has recently given some of the sources for Benedict's psychological interests at this stage of her thought.

This shift from a typology of "values of existence" to a typology of individual personality types transforms the theory of configurations from a characterization of different cultures in terms of collective *ethos* into a theory of the relations of different kinds of cultures to different personality types. If Kwakiutl culture has a "megalomaniac paranoid trend," one wants to know how many individual Kwakiutl share this trend and whether they acquired it from their culture. Benedict, quite aware that her metaphor of culture as an individual personality was turning into a theory of personality and culture, suggested definite answers to these questions implicitly in *Patterns of Culture* and explicitly in "Anthropology and the Abnormal." The gist of her answers is contained in the following paragraph from the latter work:

> I have spoken of individuals as having sets toward certain types of behavior, and of these sets as running sometimes counter to the types of behavior which are institutionalized in the culture to which they belong. From all that we know of contrasting cultures it seems clear that differences of temperament occur in every society. The matter has never been made the subject of investigation, but from the available material it would appear that these temperament types are very likely of universal recurrence. That is, there is an ascertainable range of human behavior that is found wherever a sufficiently large series of individuals is observed. But the proportion in which behavior types stand to one another in different societies is not universal. The vast majority of the individuals in any group are shaped to the fashion of that culture. In other words, most individuals are plastic to the moulding force of the society into which they are born. In a society that values trance, as in India, they will have supernormal experience. In a society that institutionalizes homosexuality, they will be homosexual. In a society that sets the gathering of possessions as the chief human objective, they will amass property. The deviants, whatever the type of behavior the culture has institutionalized, will remain few in number, and there seems no more difficulty in moulding the vast malleable majority to the "normality" of what we consider an aberrant trait, such as delusions of reference, than to the normality of such accepted behavior patterns as acquisitiveness. The small proportion of the number of the deviants in any culture is not a function of the sure instinct with which that society has built itself upon the fundamental sanities, but of the universal fact that, happily, the majority of mankind quite readily take any shape that is presented to them. (p. 196)

Restated, this theory may be summarized in terms of the following distinct propositions:

1. In every culture there is a wide range of individual temperament types (genetically and constitutionally determined) which recur universally.

2. Every culture, however, permits only a limited number of types to flourish, and they are those that fit its dominant configuration.

3. The vast majority of individuals in any society will conform to the dominant types of that society, since their temperaments will be sufficiently plastic to the moulding force of the society. These will be the "normal" personality types.

4. A minority of individuals in every society will not "fit" the dominant types, either because their temperament types are too deviant from the ruling types or because they are "insufficiently endowed." These will be the "deviants" and "abnormals."

5. The classification and distribution of "normal" and "abnormal" personality types is relative to the configurations of particular cultures which define the criteria of "normality" and "abnormality."

It does not follow from this last proposition, as is sometimes asserted, that there are no universally valid criteria of "normality" or "abnormality." As on the analogous question of "human nature" and moral values, Benedict's position is that such criteria probably exist, but we cannot be sure what they are until we have allowed for cultural relativity, and, therefore, until we have accumulated more comparative data:

> The problem of understanding abnormal human behavior in any absolute sense independent of cultural factors is still far in the future. The categories of borderline behavior which we derive from the study of the neuroses and psychoses of our civilization are categories of prevailing local types of instability. They give much information about the stresses and strains of Western civilization, but no final picture of inevitable human behavior. Any conclusions about such behavior must await the collection by trained observers of psychiatric data from other cultures. Since no adequate work of the kind has been done at the present time, it is impossible to say what core of definition of abnormality may be found valid from the comparative material. It is as it is in ethics: all our local conventions of moral behavior and of immoral are without absolute validity, and yet it is quite possible that a modicum of what is considered right and what wrong could be disentangled that is shared by the whole human race. When data are available in psychiatry, this minimum definition of abnormal human tendencies will be probably quite unlike our culturally conditioned, highly elaborated psychoses such as those that are described, for instance, under the terms of schizophrenia and manic-depressive. (*op. cit.,* p. 79)

Although very few of these propositions have survived without substantial qualification and additions, the theory which they summarize has been the starting point for almost all later developments in personality and culture theory and research. The first of Benedict's propositions is probably still acceptable with substantial modification, and the second, third, fourth, and fifth with varying degrees of modification. The collection of psychiatric data from other cultures is still far from adequate, but what there is has not yet revealed startling differences in abnormal human tendencies (e.g., Benedict and Jacks, 1954; Linton, 1956; Eaton and Weil, 1955; Kaplan and Plaut, 1956; Paul, 1955; A. Leighton *et al.,* 1957; Goldhamer, 1953; Opler, M. K., 1956).

One major series of amendments has been in the direction of complexity—both in the description of culture patterns and in the kinds and distribution of personality types. These complications have been applied even to the "simple" primitive cultures described by Benedict. Helen Codere (1956), for instance, has recently published an account of the Kwakiutl which portrays them as far more "amiable" than they are in *Patterns of Culture.* She, along with other critics, has also raised the question, whether the difference between chiefs and commoners in Kwakiutl society was understated by Benedict.

Another problem raised by the configurational theory is how the "psychological type" of the culture gets itself impressed on individuals. Today the assumption of cultural moulding of plastic temperaments has been generally replaced by an assumption of the critical importance of child-rearing experiences in the formation of adult personality (Kardiner, 1939; Eggan, 1943, 1956; Goldfrank, 1945; Erikson, 1945). This assumption, as is well known, is based on theories of learning and individual growth, and on psychoanalysis. In some of her later writings (1938, 1946a, 1949) Benedict includes some discussions of child-rearing practices without, however, committing herself to any particular psychological theory. She tends rather to stress that it is not the presence or absence of a specific practice which is important but the ways in which the practice is integrated with and expresses a particular configuration of culture. This point, quite consistent with the theory of configurations, later becomes the basis for a theory of "national character." (See the section on "National Character as Cultural Character" in this chapter.)

Despite Boas' characterization of *Patterns of Culture* as an effort to understand "the individual as living in his culture and the culture as lived by individuals," and despite the many psychological elements in the theory, there are practically no psychological data about individuals in that work. The data are predominantly cultural and social, including ceremonies, songs and poetry, social and economic organization, war practices, institutionalized attitudes, and the like. One looks in vain for the life histories and other personal documents, and the results of psychological tests, which have become the essential appurtenances of contemporary personality and cultural study. At most there is an occasional reference to the anthropologist's having asked some one a question, and brief portraits of several "abnormals."

There are at least three reasons, I think, for the neglect of psychological data in the configurational theory. It was conceived in the first instance as an explanation of cultural organization and differentiation and was extended only in midstream into a personality and culture theory; personal documents and other psychological data in culture studies were not very well known at this time (although Margaret Mead had already made them the basis of her Samoan study), and if one accepted the assumption that a vast majority of individuals in every society were so plastic as to take the mould of that society's culture pattern, it might appear superfluous to collect individual data about them, for according to this theory only the deviants would possess individuality.

This analysis is not meant as a criticism of the use of cultural data, for these are essential even when psychological data are employed. I want rather to stress that because the "psychological types" were conceived as attributes of whole cultures, it was not considered important to present evidence on the psychology of individuals, although the theory in its later forms did assert some very definite relations between the "psychological types" of whole cultures and of individuals.

Benedict and many others have used configurational theory to explain processes of cultural change. It is not, however, a historical theory except, as Boas has pointed out, "in so far as the general configuration, as long as it lasts, limits the directions of change that remain subject to it" (1934). This, to be sure, is a very important kind of effect on cultural change, but it does not account for the growth of any particular configuration, its change into another type, or the relation of such changes to changes in personality types of individuals. On these questions Benedict dropped a few tantalizing hints, for example, that a particular configuration takes its cues accidentally from the givens of biology and the environment and then grows gradually and cumulatively as an individual personality grows or as the Gothic style of architecture grew. She did not, however, elaborate these into any theory of historical change or take any serious account of history in her characterizations. The overwhelming impression given by works of this period is that configurations are timeless entities without known antecedents or consequences, but that, once established in a particular territory, they automatically become all-powerful shapers of events and personalities.

This preference for the static and the synchronic is characteristic of contemporary social anthropology and is not peculiar to the configurational theory. It may perhaps be justified because it is simpler to begin with the static, and also because in primitive cultures historical records are rare. When, however, the theory is applied to nations, the necessity for historical perspectives becomes urgent, as Kroeber has shown (1944). Even in the application of the configurational theory to primitive cultures, perhaps more can be done with the data available than has been attempted. Codere's use of travellers', missionaries', and official reports to trace changes in the Kwakiutl pattern results in a portrait, or portraits, of the Kwakiutl somewhat different from Benedict's (Codere, 1950). Hallowell and others have also shown that such materials can be used with good effect to study the relation of acculturation to persistence and change in modal personality types (Hallowell, 1942, 1946a, 1949; Caudill, 1949, 1952; Barnouw, 1950; Spindler, 1958). (See the section on "Acculturation and Change in Modal Personality Structure" in this chapter.)

These modifications of the configurational theory have been described briefly here not in order to criticize Ruth Benedict, but rather to indicate the fruitful influence of her original formulations on the further development of personality and culture theory.

BASIC PERSONALITY STRUCTURE

The psychoanalyst Abram Kardiner is chiefly responsible for the formulation of the theory of basic personality structure. Several anthropologists participated in Kardiner's seminars, and made important contributions to the theory, but the general formulation is Kardiner's. It was first presented in his book *The Individual and His Society: The Psychodynamics of Primitive Social Organization* (1939), and developed further in *The Psychological Frontiers of Society* (1945). Both books contain material of Linton's and the second has material of Cora DuBois' and James West's as well. Kardiner has also summarized his theories in a paper (1945). Cora DuBois' *The People of Alor* (1944), while it is an important independent monograph, grew out of some of the problems raised in Kardiner's seminars, and represents field research directly relevant to the theory. Ralph Linton's *The Cultural Background of Personality* (1945) should also be included as a collaborating anthropologist's attempt at a general synthesis.

The theory of basic personality structure marks an important milestone because it was one of the first systematic and explicit attempts to apply a modified psychoanalytic approach to different cultures. It consolidated the previous criticisms and research both of anthropologists (e.g., Kroeber, Malinowski, Mead, Benedict, Linton) and of psychoanalysts (e.g., Fromm, Horney, Rado, Ferenczi, W. Reich, Róheim) into a new synthesis which has been very influential on subsequent personality and culture theory and research.

The starting point of the theory is, as in Benedict's configurations, a desire to derive psychological characterizations of total cultures from cultural data. The nature of the characterization and the techniques of derivation, however, go considerably beyond configurational theory. The characterization is no longer in terms of a few "psychological types" which are descriptively fitted to the dominant values and motivations of a culture, but is given in terms of the characteristic unconscious constellations produced in individuals by the child-rearing practices and other "primary institutions" (e.g., family organization, subsistence techniques) prevailing in a culture. The aspects of the culture in which these "constellations" find expression (usually art, folklore, mythology, religion) Kardiner calls the "secondary institutions." A "basic personality structure" is then a diagnostic summary of the psychological constellations presumably generated by a culture's distinctive primary institutions and generating in turn its secondary institutions. The basic personality structure is not as such a descriptive profile of the personality types of individuals but a set of "nuclear" trends which enter as constituents into the characters of all individual personalities who have been reared under the same primary institutions.

Since "unconscious constellations" cannot be directly observed, the "basic personality structure" must be a construct inferred indirectly from cultural data. Linton describes it as "an abstraction of the same order as culture itself" (Kardiner, 1939, p. vi). "Basic personality structure," then, is an explanatory construct which tries to explain two rather different kinds of things: the integration of different institutions within a culture, at a given time and historically, and the personality resemblances among individual members of a society (what Cora DuBois and others later call the "modal personality type"). In effect the theory assimilates these two problems by asserting that it is the same "psychological coherence" which explains both the inter-relations of institutions and the distribution of personality types in a given society.

Kardiner has frequently written that he did not develop a new theory of basic personality but only presented a specific technique of "psychodynamic analysis" for deriving it in particular cultures. While this claim is a little misleading in view of the explanatory character of the concept, it does point to his own most distinctive contribution. To practice his technique Kardiner required the assistance of anthropologists with knowledge of the cultures to be analyzed. He insisted, however, on a strict division of labor between the anthropologists and the psychoanalysts in the collaboration. The anthropologists as expert informants should present the description of a culture's institutions, primary and secondary, and the psychoanalyst should take this description as data for his derivation of the basic personality structure. This procedure seems to have been generally followed in the New York seminars, and Kardiner makes a point of retaining it in his books. In the 1939 volume, Linton's description of Marquesan culture and of the Tanala of Madagascar are sharply separated from Kardiner's "psychodynamic analysis" of these cultures. The format is similar in the 1945 volume. The descriptive chapters on the Comanche, the Alorese, and Plainville are separated from Kardiner's analysis of these cultures. But there is one important difference in the later volume: Kardiner himself has written the descriptive chapters on the Comanche and the Alorese. He indicates that the Comanche chapter has been "compiled from information supplied by Ralph Linton" and the chapter on the Alorese "from seminar notes and from the book *The People of Alor.* . . ." Cora DuBois' description as it appears in the book, he says, is not a true record of this technique, since it includes "many inferences and conclusions drawn from the projective analysis" and, being written from the life cycle outward, gives an impression that personality formation can be predicted as "one ascends progressively up the life cycle." Kardiner thinks this neglects the important indicators to be found in religion, folklore, and the general "institutional set-up" (1945, p. 102).

These strictures on the proper division of labor between the anthropologist and the psychoanalyst reflect Kardiner's conception of the technique of psychodynamic analysis. They also assume importance in the later controversies concerning the mutual independence of the ethnographic and the psychological analyses.

If one could assume that specific kinds of child-rearing disciplines produced specific forms of personality reaction, and that specific kinds of (secondary) institutions derived from the unconscious representations of these reactions, one might be able, in theory at least, to infer, from descriptions of specific institutions and child-rearing practices, the specific kinds of personality reactions that intervene. This at any rate is the assumption underlying Kardiner's technique for deriving the basic personality structure of a culture. Two questions of general importance may be raised about this assumption: What are the actual steps in the application of the technique to ethnographic data? And what justification is there for assuming general causal connections between specific child-rearing practices, specific personality trends, and specific forms of art, religion and folklore?

Kardiner is quite explicit in his answer to the first question. He describes the technique as "an exercise in pathology" (1945, p. xvii). He also writes that "many of the constellations used in the reconstruction of Marquesan and Tanala culture were based on the pathology of neuroses" (1939, p. 431). He cites as an example his conclusion that the scarcity of women among the Marquesans is an important primary institution in the formation of Marquesan basic personality. He says he arrived at this conclusion by first noting that Marquesan men's fear of being eaten by women was a common theme in their folklore; on the basis of his experience with this theme among neurotics in our culture, he took it to indicate some dissatisfaction with women. Looking then at the Marquesan scarcity of women and the peculiarities of their child-rearing practices, he concluded that women as mothers are an important source of frustration to the Marquesan child and that they remain a source of frustration in other roles later on.

Kardiner's "exercise in psycho-pathology" is not a mechanical procedure or an easy one to apply. Sometimes it took Kardiner as long as four years to hit upon a satisfactory interpretation. It is a procedure, however, which involves quite general and definite operations. On the basis of Kardiner's own practice and description the following seem to be the most important steps:

1) The standardization of the reactions of adult neurotics in Western culture to specific institutions (chiefly child-rearing disciplines).

2) The generalization that the institutions assumed to be causes of neurotic reactions are also probably important loci of frustration for "normal" individuals in Western culture.

3) The identification of the reactions of whole groups exposed to similar institutional frustrations in any culture.

Step (1) represents a shift from individual to social psychiatry. It assumes that the institutional factors disclosed in psychotherapy as important for a particular individual are also probably of general etiological importance, particularly if they impinge on individuals in their early years. It also assumes that the adult's retrospective version of his childhood experiences is not significantly different from the actual experience.

Step (2) assumes that the neurotics' reactions are good indicators of the institutional source and direction of frustrations because, being more extreme than "normal" reactions, they describe the institutional pressures more accurately. It does not assume that neurotic and normal reactions are the same, but rather assumes that they are different adaptations to similar frustrating situations. The neurotic reaction is used as a clue to discover the institutional source.

Once steps (1) and (2) are taken, step (3) is not very difficult. For at this point one has a sizeable inventory of elementary "reaction types" to different kinds of frustrations induced by a variety of different institutions and needs only to discover which particular combinations apply to a given culture. Some assumptions about "human nature" are also made in this extension, but not many. Freud's theory of "instincts" and of the parallelism of the ontogenetic and the phylogenetic is dropped. What is assumed is "the phylogenetic endowment of man at birth with an ego or total personality of a very rudimentary kind, which in the process of growth and integration is constantly undergoing continuous change" (1939, p. 461). Also retained is the recognition of the basic needs of hunger, sex, and the need for protection (1939, p. 418), the capacity for repression, the existence of certain affects and attitudes, executive impulses, and attitudinized perceptions (p. 419). In addition to this trimmed version of Freud, Kardiner also accepts as "biological traits of man" gregariousness, a long period of maturation, the upright posture, prehensile hand, predominance of vision in adaptation, the capacity for speech, and the absence of a breeding season (1945, pp. 2–5). In agreement with most anthropologists, sociologists, and psychologists, he believes that "man is least dominated by inborn behavior patterns"—that "the adaptive patterns of man are acquired and that the inborn tendencies can be bent in one direction or another" (1945, p. 4).

The validity of these operations and the associated assumptions is far from self-evident. It is especially difficult to maintain that individual reactions to the same external frustrations are not uniform (1939, p. 419), and yet to reason from individualized reactions to common institutional causes. It may well be that the basic disciplines of child-rearing are the most crucial factors in the formation of basic personality structures (1939, p. 484), but this is not a conclusion that follows smoothly from clinical experience with adult neurotics.

In fairness to Kardiner, it should be said that he does not claim self-evidence for any of these steps, although he feels most confident regarding the first and argues for the validity of all. It is also important to point out that the validity of the derivation of any particular basic personality structure does not depend entirely on the validity of each of these steps. They may be regarded as ways to arrive at relevant hypotheses rather than at established generalizations of universal validity. The hypotheses would then have to find their warrant in how well they explained the "coherence" of particular cultures and in how accurately they predicted the personality profiles of "average" individuals. It is my impression that the anthropologists collaborating with Kardiner, and he himself occasionally, took this view of "psychodynamic analysis" as a technique for deriving hypothetical basic personality structures. Because they did take this view, they sought means of verification outside the framework set by the original theory. This led to new kinds of field research, new concepts of typical personality, and new tests of validity, as well as to some revisions by Kardiner of his own earlier formulations.

THE PROBLEM OF VALIDATION: MODAL PERSONALITY

The concept and term "modal personality" first assumes importance in Cora DuBois' monograph *The People of Alor, A Social-Psychological Study of an East Indian Island* (1944). One definition she there gives of the concept is that it "is the product of the interplay of fundamental physiologically and neurologically determined tendencies and experiences common to all human beings acted upon by the cultural milieu, which denies, directs, and gratifies these needs very differently in different societies" (p. 3). A second definition is in terms of the central tendencies in the variations of individual personalities:

It is quite possible that some societies permit the individual less leeway and pattern him more highly than do other societies. But in Alor both the results of test material and my own impressions indicate a wide range of variations. Ranges, however, are measured on a common base line. On such a base line data will show central tendencies that constitute the modal personality for any particular culture. (pp. 4–5)

These two definitions, although closely related, are not equivalent. The first refers to a genetic, dynamic, explanatory concept; it is "an abstraction and generalization," with the help of psychoanalytic theory, from data that are chiefly cultural. The second is a statistical concept of central tendency—a description of the "common and characteristic factors of personality in any culture" as they "might be established by a series of psychological tests and observations of cross-cultural applicability" (p. 5). The first definition approximates Kardiner's definition of "basic personality structure"; the second does not appear in the early Kardiner discussions. To avoid confusing them, let us retain Kardiner's term for the dynamic concept, and use "modal personality" only for the statistical and descriptive concept. "Modal personality" is implicit in the concept of "basic personality structure," but it emerges as an explicit concept when, as in DuBois' study, there are psychological data on individuals to summarize.

The psychological data in *The People of Alor* include eight autobiographies (four from men and four from women), thirty-seven Rorschachs (seventeen male, twenty female), responses to the Porteus maze test, word associations, and some children's drawings.

DuBois collected the psychological data because, as a participant in Kardiner's seminars in 1936 and 1937, she felt that the descriptive material used there for reconstructions of basic personality structure had been gathered for other purposes and did not give adequate description of character structure and dynamics. "It was a good exercise, but there was no opportunity to check our conclusions. Were individuals predominantly what we might suppose them to be from the institutions under which they lived, the childhood conditioning they received, the values they shared, the goals for which they strove?"

"We had talked ourselves out, and only field work could test the procedure." (p. V)

Kardiner and other participants in the seminar apparently shared this belief in the need for more data on individuals, and looked to DuBois' study as a test of the theory of "basic personality structure."

The present study by Dr. DuBois was undertaken with the foreknowledge that biographical material was essential to prove the contention that institutions affected and molded the growth of the individual in certain prescribed directions. . . . Unless such conclusions are based upon the study of biographies, any conclusions drawn from the study of institutions alone must fall into the category of guesses, more or less approximate. (Kardiner in DuBois, 1944, p. 8)

Linton thought that, before the Alor study, the concept of basic personality was only a "working hypothesis" whose "ultimate proof of validity was still lacking" (Kardiner, 1945, p. XI).

The procedure of validation, which Linton calls an "experiment," followed the earlier pattern in its first stages. When DuBois returned from her field study, she presented the ethnographic data to Kardiner's seminar. From these data Kardiner deduced, with the assistance of psychodynamic analysis, the expected basic personality structure of the Alorese. At this point two new steps were introduced to deal with the psychological data. The biographies were analyzed by Kardiner, and a Rorschach expert, Dr. Emil Oberholzer, was asked "to summarize those personality characteristics which appeared in a large majority of individuals tested" on the basis of "blind interpretations" of the Rorschach protocols, with "no exchange of information until the work was completed." When it was found that the two pictures of Alorese personality agreed on "all important points," Kardiner re-analyzed the life histories as a further check and to explain deviations in terms of atypical childhood experiences (Kardiner, 1944, p. 8; Kardiner, 1945, pp. 101–102, Linton, 1945, p. XI).

The participants in the seminar, as well as those who learned of the experiment later, generally agreed with Linton's judgment—that it "seemed to verify our earlier conclusions with respect to the reality of basic personality types, the mechanisms by which they are produced and their relations to the culture as a whole" (1945, p. XI).

The order of steps followed in the seminar is roughly followed in Kardiner's presentation of the Alorese material in his 1945 volume, but it is not quite the order followed in DuBois' monograph, which inaugurates a new style and high standard of presenting the results of personality and culture research. In that work, the results of the analysis, consisting of a "psychocultural synthesis" in which cultural analyses are combined with "the better established processes of the psychoanalytic school," are presented before the descriptive psychological data. This section, written by DuBois, makes up about a fourth of the monograph, and is designed to account for the development of Alorese modal personality. It is accompanied by a brief analysis written by Kardiner. The biographies and test results make up almost three-fourths of the volume. Each autobiography is individually analyzed by Kardiner, who also supplies a general conclusion about all of them. The material on the Rorschach was written by Oberholzer.

The procedure of validation in the Alor study consists, then, essentially in the claim to having demonstrated that modal personality types exist in the psychological data (the Rorschachs and the autobiographies), that these types coincide with one another and with the basic personality structure inferred from the cultural data, and that the methods used in the demonstration are mutually independent. This claim has been generally accepted and the procedure widely followed, not only as a method for validating basic personality construction, but as a general method for confirming inferences of typical personality and of psychological processes based on cultural data and ethnographic techniques of observation and interview.

In these extensions of the method, refinements of statistical manipulation, of sampling, and of devices to assure independence have been introduced. Many of these were suggested by the Alor study itself. The individual variability in the Alorese psychological data, for example, was as striking as the existence of common characteristics. There were important discrepancies among the results of the different methods: Oberholzer found little evidence for neurotic anxiety, while Kardiner insists this is a dominant trend. Could the different methods be strictly independent, moreover, if both cultural and psychological data were collected by the same person who, in addition, shared the theoretical framework of the psychoanalyst and was consulted both by him and the Rorschach expert in the process of interpretation? A sample of eight autobiographies and thirty-seven Rorschachs may not be sufficiently large, or sufficiently representative of a village population of 180, a village cluster of 600, and an Alorese population of 70,000. DuBois herself points out that the subjects of the autobiographies "do not represent the ideal or 'type' person of the village but represent the less successful and the 'average' " (1944, p. 191). How is this kind of "average" to be defined? Linton said that if the hypothesis of basic personality structure was correct, "the bulk of the individuals within a given society" should have the personality features ascribed to it (1945, p. xi). Does this mean a majority, a plurality, an arithmetic mean, or a mode?

These questions, and procedures designed to answer them, loom large in recent modal personality studies. There are, however, several important shifts in emphasis which come with the increasing use of psychological tests. The opinion grows that the study of modal personality by direct psychological data need not be pursued for the purpose of confirming deductions from cultural data, but is important in its own right as well as in the study of the psychology of acculturation, values, and so forth. Some have gone so far as to suggest that, since the psychological methods are more objective and quantitative, they should replace the more qualitative ethnographic method. This proposal is not workable, for as Kluckhohn and Leighton have pointed out, success in administering and analyzing the psychological tests in another culture depends upon a minimum acquaintance with the culture of the people tested, and an entirely "blind" analysis would have given markedly skewed results (*Children of the People,* p. 226–27; but see also Kluckhohn and Rosenzweig, 1949).

This conclusion is further borne out in another recent study (Gladwin and Sarason's *Truk: Man in Paradise*), where discrepancies between the psychologist's and the anthropologist's interpretations occurred because the psychologist did not know certain essential facts about the culture. This same study, however, demonstrates the value of combining psychological and ethnographic methods. Not only did the psychologist's results add important information about individuals, but they also gave the anthropologist leads to certain things in the culture which he might otherwise have overlooked. In this study also, the psychologist's analysis of the psychological data (twenty-three Rorschachs and TAT's) agreed in the main with the anthropologist's analysis of autobiographies of the same individuals and with his analysis of Trukese personality based on cultural data. There was no psychoanalyst in the Truk study; the anthropologist took the responsibility for the "psychodynamic analysis" of the culture.

Another significant innovation of the Truk study is the reversal of the direction of validating procedure: the psychologist first derives a portrait of the typical personality from the psychological data, and this is checked against the anthropologist's portrait based on observation of behavior and ethnographic data. The assumption behind this procedure is just the reverse of that used in the Alor study:

> If we assume that the psychologically derived data present a true picture of Trukese personality (in those aspects with which they deal), we would expect to find the psychological characteristics there defined also reflected in the overt behavior of the people as this is delineated through the use of anthropological techniques in the preceding chapters. Insofar as we find the personality characteristics reflected in behavior we may consider the psychological analysis to be valid; contradictions, however, for which there is no ready explanation must lead us to suspect the adequacy of both the anthropological and psychological data in the area under consideration. (Gladwin and Sarason, 1953, p. 223)

The authors (one an anthropologist and the other a psychologist) acknowledge that to begin with a derivation of personality from descriptions of behavior is an equally legitimate procedure. They prefer to give priority, however, to projective test data because they believe that this would result in "a better balanced and more complete inventory of significant psychological characteristics" (p. 223). Their choice does not imply, however, that the psychological analysis is completely independent of the ethnographic analysis nor that it can stand by itself, for they conclude, as did Kluckhohn and Leighton, that "a blind analysis of projective tests, taken alone, does not necessarily provide an adequate or complete picture of the personalities of persons of a culture other than our own" (p. 246).

It is perhaps inevitable that the increasing use of psychological data about individuals in personality and culture studies should shift the attention to problems of individual variability. This, at any rate, has been a focus in recent studies. The authors of the Truk study say they are interested in differences more than in similarities (p. 291). While they describe "typical" Trukese personality and believe that their sample, which contains 13.3% of the adult males and 14.1% of adult females on Truk, is significant, they are not interested in the sampling problem or in a precise statistical definition of the central tendencies. They concentrate instead on the variations in personality development as a function of variations in life experiences, e.g., having a parent of the same sex with whom to identify, size of household, the "times" during which one grows up, and the like.

The statistical problems raised by the "modal personality" concept have received attention in other recent studies. The results of two of these are of fundamental significance and I shall discuss them briefly.

In *The Modal Personality Structure of the Tuscarora Indians as Revealed by the Rorschach Test* (1952a), Anthony Wallace, an anthropologist, used Rorschach tests collected on the reservation near Niagara Falls, and ethnographic analysis, for a study of modal personality types. The author says that the results of the study surprised him, since, even in this small homogeneous community of six hundred, the individual variability was great. Finding common personality characteristics became a difficult problem. Wallace starts with DuBois' notion of "modal personality" as a central tendency in psychological data and develops it in rigorous statistical fashion. In order to avoid confusion with "basic personality structure" and other concepts of typical personality which include cultural variables, he goes to the other extreme of operational specificity, and defines "modal personality structure" exclusively in terms of Rorschach data and special statistical procedures:

> . . . modal personality structure is defined as that type of personality structure, formulated in terms of the Rorschach test, from which the obtained Rorschach records of more individuals are indistinguishable in certain chosen dimensions than are indistinguishable in these dimensions from any other definable type. (p. 55)

While this kind of definition calls our attention to the dependence of "modal personality" on the specific psychological tests and statistical techniques used, it has the disadvantage of being so restricted that a new concept of modal personality would have to be introduced each time a new psychological test or statistical technique was adopted. The definition is not, however, essential to the methods and results of Wallace's study, or to the two questions it was designed to answer, namely: "What is the typical Tuscarora Indian like psychologically?" "What is the type of psychological structure most characteristic of the adult Tuscarora Indians of this community, in so far as it can be inferred from the obtained Rorschach sample?"

Wallace's statistical procedure, suggested to him by a psychologist, introduces a method for deriving a group profile of psychological traits as they are actually associated in individuals, in contrast to the older method of combining mean scores into a profile of means, which may have no individual counterpart. Wallace plots a frequency distribution for each of twenty-one Rorschach personality indicators, calculates a mode for each of the twenty-one factors, and adds a standard deviation on either side of the mode to define a "modal range" for each factor. The "modal class" is then defined as consisting of those individual Rorschach records which fall within the modal range in every one of the twenty-one categories. When he analyzed the individual Rorschach records in this way, Wallace found that twenty-six out of seventy, or 37% of the sample, fell into the modal class. He also found that sixteen records (23%) "clustered about the modal type," i.e. fell into the modal range in some categories but not in all. There were twenty-eight cases (40%) which were neither *modal* nor *submodal*. Four different groups are distinguishable in this non-modal class, the largest of which accounts for 18% of the total sample.

The twenty-six modal records were then interpreted as if they were the Rorschach of a single individual (by using the mean values for the twenty-one categories, as well as qualitative clues) to produce a portrait of the modal personality structure. Wallace himself did all the calculations and interpretations, with some assistance from the Hallowells, who also knew the culture. A clinical psychologist did "blind" interpretations of some of the data.

While technically it might be argued that the 37% belonging to the "modal class" represent the largest single type, it would be difficult on the basis of the distribution of the other groups to argue that this group alone stands out as the "typical Tuscarora personality," particularly if we have to call 40% of the population non-typical and deviant.

Moreover the case is not helped by a consideration of the cultural and social relevance of the "modal type." Wallace could find no significant correlation between the presence of individuals in the modal class and their sociological roles. The closest he found to a correlation was that one small group of deviants shared the common characteristic of having highly individualized roles.

One kind of correlation between the psychological data and the cultural data does emerge: the most frequent personality traits, taken as discrete traits and not as associated in individual personalities, are also most frequently reflected in the culture. This conclusion is based on impressions and not on statistical data. Although Wallace introduces a statistical conception of "modal" culture, he does not quantify the cultural data he presents.

Using the same statistical techniques, Wallace analyzed 102 Ojibwa records collected by Hallowell east of Lake Winnipeg and found that 28.4% of the sample fell into the modal class. He interpreted these records and compared the Ojibwa profiles with the Tuscarora. While there were certain points of marked resemblance, the differences were significant. Only 4.9% of the Ojibwa fell into the Tuscarora modal class. Wallace concludes from this comparison that the two groups have psychologically different modal personalities and that these differences are a function of the cultural differences.

Another study dealing with similar problems is Bert Kaplan's *A Study of Rorschach Responses in Four Cultures* (1954). Kaplan, a psychologist, analyzed the Rorschachs of 157 adults (ages 17 to 40), half war veterans and half not, who came from four different but geographically adjacent cultural groups in northwestern New Mexico —Zuni Indian, Navaho Indian, Mormon, and Spanish American. He found the personality differences among individuals in each group greater than the differences among groups. He concluded that while "something like modal personality characteristics do indeed exist," in the sense that "there are trends closely related to cultural patterns that characterize a number of people within each group," this number "is ordinarily less than the majority," and that "large areas of personality vary without respect to cultural influence" (pp. 31–32).

Kaplan's interpretation of these results raises a provocative question about the entire notion of "modal personality" and its relation to cultural influence.

That great variability exists does not argue against the influence of culture on personality; it means merely that cultural influences do not necessarily create uniformity in a group. All individuals interact with their cultures. However human beings are not passive recipients of their culture. They accept, reject, or rebel against the cultural forces to which they are oriented. In many cultures, including our own, there exists a pattern of outward conformity and inner rebellion and deviation. It is probably correct to say that individuals seem a good deal more similar than they really are. (p. 32)

Generally speaking, the program for validating "basic personality structure," "configurational personality," and other derivations of typical personality from cultural data and social institutions has disappointed early expectations. The introduction of psychological data about individual personalities has not led to demonstrations that "a vast majority" or "the bulk" of individuals in a culture conform to a dominant personality type. Some central tendencies have been revealed in the psychological data, but the "modal types" are usually far fewer than a majority of individuals and the individual variability in types is as striking as are the similarities. While the various studies do show some agreement among results obtained by different methods, this agreement is never complete. Significant discrepancies have been found among the results of different psychological techniques, as well as between psychological and ethnographic methods. It has not proved possible, or desirable, moreover, to achieve strict independence of data and methods: "blind" interpretations of psychological data have had to be helped out with some knowledge of the culture interpreted, in order to establish applicability of tests, to administer them, and to keep interpretations from going astray. A working division of labor among anthropologist, psychoanalyst, and clinical psychologist has not prevented these different kinds of specialists from learning from one another or from pooling different theories, methods, and data in order to deal with problems which are inherently interdisciplinary. The idea that there is a unique procedure of validation, which begins with a presentation of descriptive ethnographic data and goes on to "psychodynamic analysis," then to verification by psychological data, has been abandoned in favor of multiple procedures involving alternative sequences and combinations of steps. It is now more usual to analyze the psychological data first and then to check this analysis against cultural data, than to do the reverse.

One of the most interesting questions raised by these modal personality studies concerns the significance of the discrepancies found between the psychological and the cultural results, respectively. The absence of one-to-one correlations between the two sets of results is usually taken as a failure of verification and as an indication that one or the other is "incorrect." Perhaps some of these incongruencies are objective facts, and those theories which have led us to expect isomorphic congruencies of culture and personality types are incorrect. It may well turn out that the not-quite-independent methods and data of anthropologist, psychologist, and psychoanalyst combine to yield *results* which are genuinely independent. In that case, what would be needed is a theory which will account for noncongruence of modal personality and culture as an objective fact and not merely as a result of failures in method. Explorations in this direction will be found in Inkeles and Levinson (1954), in Inkeles *et al.* (1958), and in Bendix (1952).

ACCULTURATION AND CHANGE IN MODAL PERSONALITY STRUCTURE

With few exceptions (Thomas and Znaniecki, 1917–18; Redfield, 1930, pp. 222–23; Thurnwald, 1932), the earlier approach to acculturation neglected the psychological dimension of the process and concentrated on the enumeration of discrete culture traits which did or did not change. The development of an interest in characterizing cultures in terms of "configurational personality" and of "modal personality" naturally turned attention to the problem of the relation of culture change to personality change. While the Rorschach and other projective tests were being applied to establish the "modal personality" of non-western cultures, another series of studies applied these tests to determine the psychological consequences of the cultural changes people in these cultures experienced as a result of contact with Western civilization. It is not essential in such studies to presuppose a concept of "typical personality" that is jointly validated by ethnological and psychometric data. Many of the studies bypass this assumption by seeking direct correlation between degrees or levels of acculturation as expressed in cultural terms and personality change or persistence as measured by projective tests. To the extent, however, that ethnological and psychological methods seemed to agree in validating a "modal personality type," confidence in the use of psychological tests in acculturation studies increased.

One of the first to apply projective tests to study the psychological dimension of acculturation was Hallowell. He has also made other contributions to culture and personality theory and research, including several important papers on the cultural patterning of fear, anxiety, and aggression among tribal groups (1938, 1940, 1941), as well as papers on cultural factors in the perception of space, time, and the self (1937, 1951a, 1954).

Hallowell's method for studying the effects of acculturation on modal personality is based on the systematic comparison of the Rorschach protocols of three different groups of Ojibwa Indians representing three different levels of acculturation. He first compared two of these groups living on the Berens River in Canada—the Inland group (44 subjects) and the Lakeside group (58 subjects)—and found that although there were some psychological differences between the two groups, the essential continuity of personality was unmistakable (1942). This indicated that acculturation could take place without radical change in modal personality structure. This conclusion was reinforced for Hallowell when he compared the psychological profile derived from the Rorschachs with what he pieced together from seventeenth and eighteenth century observations made by missionaries, explorers, and traders (1946b). The Berens River Ojibwa, particularly the less acculturated Inland group, seemed to match the modal personality of the aboriginal Indians. When, however, he brought into the comparison a third highly acculturated group of 115 subjects, at Lac du Flambeau, Wisconsin, some striking contrasts emerged. A core of generic traits was still recognizable as the Ojibwa modal personality among the Flambeau protocols. But the degree of psychological contrast with the Berens River groups overshadowed the differences between the Inland and Lakeside groups. Hallowell interprets the Flambeau profile as that of an "introversive personality structure pushed to the limits of its functional adequacy" and as being "thrown back on its psychological heels" (1951a). Because the records of the Flambeau children resemble those of the adults, he believes there is a kind of "frustration of maturity" among them. Using a quantitative measure of adjustment, he finds the Berens River groups show a better adjustment than the Flambeau group.

Why there is so much strain in the Flambeau group and why there is the beginning of a change in the Ojibwa modal personality, Hallowell is not sure. He does not believe the explanation lies in "acculturation" considered as an abstract and inevitable force but rather in a set of complex factors difficult to analyze and not yet very well understood. One of these may be the more rapid rates of acculturation at Flambeau which have not permitted individuals to readapt to the changing situation. Another crucial factor may be the weakening of the aboriginal value and belief systems and the lack of any positive substitute. The Flambeau Ojibwa "are attempting as best they may, to survive under conditions which, as yet, offer no culturally defined values and goals that have become vitally significant for them and which might serve as the psychological means that would lead to a more positive adjustment" (1951a).

The method of studying the modal personality changes in relation to acculturation pioneered by Hallowell on the Ojibwa has also been used by MacGregor on the Sioux (1946), by Billig, Gillin, and Davidson in Guatemala (1947–48), by Abel and Hsu with Chinese (1949), by Barnouw on the Wisconsin Chippewa (1950), by Vogt on Navaho veterans (1951), by Wallace on the Tuscarora (1952), by Caudill with Japanese (1952, 1956), and by Spindler on the Menomini (1955).

NATIONAL CHARACTER

"Our understanding of international affairs is about where our understanding of primitive peoples was before the anthropologists attempted the serious study of how primitive people learned their cultural behavior." (Benedict, 1946b)

The pressures of the second world war, led to efforts, to apply personality and culture theory and methods to the delineation of personality characteristics and processes "typical" of modern nations. Ruth Benedict and Margaret Mead were leaders in the organization of these efforts; Kluckhohn, Leighton, Gorer, and Bateson also were important contributors from the side of anthropology. Anthropologists, however, did not go it alone; they joined with historians, political scientists, sociologists, economists, and other students of national states, as well as with psychologists and psychiatrists and psychoanalysts. Studies have been published on American character (Mead, 1942; Gorer, 1948; Fromm, 1941; Riesman, 1950; Erikson, 1950; Potter, 1954), Russian character (Gorer and Rickman, 1949; Leites, 1954; Mead, 1951a; Dicks, 1952; Inkeles *et al.,* 1958), Japanese character (Gorer, 1943; Benedict, 1946a; Haring, 1946), German character (Fromm, 1936; Erikson, 1950; Dicks, 1950; Rodnick, 1948; Lowie, 1945, 1954), English character (Gorer, 1955), Hindu character (Carstairs, 1957; Narain, 1957), Balinese character (Belo, 1935; Bateson and Mead, 1942), and others.

These national character studies are an applied field insofar as they were motivated by the practical desire to know more about one's national enemies, allies, and self in war time; they nevertheless represent a natural extension of personality and culture theory, and have in turn made basic contributions to it.

Obvious obstacles were posed by the differences between modern nations and primitive tribes. Some anthropologists, who had worked on personality and culture studies in primitive cultures, were understandably reluctant to apply their methods to the enormous and heterogeneous populations of modern nations with their complex histories of social and cultural change (Linton, 1951). The sampling problem alone became formidable. Yet, as Ruth Benedict, arguing for the feasibility of "national character" studies (1946b), has pointed out, the anthropologist working on civilized nations has a head start because of the greater availability of data—statistical, political, economic, historical, and literary—and the presence of experts who have specialized on national studies.

One kind of anthropological data, that provided by direct field study, has not always been available. This practical limitation has necessitated an indirect approach, making use of previous field studies, interviews with special informants, and the study of "culture at a distance" through the analysis of folklore, literature, films, drama, political speeches and propaganda, and other cultural products (Benedict 1946b, Mead and Metraux, 1953). Even this procedure, however, does not represent so much an innovation in method as an extension of older methods. Benedict's analysis of Japanese mythology is not very different from her analysis of Zuni mythology, as Katherine Spencer has observed (1956).

The applications of personality and culture theory to the study of national character have been undertaken from several different starting points and have resulted in several different theories of national character. I shall discuss three of these: national character conceived as "cultural character," as "social character," and as "modal personality."

NATIONAL CHARACTER AS CULTURAL CHARACTER

The concept of "cultural character" has been defined by Margaret Mead as "the regularities in the intrapsychic organization of the individual members of a given society that are to be attributed to these individuals' having been reared within that culture" (Mead and Metraux, 1953, p. 33). From the extended explanation which Mead gives of the concept and from the way in which it has been used in studies with which she has been associated, one may conclude that "cultural character" is a novel synthesis of Benedict's "configurational personality" and Kardiner's "basic personality structure." The synthesis was not made in one jump or by a single individual but developed gradually and indirectly. Benedict herself applied the configurational theory to a modern nation in her study of Japan, *The Chrysanthemum and the Sword* (1946). Some of the Japanese criticism of this book— which accepts the general accuracy of the characterization but finds it a bit static and reminiscent of Sunday school sermons (Bennett and Nagai, *Japanese Journal of Ethnology,* 1949, *Appraisal,* pp. 139– 40)—simply underlines the fact that Benedict did achieve her purpose of grasping the underlying values of the Japanese ethos. The analysis in this work adds an important ingredient to Benedict's earlier use of configurational theory, by attaching great significance to certain aspects of Japanese child rearing. Many adult personality traits and the apparent contradictions in Japanese character are traced to the peculiarities of Japanese teasing, and to toilet training and discontinuities in conditioning (1946a, pp. 259, 263, 266, 271–2, 273, 286, 290–91). Even greater emphasis was placed on these child-rearing practices by Gorer, one of Benedict's co-workers, in his studies of Japanese character (1943). It is this aspect of the analysis which brings "cultural character" so close to "basic personality structure."

Yet Mead (1954b, 1955), Benedict (1949), and Gorer (1951) are essentially justified when they reply to their critics by denying that they have attributed specific causality to child-rearing practices. For when a theory of socialization is combined with configurational analysis, particular modes of child-rearing become part patterns in the total configuration of patterns. They are indeed crucial parts, from the standpoint of transmitting the configuration to the next generation, as they are then the media of communication between parents and children, the forums within which the children "learn" the character of the adults. For these reasons, child-rearing practices may give the outside observers "clues" to the adult character without being considered "causes" of that character.

Another significant ingredient in the theory of "cultural character" is the notion of thematic patterns in the interpersonal relations characteristic of a national group. This idea seems to have been originally suggested by Gregory Bateson in an early paper on national character (Bateson, 1942a). Bateson was specifically concerned with the problem of finding the "common character" in communities that have stable differentiations of social roles among their members. His solution was to look for the common character in specifically patterned relationships among the differentiated groups or individuals. These relationships are generally, but not invariably, bipolar, for example, dominance-submission, succoring-dependence, exhibitionism-spectatorship. These three happen to be examples of *complementary* relationship: if a member of one group is dominant, a member of another group will be submissive. There are also *symmetrical* relations in which the behavior of one individual will call forth similar behavior of the same kind in another. Bateson assumes that these bipolar patterns are "unitary within the individual."

> If we know that an individual is trained in overt expression of one half of one of these patterns, e.g., in dominance behavior, we can predict with certainty (though not in precise language) that the seeds of the other half—submission—are simultaneously sown in his personality. We have to think of the individual, in fact, as trained in dominance-submission, not in either dominance *or* submission. (1942a, pp. 76–77)

Bateson's theory is that different national characters differ, not in the specific themes of the relationship, since these recur, but in the proportions and combinations of themes. The Balinese, he suggests, feel that dependence and exhibitionism and high status go naturally together, whereas Europeans associate high status with succoring. He also suggested that an important qualitative difference between English and American parent-child relations could be delineated in terms of a reversed spectator-exhibitionism relationship.

In a later paper (1949), Bateson applied these ideas to an analysis of the value system of Balinese culture. The same concepts were also applied in national character studies by Margaret Mead, Ruth Benedict, Rhoda Metraux, and others (Mead and Metraux, 1953, pp. 365–397).

Gorer's study of the American character (1948) used a similar scheme for the organization and interpretation of the materials.

The chief difference between Bateson's idea and the concept of "basic personality structure" or of "modal personality type" is that he locates the common and distinctive characteristics in culturally standardized patterns of interpersonal relations among social groups, whereas the other two concepts locate them in a single pattern of traits frequently to be found associated in individuals. The particular kinds of interpersonal relations emphasized, e.g., dependence-succoring, were undoubtedly suggested by psychoanalytic theory. An analogous theory was developed by the psychiatrist Harry Stack Sullivan (1940–45, 1948). The germs of the idea, however, were already present in Bateson's study of Iatmul ethos (1935, 1936) and in Mead's study of sex and temperament among the Arapesh, Mundugumor, and Tchambuli (1935). What Bateson added is a more comprehensive idea of how several different kinds of interpersonal relations can assume functional patterns in relating culturally differentiated groups, and how these patterns may vary in different cultures.

Bateson's concept of national character as the set of culturally patterned themes recurring in interpersonal relations also adds, to his *Naven* theory of "schismogenesis" or cumulative interactions, the parent-child relationship. This relationship figures in a dual capacity: first, it is one of several kinds of interpersonal relationships manifesting the characteristic themes of the culture. From the standpoint of the growing child, however, it is also a crucial relationship, since in it he is trained in the *total* pattern of relationships characteristic of his society. The Balinese pattern of non-cumulative interaction, for example, Bateson finds in the relationship of parents and children, but he also notes that "childhood experience trains the child away from seeking climax in interpersonal relations" (1949, p. 53), and that the positive values supporting this pattern "are incorporated into the character structure during childhood" (*ibid*). In the 1958 Epilogue to the reissue of *Naven,* Bateson asserts that "the patterns of a society as a major entity can by learning be introjected or conceptualized by the participant individuals" (Bateson, 1958, p. 292). The patterns referred to in this passage include not only specific patterns of symmetrical or complementary interactions, but also the patterns of sequential change from the symmetrical to the complementary (*ibid,* p. 291).

The individual learns, according to this theory, both the particular action patterns in which he participates and the *pattern of patterns* which characterizes the society as a whole. This is not the place to discuss the details of the theory. Bateson's acknowledged model is the self-correcting causal circuit of communications theory, although other antecedents for this kind of theory can be found in George Herbert Mead's theory of "taking the role of a generalized other" and in Sapir's and Benedict's ideas about the unconscious patterning of behavior (G. H. Mead, 1934, 1956; Benedict, 1934b; Sapir, 1927).

The inclusion of the parent-child relationship, and of a theory of patterns in interpersonal relations, paves the way for the conception of "cultural character" as part of a circular system. If the child's relation to its parents is conceived as a mutually interactive system within which the parent reacts to the child's stimuli as well as stimulates the child to respond, then the theory of linear, one-way causal sequences from specific child-rearing practices to adult personality traits, postulated, for example, in the theory of basic personality structure, has to be dropped (Mead and Metraux, 1953, pp. 39–40). And when the negative feedback idea from cybernetics came along, it was assimilated to a theory of personality and culture as a circular causal system (Bateson, 1958, Epilogue). Within such a circular system "the method of child rearing, the presence of a particular literary tradition, the nature of the domestic and public architecture, the religious beliefs, the political system, are all conditions within which a given kind of personality develops" (Mead, 1951b).

Despite this assumption of circularity, many of the national character studies have concentrated on the peculiarities of child-rearing. These studies, it is true, usually deny that they impute specific causality to a specific form of swaddling or toilet training. They say that they find in a specific child-rearing practice the "clues" to the adult practice or a critical point in the communication of the cultural character to the child. These explanations are consistent with the theory of circular causality, but they reveal, as well, a certain lingering preference for psychoanalytic theories of personality formation (however modified), and a reluctance to follow through the implications of a theory of circular causality and to develop a theory of personality and culture as a complex interacting system. The reluctance is quite understandable, considering the complexities of modern nations. Yet a small beginning might be made by considering how such circular systems are affected by historical changes.

Studies of national character guided by the "cultural character" concept have been severely criticized for neglecting problems of sampling and scientific controls (Klineberg, 1944, 1949, 1950; Farber, 1950, 1955; Inkeles and Levinson, 1954; Mandelbaum, 1953). To these criticisms Mead has replied that by anthropological methods one can learn a great deal from single informants, provided that the social and cultural position of the informant is fully specified. Another reply she has given states that many of the "cultural character" studies have been concerned only with an "exploratory stage in which a set of hypotheses is developed," and not with the stages of confirmation, quantification, and experimental verification which would involve sample surveys (Mead and Metraux, 1953, p. 7; Mead, 1951b, 1953, 1955). I should like to add to these replies that because "cultural character" derives from configurational theory, which attributes "personality types" to cultures as wholes and which derives these "types" from cultural data predominantly, it does not appear to call for statistical studies of individuals. (See Benedict, 1946a, p. 16, "The ideal authority for any statement in this book would be the proverbial man in the street. It would be anybody.") Only when additional assumptions are introduced about the relation of configurational types to individual members of a culture, does it become necessary to introduce psychological data on individuals, and concepts to deal with statistical distributions, such as "modal personality type."

NATIONAL CHARACTER AS SOCIAL CHARACTER

The theory of "cultural character" assumes that in every culture a typical personality is transmitted to the young which more or less corresponds to the dominant configuration of that culture. The theory does not, however, attempt to explain the social functions of such correspondence. Nor does the theory of "basic personality structure" have much to say about such questions. In these theories, the integration and coherence of a culture is taken as a kind of ultimate "given," assumed to be essential to the well-functioning of a culture and to vary in different cultures. The relations of these culture patterns to history and to environmental changes are considered to be accidental and indirect. Erich Fromm's theory of "social character," while sharing the assumptions of these other theories about the cultural transmission of "fitting" "typical" personalities, tries, in addition, to explain the social-historical functions of the types. The explanation links the "typical" personality of a culture, or, as Fromm calls it, "the social character," to the "objective social necessities" confronting the society. To satisfy these "necessities" effectively, a society needs to translate them into character traits of the individual members so that they will *want* to do what they *have* to do. Such shared character traits constitute the "social character" of the society, and the process of translation takes place through the parents' training of the children. The parents have acquired *their* character traits either from their parents or directly, in response to changing social conditions. Fromm has made applications of this theory to Germany and to the United States (1941).

This theory has a circular and teleological tone, but it is really an at-

tempt to combine the old idea of the adaptiveness of social institutions
to environmental conditions with a modified psychoanalytic characterology. One of its starting points seems to have been Weber's theory
that industrial capitalism requires a set of disciplines which may historically have been inculcated by the acceptance of a "protestant ethic"
(Fromm 1931, 1941, 1949).

> Modern, industrial society, for instance, could not have attained its ends
> had it not harnessed the energy of free men for work in an unprecedented
> degree. He had to be molded into a person who was eager to spend most of
> his energy for the purpose of work, who acquired discipline, particularly or-
> derliness and punctuality, to a degree unknown in most other cultures. It
> would not have sufficed if each individual had to make up his mind con-
> sciously every day that he wanted to work, to be on time, etc., since any such
> conscious deliberation would have led to many more exceptions than the
> smooth functioning of society can afford. Threat and force would not have
> sufficed either as motive for work since the highly differentiated work in
> modern industrial society can only be the work of free men and not of forced
> labor. The *necessity* for work, for punctuality and orderliness had to be
> transformed into a *drive* for these qualities. This means that society had to
> produce such a social character in which these strivings were inherent. (1949,
> pp. 5–6)

Fromm does not necessarily approve of the particular adaptations and
"social characters" of particular societies. On the contrary, he makes
a point of emphasizing that the formation of any "social character"
kills individual "spontaneity" and severely restricts the opportunities
for self-realization. The process usually results in "socially patterned
defects," a "pathology of normalcy."

> It happens that, in most cultures, human relationships are greatly deter-
> mined by irrational authority. People function in our society, as in most so-
> cieties on the record of history, by becoming adjusted to their social role at
> the price of giving up part of their own will, their originality and spontaneity.
> While every human being represents the whole of mankind with all its poten-
> tialities, any functioning society is and has to be primarily interested in its
> self-preservation. The particular ways in which a society functions are deter-
> mined by a number of *objective* economic and political factors, which are
> given at any point of historical development. Societies have to operate within
> the possibilities and limitations of their particular historical situation. In order
> that any society may function well, its members must acquire the kind of
> character which makes them *want* to act in the way they *have* to act as mem-
> bers of the society or of a special class within it. They have to *desire* what
> objectively is *necessary* for them to do. *Outer force* is to be replaced by *inner
> compulsion,* and by the particular kind of human energy which is channeled
> into character traits. As long as mankind has not attained a state of organi-
> zation in which the interest of the individual and that of society are identical,
> the aims of society have to be attained at a greater or lesser expense of the
> freedom and spontaneity of the individual. This aim is performed by the
> process of child training and education. While education aims at the develop-

ment of a child's potentialities, it has also the function of reducing his independence and freedom to the level necessary for the existence of that particular society. Although societies differ with regard to the extent to which the
child must be impressed by irrational authority, it is always part of the function of child training to have this happen. (1944, p. 381)

These judgments of Fromm's are based on a "humanistic ethics" and a
social philosophy of how man's potentialities may be better realized in a
"sane society" (1948, 1955).

The theory of "social character" has been further developed and
applied in *The Lonely Crowd, A Study of the Changing American
Character* by David Riesman in collaboration with Reuel Denney and
Nathan Glazer (1950). This work introduces several important modifications in the theory and applies it to an interpretation of American
character. Fromm's basic definition of "social character" is used, but a
somewhat different typology, of "tradition-directed," "inner-directed,"
and "other-directed" types, is employed. These types are defined with
reference to different characteristic ways of assuring conformity to social
requirements—namely, following tradition, following a set of goals internalized early in life, and following the expectations of others.
Another innovation is that the "social requirements" are localized in
terms of the phase of population growth characteristic of a country.
Using F. W. Notestein's (1945) population curve of growth, Riesman
and his associates postulate that a society of "high growth potential" will
develop "in its typical members" the tradition-directed social character,
a society of "transitional population growth" will develop inner-directed
social characters, and a society of "incipient decline" will develop
"other-directed" types. An attempt is made to show that the United
States, as it becomes a society of "incipient population decline," is developing "other-directed" types among the urban middle class. These
changes are accompanied by changes in the "agents of character formation": the influence of parents and teachers, so vital in the formation
of "inner-direction," is being superseded by the influence of "peer-
groups" and the mass media, fostering "other-direction." This enlarge-
ment of the theory of socialization is another significant amendment to
Fromm's theory.

Within a particular society at any given time, different types of social
character coexist because of migration from countries in different
phases of population growth and because of differential rates of internal
change, two factors of great importance in North America. The theory
does not attempt to develop the details of the different statistical distribution of types that would result from different combinations of
these factors. In this sense it makes no predictions about "modal"
personality types or other typical values. In another volume, *Faces in*

the Crowd (1952), Riesman and others sketch individual portraits, but this is not intended as a confirming sample survey.

One thing the theory does assert is that there is a relative temporal order among the three types. The typology, in other words, has a built-in theory of historical change, something which is missing from practically all the other typologies. In this form the theory of "social character" becomes a comparative theory of social history. Some of the possible relevances of such a theory are suggested in the following picture of the "characterological struggle":

> We can picture for ourselves the last few hundred years of western history in terms of a gradual succession to dominance of each of these three types. The tradition-directed type gives way to the inner-directed, and the inner-directed gives way to the other-directed. Shifts in type of society and type of character do not, of course, occur all at once. Rather, there is an overlapping, so that within a given culture one may find groups representing all phases of the population curve and demonstrating, with more or less lag, a variety of characterological adaptations to their particular phase. This mixture is made even more various by the migration of peoples, by imperialism, and by forces that constantly throw together people of different character structures, people who "date," metaphorically, from different points on the population curve.
>
> The struggle of classes and societies may therefore be viewed, to some extent, as a struggle among different characterological adaptations to the situation created by the dominance of a given mode of insuring conformity. These character types, like geological or archaeological strata, pile one on top of the other. A cross section of society at any given time reveals the earlier as well as the later character types, the earlier changed through the pressure of being submerged by the later. One notices the dominance of tradition-directed types in Latin America, agricultural southern Europe, in Asia and Africa. One notices the dominance of inner-directed types in rural and small-town United States and Canada, in northwestern Europe, and to a degree in Central Europe. One notices an energetic campaign to introduce the inner-directed pattern in eastern Europe, in Turkey, and in parts of Asia. And one notices the beginnings of dominance by other-directed types in the metropolitan centers of the United States and, more doubtfully, their emergence in the big cities of north-western Europe. This last and newest type is spreading outward into areas where inner-direction still prevails, just as the latter is spreading into unconquered areas where tradition-directed types still hang on. (*The Lonely Crowd*, pp. 31–32)

The succession of characterological adaptations here described refers primarily to the spread of western industrialization to other parts of the world during the last two hundred years. This is undoubtedly the major focus of interest of Riesman and associates. They have studied the interaction of recent social changes with changing character types, primarily in the United States and to a lesser extent in other parts of the world (Lerner, 1958). In theory, however, the typology of social characters could be applied to other periods of history. *The Lonely Crowd* does, in fact, refer to a possible application to ancient Greece (pp. 27–29). To the extent that such application is undertaken, the theory of social character becomes a theory of cyclical and recurrent processes rather than of linear, historical change.

Applications of the theory to pre–industrial periods have not been numerous, however. One reason for this may be the absence of a detailed social psychological explanation of how a given population phase, or objective social condition, calls forth a particular kind of social character. This is a problem just beginning to receive some attention. In *People of Plenty* (1954) David Potter sketches the relation of economic abundance to the formation of American character within a historical perspective. A recent cross-cultural study shows how child training patterns adapt to a subsistence economy (Barry, Child, and Bacon, 1959).

Another aspect of the theory of social character that is being developed is the relation of social character to individual personality. Just as in the theory of basic personality structure, exploration of this relationsnip was stimulated by the use of Rorschach and other psychological tests, so the development of psychological tests for "inner-directed" and "other-directed" types is adding an individual dimension to a theory of social character that began with historically conditioned social and cultural dimensions.

NATIONAL CHARACTER, TRIBAL CHARACTER AND THE PERSONALITY OF SOCIAL GROUPS

Both the sociologically-oriented theory of "social character" and the anthropologically-oriented theory of "cultural character" are the products of efforts to extend the personality and culture theory developed for primitive cultures to modern nations. The extensions have transformed personality and culture theory and have generalized it as a theory of the "typical" personality of nations, tribes, social classes, or occupational, regional, and other significant social groups (Mead and Metraux, 1953; Riesman *et al.,* 1950). In considering whether such generalization is effective and fruitful, we note that there already are some special discussions and studies of the "typical personality" of different social groups, e.g., those of peasants (Francis, 1945; Redfield, 1956), of bureaucrats (Merton, 1940; Roe, 1947), of Indian social classes (Steed, 1955), of a Southwest regional type (Kroeber, 1947; Kluckhohn, 1954; Devereux, 1951), of rural and urban communities (Oeser, 1954a,b; Lewis, 1951; Redfield, 1955), and of the "basic personality of Western man" (Kardiner, 1945).

There are several problems in bringing these and other studies together under a single theory of "typical" personality. We can proceed on the assumption that the theory works in the same manner regardless of the nature and size of the social group. In that case it would be necessary to show how a general factor like child-rearing pattern combines with and explains occupational, status, regional, and other differentiations within a single culture or society (as, e.g., in Davis and Havighurst, 1946). Or we might assume that the general factors, child-rearing or demographic patterns, for example, do not operate directly and in similar fashion on every kind of social unit, but operate indirectly through the distinctive structures of social and cultural organization (Inkeles, 1955). A pattern of "incipient decline," for example, may not operate directly on every family to produce its alleged characterological results, but may operate indirectly through status, occupational, political, and other social groups. Under this assumption it would be necessary to develop a theory which would take account of different levels of natural, psychological, social, and cultural integration. Steward (1956) has made some suggestions in this direction, and Erikson (1950) in his studies of the Yurok and the Sioux attempted interpretations which intuitively, at least, integrate geography, individual development, society, and culture.

Lazarsfeld and Barton (1951) have provided an analysis of the differences in logical types of data that may be usefully applied to this problem of hierarchies of levels. A notable feature of their analysis is the recognition that there may be data characteristic of social units which cannot be analyzed into personal data about the component individuals, and are therefore primary characteristics of the social unit. This corresponds to the anthropologists' recognition of holistic characteristics of cultural groups.

NATIONAL CHARACTER AS MODAL PERSONALITY

In a comprehensive and brilliant critical analysis of national character studies, Inkeles, a sociologist, and Levinson, a psychologist, argue for a restriction of the "national character" concept to modal personality structure.

In our opinion, "national character" ought to be equated with modal personality structure; that is, it should refer to the mode or modes of the distribution of personality variants within a given society. "Societal requiredness" or "congeniality with the culture pattern" should not be part of the *definition* of national character. The *socially required* personality, (for example, the personalities best suited to a bureaucratic or an assertive-individualistic social structure) deserves the status of an independent though significantly related construct. Given this distinction, the degree of congruence between the modal personality structures and the psychological requirements of the social milieu emerges as an important problem for research. (Inkeles and Levinson, 1944, pp. 980–81)

If this restriction were accepted, the sample survey would be the most obvious if not the only method of study of national character.

If national character refers to modes of a distribution of individual personality variants, then its study would seem to require the psychological investigation of adequately large and representative samples of persons, *studied individually*. (*ibid.*)

Other methods, which begin with the analysis of collective documents, cultural plots and themes, standardized child-rearing practices, and other sociocultural patterns, provide leads to or at best a "hypothetical construction" of national character.

"They can never tell us with any conclusiveness what range and varieties of modal personality actually exist in a society" or lead to "adequate demonstration" of the hypothetical constructions. Only a "large-scale study of individuals" can provide these.

These arguments, it seems to me, are more persuasive on the positive side in favor of modal personality as one concept among others of "national character" than they are in their demonstration of the exclusive correctness of this conception. It is true that once the restricted definition is accepted, the methodological conclusions follow in straightforward fashion. But the case for the restriction is a debatable one. In common usage and in studies not based on personality and culture theory, "national character" frequently refers to "way of life," "ethos," and collective ideals, as well as to modal distributions (Castberg, 1954; Ginsberg, 1942; Barker, 1955; Miroglio, 1955; Smellie, 1955). Why should one particular definition be given priority?

The issues here are reminiscent of those raised by Wallace and by Gladwin and Sarason in their criticism of the earlier "basic personality structure" theories. Inkeles and Levinson are quite right to insist on a clear distinction between a descriptive, statistical concept of "modal personality," and the explanatory culture-deductive concepts of "typical personality." They are also right in questioning the assumption of simple congruence between these two orders of concepts. Once the distinction is made, however, the problem of relating the "modal personality" to the society and the culture remains, as Inkeles and Levinson clearly recognize:

Within the context defined by the title of this paper, the problem of "determinants" may be stated as follows: *What regularities in the social conditions of development—in the more or less standardized, sociocultural matrix—help determine the observed regularities (or modes) in adult personality?* (pp. 998–999)

To deal with this problem requires the introduction of such concepts as "cultural character," "basic personality," and "social character," or similar explanatory ideas. What remains of the issue, therefore, once the distinction between the descriptive psychological concepts and the explanatory socio-cultural concepts is made, is the order of procedures for deriving them in particular cases. The decision on that issue, it seems to me, rests not on the adoption of some highly restricted definition of "national character" in terms of "modal personality," but rather on the tactics of research design. Perhaps greater objectivity and mutual independence of method and data is achieved by starting at the psychological end, as Gladwin and Sarason argued. Strict independence is not possible, in any case; eventually the socio-cultural data and the psychological data have to be brought together, so perhaps the starting point does not matter too much.

Under Inkeles' direction, the Russian Research Center at Harvard has made studies of Great Russian "national character" as a set of "modal personality patterns." (See Chapter 5, below.)

> Obviously, not every Great Russian exhibits all, or even necessarily any, of these characteristics. They are, however, found frequently and regularly enough to constitute the more or less typical or modal patterns in the rank and file of the population. We do not assert that they are also characteristic for the elite. (Bauer, Inkeles, Kluckhohn, 1956, p. 135)

The psychological data for the studies were obtained from a group of Soviet refugees who had been displaced by World War II. Three hundred and thirty were given life-history interviews and sentence completion tests, and fifty-one of these took a battery of clinical tests, including the Rorschach, T.A.T., and sentence-completion tests, and several others. A sample of Americans, matched with the Russian sample on age, sex, occupation, and education, was used for comparison. Each test was analyzed separately and the results of all tests, together with "supplementary qualitative material," were used to derive an "evaluative summary" sketch of modal personality characteristics. The statistical distributions have not yet been published and the procedure was not in any case "a simple and direct translation of particular test scores into personality traits" (Inkeles, *et al.,* 1958). In fact "modal" is used in a liberal sense:

> The word modal should not be taken too literally in this context. We have relied on some test scores when only a small proportion of the sample manifested the given response or pattern of responses, if this fits with other evidence in developing a larger picture. (*ibid.*, p. 6)

After the Great Russian "national character" was derived in this fashion, an analysis was made to determine its relation to the Soviet system. This was done essentially in three different ways:

(1) by comparing the general character and policies of the Soviet system with the "modal" personality of the sample,

(2) by comparing the image of the regime entertained by the sample with the "modal personality" of the sample, and

(3) by correlating the social status (defined in terms of occupation and education) of the subjects of the sample with selected personality traits taken as indices of the "modal pattern."

The correlations showed significant class differences in the modal personality: "it is found in its relatively pure form mainly among workers and peasants, is attenuated among those upwardly mobile, and almost disappears at the top of the social hierarchy" (Bauer, *et al.,* p. 137; Inkeles *et al.,* pp. 17–20). The authors believe that these class differences are probably the result of status differences in family rearing experiences (Inkeles, *et al.,* pp. 18–19).

The conclusions of these different kinds of analyses strongly suggest "that there is a fairly massive degree of incongruence between the central personality modes and dispositions of average Russians on the one hand, and the structure of Soviet society, particularly the behavior of the regime, on the other" (Bauer, *et al.,* p. 142).

Although "acutely aware of the smallness of [the] sample," the Harvard investigators are inclined "to assume that the personality modes found in it would be found within the Soviet Union in groups comparable in nationality and occupation" (Inkeles, *et al.,* p. 19).

This "modal personality" approach to Great Russian national character contrasts strongly in method with the "cultural character" approach used by Gorer (1949, 1950a) and by Mead (1951b). In a recent searching analysis, Bell (1958) has discussed how it also differs from Leites' psychoanalytic interpretations of Bolshevik character based on published documents (Leites, 1954), and from historical and political approaches which do not use personality and culture theory.

In spite of these differences in method and concepts, the "modal personality" studies and the "cultural character" studies of the Great Russians agree in many of their results, according to Kluckhohn.

. . . Different observers and analysts, using different methods and data, are in excellent agreement among themselves—and indeed with the Russians. (Kluckhohn, 1955, p. 58)

THE PROBLEM OF VALIDATION:
COHERENCE TESTS AND CORRELATION TESTS

"Modal personality" studies are now generally regarded as the most rigorous available method of validating typical personality constructions based on cultural and institutional data. This view needs to be qualified. A "mode" is not always the most appropriate statistical measure for the variety of distributions that occur. There is also the fundamental possibility, emphasized by Kroeber (1948, pp. 587–8), that two peoples can show much the same psychological character or temperament and yet have different cultures, or that the cultures can be nearly uniform while national character differs. If this is true, then there may still be some kind of personality "typical" of each culture but not a one-to-one correspondence between culture and "modal personality." There are also special conditions when "modal personality" is simply not available as a method of validation: when, for example, the "typical personality" is attributed to the society or culture as a whole, and not distributively to individual members; or when it is attributed to individuals but not in any explicit quantitative way (Mead and Metraux, 1953, p. 15); or when there are not enough psychological data about individuals for statistical treatment.

Because of these limitations of "modal personality" as a method of validation, reliance is placed in many studies of "typical personality" on a test of "coherence" or "congruence" or "internal consistency."

> The most convincing validation still remains one of pattern, of the testing of the hypothesis for intra-cultural and intra-psychic fit. Every piece of cultural behavior is so over-determined in its systematic relationship to every other piece that any discrepancy within the material should immediately demand a revision of the delineation hypothesis established so far. (Mead, 1953, p. 659)

There is, however, not just one general test of "coherence," as the above statement seems to imply. Rather, there are almost as many as there are different kinds of theories of "typical" personality. In another statement within the same paper, Mead suggests this possibility:

> If an attempt is made to delineate national character in addition to the national culture, then the criterion of internal consistency has to be invoked in relation to some psychocultural theory of personality. (1953, p. 659)

Each particular kind of psychocultural theory has, I believe, its own special brand of internal consistency. In Benedict's configurational theory, for example, internal consistency is defined in terms of congruence of cultural items with a given pattern or type. We might call this "pattern" or "type coherence." Its recognition rests essentially on what Kroeber has called "physiognomic" judgment, and Redfield, "portraiture." Kardiner's "basic personality structure" theory implies a different kind of coherence—a coherence of specific primary and secondary institutions within a culture, conceived as antecedents and consequents of a postulated "basic personality structure." Its recognition requires isolation of specific causes and effects and their linear temporal relations. We might call this a "causal coherence." The theory of "cultural character," on the other hand, combines the requirement of "pattern coherence" with an added emphasis on the congruence between child-rearing patterns and the total configuration of the culture. But this congruence is not conceived of in this theory as implying any causal relation. The specific child-rearing practices are identified as transmissive media within the total pattern. The judgments of recognition are mainly physiognomic and stylistic.

The studies in this volume are all studies of pattern, of the stylistic interrelationships of different aspects of childhood, of the way in which in a given culture, the image of the child, the way the child is rewarded and punished, children's toys, the literature written for children, the literature written about children, the selective memories of adults about their childhood, the games children play, their fears and fantasies, hopes and daydreams, and behavior on projective tests are all systematically related to one another. (Mead in Mead and Wolfenstein, 1955, p. 13)

"Pattern coherence" also enters into the theory of "social character," particularly in the conception of society as an organized interdependent system and of the individual as an organized personality. But there is a distinctive kind of coherence implied by this theory—the coherence of social institutions and of the social character with given "objective social necessities." We might call this "functional coherence," for it requires an appraisal of the degree to which a particular society and its people are adapted to given conditions.

All these different kinds of coherence—"pattern," "causal," "functional,"—are intended to apply to single cultures or societies. It is quite conceivable that a society or culture may meet one test of coherence without meeting another. It is also important when applying these tests of coherence to bear in mind that social, cultural, and psychological "inconsistencies" are "normal" occurrences. Not every culture is equally consistent in its own terms, nor is every personality. Characters may have conflicting and even contradictory traits, societies and cultures may show class conflict, conflicts among social norms, culturally sanctioned violation of sacred norms, imaginative projections in art and mythology of anti-norms, and the like. Such conflicts and inconsistencies cannot always be reinterpreted in relation to some kind of coherence but may be brute facts that need to be recognized. They are incompatible not with coherence tests but with theories which assume too much coherence.

Whiting and Child (1953) find the tests of coherence used in the interpretation of a specific case inadequate as a method of validating the psychological hypotheses underlying personality and culture studies. While granting that a coherence test may be useful for understanding a concrete case, they feel "it never provides adequate evidence as to whether [the] hypotheses used are generally valid as general principles." In order to validate such hypotheses, "some means are needed for isolating the antecedent condition from other conditions and determining whether in fact this supposed consequent is observed with some consistency to follow or accompany it" (p. 9). Because the experimental method is not generally available for this purpose, they propose that "the correlational method" be applied cross-culturally as a method of validating general hypotheses. Whiting and Child apply the correlational method themselves to seventy-five primitive cultures, using ethnographic data from the Human Relations Area Files (for sixty-five of the cultures) and from other published sources. The underlying assumption of the study is that "by considering one set of overt customs as representing the way the typical child is treated, and another set of overt customs as representing certain overt behavior in the same person when he becomes a typical adult, these hypotheses may be used to predict that certain customs in the one set should be found to be associated with certain customs in the other set" (1953, p. 35). The hypotheses are drawn mainly from psychoanalytic theory, translated into the language of general behavior theory, and extended to refer "not just to a particular individual, but to the typical member of a society" (*ibid.*).

This correlation test of validation does not represent quite as sharp a break with the coherence tests as Whiting and Child imply. It is very similar to the "causal coherence" test of the Kardiner theory of 1939. And although Kardiner and his associates at first applied their test to individual cultures, they fully intended to multiply cases in order to get statistical correlations:

> Twenty or thirty cultures studied in the manner here delineated will offer safe ground for generalizations based on reliable comparisons. The laws which govern the psychodynamics of social change can then be approximated, if not precisely stated. (Kardiner, 1939, p. 487)

The correlation test also shares with the "causal coherence" test the problem of how to transfer individual psychological theories developed in the clinics of western culture to the customs and institutions of other cultures.

Yet there are certain respects in which the correlation test, as used by Whiting and Child, differs from all the coherence tests. The correlation test uses single cultures as units and single "typical" individuals, but this is done for statistical purposes only; no effort is made to treat cultures or personalities as organized wholes. On the contrary, the treatment is frankly limited and segmental, using only selected fragments of culture and of personality processes as variables to be correlated. They assume that only after these limited hypotheses are validated, can the more integrative interpretations of individual cultures be properly done.

Perhaps the most important difference between the coherence tests and the correlation test is that the latter is designed to validate the psychological hypotheses as general principles of behavior. This is not the aim of the coherence tests. It is true, as Whiting and Child say, that all the theories of tribal and national character make use of psychological hypotheses drawn from psychoanalysis, learning theory, maturation theory, and other sources. It is also true that all of them attach particular importance to childrearing experiences in the formation of "typical" personalities. But they have not assumed that a particular personality and culture study could validate a general psychological theory; at most a particular study might present counter-evidence to limit psychological generalizations, as Malinowski's Trobriand and Mead's Samoan studies did. The problem of validating general psychological theories has been left pretty much to the psychologist, psychoanalyst, and student of individual development. It is not surprising that Whiting and Child should assume the responsibility for this task; what is surprising is that they should attempt to do so entirely with ethnographic data, making no use whatever of psychological data on individuals. This is a validating procedure so indirect that it requires the introduction of numerous hypotheses relating the cultural to the psychological levels—as problematic as the hypotheses to be validated.

CULTURE AND THE INDIVIDUAL PERSONALITY

The true locus of culture is in the interactions of specific individuals and, on the subjective side, in the world of meanings which each one of these individuals may unconsciously abstract for himself from his participation in these interactions. Every individual is, then, in a very real sense, a representative of at least one subculture which may be abstracted from the generalized culture of the group of which he is a member. (Sapir, 1932a, p. 236)

Personality and culture studies began with an interest in understanding "the individual as living in his culture and the culture as lived by individuals." This interest, however, has lain almost dormant while preoccupation with the problem of the typical personality of tribal, national, and other social groups has dominated attention. In their earlier phase, the studies of typical personality included very little data on individuals. Only with the growing accumulation of data on individual personalities (life histories, dreams, responses to projective and non-projective tests, etc.) in different cultures has it proved useful to study the culture-individual relation cross-culturally. Such psychological data have often been collected for delineating standardized profiles, but the existence of great individual variability has stimulated a renewed interest in the data as personal documents. In this concluding section, I shall discuss some of the theoretical implications of this trend.

The expansion of psychological data and theories in personality and culture studies has tended to produce some competitiveness between psychologists and anthropologists, raising the question whether the field is not simply a branch of psychology. Implicitly there has always been a contrast between social and culture patterns on the one hand and individual behavior on the other, the former being considered the province of anthropology and sociology, the latter that of psychology. It was precisely this contrast which was blurred in the development of the hybrid field of personality and culture. How then is the hybrid related to its parent stocks, anthropology and psychology?

One basic principle of distinction was first formulated by Edward Sapir, when he wrote that:

> Our natural interest in human behavior seems always to vacillate between what is imputed to the culture of the group as a whole and what is imputed to the psychic organization of the individual himself. These two poles of our interest in behavior do not necessarily make use of different materials; it is merely that the locus of reference is different in the two cases. (1934a, p. 408)

This principle has since been restated in slightly different forms by Radcliffe-Brown (1957) Bateson (1936), Kroeber and Kluckhohn (1952), Parsons and Shils (1951), and others. Some of these restatements are probably independent of Sapir's, although most of them, including Sapir's, were probably influenced by the constructionist tendencies in the thought of James, Russell, Whitehead, and other modern philosophers. In his *Our Knowledge of the External World* (1914), *The Analysis of Mind* (1921), and the *Analysis of Matter* (1927), Russell, for example, argues that mind and matter do not differ as raw material, which is made up of "neutral" sense-data or events, but only as different logical constructions from this material.

Sapir's principle sets up a criterion for distinguishing psychology from anthropology and sociology. In itself, however, it does not explain how these different fields may be combined, as they are in personality and culture studies, into a "cultural psychology" or a "social psychology." Radcliffe-Brown, for example, although he accepts essentially the same principle, applies it to sharpen the contrast between sociology (and anthropology) and psychology. He admits the possibility of an "intermediate science" which might deal with such problems as the relation of culture to the individual, but this would have to wait upon the independent development of the laws of psychology and the laws of sociology (1957).

Here again it was Sapir's original insight which saw how personality and culture study could develop from a synthesis of psychology and anthropology into something which would be more than a post-mortem summation of the component fields:

> . . . A truly rigorous analysis of any arbitrarily selected phase of individualized "social behavior" or "culture" would show two things: First, that no matter how flexible, how individually variable, it may in the first instance be thought to be, it is as a matter of fact the complex resultant of an incredibly elaborate culture history, in which many diverse strands intercross at that point in place and time at which the individual judgment of preference is expressed [this terminology is *cultural*]; second, that, conversely, no matter how rigorously necessary in practice the analyzed pattern may seem to be, it is always possible in principle, if not in experiential fact, for the lone individual to effect a transformation of form or meaning which is capable of communication to other individuals [this terminology is *psychiatric* or *personalistic*]. (Edward Sapir, 1938, pp. 9–10)

His solution, in other words, is to suggest a systematic employment of the cultural and the individual perspectives successively or almost simultaneously upon the same body of data. Personality and culture differs from individual psychology and from the impersonal kind of anthropology in being bifocal. In practice, Sapir recognizes that some situations are seen better through the cultural lens and others through the personalistic.

> No one in his senses would wish *the alphabet* studied from this highly personalistic point of view. In plain English, it would not be worth the trouble. The total meaning of the alphabet for X is so very nearly the same as that for any other individual, Y, that one does much better to analyze it and explain its relation to other cultural patterns in terms of an impersonal or cultural or anthropological, mode of description. (*ibid.*)

Breathing is an example on the other side (1929, pp. 17–18). Even with respect to situations of this kind, however, Sapir insists on a theoretical reversibility of perspectives in order to reveal the psychological significance of cultural patterns and the cultural significance of individual behavior. The alphabet has a personal significance and breathing is to some extent culturally patterned.

> The fact . . . that X has had more difficulty in learning the alphabet than Y, or that in old age X may forget the alphabet or some part of it more readily than Y, shows clearly enough that there is a psychiatric side to even the coldest and most indifferent of cultural patterns. Even such cold and indifferent cultural patterns have locked in them psychiatric meanings which

are ordinarily of no moment to the student of society but which may under peculiar circumstances come to the foreground of attention. When this happens, anthropological data need to be translated into psychiatric terms. (1938)

Sapir's approach to the "intermediate science" is very different from Radcliffe-Brown's:

> We are not . . . to begin with a simple contrast between social patterns and individual behavior, whether normal or abnormal, but we are, rather, to ask what is the meaning of culture in terms of individual behavior and whether the individual can, in a sense, be looked upon as the effective carrier of the culture of his group. (Sapir, 1932a)

An extension of Sapir's point of view to current developments in personality and culture research would further the process of theoretical clarification and yield many leads for research problems. It would suggest, for example, that the increasing use of psychological data does not necessarily convert personality and culture into a science of individual psychology, for these data must still be related to the cultural perspective. In fact the difference between psychological data and ethnographic data consists not in their status as primary data, but in the different systems of grouping and interpretation to which they are referred. In principle, all personal documents can be related to social and cultural systems, and so be transformed into data for cultural problems (Mead and Metraux, 1953, p. 34; Kroeber, 1947; Redfield, 1958a). This is not infrequent in practice: various kinds of psychological data have been used in studies of acculturation and value change (Vogt, 1951, 1955; Hallowell, 1951b; Thomas and Znaniecki), of culturally characteristic motivations (DuBois, 1944; Aberle, 1951), and for the study of cultural transmission (Bruner, 1956a, b; Eggan, 1956), witchcraft (Kluckhohn, 1944a), and other cultural topics.

"Cultural data," in analogous fashion, can be brought into a personalistic perspective of individual psychology. The growth and change of a culture pattern, can, for example, be illuminated by studying the problem in relation to the roles of individual personalities, as Mandelbaum (1941) has done. A culture pattern like handtrembling can be related to the psychic economy of individuals (Leighton and Leighton, 1949). How an individual uses and transforms elements of a common culture may be studied in the personal use of myth in dreams (Eggan, 1955).

A striking example of the alternating use of cultural and personality perspectives is Kroeber's account of the invention of the steamboat (Kroeber, 1948). First (section 185) Kroeber tells the story in terms of the principal technological, scientific, economic, legal, and political conditions: good roads in France, canals in England, engine-builders in

England, etc. This is the impersonal cultural view of the invention. Then (section 186), he deliberately rearranges the facts in order to view them "as they relate to the individual persons involved" and the qualities that made them succeed or fail. Kroeber looks on these two accounts as "two different sets of interpretations: both significant, but neither excluding the other from being 'true' " (1948, p. 464).

It is important to remember that both sets of data always exist in the phenomena. They are necessarily intertwined, because no culture is ever operative except through and in human beings. But human beings also operate or behave only under the influence of some one culture; and their behavior has cultural effect. This double-faceting of all social or historical phenomena should never be forgotten. (*ibid.*)

In another example (section 201), Kroeber, using a study of Mandelbaum's on the Kotas (Mandelbaum, 1941), weaves the cultural and the personality perspectives into a single narrative in a series of quick jumps from one to the other. Again he feels that there is no clash or conflict between the two approaches. "Each gives a clear picture, a coherent understanding, consistent in terms of itself, or its own plane. The one level is oriented toward psychology and biography and social relations, the other toward anthropology and cultural history—or philosophy of history, if one will" (1948, p. 507). He also believes the two planes will become intrinsically relatable as our understanding of personality and its mechanisms and of culture and its mechanisms advances.

The culture and personality approach thus requires an alternating and almost simultaneous use of two different perspectives—that of culture and that of the individual person. The approach necessarily requires either a close collaboration between an anthropologist and a psychologist or, as in Sapir's case, the capacity for bifocal vision.

If Sapir's conception of the relation of culture to the individual personality is accepted, then the tests of validation which strive for strict independence of cultural and psychological data will have to be taken less seriously. For if both sets of data derive ultimately from the same order of primary data, and, if in principle at least, it is possible to place cultural data into a psychological frame of reference and psychological data into a cultural one, then the degree of actual independence between them is only of limited practical significance. When an ethnographer's description refers to "dilapidated houses," this is not only a statement of ethnographic fact; it may also become an important clue to the psychiatric interpreter for the construction of a psychological profile. Conversely, life histories, dreams, and responses to psychological tests contain in them a good deal of cultural information upon which the knowledgeable ethnographer can draw for his construction of a culture pattern. There are "culture pattern dreams" (Lincoln,

1935), and there may be "culture pattern Rorschach responses" as well. When Dollard said of Radin's pioneer Winnebago autobiography, *Crashing Thunder* (1926) that "it should be taken as an inside view of the Winnebago culture rather than as a careful analysis of a human life . . . [because] there is very little attempt at analysis and synthesis of the material or at systematic formulation of the growth of a life" (Dollard, 1945, pp. 260–63; Kluckhohn, 1945), he was not really criticizing the quality of the autobiographical data but only pointing out that the selection and organization of data were not the kind which would be required for a psychological construction of an individual's life experience.

The emphasis on "constructions," "forms of thought," and "models" is another important consequence of the Sapir approach to personality and culture theory. If the data do not carry their own labels, then constructions based on them must assume a prominent position in the development of the field. And so they have: "human nature," "configurational personality," "basic personality structure," "cultural character," "social character," even "modal personality type," are so many different constructions from similar data. The concrete individual person stands in a twofold relation to these constructions. He may on the one hand enter as a constituent of a construction and become an object of the investigation, as when the psychologist's construction of "personality" organizes selected data in terms of a constructed individual career; particular individuals may, on the other hand, enter as collaborators to the investigation, as "informants" giving testimony about the object of investigation, whether the object be individual personalities or culture patterns. Although individuals enter as informants into all personality and culture constructions (and into purely cultural constructions as well), they enter as objects only into a few constructions. "Cultural character," "social character," and "basic personality structure," for example, do not explicitly specify individuals as objects. The type statements of these constructions predicate attributes of societies and cultures as wholes, or of groups taken collectively as a class, not of individuals singly or in specific distribution.

Examples of such statements are:

Demonstrating that one is really ill and needs help is a value in Eastern European Jewish culture. (Mead and Wolfenstein, 1955, p. 15)

The Dobu are paranoid. (after Benedict, 1934)

"Modal personality" statements, on the other hand, do specify distributions of attributes among individuals within a given population, without necessarily naming them:

Thirty-seven percent of the Tuscarora Indians interviewed at Niagara Falls show personality traits that fall within the modal class. (after Wallace, 1952a)

Many of the methodological problems in personality and culture theory arise from the desire to pass too quickly from the holistic and collective type of statements to the distributive and individualistic statements, and vice versa. While a holistic or collective attribution of traits may imply that *some* individuals in the given culture or society have the attributed traits, it does not explicitly assert who or how many they are. The addition of words like "some" or "many" to the statements does not really give any additional information about individuals, as Mead recognizes (Mead and Wolfenstein, 1955, p. 15). To do that, it is necessary to add explicit assumptions relating the collective attributes to individual distributions, as Benedict did, for example, in her theory that a vast majority of individual temperaments in any society would conform to the dominant cultural configuration. It is of course possible to develop a construction entirely at the level of holistic and collective statements, without making statements about individuals at all. This was certainly the dominant trend of Benedict's and Kardiner's early work. Kardiner's criticism of such a statement as "the Dobu are paranoid" was not that it attributed paranoia to the Dobu as a class but rather that it was physiognomic and non-causal. ". . . If a group is paranoid, one ought to be able to track down those institutional forces with which all constituents make contact and which terminate in this common trait" (1939, pp. 84–85).

So long as it seemed possible to establish causal connections between "institutional forces" and the "common traits" of classes of individuals, it was not felt necessary to refer to individual biographies. Only when "basic personality structure," "configurational personality," and the other constructions added statements about individuals, did it become necessary to enlarge the theories accordingly.

Analogously, if one begins with distributional statements about individuals or with statements about specific individuals and their relations, it is not possible to pass from such statements to collective or holistic statements about the society and the culture without the introduction of special theories postulating some special relationship among the different levels of statement. In Wallace (1952a) one such special assumption is that the most frequently occurring individual traits will also manifest themselves in the culture as "master traits."

If personality and culture theory does not depend for its derivation on a unique source of data, but consists of a variety of constructions from similar bodies of data, then it is equally true that the validation of the theory does not depend on establishing correspondence with a single body of data. There is no single method of validation appropriate for all constructions; rather, the method will vary with the kind of construction, the special assumptions that go with it, and the special research procedure employed. A test of "coherence," for example, requiring physiognomic judgments of conformity to a given culture pattern, is an appropriate test for validating statements attributing holistic properties to a single culture. It is not at all an appropriate test for validating hypotheses which assert causal relations between isolable pairs of events in different cultures. Correlation tests, on the other hand, are an appropriate validating method for the latter kind of statements, but not for the former.

A sample survey yielding precise statistical distributions of traits within a specified population may be a relevant procedure for validating statements about "modal personality." It is not a relevant procedure for testing statements about "basic personality" or "cultural character" if these statements attribute personality traits to whole cultures or collective classes without specifying individual distributions. *What* is to be sampled will also vary with the kind of theoretical construction. A theory which assumes that small communities are microcosmic mirrors of larger communities will lead to the sampling of the internal structures, social and psychological, of the small communities conceived as isolable units. A theory which emphasizes the networks of external relations which bind different communities together into a larger whole will require for its testing a sampling of the structure of relations between communities (Singer, 1955). Last, a theory which concerns itself with the relation of a small number of specified individuals to one another and to their culture will accumulate a sample of many observations about just those specified individuals rather than a survey sample of observations about a large number of individuals (Mead, 1953, p. 643; Mead and Metraux, pp. 33–34; Williams, 1958).

In this sense, Mead's insistence that anthropological sampling is "a different kind of sampling in which the validity of the sample depends not so much upon the number of cases as upon the proper specification of the informant so that he can be accurately placed" (1953; Mead and Metraux, 1953, pp. 41–49) has a certain cogency in calling attention to the dependence of the sampling problem on the kind of construction. In personality and culture theory, however, it is not only the individual as informant that needs to be specified—such specification helps to establish his credibility as a witness—but also the individual as an object of the investigation, as a term in the personality and culture relationship. In this latter context, the specifications cannot be very complete or accurate at the outset of an inquiry, since all the relevant variables are not known. The specified individual cannot, either in his capacity as an informant or as an object of personality and culture study, be taken as "a perfect example, an organic representation of his complete cultural experience"; for as an informant he is fallible and as a "representative" of his culture he is a transformer as well as a mirror.

BIBLIOGRAPHY

Abel, T. M., and Hsu, F. L. K. 1949. "Some Aspects of Personality of Chinese as Revealed by the Rorschach Test," *Journal of Projective Techniques,* 13:285–301.

Aberle, D. F. 1951. "The Psychosocial Analysis of a Hopi Life-History," *Comparative Psychology Monographs,* 21:1–133.

Adcock, C. J., and Ritchie, J. E. 1958. "Intercultural Use of Rorschach," *American Anthropologist,* 60:881–92.

Adorno, T. W.; Frenkel-Brunswik, Else; Levinson, D. J.; and Sanford, R. N. 1950. *The Authoritarian Personality.* New York: Harper & Bros.

Allport, G. W. 1942. *The Use of Personal Documents.* New York: Social Science Research Council, Bull. 49.

Almond, G. A. 1950. *The American People and Foreign Policy.* New York: Harcourt, Brace & Co.

Ammar, Hamed. 1954. *Growing Up in an Egyptian Village.* London: Routledge & Kegan Paul, Ltd.

Angell, Robert. 1945. "A Critical Review of the Development of the Personal Document Method in Sociology, 1920–1940." In Gottschalk, L., Kluckhohn, C., and Angell, R., *The Use of Personal Documents in History, Anthropology and Sociology.* New York: Social Science Research Council, Bull. 53. Pp. 117–232.

Barker, E. 1955. *Britain and the British People.* (2nd ed.), London, New York: Oxford University Press.

Barker, R. G., and Wright, H. F. 1954. *Midwest and Its Children: The Psychological Ecology of an American Town.* Evanston, Illinois: Row, Peterson & Co.

Barnouw, Victor. 1950. *Acculturation and Personality Among the Wisconsin Chippewa.* Menasha, Wisconsin: American Anthropological Association, Memoir 72.

Barry, H., Child, I., and Bacon, M. K. 1959. "Relation of Child Training to Subsistence Economy," *American Anthropologist,* 61:51–63.

Bastide, Roger. 1950. *Sociologie et Psychoanalyse.* Paris: Presses Universitaires de France.

Bateson, Gregory. 1935. "Culture Contact and Schismogenesis," *Man,* 35:178–83.

———. 1936. *Naven.* Cambridge: Cambridge University Press. (2nd ed., 1958, Stanford University Press.)

Bateson, Gregory. 1942a. "Morale and National Character." In Watson, G., (ed.), *Civilian Morale*. Boston: Society for the Psychological Study of Social Issues, Second Yearbook. Pp. 74–89.

———. 1942b. "Some Systematic Approaches to the Study of Culture and Personality," *Character and Personality*, 11:76–84.

———. 1943. "Cultural and Thematic Analysis of Fictional Films," *Transactions of the New York Academy of Science*, Ser. II, 5:72–78.

———. 1944. "Cultural Determinants of Personality." In Hunt, J. McV., (ed.), *Personality and the Behavior Disorders*. Vol. II. New York: Roland Press. Pp. 714–35.

———. 1949. "Bali: The Value System of a Steady State." In Fortes, M., ed., *Social Structure: Studies Presented to A. R. Radcliffe-Brown*. London: Oxford University Press. Pp. 35–53.

Bateson, Gregory, and Mead, Margaret. 1942. *Balinese Character: A Photographic Analysis*. New York: Special Publications of the New York Academy of Sciences, Vol. II.

Bauer, Raymond, Inkeles, Alex, and Kluckhohn, Clyde. 1956. *How the Soviet System Works: Cultural, Psychological and Social Themes*. Cambridge: Harvard University Press.

Bell, Daniel. 1958. "Ten Theories in Search of Reality: The Prediction of Soviet Behavior in the Social Sciences," *World Politics*, 10:327–65.

Belo, Jane. 1935. "The Balinese Temper," *Character and Personality*, 4:120–46.

Bendix, Reinhard. 1952. "Compliant Behavior and Individual Personality," *American Journal of Sociology*, 58:292–302.

Benedict, P. K., and Jacks, I. 1954. "Mental Illness in Primitive Society," *Psychiatry*, 17:377–89.

Benedict, Ruth F. 1928. "Psychological Types in the Cultures of the Southwest." In *Proceedings of the 23rd Congress of Americanists*. Chicago: University of Chicago Press. Copyright, 1930. Pp. 572–81.

———. 1932. "Configurations of Culture in North America," *American Anthropologist*, 34:1–27.

———. 1934a. "Anthropology and the Abnormal," *Journal of General Psychology*, 10:59–80.

———. 1934b. *Patterns of Culture*. Boston: Houghton Mifflin Co.

———. 1938. "Continuities and Discontinuities in Cultural Conditioning," *Psychiatry*, 1:161–67.

———. 1946a. *The Chrysanthemum and the Sword*. Boston: Houghton Mifflin Co.

———. 1946b. "The Study of Cultural Patterns in European Nations," *Transactions of the New York Academy of Science*, Ser. II, 8:274–79.

———. 1949. "Child Rearing in Certain European Cultures," *American Journal of Orthopsychiatry*, 19:342–50.

Bennett, John W., and Nagai, Michio. 1953. "The Japanese Critique of the Methodology of Benedict's *Chrysanthemum and the Sword,*" *American Anthropologist,* 55:404–10.

Billig, O., Gillin, J., and Davidson, W. 1947–48. "Aspects of Personality and Culture in a Guatemalan Community: Ethnological and Rorschach Approaches," *Journal of Personality,* 16:153–87, 326–68.

Blumer, Herbert. 1939. "An Appraisal of Thomas and Znaniecki's *The Polish Peasant in Europe and America.*" (Critiques of Research in the Social Sciences: I.) New York: Social Science Research Council.

Boas, Franz. 1934. "Introduction," to Benedict, R., *Patterns of Culture.* Boston: Houghton Mifflin Co.

Boggs, Stephen T. 1958. "Culture Change and the Personality of Ojibwa Children," *American Anthropologist,* 60:47–58.

Bruner, Edward M. 1956a. "Primary Group Experience and the Process of Acculturation," *American Anthropologist,* 58:605–23.

———. 1956b. "Cultural Transmission and Cultural Change," *Southwestern Journal of Anthropology,* 12:191–99.

Buchanan, William, Cantril, Hadley, *et al.* 1953. *How Nations See Each Other: A Study in Public Opinion.* Urbana: University of Illinois Press.

Calpin, G. H. 1953. *The South African Way of Life.* London: Wm. Heinemann, Ltd.

Carothers, J. C. 1948. "A Study of Mental Derangement in Africans and an Attempt to Explain Its Peculiarities, More Especially in Relation to the African Attitude to Life," *Psychiatry,* 11:47–86.

Carstairs, G. Morris. 1957. *The Twice-Born: A Study of a Community of High-Caste Hindus.* London: The Hogarth Press.

Castberg, F. 1954. *The Norwegian Way of Life.* Translated by Ragnar Christophersen. (International Studies Conference.) Melbourne: Wm. Heinemann, Ltd.

Caudill, William. 1949. "Psychological Characteristics of Acculturated Wisconsin Ojibwa Children," *American Anthropologist,* 51:409–27.

———. 1952. "Japanese-American Personality and Acculturation," *Genetic Psychology Monographs,* 45:3–102.

Caudill, William, and De Vos, George. 1956. "Achievement, Culture and Personality: The Case of the Japanese-Americans," *American Anthropologist,* 58:1102–26.

Christie, R., and Jahoda, M. 1954. *Studies in the Scope and Method of "The Authoritarian Personality."* Glencoe, Illinois: The Free Press.

Codere, Helen. 1950. *Fighting with Property: A Study of Kwakiutl Potlatching and Warfare, 1792–1930.* New York: American Ethnological Society.

———. 1956. "The Amiable Side of Kwakiutl Life," *American Anthropologist,* 58:334–51.

Crawford, R. M. 1955. "The Australian National Character: Myth and Reality," *Cahiers d'histoire mondiale,* 2:704–27.

Davis, Allison, and Dollard, John. 1940. *Children of Bondage: The Person-ality Development of Negro Youth in the Urban South.* Washington: American Council on Education.

Davis, Allison, and Havighurst, R. J. 1946. "Social Class and Color Differ-ences in Child Rearing," *American Sociological Review,* 11: 698–710.

Dennis, Wayne. 1940. "Does Culture Appreciably Affect Patterns of Infant Behavior?" *Journal of Social Psychology,* 12:305–17.

Devereux, George. 1951. *Reality and Dream: Psychotherapy of a Plains Indian.* New York: International Universities Press.

Dewey, John. 1922. *Human Nature and Conduct; An Introduction to Social Psychology.* New York: Henry Holt & Co.

Dicks, H. V. 1950. "Personality Traits and National Socialist Ideology," *Human Relations,* 3:11–154.

———. 1952. "Observations on Contemporary Russian Behavior," *Human Relations,* 5:11–175.

Dollard, John. 1945. *Criteria for the Life History.* With analyses of six nota-ble documents. New Haven: Yale University Press.

Dollard, J., Miller, N. E., and Sears, R. R. 1939. *Frustration and Aggres-sion.* New Haven: Yale University Press.

Dollard, J., and Miller, N. E. 1950. *Personality and Psychotherapy.* New York: McGraw-Hill Book Co.

DuBois, Cora. 1941. "Attitudes Toward Food and Hunger in Alor." In Spier, L., *et al.,* (eds.), *Language, Culture and Personality: Essays in Memory of Edward Sapir.* Menasha, Wisconsin: Sapir Memorial Publica-tion Fund. Pp. 272–81.

———. 1944. *The People of Alor.* Minneapolis: University of Minnesota Press.

Dyk, Walter. 1938. *Son of Old Man Hat.* A Navaho Autobiography re-corded by Walter Dyk. With an introduction by Edward Sapir. New York: Harcourt, Brace & Co.

———. 1947. *A Navaho Autobiography.* New York: Viking Fund Publica-tions in Anthropology, No. 8.

Eaton, Joseph W., in collaboration with Weil, Robert J. 1955. *Culture and Mental Disorders.* Glencoe, Illinois: The Free Press.

Eggan, Dorothy. 1943. "The General Problem of Hopi Adjustment," *Ameri-can Anthropologist,* 45:357–73.

———. 1949. "The Significance of Dreams for Anthropological Research," *American Anthropologist,* 51:177–98.

———. 1952. "The Manifest Content of Dreams: A Challenge to Social Science," *American Anthropologist,* 54:469–85.

———. 1955. "The Personal Use of Myth in Dreams." In Sebeok, T. (ed.), *Myth: A Symposium. Journal of American Folklore,* 67–75.

———. 1956. "Instruction and Affect in Hopi Cultural Continuity," *South-western Journal of Anthropology,* 12:347–66.

Erikson, E. H. 1945. "Childhood and Tradition in Two American Indian Tribes." In Freud, A., and others (eds.), *The Psychoanalytic Study of the Child.* Vol. I. New York: International Universities Press. Pp. 319–50.

———. 1950. *Childhood and Society.* New York: W. W. Norton & Co.

Evans-Pritchard, E. E. 1929. "The Study of Kinship in Primitive Societies," *Man,* 29, No. 148:190–94.

Farber, Maurice L. 1950. "The Problem of National Character: A Methodological Analysis," *Journal of Psychology,* 30:307–16.

———. 1953. "English and Americans: Values in the Socialization Process," *Journal of Psychology,* 36:243–50.

———. 1955. "The Study of National Character: 1955," *Journal of Social Issues,* 11, No. 2:52–56.

Faris, R. E. L., and Dunham, H. 1939. *Mental Disorders in Urban Areas.* Chicago: University of Chicago Press.

Ford, Clellan S. 1941. *Smoke from Their Fires.* New Haven: Yale University Press.

Fortes, Meyer. 1957. "Malinowski and the Study of Kinship." In Firth, R. (ed.), *Man and Culture, An Evaluation of the Work of Malinowski.* London: Routledge & Kegan Paul. Pp. 168–72.

Francis, E. K. L. 1945. "The Personality Type of the Peasant According to Hesiod's *Works and Days: A Culture Case Study,"* *Rural Sociology,* 10:275–95.

Frank, Lawrence K. 1951. *Nature and Human Nature.* New Brunswick: Rutgers University Press.

Freud, Sigmund. 1922. *Group Psychology and the Analysis of the Ego.* London: International Psychoanalytic Press.

———. 1930. *Civilization and Its Discontents.* New York: Jonathan Cape & Harrison Smith.

Friedl, Ernestine. 1956. "Persistence in Chippewa Culture and Personality," *American Anthropologist,* 58:814–25.

Fromm, Erich. 1936. "A Social Psychological Approach to 'Authority and Family.' " In Horkheimer, M. (ed.), *Studien über Autorität und Familie.* Paris: Librairie Felix Alcan.

———. 1941. *Escape from Freedom.* New York: Farrar & Rinehart.

———. 1944. "Individual and Social Origins of Neurosis," *American Sociological Review,* 9:380–84.

———. 1948. *Man for Himself.* New York: Farrar & Rinehart.

———. 1949. "Psychoanalytic Characterology and Its Application to the Understanding of Culture." In Sargent, S. S., and Smith, Marian W. (eds.), *Culture and Personality.* New York: The Viking Fund. Pp. 1–10.

———. 1955. *The Sane Society.* New York: Rinehart.

Gerth, H., and Mills, C. W. 1953. *Character and Social Structure.* New York: Harcourt, Brace & Co.

Gesell, Arnold, Ilg, Frances, *et al.* 1943. *Infant and Child in the Culture of Today.* New York: Harper & Bros.

Gillin, John. 1939. "Personality in Preliterate Societies," *American Sociological Review,* 4:681–702.

———. 1945. "Personality Formation from the Comparative Cultural Point of View." In *Sociological Foundations of the Psychiatric Disorders of Children. Proceedings of the Twelfth Institute of the Child Research Clinic of the Woods Schools,* 12:13–34.

Ginsberg, M. 1942. "National Character," *British Journal of Psychology,* 32:183–205.

Gladwin, Thomas, and Sarason, S. B., 1953. *Truk: Man in Paradise.* New York: Viking Fund Publications in Anthropology, No. 20.

Goldfrank, Esther S. 1945. "Socialization, Personality, and the Structure of Pueblo Society," *American Anthropologist,* 47:516–39.

———. 1948. "The Impact of Situation and Personality on Four Hopi Emergence Myths," *Southwestern Journal of Anthropology,* 4:241–62.

Goldhamer, Herbert, and Marshall, Andrew. 1953. *Psychosis and Civilization.* Glencoe, Illinois: The Free Press.

Goldman, Irving. 1950. "Psychiatric Interpretations of Russian History, A Reply to Geoffrey Gorer," *American Slavic and East European Review,* 9, No. 3:151–61.

Goldschmidt, Walter. 1951. "Ethics and the Structure of Society: An Ethnological Contribution to the Sociology of Knowledge," *American Anthropologist,* 53:506–24.

Gorer, Geoffrey. 1943. "Themes in Japanese Culture," *Transactions of the New York Academy of Science,* Ser. II, 5:106–24.

———. 1948. *The American People.* New York: W. W. Norton & Co.

———. 1949. "Some Aspects of the Psychology of the People of Great Russia," *American Slavic and East European Review,* 8, No. 3:155–66.

———. 1950a. "The Concept of National Character," *Science News,* 18:105–23.

———. 1950b. "Some Notes on the British Character," *Horizon,* 20:120–121, 369–79.

———. 1951. "Swaddling and the Russians," *New Leader,* May 21, 19–20.

———. 1955. *Exploring English Character.* London: The Cresset Press.

Gorer, Geoffrey, and Rickman, John. 1949. *The People of Great Russia.* London: The Cresset Press. (New York: Chanticleer Press, 1950.)

Gottschalk, Louis. 1945. "The Historian and the Historical Document." In Gottschalk, L., Kluckhohn, C., and Angell, R. *The Use of Personal Documents in History, Anthropology and Sociology.* New York: Social Science Research Council, Bull. 53. Pp. 79–173.

Hallowell, A. I. 1937. "Temporal Orientation in Western Civilization and in a Preliterate Society," *American Anthropologist,* 39:647–70.

————. 1938. "Fear and Anxiety as Cultural and Individual Variables in a Primitive Society," *The Journal of Social Psychology*, 9:25–47.

————. 1940. "Aggression in Salteaux Society," *Psychiatry*, 3:395–407.

————. 1941. "The Social Function of Anxiety in a Primitive Society," *American Sociological Review*, 7:869–81.

————. 1942. "Acculturation Processes and Personality Changes as Indicated by the Rorschach Technique," *Rorschach Research Exchange*, 6:42–50.

————. 1945. "The Rorschach Technique in the Study of Personality and Culture," *American Anthropologist*, 47:195–210.

————. 1946a. "Some Psychological Characteristics of the Northeastern Indians." In Johnson, F. (ed.), *Man in Northeastern North America*. Andover, Massachusetts: Papers of the R. S. Peabody Foundation for Archaeology, 3:195–225.

————. 1946b. "Concordance of Ojibwa Narratives in the Published Work of Henry R. Schoolcraft," *Journal of American Folklore*, 59:136–53.

————. 1949. "Ojibwa Personality and Acculturation." In Tax, S. (ed.), *Selected Papers of the Twenty-ninth International Congress of Americanists*, 2:105–112.

————. 1950. "Personality Structure and the Evolution of Man," *American Anthropologist*, 52:159–75.

————. 1951a. "Cultural Factors in the Structuralization of Perception." In Rohrer, J. H., and Sherif, M. (eds.), *Social Psychology at the Crossroads*. New York: Harper & Bros. Pp. 164–95.

————. 1951b. "The Use of Projective Techniques in the Study of the Socio-Psychological Aspects of Acculturation," *Rorschach Research Exchange and Journal of Projective Techniques*, 15, No. 1:27–44.

————. 1953. "Culture, Personality, and Society." In Kroeber, A. L. (ed.), *Anthropology Today*. Chicago: University of Chicago Press. Pp. 597–620.

————. 1954. "The Self and Its Behavioral Environment," *Explorations*, 1:108–65.

————. 1955. *Culture and Experience*. Philadelphia: University of Pennsylvania Press.

Haring, D. G. 1946. "Aspects of Personal Character in Japan," *Far Eastern Quarterly*, 6:12–22.

————. 1949. *Personal Character and Cultural Milieu*. A Collection of Readings. Syracuse: Syracuse University Press. (Revised ed., 1956.)

Hartmann, H., Kris, E., and Loewenstein, R. M. 1951. "Some Psychoanalytic Comments on 'Culture and Personality.'" In Wilbur, G. B., and Muensterberger, W. (eds.), *Psychoanalysis and Culture*. New York: International Universities Press. Pp. 3–31.

Havighurst, R. J., and Neugarten, Bernice L. 1954. *American Indian and White Children: A Socio-Psychological Investigation*. Chicago: University of Chicago Press.

Havighurst, R. J., and Taba, Hilda. 1949. *Adolescent Character and Personality.* New York: J. Wiley.

Heinicke, C., and Whiting, Beatrice B. 1953. *Bibliographies on Personality and Social Development of the Child.* New York: Social Science Research Council.

Henry, Jules. 1948. "Anthropology and Orthopsychiatry." In Lourey, L. G., and Sloan, Victoria (eds.), *Orthopsychiatry, 1923–1948: Retrospect and Prospect.* New York: American Orthopsychiatric Association. Pp. 263–86.

Henry, Jules *et al.* 1955. "Symposium: Projective Testing in Ethnography," *American Anthropologist,* 57:245–70.

Henry, William E. 1947. "The Thematic Apperception Technique in the Study of Culture-Personality Relations," *Genetic Psychology Monographs,* 35, No. 1.

Hinkle, G. J. 1952. "The 'Four Wishes' in Thomas' Theory of Social Change," *Social Research,* 19:464–84; 20:473–77.

Hoijer, Harry (ed.). 1954. *Language in Culture.* Chicago: University of Chicago Press.

Honigmann, John J. 1954. *Culture and Personality.* New York: Harper & Bros.

Honigmann, John J., and Carrera, Richard N. 1957. "Cross-Cultural Use of Machover's Figure Drawing Test," *American Anthropologist,* 59: 650–54.

Horney, Karen. 1937. *The Neurotic Personality of Our Times.* New York: W. W. Norton & Co.

Howells, W. W. 1955. "Universality and Variation in Human Nature." In W. L. Thomas, Jr. (ed.), *Yearbook of Anthropology,* I. New York: Wenner-Gren Foundation. Pp. 227–36.

Hsu, F. L. K. 1953. *Americans and Chinese: Two Ways of Life.* New York: Henry Schuman.

Hsu, F. L. K. (ed.). 1954. *Aspects of Culture and Personality.* A symposium. New York: Abelard-Schuman.

Hughes, E. C. 1929. "Personality Types and the Division of Labor." In Burgess, W. W. (ed.), *Personality and the Social Group.* Chicago: University of Chicago Press. Pp. 78–94.

Inkeles, Alex. 1953. "Some Sociological Observations on Culture and Personality Studies." In Kluckhohn, C., Murray, H. A., and Schneider, D. M. (eds.), *Personality in Nature, Society, and Culture.* (2nd ed.). New York: Alfred Knopf. Pp. 577–92.

————. 1955. "Social Change and Social Character: The Role of Parental Mediation," *Journal of Social Issues,* 11, No. 2:12–23.

Inkeles, Alex, and Levinson, D. J. 1954. "National Character: The Study of Modal Personality and Sociocultural Systems." In Lindzey, G. (ed.), *Handbook of Social Psychology,* Vol. II. Cambridge: Addison-Wesley. Pp. 977–1020.

Inkeles, Alex, Hanfman, Eugenia, and Beier, Helen. 1958. "Modal Personality and Adjustment to the Soviet Socio-Political System," *Human Relations*, 11, No. 3:3–22.

Jahoda, M., and Christie, R. 1954. *Studies in the Scope and Method of "The Authoritarian Personality."* Glencoe, Illinois: The Free Press.

Japanese Journal of Ethnology. 1949. "The Problems Raised by *The Chrysanthemum and the Sword.*" 14, No. 4:1–35.

Jones, Ernest. 1924. "Psychoanalysis and Anthropology," *Journal of the Royal Anthropological Institute,* 54:47–66.

———. 1925. "Mother-Right and the Sexual Ignorance of Savages," *International Journal of Psychoanalysis,* 6:109–130.

Joseph, Alice, and Murray, Veronica F. 1951. *Chamorros and Carolinians of Saipan: Personality Studies.* With an analysis of the Bender Gestalt texts by Lauretta Bender. Cambridge: Harvard University Press.

Joseph, Alice, Spicer, R. B., and Chesky, Jane. 1949. *The Desert People.* Chicago: University of Chicago Press.

Kaplan, Bert. 1954. *A Study of Rorschach Responses in Four Cultures.* Cambridge: Papers of the Peabody Museum of American Archaeology and Ethnology, Harvard University, 42, No. 2.

Kaplan, Bert, and Plaut, Thomas F. A. 1956. *Personality in a Communal Society: An Analysis of the Mental Health of the Hutterites.* Lawrence, Kansas: University of Kansas Publications, Social Science Studies.

Kardiner, Abram. 1939. *The Individual and His Society.* With a foreword and two ethnological reports by R. Linton. New York: Columbia University Press.

———. 1944. Introduction to DuBois, Cora, *The People of Alor.* Minneapolis: University of Minnesota Press.

———. 1945. "The Concept of Basic Personality Structure as an Operational Tool in the Social Sciences." In Linton, R. (ed.), *The Science of Man in the World Crisis.* New York: Columbia University Press. Pp. 107–22.

Kardiner, Abram, with the collaboration of Linton, R., DuBois, Cora, and West, J. 1945. *The Psychological Frontiers of Society.* New York: Columbia University Press.

Kardiner, Abram, and Ovesey, L. 1951. *The Mark of Oppression.* New York: W. W. Norton & Co.

Klineberg, Otto. 1944. "A Science of National Character," *Journal of Social Psychology,* 19:147–62.

———. 1949. "Recent Studies of National Character." In Sargent, S. S., and Smith, Marian W. (eds.), *Culture and Personality.* New York: The Viking Fund. Pp. 127–38.

———. 1950. *Tensions Affecting International Understanding.* New York: Social Science Research Council, Bull. 62.

Kluckhohn, Clyde. 1941. "Patterning as Exemplified in Navaho Culture." In Spier, L., *et al.* (eds.), *Language, Culture, and Personality: Essays in*

Memory of Edward Sapir. Menasha, Wisconsin: Sapir Memorial Publication Fund. Pp. 109–30.

———. 1944a. *Navaho Witchcraft.* Cambridge: Papers of the Peabody Museum of American Archaeology and Ethnology, Harvard University, 22, No. 2.

———. 1944b. "The Influence of Psychiatry on Anthropology in America during the Past One Hundred Years." In *One Hundred Years of American Psychiatry.* New York: Columbia University Press. Pp. 569–617.

———. 1945. "The Personal Document in Anthropological Science." In Gottschalk, L., Kluckhohn, C., and Angell, R. *The Use of Personal Documents in History, Anthropology and Sociology.* New York: Social Science Research Council, Bull. 53. Pp. 79–173.

———. 1946. "Personality Formation Among the Navaho Indians," *Sociometry,* 9:128–32.

———. 1947. "Some Aspects of Navaho Infancy and Early Childhood." In Róheim, G. (ed.), *Psychoanalysis and the Social Sciences.* Vol. I. New York: International Universities Press. Pp. 37–86.

———. 1948. *Personality in Nature, Society and Culture.* New York: Alfred Knopf. (2nd ed. 1955).

———. 1949. "Personality in Culture." In Kluckhohn, C., *Mirror for Man.* New York: Whittlesey House, McGraw-Hill. Pp. 196–227.

———. 1953. "Universal Categories of Culture." In Kroeber, A. L. (ed.), *Anthropology Today.* Chicago: University of Chicago Press. Pp. 507–23.

———. 1954. "Southwestern Studies of Culture and Personality," *American Anthropologist,* 56:685–707.

———. 1955. "Recent Studies of the 'National Character' of Great Russians," *Human Development Bulletin.* Chicago: Committee on Human Development, 6th Annual Symposium. Pp. 39–60.

———. 1956. "The Impact of Freud on Anthropology," *Bulletin of the New York Academy of Medicine,* 32:903–7.

Kluckhohn, Clyde, and Leighton, Dorothea. 1946. *The Navaho.* Cambridge: Harvard University Press.

Kluckhohn, Clyde, and Morgan, W. 1951. "Some Notes on Navaho Dreams." In Wilbur, G. B., and Muensterberger, W. (eds.), *Psychoanalysis and Culture: Essays in Honor of Géza Róheim.* New York: International Universities Press. Pp. 120–31.

Kluckhohn, Clyde, and Murray, Henry A. (eds.). 1948. *Personality in Nature, Society, and Culture.* New York: Alfred A. Knopf. (2nd ed. with David M. Schneider, 1953.)

Kluckhohn, Clyde, and Rosenzweig, Janine C. 1949. "Two Navaho Children over a Five-Year Period," *American Journal of Orthopsychiatry,* 19:266–78.

Kroeber, A. L. 1920. *"Totem and Taboo:* An Ethnologic Psychoanalysis," *American Anthropologist,* 22:48–55.

————. 1939. *"Totem and Taboo* in Retrospect," *American Journal of Sociology,* 45:446–57.

————. 1940. "Psychosis or Social Sanction," *Character and Personality,* 7:204–15. (Reprinted in Kroeber, A. L., *The Nature of Culture.* Chicago: University of Chicago Press, 1952. Pp. 310–19.)

————. 1944. *Configurations of Culture Growth.* Berkeley and Los Angeles: University of California Press.

————. 1945. "The Use of Autobiographical Evidence." Pp. 318–22 of "A Yurok War Reminiscence," *Southwestern Journal of Anthropology,* 1:318–32. (Reprinted in Kroeber, A. L., *The Nature of Culture.* Chicago: University of Chicago Press, 1952. Pp. 320–22.)

————. 1947. "A Southwestern Personality Type," *Southwestern Journal of Anthropology,* 3:108–13.

————. 1948. *Anthropology.* New York: Harcourt, Brace & Co. (Rev. ed.)

————. 1955. "On Human Nature," *Southwestern Journal of Anthropology,* 11:195–204.

Kroeber, A. L. (ed.). 1953. *Anthropology Today.* Chicago: University of Chicago Press.

Kroeber, A. L., and Kluckhohn, Clyde. 1952. *Culture, A Critical Review of Concepts and Definitions.* Cambridge: Papers of the Peabody Museum of American Archaeology and Ethnology, Harvard University, 47, No. 1.

La Barre, Weston. 1945. "Some Observations on Character Structure in the Orient: The Japanese," *Psychiatry,* 8:319–42.

————. 1946. "Some Observations on Character Structure in the Orient: The Chinese," *Psychiatry,* 9:375–95.

————. 1948. "Columbia University Research in Contemporary Cultures," *Scientific Monthly,* LXVII, No. 3:239–40.

————. 1958. "The Influence of Freud on Anthropology," *The American Imago,* 15:275–328.

Langer, William C. 1958. "The Next Assignment," *The American Imago,* 15:275–328.

Lasswell, Harold D. 1930. *Psychopathology and Politics.* Chicago: University of Chicago Press.

————. 1931. "A Hypothesis Rooted in the Preconceptions of a Single Civilization Tested by Bronislaw Malinowski." In Rice, S. A. (ed.), *Methods in Social Science: A Case Book.* Chicago: University of Chicago Press. Pp. 480–88.

————. 1935. *World Politics and Personal Security.* New York: McGraw-Hill Book Co.

————. 1937. "The Method of Overlapping Observation in the Study of Personality and Culture," *Journal of Abnormal and Social Psychology,* 32:240–43.

————. 1939. "The Contribution of Freud's Insight Interview to the Social Sciences," *American Journal of Sociology,* 45:375–90.

Lasswell, Harold D. 1948. *Power and Personality*. New York: W. W. Norton & Co.

Lazarsfeld, Paul F., and Barton, A. H. 1951. "Qualitative Measurement in the Social Sciences: Classification, Typologies, and Indices." In Lerner, D., and Lasswell, H. (eds.), *The Policy Sciences*. Stanford: Stanford University Press. Pp. 155–92.

Leighton, Alexander H., Clausen, John A., and Wilson, Robert N. (eds.). 1957. *Explorations in Social Psychiatry*. New York: Basic Books, Inc.

Leighton, Alexander H., and Leighton, Dorothea C. 1944. *The Navaho Door, An Introduction to Navaho Life*. Cambridge: Harvard University Press.

————. 1949. *Gregorio, The Hand-Trembler: A Psychobiological Study of a Navaho Indian*. Cambridge: Papers of the Peabody Museum of American Archaeology and Ethnology, Harvard University, 40, No. 1.

Leighton, Dorothea, and Kluckhohn, Clyde. 1947. *Children of the People: The Navaho Individual and His Development*. Cambridge: Harvard University Press.

Leites, Nathan. 1947. "Trends in Affectlessness," *The American Imago*, 4:89–112.

————. 1948. "Psycho-cultural Hypotheses About Political Acts," *World Politics*, 1:102–119.

————. 1954. *A Study of Bolshevism*. Glencoe, Illinois: The Free Press.

Leites, Nathan, and Bernaut, Elsa. 1954. *Ritual of Liquidation: The Case of the Moscow Trials*. Glencoe, Illinois: The Free Press.

Leites, Nathan, and Wolfenstein, Martha. 1947. "An Analysis of Themes and Plots," *Annals of the American Academy of Political and Social Science*, 254:41–48.

Lerner, Daniel. 1958. *The Passing of Traditional Society*. Glencoe, Illinois: The Free Press.

Lewin, K. 1948. "Some Social Psychological Differences Between the United States and Germany." In Lewin, Gertrud (ed.), *Resolving Social Conflicts: Selected Papers on Group Dynamics, 1935–1946*. New York: Harper & Bros. Pp. 3–33.

Lewis, Oscar. 1951. *Life in a Mexican Village: Tepoztlan Restudied*. Urbana: The University of Illinois Press.

Li An-che. 1937. "Zuni: Some Observations and Queries," *American Anthropologist*, 39:62–76.

Lincoln, J. S. 1935. *The Dream in Primitive Cultures*. London: The Cresset Press.

Lindesmith, A. R., and Strauss, A. L. 1950. "A Critique of Culture-Personality Writings," *American Sociological Review*, 15:587–600.

Linton, Ralph. 1945. *The Cultural Background of Personality*. New York: Appleton-Century-Crofts.

————. 1949. "Problems of Status Personality." In Sargent, S. S., and Smith, Marian W. (eds.), *Culture and Personality*. New York: The Viking Fund. Pp. 163–73.

————. 1951. "The Concept of National Character." In Stanton, A. H., and Perry, S. E. (eds.), *Personality and Political Crisis*. Glencoe, Illinois: The Free Press. Pp. 133–50.

————. 1956. *Culture and Mental Disorders*. George Devereux, (ed.) Springfield, Illinois: Charles C. Thomas.

Little, Kenneth L. 1950. "Methodology in the Study of Adult Personality," *American Anthropologist*, 52:279–82.

Lowie, Robert H. 1945. *The German People, A Social Portrait to 1914*. New York: Farrar & Rinehart.

————. 1954. *Toward Understanding Germany*. Chicago: University of Chicago Press.

MacGregor, Gordon. 1946. *Warriors Without Weapons*. Chicago: University of Chicago Press.

Malinowski, Bronislaw. 1927. *Sex and Repression in Savage Society*. New York: Harcourt, Brace & Co.

————. 1929. *The Sexual Life of Savages*. New York: Halcyon House.

Mandelbaum, David G. 1941. "Social Trends and Personal Pressures: The Growth of a Culture Pattern." In Spier, L., *et al.*, (eds.), *Language, Culture, and Personality: Essays in Memory of Edward Sapir*. Menasha, Wisconsin: Sapir Memorial Publication Fund. Pp. 219–238.

————. 1953. "On the Study of National Character," *American Anthropologist*, 55:174–87.

McClelland, D. C., and Friedman, G. A. 1952. "A Cross-Cultural Study of the Relationship between Child-Training Practices and Achievement Motivation Appearing in Folk-Tales." In Newcomb, T. M., Hartley, E. L., and Swanson, G. E. (eds.), *Readings in Social Psychology*. New York: Henry Holt & Co. Pp. 243–49.

McGranahan, D. V., and Wayne, I. 1948. "German and American Traits Reflected in Popular Drama," *Human Relations*, 1:429–55.

McQuown, Norman. 1957. "Linguistic Transcription and Specification of Psychiatric Interview Materials," *Psychiatry*, 20:79–86.

Mead, George Herbert. 1934. *Mind, Self, and Society*. Edited by C. W. Morris. Chicago: University of Chicago Press.

————. 1956. *The Social Psychology of George Herbert Mead*. Selected Writings of an American Pragmatist. Edited by Anselm Strauss. Chicago: University of Chicago Press.

Mead, Margaret. 1928. *Coming of Age in Samoa*. New York: Wm. Morrow & Co.

————. 1930. *Growing Up in New Guinea*. New York: Wm. Morrow & Co.

————. 1935. *Sex and Temperament in Three Primitive Societies*. New York: Wm. Morrow & Co.

————. 1937. (ed.), *Cooperation and Competition among Primitive Peoples*. New York: McGraw-Hill Book Co.

————. 1939. *From the South Seas*. New York: Wm. Morrow & Co. Copyright 1928, 1930, 1935, 1938 by Margaret Mead.

Mead, Margaret. 1940. "Social Change and Cultural Surrogates," *Journal of Educational Psychology*, 14:92–110.

———. 1941. "Review of Abram Kardiner: *The Individual and His Society*," *American Journal of Orthopsychiatry*, 11:603–5.

———. 1942a. *And Keep Your Powder Dry: An Anthropologist Looks at America*. New York: Wm. Morrow & Co.

———. 1942b. "Anthropological Data on the Problem of Instinct," *Psychosomatic Medicine*, 4:396–97.

———. 1946. "Research on Primitive Children." In Carmichael, L. (ed.), *Manual of Child Psychology*. New York: J. Wiley. Pp. 667–706.

———. 1947a. "The Concept of Culture and the Psychosomatic Approach," *Psychiatry*, 10:57–76.

———. 1947b. "The Application of Anthropological Technique to Cross National Communication," *Transactions of the New York Academy of Science*, Ser. II, 9:133–52.

———. 1947c. "The Implications of Culture Change for Personality Development," *American Journal of Orthopsychiatry*, 17:633–46.

———. 1947d. "On the Implications for Anthropology of the Gesell-Ilg Approach to Maturation," *American Anthropologist*, 49:69–77.

———. 1949a. "Character Formation and Diachronic Theory." In Fortes, M. (ed.), *Social Structure: Studies Presented to A. R. Radcliffe-Brown*. Oxford at the Clarendon Press. P. 18.

———. 1949b. *Male and Female: A Study of the Sexes in a Changing World*. New York: Wm. Morrow & Co.

———. 1951a. *Soviet Attitudes Toward Authority*. New York: McGraw-Hill Book Co.

———. 1951b. "The Study of National Character." In Lerner, D., and Lasswell, H. D. (eds.), *The Policy Sciences*. Stanford: Stanford University Press. Pp. 70–85.

———. 1951c. "Columbia University Research in Contemporary Cultures." In Guetzkow, H. (ed.), *Groups, Leadership and Men*. Pittsburgh: Carnegie Press. Pp. 106–18.

———. 1952. "Some Relationships between Social Anthropology and Psychiatry." In Alexander, F. and Ross, H. (eds.), *Dynamic Psychiatry*. Chicago: University of Chicago Press. Pp. 401–48.

———. 1953. "National Character." In Kroeber, A. L. (ed.), *Anthropology Today*. Chicago: University of Chicago Press. Pp. 642–67.

———. 1954a. "Some Theoretical Considerations on the Problem of Mother-Child Separation," *American Journal of Orthopsychiatry*, 24: 471–83.

———. 1954b. "The Swaddling Hypothesis: Its Reception," *American Anthropologist*, 56:395–409.

———. 1955. "Effects of Anthropological Field Work Models on Interdisciplinary Communication in the Study of National Character," *Journal of Social Issues*, 11, No. 2; 3–11.

————. 1956. *New Lives for Old: Cultural Transformation—Manus, 1928–1953.* New York: Wm. Morrow & Co.

————. 1959. *An Anthropologist at Work, Writings of Ruth Benedict.* Boston: Houghton Mifflin Co.

Mead, Margaret, and MacGregor, Frances C. 1951. *Growth and Culture.* New York: G. P. Putnam's Sons.

Mead, Margaret, and Metraux, Rhoda. 1953. *The Study of Culture at a Distance.* Chicago: University of Chicago Press.

Mead, Margaret, and Wolfenstein, Martha (eds.). 1955. *Childhood in Contemporary Cultures.* Chicago: University of Chicago Press.

Merton, Robert K. 1940. "Bureaucratic Structure and Personality," *Social Forces,* 18:560–68.

Metraux, Rhoda, and Mead, Margaret. 1954. *Themes in French Culture; a Preface to a Study of French Community.* Stanford: Stanford University Press.

Miller, N. E., and Dollard, John. 1941. *Social Learning and Imitation.* New Haven: Yale University Press.

Miroglio, A. 1955. "Géographie psychologique et psychologie des peuples," *Revue Psychologique des Peuples,* 10:201–6.

Morgan, William. 1932. "Navaho Dreams," *American Anthropologist,* 34:390–405.

Morris, Charles W. 1947. "Individual Differences and Cultural Patterns." In Bryson, L., Finkelstein, L., and MacIver, R. M. (eds.), *Conflicts of Power in Modern Culture.* New York: Conference on Science, Philosophy and Religion in Their Relation to the Democratic Way of Life, Inc. Pp. 74–84.

————. 1956. *Varieties of Human Value.* Chicago: University of Chicago Press.

Mowrer, O. H., and Kluckhohn, Clyde. 1944. "Dynamic Theory of Personality." In Hunt, J. McV. (ed.), *Personality and the Behavior Disorders.* Vol. I. New York: Ronald Press. Pp. 69–135.

Muensterberger, Warner. 1951. "Orality and Dependence: Characteristics of Southern Chinese." In Róheim, G., *et al.* (eds.), *Psychoanalysis and the Social Sciences,* III. New York: International Universities Press. Pp. 37–69.

Murdock, G. P. 1949. "The Science of Human Learning, Society, Culture, and Personality," *Scientific Monthly,* 49:377–81.

Murphy, Gardner. 1947. *Personality.* New York: Harper & Bros.

————. 1953. *In the Minds of Men.* New York: Basic Books, Inc.

Murray, H. A., *et al.* 1938. *Explorations in Personality.* New York: Oxford University Press.

Nadel, S. F. 1937a. "Experiments on Culture Psychology," *Africa,* 10:421–35.

————. 1937b. "A Field Experiment in Racial Psychology," *British Journal of Psychology,* 28:195–211.

Nadel, S. F. 1937c. "The Typological Approach to Culture," *Character and Personality,* 5:267–84.

―――. 1951. *The Foundations of Social Anthropology.* London: Cohen & West, Ltd.

―――. 1952. "Witchcraft in Four African Societies: An Essay in Comparison," *American Anthropologist,* 54:18–29.

―――. 1956. "Culture and Personality: A Reexamination," *Medical Journal of Australia,* December 8.

Narain, Dhirendra. 1957. *Hindu Character (A Few Glimpses).* Bombay: University of Bombay Publications, Sociology Series, 8.

Newcomb, Theodore M., Hartley, Eugene L., *et al.* (eds.). 1947. *Readings in Social Psychology.* New York: Henry Holt & Co. (Rev. ed., 1952., with Swanson, G. E.)

New Directions in the Study of National Character. 1955. *Journal of Social Issues,* 11, No. 2.

Notestein, F. W. 1945. "Population—The Long View." In Schultz, T. W. (ed.), *Food for the World.* Chicago: University of Chicago Press. Pp. 36–57.

Oeser, O. A., and Emery, F. E. 1954. *Social Structure and Personality in a Rural Community.* New York: Macmillan Co.

Oeser, O. A., and Hammon, S. B. (eds.). 1954. *Social Structure and Personality in a City.* New York: Macmillan Co.

Ombredane, A., *et al.* 1957. *Etude psychotechnique des Baluba.* Brussels: Memoires de l'Academie des sciences coloniales, sciences morales, 8. N.S. 6:5.

Opler, Marvin K. 1956. *Culture, Psychiatry, and Human Values.* Springfield, Illinois: Charles C. Thomas.

Opler, Morris E. 1936a. "An Interpretation of Ambivalence of Two American Indian Tribes," *Journal of Social Psychology,* 7:82–116.

―――. 1936b. "Some Points of Comparison and Contrast Between the Treatment of Functional Disorders by Apache Shamans and Modern Psychiatric Practice," *American Journal of Psychiatry,* 92:1371–87.

―――. 1941. *An Apache Life-way.* Chicago: University of Chicago Press.

Orlansky, Harold. 1949. "Infant Care and Personality," *Psychological Bulletin,* 46:1–48.

Park, Robert E. 1931. "The Sociological Methods of William Graham Sumner, and of William I. Thomas and Florian Znaniecki." In Rice, S. A. (ed.), *Methods in Social Science: A Case Book.* Chicago: University of Chicago Press. Pp. 154–73.

Parsons, Talcott. 1950. "Psychoanalysis and the Social Structure," *Psychoanalytic Quarterly,* 19:371–84.

Parsons, Talcott, and Shils, E. A., *et al.* 1951. *Toward a General Theory of Action.* Cambridge: Harvard University Press.

Paul, Benjamin D. 1953. "Mental Disorder and Self-regulating Processes in Culture: A Guatemalan Illustration." In *Interrelations Between the Social*

Environment and Psychiatric Disorders. New York: Milbank Memorial Fund. Pp. 51–67.

Paul, Benjamin D. (ed.). 1955. *Health, Culture and Community.* New York: Russell Sage Foundation.

Piers, Gerhart, and Singer, Milton. 1953. *Shame and Guilt: A Psychoanalytic and a Cultural Study.* Springfield, Illinois: Charles C. Thomas.

Pitt-Rivers, G. H. L. F. 1924. "Some Problems in Mental Anthropology and the Problem of Civilization," *Australasian Association for the Advancement of Science,* Wellington Meeting (1923), 497–517.

Plant, James S. 1937. *Personality and the Cultural Pattern.* New York: The Commonwealth Fund.

Potter, David M. 1954. *People of Plenty.* Chicago: University of Chicago Press.

Qureshi, I. Q. 1956. *The Pakistani Way of Life.* London: Wm. Heinemann, Ltd.

Radcliffe-Brown, A. R. 1957. *A Natural Science of Society.* Glencoe, Illinois: The Free Press, and the Falcon's Wing Press.

Radin, Paul. 1913. "Personal Reminiscence of a Winnebago Indian," *Journal of American Folklore,* 26:293–318.

Radin, Paul (ed.). 1926. *Crashing Thunder, The Autobiography of an American Indian.* New York: D. Appleton & Co.

Redfield, Robert. 1930. *Tepoztlan, A Mexican Village.* Chicago: University of Chicago Press.

———. 1955a. *The Little Community:* Viewpoints for the Study of a Human Whole. (The Gottesman Lectures, Upsala University.) Chicago: University of Chicago Press.

———. 1955b. "Society and Culture as Natural Systems" (The Huxley Memorial Lecture, 1955), *Journal of the Royal Anthropological Institute,* 85:19–32.

———. 1956. *Peasant Society and Culture.* Chicago: University of Chicago Press.

———. 1957. "The Universally Human and the Culturally Variable," *Journal of General Education,* 10:150–60.

———. 1959. "Anthropological Understanding of Man." *Anthropological Quarterly,* vol. 32, No. 1:3–21.

———. In press. "Thinker and Intellectual in Primitive Society." In a projected memorial volume for Paul Radin. New York: Columbia University Press.

Redfield, Robert, and Villa, Alfonso R. 1934. "A Village Leader, a Native Autobiography." In Redfield, R., and Villa, A. R. *Chan Kom.* Washington: Carnegie Institution, Publication 448. Pp. 212–230.

Richards, Audrey. 1932. *Hunger and Work in a Savage Tribe.* London: Allen & Unwin, Ltd.

Riesman, David. 1953. "Psychological Types and National Character," *American Quarterly,* 5:325–43.

Riesman, David, Denney, Reuel, and Glazer, Nathan. 1950. *The Lonely Crowd: A Study of the Changing American Character.* New Haven: Yale University Press.

Riesman, David, and Glazer, Nathan. 1952. *Faces in the Crowd: Individual Studies in Character and Politics.* New Haven: Yale University Press.

Rivers, W. H. R. 1926. *Psychology and Ethnology.* New York: Harcourt, Brace & Co.

Rodnick, David. 1948. *Postwar Germans.* New Haven: Yale University Press.

Roe, Anne. 1947. "Personality and Vocation," *Transactions of the New York Academy of Science,* Ser. II, 9:257–67.

Róheim, Géza. 1932. "Psychoanalysis of Primitive Cultural Types," *International Journal of Psychoanalysis,* 13:1–224.

———. 1950. *Psychoanalysis and Anthropology.* New York: International Universities Press.

Russell, Bertrand. 1914. *Our Knowledge of the External World.* New York: Humanities Press, Inc.

———. 1921. *The Analysis of Mind.* New York: Macmillan Co.

———. 1927. *The Analysis of Matter.* New York: Dover Publications.

Sachs, Wulf. 1937. *Black Hamlet,* The Mind of an African Negro Revealed by Psychoanalysis. London: Geoffrey Bles.

Sapir, Edward. 1921. "The Life of a Nootka Indian," *Queens Quarterly,* 28:232–43; 351–67. (Reprinted in Parsons, E. C. (ed.), *American Indian Life.* New York: B. W. Huebsch, 1922.)

———. 1924. "Culture, Genuine and Spurious," *American Journal of Sociology,* 29:401–29; Pt. 2, *The Dalhousie Review* (1922), *q.v.;* Pt. 1 (under the title "Civilization and Culture"), *The Dial* (1919), *q.v.*

———. 1926. "Speech as a Personality Trait," Illinois Society for Mental Hygiene *Health Bulletin.*

———. 1927. "The Unconscious Patterning of Behavior in Society." In Dummer, E. S. (ed.), *The Unconscious: A Symposium.* New York: Alfred Knopf. Pp. 114–42.

———. 1932a. "Cultural Anthropology and Psychiatry," *Journal of Abnormal and Social Psychology,* 27:229–42.

———. 1932b. "Group." In Seligman, E. R. A. (ed.), *Encyclopaedia of the Social Sciences,* Vol. 7. New York: Macmillan Co. Pp. 178–82.

———. 1934a. "The Emergence of the Concept of Personality in a Study of Cultures," *Journal of Social Psychology,* 5:408–15.

———. 1934b. "Personality." In Seligman, E. R. A. (ed.), *Encyclopaedia of the Social Sciences,* Vol. 12. New York: Macmillan Co. Pp. 85–87.

———. 1937. "The Contribution of Psychiatry to an Understanding of Behavior in Society," *American Journal of Sociology:* 42, 862–70.

———. 1938. "Why Cultural Anthropology Needs the Psychiatrist," *Psychiatry,* 1:7–12.

————. 1949. *Selected Writings of Edward Sapir.* Edited by David Mandelbaum. Berkeley and Los Angeles: University of California Press.

Sargent, S. S., and Smith, Marian W. (eds.). 1949. *Culture and Personality.* (Proceedings of an Inter-Disciplinary Conference Under the Auspices of the Viking Fund, November 7–8, 1947.) New York: Viking Fund.

Schneider, David M. 1954. "The Social Dynamics of Physical Disability in Army Basic Training." In Kluckhohn, C., and Murray, H. A. (eds.), with the collaboration of Schneider, D. M., *Personality in Nature, Society, and Culture.* New York: Alfred Knopf. Pp. 386–97.

————. 1955. Review of Gladwin, T., and Sarason, S. B., *Truk: Man in Paradise, American Anthropologist,* 57:1098–1101.

————. 1957. "Political Organization, Supernatural Sanctions and the Punishment for Incest on Yap," *American Anthropologist,* 59:791–800.

Sears, R. R., Maccoby, E. E., and Levin, H. 1957. *Patterns of Child Rearing.* Evanston, Illinois: Row, Peterson & Co.

Seligman, C. G. 1924. "Anthropology and Psychology: A Study of Some Points of Contact," (Presidential Address) *Journal of the Royal Anthropological Institute,* 54:13–46.

————. 1932. "Anthropological Perspective and Psychological Theory," (The Huxley Memorial Lecture for 1932), *Journal of the Royal Anthropological Institute,* 62:193–228.

Sewell, W. H. 1952. "Infant Training and the Personality of the Child," *American Journal of Sociology,* 58:150–59.

Shub, Boris. 1950. "The Soviets Expose a Baby," *New Leader,* June 17, 11–12.

Sikkema, Mildred. 1947. "Observations on Japanese Early Child Training," *Psychiatry,* 10:423–32.

Simmons, Leo W. (ed.). 1942. *Sun Chief.* New Haven: Yale University Press.

Singer, Milton. 1955. "The Cultural Pattern of Indian Civilization: A Preliminary Report of a Methodological Field Study," *Far Eastern Quarterly,* 15:23–36.

———— and Piers, Gerhart. 1953. See Piers.

Slotkin, J. S. 1951. *Personality Development.* New York: Harper & Bros.

————. 1953. "Social Psychiatry of a Menomini Community," *Journal of Abnormal and Social Psychology,* 48:10–16.

Smellie, K. B. 1955. *The British Way of Life.* London: Wm. Heinemann, Ltd.

Smith, Marian W. 1952. "Different Cultural Concepts of Past, Present, and Future, A Study of Ego Extension," *Psychiatry,* 15:395–400.

Spencer, Katherine. 1956. "Mythology and Values: An Analysis of Navaho Chantway Myths," *Memoirs of the American Folklore Society.*

Spindler, G. D. 1948. "American Character Structure as Revealed by the Military," *Psychiatry,* 11:275–81.

————. 1952. "Personality and Peyotism in Menomini Indian Acculturation," *Psychiatry,* 15:151–59.

Spindler, G. D. 1955. *Sociocultural and Psychological Processes in Menomini Acculturation.* Berkeley and Los Angeles: University of California Publications in Culture and Society, No. 5.

Spindler, Louise, and Spindler, George. 1958. "Male and Female Adaptations in Culture Change," *American Anthropologist,* 60:217–33.

Spiro, M. E. 1950. "A Psychotic Personality in the South Seas," *Psychiatry,* 13:189–204.

———. 1951. "Culture and Personality; the Natural History of a False Dichotomy," *Psychiatry,* 14:19–46.

———. 1952. "Ghosts, Ifaluk, and Teleological Functionalism," *American Anthropologist,* 54:497–503.

———. 1954. "Human Nature in Its Psychological Dimensions," *American Anthropologist,* 56:19–30.

———. 1955. "Education in a Collective Settlement in Israel," *American Journal of Orthopsychiatry,* 25:283–92.

———. 1958. *Children of the Kibbutz.* Cambridge: Harvard University Press.

Steed, Gitel P. 1955. "Notes on an Approach to a Study of Personality Formation in a Hindu Village in Gujarat." In Marriott, M. (ed.), *Village India.* Chicago: University of Chicago Press. Pp. 102–44.

Stendler, C. B. 1950. "Sixty Years of Child-Training Practices," *Journal of Pediatrics,* 36:122–36.

Steward, Julian, *et al.* 1956. *The People of Puerto Rico.* Urbana: University of Illinois Press.

Straus, Jacqueline H., and Straus, M. A. 1953. "Suicide, Homicide, and Social Structure in Ceylon," *American Journal of Sociology,* 58:461–69.

Sullivan, Harry Stack. 1940–1945. *Conceptions of Modern Psychiatry.* Washington, D.C.: William Alanson White Psychiatric Foundation. (Reprinted from *Psychiatry,* 3, No. 1, 1940, and 8, No. 2, 1945.)

———. 1948. "Towards a Psychiatry of Peoples," *Psychiatry,* 11:105–16.

Swadesh, Morris. 1948. "Motivations in Nootka Warfare," *Southwestern Journal of Anthropology,* 4:76–93.

Swartz, Marc J. 1958. "Sexuality and Aggression on Romonum, Truk," *American Anthropologist,* 60:467–86.

"Symposium on Projective Testing in Ethnography." 1955. *American Anthropologist,* 57, No. 2, Part 1.

Tax, S., Eiseley, L. C., Rouse, I., and Voegelin, C. F. (eds.). 1953. *An Appraisal of Anthropology Today.* Chicago: University of Chicago Press.

Thomas, W. I., and Znaniecki, F. 1917–18. *The Polish Peasant in Europe and America.* Boston: Richard Badger. (1927, New York: Alfred Knopf.)

Thompson, Laura, and Joseph, Alice. 1944. *The Hopi Way.* Chicago: University of Chicago Press.

Thorpe, W. H. 1956. *Learning and Instinct in Animals.* Cambridge: Harvard University Press.

Thurnwald, R. C. 1932. "The Psychology of Acculturation," *American Anthropologist,* 34:557–69.

Tinbergen, N. 1951. *Study of Instinct.* Oxford and London: Oxford University Press.

Tooth, Geoffrey. 1950. *Studies in Mental Illness in the Gold Coast.* London: Colonial Research Publication, No. 6.

Turi, Johan. 1931. *Turi's Book of Lapland.* Edited and translated into Danish by Emilie Demant Hatt. Translated from the Danish by E. Gee Nash. London: Jonathan Cape.

Underhill, Ruth. 1936. *The Autobiography of a Papago Woman.* Menasha, Wisconsin: American Anthropological Association, Memoir 46.

Underwood, Frances W., and Honigmann, Irma. 1947. "A Comparison of Socialization and Personality in Two Simple Societies," *American Anthropologist,* 49:557–77.

Vogt, E. Z. 1951. *Navaho Veterans: A Study of Changing Values.* Cambridge: Papers of the Peabody Museum of American Archaeology and Ethnology, Harvard University, 41, No. 1.

————. 1955. *Modern Homesteaders: The Life of a Twentieth-Century Frontier Community.* Cambridge: Belknap Press of the Harvard University Press.

Volkhart, E. H. 1951. *Social Behavior and Personality.* New York: Social Science Research Council.

————. 1953. "Aspects of the Theories of W. I. Thomas," *Social Research,* 20:345–57.

Wallace, A. F. C. 1952a. "The Modal Personality Structure of the Tuscarora Indians as Revealed by the Rorschach Test," *Bulletin, Bureau of American Ethnology,* No. 150.

————. 1952b. "Individual Differences and Cultural Uniformities," *American Sociological Review,* 17:747–50.

————. 1958. "Dreams and the Wishes of the Soul: A Type of Psychoanalytic Theory among the Seventeenth-Century Iroquois," *American Anthropologist,* 60:234–48.

Warner, W. Lloyd. 1953. *American Life: Dream and Reality.* Chicago: University of Chicago Press.

Weakland, John Hast. 1950. "The Organization of Action in Chinese Culture," *Psychiatry,* 13:361–70.

Weisskopf, W. A. 1951. "Industrial Institutions and Personality Structure," *Journal of Social Issues,* 7, No. 4; 1–6.

White, Leslie A. 1925. "Personality and Culture," *The Open Court,* 39:145–49.

————. 1947. "Culturological vs. Psychological Interpretations of Human Behavior," *American Sociological Review,* 12:686–98.

Whiting, John W. M. 1941. *Becoming a Kwoma.* New Haven: Yale University Press.

Whiting, John W. M. 1954. "The Cross-Cultural Method." In Lindzey, G. (ed.), *Handbook of Social Psychology*, Vol. I. Cambridge: Addison-Wesley. Pp. 523–31.

Whiting, J. W. M., and Child, I. L. 1953. *Child Training and Personality.* New Haven: Yale University Press.

Wilbur, George B., and Muensterberger, Warner (eds.). 1951. *Psychoanalysis and Culture.* New York: International Universities Press.

Williams, Roger. 1958. "The Improper Study of Mankind," *The Texas Quarterly,* 1, No. 1; 16–32.

Wolfe, Bertram D. 1951. "The Swaddled Soul of the Great Russians," *New Leader,* January 29, 15–18.

Wolfenstein, Martha. 1953. "Trends in Infant Care," *American Journal of Orthopsychiatry,* 33:120–30.

Wolfenstein, Martha, and Leites, Nathan. 1950. *Movies: A Psychological Study.* Glencoe, Illinois: The Free Press.

———. 1955. "Trends in French Films," *Journal of Social Issues,* 11, No. 2; 42–51.

Yap, P. M. 1951. "Mental Diseases Peculiar to Certain Cultures: A Survey of Comparative Psychiatry," *Journal of Mental Science,* 97:313–27.

———. 1952. "The Latah Reaction: Its Pathodynamics and Nosological Position," *Journal of Mental Science,* 98:515–64.

Zborowski, Mark. 1953. "Cultural Components in Attitudes Towards Pain," *Journal of Social Issues,* 8, No. 1; 16–31.

Zborowski, Mark, and Herzog, Elizabeth. 1952. *Life Is with People, The Jewish Little Town in Eastern Europe.* New York: International Universities Press.

II

SOCIAL THEORY AND PERSONALITY

About the Chapter

This chapter by Dr. Spiro, and subsequent chapters by Drs. Wallace, Devereux, and Parsons, attempt to define the primary theoretical issue of culture and personality study. Dr. Spiro's chapter places the field directly in relationship to the central issue in social science, the explanation of social cohesion and functioning. He sees personality as the organized system of motivational tendencies of the person. The motivations are deemed to be crucial variables in the functioning of social systems. Dr. Spiro further analyzes the nature of the social scientist's interest in personality processes and provides a framework for a specification of those aspects of personality with which the social scientist is directly concerned.

About the Author

MELFORD E. SPIRO is Professor of Anthropology at the University of Washington. He is on the Board of Directors of the Social Science Research Council. In 1958–59 he was a Fellow at the Center for Advanced Study in the Behavioral Sciences. He has done field work in Ifaluk (Micronesia) in 1947–48 and in Kiryat Yedidim (Israel) in 1951–52. His current research under a fellowship from the National Institute of Mental Health is in cross-cultural study of religion. His major interests are in comparative religion, culture and personality, theory of social systems, and cultures of Southeast Asia. *Children of the Kibbutz* is his most recent publication.

Acknowledgments

The following individuals who, of course, are not responsible for the content of this chapter, gave the author the benefit of their generous criticisms: Cora DuBois, Dorothy Eggan, Clifford Geertz, John Honigmann, Thomas Kuhn, Kaspar Naegele, George P. Murdock, Richard Rudner, George Spindler, and Jan Waterhouse. The Center for Advanced Study in the Behavioral Sciences provided the leisure and stimulation which made this chapter possible.

2

Social Systems, Personality, and Functional Analysis

MELFORD E. SPIRO

University of Washington

INTRODUCTION

When anthropology was primarily interested in culture history, the question of how societies get their members to behave in conformity with cultural norms was of small concern. But when anthropology became interested in the problem of how societies operate, this question became—and has remained—salient, not only for culture-and-personality theorists but for other anthropologists as well. "Our great problem as anthropologists," says Firth, is ". . . to translate the acts of individuals into the regularities of social process" (1954, p. 11).

Since social systems are attributes of society and personality systems are attributes of individuals, it was formerly assumed, both by anthropologists and by psychologists, that there was little relationship between "the acts of individuals" and the "regularities of social process." Before the development of culture-and-personality studies, this assumption seemed reasonable. First, although there is but one social system for a society, there are as many personalities as there are members of society. Secondly, since social systems are normative, their constituent activities are prescribed; but since personality systems are conative, their activities are

93

motivated. Finally, social systems serve social functions, while personalities serve individual functions. In short, although the functions of social systems are served by the activities of individuals, these activities were not seen as serving personal functions. Hence, older theories of cultural conformity [1] and social control ignored personality as an irrelevant variable.

Classical cultural determinism, for example, attributed efficient causation to the cultural heritage—people perform this or that activity of the social system "because it's part of their culture." Although this theory represents an advance over still older biologistic theories, it begs the very question which is to be answered. As Nadel has put it: ". . . little is gained [in the study of social control] by adducing the force of custom and tradition, that is, the sheer inertia of habitual behavior and inherited practice" (1953, p. 266). The mere existence of a cultural heritage does not imply that it will be inherited; or, if inherited, that behavior will be in conformity with its requirements. The notion that cultural behavior is inherited automatically from the cultural heritage is probably based on a confusion ultimately derived from Tyler's omnibus definition of culture (1874, p. 1). For it would seem that the model upon which the inheritance of cultural behavior is based, is the inheritance of, for example, tools, paintings, and houses—all of which are, of course, inherited automatically, without either effort or motivation. Culture behavior, too, is transmitted from a previous generation; but it is inherited by learning, and not merely by being handed down.

Another answer to the problem of cultural conformity is provided by the social sanctions theory. According to this theory, compliance with cultural norms is achieved through positive and negative sanctions—rewards and punishments—which function as techniques of social control. Although the use of sanctions is probably universal, the thesis that cultural conformity is achieved primarily or exclusively through the use of social sanctions rests, at least implicitly, on two demonstrably false assumptions. These are the Rousseauist assumption that culture is necessarily frustrating, and the super-organistic assumption that cultural norms "exist" in the cultural heritage, but are not internalized by the members of society.

Agreeing with the first, but disagreeing with the second of the above two assumptions, a third theory of cultural conformity views compliance with cultural norms as a function, primarily, of their internalization within personality. Although cultural norms are, indeed, internalized, and although conscience does play an important part in achieving cultural conformity, this theory too is but a partial theory for, as we shall attempt to show, social control is frequently achieved without the necessity for norm internalization.

Culture-and-personality studies suggest that though there is a large measure of truth in these theories, cultural conformity is most frequently achieved because social systems satisfy personality needs. This chapter, then, will attempt to show that there is an intimate relationship between social systems and personality: social systems operate by means of personality, and personality functions by means of social systems. Many of the social functions of social systems can be served only when this intimate relationship obtains.

HUMAN SOCIAL SYSTEMS: THE PROBLEM

Unlike other social animals, the social system of any particular human society cannot be predicted from a knowledge of the species (*Homo sapiens*) of which the society is a member. Nevertheless, since human social systems are rooted in man's biological nature, any discussion of the generic attributes of these systems must take its departure from certain biological dimensions of human existence. From a comparative biological perspective a human social system may be viewed as a functional requirement of human life. Ultimately it stems from the psychobiological needs of, what the biologist terms, a generalized, fetalized (Bolk, 1929), and highly plastic (Montagu, 1951, pp. 368–375) primate. Here we can only point to the consequences of these biological attributes for human social systems. (But cf. LaBarre, 1954; Róheim, 1943.)

The combination of man's mammalian drives (hunger, sex, etc.) and his plastic hominoid constitution (paucity of instincts) requires that means of drive-reduction be learned. Again, the combination of man's organic needs (protection against weather, predatory beasts, etc.) and his hominoid constitution (generalized and fetalized) requires learned methods of protection and adaptation. Moreover, man's prolonged primate dependency and his primate sexual behavior (lack of a breeding season) combine to produce the relatively permanent bi-parental family, and—by extension—larger collectivities (societies) consisting of two or more families. In the absence, however, of an instinctual base—shopworn comparisons of human with insect societies (Wheeler, 1928) are still much to the point—human social life demands that forms of social interaction, methods of social cooperation, techniques of conflict resolution, and the like be learned. But this is not enough. Social existence is necessarily an orderly and regulated existence. Unless the members of a group are able to predict with some probability far greater than chance the behavior of other members of the group with whom they interact, social action, let alone interaction, would be all but precluded. Hence, man must not only learn the various kinds of behavior patterns mentioned above, but these learned behavior patterns must be prescribed by

society and shared with others. The configuration of these socially prescribed, learned, shared and transmitted behavior patterns which medi-
ate and facilitate social relationships constitutes the social system of a human society. We are here only concerned with those characteristics which
make social systems necessary for human survival. We are not concerned
with those characteristics—a complex brain and central nervous system
and the symbolic behavior to which they give rise (White, 1940; Mead,
1934; Langer, 1942; Cassirer, 1944; Hallowell, 1950)—which make
their invention and transmission possible.

To conclude: since man is a generalized, fetalized, and plastic animal
and since everywhere he is necessarily social, a typically human existence
depends on the existence of socially shared behavior patterns which satisfy his (1) biological needs, (2) those group needs that are an invariant
concomitant of social life (Aberle, 1950) and (3) those emotional
needs that develop in the interaction between biology and society. In
this evolutionary perspective a social system may be viewed as an "instrumental apparatus" (Malinowski, 1944) for the satisfaction of these
needs. Social systems, then, have three types of functions. They promote
the physical survival of society and of its constituent members (adaptive
functions); they contribute to the persistence of the social structure of a
society and, hence, to orderly social interaction (adjustive functions);
they promote social solidarity by the reduction of inter- and intra-per-
sonal tension (integrative functions).

This is not to say, of course, that all aspects of every social system
are functional, or that all social systems are equally functional, or that
any social system is functional to the same degree for all the members
of, or groups within, a society. The collapse of some social systems, the
oppressive means used by powerful groups within a society to preserve
others, the repeated history of successful and of unsuccessful rebellions
against still others—all these testify to the powerful dysfunctional forces
operative in some, and potential in all, social systems. But these observations serve to confirm, rather than to confute, the major thesis. Social
systems have vital functions; that these functions be served is their
raison d'être. If they are not served, to a greater or lesser degree, the
social system will, in the long-run, be modified, or the society will not
survive.

Before proceeding with this discussion, it is necessary to emphasize
an obvious characteristic of human social systems that is frequently ob-
scured by the ambiguity of the word "learned," an ambiguity that sometimes leads to hasty generalizations from small-group experiments to social behavior in society. When it is observed that human social systems,
as well as all other aspects of culture, are learned, the word "learned"
has one meaning in a phylogenetic, and another in an ontogenetic con-

text. "Learned" in a phylogenetic context means invented or discovered; "learned" in an ontogenetic context means acquired. Thus, the hypothetical *Ur-mensch* of the Paleolithic was, culturally viewed, a *tabula rasa*. The adaptive, adjustive, and integrative requirements of his society had to be satisfied by behavior patterns of his own invention and discovery. Succeeding generations of human societies have also, to be sure, invented and discovered behavior patterns, and their incorporation into the configuration of existing behavior patterns (which comprise their social systems) is one of the unique dimensions of culture—its cumulativeness. For the most part, however, all generations subsequent to the hypothetical Ur-generation of a society have *acquired* their social systems from a previous generation, rather than inventing or discovering them themselves. In short, the social system of any generation represents, in part, the cultural heritage of the succeeding generation; the social system of the latter, is acquired from the social system of the former.

Social systems, like any other large configuration, can be—and for certain purposes must be—broken down into smaller components. These units, proceeding from the largest to the smallest, are generally termed sub-systems, institutions, roles. Thus, every social system includes an economic system—an organized means for the production, consumption, and distribution of goods and services; a kinship system—an organization of behavior within the family and among kinsmen; a political system—a sanctioned means for the acquisition and use of legitimate power, and so forth. The universality of these sub-systems is sometimes referred to as "the universal culture pattern" (Wissler, 1923, Ch. 5).

Each of these broad categories can usually be classified, in turn, into smaller units. It is rare for any one type of social group within society to perform all the activities which comprise any of these broad sub-systems. Thus the kinship system may embrace the activities of nuclear families, lineages and clans; or the economic system may include the activities of trade unions, banks, factories, and accounting firms. In short, since any society is differentiated and, therefore, consists of many types of social groups, and since each type serves different functions, either for its own members or for those of other social groups, each type of group performs different activities. The configuration of activities which characterizes these different types of groups may be termed an "institution." Thus the activities of the members of the family, *qua* family members, may be termed the "family institution"; the activities of the members of the lineage, *qua* lineage members, may be termed the "lineage institution." Since, collectively, these institutions comprise the kinship system of a society, each may be termed a kinship institution.

Although each type of social group within a society is characterized by a different institution, its constituent members do not, *qua* members, perform the same activities. Each type of group, like the entire society of which it is a part, is structurally differentiated so that various members of the group occupy different positions within the group. Within the family, for example, different members may occupy such positions as father, mother, son, or daughter. Since each position ("status") within the group is associated with one (Linton, 1936) or more (Merton, 1957) sets of activities ("roles"), each institution may be broken down into its constituent roles. Thus the set of activities which comprises the role of father varies from that which comprises the role of mother. Each is a family role; collectively they comprise the family institution. The role, then, is the smallest unit of the social system; the operation of the social system, ultimately and most directly, depends on the proper performance of roles.

To sum up: the survival of a society depends on the operation of its social system; a social system is comprised of sub-systems which, in turn, are comprised of institutions; the functions of these institutions are served only if their constituent roles are performed. In turn, this requires the recruitment of individuals for the various statuses which comprise the social structure. If these propositions are valid, we are brought back to the central issue of this chapter—the problem of cultural conformity. How does society induce its members to perform roles—those that are instrumental to the attainment of a status, as well as those that are entailed by the occupancy of a status? (Nadel, 1957, Ch. 2, has suggested the terms "recruitment roles" and "achievement roles" to refer to these different types of roles.) This problem is best understood against the background of infra-human societies.

Among lower social animals there is a remarkably high correlation between species and social systems. If the environment is held constant, the description of the social system of one society within a species is more or less descriptive of all other societies within the species. Thus, if one knows the species to which a particular subhuman organism belongs, one can predict with high accuracy and with great detail the social system (assuming that it is social) in which it participates (Hine and Tinbergen, 1958; Thompson, 1958; Mayr, 1958). It is quite meaningful, therefore, to speak of species-specific social systems among lower animals.

But though it is meaningful to speak of the red deer social system (Darling, 1937) or the howling monkey social system (Carpenter, 1934) it is not at all meaningful, except on the highest level of generality, to speak of *the* human social system. Man differs dramatically from all other social mammals in the great variety of his intra-species social system differences. Indeed, the magnitude of social system differences within the human species may be as great as the magnitude of difference among animal species. Thus, for example, while the mating pattern of an entire mammalian species may be characterized, and thus distinguished from other species, by monogamy (e.g., gibbons—Carpenter, 1940) or polygyny (e.g., baboons—Zuckerman, 1932) or group marriage (e.g., howling monkeys—Carpenter, 1934), such generalizations apply in the case of humans only to societies within the species and not to the species as a whole. Hence, the fact that one human society practices monogamy, or has patrilineal descent, or is governed by hereditary chiefs, or is stratified by caste, does not enable us to predict that other societies within the species will have the same marriage, descent, political or stratification systems. In short, if one knows that a particular organism belongs to the human species, one cannot predict in any detail the social system in which he participates even if the physical environment is specified. Thus, though paired groups such as California Indians and modern California Americans, pre-contact Hawaiians and the contemporary inhabitants of Hawaii, Alaskan Eskimos and contemporary modern Alaskans have occupied the same physical environment, their respective social systems are radically different.

It is a reasonable inference, then, that though much of the social behavior of animals is not instinctive (Beach, 1955; Lehrman, 1953)—as was formerly believed to be the case—so that each generation of social animals may learn a large percentage of its behavior patterns and social roles from a preceding generation, the range of species plasticity is so narrow that any animal has little alternative, if he is to learn at all, but to learn the behavior patterns which he is taught. What he *must* learn in order to participate in his society's social system and what he *can* learn are for the most part identical. Since humans, on the other hand, are highly plastic, what an individual *must* learn in order to participate in the social system of his society is not at all identical with what he *can* learn; for what he is taught represents, as the cross-cultural record clearly reveals, but one alternative among a large number of behavior patterns and roles which he is potentially capable of learning or, at least, of thinking of learning.

Since humans are so enormously plastic it is not enough, if human social systems are to function properly, that social roles and the behavior patterns of which they are comprised be socially learned, shared, and transmitted; it is also necessary that these roles be prescribed (Newcomb, 1950, Ch. 3). For, since what a person *must* do in order to participate in a given social system is not identical with what he *can* do, it may be inconsistent with what he would *like* to do. Hence in the process of socialization children are not only taught how to behave, but they are taught that the ways in which they are taught to behave are the ways in which they ought to behave. In short, "every human social order," as Hallowell has put it, "operates as a moral order" (1950, p. 169). This normative, or cultural dimension (Spiro, 1951, pp. 31–36) of the human social system is for humans the functional equivalent of restricted plasticity for lower animals. It is the basis for relatively uniform and, therefore, predictable role behavior. (The psychological basis for the emergence of a moral dimension in experience—the self—is discussed in Hallowell, 1954.)

But this analogy cannot be pressed too far, and it is precisely at the point where it breaks down that human societies are uniquely different from animal societies. Since there is always a potential conflict between duty and desire, between cultural heritage and personality, this potentiality—which gives special poignancy to the human situation—sets the problem of our present inquiry: how do human societies get their members to behave in conformity with cultural norms? Or, alternatively, how do they induce their members to perform culturally prescribed roles?

It is at this juncture in the analysis that the concept of personality becomes salient for the understanding of human social systems, for it is in the concept of *role* that personality and social systems intersect. If personality is viewed as an organized system of motivational tendencies, then it may be said to consist, among other things, of needs and drives. Since modes of drive-reduction and need-satisfaction in man must be learned, one of the functions of personality is the promotion of physical survival, interpersonal adjustment, and intrapersonal integration by organizing behavior for the reduction of its drives and the satisfaction of its needs. If some of these needs can then be satisfied by means of culturally prescribed behavior—if, that is, social roles are capable of satisfying personality needs—these needs may serve to motivate the performance of the roles. But if social systems can function only if their constituent roles are performed, then, in motivating the performance of roles, personality not only serves its own functions but it becomes a crucial variable in the functioning of social systems as well. This is the thesis which will be explored in this chapter.

EXTRINSIC CULTURAL MOTIVATION

Since role behavior is a sub-class of learned behavior, we may begin our discussion by asking under what conditions any learned behavior pattern is emitted. Many—but not all—behavioral scientists [2] seem to agree that behavior occurs when the contemplated action is believed by the actor to be rewarding. An act is performed when a person wants something and when he has reason to expect that the performance of the act will supply his want. A simple ontogenetic model can illustrate how this expectation is established.

The ontogenetic model begins with a "drive"—that is, with some felt tension or discomfort. "Drive" is used here in a psychological, not a

physiological, sense, for even the biological drives are significant for behavior only if they function as psychological stimuli; hence, "felt tension
or discomfort." Behavior in an infant or in a naïve experimental animal
is instigated by the desire to "reduce" the drive. But since the drive is
still uncanalized (Murphy, 1947, Ch. 8)—it has no goal, no cathected
object—behavior approaches randomness. By trial-and-error some object or event, which has the property of reducing the drive, is chanced
upon; the drive is gratified; homeostasis is restored. If this sequence is
repeated a sufficient number of times, the drive-reducing object or event
becomes a "goal" and the act which is instrumental to the attainment of
the goal becomes a behavior pattern. An expectation of gratifying a drive
by means of the goal attained by the behavior pattern has been established.

Using this psychological model two simple questions concerning behavior may be answered. Why does a naïve organism behave at all? Because it has a drive. Why, after experience or training, does it behave in
this, rather than in some other, way? Because it has learned that this way
attains goals which are rewarding, *i.e.,* drive-reducing. It should be emphasized, of course, that "drive" refers to both innate and acquired drives,
and that rewards need not be "physical" nor need they be administered
by others. The rewards for exploratory and cognitive activity are frequently—even in the case of lower primates (Harlow, 1953)—inherent
in the very act of exploration or intrinsic to the solution of a problem. It
should also be emphasized that no assumption is made concerning fixed
homeostatic states such that the achievement of drive-reduction leads to
relative quiescence until the drive is reactivated. It is assumed, on the
contrary, that there is always some discrepancy between achievement
and aspiration levels (Lewin, *et al.,* 1944) so that present goal achievement may become but a temporary way-station for contemplated further
and different goal achievement. It *is* assumed, however, that drives *are*
motivational variables and, although not every act is instigated by the
anticipation of drive-reduction, that every drive must eventually be reduced, either directly or indirectly.

Can this psychological model help us to understand cultural behavior,
in general, or the performance of the constituent roles of a social system,
in particular? At first, the answer might appear to be negative. For social
roles, it will be remembered, are not discovered at random by each individual, and social systems are not invented *de novo* by each generation.
On the contrary, since the social system of any generation is in the main
acquired from its cultural heritage, from a previous generation, the goals
which are attained by the performance of roles are either sanctioned or
prescribed.[3] The roles which are instrumental for the attainment of these
goals are prescribed. In short, since social systems are normative systems,

social roles—unlike other learned behavior patterns—very likely are performed not because they are rewarding but because they are mandatory.

It is this imperative dimension of human social systems that has led many social theorists to interpret cultural conformity as a function, primarily, of special techniques of social control. Since social systems have vital social functions, which are served only if their constituent roles are performed, their operation requires that individuals behave in culturally desirable, rather than in personally desired, ways. The proponents of this theory see little relationship between personal motivation and cultural behavior. Conformity to cultural norms, they believe, is not a matter of personality drives primarily, but of social sanctions.

All societies, of course, employ social sanctions as a means of achieving social control, though the specific techniques and agents of control may differ from society to society. Thus, the sanctions may consist in quite different kinds of rewards or punishments. Similarly the agents who administer these sanctions (agents of control) may be one's peers who exercise control through the ubiquitious (informal) techniques of public opinion—shame and praise. This may be termed "alter-ego" control. Alternatively, the agents may be one's superiors, who exercise control through numerous (formal) techniques of public recognition and punitive sanctions available to constituted authority. This may be termed "super-alter" control. These superiors, it might be added, may be natural or supernatural beings, and they may possess natural or supernatural authority.

It should be obvious, however, that even a social sanctions theory of social control, despite the anti-psychological bias of many of its proponents (Radcliffe-Brown, 1957, pp. 45–52), is essentially a motivational theory. No social sanction can *compel* a person to conform; it can only *motivate* him to do so. As Radcliffe-Brown himself observes (1933, p. 531), "The sanctions existing in a community constitute motives in the individual for the regulation of his conduct in conformity with usage." Thus the positive sanction of material reward does not *compel* a person to perform an economic role; rather, it *motivates* him to perform it because the material reward serves as a goal to reduce some drive such as hunger or prestige. Similarly malicious gossip or a jail sentence can induce a person not to steal only if either of these negative sanctions are painful to him; if incarceration or gossip were not painful, they could not compel him to conform to the injunction. Unless the members of society have certain personality drives which can be reduced by acquiring positive, and avoiding negative, sanctions, it is unlikely that these sanctions would serve as techniques of social control. In short, social sanctions serve as techniques of social control because they function as motivational variables.

If social sanctions become incentives for action because of their cathexes as personal (positive or negative) goals, their efficacy may be explained in terms of our psychological model. They function as anticipated rewards or punishments. Since these rewards and punishments are extrinsic to the performance of a role, and since they are administered by persons other than the actor, this type of cultural motivation [4] may be termed "extrinsic cultural motivation," and this type of social control may be termed "extrinsic social control."

To the extent that all societies employ extrinsic social control in some degree as a means of achieving cultural conformity, personality motivation enables the social system to serve its vital social functions. Though the performance of roles may be motivated by the fear of punishment or the desire for rewards, their social functions are served regardless of the personal motives for their performance. Even if social sanctions were the primary technique of social control, analysis of cultural conformity could not avoid the concept of personality.

Although extrinsic social control is universal, it does not follow that its importance in achieving cultural conformity is paramount. Social sanctions may be necessary in order to achieve the conformity of some individuals in some societies almost all of the time, and of most individuals in any society some of the time. Moreover, they are necessary to resolve those conflicts that frequently arise between two persons or groups, both of whom are behaving in conformity with the cultural norms. It is probably safe to assume, however, that this type of control is only rarely the primary type in any society; it is most prevalent in those historical periods of a society which are characterized by anomie. Thus, it is typically found as a primary type of control in transitional periods in which changes, either in tension-producing or tension-reducing social institutions seriously restrict the possibility of satisfying personality needs by culturally stipulated techniques (Sapir's, 1924, "Spurious culture"). In the long run, however, further changes in the social system will restore its tension production-reduction balance (Henry, 1953, p. 154), so that extrinsic control is no longer primary; or the psycho- and sociopathology that result from this cultural pathology will become so extensive that social life is no longer viable.

INTRINSIC CULTURAL MOTIVATION

Personal Motives and Manifest Social Functions

If social sanctions are not the primary means of achieving cultural conformity, it is because social roles, though prescribed, satisfy personality needs. Fromm is undoubtedly correct when he writes:

In order that any society may function well, its members must acquire the kind of character which makes them *want* to act in the way they *have* to act as members of the society . . . They have to *desire* what objectively is *necessary* for them to do. (1944, p. 381)

In order to understand this transformation of duty into desire we must first understand how the normative dimension of human social systems serves to qualify our psychological model. In this model, it will be recalled, behavior is instigated initially by the desire to reduce a drive, and any object or event which serves this end will do. Subsequently those objects or events which gratify the drive may become cathected so that they function as goals. When this happens behavior is motivated by the desire not merely to gratify a drive, but to gratify it by attaining a particular goal. Canalization, as Murphy (1947, Ch. 8) has termed this process of drive-goal connection, is characteristic of much motivation. But cultural motivation is unique in that these canalizations are ordained by the cultural heritage prior to individual experience instead of arising in the context of individual experience. By stipulating that only a limited, out of a potentially large, number of objects or events may serve as goals for drives, and by prohibiting all others, the cultural heritage insists that if a drive is to be gratified at all, it must be gratified by means of these stipulated prescribed or sanctioned goals. Thus, though a New Guinea headhunter must bring home a head if he is to gratify his prestige drive, an Ifaluk must not; and though an American is permitted to gratify his hunger drive by eating roast beef, a Hindu is not.

If the goal of a behavior pattern is distinguished from its drive, much of the dramatic diversity found in the cross-cultural record reflects the diversity, not of man's "nature," but of his history and of his cognitive ingenuity. Since man is enormously plastic, a large variety of goals may, potentially, reduce the same drive. In the absence of biologically rigid drive-goal connections, different societies, as a function of their unique histories and ecologies, have "chosen" different goals for the same drives as well as different roles for the attainment of these goals. The resultant diversity in goals has led some anthropologists to insist that each culture is not only *sui generis* but that cross-cultural generalizations are impossible to achieve. Such a position is, functionally viewed, wide off the mark. Although cultural goals are parochial, most human drives—because of their rootedness in a common biology and in common conditions of social life—are probably universal. Hence, it is generally not too difficult to demonstrate (on a fairly high level of generality, of course) that the quite diverse goals of different societies, as well as the roles which are instrumental for their attainment, are functionally equivalent; they serve to gratify the same drives (Murphy, 1954, pp. 628–631).

But the fact that goals are prescribed does not imply—as some theorists take it to imply—that they do not or cannot gratify drives. On the contrary, culturally prescribed goals may be as rewarding as non-prescribed goals. By prescribing goals the cultural heritage does not frustrate drives, it merely limits the number of ways in which they may be gratified. To be sure, since man has few instincts, he must learn to perceive the pre- scribed goals as rewarding. But this is the function of child-training. In the process of socialization, children acquire not only drives, but they ac- quire goals as well; they learn which objects or events—the culturally prescribed goals—are drive-reducing. In short, socialization systems— by techniques which cannot be described here—are institutionalized means for transforming culturally-stipulated goals into personally- cathected goals (Erikson, 1950; Whiting and Child, 1953). If the per- sonal cathexis of a stipulated goal is termed a "need," it is apparent that a need-satisfaction model is more appropriate than a drive-reduction model as a description of cultural motivation. For in general once a prescribed goal is sufficiently cathected, that goal which is culturally viewed as the only desirable, if not the only possible, goal for the gratification of a drive, becomes personally viewed as the most desired goal. Indeed, in some in- stances it, and no other, is perceived as drive-reducing, so that drive- frustration may be preferred to drive-reduction by non-cathected goals. An Orthodox Hindu, for example, refuses to eat beef, not only because it is prohibited, but because it is not desired; the very notion of eating beef may be disgusting to him. Hence the paradox: although evolution has produced a species characterized by the absence of drive-goal in- variants, culture produces personalities who behave as if there were. For after cultural goals are cathected, human beings sometimes behave as if *their* drive-goal connections were the only ones possible.

To conclude: social roles, like other types of learned behavior, are per- formed if they are rewarding. But if the culturally stipulated goals, which are attained by their performance, are cathected, behavior is motivated by the expectation of attaining a goal not by the desire to reduce a drive. To be sure, the goal is desired because its attainment produces drive- reduction; if it did not, it would not, in the long run, continue to be de- sired. But this is precisely the point of the "need" concept: it looks, so to speak, in two directions. On the one hand it affirms that drive-reduction is rewarding, so that acts that do not reduce drives are not performed. On the other hand, it denies that the desire to reduce a drive is a sufficient explanation of cultural motivation; for when culturally stipulated goals are sufficiently cathected, action is motivated (with the possible exception of extreme deprivation) by the expectation of attaining these cathected goals.[5]

It is now perhaps clear how cultural imperatives can become personal desires—how, in short, people can want to perform social roles. If the performance of social roles does in fact attain those culturally stipulated goals for whose attainment they are intended by the cultural heritage, and if these goals have been cathected by the members of society, these roles are performed because of the desire to attain these goals. In short, although social roles are prescribed by the cultural heritage, their performance is motivated by the expectation of satisfying personality needs. Though these roles must be performed so that their functions for society can be served, individuals desire to perform them because personal functions are thereby served.[6] Thus, for example, the American army serves an important adaptive function for American society by defending its people against foreign enemies. Should an individual American become identified (in the psychoanalytic sense) with his society, he will internalize this function as a personal drive and, therefore, he might cathect this stipulated goal as a personal goal. Should this happen he may be motivated to become a soldier and to perform its prescribed role because its performance satisfies a personality need. In short, if the social function of a role is internalized as a personal drive, its performance, which is intended to serve a social function, serves a personal function—albeit unintentionally—as well. Diagrammatically, this can be represented thus:

need ———▶performance of role ⟨ ⟶ personal function (unintended)
                                   ⟶ social function (intended)

But if cultural goals are cathected as personal goals only when social functions are internalized as personal drives, the number of roles whose performance can serve personal functions would be small indeed. Indeed, it is precisely because the social functions of roles only rarely become personal drives that some theorists have stressed the importance of social sanctions as a means, *par excellence,* of assuring cultural conformity. And surely the argument is plausible. For if a role has a social function, and if the serving of its function is not a personality need, how can its performance be motivated by the expectation of satisfying a personality need?

This argument, however plausible, neglects to consider still another possibility. Stipulated goals may be cathected, and therefore social roles performed, although social functions are not internalized; and social functions may be served, although they are unintended. As Kroeber, generalizing from his analysis of religious change among the Kota, has put it: "In manipulating their culture for their personal ends, the participants often produce a cultural effect that may be enduring, as well as attaining their individual goal or tension reliefs" (1948, p. 507).

This can happen in two ways: when personal and social functions are members of the same functional class, and when they are members of different functional classes. Both of these ways, beginning with the first, can be illustrated by returning to the soldier role and the motives for its performance. Since individuals exist *qua* members of society as well as *qua* individuals, their welfare is frequently dependent upon the welfare of society. Thus, though an individual may not internalize the adaptive (social) function of the soldier role as a personal drive, he may nonetheless, if he believes that his personal survival depends on the survival of his society, cathect its goal of national defense; and he may then be motivated to perform the role in order to satisfy this personality need. But since the social (adaptive) function of the soldier role consists in the summation of its personal (adaptive) functions for individuals, the performance of the role not only serves a personal function, but it serves its social function as well—albeit unintentionally.

There is still another way in which culturally stipulated goals can become personality needs. Not everyone who becomes a professional soldier, for example, is motivated to achieve or to perform this role in order to defend either himself or his society from enemy attack. Since the promotion of national defense is, at least in our society, one means for the attainment of prestige and power, this culturally stipulated goal may become the cathected goal for the reduction of these drives. The performance of the soldier's role may then be motivated by the expectation of satisfying power and prestige needs. Nevertheless though the personal functions (integrative and adjustive) and social function (adaptive) of the role are members of different functional classes, and though its performance is intended to serve personal functions, its social function—although unintended—is served as well. Diagrammatically, these last two cases can be represented thus:

$$\text{need} \longrightarrow \text{performance of role} \begin{cases} \longrightarrow \text{personal function (intended)} \\ \longrightarrow \text{social function (unintended)} \end{cases}$$

To sum up, any act may be viewed from at least two perspectives: motive and function. The motive of an act is the consequence, either for the actor or for society, which is intended by its performance; its function is the actual consequence of its performance, either for the actor or for society. Functions may be positive or negative; that is, the consequence of an act may contribute to the welfare of the actor or of society or it may detract from their welfare. (We are here concerned with positive functions only, and the generic term, "function," refers to positive function exclusively.) Finally acts have intended and unintended functions. That is, the consequence of an act may be the consequence which was intended by its performance, or it may be one which was not intended by its performance. Since social roles have social functions, and since acts are performed only if they have personal functions, it has often been assumed that there is little intrinsic relationship between personality needs and the performance of roles except in those few instances in which an act is intended to serve both personal and social functions. A soldier, for example, might be motivated to play his role because he intended to serve both himself and his country.

But if acts can have unintended as well as intended consequences, it is possible for personal and social functions to be served in the performance of the same acts or roles. And this can happen in two ways: when their personal functions are intended and their social functions are unintended, and when their personal functions are unintended and their social functions intended. In either event since the performance of the roles serves personal as well as social functions, their performance is motivated—without the operation of social sanctions—because they satisfy personality needs. Since these needs consist in the personal cathexes of culturally stipulated goals, the performance of social roles is effected by, what may be termed, "intrinsic cultural motivation." Alternatively, the cultural conformity which results from this type of motivation is achieved by "intrinsic social control," for the control function is, as it were, built into the very fabric of the role. By satisfying personality needs, its performance is assured, and its social functions performed, without the necessity for sanctions extrinsic to the role or for agents external to the actor.

Personal Motives and Latent Social Functions

Thus far it has been contended that personality plays an important part in the operation of social systems because, by motivating the performance of social roles, it enables the social system to serve its social functions. The discussion, however, has dealt with the manifest functions of roles exclusively, that is, with those social functions which, whether intended or unintended by the members of society, are recognized by them. But social systems, have latent functions as well, and sometimes their latent functions are more important for society than their manifest functions. It is here, moreover, that personality is uniquely important for the functioning of society.

If manifest functions are those consequences of role performance which are recognized by the members of society, latent functions are those consequences which—whether intended or unintended—are not recognized by them.[7] That the paradox of an intended but unrecognized function is apparent rather than real, becomes clear when one considers that motives may be unconscious, as well as conscious. In short, manifest (recognized) functions are served by the performance of roles when at least one of the motives for their performance is conscious; latent (unrecognized) functions are served when at least one of the motives for their performance is unconscious. Hence, before analyzing latent functions, it is necessary to examine the concept of unconscious motive.

If the motive for behavior consists in an intention to satisfy a need by performing a particular act (and if a need consists in a drive and a goal), a motive may be unconscious, i.e., unrecognized, in any one or all of these three dimensions. Thus a drive, its goal, and the desired means for the attainment of the goal may all be unconscious. With the exception of neurotic, i.e., idiosyncratic, repression, if any or all of these dimensions of a motive are unconscious in a typical member of a society, the motive has generally been rendered unconscious because of a cultural prohibition or because of its systematic frustration. In the latter case, since need-frustration as well as the memory of need-frustration are painful, repression of the frustrating experience as well as of the need is one possible defense against pain. We shall confine the discussion to the former basis for repression. Thus, for example, the cultural heritage may prohibit any reduction of the sex drive, as in sacerdotal celibacy; or it may prohibit a desired goal for its reduction, such as intercourse with kinsmen who fall within the boundaries of the incest taboo; or it may prohibit a desired means for the attainment of the goal, such as some "perverted" technique of sexual relations. In short the cultural heritage not only provides means of need-satisfaction for an animal without in-stinctive means for drive-reduction, but—by prescribing these means—it prohibits other means which this relatively plastic and imaginative animal may come to prefer. Moreover it may completely prohibit any conceivable (manifest) expression or reduction of certain drives.

But motives do not disappear simply because they are prohibited. Even if the cultural prohibition is internalized as a personal norm, the culturally prohibited canalization may continue to persist as a personally preferred canalization, and the culturally prohibited drive may continue to seek ex-pression. The resultant incompatibility between internalized norm and personal desire leads to inner conflict which must be "handled" in some way. If these personally preferred, but culturally prohibited, canalizations are stronger than the internalized cultural prohibition, they may be ex-pressed directly. If, then, the resultant behavior is categorically pro-hibited, it is deemed criminal or psychologically aberrant (depending on the culture) by the members of society. Alternatively, if the behavior is culturally aberrant, but not clearly prohibited, it may be viewed as a cultural innovation—that is, as a new, but culturally acceptable, behavior pattern.

On the other hand, should the internalized cultural prohibition be stronger than the personal desire, the inner conflict may be resolved by repressing the desire. The prohibited motive, in short, becomes un-conscious. But unconscious as well as conscious motives seek expression and satisfaction. They may be expressed (and satisfied) in neurosis and psychosis; in private fantasy (day-dreams and night dreams); in sym-bolic, but culturally creative, ways (artistic and scientific work); or, and more germane to this chapter, in the performance of culturally prescribed roles. Since unconscious motives cannot be satisfied directly—if they could they would not be unconscious—they may thus seek indirect satisfaction in the performance of culturally sanctioned behavior. In short, in addition to its conscious motivation, culturally sanctioned behavior, including role behavior, may be unconsciously motivated as well. Since, in the latter case, the performance of a role is motivated by an unconscious as well as by a conscious intention of satisfying a need, the role may have unrecognized though intended personal functions; and these, in turn, may produce unrecognized and unintended social functions. This thesis may be illustrated by examples from two societies: warfare among the Sioux Indians of the American Plains, and religion among the Ifaluk of Micronesia.

Diagrammatically, the relationship between the motives for the performance of the Sioux warrior role and its various personal and social functions can be represented thus:

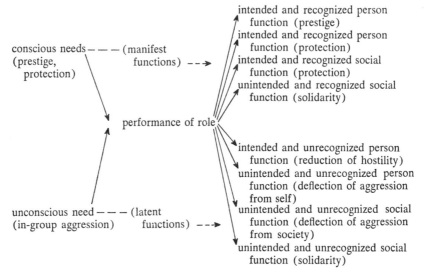

conscious needs – – – (manifest
(prestige,   functions) – –➤
  protection)

performance of role

unconscious need – – – (latent
(in-group aggression)   functions) – –➤

intended and recognized person
  function (prestige)
intended and recognized person
  function (protection)
intended and recognized social
  function (protection)
unintended and recognized social
  function (solidarity)

intended and unrecognized person
  function (reduction of hostility)
unintended and unrecognized person
  function (deflection of aggression
  from self)
unintended and unrecognized social
  function (deflection of aggression
  from society)
unintended and unrecognized social
  function (solidarity)

Sioux warfare was motivated by two conscious needs: prestige and protection from enemies. In satisfying these needs for prestige and protection, warfare served manifest personal (integrative) and social (adaptive) functions. It may be assumed, it served an unintended (integrative), but manifest social function, as well—the promotion of social solidarity by the creation of *esprit de corps* among the warriors.

But the "choice" of warfare as a preeminent institutionalized means of obtaining prestige leads us to suspect that the conscious motives for the performance of the warrior role, though genuine, were not its only motives. Warfare is an aggressive activity. Why did the Sioux act aggressively when the objective threat from the enemy was slight? Sioux war parties, it will be recalled, attacked rather than defended; they preferred to attack when their "enemies" were least prepared, that is, when they constituted no threat; young bucks had to be restrained from going on the warpath, rather than having to be encouraged to do so. And why did they seek prestige through aggression when, as the cross-cultural record reveals, there are many non-aggressive roles through which prestige can be obtained? Sioux warfare apparently was motivated not only by the conscious needs of prestige and protection, but by yet another, unconscious, motive—hostility against their fellows.

As is the case in most societies, Sioux socialization, as well as the conditions of adult Sioux social life, created in each new generation a motive for aggression against their fellows (Erikson, 1939, 1945). Like most societies, moreover, the cultural heritage of the Sioux prohibited physical aggression against the in-group. However, only one of the three dimensions of this motive was prohibited. Neither the drive itself (hostility) nor the means of its reduction (physical aggression), but only its object (the in-group), was prohibited. It was assumed, then, that the specific dimension of physical aggression against *fellows* was repressed, i.e., rendered unconscious. But by displacing hostility from the in- to the outgroups, this motive could now be expressed. This motive, one may suggest, sought satisfaction in, and was therefore important in the motivation of, Sioux warfare. In addition to their motives of prestige and protection, Sioux war parties were also motivated by aggression. In satisfying this motive, the warrior role served a latent personal function (integration), as well as its manifest personal and social functions.

When the performance of roles is motivated by unconscious needs, it serves unintended and unrecognized social functions as well as intended but unrecognized personal functions. What possible unintended and unrecognized function for society was served by the Sioux institution of warfare? By displacing hostility, and its subsequent aggression, in warfare against the outgroup, the warrior role protected Sioux society from the aggression of its own members (adaptive function). Had the original hostility not been displaced and subsequently gratified in socially sanctioned aggression, it might have sought undisguised and, therefore, socially disruptive expression. It might have sought expression in other ways as well. Indeed, Erikson interprets the sun dance, and its painful consequences for its participants—staring into the sun and tearing of skewers from their flesh—as the turning of aggression inward. It might be suggested, then, that in the absence of war, even more aggression would have been turned against the self. Hence, the performance of the warrior role served a latent, unintended personal function, as well as its latent unintended social function.

But to return to the social functions of Sioux warfare: by deflecting hostility from in- to out-group, the preponderance of positive over negative sentiments concerning the members of the group was increased, thereby promoting in-group solidarity (integrative function). Neither of these unintended and unrecognized social functions would have been served had the performance of the warrior role been motivated exclusively by the motives of prestige and protection. Moreover, those anthropologists who are unaware of, or uninterested in, the latent personal functions of roles—because unaware of, or uninterested in, unconscious motives—would remain ignorant of the important latent social functions which are served by this role, and of the general functional significance of Sioux warfare within the total social system.

The second example of the relationship between unconscious motives and social functions not only illustrates the importance of unconscious motivation in the functioning of social systems, but it also illustrates how a society and its social system may be affected by the intrinsic motivation of another cultural system—religion. Most public religious rituals in the Micronesian atoll of Ifaluk are either therapeutic or prophylactic in nature; they are designed to maintain or restore health by exorcising malevolent ghosts (who cause illness by possessing their victims), or by preventing these ghosts from executing their intentions in the first place. It is not within the province of social science to decide whether one of the manifest, intended, functions of these rituals—defeat of the ghosts—is served; the Ifaluk, of course, believe that it is. But these rituals serve other manifest functions to which the behavioral scientist can testify. By their performance the twin fears of illness and of attack by ghosts are reduced (manifest intended personal function), and by assembling and acting in concert for the achievement of a common end, good fellowship is strengthened (manifest unintended social function).

But the performance of these rituals requires another motive in addition to its therapeutic motive. These are aggressive rituals in which malevolent ghosts are attacked and, it is hoped, routed. It requires little insight to infer that hostility, as well as fear, motivates the performance. Indeed, the Ifaluk are quite consciously hostile toward the ghosts. But though consciously hostile to ghosts, the Ifaluk, like all people, have occasion to be hostile to their fellows, particularly to their close kinsmen. By displacing hostility from fellows to ghosts, their hostility is acceptable, and their subsequent aggressive motive can be gratified in a socially sanctioned manner in the performance of these rituals (Spiro, 1953a). A latent personal function (integrative) of these rituals, then, consists in the opportunity which their performance affords for the satisfaction of this aggressive need.

As in the Sioux example, however, the performance of these rituals also serves a latent unintended social function, one which is vital for this society. The Ifaluk social system, based on the strongly held values of sharing, mutual aid, and kindliness, is highly cooperative. If the Ifaluk were unable to express aggression symbolically in ritual, it is not improbable that their hostility would eventually seek direct expression. If this were to happen, the probability of physical survival on an atoll, six-tenths of a mile square, would be effectively reduced. By serving to deflect aggression onto malevolent ghosts, the performance of these rituals effectively increases the chances for survival. Moreover, as in the case of the Sioux, the belief in malevolent ghosts, which permits the displacement of hostility from the in-group to the wicked out-group, assures the persistence of the warm sentiments which the Ifaluk harbor towards each other. Hence the psychological basis for their cooperative social system —probably the only kind of system which is viable in this demographic-ecological balance—is preserved. In short, by serving its latent personal function, this ritual is also able to serve the latent social functions of promoting the group's survival and of preserving the viability of its social system (Spiro, 1952).

Diagrammatically, the relationship between the motives for the performance of Ifaluk rituals, which attack and exorcise malevolent ghosts, and their personal and social functions can be represented in the following way:

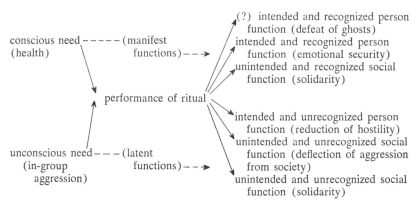

This discussion of unconscious motives, and of the latent social functions served by social roles (and other types of cultural behavior) whose performance is motivated by them, has been somewhat extended because, with the exception of culture-and-personality research, they are ignored in most analyses of social systems. Unconscious motives are frequently dismissed by social scientists as irrelevant to an understanding of society. "Oh," it is often said, "these unconscious motives may be important for personality, but we're interested in the study of society." This analysis has attempted to demonstrate that anyone interested in society should also be interested in unconscious motives. They are as important for the student of society as for the student of personality, not only because they motivate the performance of social roles but because the latent social functions which they enable these roles to serve are often more important than those which are served under conscious motivation. It should be emphasized, however, that unconscious motives, however important, are not the only motives of behavior, that conscious motives are not merely rationalizations. Though this may sometimes be the case, the assumption that only unconscious motives are genuine is as fallacious as the contrary assumption. If the conscious motives of Sioux warfare and Ifaluk ritual are not sufficient explanations for their performance, neither are the unconscious motives: both are necessary, both are genuine, neither is sufficient. To assume that only unconscious motives are genuine is to perpetuate that vulgar interpretation of psychoanalytic theory in which schoolteaching, for example, is "nothing but" the sublimation of an unconscious sexual motive, or surgery is "nothing but" the displacement of unconscious aggression.

Theories of social systems that ignore unconscious motives are not only truncated, but when social analyses which are based on such theories are applied by administrators, they often lead to unfortunate results. If we were to assume, for example, that Sioux warfare or Ifaluk religious rituals are means merely for obtaining prestige or reducing anxiety concerning illness respectively, and that by achieving these ends they also promote social solidarity—the typical social anthropological functionalist analysis —then it is a fair administrative conclusion that these "savage" and "superstitious" practices can be abolished without harm to society as long as the "civilized" practices with which they are replaced are their functional equivalents, as long, that is, as the new practices are also means for obtaining prestige, for reducing anxiety concerning illness, and for promoting social solidarity. But despite these good intentions, the new practices are *not* the functional equivalents of the old if they do not serve, as well, the latent personal function of displacing unconscious hostility. Unless this function is achieved, substitutes cannot serve the latent social function of deflecting aggression from the in-group. Hence, this unconscious motive may seek expression in numerous dysfunctional ways— dysfunctional both for individuals and society. It may be expressed directly, leading to crime, or indirectly, leading to drunkenness, etc.; it may be inverted, leading to anxiety and depression ("race suicide"), and so forth. By ignoring the importance of unconscious motivation in social behavior, the attempt of well-intentioned administrators (acting upon the findings of psychologically uninformed researchers) to substitute "unobjectionable" for "objectionable" native practices has often been a history of grave disappointments to the administrator and sordid results for the natives.

It should be strongly emphasized that although personality needs are satisfied in and therefore motivate the performance of social roles, a person's personality cannot necessarily be inferred from a knowledge of the roles he performs. In the first place, although this chapter is concerned with the relationship between personality and the social system, it is obvious that only part of the personality is relevant to and is expressed through the social system. The relationship between personality and other cultural systems (religion, art, science, etc.), as well as those private aspects of personality that are not caught up in the sociocultural net (Murphy, 1958, part 3), are deliberately ignored. In short, a description of a person's various social roles would not lead to an exhaustive description of his personality.

More important, however, for our purposes, a knowledge of a person's social roles would not even lead to an accurate prediction of those aspects of his personality that are caught up in their performance. For, as this section has attempted to show, since different goals may be cathected by the same drive and since different roles may be instrumental for the attainment of the same goal, "a high degree of role differentiation," as Kaplan has put it, does not necessarily require "a similar degree of differentiation at the personality level" (1957, p. 100). At the same time, since the same goal may be cathected by different drives, and since the same role may be instrumental for the attainment of different goals, a high degree of personality differentiation does not necessarily require a similar degree of differentiation at the social system level. Thus, (1) different drives may be canalized by the same goal, which is attained by the performance of the same role; (2) the same drive may be canalized by different goals, which are attained by the performance of different roles; and (3) different drives may be canalized by the same goal which is attained by the performance of different roles. These alternatives are shown in the following diagrams.

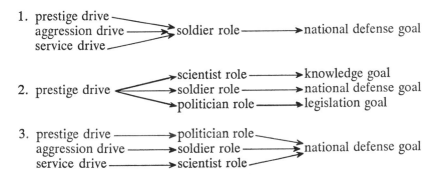

But if this is true within a society, it is equally true among societies. Since there are fewer drives in man than there are goals in all his societies, and since there are fewer goals in all human societies than there are roles in their social systems, it is reasonable to expect fewer modal personality systems than social systems. On the other hand, since drives, goals, and roles may vary independently of each other, it is possible for different modal personality systems to be associated with similar social systems, and for similar modal personality systems to be associated with different social systems.

If this is so the student of social systems, who is interested in their motivational well-springs, must at the same time be a student of personality; and statements about the relationships between personality and social systems must be based on personality investigations, and not inferred from a description of social systems (Inkeles and Levinson, 1954). Personality investigation may entail the use of psychological instruments, such as projective tests (Hallowell, 1955), the analysis of dreams (Eggan, 1952), the collection of life histories (Kluckhohn, 1945), and depth interviewing. It may also be based, however, on the observation of behavior when viewed from the perspective of, and interpreted in terms of, psychodynamic personality theory. For if the same set of activities can serve both personal and social functions, the same set of activities may be viewed from a personality perspective (as a means for serving personal functions) or from a social system perspective (as a means for serving social functions). If one's focus is on society and on those adaptive, adjustive, and integrative prerequisites of a viable social life, a given set of activities is analyzed as a role within the social system. If, on the other hand, one's focus is on an individual and on the adaptive, adjustive, and integrative prerequisites of a viable individual life, the same set of activities is analyzed as a means for satisfying the needs of the personality system. This last technique uses a powerful, but rare instrument—a sensitive observer.

INTERNALIZED CULTURAL MOTIVATION

Since intrinsic cultural motivation is based on the personal cathexis of culturally stipulated goals, it obviously cannot serve as a technique of social control when these goals are not cathected. There are various conditions which reduce the probability of goal cathexis. The following are probably most important: (a) the goals of many taboos and prohibitions, since they lead to frustration, may increase rather than reduce the intensity of drives (Freud, 1930); (b) in societies undergoing rapid culture change, many new goals will not reduce extant drives (Hallowell, 1945); (c) a similar situation will obtain in the case of subordinate groups, whose culture has largely been imposed by a dominant group; (d) cathexis may be withdrawn from previously cathected goals because of the realization that they cannot be achieved (Merton, 1938).

Even when goals are cathected it does not necessarily follow that the culture patterns or roles that attain them will be performed. There are other possibilities. Though the goal is desired, the role which is prescribed for its attainment may be odious. Thus, though everyone may desire clean public latrines, no one may desire to perform the role of latrine attendant. Again, a non-sanctioned means for the attainment of a desired goal may be perceived as more efficient or as less burdensome than the sanctioned role. Similarly, the cultural goal may be scarce, so that not all who strive for its attainment can be successful. Hence, competitive anxiety may motivate the performance of proscribed, but more efficient, techniques. Finally, the social structure, particularly in a stratified society, may effectively preclude certain categories of persons from performing the roles which attain the goals (Merton, 1938).

In all of these situations social conformity will be achieved only by some technique of social control other than—or in addition to—intrinsic cultural motivation. Extrinsic social control is one such technique; but it is not the only one. For the importance of personality needs in the motivation of social roles is not restricted to intrinsic cultural motivation. The latter type of motivation is ultimately based on two kinds of personality needs—id and ego needs, in psychoanalytic vocabulary. But personality has superego needs as well; and many roles may be performed (though id and ego are not satisfied, and may even be frustrated) because their performance satisfies superego needs.

If roles are motivated by the expectation of satisfying superego needs, social control is achieved by, what we may term, "internalized cultural motivation." For cultural conformity in this instance is achieved, not through external sanctions (extrinsic control), nor by intrinsic goals (intrinsic control), but by internalized norms. To put it in terms we have been employing, if extrinsic control is achieved (in the case of positive sanctions) by the cathexis of the social sanction, and if intrinsic control is achieved by the cathexis of the cultural goal, internalized control is achieved by the cathexis of the cultural norm.

There has been a great deal of discussion concerning the internalization of norms. Some writers, following Ruth Benedict (1946, pp. 222–227, 288–289), have suggested that norm-internalization is a phenomenon restricted to certain types of societies and absent from others. Cultures which give rise to norm-internalization are termed "guilt-cultures," for cultural conformity is motivated by guilt. Those which do not produce norm-internalization are termed "shame-cultures," for the members of society conform to cultural norms only when their fellows are present to shame them. Hence, in societies with shame cultures extrinsic control is necessary to ensure cultural conformity—assuming that the performance of roles is not intrinsically motivated.

Although shame obviously operates as a control technique in any society, the validity of this shame culture—guilt culture dichotomy is open to question (Piers and Singer, 1953). Since social systems are, to a great extent, normative—many of their constituent roles and goals are prescribed by the cultural heritage—it is improbable for the members of any society not to have internalized these norms. If norms were not internalized, parents would have none to transmit to their children because, *ex hypothesi,* they would not have internalized any in the course of their own socialization. Further, if no one has internalized the norms, who, in societies with shame cultures, would do the shaming? The existence of agents of shame implies that at least some members of society have internalized at least some norms.

In short, one may argue that although in any society there may hypothetically be some individuals who have internalized very few norms (the so-called psychopaths), and many individuals who have not internalized some of the norms, in all societies most individuals not only (a) learn *about* their cultural norms, but they also (b) accept them, (c) evaluate their own acts in accordance with them, and (d) experience anxiety ("moral anxiety") should they desire to violate them. This anxiety serves as an important deterrent to norm violation. Indeed, even in societies whose cultures correspond most closely to the description of the ideal shame culture, ". . . blame, ridicule, or holding up to shame are controls only if they express commonly accepted values and correspond to the promptings of the superego" (Nadel, 1953, p. 272).

How does this moral anxiety develop? And what does it represent? To answer the second question first, this anxiety presumably represents the largely unconscious expectation of punishment, as distinguished from the rational, conscious fear of being punished. This distinction must be explained.

The individual who has internalized a norm, and not merely learned about it, perceives his anticipated violation of it as a transgression and hence as deserving of punishment. This perception induces anxiety (the anticipation of punishment). The mere intention of committing an act which he himself labels as a "transgression," or of not performing an act which he deems compulsory, leads him to expect that his behavior (which in his eyes is deserving of punishment) will in some way be punished. Where the individual believes that punishment is his due, "expectation of punishment" is but another term for "moral anxiety."

On the other hand, the individual who has merely learned about the norm, but has not internalized it, suffers no moral anxiety as a consequence of his anticipated violation of it. Because he himself has not internalized the norm, he does not (though others may) consider his anticipated violation to be deserving of punishment, since he does not consider his act to be "wrong." In short, he experiences no moral anxiety. He may, of course, experience considerable anxiety about the punishment which would be meted out to him were he caught. In moral anxiety, however, it is not the fear that one might be punished if caught, but the belief that one merits punishment that evokes anxiety.

Moral anxiety, therefore, has both drive and cue properties. It informs the individual that his anticipated behavior is wrong (worthy of punishment), and that its performance will lead to punishment; and it motivates him to reduce the anxiety by refraining from transgression. Hence, the anxiety serves as a motive for conformity.

Since moral anxiety is not innate, how is it acquired? So far as our present knowledge permits, we may suggest that it arises out of certain universal features of human socialization systems. In all societies, agents of socialization are not only trainers, but they are also nurturers, satisfying the child's most important need—the need for love. To the extent that these agents employ rewards and punishments as part of their training methods, and to the extent that such rewards and punishments are, for the child, symbolic of their love, the child is motivated to comply with the demands of these "significant others" (Mead, 1934) in order to obtain their love or, conversely, to preclude its withdrawal. Through their ability to give and withhold love, the child not only learns what the agents of socialization judge to be good and bad behavior, but he also learns to concur in their judgment; in short, he models his behavior in accordance with their norms. He learns to accept their judgment as his own because behavior which these significant others judge to be bad is indeed "bad" *for him*—it leads to the withdrawal of love (punishment) by those whose love he so strongly desires. Since he agrees that certain acts are "bad," and therefore deserving of punishment, his mere intention to transgress leads to the anticipation of punishment (moral anxiety). He has developed a superego, or a conscience.

But having questioned the validity of one distinction—that between shame and guilt cultures—it is necessary to introduce another. The superego has been implicitly defined operationally as the configuration of those expectations of punishment, experienced as anxiety (either conscious or unconscious) that are evoked by the anticipated violation of an internalized cultural norm. But we have not yet specified the agent of punishment, the "significant other" from whom punishment (withdrawal of love) was originally expected. Two types of superego, based on the agent of anticipated punishment, can be distinguished. This agent may be outside the individual or "within" him. It is our hypothesis that societies in which the child is trained by only a few agents of socialization, who themselves administer punishments, produce individuals who not only internalize the norms of the socializing agent but who "introject" the agent as well. This introjected figure, then, is the significant other for such individuals and it is withdrawal of its "love" that constitutes the anticipated punishment. Since this punishment, when it comes—and it comes after the transgression is committed—is experienced as guilt ("pangs of conscience"), this type of superego may be termed "guilt-oriented."

Other societies, we believe, in which the child is trained by a number of socializing agents, or in which the trainers discipline the child by claiming that other agents will punish him, do not produce individuals with "guilt oriented" superegos. For, though these individuals internalize the norms of the socializing agents, they do not introject the agents themselves. Since the significant others continue to remain external, it is withdrawal of the love of others that constitutes the anticipated punishment. Because this punishment, when it comes, is experienced as shame, this type of superego may be termed "shame-oriented." Of course, these two types of superego represent the polar extremes, conceived as ideal types, of a superego continuum. Most superegos would represent admixtures of the two, weighted toward one or the other end of the continuum.

A shame- no less than a guilt-oriented superego constitutes a conscience. By producing anxiety concerning anticipated punishment, both types inform the individual that his anticipated behavior is wrong, and both motivate him to refrain from transgressing a norm, whether others are present or not. Nevertheless, they function differently after a transgression has occurred. A person with a guilt-oriented superego suffers guilt when he transgresses, even if no one perceives his transgression, because the agent of punishment (the introjected figure) is always with him. However, a person with a shame-oriented superego does not suffer shame when he transgresses unless others witness his transgression, for no agent of punishment (the external others) is present. Instead of experiencing *actual* punishment (shame), he continues to anticipate punishment; he suffers from anxiety.[8] This anxiety may be so painful that it may lead some persons who live in societies with so-called shame-cultures to commit suicide. Incidentally, this fact is sufficient to cast doubt on the validity of the shame-culture guilt-culture dichotomy. The Japanese, who allegedly have a shame-culture, may be driven to suicide when they perceive themselves to have lost face, even in the absence of any other perceiver. In the terms we have been employing, the Japanese would be said to have shame-oriented superegos; they experience anxiety when they anticipate performing a forbidden act or not performing a prescribed act. After committing the transgression, they continue to anticipate punishment, anxiety mounts, and suicide represents the last desperate attempt to remove the anxiety.

To conclude, then, regardless of the type of superego that is preponderant in the personalities of the members of any society, cultural conformity is frequently achieved by means of internalized cultural motivation. Though the goal attained by the performance of a role may not be cathected, and though a means other than the prescribed role may be preferred, the role may nevertheless be performed (and its social functions thereby served) without the necessity for extrinsic control. If the members of society have cathected and internalized their cultural norms, conformity with these norms serves to reduce the drive of moral anxiety. In short, in internalized, as well as in intrinsic, cultural motivation the members of society have acquired "the kind of character which makes them *want* to act in the way they have to act . . ."

CONCLUSIONS

In the past, when the behavioral sciences were still reacting against instinctivist theories of social behavior, the relationship between social system and personality was viewed as primarily asymmetrical. Personality was viewed as a relatively passive agent—affected by, but not affecting, the social system. Faris (1937, ch. 3), for example, refers to personality as the "subjective aspect of culture." Recent work in culture-and-personality, however, has tended to conceive of the social system—personality relationship as more nearly symmetrical. These studies have suggested that although personality is, indeed, affected by the social system, the social system, in turn, is affected by personality.

This changing conception of the relationship between personality and social system has had its influence on the study and analysis of social systems by culture-and-personality theorists. Instead of merely asking how the social system influences the development and structuring of personality, we are now equally interested in how personality affects the functioning of social systems. And, in general, it seems to be agreed that there is feed-back between social system and personality such that the social system creates those personality needs which, in turn, are satisfied by and motivate the operation of the social system (Kardiner, 1939). Since society has but one social system, while the component members of society have different personalities, this feed-back is effected because the component roles of the social system can satisfy different needs, and its socialization system produces common needs, or a modal personality (DuBois, 1944).

This chapter has been exclusively concerned with the impact of personality on the social system, and specifically on the importance of personality for the motivation of role performance. Since the social system can serve its functions for society only if its component roles are performed, every society is confronted with the problem of social control—the problem of getting people to behave in conformity with cultural norms. By supplying the psychological basis for cultural motivation, personality is a vital instrument in society's attempt to achieve social control. It serves as such an instrument in three ways.

In the first place, although society provides sanctions as a means for achieving social control, these sanctions are effective only if the members of society have drives which can be reduced by the attainment of these goals. If this is the case these sanctions are cathected, and thereby become personality needs which motivate role performance. Second, if the cultural norms, which prescribe the performance of the role, are internalized by the members of society, non-conformity induces anxiety. Since this anxiety can be reduced by the performance of the role, conformity with these norms becomes a need which motivates role performance. Finally, the prescribed goals which are attained by role performance are, themselves, cathected and, hence, serve as personality needs to motivate the performance of roles.

These three types of control have been termed, extrinsic, internalized, and intrinsic, respectively. We may summarize their differences and similarities, as follows: (a) In extrinsic control which is based on positive social sanctions, and (b) in intrinsic control which is based on manifest personal functions, the performance of roles is motivated by the desire to obtain a rewarding goal—either the cathected social sanction or the cathected goal of the role. (c) In extrinsic control which is based on negative social sanctions, (d) in internalized control, and (e) in intrinsic control which is based on latent personal functions, the performance of roles is motivated by the desire to avoid pain—in the forms of physical or social punishment, moral anxiety, or unrelieved needs, respectively.

NOTES

1. The concept, "cultural conformity," is here taken to mean, behavior which is in conformity with cultural norms. Hence, "cultural conformity," as used in this chapter, is to be distinguished from "social conformity," which refers to behavior which is in conformity with the behavior of others. In a fully integrated and relatively unchanging society it would be difficult to distinguish between these two types of conformity: the behavior of others would be more or less identical with the requirements of the cultural heritage. In a somewhat less integrated and rapidly changing society (such as our own) the distinction between these two types of conformity is clearer; Riesman's (1950) other-directed individuals, for example, represent social conformity rather than (or more than) cultural conformity. In either case, though it might be difficult to distinguish between these types of conformity

in overt behavioral terms, it is not at all difficult to distinguish between them in motivational terms. Social conformity is motivated by the desire to conform to the behavior of others; cultural conformity, by the desire to conform to cultural norms. Cultural conformity, as we shall attempt to show, is a requisite for the functioning of human social systems, whereas social conformity is not.

2. This discussion is based primarily on psychoanalytic (Rapaport, 1951) and behavior theory (Miller and Dollard, 1941; Tolman, 1951). Despite the differences among contemporary psychological theorists, almost all agree that reward—different terms are used to refer to the same concept—is a crucial motivational variable (Nebraska Symposia on Motivation, 1953, V. 1, ff.). They differ primarily in their analysis of its referents and its properties. It is with respect to performance, not to learning, that the notion of reward is here held to be crucial.

3. "Sanctioned" goals are goals which are culturally approved; "prescribed" goals are goals which are culturally mandatory. Thus, though all prescribed goals are sanctioned, not all sanctioned goals are prescribed. The goal of achieving the status of physician, for example, is a sanctioned, not a prescribed, goal in our culture. That is, we approve of those who aspire to achieve the goal, but we do not expect everyone to aspire to it. On the other hand the goal of curing patients is not only a sanctioned, but a prescribed goal for physicians. From now on the expression, "culturally stipulated" will be used to embrace both "sanctioned" and "prescribed."

4. The motivation for the performance of social roles is termed "cultural motivation" because these roles are *culturally* sanctioned and prescribed.

5. This notion of "need" is almost identical with the notion of "need-disposition" in Parsons' action theory (Parsons and Shils, 1951, pp. 114–120). There are other points of convergence, as well, between the limited formulations of this chapter and those of Parsons (Parsons and Shils, 1951, parts 1 and 2; Parsons, 1951, chs. 1–3, 6–7). The serious student of the relationship between social system and personality is urged to read these two important volumes.

6. For a preliminary typology of functionalism, see Spiro, 1953. For a detailed analysis of functionalism as "functional consequence," see Merton, 1949. For illuminating discussions of functionalism, based on Merton's analysis, see Nagel, 1957, ch. 10, and Hempel, 1959. For a general review of recent functionalist theory and research, see Firth, 1955.

7. Merton (1949), whose now-classic analysis of functionalism remains the incisive treatment of this subject, and who first introduced the terms "manifest" and "latent" into functional analysis, ignored a potentially powerful mode of analysis by merging "intention" and "recognition." As he defines them, manifest functions are those which are both intended and recognized, while latent functions are those which are neither intended nor recognized. Since manifest functions—as we have seen—may be unintended, and since latent functions—as we shall see—may be intended, intention and recognition may vary independently.

8. For an empirical demonstration of this process, see Spiro, 1958, ch. 15, from which part of this discussion, with permission of the publisher, is taken.

BIBLIOGRAPHY

Aberle, D. F., *et al.* 1950. "The Functional Prerequisites of a Society," *Ethics*, 9:100–111.

Beach, F. 1955. "The Descent of Instinct," *Psychological Review*, 62:401–10.

Benedict, R. 1946. *The Chrysanthemum and the Sword*. Boston: Houghton Mifflin.

Bolk, L. 1929. "Origin of Racial Characteristics in Man," *American Journal of Physical Anthropology*, 13:1–28.

Carpenter, C. 1934. "A Field Study of the Behavior and Social Relations of the Howling Monkeys (*Alouatta paliata*)," *Comparative Psychology Monographs*, vol. 10.

Carpenter, C. 1940. "A Field Study in Siam of the Behavior and Social Relations of the Gibbon (*Hylobates lar*)," *Comparative Psychology Monographs*, vol. 16.

Cassirer, E. 1944. *An Essay on Man*. New Haven: Yale University Press.

Darling, F. 1937. *A Herd of Red Deer*. London: Oxford University Press.

DuBois, C. 1944. *The People of Alor*. Minneapolis: University of Minnesota Press.

Eggan, D. 1952. "The Manifest Content of Dreams: A Challenge to Social Science," *American Anthropologist*, 54:469–85.

Erikson, E. H. 1939. "Observations on Sioux Education," *Journal of Psychiatry*, 7:101–56.

———. 1945. "Childhood and Tradition in Two American Indian Tribes," *Psychoanalytic Study of the Child*, 1:319–50.

———. 1950. *Childhood and Society*. New York: Norton.

Faris, E. 1937. *The Nature of Human Nature*. New York: McGraw-Hill.

Firth, R. 1954. "Social Organization and Social Change," *Journal of the Royal Anthropological Institute*, 84:1–20.

———. 1955. "Function," *Yearbook of Anthropology*, 1:237–258.

Freud, S. 1930. *Civilization and its Discontents*. New York: J. Cape and H. Smith.

Fromm, E. 1944. "Individual and Social Origins of Neurosis," *American Sociological Review*, 9:380–84.

Hallowell, A. 1945. "Sociopsychological Aspects of Acculturation," in Linton, R. (ed.), *The Science of Man in the World Crisis*. New York: Columbia University Press.

———. 1950. "Personality Structure and the Evolution of Man," *American Anthropologist*, 52:159–173.

———. 1954. "The Self and Its Behavioral Environment," *Explorations*, 2:106–165.

———. 1955. "The Rorschach Test in Culture and Personality Studies," in Klopfer, B. *et al.*, *Developments in the Rorschach Technique*, vol. 2, Yonkers-on-Hudson: World Book Company.

Harlow, H. 1953. "Motivation as a Factor in the Acquisition of New Responses," *Nebraska Symposia in Motivation*, 4:24–49.

Hempel, C. 1959. "The Logic of Functional Analysis," in Gross, G. (ed.), *Symposium on Sociological Theory*. Evanston: Row, Peterson and Co.

Henry, J. 1953. "Towards a System of Socio-Psychiatric Invariants: A Work Paper," *Journal of Social Psychology*, 37:133–161.

Hilgard, E. 1956. *Theories of Learning*. New York: Appleton-Century-Crofts.

Hine, R. and Tinbergen, N. 1958. "The Comparative Study of Species-Specific Behavior," in Roe, A. and Simpson, G. (eds.), *Behavior and Evolution*. New Haven: Yale University Press.

Inkeles, A. and Levinson, D. 1954. "National Character: The Study of Modal Personality and Sociocultural Systems," in Lindzey, G. (ed.), *Handbook of Social Psychology*. Cambridge: Addison-Wesley.

Kaplan, B. 1957. "Personality and Social Structure," in Gittler, J., *Review of Sociology, Analysis of a Decade*. New York: John Wiley and Sons.

Kardiner, A. 1939. *The Individual and His Society*. New York: Columbia University Press.

Kluckhohn, C. 1945. "The Personal Document in Anthropological Science," in Gottschalk, L., Kluckhohn, C., and Angel, R. *Use of Personal Documents in History, Anthropology, and Sociology*. Social Science Research Council, Bull. no. 53.

———, and Murray, H., with the collaboration of Schneider, D. 1953. *Personality in Nature, Society, and Culture*. New York: Knopf.

Kroeber, A. L. 1948. *Anthropology*. New York: Harcourt, Brace.

Langer, S. 1942. *Philosophy in a New Key*. Cambridge: Harvard University Press.

La Barre, W. 1954. *The Human Animal*. Chicago: University of Chicago Press.

Lehrman, D. 1953. "A Critique of Konrad Lorenz' Theory of Instinctive Behavior," *Quarterly Review of Biology*, 28:337–363.

Lewin, K., Dembo, T., Festinger, L., and Sears, P. 1944. "Level of Aspiration," in Hunt, J. (ed.), *Personality and the Behavior Disorders*. New York: Ronald Press.

Linton, R. 1936. *The Study of Man*. New York: Appleton-Century.

Malinowski, B. 1944. *A Scientific Theory of Culture*. Chapel Hill: University of North Carolina Press.

Mayr, E. 1958. "Behavior and Systematics," in Roe, A. and Simpson, C. (eds.), *Behavior and Evolution*. New Haven: Yale University Press.

Mead, G. 1934. *Mind, Self, and Society*. Chicago: University of Chicago Press.

Murphy, G. 1947. *Personality: A Biosocial Approach to Origins and Structure*. New York: Harper.

Murphy, G. 1954. "Social Motivation," in G. Lindzey, *Handbook of Social Psychology.* Cambridge: Addison-Wesley.

———. 1958. *Human Potentialities.* New York: Basic Books.

Nadel, S. F. 1953. "Social Control and Self-Regulation," *Social Forces,* 31:265–273.

———. 1957. *The Theory of Social Structure.* London: Cohen and West.

Nagel, E. 1957. *Logic Without Metaphysics.* Glencoe, Ill.: The Free Press.

Nebraska Symposia on Motivation. 1953. Jones, M. R. (ed.), Lincoln: University of Nebraska Press.

Newcomb, T. M. 1950. *Social Psychology.* Dryden: New York.

Parsons, T. 1951. *The Social System.* Glencoe, Ill.: The Free Press.

——— and Shils, E. 1951. *Toward a General Theory of Action.* Cambridge: Harvard University Press.

Piers, G. and Singer, M. B. 1953. *Shame and Guilt: A Psychoanalytic and a Cultural Study.* Springfield: Charles C. Thomas.

Radcliffe-Brown, A. R. 1933. "Sanctions, Social," *Encyclopedia of the Social Sciences,* 13:531–34.

———. 1957. *A Natural Science of Society.* Glencoe, Ill.: The Free Press.

Rapaport, D. 1951. "The Conceptual Model of Psychoanalysis," *Journal of Personality,* 20:56–81.

Riesman, D. 1950. *The Lonely Crowd.* New Haven: Yale University Press.

Róheim, G. 1943. *The Origin and Function of Culture.* New York: Nervous and Mental Disorder Monograph Series, Vol. 63.

Sapir, E. 1924. "Culture, Genuine and Spurious," *American Journal of Sociology,* 29:401–429.

Spiro, M. E. 1951. "Culture and Personality: The Natural History of a False Dichotomy," *Psychiatry,* 14:19–46.

———. 1952. "Ghosts, Ifaluk, and Teleological Functionalism," *American Anthropologist,* 54:497–503.

———. 1953a. "Ghosts: An Anthropological Inquiry into Learning and Perception," *Journal of Abnormal Social Psychology,* 48:376–382.

———. 1953b. "A Typology of Functional Analysis," *Explorations,* 1:84–95.

———. 1958. *Children of the Kibbutz.* Cambridge: Harvard University Press.

Thompson, W. 1958. "Social Behavior," in Roe, A. and Simpson, G. (eds.), *Behavior and Evolution.* New Haven: Yale University Press.

Tolman, E. C. 1951. *Collected Papers in Psychology.* Berkeley and Los Angeles: University of California Press.

Tylor, E. B. 1874. *Primitive Culture.* Chicago: Brentano.

Wheeler, W. M. 1928. *The Social Insects—Their Origin and Evolution.* New York: Harcourt, Brace.

White, L. 1940. "The Symbol: The Origin and Basis of Human Behavior," *Philosophy of Science*, 7:451–463.

Whiting, J. W. M. and I. Child. 1953. *Child Training and Personality*. New Haven: Yale University Press.

Wissler, C. 1923. *Man and Culture*. New York: Thomas Y. Crowell.

Zuckerman, S. 1932. *The Social Life of Monkeys and Apes*. New York: Harcourt, Brace.

About the Chapter

Dr. Wallace's chapter considers the psychological characteristics upon which the unity of human social groups is based. He asks what makes communication and orderly behavior possible and advances a theory which, in its emphasis on common cognitive processes, has important implications for personality study and for a theory of cross-cultural communication. He accepts the existence of a high degree of motivational diversity even within the same groups and explains group unity in terms of the possibilities of organization and coordination inherent in human nature.

About the Author

ANTHONY F. C. WALLACE is currently Director of Clinical Research at the Eastern Pennsylvania Psychiatric Institute, and Visiting Research Associate Professor in the Department of Anthropology, University of Pennsylvania. In 1956–1957, he was a member of the Committee on Disaster Studies of the National Research Council. His major fields of interest are culture and personality, culture and religion and ethnohistory of the northeastern Indians. He is author of *King of the Delaware: Teedyuscung, 1700–1763; Tornado in Worcester;* and numerous contributions covering a wide area from visionary experience to mathematical logic.

Acknowledgments

This chapter is based in part on research conducted under Grants M-883 and M-1106 from the National Institute of Mental Health, U.S. Public Health Service, and Grant 1769 (Penrose Fund) from the American Philosophical Society. Personal acknowledgment is due to the author's colleagues, John Atkins, James Casby, and Dr. Nathan Fine, who gave valuable assistance in the development of the logical and mathematical schemata; to Dr. Harold A. Rashkis, for insightful discussion of organizational functions in cognitive processes; and to the author's assistants, Mrs. Josephine H. Dixon and Mrs. Arlene Fonaroff, who read and abstracted certain source materials and typed the manuscript.

3

The Psychic Unity of Human Groups

ANTHONY F. C. WALLACE

Eastern Pennsylvania Psychiatric Institute
and
University of Pennsylvania

What must people have in common, psychologically, in order to live together in culturally organized social groups?

On the answer to this question will depend, in part, our expectations, not only for communicating more adequately with our own close kin and neighbors, but also for a reasonably orderly and humane world society. For the kind of psychological nature that is necessary and sufficient to a cultural way of life may set limits, broad or narrow, on the kind of life that culture can provide. The question is, of course, not certainly answerable. (To *know* that a question is completely answerable would make it trivial to ask.) A number of generations of poets, philosophers, politicians, religious reformers, and, finally, humane scientists have searched for the answer with but indifferent results.

We scientists have come latest upon the scene; our tools are sharp and our hopes are bright, but we are sometimes a little provincial in the ways in which we formulate problems. The scientist starts with the knowledge that everywhere men satisfy their needs in culturally organized social groups. He tends to work back from this datum to propositions about what these needs are, and what the motives are that give these needs cognitive form. Then he may assume, rather blithely, that if on some level of abstraction the needs are the same and the culture is the same, then the motives must be the same. The enthusiastic religious leader and the fanatical political reformer think along the same lines: they take the group as given, and declaim that its continued existence requires the sharing of motives.

The humanist—the poet, the novelist, the dramatist, the historian—has tended to approach the question with a sense of tragedy (or humor) at the paradox, so apparent to him, that despite the continuing existence of the culture and the group, the individual is always partly alone in his motivation, moving in a charmed circle of feelings and perceptions which he cannot completely share with any other human being. This awareness of the limits of human communication, of the impossibility, despite all the labor of God, Freud, and the Devil, of one man fully understanding another, of the loneliness of existence, is not confined to any cult of writers; it is a pan-human theme. Shylock can declare:

> I am a Jew. Hath not a Jew eyes? hath not a Jew hands, organs, dimensions, senses, affections, passions? fed with the same food, hurt with the same weapons, subject to the same diseases, healed by the same means, warmed and cooled by the same winter and summer, as a Christian is? If you prick us, do we not bleed? if you tickle us, do we not laugh? if you poison us, do we not die? and if you wrong us, shall we not revenge?

But in the play at last, his common humanity avails Shylock nothing; his motives—the form in which his common humanity expresses itself—are portrayed (for Christians) as being so incomprehensibly perverse in greed and bitterness as to justify his being stripped of his daughter, his wealth, and even his religion. And yet, it is not his punishment but the gulf in understanding between Shylock and his persecutors, and the impossibility of a mutual knowledge, which excite sympathy. This theme of motivational loneliness, it need hardly be added, has been found to be as poignantly relevant to the relations of mothers and daughters, fathers and sons, husbands and wives, within the group, as to dealings among strangers.

From the standpoint of the humanist and, for that matter, of any individual in solitude, the narrow scientists' ponderous deductions of panels of common human drives, instincts, emotions, needs, tensions, affects, and whatnot, appear to be merely a sterile cataloguing of the obvious. To be sure, all men—Jews and Christians, males and females, young and old—experience substantially the same feelings. But this merely recognizes the mammalian nature of man. To say that human culture depends on love, lust, fear, and hate would be no more significant than to say that it depends on hearts, lungs, livers, and kidneys. But when the scientist claims that all men, or at least all members of the same culturally organized group, must share a common panel of interests and motives (ideal states-of-affairs to which strong affects are attached), the humanist can only raise his eyebrows and smile a wry smile at the naïvety of scientism.

Thus, for the humanistic scientist, the intriguing aspect of the problem of the psychic unities must rest precisely in the paradox that cultures do exist, and societies do survive, despite the diversity of the interests and motivations of their members, the practical impossibility of complete interpersonal understanding and communication, and the unavoidable residuum of loneliness that dwells in every man. The technique for the unraveling of the paradox would seem to lie in abandoning the assumption that motivational unity is necessary for social coordination. Instead, those rational functions must be defined which make it possible for persons of diverse motivations to perform the cognitive tasks necessary to the maintenance and expansion of culture. Only when this is done, shall we be in a position to investigate the manner in which individuals organize their own motivations, and their perceptions of the motivations of others and of others' perceptions of them, in such a fashion as to maximize both the meaningfulness of individual experience and the organization of the social group.

This chapter will present some considerations for a general theory relating the cognitive processes of individuals to the cultural organization of groups. For the purpose of anthropological analysis of culture-and-cognition relationships, the most convenient psychological model is one in which the individual organism is conceived to maintain an extensive set of learned meanings. A mazeway—the organized totality of learned meanings maintained by an individual organism at a given time —is the cognitive map of the individual's private world regularly evoked by perceived or remembered stimuli. Mazeway includes motivation but also includes much cognitive content that is not motivationally weighted. Meaning, degree of meaningfulness, and quantity of organization will be defined in this chapter by formal schemata based respectively on a logico-mathematical development of componential analysis, and on the mathematical theory of information. These schemata are intended to replace extended and ambiguous essays on the meaning of words like "meaning" and "organization." The full "meaning" of a stimulus includes the entire train of associated semantic matrices (which are parts of the mazeway) evoked by that stimulus, including the cognitive representation of discriminable features of the stimulus and of related motivations, possible responses, and chosen response. Such "meaning" may be conscious but is not necessarily so, either in whole or in part. Societies of organisms will be, to a greater or lesser degree, culturally organized if the organisms are sufficiently proximate and sufficiently capable of learning so that their mazeways will contain either identical or merely equivalent [1] meanings for standard stimuli. Culture, personality, modal personality structure, and national character are treated as abstractions from mazeway. It is suggested that a tendency toward maximizing the quantity of meaning, and organization of meaning, in cognitive structure is exhibited in organic behavior.[2]

CULTURAL NATURE: THE PSYCHOLOGICAL PREREQUISITES OF CULTURE

The anthropologist can, from his knowledge of culturally organized systems of behavior, contribute possibly unique insights into psychological function by writing certain functional specifications for a human brain based on a knowledge of the tasks which a cultural mode of existence requires that brain to perform. From this standpoint let us discuss the general concept of "cultural nature:" those psychological properties, determined by physical constitution, but not necessarily specific to a human or even hominid constitution, which seem to be necessary and sufficient conditions for a society to be culturally organized. By "psychological properties" I mean properties (including learned properties) of the behavior of the central nervous system, such as cognitive processes or content, knowledge of which will enable the observer to predict the individual organism's response to specified internally or externally originated stimuli. By culture I mean those sets of equivalent or identical learned meanings by which the members of a society do in fact define stimuli. Culture, in this usage, thus is not behavior nor products of behavior but inferences—from observation of stimulus and response sequences—concerning cognitive content (mazeway) maintained by one or more of a group of interdependent organisms. A culturally organized society is accordingly one whose organization (or "integration," to use Schneirla's term) depends heavily upon the patterned relationship of the meanings of stimuli learned by members of the society.

Not all societies are culturally organized. Some species do not maintain any recognizable cultural organizations at all; "society," in fact, does not require "culture." But culture is not therefore species-bound and confined to man. A culturally organized society may be participated in by any organism which learns a set of meanings sufficiently extensive for his participation to be rewarding both to himself and to his associates. A non-culturally organized society requires only "instinctive" appropriateness of behavior. By implication, then, culturally-organized societies are no more apt to be species-limited than societies (such as those of non-mammalian vertebrates, invertebrates and plants) whose integration is more largely dependent on genetically acquired "instincts" or "tropisms."

The suggestion of the irrelevance of culture to species *per se* has several justifications. Let us consider the fact that a number of non-human species do participate in human society. The extent of their participation is, of course, so limited and specialized that human beings do not concede them "membership in human society" nor, conventionally, a capacity for culture. This official refusal to allow the participation of other species in human society to be dignified by the extension to them of the terms "human" and "culture" is, however, conventionally disregarded in such contexts as the relation between a pet, such as a cat, and its owner, or between a work-animal, such as a horse, and its master. Also, many groups of non-human creatures possess what seem to be rudimentary cultures. For instance, birds, cats, dogs, apes, and monkeys learn and transmit over generations local social arrangements (cf. Hallowell, 1956). Efforts to state the essence of the difference between man and animal by invoking "culture" have not been convincing; Hallowell has even proposed a term, "proto-culture," to denote the cultures of pre-*sapiens* hominids. I would suggest that the term "proto-culture" be extended, in order to liberate the concept from an anatomically based taxonomy, to include any species in which the structure of social groups depends upon inter-generational learning. All of this emphasizes the proposition that the identification of "cultural nature" with "human nature" is not desirable and that "human nature" should be considered as just one kind of "cultural nature."

As an *entree* to the problem of defining the psychological properties prerequisite to and sufficient for participation in a culturally organized society, let us examine a fictitious species which commonly goes under the label of "intelligent life on other planets" and which, both in science fiction and in sober speculation (Mead *et al.,* 1958), is regarded as eminently capable of sharing in a super-culture with *Homo sapiens.* What psychological properties must this species possess in order that we humans consider it to be "intelligent" and capable of participation in some sort of culturally organized meta-society with ourselves?

Let us suppose that human space explorers briefly visit a planet which is inhabited by a variety of living things. Some specimens are collected. Anatomically they are bizarre to human eyes; even their biochemistry is grossly alien. Nevertheless, they are observed to ingest and to excrete matter, and *in vitro* studies indicate that their tissues conduct metabolic processes. Anatomical examination reveals the existence of tissues which suggest a central nervous system including receptors, a "brain," and effectors, and of tissues which resemble a muscular structure. If, on psychological examination, it is found that these creatures can learn, we may infer their ability to perform several psychological functions: (1) perception; (2) memory (including fantasy, here conceived as reorganized memory data); (3) discrimination between perceptual and remembered stimuli; (4) continuous selective attention to sets of perceptual and/or remembered stimuli; (5) discrimination among sets of perceptual and/or remembered stimuli with respect to their "meaning" (including their value on some affective dimension); (6) a capacity for matching meanings of perceptual and/or remembered stimuli to overt responses. If the creatures can perform these functions sufficiently well to learn tasks of the complexity mastered by domestic animals, or by animals with proto-culture, we may say by rule of thumb that they are capable of participating with human beings in a meta-culture.

Because no particular set of instincts is necessary to cultural nature, we have not alluded to particular "instincts" (or "drives," "needs," "organic demands," etc.) although particular instincts have often been regarded as essential aspects of human nature (see Goldenweiser, 1933; Murdock, 1945; Bartlett, 1923). Even casual reflection will reveal that "the human instincts" are certainly not shared by all organisms which participate in "human" culture. Let us take the "instincts proper" attributed to man in a recent work based on comparative ethology (Fletcher, 1957). They are: breathing, eating and drinking, temperature control, sleep, rest, care for comfort of body surfaces, fear, excretion, play, curiosity, hunting, eroticism, sexual fighting and jealousy, parental activity, home-maintenance. None are peculiar to man; they are generalized mammalian behavior categories, and are consequently no more determinate of human culture than the backbone or the maternal placenta. While any human society may depend on most of its individual members possessing all of these instincts (assuming, for the sake of argument, that the behaviors are indeed all instinctive), an individual organism can not only survive but make valued social contributions in the context of a cultural organization without experiencing a number of them. Victims of disease and injury, persons with congenital anomalies of bodily structure or chemistry, persons with sex or age-specific limitations of instinctual motives, and various animals with mutilated genital and other organs can and do participate effectively in human culture. One cannot, then, say that any particular set of instinctively governed behaviors, any more than a special type of anatomy, is necessary to culture *per se,* even though it may be an empirical fact that all, or most, of the members of some particular society do share certain anatomical features and certain instincts (which then, as anthropology and other disciplines commonly observe, are modulated and satisfied by culturally restricted patterns of behavior). Culture is rarely defined with respect to instinct, although it is very often defined with respect to learning (Wissler, 1923; Murdock, 1945; Kroeber and Kluckhohn, 1952).

The "degree" to which organisms must be able to perform the functions listed above before a culture of human proportions emerges, including an extensive body of tools and an elaborate language, is a difficult question to answer in the present state of knowledge. Ultimately, we shall be able to state this parameter in terms of the complexity of the cognitive tasks which an organism can learn and reliably perform. Some initial insight may be gained from considering the phenomenology of psychosis among human beings. The participation of a psychotic individual in his culture is defective. We may define a psychotic person as one who so frequently commits culturally defective acts as to lead his fellows or himself to limit his participation in culturally organized society. An act may be defined as socially psychotic whenever, but only when, three conditions are satisfied: (1) the response of the actor is not included in the range of responses culturally defined as appropriate to the stimulus; (2) the situation to which the act is a response has been given a meaning by the actor which does not include culturally essential criteria because the actor is unable to entertain a meaning sufficiently complex; and (3) the actor has in the past regularly given "correct" cultural meanings and responses. Both the cultural meaning of, and the cultural response to, the situation, may be relatively simple in comparison with the richness of the individually experienced meaning of the individually expressed normal response; the non-psychotic individual meaning and response are thus sub-types of the cultural meaning and cultural response. The psychotic meaning and response are too limited to be sub-types at all. This definition excludes the mentally deficient who has never learned the correct cultural meaning or response; the newly arrived alien whose meanings and responses, despite apparent inappropriateness, are complex and appropriate to his own culture; the criminal, who is sharply aware of the cultural meaning but deliberately makes an unsanctioned response in order to obtain private advantage; and the neurotic, whose meaning is included in the cultural meaning of the situation but whose response either is not included in the appropriate cultural response, or who responds culturally but experiences severe anxiety and discomfort.

With respect to the six functions mentioned above, it is likely that serious chronic interference with the performance of any one function amounts to a mental disorder. For human beings, it would appear superficially that the most vulnerable of the functions are the perception-vs.-memory discrimination function and the capacity for construing semantic relationships. When the former function fails, the organism may be described as "hallucinating." In regard to the second function, psychiatrists and psychologists have for years explained certain deficiencies of language and thought in schizophrenia as being the result of a relative inability of the schizophrenic to perform complex operations with abstractions or "concepts." Von Domarus (1954) and his disciple Arieti (1955, 1956) have gone so far as to postulate a "paleologic," supposedly common to schizophrenics, children, and primitive people, which differs in quality from the classical Aristotelian logic in that "identity" in paleologic is given by the identity of the predicates rather than of the subjects (or arguments). In the "correct" form, if the argument is that x is a p, and that y is also a p, one cannot say that x is identical with y. In Von Domarus' paleologic, however, one can say that x is identical with y if x is a p and y is a p. The force of Von Domarus' distinction depends entirely upon the analyst's ability to consider that there is at least one other predicate q such that x is a q and y is not a q. In this event, of course, x is not identical to y. But, if in fact the only statements that can be made about x and y are p(x) and p(y) (if no statement, in other words, is *possible* about spatial and temporal separation, or any other conceivably distinguishing feature), then x does indeed have to be regarded as being identical with y, since no distinguishing predicate can be introduced. Thus the "paleologic" of Von Domarus would appear to be the same old formal logic, operating, in psychotic thinking, with a drastically limited range of predicates. The attribution of paleologic to children and primitives appears to be even less justified than its attribution to schizophrenics.

The principle of limited predicates leads to an interesting speculation, however. The number of predicates which can enter effectively into a consideration of x and y during a given period of time may be a function of either the temporal span or the complexity span of attention. Anything which restricts the span of attention must restrict the individual's ability to perform continuous semantic or other logical operations involving a large number of predicates. Evidently, in order for an individual to participate satisfactorily in a culturally sanctioned transaction, he must be able to attend, during the duration of the transaction, to the entire relevant repertoire of cultural meanings and cultural responses: i.e., he must be able to maintain cognitive representations of a number of predicates simultaneously and continuously (whether consciously or not). If, for example, the individual is discussing a serious pending business transaction with his partner, and the discussion requires several hours, he must have under attention during the whole of that time (with only fleeting lapses) the cultural meaning of the whole situation and the boundaries of culturally permissible responses. Otherwise his behavior will appear bizarre, "crazy," to his partner. In humans, it seem to be particularly scope and continuity of attention, rather than memory, sensory perception, logical form, or affective sensitivity, which fail in varying degrees in psychosis. (Hallucination is a poor index of psychosis: not all psychotics hallucinate, and many non-psychotics do so under a variety of conditions.) In extreme cases, attention span is apparently so brief that sensation becomes virtually divorced from meaning; the victim is unable to assign meaning to experience beyond distinguishing between small and large objects, and is unable to make more complex responses than an almost automatic placing of small objects in the mouth (Arieti, 1955). Full participation in a culturally organized society of human proportions becomes impossible long before this level of de-semantication is reached, however.

In summary, then, I have suggested that "cultural nature" has nothing in particular to do with anatomy, instincts, motivations, or even a uniquely *human* set of cognitive capacities. Culture as such is not a species-associated phenomenon, and all organisms capable of culture can participate in some common meta-culture. Capacity for learning is capacity for culture. And the degree of learned capacity depends upon the fineness of sensory perception and the flexibility of motor execution, the amplitude and reliability of memory, the scope and the stability of attention, and the semi-automatic processing of sensory inputs by a semantic process which gives meaning to experience and matches that meaning to response. A group of social organisms possessing this basic mechanism will produce a culture whatever their species.

This view stands in sharp opposition to theories which make the sharing of interests and motivations a central requirement for common cultural participation. In our conception, while motivational content may, as a matter of fact, be more or less fully shared, this sharing is neither a necessary nor a sufficient condition for the existence of a cultural organization. The extent of sharing of motivational content, and the extent to which specific acts are dependent upon specific motivations, thus becomes a matter for empirical investigation rather than an article of faith. The attitudes of individuals and groups toward motivational unity also provide an interesting subject for study. In some groups, particularly those involved in new religious and political movements—in fact, in revitalization movements in general—there probably will be a strong insistence on the virtue, even the necessity, of motivational unity. In other groups, particularly in old, stable, and sophisticated institutions—this does not necessarily imply high technological development—motivational unity will be less important than reliability of performance, however motivated, of those minimal tasks necessary to cultural and group continuity. Whatever else the individual does with his spare time, for whatever reasons, is his own business, and is justifiable by its cathartic or recreative value, and its potentiality for useful in-novation. A useful index of the cultural sophistication of a person might be a function of the number of different motivations conceivable to him as co-existing in some single social system or institution.

CULTURE AND MAZEWAY

When in the 1930's anthropologists first began seriously to investi-gate the relationship between cultural and personality processes, they encountered a curious semantic dilemma. The concept *personality* re-ferred to psychological structures which were motivational—*i.e.,* they were both affective and cognitive. But the term was in itself ambigu-ous about the relationship between affect and cognition. In fact, a prob-lem of basic research in personality has been to define the rules govern-ing that relationship. *Personality,* furthermore, was an individual concept. *Culture,* on the other hand, insofar as it referred to psychological structures, was primarily a cognitive and not an affective or motiva-tional concept. It described sequences of action, criteria of choice, pat-terns of coordination, and so forth, which had cognitive status for the members of a group whose affective status was a "personality" ques-tion. Furthermore, *culture* was a group concept. In sum, *personality* was an affective-cognitive and individual concept; *culture* was a cognitive and group concept. Relationships between culture and personality were therefore awkward to discuss: the two concepts, like the gingerbread dog and the calico cat in the children's jingle who ate one another up, were mutually incorporating on different dimensions.

The anthropologist responded intuitively to this dilemma. First, he be-lieved that affective processes were dynamically related to the cogni-tive tasks he described under the rubric *culture.* Second, one or both of the concepts had to be redefined if the semantic tangle was to be elimi-nated. Sometimes he redefined the concept of culture so that it, too, in one of its senses, was a motivational (affective-cognitive) and an indi-vidual concept. And sometimes he redefined both culture and personal-ity so that, in one sense of each, both were affective-cognitive and group, and in another sense of each, both were affective-cognitive and individual. Both redefinitions were rationalized by the argument that culture and personality were "really" the same in substance, that there was no ontological difference between them, that they formed, not a dichotomy, but a tautological equivalence (Spiro, 1951).

The desirability of these tautological redefinitions is open to grave doubt, however, despite their convenience in theoretical discussion. Operationally, culture and personality have been and still are two dis-tinct bodies of phenomena; their description depends on different observations, and must in fact do so unless studies of their inter-relationships are to be entirely circular, *via* the "cultural-deductive" method whereby personality is merely a re-description of culture and *vice versa* (Wallace, 1952). Furthermore, cultural and personality data are relatable only by means of correlations and associations far smaller than unity. They display no one-to-one correspondence such that, given a cultural description, one can infallibly predict what the personality data will show. In other words, except in the use of the cultural-deductive method, cultural and personality data are not only not tautologically equivalent, they are not even materially equivalent.

A second solution of the semantic dilemma, which avoids the risks inherent in manufacturing new tautologies out of old concepts, is to introduce a new concept. In several publications (Wallace, 1956a, 1956b, 1957) I have suggested that the conceptual armamentarium of the anthropologist requires such a new concept. It should be somewhat different from, but related to, the concept of personality, in order to deal adequately with those cognitions of individuals the abstractions of which are culture. The meaningfully organized totality of learned cognitive representations of people, things, processes, and values held at a given time by an individual I have termed "mazeway." This totality includes precisely the *kind* of category which the anthropologist employs when he is dealing with the organized totality of statuses, artifacts, customs, laws, language, moral values, and so forth which he attributes to a society as its "culture" (see Sapir, 1949, p. 515). Thus, the description of how Iroquois Indian men make wooden masks has as its counterpart the description of how an individual Iroquois Indian man makes wooden masks. The complex of meanings which determine the sculpturing and painting activity of the mask-maker involves such things as knowing ways to discriminate kinds of wood, selection of tools to use for various parts of the work, the techniques for sharpening drills, an adequate manner of mixing paint, the boundaries of design variation among acceptable masks, and so forth. This cognitive equipment of the individual mask-maker is not, in any useful sense of that word, an attribute of his "personality." Personality is a valuable concept, on a higher level of abstraction, for certain broad and stable attributes of a mazeway, organized around major motives, such as (to use the same example) a tendency to prefer making masks to plowing fields, because mask-making is associated with a deeply felt commitment to an Indian identity. Similarly, the simple notion that to light a cigarette one must touch its end to a flame or a red-hot surface while drawing air through the cylinder is not a personality attribute. It is an element of mazeway and also an element of culture. Whether or not I like to smoke may well be termed a personality characteristic, however, just as an emphasis on the providing of many tension-reducing oral play activities, like tobacco, mid-morning coffee, candy, pop-corn, and chewing gum may be described as a (perhaps minor) theme in my culture. Personality, an abstraction from mazeway, thus is parallel to such abstractions from culture as "themes," "national character," and "ethos." Modal personality, correspondingly, is an abstraction from personality, parallel to culture as an abstraction from mazeway. The relationships are exemplified in the following diagram (Fig. 1):

FIG. 1: RELATIONSHIP OF CONCEPTS IN CULTURE
AND PERSONALITY

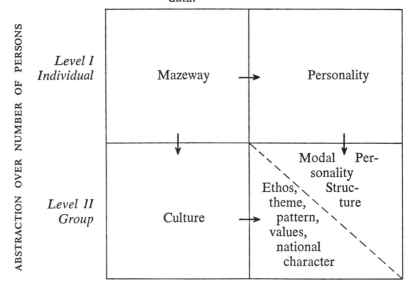

ABSTRACTION OVER CATEGORIES

	Level 1	*Level 2*
	Concrete, detailed, map of cognitive "world" including motives as cognitive data.	Complex patterns abstracted and generalized.
Level I *Individual*	Mazeway ⟶	Personality
Level II *Group*	Culture ⟶	Ethos, theme, pattern, values, national character Modal Personality Structure

(ABSTRACTION OVER NUMBER OF PERSONS)

The elements of mazeway are the totality of what has been learned and is now known. But it is a totality which possesses an organization, a structure, that is not wholly inherent in the separate learnings themselves, but has been formed by such processes as generalization, logical analysis, and imagination reconstructing learned materials in memory. Whatever the relationship between the individual learnings and mazeway *Gestalt,* however, by virtue of the learning process the individual members of a society will learn to predict one another's behavior. They will maintain a set of mutually equivalent (not necessarily identical) learned meanings for stimuli which are continuously available, during all of their transactions, as statements of the boundaries and conditions of their mutual behavior. Thus the statement that given learning capacity, the members of a society will produce a culture, has as its corollary the statement that the members of that society will individually possess mazeways whose contents, including mutually predictive cognitions, are equivalent. In other words, the culture concept implies a Principle of Mazeway Equivalence for members of a culturally organized social group.

This view does not require that motivational content be shared in order that cultural organization exist, but only that cognitive content be equivalent, and thus mutually predictable. Motivation, of course, is experienced subjectively as one kind of data which has been given meaning by incorporation into mazeway, and motivation may be attributed to others (often very inaccurately).

One further psychological component of cultural nature must be postulated at this point to account for certain aspects of both psychological and cultural dynamics. This component is a primary association of pleasure with maximal complexity and orderliness of the mazeway, and of discomfort with minimal complexity and order (see Wallace, 1956a and 1957; Hebb, 1944). This association makes it possible to learn, and to be motivated, to increase mazeway organization. In simpler language, organisms possessing cultural natures (and perhaps all organisms) act in such ways as to maximize the meaningfulness of experience: they follow a Principle of Maximal Meaning. This principle has, as its consequence, such dynamic phenomena as growth and revitalization in both psychological and cultural systems. It may indeed be a function in mental economy whose affective intensity in man is in large measure responsible for those extraordinary reciprocating evolutions of culture and brain which the newer paleontology finds it difficult to explain by a principle of Darwinian natural selection alone (Eiseley, 1958). It suggests, indeed, that in an operational sense, as biological and cultural evolution has proceeded, the universe has become more meaningful. And it leads us to a consideration of the formal structure of "meaningfulness" as a property of experience essential to an understanding of individual participation in culturally organized society.

TOWARD AN ANTHROPOLOGICAL THEORY OF MEANING

Anthropologists have always been interested in the phenomenon of meaning. On its simplest level this interest is evoked by the necessity of translating unfamiliar linguistic and other behavior into a scientific language. The anthropologist must always ask: What does this event "mean" in *my* language? The problem of making adequate translation leads directly to inquiry into the nature of meaning itself. On a more advanced level, the anthropologist must constantly keep in mind that meaning is culturally relative. Hallowell in particular has repeatedly pointed out, and emphasized, that the meanings of standard stimuli vary from group to group, depending on the nature and degree of cultural definition. The semantic structure of experience, in effect, depends on culture, whether the experience be that of seeing a Rorschach ink-blot, or of hearing a sound in the woods at night (Hallowell, 1955). Nevertheless, in spite of the cultural relativity of the *content* and perhaps *degree* of meaning of standard stimuli, it is possible that the cognitive *process* of perceiving and learning the meanings of stimuli, and of relating these meanings in thought, follows constant laws irrespective of culture, and, indeed, of species. The Whorfian and other hypotheses of extreme cultural relativism (Whorf, 1956; Hoijer, 1954; Levi-Strauss *et al.,* 1953) assert a radical dependence of the very form of rationality upon the local structure of language. But it seems more likely that the elemental notions which are the common base of the various logical and semantic calculi—notions of "not," of "and," of "and/or," of "identically equal," of "equivalent," of "order," and the like—are symbolic representations of processes intrinsic to such evidently universal psychic functions as discrimination, conditioning, and the generalization of learning. Indeed, a radical linguistic relativism would probably be, by its own axioms, not only incapable of proof but incapable of being described. Logical processes, and a few axioms based upon their combinations, have been regarded by mathematicians and philosophers like George Boole (1854) as "laws of thought" which are universal, certainly for mankind, and possibly for any organism which can learn.

In a recent development of major importance to anthropology, efforts have been made by anthropologists and linguists (Goodenough, 1956; Lounsbury, 1956; Wallace and Atkins, 1960) to adapt the technique of componential analysis from phonemics to serve as a semantic calculus for the explication of the meanings of kinship terms and other culturally patterned behavior. These efforts are justifiable only under the premise that the meaning of behavior (whatever the language and culture of the speaker) is contained in a particular and universal type of logicosemantic cognitive structure. Under such a premise, the meaning of *any* culture's terms can be analyzed with the same type of structure as a model, without doing violence to the principle of cultural relativity of content. Since the matrices of definitive and connotative learned meaning which constitute the elements of mazeway, and therefore of culture and personality, can be considered as being formed according to this model, a brief and general description of its structure will be given here.

The fundamental and intuitive idea on which the semantic calculus is based is a simple one: that the signification of a "term" (which may be an extrinsic linguistic symbol, such as a word, or any other overt behavior) is given by a particular pattern of predicates which evoke, or are evoked by, that term. A predicate is a symbol for the common property of the members of a class. In the technique of componential analysis, the various criteria (predicates) relevant to the definition of the terms in a lexicon are conceived as values on dimensions, and a semantic space is defined as the product of the several dimensions, such that each cell in the space represents a unique combination of values, one from each dimension. Each term can then be mapped onto the space by stating to which combination or combinations of the criteria it corresponds. When all the terms have been so mapped, their logico-semantic relationships can be explicitly stated.[3] Thus one of several possible analyses of the definitional meanings of several Trukese kinship terms may be graphically represented on a semantic space as follows (Fig. 2):

FIG. 2: COMPONENTIAL MATRIX OF TRUKESE KINSHIP TERMS
(MODIFIED FROM GOODENOUGH, 1956)

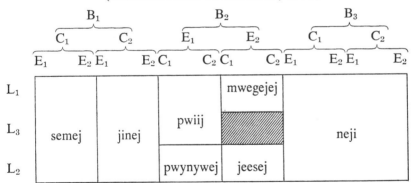

DIMENSIONS
  B (seniority of generation)
    B_1 (senior), B_2 (same)
  C (sex of relative)
    C_1 (male), C_2 (female)
  E (sex relative to ego's sex)
    E_1 (same), E_2 (opposite)
  L (degree of affinal removal)
    L_1 (consanguineal), L_2 (one), L_3
    (two)

34 cells are occupied by 7 terms shown.

2 cells ($B_2E_2L_3$) are not occupied by any of the 7 terms shown.

All 36 cells are occupied by an 8th term *tefej* ("kinsman"), not shown.

Now, inspection of the paradigm of Trukese terms displayed in Fig. 2 reveals an interesting feature: when each cell is plotted to contain the same area, the areas occupied by the several terms are not equal because the number of cells occupied by the terms are not equal. This inequality is determined by the variation in the levels of specificity of the terms themselves: terms which are highly specific, which "answer" many questions, occupy the minimal areas, while more general terms, which "answer" only one or two questions, occupy larger areas. All this suggests that the quantity of semantic information given by a term, or a set of terms, may be measured by a function of the number of cells in its semantic space and of the number of cells in the sub-space corresponding to the term or terms (see Shannon and Weaver, 1949, and Bar-Hillel and Carnap, 1954).[4]

This leads us, at last, to precisely the point to which I intended to come: a concept of degree of meaningfulness of experience. We conceive of the meaningfulness of experience as being limited by the quantity of semantic information contained in the semantic spaces available for defining sensory stimuli (including affects), and as varying with the complexity of the patterns of stimulation. If an individual is unable to maintain a varied and extensive set of semantic spaces continuously available for the definition of sensory situations, not only will his experiences be introspectively barren, but (if the poverty of predicates is severe) he will be unable to maintain matrices complex enough even to include all the relevant dimensions of cultural meaning demanded by his society. For cultural participation requires that the individual be capable of maintaining mazeway sets complex enough to accommodate the minimal cultural definitions of stimuli necessary to performance of the cognitive tasks required by the culture.

HUMAN NATURE

The question was raised, in the preceding section, of how much semantic capacity is necessary for full participation in a given culturally organized *human* society. The question thus returned us to the problem of defining the human variety of cultural nature. Before continuing with the discussion of meaning and experience in human nature let us pause briefly to consider the existing literature which approaches the matter from a different point of view.

There exists an extensive but curiously unsatisfying special literature on the nature of human nature. Until recent years, much of it was singularly barren of description. Bastian, Morgan, Tylor and others concerned with explaining the psychological basis both of a unilinear cultural evolution, and of extensive diffusion, found it necessary to postulate a psychic unity for man. But they rarely descended to describing in any detail what it was that was uniform (see Lowie, 1937). Later theorists emphasized the universality and importance of learning in the mediation of instinctual drives (Wissler, 1923; Murdock, 1945) as the psychological *sine qua non* of culture. Other writers have been less concerned with the uniformity of the human mind than with its uniqueness. Man has been described as the only symbol-using, tool-making, culture-building animal; "symboling" in particular (to use White's expression) has appealed to the searcher for the essence of man's uniqueness (Cassirer, 1944; White, 1949; Bidney, 1953; Spiro, 1951, 1954). The concern with uniqueness has posed something of a dilemma for anthropology. On the one hand the facts of comparative anatomy and the fossil record demonstrate man's physical affinities with the rest of the animal kingdom. On the other hand, man's behavior —particularly his culture-producing behavior, of which he is so extremely proud—insofar as it is unique, has separated him sharply in some spiritual or psychological dimension. Such an awkward discontinuity between man and his primate relatives has troubled paleontologists (cf. Eiseley, 1958) and cultural anthropologists alike (Hallowell, 1956). Hallowell (1956) has recently stated the problem sharply in his paper on the "Cultural and Psychological Dimensions of a Human Existence." As noted earlier, he has suggested the term "proto-culture" to refer to the cultural achievements of non-*sapiens* hominids. Since "proto-culture" is, after all, culture, he has in effect denied to modern man the exclusive proprietorship of those psychological faculties which are necessary to a cultural mode of life. Correspondingly, Eiseley (1956) has suggested that many of the distinctively human features of our cerebral anatomy are of extremely recent origin, more recent than the cultural remains of the lower and middle Paleolithic. Dobzhansky and Montague (1947), Tappen (1953), and others have suggested that the human mentality is itself a product of selection for educability and intelligence under cultural conditions.

Perhaps the most elaborate effort to describe human nature in an anthropological context has been undertaken by psychoanalysts and psychoanalytic anthropologists (Fenichel, 1945; Fromm, 1951; Róheim, 1943; Devereux, 1945, 1956; LaBarre, 1954, 1958). Based essentially on considerations of human sexual and aggressive instincts (in rather special and abstract senses of those terms) and of human anatomy, physiology, and the universal culture pattern, the psychoanalytic tradition utilizes comparative data on psychopathology, dreams, and religious myths and ritual to support universalistic propositions about human motivational content and process. There are propositions about a universal symbolic language of dreams, myth, ritual, and expressive behavior generally; propositions about universal neurotic structures (Oedipal conflict, sibling rivalry, castration anxiety); propositions about universal mental functions (the Ego-Id-Super Ego and the Conscious-Preconscious-Unconscious trichotomies, and the various mechanisms of defense); and propositions about universal fears, delusions, and fantasies concerning fundamental human experiences like eating, excretion, sleep, dreams, birth, death, sexual function, conception, and so forth. There would hardly seem to be much room for doubt about the universality of the mechanisms of defense and of certain processes involved in the psychological dynamics of various emotional disorders, such as the very tendency of insecure persons to insist on the motivational identity of their friends, or their enemies. The difficulty, as far as psychic unity is concerned, again, lies in motivational content. The problem here is not so much the unreasonableness of supposing that *some* minimal core of cognitive experience, of meaning, is universal with regard to basic and nearly universal physiological needs, but of separating what *is* universal from what might be, but in fact is not universal but merely common, or even rare, although discoverable in a wide range of societies. The criterion that seems to be involved is level of specificity. Pan-human, psychically universal meanings should in general be abstract or simple, involving few dimensions, in comparison with the meanings attributable to individual cultures, and, even more emphatically, in comparison with the meanings entertained by individual persons, which will be much richer, more detailed, more concrete and idiosyncratic.

The notion of semantic information offers a way of approaching the problem by defining human nature, as opposed to generalized primate or mammalian nature, as a level of semantic capacity minimally adequate to the performance of the cognitive tasks required by known human cultures. Such a level of semantic capacity should function as a lower boundary on the complexity and degree of organization of the motivations, as well as of other mazeway content, and thus should determine the boundary between human and non-human levels of personality organization. As suggested earlier, the determination of this boundary is highly relevant to the definition of mental disorders. Preliminary findings in studies being conducted by me and my associates, for instance, suggest that folk social typologies (i.e., non-scientific taxonomies, such as kinship terminologies, categories of military rank, etc.) contain, irrespective of the language, about four bits of semantic information per most specific level of concept in a lexicon. That is to say, proper use of the most specific concepts for which there are conventional terms requires, within the context of the relevant lexicon, the equivalent of about four binary discriminations. Whether or not the figure of four will be found to be a constant for folk typologies in all languages, we feel that we now have a grip on the operational problem of defining the complexity of the cognitive task. At present we are extending the theory and procedures in the direction of a formal calculus which will make possible the analysis of both semantic and pragmatic sequences in terms of quantity of semantic information.

Such categories of human cognitive content as concept of self, self-evaluation, morality, and the development of language, may be the inevitable precipitates of brains with high levels of semantic capacity operating in social groups.

EQUIVALENCE, IDENTITY, AND THE DISTRIBUTION OF PSYCHOLOGICAL CHARACTERISTICS

Let us now turn to a more detailed consideration of the distribution of mazeway, personality, and motivational content.

Sometimes we regard human societies as populations and not as groups when we make psychological statements. A population of individuals may be described without reference to their interrelationships; but a group cannot be considered apart from its organizational structure. Thus physical, demographic, or personality characteristics of the members of a population can be stated, explicitly or implicitly, as a statistical distribution on one or more dimensions. To the extent that the data permit, some measure or estimate of central tendency can be calculated which will allow the attribution of some value or range on one or more dimensions to the entire population, or a specified sub-population. The logical form of such an operation is simple enough: the researcher wants to be able to select a sub-set of individuals from the population to whom, with a known degree of confidence, an identical predicate can be applied. The sub-set may or may not be the entire population. The definition of the predicate is usually related to the distribution by the requirement that its probability value lie within a standard confidence limit (e.g., .95 or .99). The final product is a statement of the form: for all members x of the population X, any given x is a p, with a probability greater than k.

Now most modal personality statements are of this kind. The inference to be drawn is that if the statement is true, then almost all the x's have in common some mazeway element (motivational or personality attribute) p. If p represents "introversion," for example, then almost all x's are asserted to be "introverts" (however loosely p may be defined) and non-p's are "deviants" from the norm. The identification of predicates which are identical for almost all of a population is in part the aim of ethnography, of modal personality investigation, and of the analysis of language. We shall return to the relevant methodological problems shortly.

Such predicates, applicable to all or almost all members of a population, are too rare to be adequate for the psychological analysis of that population as a group. As an elementary consideration will reveal: most culturally organized groups not merely permit but require that their members perform different roles and address themselves to different interests. By our theory, this implies that the mazeways of participants in an interaction situation are in general semantically different. Thus the relationship among the mazeway definitions (p, q, . . .) by any groups of organisms (x, y, . . .) of a given stimulus situation will, semantically, be one of various combinations of equivalence, contrariety, implication (which, in the form of a partial ordering, defines the property of scaling), and independence (in the logical sense, which corresponds to the empirical situation of correlation significantly greater than zero and less than unity).

All of these relations are interesting, but perhaps the most important relationship, for the purposes of psycho-cultural analysis, is that of approximate equivalence. Two propositions are equivalent when the truth of either one implies the truth of the other [if $p(x)$, then $q(y)$, and if $q(y)$, then $p(x)$]; the two propositions themselves may contain very different predicates. Approximate equivalence is recognizable empirically when the correlation or association between two phenomena under some constant condition approaches unity. Social structure depends, not on the identity of predicates, but on the near equivalence of propositions concerning tasks and motivations. Indeed identity of predicates representing tasks and motives would be possible only in a social structure resembling that of a horde of lemmings. It is important to note that the concept of complementary distribution, which linguists have employed effectively in descriptive structural linguistics, is a special case of paired equivalence, having the form: if $p_1(x)$, then $q_1(y)$ and not $q_2(y)$; if $p_2(x)$ then $q_2(y)$ and not $q_1(y)$; if $q_1(y)$, then $p_1(x)$ and not $p_2(x)$; if $q_2(y)$, then $p_2(x)$ and not $p_1(x)$. The recognition of complementary distributions is also used as a primary methodological tool in Goodenough's type of structural analysis of the "rules" of culture (Goodenough, 1951).

We shall now generalize the Principle of Mazeway Equivalence: *the members of a culturally organized group maintain mazeways whose content is equivalent, but rarely identical, over wide situational parameters.* Since contents are equivalent, they are as reliably predictable as if they were identical. But because they are not identical, statistical generalizations concerning central tendencies of content may reveal only very limited congruence. This, I believe, is the major limitation on statistical efforts to describe the substance of the cognitive and motivational unity of human cultural groups, on a level of specificity below cultural or human nature. Furthermore, the magnitude of the statistical task necessary to establish semantic equivalence is altogether formidable. This may also be a reason why the more intuitive students in this field, like Margaret Mead and her co-workers, find so little use in statistical generalization. For the essence of culturally relevant psychological "pattern," as I understand Mead's sense of that term, lies in the apprehension of equivalences rather than of identities. It is indeed the equivalence of mazeways, rather than their identity, which makes possible culturally organized society. The formulation of "end-linkage" (i.e., of complementary patterns) by Bateson and others in *The Study of Culture at a Distance* (Mead and Metraux, 1953) represents this approach, albeit in a language somewhat less formal than the one employed here, and less exact than the analysis of complementaries performed by Goodenough (Goodenough, 1956).

We now return to the methodological problems encountered in the search for identities. It is possible to discover some descriptive predicates in mazeway of personality data which are identical for all or almost all of a population, or for all or almost all of a sub-group of a population. The statistical problem has been discussed at some length in an earlier monograph (Wallace, 1952). Very briefly, it is presented by two empirical observations: first, that few universally appropriate predicates can be discovered in any body of data concerning the individual members of a culturally defined population, and these few may be trivial; and second, the more complex a compound predicate is, the smaller the proportion of the population for which that compound predicate will be true. The statistical difficulty is further increased by whatever unreliability is associated with the chosen method of observation and coding, and by problems of sampling. Sampling problems in modal personality investigation may be readily enough overcome when the population is small (a few hundred persons, perhaps) and the observations required are simple and brief. But when the population is large (and populations of up to hundreds of millions of persons have been approached) and the observations are, let us say, of the psychoanalytic sort which require tens or hundreds of hours of interviewing under special conditions of privacy, with extended time also required for analysis —then the problem of making significant statistical abstractions becomes truly formidable. These sampling problems, furthermore, cannot be shrugged off by arguing that the individuals selected can be accurately characterized in regard to their social position. The impracticability of characterizing all individuals in large populations is precisely the reason why a sample is selected in the first place.

Granted, however, that problems of observation, coding, and sampling are overcome, the task resolves itself into developing methods of stating which predicates can be applied to which sub-sets of the population with what degree of confidence. The simplest technique is to proceed dimension by dimension, discovering the frequency distribution, point of central tendency, and measure of dispersion for each dimension independently. This will yield conclusions of the following kind: 92 per cent of the X population are p, 49 per cent of X are q, 71 per cent of X are r. But unhappily these observations do not indicate how many of the p's are also q's, how many p's and q's are also r's, and so forth. Indeed, in the above case, *not more* than 49 per cent, and *not less* than 12 per cent, can be simultaneously p and q and r. Evidently, furthermore, we can identify eight structural psychological types on this matrix of three binary dimensions: pqr, $\bar{p}qr$, $p\bar{q}r$, $pq\bar{r}$, $\bar{p}\bar{q}r$, $\bar{p}q\bar{r}$, $p\bar{q}\bar{r}$, $\bar{p}\bar{q}\bar{r}$. If we are interested in structure, we are then interested in the frequency with which a given compound predicate (such as pqr) is to be found in a population. Since a predicate matrix of, say, twenty binary dimensions (a much less complex matrix than is actually employed in Rorschach analysis) will yield up to 1,048,576 structural types, the uniformity of the population on each dimension must be impressive, or the types must be very crudely defined, before any one type is likely to acquire prevalence over any substantial proportion of the group, and before any conveniently small sample will be informative. Various methods of statistical analysis of the multi-dimensional modalities of population characteristics are available: factor analysis by one technique or another, which depends on the computation of coefficients of correlation; trial-and-error sorting of the sample by types; and the modal technique described in the previously mentioned monograph (Wallace, 1952). Simple, separate calculations of measures of central tendency on numerous dimensions are unsatisfactory if the dimensions are considered to be structurally related, as is often the case with psychological data, or if the question of relationship is being raised in the investigation.

Turning now to the methodological problems of the analysis of equivalence, we find an equally formidable task. The problem here is to discover a unity in pattern rather than a unity in uniformity. In formal terms, we are now not seeking to say of the X population that each x is a p, or a q, or a pq, or a pqr, but rather that whenever the stimulus is N, then whenever x_1 is a p, x_2 is a q, . . . , and x_n is an s. Let us put the matter in Rorschach terms, for the sake of example. The standard analysis is of the form: if the response to Card N of x_1 is p, of x_2 is q, . . . , of x_n is s, and x_1, x_2, . . . , x_n give the "same (in whatever coding system we employ) response, then $p = q = \ldots = s$, and we say, in brief, that all the x's are p's. But the equivalence analysis (retaining the same symbols) would be of the form: if x_1, x_2, . . . x_n give "different" responses to Card N, but x_1 regularly responds with p, x_2 with q, . . . , and x_n with s, then $p(x_1) \leftrightarrow q(x_2) \leftrightarrow . . . \leftrightarrow s(x_n)$, and we can say in brief that the x's may be predicated by a system of equivalent meaning-sets p, q, . . . , s.

To give a crude example, if all the males in the sample saw Card 1 as a flying bat, scored FM, and all the females saw it as a fuzzy skin cut to look like a bat, scored Fc, then we might say that the male and female responses were equivalent even though they might contribute to a considerably different psychological interpretation for males and females. This I suggest is the psychological test analogue to the equivalence of mazeways in culturally organized societies.

In "real life," however, the standard stimulus will not be an ink-blot but a situation, and there are various kinds of equivalence-structures which empirical reality may approximate, in addition to the complementary distribution model we mentioned earlier, and the psychological test model mentioned above. Consider a group of airmen at a defense airbase. At the sound of the claxon, they run to their aircraft, each taking an assigned seat, and commence the performance of their various highly specialized roles. There is one stimulus—the claxon—but its meaning, and the consequent responses, are different for each man. Nevertheless, the meanings—and the responses—can be defined as equivalent because *whenever* the claxon sounds, each responds in the same way that he had before. It is this equivalence of meanings which makes possible that coordinated specialization of responses to standard stimuli which is achieved in culturally organized societies.

Equivalence analysis of social behavior, however, will rarely find so simple a case as that offered by a well-organized system of highly trained specialists each of whom is able to make extended but socially coordinated responses to a stimulus without reference to the actions of his colleagues. More commonly, each overt event in the sequence serves as a stimulus to all participants (including the actor himself, *via* "feedback"), each of whom defines the new situation differently and produces a response. A simple example of this kind of system would be an evenly-matched pair of people playing a game of tennis: the velocities of the ball and of the players are the common stimulus sequence, and the responses of the competitors approximate equivalence with respect to footwork and stroking. To the extent that the meanings are equivalent, the grouped responses will be "organized."

The discovery and description of such semantic and overt behavioral equivalences is done formally or informally by the anthropologist whenever he describes how a group of people carry out some joint activity, such as a religious ritual, a war-raid, a fishing expedition, and the like. It is implicit in the analysis of kinship and other types of cultural structures, by both anthropologists and sociologists. It is my impression, however, that it is but rarely undertaken in psychologically oriented investigations, although exceptions can be adduced: the theory of complementary needs in mate selection, certain aspects of psychoanalytic theory of interpersonal relations, and so forth. Evidently the statistical problem here is to establish high-order correlations or associations between different predicates describing the responses of different persons over a series of temporally successive presentations of the "same" stimulus sequence or of different categories of persons independently but approximately simultaneously exposed once to the "same" stimulus sequence. Such equivalence analysis would go farther, I suspect, in revealing the psychological structure of groups than the search for identities which has so largely occupied our efforts until now. Furthermore, equivalence analysis will reveal differences between groups which identity analysis may gloss over. Two populations may be very similar in the uniformities which they display, and yet differ sharply in the nature and relationship of their equivalence groups.

Let us now summarize some of the implications of the foregoing rather complex train of discussion of the relationship between frequency distribution and structure. While a few identities of mazeway content may be discoverable in any given group, such as a culturally organized society, or population, such as all human beings, they will be difficult to observe, both for the scientist and for the individual in society. Societies in general must depend for their structure on equivalences rather than identities of mazeway content. It is difficult to go beyond this, at the present state of knowledge, to a statement of the actual relationship between frequency distribution and equivalence structure in a group of particular content categories. But for the sake of further defining the sort of questions at issue, we may offer some hunches. Mazeway content might, for instance, be divided analytically into two dimensions of cognitive data: goal states, and instrumental cognitive tasks. Social groups can be characterized on a combined dimension of group restriction—localization and specificity of function— from intra-societal role groups—all persons within a given society who play some common role or roles, determined by age, sex, training, or whatever—through band or community, to intra-societal class, caste, ethnic group, region, or interest group, to political group, to culture-area and trans-political social types, and finally, to humanity as a whole. Within any such grouping, any set of predicates descriptive of mazeway content can be characterized with respect to both frequency distribution and equivalence structure.

Culture can be conveniently defined as the complete equivalence structure of mazeway content characteristic of a group. Other categories, however, are less global in content than culture and mazeway, and also may refer either to individuals or to groups or both. Among such categories let us consider five in particular: goal state; cognitive task; motivation; values; and personality. A motivation is a combination of a goal state and a cognitive task; values are classes of goal states, and personalities are equivalence structures of classes of stimuli and motivations whose locus is the individual. Although we assume that for most practical purposes both affects and cognitive processes are nearly identical for all members of all the groups named, this is not the case with the five special concepts. On the localization-specificity dimension, the more restricted the group, the larger the proportion of identical cognitive task, goal state, and motivational elements to those which are not identical but are equivalent or independent, and the larger the proportion of equivalent to independent. In general, furthermore, the rank order of proportion of identity to nonidentity and of equivalence to independence, is constant for cognitive task, goal state, and motivation, in that order, in all groups. Values and personality, while they also follow the same role of proportionality with respect to the group restriction dimension, are more difficult to place in rank order, because they include abstractions on a variety of levels.

My intuition, however, would be that it is precisely in personality and motivation—the combinations of ends and means—in which men differ most from one another, and are least predictable, and that it is in cognitive tasks, goals, and values that they have most in common, and are most predictable.

ORGANIZATION AND THE STUDY OF PROCESSES OR TYPES OF EVENTS

In the field of psychological processes relevant to an understanding of the psychic unity of culturally organized human groups, we find a host of problems refractory to analysis because of the inconveniences imposed by temporal extension. Temporal extension in psychological process may be observed over ranges from milliseconds (e.g., for an event of synaptic transmission) to hundreds or even thousands of years (e.g., for the "life-history" of a concept). Neglecting the extremes and devoting our attention to processes which occur within the life-span of an individual, we find such processes as personality development, enculturation, acculturation, psychotic episode, religious conversion and inspiration, revitalization movements, the disaster syndrome, and the like, which in general occupy sufficient time to require analysis in terms of stages. Major sub-disciplines and special subject areas within psychology, psychiatry, anthropology, and other behavioral sciences concern themselves with one or another of these fields, both on pan-human and particular-culture levels of generalization.

Methodology in these areas is still relatively primitive. Because of the duration and phenomenological complexity of these types of events, continuous first-hand observation is difficult to arrange, and the investigator is often forced to rely on historical and autobiographical data whose reliability, completeness, and standardization is low. Sampling is awkward because the universe of events is difficult to define. Typologies are hazardously constructed because of the extreme complexity of the dimensions.

In an effort to simplify the conceptual model, a general tactic in such research is to formulate as early as possible, an ideal set of stages and a matrix of dimensions for the description of each stage. Thus Piaget, working on the intellectual development of children, and Gesell and his colleagues, concerned with behavior generally, organize their material by stages; psychoanalysis emphasized stages of psychosexual development, of ego function, and so forth; learning theorists arrange the events of a learning sequence stage-wise, from "drive" to "extinction." In my own work, stages in the evolution of types of events—in disasters and in revitalization movements, in particular—have been a major methodological tool.

The aim of stage-description in processual analysis is to state that a particular stage sequence on a given matrix of dimensions is universal, or at least highly probable, for all organisms of a certain type (e.g., for all humans, or for all members of some society) under a given limited set of conditions. But, unless the process is a simple partial ordering (a unilinear scale), different events are possible at each stage. If the outcome at each stage is to some degree dependent on the outcome in the preceding stage or stages, and if this dependence can be expressed as a set of conditional probabilities, then the sequence has the general mathematical form of a stochastic process. In an area of interest to behavioral science, information theory is based on stochastic processes; the analysis of learning as a stochastic process has been undertaken by Bush and Mosteller (1955) and others. The importance of these processes to us, however, lies in the circumstance that such processes may be analyzed with respect to their quantity of organization.

The concept of a *quantity of organization* is centrally important in any consideration of the psychic unity of culture-maintaining groups. Cultures, like the physical bodies of their executors, are not static: they evolve, over long periods of time, and they oscillate, during briefer periods, between states of climax and states of disorganization. While for some purposes it is not necessary, or even desirable, to invoke psychological processes in the analysis of culture change, it is necessary to do so for any general behavior theory which relates levels of abstraction. One overtly observable process which it is important to explain in such a theory of behavior is the tendency of living things to maintain and increase the quantity of organization in the field which they and their environment together constitute. This process is connoted by such terms as evolution, growth, and adaptation. It is convenient to think of this process as depending upon a "drive" to increase the quantity of organization in the mazeway—i.e., in the organism's cognitive representation of the phenomenological field. Such a "drive" is evident in behavioral processes like learning, curiosity, play, fantasy, emotional maturation, the desire for health, and the urge to master and control both self and environment.

The measure of organization of a system should increase both with the orderliness of the system and with its complexity.[5] Complexity should be clearly distinguished from size (e.g., one would not say that a large pattern is more complex than a perfect replica of smaller size). Complexity essentially is a function of the number of possible events within the system. Orderliness, on the other hand, is a function of the relative probability of these events. This argument agrees with intuition. When we refer to a system as "highly organized" we mean that it is highly predictable; if we observe A, we can be reasonably certain that we will find B rather than some alternative. Conversely with a "disorganized" system, we are very uncertain whether we will find B or not if A is observed. In other words, organization is inversely related, in our intuitive apprehension, to uncertainty (information). Also, when we compare "large organization" and "small organization," we use complexity (or, more exactly, that complexity that is associated with large numbers of people) as another, different, and equally intuitive measure of the organization quantity. One kind of stochastic process, the periodic Markov chain (Feller, 1950), appears to be a suitable elementary model for the representation of any process or phenomenon whose stages or aspects may be repeatedly observed in a fixed order.

I shall not undertake here to describe the method (see Miller, 1952) for obtaining the stable distribution of probabilities of the joint events (E_i) in a periodic Markov chain; it is sufficient to note that the periodic Markov chain $A_iB_jC_k$ . . . N_mA_r . . . generates an aperiodic Markov chain in (E_j) and in (E_i, E_j). The basic information function as defined by Shannon (1949) for aperiodic Markov processes is:

1.1
$$H(j) = -\sum_j P(j) \log_2 P(j)$$

For joint events (E_i, E_j) in aperiodic processes of the type considered here, the expression takes the form:

1.2
$$H(E_i, E_j) = -\sum_{E_i, E_j} P(E_i, E_j) \log_2 P(E_i, E_j).$$

The measure H gives the average entropy (information) of the process per joint event. The measure of the average entropy per event is given by:

1.3
$$H(E_j) = -\sum_{E_i, E_j} P(E_i) \cdot P(E_j \mid E_i) \cdot \log_2 P(E_j \mid E_i).$$

where

1.4
$$P(E_j \mid E_i) = \frac{P(E_i, E_j)}{P(E_i)}.$$

The significance of the measure H for this study lies in the fact that it is a function of the predictability of the process: the more predictable the process, the lower the value of H. One may take (1.3) as the fundamental measure for our purposes.

As I have argued, the measure of organization should be a function of both the orderliness and the complexity of the system. The measure of the orderliness of the system may be conceived in the following way: H, the average amount of information produced by the system at event E_j, can vary from zero (for a completely deterministic system) toward some finite limit (as the system approaches complete randomness). The difference between the maximum possible information output, and the actual information output, is the amount of information which the system retains.

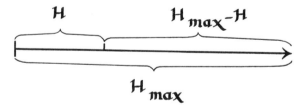

The ratio $\dfrac{H_{max} - H}{H_{max}}$ is the measure of the relative orderliness of the system.

The ratio $\dfrac{H}{H_{max}}$ is defined by Shannon as the relative entropy, and $\left(1 - \dfrac{H}{H_{max}}\right)$ as the redundancy.

The measure of the complexity of the system may be conceived in the following way: let the number of possible events E_j in the system be represented by N, and let the measure of complexity be $\log_2 N$, so that for each doubling of the number of possible system events, the measure of complexity increases by one.

If we now define the measure of quantity of organization in a system as the product of the measure of its relative orderliness by the measure of its complexity, we have

2.1
$$O = \log_2 N\left(\frac{H_{max} - H}{H_{max}}\right).$$

But $H_{max} = \log_2 N$. Therefore,

2.2
$$O = H_{max} - H.$$

Equation (2.2) defines the fundamental measure of quantity of organization.

The argument of this section may be summarized in a Principle of Maximal Organization. This principle asserts that an organism acts in such a way as to maximize, under existing conditions, and to the extent of its capacity, the amount of organization in the dynamic system represented in its mazeway; that is to say, it works to increase both the complexity and the orderliness of its experience. Such a mode of action should simultaneously maximize intra-psychic and group organization.

CONCLUSIONS

This inquiry began by asking what people must have in common, psychologically, in order to live together in culturally organized social groups. After initially questioning whether motivational uniformities are a necessary condition for a cultural way of life, I proceeded to outline a theory relating the cognitive structures of individuals to the cultural organization of groups. This theory emphasizes the importance of capacity to learn and to maintain a semantic organization (mazeway) sufficiently complex to permit the performance of the cognitive tasks required by the culture. Semantic process was defined operationally by the procedures of componential analysis. It was emphasized that this type of cognitive process permits cultural participants to act on the basis of perceived semantic equivalences, without a necessary uniformity of motivation, and that, in fact, motivational uniformity would make social structure of a human kind impossible. Next, I examined the methodological problems involved in the investigation of the distribution of motivational and other cognitive content of mazeway from the standpoints of identity and equivalence analysis. Finally, I suggested that a primary drive to increase the quantities of meaning and organization in mazeway should be postulated in order to conceptualize as non-problematical the tendency for behavioral systems, like culture and personality, to evolve in the direction of increased organization.

The viewpoint expressed throughout the discussion, that motivational uniformity is neither demonstrable nor necessary to social coordination, has an evident bearing on the problems of cross-cultural communication and of defining desirable social systems including, ultimately, a world organization. It seems characteristic of reformist, authoritarian political and religious movements to insist strongly on the importance of an almost complete motivational uniformity as a condition for the achievement of the ideal society. To the extent that social scientists also are convinced that this is the case, they are sharing in one of the illusions characteristic of new movements of thought. Intuitive humanistic perception, the data available in existing monographs, and methodological considerations all reveal that motivational uniformity is not only unnecessary (and is even antithetical) to the development of highly organized civilizations, but is also not empirically observed or observable in human behavior, by either scientist or the individual in culture. This does not mean, of course, that all men do not have in common a set of basic affective and cognitive processes, but only that the semantic content which these processes produce must be highly diverse, and the more diverse the larger the size and complexity of the group.

Thus the most effective base for cross-cultural communication, in the long run, would seem to be the assumption by all parties concerned that social coordination is entirely feasible, given the common possession of a cultural nature, without uniformity of motive or interest. This is, in fact, precisely the achievement of the cultural mode of organization. Such an assumption lies at the root of such notions as the ideas of justice, of law, of convention, and of a minimally necessary behavioral conformity without sacrifice of individuality, which have been associated with the concept of "freedom" in sophisticated civilizations. Without such an assumption, indeed, motivational diversity is merely hidden, under mutual illusions of motivational identity (and mutual suspicions of "disloyalty"), by the ritualization of all expression, by the frustration of the drive for maximal meaning and organization of experience, and by the blocking of the evolution of human personalities and cultures. Neither order nor complexity can be immolated on the other's altar without violating the laws of cultural nature.

NOTES

1. The concepts of identity and equivalence, which are used extensively in this paper, are formal logical concepts. They may be applied to predicates, which are the descriptive elements of propositions (for instance, in the proposition, "The table is round," "is round" is the predicate). Two symbols, 'p' and 'q,' are said to stand for identical predicates only if the predicates are one and the same. The two symbols 'p' and 'q' are said to stand for strictly equivalent predicates if, whenever p is true, q is true also, and whenever q is true, p is true. Evidently identity implies equivalence; but equivalence does

not imply identity. Tautological equivalence is established by definitions. Empirical data may reveal that under some conditions two variables (two sets of predicates) approach equivalence, over certain values of each, by virtue of the fact that whenever a particular value of one variable is true, some particular corresponding value of the other variable is true. The discovery of this kind of non-tautological or material equivalence, expressible in statistical associations and mathematical functions like differential equations, is a main object of scientific research.

2. Some readers may feel discomfort at an attempt to treat cognition independently of motivation. They may justly point out, with Mannheim (1936), that human cognition rarely if ever occurs in a complete motivational vacuum. Nevertheless, it is important to distinguish between "pure" cognition and motivational cognition in order to consider their respective bearings on culture. Scientific analysis frequently requires the conceptual separation of elements which in experience are inextricable. An obvious example from physics is the formulation of the laws of motion of two bodies, gravitationally independent of other bodies, in a perfect physical vacuum: an experimentally impossible condition.

3. It is not desirable to go farther into the theory of componential analysis here, since that would require an extended technical discussion in the language of symbolic logic and set theory which would be out of place in this context. It may however be noted that there are several other logical systems available for the formal exhibition of semantic relations: for instance, Morris' "semiotic" (Morris, 1955), and Carnap's calculus of state-descriptions (Carnap, 1955). With the assistance of John Atkins, I have made some progress in formulating a semantic calculus based on propositional logic and set theory. Our calculus, we believe, accurately represents the intuitive operations of linguists, anthropologists, and other behavioral scientists when they perform componential and other kinds of semantic analysis, and must, indeed, be postulated in order to justify these operations rationally. Furthermore, this calculus promises to be useful in designing more efficient scientific taxonomies. We believe also that this approach is compatible with the theory of logical nets—based on the simple propositional calculus—which underlies the efforts of certain mathematicians to describe the data-processing functions of the brain (cf. George, 1958). This calculus is not related to that of Osgood (1957) whose "semantic differential" deals with connotative rather than definitive meaning.

4. Semantic information (H_{sem}) is distinguished from statistical information (H_{stat}) by the property that H_{sem} of a term is a function solely of the ratio of the number of cells corresponding to the term to the number of cells in the space on which the term is defined. H_{stat} of a term, on the other hand, is a function solely of the relative conditional probability within the lexicon of the term's occurrence in a sequence of terms. A lexicon (L) contains u terms l, each of which is defined by a subset of w cells in a space (M) of v cells. The following definitions refer to H_{sem}:

Def. 1. Each of the v cells m in semantic space (M) contains a quantity of semantic information which is equivalent to $(-\log_2 \frac{1}{v})$;

$$H_m = -\log_2 \frac{1}{v}.$$

Def. 2. The quantity of semantic information H_M contained in the space (M) is equivalent to the sum of the quantities of semantic information contained in the v individual cells;

$$H_M = -v \log_2 \frac{1}{v}.$$

Def. 3. The quantity of semantic information H_1 conveyed by a term 1 is equivalent to the sum of the quantities of semantic information contained in the w cells which define 1;

$$H_1 = -w \log_2 \frac{1}{v}.$$

Def. 4. The quantity of semantic information H_L conveyed by the lexicon (L) is equivalent to the sum of the quantities of semantic information conveyed by the u individual terms 1;

$$H_L = \overset{u}{\underset{1}{\Sigma}} H_1.$$

5. The multiplicative relation of order and complexity is one criterion, among others, which distinguishes organization measure from Birkhoff's "aesthetic measure," which also is a function of order and complexity (M = O/C) (see Birkhoff, 1933). Coon's concept of "level of complexity," which he applies to cultures, concerns complexity alone and implicitly assumes constant order (see Coon, 1948).

BIBLIOGRAPHY

Arieti, S. 1955. *Interpretation of Schizophrenia*. New York: Robert Brunner.

————. 1956. "Some Basic Problems Common to Anthropology and Modern Psychiatry," *American Anthropologist*, 58:26–39.

Bar-Hillel, J., and Carnap, R. 1954. "Semantic Information," *British Journal for the Philosophy of Science*, 4:147–157.

Bartlett, H. C. 1923. *Psychology and Primitive Culture*. New York: Macmillan Co.

Bidney, D. 1953. *Theoretical Anthropology*. New York: Columbia University Press.

Birkhoff, G. 1933. *Aesthetic Measure*. New Haven: Yale University Press.

Boas, F. 1911. *The Mind of Primitive Man*. New York: Macmillan Co.

Boole, G. 1854. *The Laws of Thought*. New York: Reprinted by Dover Publications, Inc.

Bush, R. R., and Mosteller, F. 1955. *Stochastic Models for Learning*. New York: John Wiley & Sons, Inc.

Carnap, R. 1955. "Foundations of Logic and Mathematics," *International Encyclopedia of Unified Science*, 1:141–213.

Cassirer, E. 1944. *An Essay on Man*. New Haven: Yale University Press.

Coon, C. S. 1948. *A Reader in General Anthropology*. New York: Henry Holt.

DeLaguna, G. 1949. "Culture and Rationality," *American Anthropologist,* 51:379–391.

Devereux, G. 1945. "The Logical Foundations of Culture and Personality Studies," *Transactions of the New York Academy of Sciences,* 7, series 2; 110–130.

———. 1956. "Normal and Abnormal: The Key Problem of Psychiatric Anthropology," in Casagrande, J. B. and Gladwin, T. (eds.), *Some Uses of Anthropology: Theoretical and Applied,* 23–49. Washington, D.C.: Anthropological Society of Washington.

Dobzhansky, T., and Montagu, M. F. Ashley. 1947. "Natural Selection and the Mental Capacities of Mankind," *Science,* 105:587–590.

Domarus, E. von. 1954. "The Specific Laws of Logic in Schizophrenia," in Kasanin, J. S. (ed.), *Language in Thought and Schizophrenia,* 104–114. Berkeley and Los Angeles: University of California Press.

Eiseley, L. 1956. "Fossil Man and Human Evolution," in Thomas, W. L. (ed.), *Current Anthropology,* 61–78. Chicago: University of Chicago Press.

———. 1958. *Darwin's Century.* New York: Doubleday & Co.

Feller, W. 1950. *An Introduction to Probability Theory and Its Applications;* v. 1. New York: John Wiley & Sons.

Fenichel, O. 1945. *The Psychoanalytic Theory of Neurosis.* New York: W. W. Norton Co.

Fletcher, R. 1957. *Instinct in Man in the Light of Recent Work in Comparative Psychology.* New York: International Universities Press.

Frank, L. K. 1951. *Nature and Human Nature.* New Jersey: Rutgers University Press.

Fromm, E. 1951. *The Forgotten Language.* New York: Rinehart & Co., Inc.

George, F. H. 1958. "Machines and the Brain," *Science,* 127:3309, 1269–74.

Goldenweiser, A. 1933. *History, Psychology and Culture.* New York: Knopf.

Goodenough, W. 1956. "Componential Analysis and the Study of Meaning," *Language,* 32, 1:195–216.

———. 1951. *Property, Kin, and Community on Truk.* New Haven: Yale University Press.

Hallowell, A. I. 1950. "Personality Structure and the Evolution of Man," *American Anthropologist,* 52:159–73.

———. 1955. *Culture and Experience.* Philadelphia: University of Pennsylvania Press.

———. 1956. "The Structural and Functional Dimensions of a Human Existence," *Quarterly Review of Biology,* 31:88–101.

Hebb, D. O. 1949. *Organization of Behavior: A Neuropsychological Theory.* New York: John Wiley & Sons.

Hoijer, H., (ed.). 1954. *Language in Culture* (American Anthropologist Memoir 79).

Kasanin, J. S., (ed.). 1954. *Language and Thought in Schizophrenia.* Berkeley and Los Angeles: University of California Press.

Kluckhohn, C. 1953. "Universal Categories of Culture," in Kroeber, A. L., (ed.), *Anthropology Today*, 507–523. Chicago: University of Chicago Press.

Kroeber, A. L. 1955. "On Human Nature," *Southwestern Journal of Anthropology*, 11:195–204.

Kroeber, A. L., and Kluckhohn, C. 1952. *Culture: A Critical Review of Concepts and Definitions*. Papers of the Peabody Museum, XLVII, no. 1. Cambridge: Harvard University Press.

La Barre, Weston. 1954. *The Human Animal*. Chicago: University of Chicago Press.

———. 1958. "The Influence of Freud on Anthropology," *American Imago*, 15:275–328.

Langer, S. K. 1942. *Philosophy in a New Key*. Cambridge: Harvard University Press.

Levi-Strauss, C., Jakobson, R., Voegelin, C. F., and Sebeok, T. A. 1953. *Results of the Conference of Anthropologists and Linguists*. Baltimore: Waverly Press.

Lounsbury, F. G. 1956. "A Semantic Analysis of the Pawnee Kinship Usage," *Language*, 32:158–194.

Lowie, R. H. 1937. *History of Ethnological Theory*. New York: Farrar & Rinehart.

Mannheim, Karl. 1936. *Ideology and Utopia*. New York: Harcourt, Brace (reprint).

Mead, M. 1948. "Anthropological Data on the Problem of Instinct," in Kluckhohn, C. and Murray, H. (eds.), *Personality in Nature, Society, and Culture*, 109–112. New York: Knopf.

Mead, M., and Metraux R., (eds.). 1953. *The Study of Culture at a Distance*. Chicago: University of Chicago Press.

Mead, M., Michael, D. N., Lasswell, H. D., and Frank, L. K. 1958. *Man in Space: A Tool and Program for the Study of Social Change*. (Annals of the New York Academy of Sciences, 72:165–214.)

Miller, G. A. 1952. "Finite Markov Processes in Psychology," *Psychometrika*, 17:149–167.

Morgan, L. 1877. *Ancient Society*. Chicago: Charles H. Kerr.

Morris, C. W. 1955. "Foundations of the Theory of Signs," *International Encyclopedia of Unified Science*, 1:79–137.

Murdock, G. P. 1945. "The Common Denominator of Culture," in Linton, R. (ed.), *The Science of Man in the World Crisis*, 123–142. New York: Columbia University Press.

Osgood, C. E. 1952. "The Nature and Measurement of Meaning," *Psychological Bulletin*, 49:197–237.

———. 1957. *The Measurement of Meaning*. Urbana: University of Illinois Press.

Rashkis, H. A. 1957. "A General Theory of Treatment in Psychiatry," *Archives of Neurology and Psychiatry*, 78:491–99.

Redfield, R. 1952. "Primitive World View," *Proceedings of the American Philosophical Society*, 96:30–36.

Róheim, G. 1943. *The Origin and Function of Culture.* (Nervous and Mental Disease Monographs, No. 69.)

Sapir, E. 1949. *Selected Writings of Edward Sapir in Language, Culture, and Personality,* Mandelbaum, D. G. (ed.). Berkeley and Los Angeles: University of California Press.

Shannon, C. E., and Weaver, W. 1949. *The Mathematical Theory of Communication.* Urbana: University of Illinois Press.

Spiro, M. E. 1951. "Culture and Personality, The Natural History of a False Dichotomy," *Psychiatry*, 14:19–40.

———. 1954. "Human Nature in Its Psychological Dimensions," *American Anthropologist*, 56:19–29.

Tappen, N. C. 1953. "A Mechanistic Theory of Human Evolution," *American Anthropologist,* 55:605–07.

Tylor, E. B. 1871. *Primitive Culture,* 2 vols. London: J. Murray.

Wallace, A. F. C. 1952. *Modal Personality of Tuscarora Indians.* Bureau of American Ethnology Bulletin 150, Washington, D.C.

———. 1956a. "Mazeway Resynthesis: A Biocultural Theory of Religious Inspiration," *Transactions of the New York Academy of Sciences*, 18, series 11:626–38.

———. 1956b. "Revitalization Movements," *American Anthropologist*, 58: 264–81.

———. 1956c. *Tornado in Worcester.* Washington, D.C.: National Academy of Sciences, National Research Council.

———. 1957a. "Mazeway Disintegration: The Individual's Perception of Socio-Cultural Disorganization," *Human Organization,* 16:23–27.

———. 1957b. "Study of Processes of Organization and Revitalization of Psychological and Socio-cultural Systems, Based on a Comparative Study of Nativistic Religious Revivals," *Yearbook of the American Philosophical Society,* 310–11.

———, and Atkins, John. 1960. "The Meaning of Kinship Terms," *American Anthropologist,* 62:58–80.

White, L. 1949. *The Science of Culture.* New York: Farrar, Straus & Co.

Whorf, B. L. 1956. *Language, Thought and Reality: Selected Writings of Benjamin Lee Whorf,* Carroll, J. B. (ed.). Cambridge: Technology Press.

Wissler, C. 1923. *Man and Culture.* New York: Thomas Y. Crowell.

Wundt, W. 1916. *Elements of Folk Psychology.* New York: Macmillan Co.

About the Chapter

The problem of personality development or socialization occupies a key position in culture and personality theory. In this chapter Dr. Parsons defines a variety of processes in socialization which produce the kind of personality processes that support the individual's appropriate participation in society. Unlike the psychologist who is concerned with how personality becomes what it is, Dr. Parsons' interest centers on how personality becomes shaped so that it motivates the kind of behavior that society requires. This development, which is seen in relationship to Freud's theory of object relations, is held to involve the organization of the motivational system through three processes: identification, object-cathexis and internalization.

About the Author

TALCOTT PARSONS is Professor of Sociology at Harvard University. He received his A.B. from Amherst College and his Ph.D. from the University of Heidelberg, Germany. In earlier years he taught economics as well as sociology. He was formerly Chairman of the Department of Sociology at Harvard and from 1946–56 was Chairman of the Department of Social Relations there. He was Visiting Professor of Social Theory at the University of Cambridge in 1953–54, and was a Fellow at the Center for Advanced Study in the Behavioral Sciences in 1957–58. He has written *Structure of Social Action; Essays in Sociological Theory; Toward a General Theory of Action* (with collaborators); *The Social System, Working Papers in the Theory of Action* (with collaborators); *Family, Socialization and Interaction Process* (with R. F. Bales); *Economy and Society* (with N. J. Smelser); and *Structure and Process in Modern Society*.

Acknowledgment

The bulk of this chapter, in substantially the same form, first appeared in *Psychiatry* 21, 4, Nov. 1958 (copyright 1958 by the William Alanson White Psychiatric Foundation, Inc.), and is published here by permission. However, new material has been added in the first part of the chapter.

4

Social Structure and the Development
of Personality

TALCOTT PARSONS
Harvard University

In the United States the ideological needs of the intellectual classes have led to an interpretation of Freud's work which places primary emphasis on the power of the individual's instinctual needs and the deleterious effects of their frustration. On the occasion of the recent centenary of Freud's birth there were a number of statements to this effect.[1] They viewed Freud mainly as a psychologist who tended to bring psychology closer to the biological sciences. Accordingly, the relation of the individual personality to society and culture is relatively unimportant, except as society and culture constitute agencies of the undesirable frustration of man's instinctual needs.

There is, however, another side to Freud's thinking, which became, I think, progressively more prominent in the course of the complicated evolution of his theoretical scheme through time. It culminated in the works dealing with the structural differentiation of the personality into id, ego and superego, and in Freud's late treatment of anxiety. This trend concerns two main themes: the problem of the *organization* of the personality as a system, and the relation of the individual to his social surroundings especially in the course of his personality development. In

165

psychoanalytic terminology, this is the field of "object relations"—the most important area of articulation between the psychoanalytic theory of the personality of the individual and the sociological theory of the structure and functioning of social systems.

This latter aspect of Freud's thought will form the subject-matter of this chapter.[2] It is my main thesis that there is, in the structure of Freud's own theoretical scheme, a set of propositions which can, with relatively little reinterpretation, be very directly integrated with the sociological analysis of the family as a small scale social system. Further, these propositions can be applied to the problems of the child's transition from membership mainly in his own family to participation in wider circles which are not, in societies like ours, mainly organized in terms of kinship. Freud's own contribution here centers mainly in the earlier stages of socialization, through the oedipal resolution. But the same basic principles of analysis can be extended to the later stages.

The most important of Freud's concepts in this respect are identification, object-cathexis, internalization or introjection, and the superego. Most attention has been given to the concept of the superego. Though many difficult problems of interpretation cluster about that concept, it undoubtedly refers to the internalization—becoming a constitutive part of the structure of the personality itself—of aspects of the normative culture of the society in which the individual grows up.

Very important clues are given by the remarkable convergence, in these respects, between Freud's views on internalization and those developed, independently and at nearly the same time in sociological quarters, by Emile Durkheim in France and by C. H. Cooley and G. H. Mead in the United States. This convergence is one of the few truly momentous developments of modern social science, comparable perhaps to the convergence between the studies of experimental breeding in the tradition of Mendel and the microscopic studies of cell division from which the conceptions of the chromosomes as the vehicles of biological heredity developed. The two together produced the modern science of genetics.

The fundamental principle on which Freud's idea of the superego was based, can be extended, not merely across disciplines to the sociological treatment of the relations between social structure and personality, but within the personality, to the constitution of its other sectors and structural components. Some have tended to treat the superego as a very special case within the personality, as the only point at which the norms of the culture enter into it. A major objective of the present chapter, however, is to show that the whole logic of Freud's later position implies that the same is true for the structure of the ego also. Indeed it follows from Freud's whole main treatment of the process of socialization—

and, at least at one point, was explicitly stated in his writings (see passage quoted on p. 193)—that the major structure of the ego is a precipitate of the series of object relations which the individual has experienced in the course of his life-history. Internalization of the sociocultural environment provides the basis, not merely of one specialized component of the human personality, but of what, in the human sense, is its central core. In the light of the main traditions of modern psychology this is a very radical position, so radical that its import has not yet been very widely appreciated.

The final question inevitably arises as to whether even the third of Freud's famous three subsystems of the personality, the id, should be completely exempted from this central interpretation of the importance of object relations and internalization. In the final section of the chapter, I shall argue very briefly that the interpretation of the id as a manifestation of "pure instinct" is, in Freud's own terms, untenable. Though it is the primary channel of transmission of instinctual energy and more particularized impulses into the personality, it also is structured through internalized object-relations. It involves above all the residues of the earliest object relations of the life history of the individual, which have had to be rather drastically reorganized in the course of later life-experience.

In order to provide a frame of reference in which to approach the interpretation and to some extent, I hope, the extension of Freud's ideas in the field of object relations, it should be useful to give a broad outline of the relations of the basic categories of the phenomena or factors involved in the behavior of human organisms as they appear in the light of contemporary social science.

The essential point in this framework which I have called the "theory of action" is that one can distinguish four systems; namely (1) the organism, in that aspect most directly concerned with the energy and the facilities involved in behavior; (2) the personality, or the psychological systems concerned with the situation-oriented behavior of the individual organism; (3) the social systems generated by the interaction of a plurality of acting persons; and finally (4) the cultures developed in and through interaction but also regulating its processes. All four of these must be regarded as analytically distinguishable systems which are not mutually reducible in the analytical-theoretical sense to terms of each other. This is, at the same time, both a theoretical and a substantive view. It maintains that, in the course of organic evolution, those aspects of the organism directly involved in the mechanisms of behavior have come to be differentiated from those involved in the transmission of inheritance through the genes, and from those involved in the more "vegetative" functions (see Alexander, 1950) of the organism which entail interchanges with the environment on bio-chemical levels such as nutrition-elimination and respiration.

I should like then to refer to the "behavioral organism" as consti-tuting a system conceived to stand in relations of interdependence with the other three systems of action, the personality of the individual, the social system and the cultural system. The personality is conceived as an analytically independent system, constituted by the *behavior* of the single living organism itself; in other words it is always conceived in relation to objects in the environment other than the organism of reference.[3] The social system then is generalized by a plurality of living organisms (and personalities) interacting with each other. A particular social system may, of course, "engage" only a part of the personality of a living or-ganism, first because objects other than other persons are important to personalities, and second because the same personality may be, indeed on differentiated levels always is, engaged in interaction in a plurality of different systems of social interaction; a person has, as sociologists say, a plurality of roles. Finally, cultural systems must also be treated as independent not only of social systems, but of the other two, in the same basic analytical sense in which they are independent of each other. One basis of this analytical independence is that the *same* system of cultural components may be involved in, and regulate, action in a plural-ity of distinct social systems. Furthermore, the basis of their integra-tion is different in that cultural integration concerns the pattern-com-ponents in their relations to each other on the level of meaning rather than the mutual adjustment of the congruence of the actor-units as such, which is the focus of integration of social systems.

What then can be said about the relations of these four systems to each other? They must, of course, be considered to be interdepend-ent; processes in any one will partially determine and, in turn, be de-termined by processes in each of the others. But even more than that, they must be considered on some level to be subsystems of a single more comprehensive system—what some of us have been calling a system of *action*. What is a system of action?

It is constituted by the behavior of living organisms. For some pur-poses on all levels, and for all purposes on the lowest level of the dif-ferentiation and organization of behavior, this behavior can be treated as a *single* system. This is essentially what is done on the "stimulus-response" level of psychological analysis, and in some cases in other types of study of animal behavior. But particularly on the human socio-cultural levels it becomes essential to discriminate different types of subsystems of this more general system. Methodologically this is necessary because in analyzing more differentiated and complex phe-nomena we face two alternatives. One is the introduction into our analysis, *ad hoc,* of more and more distinct variables. Up to a point this may add to the empirical realism of an analytical scheme. But as the number of variables grows, the possibilities of analytical inference with respect to their interrelations diminish very rapidly. The only logical alternative to this scientifically self-defeating procedure, is to repeat essentially the same basic analysis of systems at many different levels in application to many different systems and subsystems. This, essentially, was Freud's procedure and it is the one I shall follow in this chapter.

Action, then, is the set of processes by which the relations between organisms and their situations of action come to be organized and regulated. The focus of this organization and regulation is the building up of systems of the *meanings* of objects as signs or symbols so that the "reaction" of the organism to the presence or expected presence of a given object or class of objects in the situation becomes organized and stabilized.

Since reactions to objects become stabilized in patterned ways, we can speak of action as being inherently "goal-directed" in the sense that there are *optimum* relations to given objects. When such optimum relations are disturbed, the organism-object system will tend to change its state in the direction of the optimum. Secondly, action as process is fundamentally and inherently dependent on learning. Of course, the major anatomical structures involved in behavior are laid down in the genetic constitution of the organism. But the most essential property of the higher organisms is their adaptive capacity. High adaptive capacity in the individual organism and rigid specification of behavior patterns on a constitutional basis are inherently incompatible. The distinctive feature of human organisms is a hereditary constitution which provides a high capacity for learning. Certainly man has gone a significant step beyond any other species in this respect. This means, as Freud, far more than most psychologists even today, says, that the "instinctual" basis of behavior must be highly *nonspecific,* and that the primary specific patterns of behavior are *learned* by the individual. It is of particular importance that primary *life-goals* must be treated as learned.

PERSONALITY AND SOCIAL SYSTEM

Let us now take up the two subsystems of action which are most critical for our present purposes, personality and social system. Relative to the organism, the personality may be regarded as a system of mechanisms of control. It is the set of ways in which organized patterns of learned response to objects in the situation operate to control the organism's goal-directed and adaptive activity. The personality thus mediates between the organism and the environment in which it lives.

The facilities utilized by the organism in its life processes come to it to a large extent in forms, in timing sequences, etc. organized through the action of the personality. For example, human beings must as organisms be adequately fed, but *what* they eat, at what times, in what circumstances, and how secured, are mediated through personality controls. Respiration is a vital function relatively little subject to personality control on a routine basis, but personality intervention is very prompt when there is an interference with respiratory function.

Conversely, the organism is, for the personality, the source of the energy, or in the most general sense "motivation," and also the primary immediate source of facilities for the achievement of personality goals. Besides the underlying energy-producing "power house" of the organism, these facilities may be classified as information processing facilities (such as organs of perception), as instrumentalities for securing rewards (e.g., musculo-skeletal mechanisms), and integrative-storage facilities (such as the central nervous system which serves as memory and paramount control organ).

Later, I shall have something further to say about the relations of organism and personality. But first let us discuss the most essential relations of personality and social systems. The focal point is that, for man at any rate, as Freud made clear, the most critically important objects in the situation are other human beings. It is the exposure of the human infant to *other* human beings, particularly the mother, in a special kind of *social* relationship, which lays down the genetic basis of the development of his personality.

Secondly, the essential feature of the relation of the child to others lies in his dependence on the relationship to the mother for the basic *rewards* involved in the attainment of his goals or the gratification of his wishes. Third, it is inherent in the *interactive* character of human social relationships that there should be a *contingent* element in the relationship. The securing of the essential rewards is made contingent on the child's performance in areas and in respects *other* than the process of organic gratification itself. This contingency of reward is the basic source of leverage for motivating the process of learning.

Two further points are critical in this connection. One is that, as already stated, the *goals* of the human individual in the human personality sense, are not primarily given in his biological constitution, but must be learned in the process of socialization. The other is that not only are other human beings, as discrete objects, individually and severally the most significant objects in the child's, and indeed any human being's, situation of action, but the *system of relationships* in which these objects stand to each other, and which includes the child himself, constitutes the most fundamental *structure* of the situation or environment in which his action takes place. A child, throughout his life cycle, is never exposed to just one person or "social object" but always to structured *systems* of social objects. In this sense the social system (or systems) in which he participates always constitutes the essential environment of any personality in its action processes, so far as this system operates on the social interaction level, rather than in relation to the individual's own organism, and the bodies of others.

Finally, something needs to be said about the status of the cultural system relative to the other three. Its focus is the cultural pattern component of all action—the system of the *meanings* of the objects experienced by individuals. Meanings, like object relations, are primarily learned. Moreover there is an immensely heavy premium on the importance of the respects in which meanings are *shared* with other individuals; only through meeting this criterion can such meanings facilitate the processes of communication. Meanings, looked at from the point of view of the individual, define *norms* governing action. This conclusion follows from the primary significance of the *social object* whose reaction to ego's action is the prototypical example of meaning. The meaning of ego's own actions is essentially the codification of the set of *consequences* for him that his own action evokes in relation to the environment. But if the objects concerned are also actors in the same social system, the meanings can be stabilized only if ego recognizes alter's *expectations* of action as a *norm* which should govern his action and vice versa. *Complementarity* of expectations, then, is the basis of the *commonness* of norms. These common norms, or values, constitute the cultural core of any system of social interaction. As part of the total system of action, the cultural system is that aspect which is oriented to the maintenance of such a set of common values in the system.

I have noted that relative to the organism the personality may be conceived as a system of controlling agencies. Essentially the same relation is repeated as we follow through the relations of personality to the other subsystems of action. Social systems, that is, in certain essential respects control personalities, and cultural systems in some respects control social systems. There is a *hierarchy* of control relations.

The distinction between the aspects of the system of action centering on the individual and his behavior on the one hand, and the transindividual factors of society and culture on the other hand, is a very old one. In one major tradition at least, it stems from the problems of Darwinian biology as applied to human behavior. More recently it has seemed necessary to draw lines within each of the two categories resulting from that distinction—namely between cultural and social systems on the one hand, between organism and personality on the other.

The importance of the latter distinction will be strongly stressed in what follows. It is emergent in Freud's own work and was progressively more strongly stressed.[4] This distinction is crucial to the understanding of the place of the theory of instincts in Freud's total psychological theory, and to the whole problem of the role of pleasure and of eroticism. The main emphasis in my analysis, however, will be on the relations between personality and social system. I believe that, while the main content of the structure of the personality is derived from social systems and culture through socialization, the personality becomes an independent system through its relations to its own organism and through the uniqueness of its own life-history experience; it is not a mere epiphenomenon of the structure of the society. There is, however, not merely interdependence between the two, but what I call *interpenetration*. From the sociological side the essential concept of *role* designates this area of interpenetration. From the personality side a corresponding concept of *relational needs* may be used. The psychoanalytically central need for love may serve as an example.

THE ORAL STAGE AND THE PROCESS OF IDENTIFICATION

Let us now turn to Freud's theory of object relations. Following up my initial remarks about instinct, it may be said that there are two main directions of thinking about the nature of personality development. One may be illustrated by analogy with the plant where the main qualities of the mature organism—for example, the number and qualities of wheat grains produced, or the brilliance and shape of the flowers—are predetermined in the genetic constitution of the species. There will be differences in outcome as a function of the favorableness or unfavorableness of the environment within which development takes place. The *main pattern,* however, is not determined by this process of interaction with the environment, only the degree of excellence with which it "comes out." The other direction of thinking sees the genetic constitution as a *nonspecific* base from which the pattern of the adult personality will be evolved.[5] The main pattern-setting components are not so much the genetic elements, but are the *values* of the culture and the *meanings* of social objects experienced in the course of personality development.

These two directions of thinking are not mutually exclusive. Their differences are primarily a matter of relative emphasis. It is my contention that the main significance of Freud's work for the social sciences consists in the seriousness and the fruitfulness with which he explored the *second* direction of thinking. This is not to say that the theory of object relations is "more important" than the theory of instincts. Rather, in Freud's treatment of human personality, object relations acquire a quite different order of significance than they do in botany. This line of thinking colors Freud's whole theory of personality including the theory of instincts.[6]

As noted above, three fundamental concepts in Freud's theory bear most directly on the problem of object-relations, namely identification, object-cathexis (or object-choice) and internalization or "introjection." Freud associated these concepts particularly, though by no means exclusively, with three different levels of the process of socialization. The first, identification, referred in the first instance to the relation established between mother and child in the oral phase. The second, object-cathexis, was used preponderantly to characterize the relation of mother and child in the later phase standing between the oral and the oedipal, while the third, internalization or introjection, referred mainly to the process of establishment of the superego in the oedipal phase. It will be my thesis that each of these concepts, in different ways, designates an aspect of the integration of the personality of the individual in a social system, an integration which is characterized by a particular process of *learning* in a particular context of object-relations.

Therefore, I suggest: first that Freud tended to confuse the genetic and the analytical uses of these concepts and, second, that for the theory of personality in general, the analytical meaning of them is more important than the genetic.[7]

In order to establish a basis for clarifying some theoretical implications of Freud's treatment of these processes, I shall attempt to sketch them in my own terms, though with continual references to Freud. Freud, in common with many other writers, maintained [8] that the starting point for the process of socialization, was the action of persons responsible for gratifying the child's constitutionally given organic needs —in the first instance the mother. Though there is a plurality of such needs, in the earliest phases, that for nutrition is presumably paramount. In addition, however, the mother is the primary object for gratification of a series of instinctual responses at the behavioral level.

The psychological importance of physiological dependence on a human agent hinges only partly on the adequacy of the "satisfaction" the agent gives to the inborn needs. It also depends on physiological mechanisms by which the feeling of satisfaction is experienced as a *reward* in the form of internal organic pleasure.[9] Satisfaction cannot acquire this meaning, unless the child learns that instinctual gratifications are in some sense *contingent, both* on the action of the mother, *and* on that of the child. To take one instinctual response for illustration, it seems to be established that there is an inborn sucking response, but the child early learns to suckle better than he is equipped to do by sheer "instinct." He learns motions of the lips, posture, when to exert effort and when to relax (see Grinker, 1953). The amount of milk he gets and the ease with which he gets it are contingent to an appreciable degree on his own goal-oriented action. This holds true apart from any influence he may exert on when and under what circumstances the breast or bottle will be presented to him. These factors he can also learn to influence through crying and other procedures.

On the mother's side also, feeding a baby is by no means purely "instinctive" but involves elements of skill and of "intentional" (not necessarily conscious) regulation. She tries to "get him" to nurse properly. She can influence this through her manner of holding the baby, through her sensitivity to his "need to rest," through judgment as to how far to "force" him, as to when he has "had enough." In addition, it is clearly she who is the primary agent of imposition of any sort of schedule on the timing of feeding. It is she who determines the "picking up" and the "setting down" of the baby, the way he is dressed, covered, bathed, cleaned, etc., along with the feeding.

Thus even at this very elementary level, the relations between mother and infant constitute a genuine process of *social interaction* of which "care" in the sense of sheer attending to physiological needs, is clearly only one component. The child, from the beginning, is to some degree an active agent who "tries" to do things and is rewarded or punished according to his "success" in doing them. Obviously the degree to which this is true increases rapidly with time. The mother, on her side, actively manipulates the situation in which this learning process takes place. However genuine the process of interaction as such, she is in the overwhelmingly predominant position of power, as manifested in her capacity to control the timing of feeding and other acts of care, indeed the whole setting of the experience.

Whatever the relation between the mother's agency in caring for basic metabolic needs and whatever the child's own instinctual responses on the behavioral level, this agency is the primary factor in developing an attachment to her as an object. The *organization* of the emerging motivational system is a function, not simply of the needs of the child, but of the way in which the mother's responses to these needs have themselves been organized.[10]

Translating these familiar psychological facts into sociological terms the essential consideration is that the infant in the first few weeks, if not days, of life, comes to be integrated into a social system. There are built up relatively definite expectations of his behavior, not only in the predictive, but in the normative sense. He nurses "well" or "badly"; he cries only when he "should" and is quiet the rest of the time, or he cries "when there isn't any good reason." Inevitably, the behavior of adults takes on the character of rewarding him for what *they* feel to be "good" behavior, and punishing him—including omission of reward—for what they feel to be bad behavior, and otherwise manipulating sanctions in relation to him.

From the point of view of the infant, there are two particularly crucial aspects which present cognitive problems to him. The first is the problem of "understanding" conditions on which his gratifications and frustrations depend. What are the cues, or conditional stimuli, which indicate the direction of consequences for him, if he acts in a given way? From the psychology of learning we know that it does not require any high level of "rationality" or "higher mental process" for significant learning to take place if certain modes of action consistently produce rewards, while others do not. The second basic problem to him is the focus of *organization* of this system of cues. This is not simply the question of what specific cues indicate probable gratification or deprivation of specific needs, but rather, of what general *formula* of action can improve the chances of generalized gratification.

Here again, it is not necessary to assume any rationalistic hypotheses. If the pattern of sanctions imposed is *consistent* over a range of more specific actions, we may assume that there will be generalization from the more specific items to the *pattern*.[11] Thus, where the child "tries" to nurse properly in the sense of "cooperating" with the mother, he is more likely to be gratified. In a way, she presents cues and supplementary rewards. It is not a very long step from this level to think of the organized pattern of sanctions in terms of the *intentions* of the mother. The significance of this step derives from the fact that there is generally a *single* primary agent of early child care,[12] and that in a variety of significant respects, the actions of this agent come to be *contingent* on what the child does. In these circumstances, the learning of the *meaning* of a cue is, I think, synonymous with the imputation of intention to the agent.

The concept of intention as here used involves two central components. The first is the *contingency* of what alter (the agent of care) does on what ego (the child) has done or is expected to do, so that alter's action may be treated as a *sanction* in relation to ego's action. The second is the component of generalization. There exist not merely discrete, disconnected sanctions, but a *pattern* of sanctions. This pattern is relatively systematic and organized and eventually leads to the learning of a complementary pattern of responses which is also organized and generalized. In its relation to discrete, particularized acts on either side of the interaction process, the pattern component of the sanction system acquires the character of a set of values or norms. These norms define the relation between acceptable, rewarded behavior on the one hand, and unacceptable, nonrewarded or punished behavior on the other.

Because of the immense inequality of the power relationship, the most important change brought about by this early phase of the process of interaction is the change in the personality of the child. Presumably there is also some change in the personality of the mother. The primary change in the child is the introduction of a new level of *organization* into his behavior system. It is a new level of capacity for organized behavior in the external world, for successfully attaining his goals and for coping with a variable situation. Internally, it is a new level of organization of his motivational or instinctual impulses or needs. A system of *control over* these impulses is introduced and a pattern provided for their utilization in the interest of the newly learned goals and interests. In Freud's famous metaphor (1933),[13] this new organization derived from contact with objects, the ego, was likened to a rider on the impulse system, the id, a horse which may ordinarily do the rider's bidding, but on occasion may be difficult or impossible to control.

The essential point here is that this system of internal control over the child's own instinctual or impulse system has become established through a generalized pattern of sanctions imposed by the mother. The child learns to respond, not simply to specific proffered rewards, but to "intentions" and thereby to "conform" with her wishes or expectations. In so doing he has learned a new *generalized goal.* It is no longer simply to gratify his constitutionally given instinctual needs, especially for food, but to "please" his mother. It is the attainment of this new level of generalized organization of the motivation of behavior, including a new goal, which I think Freud primarily designated as *identification.* This is a mode of *organization* of the ego with reference to its *relation* to a social object. We can clearly say that, *at the same time,* it is learning to act in conformity with a set of norms.

Let me sum up the main characteristics of this basic learning process. It depends on the establishment of a determinate set of relations between inborn mechanisms of the organism, on both metabolic and behavioral levels, and stimuli from the environment. There are particularities, of organic and instinctual gratification and of practices of care; but equally on both sides there is *generalization.* For the learning infant the most important vehicle of generalization probably is the pleasure mechanism,[14] not to be confused with sheer organic or instinctual gratifications in the particularized sense. On the environmental side it is the *patterning* of the system of sanctions which constitutes the element of generalization.

It is the *correspondence* of these two patterns of generalization which is the essential basis on which a new motivational structure—the ego— is built up. Important as this correspondence of pattern is, it is also essential to discriminate between these two references. The external, environment-oriented process, which may be called "goal-gratification," concerns the relation of the child to a social object outside itself. The internal, organism-oriented process concerns his relation to a generalized neurological mechanism by which a plurality of gratifications is organized to produce or maximize what we have come to call pleasure.

Freud speaks of the ego as an organization established through learning to govern the *relations* between internal organic processes and the environment. *Externally,* the goal of the ego must be the attainment of goal-gratifications—the establishment of optimal *relations* to environmental objects. *Internally,* we may speak of the ego—which Freud treated as originally a subsystem of the id—as oriented to the maximization of pleasure. The external situation and the internal physiological system are to an important degree independent of each other. This fact is the fundamental basis of Freud's contention that the pleasure principle and the reality principle must be treated as analytically independent. At the same time their integration is the most fundamental condition of the functioning of a personality as a system at this nodal point of articulation between the organism and the external world.

Freud's commonest formula for instinctual impulse (governed by the pleasure principle) is that it is the "representative" of the needs of the organism to the psychic apparatus—the ego.[15] This formula is acceptable for our analysis. The most crucial part of "reality" even at the oral level, and predominantly from then on, is *social*. It is "mother" as a social object, acting in a role in a system of social interaction.

Even at the oral level one aspect of reality is non-social, e.g., milk as food-object. But in terms of learning and of personality development it is the *agency* of the mother as the source of the milk which organizes the learning process. It is in terms of generalization that the social qualities of the significant object become crucial.

Let us look at the structure of this aspect of the mother-child system. Identification implies that the child's basis of "interest" in the mother is, after a time, no longer exhausted by the fact that she acts as an instrumentality of discrete organically or instinctually significant goal-gratifications such as food or clinging. *She, as role-person, becomes* on a higher level a meaningful object. Inevitably, in the learning process, the meaning of the mother as object must be established *through generalization* from gratification (and deprivation) experiences on non-social levels. But once this meaning has become established, then in a sense the tables are turned. The discrete, instinctually significant gratifications and deprivations become *symbols* of the intentions or attitudes of the mother. Food then is no longer sought only because it produces the organic pleasure specific to alimentary stimulation. Perhaps just as important, it is no longer rejected simply because of alimentary discomfort associated with it. More generally, a primary, indeed *the* primary goal of the developing personality, comes to be to secure the favorable attitude, as it is often called, the *love* of the mother. Specific gratifications on lower levels then have become part of an *organization* on a wider level. Their primary meaning derives from their relation to the paramount goal of securing or maximizing love. Indeed, it seems a legitimate interpretation of Freud to say that only when the *need for love* has been established as the paramount *goal* of the personality can we say that there is a genuine ego present. This need then, in an important sense, comes to *control* the ontogenetically older goal-needs of the organism including, eventually, that for pleasure. There must be provision for the adequate gratification of the latter, but at the same time, they must each take their place in an organized *system* of gratifications.

What, now, of the internal aspect at the level of oral generalization? Undoubtedly one of Freud's greatest discoveries was the significance of childhood eroticism and its tracing back to the oral stages of development.[16] I have suggested that the integration of external and internal references, of reality principle and pleasure principle, is the most important single condition of attainment of an organized ego. Though Freud was not able to spell out its physiological character very far, I think that his discovery of childhood eroticism is essentially the discovery of a built-in physiological mechanism of the *generalization* of internal reward, which matches the generalization of external goal-gratification. Erotic pleasure seems to be essentially a diffuse generalized "feeling" of organic well-being which is not attached to any one discrete instinctual need-fulfillment. When hungry, feeding produces gastric pleasure, when cold, being warmed produces another specific feeling of pleasure, as does clinging, etc. But erotic pleasure is not as such dependent on *any one* of these or *any specific combination* of them. The mouth, Freud held, is an erogenous zone. This means that oral stimulation through sucking is one important, specific source of this more generalized erotic pleasure. The essential points about oral stimulation are two: first it produces a pleasure which is *independent* of that produced by the ingestion of food, e.g., through sucking as such, and second, this pleasure is capable of generalization to a higher level. Organically the main manifestation of oral eroticism seems to be the capacity for pleasure in diffuse bodily contact. This is connected by generalization with stimulation of the mouth,[17] so that holding, fondling, and the like, produce pleasure as a fundamental type of generalized reward.

Certain capacities of the organism thus operate as mechanisms which facilitate the generalization of cathexis, and hence of goals, from the goal-objects which immediately gratify particularized needs, to the *agent* of these gratifications (treated as an organized system of sanctioning behavior). Eroticism, whatever the physiological processes involved,[18] is a mechanism of internal reward by which fixation on the more specific instinctual gratifications is overcome in favor of pleasure in the diffuse and generalized *relationship* to a nurturing social object.

This establishment of an organized ego in the personality through a pattern of sanctions designates essentially what Freud meant by identification. Several of Freud's own formulations of the concept stress the striving to be *like* the object. This emphasis requires elucidation and some qualification. Only in a very qualified sense can we say that an infant learns to be like his mother. The important sense, for us, is that he learns to play a social role *in interaction* with her. His behavior (hence his motivation) is organized according to a generalized pattern of norms. These norms define shared meanings of the acts which are internalized in terms of values and norms. Together, that is, mother and child come to constitute a *collectivity* in a strict sociological sense. But this does not mean that the two members of the collectivity are alike in the sense that they play identical roles; on the contrary their roles are sharply differentiated as are the norms which define the respective expectations. In the light of these considerations I should like to speak of identification as the process by which a person comes to be inducted into membership in a collectivity through learning to play a role complementary to those of other members in accord with the pattern of values governing the collectivity. The new member comes to be *like* the others with respect to their common membership status and to the psychological implications of this, above all the common internalized values. Psychologically the essential point is that the process of ego development takes place through the learning of social roles in collectivity structures. Through this process the normative patterns of the collectivity in which a person learns to interact become part of his own personality and define *its* organization.[19]

OBJECT CHOICE AND INTERNALIZATION

The other two of Freud's basic concepts in this area are object-choice or cathexis, and internalization, or what is sometimes called by Freud's translators "introjection."[20] I have emphasized that for the infant the mother is a *social* object and becomes the most important part of his "reality,"—the environment external to him. But though he comes to be profoundly "attached" to her (i.e., to "cathect" her as an object) the infant can scarcely be said to have "chosen" her. Object choice is an act of the ego, and the neonate does not yet have an ego. He can be rejected by the mother, but he can neither choose nor reject her at first.

In the phase of primary identification the infant is in the process of learning a role in, and the values of, a collectivity. There is of course an essential element of spontaneity or autonomy in response to the actions of alter. But the motivation to action which is in conformity with the expectations of the new role is still directly dependent on the sanctions appropriate to the learning process. There is a period of capacity to fulfill alter's expectations in anticipation of reward. This period precedes the development of the capacity autonomously to implement the newly learned values in the absence of the accustomed goal-gratification rewards. Freud clearly recognizes this when he speaks of identification as having fully taken place only when the object has been renounced or lost.[21]

The process of learning a role vis-à-vis the mother,[22] as we have seen, involves at least *two levels* of generalization and organization. The *pattern* of sanctions imposed by the mother incorporates and expresses the *higher* of these two levels. Successful identification enables the individual to implement this higher pattern level in his own autonomous behavior and not merely in response to the expected rewards of another. This capacity to implement independently is perhaps the most important respect in which the child has through identification come to be like the mother.

If, however, action in accordance with the newly acquired value-pattern is to be reality-directed, it must establish goals in relation to objects. The object world is not to be treated merely as given, taking over the care of the helpless infant. Rather, the new ego actively "tries out" its capacity for organized behavior in its object-environment. Object-choice, in Freud's sense, is the "spontaneous" investment by the ego of libido in seeking attachment to an object in the external world.

Typically, at the first main stage of this process, the object "chosen" is the same concrete person, the mother, who was the primary agent of care in the oral phase. But it is a mother who comes to play a different *role* vis-à-vis her child. She shifts from rewarding his conformity with the minimum expectations of being a "good child" to rewarding his attempts to perform above that minimum. His role shifts, in turn, from an emphasis on ascription to one on achievement. The minimum base is taken for granted, but beyond that his rewards depend far more heavily on *how well* he performs.

There is a sense in which this shift involves a turning of the tables. If the *diffuse* attitude of the mother toward her child in the oral phase could be called love, then we may say that by his identification the child has become capable of displaying and acting upon a similar attitude toward another object. He can love an object, normally his mother.

If the child's need to love and be loved is strongly attached to an object, then this object gains a very strong point of leverage for motivating him to new levels of achievement. The mother not only dispenses specific rewards for specific performances, but she can treat these as *symbols* of her reciprocation of his love.

It is undoubtedly significant that the period when the love-attachment to the mother is paramount, is the period of the learning of the basic *skills* of action. Pre-eminent among these are learning to walk, which is, in a sense, the foundation of the whole complex of motor skills, and learning to talk, which is the foundation of skills in communication. Object-choice thus is the motivational foundation of that aspect of socialization in which basic performance patterns are learned. The diffuse attachment to the object of cathexis is the basis for the motivational meaning of the more specific rewards of specific performances.

It is worth while here to note the double reference of the category of meaning. In speaking of the process by which identification is established, I referred to the organized pattern of sanctions as establishing the meaning of the specific acts of the child, and of the mother. This was the factor of generalization in the process of interaction as such. Now, in speaking of the process of achievement-learning, I refer to the diffuse love-attachment as the primary reference of the meaning of particular rewards—and of course of ego's own acts of performance in relation to these rewards. This, essentially, is what is meant by the internalization of a value-pattern: it comes to define meanings for the personality system as such. The first set of meanings is organized about the sanctions applied to the child, the second about a set of performances he has spontaneously tried out and learned successfully to complete.

Freud's concept of object cathexis designates the primary basis on which *one* type of process of differentiation in the structure of the personality takes place.[23] The base-line starting point for this process is the "internalized mother" established through the previous identification. But from this base comes to be differentiated an autonomous subsystem of the personality oriented to active manipulation of the object-world. The dependency component of the personality then becomes the restructured residue of the internalized mother, which gives a more diffuse and generalized *motivational* meaning to the specific acts and rewards involved in the exercise of motor and communication skills. On the other hand, the "self," or the ego in a more differentiated sense than at the oral level, assumes the role of autonomous initiative in the performance process.

The great increases in performance capacity which occur in this pre-oedipal love-attachment period lead to an immense widening of the child's range of contacts with the world in which he lives. He is continually engaged in trying out new motor skills and in learning about his world, both by direct observation and by insistent questioning through the newly learned medium of language.

In the phase of infancy the mother plays a role determined to a very important degree by her commitment to roles other than that of mother of this particular child: her relation to her husband, to older siblings of the infant, to the family-household and to various extrafamilial responsibilities. In infancy these other involvements of the child's mother appear to him mainly as sources of restrictions on her exclusive devotion to him. But with growing mobility and wider ranges of communication, the other persons to whom his mother is related become more and more clearly defined objects to him also. Though he has various relations to extrafamilial persons, typically it is the other members of his family, his father and his siblings—including perhaps by now a younger sibling—which form the primary focus of this new structuring of the situation in which he acts and learns.

Gradually, a new phase in the processes of identification emerges. This time, its focus is the assumption of membership in the child's total nuclear family of orientation. This is a far more complex process than the original identification with the mother. It involves at least three such identifications which are interdependent but also are partially independent, namely identification with the family as a collectivity, identification defined in terms of sex with those family members of his own sex, and identification by generation as defined by himself and his siblings as contrasted with the parents.

The child must now internalize a *higher level* of generality and/or organization in his personality system. In his relation with his mother he has already learned the fundamentals of reciprocal role-behavior in a *diadic* relationship, the simplest type of social system. In this relationship the most fundamental question is that of the balance between dependency and autonomy, the ranges within which the child can take independent initiative and within which on the other hand, he must give way to the wishes and sanctions of his role-partner. We may say that the circumstances of early socialization have stacked the cards in favor of dependency. Therefore, the problem of *independence training* is a focal one in the pre-oedipal period.

In the oedipal period the child begins to have a plurality of diadic relations: to mother, to father, to sister, to brother, but these in turn must be organized into a higher-order system, the family as a whole. It is in this context that Freud most prominently raises the problems of the superego and its place in the personality. I have mentioned the way in which he treats identification with the mother as producing an internalized base from which object choices are made. In a parallel way he speaks of the superego as providing, for the latency period and later, the internal surrogate of the *parental function* as it operated in the control of the pre-oedipal child (see Freud, 1933, p. 91).

During the primitive mother-identification the situation was sociologically very simple because the child was primarily related to a single person as object. The essential points were that it was a social object, and that mother and child together formed a collectivity. Now the situation has become much more complex, but nevertheless the same basic principles obtain. What Freud refers to as the parental function may be interpreted to mean a function in the family as a system. Moreover it includes the functions of *both* parents as what, sociologically, may be called the "leadership coalition" of the family. Seen in these terms, *the family* is an object with which the child identifies. Through this identification he now becomes a full-fledged member of that family. He and its other members come to constitute a collectivity which, if not new, is at least, through his altered status and the adjustments made by other members, a changed one.

The superego, then, is primarily the *higher-order* normative pattern governing the behavior of the different members in their different roles in the family as a system. It is first impressed upon the child through the pattern of sanctions applied to his behavior, through rewards and punishments. If the family is at all well integrated, these sanctions, though administered by all the members of the family in different ways, have a certain coherence as a system which derives mainly from the coordinated leadership roles of the two parents. Therefore a new element of organization is introduced into the personality by this process of identification. It is an organization on a higher level of generality and complexity than before, which gives the child new goals and values.

Through this process the child comes to be "like" the object of his identification in the same essential sense, and with the same qualifications, as he came to be like his mother at the earlier stage of identification. He has acquired a pattern of orientation which he holds in common with the other, more socialized members of his family. When this pattern has been internalized he can act in relation to the extrafamilial world, in terms of that pattern without reference to the continuing administration of the earlier pattern of external sanctions. In the same sense in which for the post-oral child, the oral mother became a "lost object," for the latency child his family of orientation eventually becomes a lost object. The completion of this process normally occurs in late adolescence.

Within the family, the child's role has become far more complex than it was earlier; he has as many subroles as there are diadic relations to other family members. But from the point of view of the wider society, he plays only *one* role, namely that defined by his age-status as latency-period child of his family, and by his sex.[24]

SEX ROLE, EROTICISM AND THE INCEST TABOO

One aspect of the greater complexity of the new system of identifications and object-relations is the fact that the child cannot identify indiscriminately with all the available objects of his nuclear family. Two of the subsidiary identifications within the nuclear family, by sex and by generation, are to become structurally constitutive for his status in the wider society, and these are cross-cutting. It is essential to the understanding of the differential impact of the oedipal situation on the sexes that for the boy the tie to his mother, the original object of identification and of subsequent object-cathexis, is not included in either of these new identifications, whereas for the girl the tie to the mother is included in the identification by sex.

Hence the girl can, in relation to her mother, repeat on a higher level the infantile identification. She can, to a degree, take over the mother's role, which she does as an apprentice in the household and, in phantasy, in doll-play. She is, however, precluded from taking over the mother role in relation to the father by her categorization as belonging to the child generation.

The boy, on the other hand, must break radically with his earlier identification pattern. He cannot turn an object-cathexis into an identification except on the familial level which has to be shared with the other members. The mother has been the boy's primary object of cathexis and previously of identification. But he is blocked by the importance of the sex categorization from identifying with her in intrafamilial function and he is blocked by the generation categorization from taking a role like the father's in relation to her. Moreover, the father is a more difficult object of identification for a child because so much of his role is played outside the household. Considerations such as these seem to be as important in explaining the boy's ambivalent attitudes toward the father as is the boy's subjection to his father's authority. The authority factor is only one component in a larger complex. It is not, as has often been held, the one central factor which overshadows all others. The authority factor does explain, however, why the child, at the oedipal period begins to have much more important relations outside his family. In a sense, the father is the primary representative of the family in the outside society, and vice versa of the latter in the family.

Another important complexity in the identification situation in the oedipal period is that the ascribed identification is *selective*—except for the overall familial identification—among the members of the family. The very important possibilities of object choice of the child for the parent of opposite sex and vice versa are *excluded* from the main formal identification structure. They are relegated to the status of "secondary" or informal attachments which, if they become too strong, can become both disruptive of the family as a system and distorting factors in the personality development of the child.

This relates to two fundamental and interrelated sociological problems in which Freud took a considerable interest—those of the roles of the sexes, and of the incest taboo. Freud was clear and insistent about the existence of what he called constitutional bisexuality. He believed that the motivational structure of sex role was importantly influenced by the individual's object-relations in the course of his life-history. We may go further and say that the learned aspect of sex role provides an essential condition for the maintenance of the family as an integral part of the social structure, and hence of its functions in the socialization of the child.

The feminine role is primarily focused on the maternal function which, through the *combination* of instrumental child care and love, seeks to provide a suitable object for the child's earliest identification, and subsequently his autonomous object-cathexis. The agent of these functions must be anchored in an organizational unit of the larger society; otherwise the leverage for socialization beyond the earliest stage would not be adequate. The family which, in its membership, includes an adult male, is of course the usual unit.

The masculine role, on the other hand, is not primarily focused on socialization, but on the performance of function in the wider society, economic, political or otherwise. If boys are to achieve in this arena they must make the proper set of transitions between the intrafamilial context of early socialization and the larger societal context. The coalition of the *two* parents in the family leadership structure is the main sociological mechanism which makes this possible (see Bales, 1953, Chapter 4). Clearly, also, the relation of girls to their fathers, and hence to men in general, is just as important as that of boys to their mothers in balancing these forces.

Consideration of the incest taboo brings us back to the role of eroticism in the socialization process. Throughout the oral stage, the stage of first main object-choice and the oedipal stage, the main principle operating in the socialization process is internalization of cultural patterns of the organization of behavior. It takes place through successive identifications on progressively higher levels of generalization. These new identifications lead to new object-choices and new definitions of goals in relation to these objects.

At the oral level, eroticism is primarily significant because it provides a vehicle for the generalization of reward in its internal physiological aspect. There seems to be a duality of levels of the object relation to the mother which can be matched with a duality of hedonistic rewards which makes oral eroticism so important. I am not competent to follow the subsequent course on a physiological level. With a difference, there is probably a repetition of this pattern in the "phallic" stage. The erotization of the genital organs at this stage is presumably partly instinctive and partly learned, either through masturbatory activities or through some kind of adult stimulation, or both.

At this period, the differentiation of personalities by sex role becomes of critical significance for the first time. The genital organs are clearly the primary anatomical differentiae by sex, particularly in the prepubertal period. Hence they are particularly appropriate as *symbols* of sex-identification. The erotic gratification attained through genital stimulation constitutes a type of internal pleasure which can become directly associated with learning to act *in the role* of a member of the appropriate sex group. The diffuse sense of bodily well-being which is the critical feature of erotic gratification in its generalized aspect may then come to be associated with proper fulfillment of the expectations of sex role.

These considerations are essential as background for the discussion of the incest taboo. Eroticism, I have suggested, operates on two levels: through the stimulation of one or more specific erogenous zones and through the induction of a diffuse sense of bodily well-being, through affectionate physical contact with another person. In the case of identification with the mother, the primary object of identification is a single person. Physical contact with her, being caressed or fondled, remains the prototype of erotic gratification on the more generalized level.

In the oedipal period, the significant object for identification is not a human individual, but a collectivity. Tender physical contact with a complex collectivity is clearly not possible. Thus eroticism cannot play the same role as a socialization mechanism as it did in the pre-oedipal period. Indeed, the necessity to achieve a fundamental identification without the help of this internal reward constitutes one of the main sources of strain in this stage. This, more than the punishing aspects of paternal authority, may be why the superego stands out as being peculiarly "impersonal" and in some respects threatening.

In the process of socialization, the incest taboo functions primarily as a mechanism by which the child is both forced and enabled to internalize value systems of a *higher order* than those which can be exclusively embodied in a diadic two-person relation or in a social system as simple and diffuse as the nuclear family. The inherent tendency of erotic relations is to reinforce solidarity *à deux,* to give the single person an object priority over the larger collectivity or system of collectivities in which the diad is embedded. To internalize these higher-order value-systems the child must learn, in the requisite contexts, to do without the crutch of erotic gratification.

Looked at from the point of view of the society as a system, the incest taboo has another order of functional significance, closely linked with the above. This concerns the importance of maintaining a diversity of cultural patterns on the lowest level of internalization in personalities, so that their combinations on the higher levels of generality can support the high-level patterns without too strong a tendency to "reduce" them to a less general common denominator. The incest taboo insures that new families of procreation will be set up by persons socialized in two distinct families of orientation. The culture internalized in the early stages by the children of the new family will then have a dual origin, and will in certain respects constitute a new variant a little different from either of the parental ones. The argument is not that the process of crossing of familial cultures will reduce them to greater uniformity. On the contrary, by *preserving variability* at the lower levels of generality it protects against the establishment of a uniformity which might lessen the pressure to achieve higher levels of generality capable of including *all* the variable versions.

Another aspect of the problem which ties these two together is the bearing of the incest taboo on the internal structure of the nuclear family. The erotic relation of the parents to each other is a primary focus of their solidarity. Its exclusiveness tends to symbolize their solidarity vis-à-vis third persons—even the small child. As the child becomes more active and develops higher capacities for performance there is a strong pressure for him to develop or reinforce erotic relationships to both parents, in different ways. The developing importance of sex as an ascribed focus of status then fosters attachment to the parent of the opposite sex, thereby implicitly challenging the relationship to the parent of the same sex. In the face of this competition, the erotic solidarity of the parents tends to lead to rejection of these advances. This forces the child's *primary* new identification into the mold of member of the family as a whole, and his sex and generation roles within it. It does not allow him to concentrate on a single diadic relation *within* the family. He is forced to a higher *level* of value-internalization than that governing *any* diadic relation. It thus prepares him, in his latency period and in subsequent orientations outside his family, to internalize still higher-level patterns of value.

These considerations alone do not adequately account for the brother-sister aspect of the incest taboo. While this is the weakest of the taboos within the nuclear family, it is none the less very strong. I believe that this version of the taboo is internalized, at least in part, by emphasis on the factor of *generation* as an institutionalized status-component. Erotic relations to parents are prohibited because they are inadmissible in the *age*-status of the oedipal child. He is too old for infantile erotic gratifications, and too young for adult. He must be classed with the parent of the same sex with respect to sex, but cannot presume to the adult privilege of genital eroticism. The identifications with the family as a whole and by sex create a configuration in his environment which leaves no place for an erotic relation to a sibling or even another person of the opposite sex. Two siblings having both internalized the same "generalized parent" cannot maintain the internalized generation differentiation as well as when their parental figures are independent.

More generally, in one major aspect the significance of the oedipal transition lies in the fact that the child reaches a level of internalized values and a complex structure of identifications, which enables him to dispense with erotic rewards as a primary mechanism of further socialization. The basic difference between the pre-oedipal stages within the family and the post-oedipal stages mainly outside it, lies in the fact that in the former, identification and object-choice involve an erotic attachment to a primary personal object, whereas later they do not. This shift is, as we have seen, essential if the internalization of social value systems on high levels of generality is to be achieved.[25]

The immediately pre-oedipal attachment of erotic significance to sex-role, and the symbolization of this by the awakening of genital eroticism at the phallic level, has laid the foundations for the formation later by the individual, through his marriage, of a new family in which he or she will play conjugal and parental roles. In the new family, erotic attachment will form one primary component in the solidarity of the parental pair, a solidarity which is the essential prerequisite of their successful performance of their socialization function. But the erotic need, thus restructured, is allowed expression only in the context of an adult character structure in which the higher-level value-patterns have had an opportunity to develop and consolidate their position. It is only through this non-erotic component of the individual's personality structure that parents have a sufficiently strong superego and a sufficiently mature ego to be able to serve as a model for identification for their children, and that socialization beyond the stages of early childhood becomes possible.

In the light of these considerations Freud's famous view about the sexual genesis of all the neuroses may perhaps be interpreted in current socio-psychological terms. The most important point is that the personality structure, as a precipitate of previous identifications and of lost objects, develops by a process of *differentiation* from the earliest and simplest identification with the mother. Both this early relationship of identification and the succeeding object-choice relationship contain in their motivation an essential erotic component. Without the element of erotic attachment there could not have existed sufficient motivational leverage to bring about the learning processes involved in the identification and in the performance learning later based upon it. The erotic needs thus built up are never extinguished but remain permanent parts of the personality structure.

Neuroses, like other disturbances of personality functioning, involve important regressive components because the more generalized *motivational* structures—as distinguished from social values where the order of generality is the reverse—are laid down in early childhood. Regression to deep enough levels then will always involve motivational structures in which erotic needs form an essential component. Hence in a neurosis which pervades the personality as a whole, an erotic component will always be present, not to say prominent. By the same token, in so far as the etiology of the neurosis goes back to early childhood experiences—which if it is pervasive enough will always be the case—there will of necessity, be a prominent component of erotic disturbance.

This does not mean that "all motivation is in the last analysis sexual." Rather, on the genetically earliest and hence in one sense most fundamental levels, the sexual (or better erotic) element is always prominently involved, both symptomatically and etiologically. This does not in any way contradict the importance of the capacity to develop and operate motivational structures which are *not* primarily oriented to erotic gratifications, but rather to impersonal or "affectively neutral" patterns of behavior. This occurs by the process which Freud usually referred to as sublimation.[26]

POST-OEDIPAL OBJECT-RELATIONS

Let us now return to a brief discussion of the post-oedipal sequence of development. Freud treated the relation between oedipal and latency periods as essentially parallel to the earlier oral and object-choice periods. The oedipal period involves an identification process through which the "parental function" is internalized to form the superego. The identification, I have argued, must be interpreted to refer to membership in the nuclear family as a collectivity, and within that, with the child's own sex and generation roles. But once this process of identification has been completed, the child can turn to a new process of object-choice, this time in relationships primarily outside his family of orientation. What may be called his "dependency base" still remains inside that family; he "lives" with his parents and siblings and they remain responsible for his subsistence and general protection. Moreover, his place in the community is still defined primarily by his family membership.

But from this base, which is analogous to his identification with his mother at the earlier period, the child ventures out to establish important relations outside the family. In a differentiated society of the modern Western type this occurs typically in two overlapping contexts— the school, in which his formal education begins, and the informal "peer group," usually composed of age-mates of his own sex (see Parsons, 1959). There are two particularly prominent features of these new object-relations. First, none of them is overtly erotic in content or tone— hence Freud's concept of "latency." Second, for the first time, the pattern of relationship is not ascribed in advance. Age and sex status are ascribed, but not the level of performance and the rewards for it which the child may gain in the school and in his relations with his peers. He is exposed, within the limits permitted in the community, to open competition with his age-peers. A significant structuring of the social groups in question will result which is independent of the structure of the families from which the competitors come.[27]

This structuring seems to revolve about two main axes. The first is the learning of achievements which can be evaluated by universalistic standards. The prototype of these achievements is the mastery of the intellectual content of the school curriculum; but other things like athletic prowess fall into the same category. It is certainly of first-rate significance that the foundations of the more abstract skills involved in intellectual function are laid down in the latency period, notably the use of *written* language and the skills of abstract reasoning, as Piaget has so fully shown.

The second axis is the establishment of position in more or less organized groups where status is not ascribed in advance. The focus is on such roles as leadership and followership, and on primarily task-oriented or primarily integrative roles in relation to one's fellows. The contexts in which this learning takes place range all the way from the school class itself, under the direct supervision of the teacher, to wholly informal peer activities entirely removed from adult participation.

It is a striking fact, perhaps particularly striking in the United States with its tradition of coeducation in the schoolroom, that in the latency period the peer group is overwhelmingly a *one*-sex peer group. The child is here "practicing" his sex role in isolation from the opposite sex. When this isolation begins to break down and cross-sex relations assume a prominent place, this is in itself a sign of the approach of adolescence. With this a further differentiation begins to take place, namely into first a sphere in which erotic interests are revived, which leads over into marriage and eventually the family of procreation, and second a sphere of organizations and associations where the direct expression of erotic interests remains tabooed.[28] The essential point is the existence of a discrimination between the contexts in which erotic interests are treated as appropriate from those in which they are not. Their appropriateness is clearly confined to a single role-complex within a much larger context, most of which is treated as non-erotic.

It is my principal thesis that, in the analysis of object relations, there is complete continuity in the basic conceptual framework appropriate to identification in the oral stage, and of object-choice in the post-oral stage on the one hand, and the analysis of latency period and adolescent socialization on the other. The learning of roles in school and peer group occurs through the mechanisms of object-choice, motivated by prior identifications. But, in the first instance, it is now much more clearly collectivities rather than persons which are the most significant objects. Just as within the nuclear family significant new diadic relations besides the relation to the mother develop and influence the child's personality development, so in school and peer groups significant new diads form, with the teacher and with particular age-mates. But the significance of these diads must be understood *within the context of the new collectivity structures* in which the child is in process of learning to play a role, or a complex of roles.

Similarly, this later process of object-choice leads to a new set of identifications, which involve the collectivity-types outside his family in which the child acquires memberships and roles. As in the case of the mother-child diad and of the nuclear family, he internalizes the values of these collectivities as part of the process of identification with them and assumption of a role in them. The differences lie in the greater diversity of memberships the child acquires, the higher level of generality of the values he internalizes, and the mechanisms of the learning process. One of the most striking features of the differences is the absence of erotic rewards made possible by the more highly differentiated and organized personality structure with which the post-oedipal child approaches his object relations. The regressive associations of erotic experience would militate against attaining the higher disciplines which have now become necessary.

By the completion of the major phase of adolescence, the normal child has, outside the family of orientation, achieved identification with four main types of collectivity, and has hence internalized their values and become capable of pursuing the goals appropriate to them independent of the detailed pattern of sanctions which have operated during the internalization process. These are represented by (1) the subsociety of his age-peers as a whole, i.e., the values of the so-called "youth culture," (2) the school, which is the prototype of the organization dedicated to the achievement of a specified goal through disciplined performance, (3) the peer-association, the prototype of collective organization to satisfy and adjust mutual interests, and (4) the newly emerging cross-sex diad, which is the prototype of the sole adult relationship in which erotic factors are allowed an overt part.

These identifications, which are normally achieved in adolescence, form the main basis in personality structure on which adult role-participations are built. Through at least one further major step of generalization of value-level, participation in the youth culture leads over to participation in the values of the society as a whole. The participation in the school leads over into the adult occupational role with its responsibility for a productive contribution, for independent choice of occupation, and for self-support in the role. The peer-association identification leads over into the roles of cooperative association memberships in a variety of fields, of which the role of citizen in a democratic society is perhaps the most important. Finally the "dating" pattern of adolescence leads over to marriage and to the assumption of parental responsibilities in the family of procreation.

I emphasize this continuity from the objects of identification in childhood to the role and collectivity structure of the adult society in order to bring out the central point of the whole analysis. This is that Freud's theory of object-relations is essentially an analysis of the relation of the individual to the *structure of the society* in which he lives. Freud analyzed this relation from the point of view of the individual rather than from the point of view of the structure of the social systems concerned. His perspective also was primarily developmental in the psychological sense. Sociologically stated, he was mainly concerned with the processes by which the individual comes to acquire membership in social collectivities, to learn to play roles in them, and to internalize their values. Moreover, he was most interested in the identifications entered into in early childhood.

But straight through, the process of identification, of object-choice and of internalization are processes of relating the individual to and integrating him in the social system and through it, the culture. Since this process is a relational matter, eventually technical analysis has to be applied to both sets of relata as well as to the relationship itself. Had Freud lived long enough to enter more deeply into the technical analysis of the object-systems to which the individual does become related, he would inevitably have had to become in part a sociologist, for the structure of this object system *is*—it is not merely "influenced by"—the structure of the society itself. Essentially Freud's theory of object-relations is a theory of the relation of the individual personality to the social system. It is a primary meeting ground of the two disciplines of psychology and sociology.

CONCLUSION

If the importance of the individual's object-relations in the course of his life-history is as great as it seems to be, then the significance of internalized social objects and culture cannot, as some psychoanalysts have tended to assume, be confined mainly to the content of the superego. On the contrary since, with all his emphasis on its differentiation, Freud consistently treated the human personality as an integrated system, it ought to permeate the whole system, and not be confined to one restricted part of it.

In certain respects the ego should provide the key test case of this hypothesis. Indeed the increasing attention of Freud himself in his later years to problems of ego psychology, a tendency which has been considerably further developed in the work of such authors as Hartmann and Kris, seems to be closely related to his increasing attention to the field of object relations. At the same time I do not think that the id should be exempted from the logic of this development.

Since the ego is the primary location of interchange between the personality and the outside world of reality, and since the most important aspect of reality itself is social, the conclusion is inescapable that the ego is "socially structured." It is a particularly welcome confirmation of this hypothesis, much of which has been worked out from a sociological point of view, that Freud himself explicitly recognized this conclusion. The most striking passage I have found deserves to be quoted at length.

> When it happens that a person has to give up a sexual object, there quite often ensues a modification in his ego which can only be described as a reinstatement of the object within the ego, as it occurs in melancholia; the exact nature of this substitution is as yet unknown to us. It may be that by undertaking this introjection, which is a kind of regression to the mechanism of the oral phase, the ego makes it easier for the object to be given up or renders that process possible. It may even be that this identification is the sole condition under which the id can give up its objects. At any rate, the process, especially in the early phases of development, is a very frequent one, and *it points to the conclusion that the character of the ego is a precipitate of abandoned object-cathexes* and that it contains a record of past object-choices.[29] (1935, p. 36, italics added)

It can, then, quite safely be said that object-cathexes and identifications do not, in Freud's own mature view, simply "influence" the development of the ego, in the sense in which environmental temperature or moisture influences the growth of a plant, but that the structure of the object-relations a person has experienced is directly *constitutive* of the structure of the ego itself.

If the ego can be regarded as a precipitate of abandoned object-cathexes, there does not seem to be any serious doubt that the superego is primarily social and cultural in origin. Indeed this has been clearly recognized by psychoanalysts from the introduction of the concept by Freud. Freud's formula that it represents the "parental function" is to my mind the most adequate one. He also quite explicitly refers to it as the focus of "that higher nature" representing the "moral, spiritual side of human nature," (1935, pp. 46–7) which we have "taken into ourselves" from our parents.

The role of the id has been focal to the issue with which the present discussion started, namely the relative importance of "instinctive" as compared with cultural, social and other "environmental" influences in the motivation of personality. The concept of the id in Freud's later work is of course one primary heir, though by no means the only one, of such concepts as the unconscious, the primary process and the libido in his earlier work. Furthermore in the strong enthusiasm of discovery the id tended to be contrasted as sharply as possible with the ego which seemed to be the closest of all the components of the personality to traditionally rationalistic common sense. Freud sometimes makes extreme statements of this contrast when he speaks of the id as entirely lacking in organization (see e.g., 1933, p. 103).

Against the tendency to highlight the conflicts between the ego and id must be set the conception of the ego as a system of control, as implied in the metaphor of the horse and rider. Furthermore, the id is treated at many points in specific relation to the pleasure *principle,* and we have seen a variety of reasons for assuming that pleasure is an organizing mechanism which integrates diverse motives at lower levels of organization.

A still further consideration is the progressive increase in the generality which Freud attributed to the basic instinctual urges, ending up with only a single underlying duality. This is not inconsistent with Bowlby's views of the importance in more specialized contexts of various more particularized instinctual responses. But it does imply that, from a very early phase of development, the basic *organization* of the motivational system cannot be derived from instinctual sources, but must resort to identifications and internalized objects.

It is my own view that the distinction between instinctual and learned components of the motivational system cannot legitimately be identified with that between the id on the one hand, the ego and superego on the other. I believe that the two distinctions cut across each other. The id like the other subsystems, is organized about its experience in object relations. It differs, however, in two fundamental respects from the other subsystems. First it is oriented, as the other two are not, to the individual's own organism as object. This seems to me to be the essential significance of the *pleasure* principle as the governing principle of the id. Secondly, however, the object-cathexes which are constitutive of the structure of the id are predominantly those of the earlier phases of the process of socialization. In any internal conflicts involving the problem of regression, id-drives represent the regressive side of the conflict.

However much it may be true that to advance beyond certain early levels of development it is necessary to transcend the fixation on these early cathexes, and however much the mature personality must effectively control them through ego and superego mechanisms, it still remains true that these are particular cases of identification and internalized objects, not the leading example of motivation in their absence.

Thus it seems to me that the general principles involved in the significance of object-relations through identification, object-cathexis and internalization, must be extended to the *whole* psychoanalytic theory of personality. Indeed, though he had not ironed out all the inconsistencies in his treatment, nor reconciled many earlier with later statements, in his latest phase of development Freud himself had, in all essential respects, come to this position.

There are two particular virtues of this position when seen in a more general setting than is often done. First, it formulates psychoanalytic theory in a set of terms where direct and detailed articulation with the theory of social systems is enormously facilitated. This is of the first importance to the theory of the motivation of social behavior and hence, in my opinion, an essential prerequisite of the advance of sociology. But at the same time there are reciprocal benefits for psychoanalysis, for example, in enabling it to do far greater justice to the problem of the senses which requires that personality theory take account of variations in the structure of the social systems on which it impinges.

On a still more general level, this view should do much to relieve discussion of psychoanalytic theory from involvement in a false dilemma through its use of the categories of heredity and environment. As has by now become clear in general biology, the main question is not whether or how much one or the other factor influences outcomes. The trend is strongly away from a "predominant factor" explanation of the phenomena of life toward a more analytical one. Analytically conceived variables, except for limiting cases, are always *all* important. The salient technical problems concern their clear definition and analysis of their intricate modes of *interrelationship* with each other. This chapter is intended as a contribution to what I conceive to be the major trend of psychoanalytic theory in this direction.

NOTES

1. Notable ones were made by Lionel Trilling (1955), and by Alfred Kazin (1956). It is perhaps significant that this view is particularly strong in literary circles.

2. This chapter belongs in a series of my own writings on the relations between psychoanalytic theory and the theory of social systems. The most important of these are: "Psychoanalysis and the Social Structure" (1950); "The Superego and the Theory of Social Systems" (1952); "Psychoanalysis and Social Science" (1954); *Twenty Years of Psychoanalysis; Family, Socialization and Interaction Process* (1955); "The Incest Taboo in Relation to Social Structure and the Socialization of the Child" (1954); and "An Approach to Psychological Theory in Terms of the Theory of Action" (1958).

3. Of course, from the point of reference of the personality as system, the organism, that is the person's own body, is itself an object of his situation.

4. See Lord Adrian, 1953. This stands in contrast to the interpretation of many other commentators, less qualified in biology than Lord Adrian. Compare also the formula that the instinct is the "representative" of the needs of the organism to the "psychic" apparatus.

5. This, for example, is clearly what happens in learning intellectual content. Such learning requires "capacity"; but a textbook of algebra, for example, to one not previously trained in the subject, is not just a "relatively favorable influence" on the outcome; it is the primary source of the content of the learned pattern.

6. In this connection I am particularly indebted to a paper by Dr. John Bowlby, "The Nature of the Child's Tie to its Mother," 1958, and to personal discussions with Dr. Bowlby. The most essential point for our purposes is that there are two main levels in Freud's treatment of the problem of instinct. One tended to predominate in his earlier work, the other in the later. The first is closer to the main biological tradition in emphasizing relatively specific inborn patterns of behavior which do not need to be learned. It is a type of mechanism prominently emphasized by current "ethologists" like Lorenz and Tinbergen. Bowlby emphasizes five such "instinctual responses," as he calls them, which figure prominently in the first year or so of life, namely sucking, crying, smiling, clinging and following. The second level concerns the more diffuse "motivational energy" which is particularly involved in Freud's later conception of the id.

The role attributed by Bowlby to the more specific instinctual responses does not seem to me to be incompatible with the general thesis of this chapter. That these and other patterns are definitely inborn is certain. But the higher level of organization of the behavioral system, which we think of as the personality, cannot be derived from the organization of these responses without reference to the influence of object relations exerted in the course of the process of socialization. It has, however, been necessary to revise a number of statements made in an earlier draft of this chapter in the light of these considerations. Essentially the "instinctual responses" may be thought of as a set of mechanisms of behavior which operates at a level intermediate between the metabolic needs of the organism, on which Freud himself and many later psychoanalysts have laid such great emphasis, and the higher order mechanisms of control of behavior through internalized objects.

7. There is a notable parallel in this respect between Freud and Durkheim. Though the empirical subject-matters of their concern are far apart. Durkheim, in his discussion of the relations of mechanical and organic solidarity, particularly in his *Division of Labor,* tended to treat these concepts as associated with stages in the evolution of social systems. He also tried to put them in the context of an analytical theory of social systems. See my paper, "Durkheim's Contribution to the Theory of the Integration of Social Systems."

8. The thesis is perhaps most clearly stated in *The Problem of Anxiety.*

9. In this connection I am particularly indebted to the work of James Olds who strongly emphasizes the independence of pleasure-reward mechanisms from the instinctual needs. Frustration of the latter is closely associated with pain and other compulsion mechanisms. See Olds, 1958.

10. Part, however, of the mother's position vis-à-vis the child is determined by the fact that third parties are always involved in the relationship. Typically there is a father also present in the situation; he may not participate very actively in early child care, but the fact that the mother "lives with" him in a common household greatly affects her treatment of her child. There may also be older siblings. Then of course this family is a part of a larger society which imposes both relational constraints and a set of values which, among many other things, set certain norms for what is considered *proper* treatment of infants.

11. The presumption is that the generalized pleasure mechanism plays a crucial part in this learning process and is a primary reason for the importance of childhood eroticism.

12. This proposition needs qualification for certain types of variability in the structure of social situations (i.e., kinship systems).

13. It goes without saying that in terms of "motivational force" the id is "stronger" than the ego, as a horse is far stronger than its human rider. The ego, however, is not an energy system but a "cybernetic" type of *control* system. For this function relatively little energy is needed.

14. For some purposes it may well be necessary to distinguish different kinds of pleasure; thus, erotic pleasure may be a special type.

15. In somewhat different and more strictly theoretical terms we might say that it constitutes an *input* from the organism to the personality system.

16. My own previous views on eroticism and its functions have been stated most fully in "The Incest Taboo . . . ," 1954.

17. It may be that a special connection is thus established between the independent instinctual responses of sucking and clinging. Such a connection between discrete gratifications would imply a generalized medium analogous to money in social systems. It is as such a medium that I conceive pleasure. (See Olds, 1958.)

18. Olds's work implies that they operate at the level of the central nervous system, not of the "erogenous" peripheral areas alone.

19. Freud (1935) clearly recognized the duality of being both like and unlike the object in speaking of the boy's identification with the father, and the girl's with her mother in the oedipal period.

20. The German term used by Freud is *Introjektion*.

21. *The Ego and the Id*, pp. 36–7.

22. Throughout this discussion I speak of the mother as the primary object of cathexis. More strictly one should refer to a "generalized parent" since before the oedipal transition presumably the category of sex has not yet been fully internalized, nor the agency-roles of the two parents fully discriminated.

23. I have analyzed this elsewhere at considerably greater length than is possible here. See Parsons and Bales, (1955) especially Chapter II. This book may be used for general reference though my views have changed in a few respects since its writing.

24. See Merton (1957), for an excellent discussion of the complexity of role-constellations.

25. The taboo on homosexuality is dynamically closely related to that on incest. It applies, however, mainly to emancipation from the latency-period one-sex peer group, not from the family of orientation. Homosexuality would be the most tempting latency-period form of eroticism.

26. Freud's own analysis of these processes is, in my opinion, considerably less satisfactory than his analysis of the earlier ones.

27. On the sociological significance of this transition see S. N. Eisenstadt (1956), especially Chapters I and III.

28. Same-sex friendship seems to occupy an intermediate position between these two types. See Eisenstadt (1956), p. 43.

29. The relation of this passage to Freud's late view of the role of anxiety in *The Problem of Anxiety* as concerned primarily with the fear of object-loss, is clear.

BIBLIOGRAPHY

Adrian, Lord. 1953. "Review of Jones, E. *The Life and Work of Freud*," *The Observer*. London. Vol. I. November.

Alexander, F. 1950. *Psychosomatic Medicine*. New York: Norton.

Bales, R. F. 1953. "The Equilibrium Problem in Small Groups," in Parsons, T., Bales, R. F. and Shils, E. A. *Working Papers in the Theory of Action*. Glencoe: The Free Press.

Bowlby, John. 1958. "The Nature of the Child's Tie to His Mother," *International Journal of Psycho-analysis*, Vol. 39, Pt. V.

Eisenstadt, S. N. 1956. *From Generation to Generation*. Glencoe: The Free Press.

Freud, S. 1933. *New Introductory Lectures on Psycho-analysis*. New York: Norton.

———. 1935. *The Ego and the Id*. London: Hogarth.

———. 1936. *The Problem of Anxiety.* New York: Norton.

Grinker, R. 1953. *Psychosomatic Research.* New York: Norton.

Kazin, A. 1956. "The Freudian Revolution Analyzed," *New York Times Magazine,* May 6, p. 22.

Merton, R. K. 1957. "The Role Set," *British Journal of Sociology,* 8:2.

Olds, J. 1958. "Self Stimulation of the Brain," *Science,* Feb. 14, 127:315–24.

Parsons, T. 1950. "Psychoanalysis and the Social Structure," *Psychoanalytic Quarterly,* 19:371–94.

———. 1952. "The Superego and the Theory of Social Systems," *Psychiatry,* 15:15–25.

———. 1954a. "Psychoanalysis and Social Science," in Alexander and Ross (eds.), *Twenty Years of Psychoanalysis.*

———. 1954b. "The Incest Taboo in Relation to Social Structure and the Socialization of the Child," *British Journal of Sociology,* June, pp. 101–17.

———. 1958. "Durkheim's Contribution to the Theory of the Integration of Social Systems," in Wolff, K. (ed.) *Volume Honoring the Centenary of Emile Durkheim.* Ohio State University Press.

———. 1959a. "An Approach to Psychological Theory in Terms of the Theory of Action," in Koch, S. (ed.), *Psychology, A Science.* Vol. III. New York: McGraw-Hill.

———. 1959b. "The School Class as a Social System," *Harvard Educational Review,* Fall, 1959.

Parsons, T. and Bales, R. F. 1955. *Family, Socialization and Interaction Process.* Glencoe: Free Press.

Parsons, T., Bales, R. F. and Shils, E. A. 1953. *Working Papers in the Theory of Action.* Glencoe: Free Press.

Parsons, T. and Shils, E. A. 1951. *Toward a General Theory of Action.* Cambridge: Harvard University Press.

Trilling, L. 1955. *Freud and the Crisis of Our Culture.* Boston: Beacon Press.

About the Chapter

In relationship to the more theoretical chapters in this section, this chapter may be regarded as a case study. It is a prototype of researches linking modal personality to the functioning of a social system. The authors compare their Russian sample with an American control group. Their analysis is divided into a description of Russian modal personality trends and an analysis of the relationship of these trends to the needs and pressures of the Soviet socio-political system. Particular attention is given to congruence between personality modes and social systems and the implications of incongruence for the functioning of the Soviet system.

About the Authors

ALEX INKELES is Professor of Sociology at Harvard University, and Director of Studies in Social Relations at the Russian Research Center. He is the author of *Public Opinion in Soviet Russia,* and co-author of *How the Soviet System Works* and *The Soviet Citizen.* The inter-relations of personality and social structure are at the center of his research interests, and he is currently engaged in comparative studies of the social-psychology of industrial societies.

EUGENIA HANFMANN is Professor of Psychology and Director of the Student Counseling Center at Brandeis University. She is a diplomate of the American Board of Examiners in the specialty of Clinical Psychology. She obtained her Ph.D. in Psychology from the University of Jena in 1927. She has done research, teaching and clinical work at Smith College, Worcester State Hospital, Mount Holyoke College, the Office of Strategic Services and Harvard University. Her special research interests are in the fields of disturbances of thinking, personality dynamics and projective techniques.

HELEN BEIER studied at the Universities of Munich, Jena, London, Berlin, and in 1933 received her doctoral degree in psychology from the University of Danzig. She holds the position of Instructor in Psychology in the Department of Psychiatry of Boston University, as well as that of Chief Psychologist in the Child Guidance Center of the Boston City Hospital. She formerly did research at the Russian Research Center at Harvard.

Acknowledgments

This chapter, in slightly different form, was published first in *Human Relations,* XI, 1, 1959. The authors wish to express their warm appreciation for the prolonged support of the Russian Research Center at Harvard. Revisions were made by the senior author while he was a Fellow of the Center for Advanced Study in the Behavioral Sciences; the Center's support is gratefully acknowledged.

5

Modal Personality and Adjustment to the Soviet Socio-Political System

ALEX INKELES, *Harvard University*

EUGENIA HANFMANN, *Brandeis University*

HELEN BEIER, *Boston University*

Two main elements are encompassed in the study of national character.[1] The first step is to determine what modal personality patterns, if any, are found in a particular national population or in its major sub-groups. In so far as such modes exist, one can go on to the second stage: studying the interrelations between the personality modes and various aspects of the social system. Even if the state of our theory warranted the drafting of an "ideal" research design for studies in this field, they would require staggering sums and would probably be beyond our current methodological resources. We can, however, hope to make progress through more restricted efforts. In the investigation reported here we studied a highly selected group from the population of the Soviet Union, namely, former citizens of Great Russian nationality who "defected" during or after World War II. Attention is focused mainly on one aspect of the complex interrelations between system and personality: our subjects' participation in and adjustment to their Communist socio-political order.[2] We found that certain personality modes were outstanding in the group, and believe that we can trace their significance for our subjects' adjustment to Soviet society.

201

SAMPLE AND METHOD

An intensive program of clinical psychological research was conducted as part of the work of the Harvard Project on the Soviet Social System.[3] The Project explored the attitudes and life experiences of former Soviet citizens who were displaced during World War II and its aftermath and then decided not to return to the USSR. Almost 3,000 completed a long written questionnaire, and 329 undertook a detailed general life history interview. The individuals studied clinically were selected from the latter group. Criteria of selection were that the interviewee seemed a normal, reasonably adjusted individual who was relatively young, had lived most of his life under Soviet conditions, and was willing to undertake further intensive interviewing and psychological testing.

The group studied clinically included 51 individuals, 41 of whom were men. With the exception of a few Ukrainians, all were Great Russians. Almost half were under 30, and only 8 were 40 or older at the time of interview in 1950, which meant that the overwhelming majority grew up mainly under Soviet conditions and were educated in Soviet schools. Eleven had a minimum education of 4 years or less, 22 had between 4 and 8 years, and 18 had advanced secondary or college training. The group consisted predominantly of urban residents. But if those who had moved from the countryside to the city were included with the rural, then approximately half fell in each category. As might be expected from the education data, the group included a rather large proportion of people in high status occupations, with 11 professionals and members of the intelligentsia, 7 regular army officers, and 9 white collar workers. Sixteen were rank and file industrial and agricultural workers, and 5 rank and file army men. In keeping with the occupational pattern but running counter to popular expectations about Soviet refugees, a rather high proportion were in the Party (6) or the Young Communist League (13). Again running counter to popular expectations about refugees, the group was not characterized by a markedly high incidence of disadvantaged family background as reflected either in material deprivation, the experience of political arrest, or other forms of repression at the hands of the regime. Ten were classified as having been extremely disadvantaged, and 15 as having suffered minor disadvantage.

All of the Soviet refugees have in common their "disaffection" from Soviet society. The clinical group included mainly the more "active" defectors, who left Soviet control on their own initiative rather than the "passive" who were removed by force of circumstance. Thirty-four had deserted from the military[4] or voluntarily departed with the retreating German occupation armies. In general, however, the clinical group was not more vigorously anti-Communist than the other refugees. They overwhelmingly supported the principles of the welfare state, including government ownership and state planning, and credited the regime with great achievements in foreign affairs and economic and cultural development. They refused to return for much the same reasons given by other refugees: fear of reprisal at the hands of the secret police, memories of former oppression, opposition to institutions like the collective farm, or resentment of the low standard of living and the absence of political freedom. In psychological adjustment, finally, they seemed to reflect fairly well the tendency toward adequate adjustment which characterized the refugees as a whole.

With regard to the parent refugee population, then, the clinical group was disproportionately male, young, well educated, well placed occupationally and politically, and "active" in defecting.[5] In its internal composition, the sample was also unbalanced in being predominantly male. Otherwise the sample gave about equal weight to those over and under 35, manual and white collar occupations, urban or rural backgrounds, and education above or below the advanced secondary level.

Each respondent was interviewed about his childhood experience, some aspects of his adult life, and his adjustment to conditions in a displaced persons camp. Each took a battery of tests which included the Rorschach, TAT, a sentence completion test of 60 items, a "projective questions" test including 8 of the questions utilized in the authoritarian personality study, and a specially constructed "episodes" or problem-situations test. We regard the use of this battery of tests as a matter of special note, since most attempts to assess modal tendencies in small scale societies have relied upon a single instrument, particularly the Rorschach. The various tests differ in their sensitivity to particular dimensions or levels of personality, and differentially reflect the impact of the immediate emotional state and environmental situation of the subject. By utilizing a series of tests, therefore, we hope that we have in significant degree reduced the chances that any particular finding peculiar to the special combination of instrument, subject, and situation will have been mistakenly interpreted as distinctively Russian. In addition, the use of this battery enables us to test our assumptions in some depth, by checking for consistency on several tests.

Each test was independently analyzed according to fairly standard scoring methods, and the results reported separately.[6] In reporting their results, however, each set of analysts made some observations on the character traits which seemed generally important to the group as a whole. Further, in drawing these conclusions the analysts made use of a criterion group of Americans matched with the Russian sample on age, sex, occupation, and education. The availability of such test results posed a challenge as to whether or not these general observations, when collated and analyzed, would yield any consistent patterns for the group as a whole.

To make this assessment we selected the eight major headings used below as an organizing framework. We believe that they permit a fairly full description of the various dimensions and processes of the human personality, and at the same time facilitate making connections with aspects of the social system. These categories were, however, not part of the design of the original clinical research program, and were not used by the analysts of the individual instruments. While this circumstance made for lesser comparability between the tests, it forestalled the slanting of conclusions to fit the analytic scheme. The statements in the conclusions drawn by the analysts of each instrument were written on duplicate cards, sorted, and grouped under all the categories to which they seemed relevant. The evidence with regard to each category was then sifted and weighed. Where there were ambiguous findings the original tables were re-examined for clarification. Relevant impressions based on the interviews were also used. Similarities and differences between those in our sample and the matching Americans aided in grasping the distinctive features of the Russian pattern. On this basis a characterization of the group was developed under each heading of the analytic scheme.

It should be clear that the sketch of modal personality characteristics presented below is not a simple and direct translation of particular test scores into personality traits. Rather, it is an evaluative, summary statement, following from the collation and interpretation of conclusions drawn from each test, conclusions which were in turn based both on test scores and supplementary qualitative material. The word "modal" should not be taken too literally in this context. We have relied on some test scores when only a small proportion of the sample manifested the given response or pattern of responses, if this fit with other evidence in developing a larger picture. In stating our findings we have been freer with the evidence than some would permit, more strict than others would require. We attempted to keep to the canons of the exact method, without neglecting the clinical interpretations and insights. In this way we hoped to arrive at a rich and meaningful picture of the people studied, a picture that would provide an adequate basis for an analysis of their adjustment to the socio-political system.

BRIEF SKETCH OF RUSSIAN MODAL PERSONALITY CHARACTERISTICS

1. Central Needs [7]

Since all human beings manifest the same basic needs, we cannot assert that some need is unique to a given national population. Among these universal needs, however, some may achieve greater strength or central importance in the organization of the personality, and in this sense be typical of the majority of a given group.

Probably the strongest and most pervasive quality of the Russian personality which emerged from our data was a need for *affiliation*. By this we mean a need for intensive interaction with other people in immediate, direct, face-to-face relationships, coupled with a great capacity for having this need fulfilled through the establishment of warm and personal contact with others. Our subjects seemed to welcome others into their lives as an indispensable condition of their own existence, and generally felt neither isolated nor estranged from them. In contrast to the American subjects, the Russians were not too anxiously concerned about others' opinion of them and did not feel compelled to cling to a relationship nor to defend themselves against it. Rather, they manifested a profound acceptance of group membership and relatedness. These orientations were especially prevalent in test situations dealing with relations between the individual and small face-to-face groups such as the family, the work team, and the friendship circle.

Closely linked with the need for affiliation is a need for *dependence* very much like what Dicks (1952) spoke of as the Russians' "strong positive drive for enjoying loving protection and security," care and affection. This need shows not only in orientation towards parents and peers, but also in the relations with formal authority figures. Unlike Dicks, we did not, however, find a strong need for submission linked with the need for dependence. In addition there is substantial evidence for the relatively greater strength of *oral* needs, reflected in preoccupation with getting and consuming food and drink, in great volubility and in emphasis on singing. These features are especially conspicuous by contrast with the relative weakness of the more typically compulsive puritanical concern for order, regularity and self-control. However, our data do not permit us to stress this oral component as heavily as does Dicks, who regards it as "typical" for the culture as a whole.

Several needs rather prominent in the records of the American control group did not appear to be of outstanding importance in the personality structure of the Russians. Most notable, the great emphasis on *achievement* found in the American records was absent from the Russian ones. Within the area of interpersonal relations our data lead us to posit a fairly sharp Russian-American contrast. Whereas the American records indicate great strength of need for *approval* and need for *autonomy*, those needs were rather weakly manifested by the Russians. In approaching interpersonal relations, our American subjects seemed to fear too close or intimate association with other individuals and groups. They often perceived such relations as potentially limiting freedom of individual action, and therefore inclined above all to insure their independence from or autonomy within the group. At the same time the Americans revealed a strong desire for recognition and at least formal acceptance or approval from the group. They are very eager to be "liked," to be regarded as an "all right" guy, and greatly fear isolation from the group. Finally we noted that certain needs important in other national character studies were apparently not central in either the American or the Russian groups. Neither showed much need for dominance, for securing positions of superordination or for controlling or manipulating others and enforcing authority over them. Nor did they seem markedly distinguished in the strength of hostile impulses, of desires to hurt, punish, or destroy.

2. Modes of Impulse Control

On the whole the Russians have relatively *high awareness* of their impulses or basic dispositions—such as for oral gratification, sex, aggression, or dependence—and rather *freely accept* them as something normal or "natural" rather than as bad or offensive.[8] The Russians showed evidence, furthermore, of *giving in* to these impulses quite readily and frequently, and of *living them out*. Although they tended afterwards to be penitent and admit that they should not have "lived out" so freely, they were not really punitive towards themselves or others for failure to control impulses. Of course, this does not mean complete absence of impulse control, a condition which would render social life patently impossible. Indeed, the Russians viewed their own impulses and desires as forces which needed watching, and often professed the belief that the control of impulses was necessary and beneficial. The critical point is that the Russians seemed to rely much less than the Americans on impulse control to be generated and handled from within. Rather, they apparently felt a need for aid from without in the form of guidance and pressure exerted by higher authority and by the group to assist them in controlling their impulses. This is what Dicks referred to as the Russian's desire to have a "moral corset" put on his impulses. The Americans, on the other hand, vigorously affirm their ability for *self*-control, and seem to assume that the possession of such ability and its exercise legitimates their desire to be free from the overt control of authority and the group.

In this connection, the review of individual cases revealed a relative lack of well developed *defensive structures* in many of the Russian subjects. Mechanisms which serve to counteract and to modify threatening feelings and impulses—including isolation, intellectualization and reaction formation—seem to figure much less prominently among them than among the Americans. The Russians had fewer defenses of this type and those they had were less well established.

3. Typical Polarities and Dilemmas

Within certain areas of feelings and motives individuals may typically display attitudes and behavior that belong to one or the opposite poles of the given variable, or else display a preoccupation with the choice of alternatives posed by these poles. Such preoccupation may be taken to define the areas of typical dilemmas or conflicts, similar to the polarized issues, such as "identity vs. role diffusion" and "intimacy vs. isolation," which Erikson (1950) found so important in different stages of psychological maturation.

In our Russian subjects we found a conscious preoccupation with the problem of *trust vs. mistrust* in relation to others. They worried about the intentions of the other, expressing apprehension that people may not really be as they seem on the surface. There was always the danger that someone might entice you into revealing yourself, only then to turn around and punish you for what you have revealed. Another typical polarity of the Russians' behavior is that of *optimism vs. pessimism,* or of faith vs. despair. One of our projective test items posited the situation that tools and materials necessary for doing a job fail to arrive. In responding to this item our Russian subjects tended to focus on whether the outcome of the situation will be good or bad for the actor, while the Americans at once sprang into a plan of action for resolving the situation. Finally, we may include under the typical polarities of the Russians' attitude that of *activity vs. passivity,* although in the case of this variable we found little indication of a sense of a conscious conflict. However, the subjects' choices of alternatives in the projective tests tended to be distributed between the active and the passive ones, while the Americans' preference for the active instrumental response was as clear-cut and strong as was their generally optimistic orientation.

The pronounced polarities of the Russians' orientation lend support to Dicks's assertion that "the outstanding trait of the Russian personality is its contradictoriness—its ambivalence" (1952, p. 168). Two qualifications, however, must be kept in mind. First, the strength of our Russian subjects' dilemmas may have been greatly enhanced by the conditions of their lives, both in the Soviet Union and abroad. Second, the American subjects also show some involvement in problematic issues, though the issues were different from the Russian ones. Thus the problem of "intimacy vs. isolation" or "autonomy vs. belongingness" to which we have already alluded, seemed a major dilemma for Americans but not for the Russians.

4. Achieving and Maintaining Self-Esteem

In their orientations toward the self, the Russians displayed rather low and *unintense self-awareness* and little painful self-consciousness.

They showed rather high and *secure self-esteem,* and were little given to self-examination and doubt of their inner selves. At the same time they were not made anxious by examination of their own motivations or that of others, but rather showed readiness to gain insight into psychological mechanisms. The American pattern reveals some contrasts here, with evidence of acute self-awareness, substantial self-examination and doubting of one's inner qualities.

We were not able to discern any differences between Americans and Russians in the relative importance of *guilt* versus *shame* as sanctions. There were, however, some suggestive differences in what seemed to induce both guilt and shame. The Americans were more likely to feel guilty or shamed if they failed to live up to clear-cut "public" norms, as in matters of etiquette. They were also upset by any hint that they were inept, incompetent, or unable to meet production, sports, or similar performance standards. The Russians did not seem to be equally disturbed by such failures, and felt relatively more guilty or ashamed when they assumed that they had fallen behind with regard to moral or interpersonal behavior norms, as in matters involving personal honesty, sincerity, trust, or loyalty to a friend. These latter qualities they value most highly and they demand them from their friends.

5. Relation to Authority [9]

Our clinical instruments presented the subjects with only a limited range of situations involving relations with authority. No pronounced differences in basic attitudes between Russians and Americans appeared, except that Russians seemed to have more fear of and much less optimistic expectations about authority figures. Both of these manifestations might, of course, have been mainly a reflection of their recent experiences rather than of deeper-lying dispositions. Fortunately, we can supplement the clinical materials by the life history interviews which dealt extensively with the individual's relations with authority. A definite picture emerges from these data. Above all else the Russians want their leaders—whether boss, district political hack,. or national ruler—to be warm, nurturant, considerate, and interested in the individuals' problems and welfare. The authority is also expected to be the main source of initiative in the inauguration of general plans and programs and in the provision of guidance and organization for their attainment. The Russians do not seem to expect initiative, directedness, and organizedness from an average individual. They therefore expect that the authority will of necessity give detailed orders, demand obedience, keep checking up on performance, and use persuasion and coercion intensively to insure steady performance. A further major expectation with regard to the "legitimate" authority is that it will institute and enforce sanctions designed to curb or control bad impulses in individuals, improper moral practices, heathen religious ideas, perverted political procedures, and extreme personal injustice. It is then the government which should provide that "external moral corset" which Dicks says the Russian seeks.

An authority which meets these qualifications is "good" and it does what it does with "right." Such an authority should be loved, honored, respected, and obeyed. Our Russian subjects seemed, however, to expect that authority figures would in fact frequently be stern, demanding, even scolding and nagging. This was not in and of itself viewed as bad or improper. Authority may be, perhaps ought to be autocratic, so long as it is not harshly authoritarian and not totally demanding. Indeed, it is not a bad thing if such an authority makes one rather strongly afraid, makes one "quake" in expectation of punishment for trespassing or wrongdoing. Such an authority should not, however, be arbitrary, aloof, and unjust. It should not be unfeeling in the face of an open acknowledgment of one's guilt and of consequent self-castigation. Indeed, many of our subjects assumed that authority can in fact be manipulated through humbling the self and depicting oneself as a weak, helpless person who needs supportive guidance rather than harsh punishment. They also assumed that authority may be manipulated by praise or fawning, and seduced through the sharing of gratificatory experiences provided by the supplicant—as through the offer of a bottle of liquor and the subsequent sharing of some drinks. Russians also favor meeting the pressure of authority by evasive tactics, including such devices as apparently well-intentioned failure to comprehend and departures from the scene of action.

Throughout their discussions of authority our respondents showed little concern for the preservation of precise forms, rules, regulations, exactly defined rights, regularity of procedure, formal and explicit limitation of powers, or the other aspects of the traditional constitutional Anglo-Saxon approach to law and government. For the Russians a government which has the characteristics of good government listed above, justifies its right to rule by virtue of that performance. In that case, one need not fuss too much about the fine points of law. By contrast, if government is harsh, arbitrary, disinterested in public welfare—which it is apparently expected to be more often than not—then it loses its right to govern no matter how legal its position and no matter how close its observance of the letter of the law.

6. Modes of Affective Functioning

One of the most salient characteristics of the Russian personality was the high degree of their *expressiveness* and emotional aliveness. On most test items the Russian responses had a stronger emotional coloring, and covered a wider range of emotions than did the American responses. The Russians' feelings were easily brought into play, and they showed them openly and freely both in speech and in facial expression, without much suppression or disguise. In particular they showed a noticeably greater *freedom and spontaneity in criticism* and in the expression of hostile feelings than was true for the Americans. There were, further, two emotions which the Russians showed with a frequency far exceeding that found in the Americans—*fear,* and *depression* or despair. Many of the ambiguous situations posited in the tests were viewed by them in terms of danger and threat, on the one hand, and of privation and loss on the other. Undoubtedly this was in good part a reflection of the tense social situation which they had experienced in the Soviet Union, and of their depressed status as refugees, but we believe that in addition deeper lying trends were here being tapped. These data provide some evidence in support of the oft noted prevalence of depressive trends among the Russians.

7. Modes of Cognitive Functioning

In this area we include characteristic patterns of perception, memory, thought, and imagination, and the processes involved in forming and manipulating ideas about the world around one. Of all the modes of personality organization it is perhaps the most subtle, and certainly in the present state of theory and testing one of the most difficult to formulate. Our clinical materials do, however, permit a few comments.

In discussing people, the Russians show a keen *awareness of the "other"* as a distinct entity as well as a rich and diversified recognition of his special characteristics. Other people are usually perceived by them not as social types but as concrete individuals with a variety of attributes distinctly their own. The Russians think of people and evaluate them for what they are rather than in terms of how they evaluate ego, the latter being a more typically American approach. The Russians also paid more attention to the "others'" basic underlying attributes and attitudes than to their behavior as such or their performance on standards of achievement and accomplishment in the instrumental realm.

Similar patterns were evident in their perception of interpersonal situations. In reacting to the interpersonal relations "problems" presented by one of the psychological tests they more fully elaborated the situation, cited more relevant incidents from folklore or their own experience, and offered many more illustrations of a point. In contrast, the Americans tended more to describe the formal, external, characteristics of people, apparently being less perceptive of the individual's motivational characteristics. The Americans also tended to discuss interpersonal problems on a rather generalized and abstract level. With regard to most other types of situation, however, especially problems involving social organization, the pattern was somewhat reversed. Russians tended to take a rather broad, sweeping view of the situation, *generalizing* at the expense of details, about which they were often extremely vague and poorly informed. They seemed to feel their way through such situations rather than rigorously to think them through, tending to get into a spirit of grandiose planning but without attention to necessary details.

8. Modes of Conative Functioning

By conative functioning we mean the patterns, the particular behavioral forms of the striving for any valued goals, including the rhythm or pace at which these goals are pursued and the way in which that rhythm is regulated. In this area our clinical data are not very rich. Nevertheless, we have the strong impression that the Russians do not match the Americans in vigor of striving to master all situations or problems put before them. Rather, problems are met primarily through adaptive instrumental orientations. Though by no means listless, Russians seem much more *passively accommodative* to the apparent hard facts of situations. In addition, they appeared less apt to persevere systematically in the adaptive courses of action they did undertake, tending to backslide into passive accommodation when the going proved rough. At the same time, the Russians do seem capable of great bursts of activity, which suggests the bi-modality of an *assertive-passive pattern* of strivings in contrast to the steadier, more even, and consistent pattern of strivings among the Americans.

To sum up, one of the most salient characteristics of the personality of our Russian subjects was their emotional aliveness and expressiveness. They felt their emotions keenly, and did not tend to disguise or to deny them to themselves, nor to suppress their outward expression to the same extent as the Americans. The Russians criticized themselves and others with greater freedom and spontaneity. Relatively more aware and tolerant of impulses for gratification in themselves and others, they relied less than the Americans on self-control from within and more on external socially imposed controls applied by the peer group or authority.

A second outstanding characteristic of the Russians was their strong need for intensive interaction with others, coupled with a strong and secure feeling of relatedness to them, high positive evaluation of such belongingness, and great capacity to enjoy such relationships. The image of the "good" authority was of a warm, nurturant, supportive figure. Yet our subjects seemed to assume that this paternalism might and indeed should include superordinate planning and firm guidance, as well as control or supervision of public and personal morality, and if necessary, of thought and belief. It is notable, in this connection, that in the realm of conative and cognitive functioning orderliness, precision of planning and persistence in striving were not outstandingly present. Such qualities were rather overshadowed by tendencies toward over-generalizing, vagueness, imprecision, and passive accommodation. Countering the image of the good authority, there was an expectation that those with power would in fact often be harsh, aloof, and authoritarian. The effect of such behavior by authority is alienation of loyalty. This fits rather well with the finding that the main polarized issues or dilemmas were those of "trust vs. mistrust" in relations with others, "optimism vs. pessimism," and "activity vs. passivity," whereas the more typically American dilemma of "intimacy vs. isolation" was not a problem for many Russians.

Though strongly motivated by needs for affiliation and dependence and wishes for oral gratification—in contrast to greater strength of needs for achievement, autonomy, and approval among the Americans —our Russian subjects seemed to have a characteristically sturdy ego. They were rather secure in their self-estimation, and unafraid to face up to their own motivation and that of others. In contrast to the Americans, the Russians seemed to feel shame and guilt for defects of "character" in interpersonal relations rather than for failure to meet formal rules of etiquette or instrumental production norms. Compared to the Americans, however, they seemed relatively lacking in well developed and stabilized defenses with which to counteract and modify threatening impulses and feelings. The organization of their personality depended for its coherence much more heavily on their intimate relatedness to those around them, their capacity to use others' support and to share with them their emotions.

RELATIONS OF MODAL PERSONALITY AND THE SOCIO-POLITICAL SYSTEM

In the following comments we are interpreting "political participation" rather broadly, to cover the whole range of the individual's role as the citizen of a large-scale national state. We therefore include his major economic and social as well as his specifically political roles. This may extend the concept of political participation too far for most national states, but for the Soviet Union, where all aspects of social life have been politicized, it is the only meaningful approach. Specifically, the questions to which we address ourselves are as follows:

Assuming that the traits cited above were widespread among the group of Great Russians studied by our project, what implications would this have for their adjustment to the role demands made on them by the social system in which they participated? To what extent can the typical complaints of refugees against the system, and the typical complaints of the regime against its own people, be traced to the elements of non-congruence between these personality modes and Soviet social structure?

A full answer to these questions would involve us in a much more extensive presentation and a more complex analysis than is possible here. We wish to stress that our analysis is limited to the Soviet socio-political system as it typically functioned under Stalin's leadership, (Bauer, Inkeles and Kluckhohn, 1956; Fainsod, 1953) since this was the form of the system in which our respondents lived and to which they had to adjust. To avoid any ambiguity on this score we have fairly consistently used the past tense. We sincerely hope that this will not lead to the mistaken assumption that we regard the post-Stalin era as massively discontinuous with the earlier system. However, to specify in any detail the elements of stability and change in post-Stalin Russia, and to indicate the probable effects of such changes on the adjustment of Soviet citizens to the system, is beyond the scope of this chapter. As for the personality dimensions, we will discuss each in its relations to system participation separately, rather than in the complex combinations in which they operate in reality. Only those of the personality traits cited above are discussed that clearly have relevance for the individual's participation in the socio-political system.

Need Affiliation

Virtually all aspects of the Soviet regime's pattern of operation seem calculated to interfere with the satisfaction of the Russians' need for affiliation. The regime has placed great strains on friendship relations by its persistent programs of political surveillance, its encouragement and elaboration of the process of denunciation, and its assignment of mutual or "collective" responsibility for the failings of particular individuals. The problem was further aggravated by the regime's insistence that its elite maintain a substantial social distance between itself and the rank-and-file. In addition, the regime developed an institutional system which affected the individual's relations with others in a way that ran strongly counter to the basic propensities of the Russians as represented in our sample.

The desire for involvement in the group and the insistence on loyalty, sincerity, and general responsiveness from others, received but little opportunity for expression and gratification in the tightly controlled Soviet atmosphere. Many of the primary face-to-face organizations most important to the individual were infiltrated, attacked, or even destroyed by the regime. The breakup of the old village community and its replacement by the more formal, bureaucratic, and impersonal collective farm is perhaps the most outstanding example, but it is only one of many. The disruption and subordination to the state of the traditional family group, of the Church, the independent professional associations and the trade unions are other cases in point. The regime greatly feared the development of local autonomous centers of power. Every small group was seen as a potential conspiracy against the regime or its policies. The system of control required that each and all constantly watch and report on each other. The top hierarchy conducted a constant war on what it scornfully called "local patriotism," "back scratching" and "mutual security associations," even though in reality it was attacking little more than the usual personalizing tendencies incidental to effective business and political management. The people strove hard to maintain their small group structures, and the regime persistently fought this trend through its war against "familieness" and associated evils. At the same time it must be recognized that by its emphasis on broad group loyalties, the regime probably captured and harnessed somewhat the propensities of many Russians to give themselves up wholly to a group membership and to group activity and goals. This is most marked in the Young Communist League and in parts of the Party.

Need Orality

The scarcity element which predominated in Soviet society, the strictly rationed economy of materials, and men, and the physical requirements of daily life seem to have aroused intense anxieties about further oral deprivation which served greatly to increase the impact of the real shortages which have been chronic to the system. Indeed, the image of the system which most individuals in our sample held is very much that of an orally depriving, niggardly, non-nurturant leadership. On the other hand, the regime can hope to find a quick road to better relations with the population by strategic dumping or glutting with goods. To some extent, this was attempted during the period of Malenkov's ascendancy, although perhaps more in promise than reality.

Need Dependence

The regime took pride in following Lenin in "pushing" the masses. It demanded that individuals be responsible and carry on "on their own" with whatever resources were at hand. It clamored for will and self-determination (see Bauer 1952). Clearly, this was not very congruent with the felt need for dependent relations. At the same time certain aspects of the regime satisfied the need for dependence. The popular image of the regime as one possessed of a strong sense of direction fits in with this need. Similarly emphasis on a massive formal program of social-welfare measures helped, even if they were not too fully implemented.

This directedness has a bearing also on the problem of submission. Although the regime had the quality of a firm authority able to give needed direction, it did not gain as much as it might because it was viewed as interested in the maximation of power *per se*. This appears to alienate the Russian as represented in our sample.

The Trust-Mistrust Dilemma

Everything we know about Soviet society makes it clear that it was extremely difficult for a Soviet citizen to be at all sure about the good intentions of his government leaders and his immediate supervisors. They seemed always to talk support and yet to mete out harsh treatment. This divided behavior pattern of the leadership seemed to aggravate the apparent Russian tendency to see the intentions of others as problematical. It intensified the dilemma of trust-mistrust. On the basis of our interviews one might describe this dilemma of whether or not to grant trust as very nearly *the* central problem in the relations of former Soviet citizens to their regime. The dilemma of optimism vs. pessimism, of whether outcomes will be favorable or unfavorable, presents a very similar situation.

The Handling of Shame

The regime tried exceedingly hard to utilize public shame to force or cajole Soviet citizens into greater production and strict observance of the established rules and regulations. Most of our available public documentary evidence indicates that the regime was not outstandingly successful in this respect. Our clinical findings throw some light on the reason. The regime tried to focus shame on nonperformance, on failures to meet production obligations or to observe formal bureaucratic rules. To judge by the clinical sample, however, the Russian is little shamed by these kinds of performance failures, and is more likely to feel shame in the case of moral failures. Thus, the Soviet Russian might be expected to be fairly immune to the shaming pressures of the regime. Indeed, the reactions of those in our sample suggest the tables often get turned around, with the citizen concluding that it is the regime which should be ashamed because it has fallen down in these important moral qualities.

Affective Functioning

The general expansiveness of the Russians in our sample, their easily expressed feelings, the giving in to impulse, and the free expression of criticism, were likely to meet only the coldest reception from the regime. It emphasized and rewarded control, formality, and lack of feeling in relations. Discipline, orderliness, and strict observance of rules are what it expects. Thus, our Russian subjects could hope for little official reward in response to their normal modes of expression. In fact, they could be expected to run into trouble with the regime as a result of their proclivities in this regard. Their expansiveness and tendency freely to express their feelings, including hostile feelings, exposed them to retaliation from the punitive police organs of the state. And insofar as they did exercise the necessary control and avoided open expression of hostile feelings, they experienced a sense of uneasiness and resentment because of this unwarranted imposition, which did much to color their attitude to the regime.

Conative Functioning

The non-striving quality of our Russian subjects ties in with the previously mentioned characteristics of dependence and non-instrumentality. The regime, of course, constantly demanded greater effort and insisted on a more instrumental approach to problems. It emphasized long-range planning and deferred gratification. There was a continual call for efforts to "storm bastions," to "breach walls," "to strive mightily." With the Russian as he is represented in our sample, it does not appear likely that the regime could hope to meet too positive a response here; in fact it encountered a substantial amount of rejection for its insistence on modes of striving not particularly congenial to a substantial segment of the population. Indeed, the main influence may have been exerted by the people on the system, rather than by the system on them. Soviet official sources have for many years constantly complained of the uneven pace at which work proceeds, with the usual slack pace making it necessary to have great, often frenzied, bursts of activity to complete some part of the Plan on schedule, followed again by a slack period. It may well be that this pattern results not only from economic factors such as the uneven flow of raw material supplies, but that it also reflects the Russian tendency to work in spurts.

Relations to Authority

In many ways the difficulties of adjustment to the Soviet system experienced by our subjects revolved around the gap between what they *hoped* a "good" government would be and what they *perceived* to be the behavior of the regime. Our respondents freely acknowledged that the Soviet leaders gave the country guidance and firm direction, which in some ways advanced the long-range power and prestige of the nation. They granted that the regime well understood the principles of the welfare state, and cited as evidence its provision of free education and health services. The general necessity of planning was also allowed, indeed often affirmed, and the regime was praised for taking into its own hands the regulation of public morality and the conscious task of "raising the cultural level" through support of the arts and the encouragement of folk culture.

Despite these virtues, however, the whole psychological style of ruling and of administration adopted by the Bolsheviks seems to have had the effect of profoundly estranging our respondents. A great gulf seemed to separate the rulers and the ruled, reflected in our respondents' persistent use of a fundamental "we"—"they" dichotomy. "They" were the ones in power who do bad things to us, and "we" were the poor, ordinary, suffering people who, despite internal differences in status or income, share the misfortune of being oppressed by "them." Most did not know that Stalin had once asserted that the Bolsheviks could not be a "true" ruling party if they limited themselves "to a mere registration of the sufferings and thoughts of the proletarian masses." (Stalin, 1933) Yet our respondents sensed this dictum behind the style of Soviet rule. They reacted to it in charging the leaders with disinterest in individual welfare and extraordinary callousness about the amount of human suffering engendered in carrying out their plans. Our subjects saw the regime as harsh and arbitrary. The leaders were characterized as cold, aloof, "deaf" and unyielding to popular pleas, impersonal and distant from the people's problems and desires. The regime was seen not as firmly guiding but as coercive, not as paternally stern but as harshly demanding, not as nurturant and supportive but as autocratic and rapaciously demanding, not as chastening and then forgiving but as nagging and unyieldingly punitive.

The rejection of the regime was however by no means total, and the Bolshevik pattern of leadership was in many respects seen not as totally alien but rather as native yet unfortunately exaggerated. This "acceptance" did not extend to the coldness, aloofness, formality, and maintenance of social distance which were usually rejected. It did, however, apply to the pressures exerted by the regime, which were felt to be proper but excessive. Coercion by government was understandable, but that applied by the regime was not legitimate because it was so harsh. The scolding about backsliding was recognized as necessary, but resented for being naggingly persistent and caustic. And the surveillance was expected, but condemned for being so pervasive, extending as it did even into the privacy of one's friendship and home relations, so that a man could not even hope to live "peacefully" and "quietly." The elements of acceptance within this broader pattern of rejection have important implications for the future of the post-Stalin leadership. They suggest that the regime may win more positive support by changing the mode of application of many of its authoritarian and totalitarian policies without necessarily abandoning these policies and institutions as such.

Indeed in watching the public behavior of men like Khrushchev and Bulganin one cannot help but feel that their style of leadership behavior is much more congenial to Russians than was that of Stalin.

The preceding discussion strongly suggests that there was a high degree of incongruence between the central personality modes and dispositions of many Russians and some essential aspects of the structure of Soviet society, in particular the behavior of the regime. Most of the popular grievances were clearly based on real deprivations and frustrations, but the dissatisfactions appear to be even more intensified and given a more emotional tone because they were based also on the poor "fit" between the personality patterns of many Soviet citizens and the "personality" of the leaders as it expressed itself in the institutions they created, in their conduct of those institutions and the system at large, and in the resultant social climate in the USSR.

SOCIAL CLASS DIFFERENTIATION

Since personality traits found in the Russian sample are merely modal rather than common to the group at large, it follows that subgroups can meaningfully be differentiated by the choice of appropriate cutting points on the relevant continua. As a way of placing the individuals in our sample on a common scale, three elements from the total range of characteristics previously described were selected. They were chosen on the grounds that they were most important in distinguishing the Russians as a group from the Americans, and also because they seemed meaningfully related to each other as elements in a personality syndrome. The three characteristics were: great strength of the drive for social relatedness, marked emotional aliveness, and general lack of well developed, complex, and pervasive defenses. The two clinicians rated all cases for a combination of these traits on a three point scale. Cases judged on the basis of a review of both interview and test material to have these characteristics *in a marked degree* were placed in a group designated as the "primary set." Individuals in whom these characteristics were clearly evident but less strongly pronounced, were designated as belonging to a "variant" set. The "primary" and "variant" sets together constitute a relatively homogeneous group of cases who clearly revealed the characteristics which we have described as "modal." All the remaining cases were placed in a "residual" category, characterized by markedly stronger development of defenses, and in most instances also by lesser emotional expressiveness and lesser social relatedness. This group was relatively the least homogeneous of the three because its members tended to make use of rather different combinations of defenses without any typical pattern for the set as a whole. Subjects placed in the "residual" group appeared to differ more from those in the "variant" set than the "primary" and the "variant" sets differed from each other. However, even the "residual" pattern was not separated from the others by a very sharp break: emotional aliveness and relatedness to people was present also in some members of this group.

Each of our 51 cases was assigned to one of four social status categories on the basis of occupation and education. All those in group A were professionals and higher administrative personnel most of whom had university training, and all those in the D group were either peasants, or unskilled or semi-skilled workers with no more than five years of education. Placement in the two intermediary categories was also determined by the balance of occupation and education, group B consisting largely of white collar workers and semi-professional and middle supervisory personnel, and group C of more skilled workers with better education.

Table 1 gives the distribution of cases among the three personality types within each of the four status groups. It is evident that the primary pattern has its greatest strength in the lower classes, becomes relatively less dominant in the middle layers, and plays virtually no role at all in the top group. The "residual" pattern predominates at the top level and is very rare among peasants and ordinary workers.

Table 1

STATUS DISTRIBUTION OF PERSONALITY
TYPES AMONG FORMER SOVIET CITIZENS

		Personality Type		
Status	*primary*	*variant*	*residual*	*total*
A	—	1	12	13
B	2	8	6	16
C	3	4	2	9
D	8	3	2	13
total	13	16	22	51

The distinctive patterns of adjustment to the Soviet system by the various socio-economic groups are discussed in detail in another publication (Inkeles and Bauer 1959). Here we restrict ourselves to a few general observations. First, we wish to stress that, as our interviews indicate, both the more favored and the rank-and-file share substantially the same range of complaints against the regime, find the same broad institutional features such as the political terror and the collective farm objectionable, and view the same welfare features such as the system of education and free medical care as desirable. In spite of these common attitudes, our data suggest that personality may play a massive role with regard to some aspects of participation in and adjustment to the socio-political system. The educational-occupational level attained and/or maintained by an individual in an open-class society is one of the major dimensions of such participation. This is particularly the case in the Soviet Union where professional and higher administrative personnel are inevitably more deeply implicated in the purposes and plans of the regime, are politically more active and involved, and are subjected to greater control and surveillance. It seems plausible that persons in whom the affiliative need was particularly strong, expressiveness marked and impulse control weak, and the defensive structures not well developed or well organized, would be handicapped in competition for professional and administrative posts in any society; they certainly could not be expected to strive for or to hold on to positions of responsibility in the Soviet system.

The pattern of marked association between certain traits of personality and educational-occupational level clearly invites a question as to whether the personality really affected the level attained and held, or whether the appropriate personality traits were merely acquired along with the status. This question raises complex issues which we cannot explore here. We do wish to point out, however, that the characteristics on which our psychological grouping was based belong to those that are usually formed at an early age and are relatively long enduring and resistant to change. At first glance this affirmation of the early origins of the patterns described seems to be inconsistent with their observed association with educational-occupational level. However, the contradiction exists only if one assumes that obtaining a higher education and a superior occupation in Soviet society is a matter either of pure chance or exclusively of ability, unrelated to family background and the person's own attitudes and strivings. The data on stratification and mobility in Soviet society show, however, that persons born into families of higher social and educational level have a much better chance than do others to obtain a higher education and professional training (Feldmesser, 1953; Inkeles, 1950). Consequently, many people of the professional and administrative class grew up in families of similar status, and in those families were apparently reared in a way different from that typical of the peasant and worker families (see Rossi, 1954). Presumably, this produced enduring effects on their personality, which were important prior to exposure to common educational experiences.

In addition, mobility out of the lower classes may have been mainly by individuals whose personality was different, for whatever reason, from that of the majority of their class of origin. Such differences can easily express themselves in a stronger drive for education and for a position of status. We must also allow for the role played by the regime's deliberate selection of certain types as candidates for positions of responsibility. Finally, there is the less conscious "natural selection" process based on the affinity between certain personality types and the opportunities offered by membership in the elite and near elite categories. In this connection we are struck by the relative distinctness of the highest status level in our sample, since only one person with either of the two variants of the modal personality of the rank and file shows up among them. These results bear out the impression, reported by Dicks, of radical personality differences and resultant basic incompatibilities between the ruled population and the rulers. The latter, we assume, are still further removed from the "modal pattern" than are our subjects in the elite group.

We have yet to deal with the question of how far our observations concerning a group of refugees can be generalized to the Soviet population and *its* adjustment to the Soviet system. The answer to this question depends in good part on whether personality was an important selective factor in determining propensity to defect among those in the larger group who had the opportunity to do so.[10] It is our impression that personality was not a prime determinant of the decision not to return to Soviet control after World War II. Rather, accidents of the individual's life history such as past experience with the regime's instruments of political repression, or fear of future repression because of acts which might be interpreted as collaboration with the Germans, seem to have been the prime selective factors. Furthermore, such experiences and fears, though they affected the loyalty of the Soviet citizen, were not prime determinants of his pattern of achievement or adjustment in the Soviet socio-political system. The refugee population is not a collection of misfits or historical "leftovers." It includes representatives from all walks of life and actually seemed to have a disproportionately large number of the mobile and successful.

Though we are acutely aware of the smallness of our sample, we incline to assume that the personality modes found in it would be found within the Soviet Union in groups comparable in nationality and occupation. We are strengthened in this assumption by several considerations. First, the picture of Russian modal personality patterns which emerges from our study is highly congruent with the traditional or classic picture of the Russian character reported in history, literature and current travellers' accounts.[11] Secondly, much of the criticism directed by the regime against the failings of the population strongly suggests that some of the traits we found modal to our sample and a source of strain in its adjustment to the system are widespread in the population and pose an obstacle to the attainment of the regime's purposes *within* the U.S.S.R. Third, the differences in personality between occupational levels are consistent with what we know both of the general selective processes in industrial occupational systems and of the deliberate selective procedures adopted by the Soviet regime. Because of the methodological limitations of our study, the generalization of our findings to the Soviet population must be considered as purely conjectural. Unfortunately we will be obliged to remain on this level of conjecture as long as Soviet citizens within the U.S.S.R. are not accessible to study under conditions of relative freedom. We feel, however, that, with all their limitations, the findings we have reported can be of essential aid in furthering our understanding of the adjustment of a large segment of the Soviet citizens to their socio-political system and of the policies adopted by the regime in response to the disposition of the population.

NOTES

1. For a discussion of the basic issues and a review of research in this field see Inkeles, A. and Levinson, D. J. (1954).

2. For analysis of another aspect of the psychological properties of this group, see Hanfmann, 1957.

3. The research was carried out by the Russian Research Center under contract AF No. 33(038)–12909 with the former Human Resources Research Institute, Maxwell Air Force Base, Alabama. For a general account of the purposes and design of the study see: Bauer, Inkeles and Kluckhohn, 1956. The clinical study is described by Hanfmann and Beier, 1958.

4. This was in part a result of our selection procedure. The larger project was particularly interested in post-war defectors, almost all of whom came from the Soviet military occupation forces in Germany. Half of the men fell in that category.

5. The young post-war defectors on the whole did prove to be less stable and more poorly adjusted. Apart from their adjustment or "integration," however, they shared with the rest of the sample much the same range of outstanding personality traits. Therefore, no further distinctions between that group and the rest are discussed in this chapter. See Hanfmann and Beier, 1958.

6. See Hanfmann and Getzels, 1955, for a detailed report on the "Episodes Test." A brief account of results on the Projective Questions has also been published in Beier and Hanfmann, 1956. Some of the TAT results are described in Rosenblatt, 1960. The other results were described in the following unpublished reports of the Project, which may be examined at the Russian Research Center: "Some Systematic Patterns of Relationship between Personality and Attitudes among Soviet Displaced Persons," by Marc Fried, October 1954, 133 pages; "Relationships between Personality and Attitudes among Soviet Displaced Persons: A Technical Memorandum on the Derivation of Personality Variables from a Sentence Completion Test," by Marc Fried and Doris Held, August 1953, 125 pages; "A Comparative

Analysis of the Responses to a Sentence Completion Test of a Matched Sample of Americans and Former Russian Subjects," by H. E. Roseborough and H. P. Phillips, April 1953, 80 pages.

7. See H. Murray, 1938. We do not strictly follow Murray in our use of the "need" terminology.

8. Such a statement must of course always be one of degree. We do not mean to say that such threatening impulses as those toward incest are present in the awareness of Russians or are accepted by them more than by Americans.

9. Relations to authority may be thought of as simply one aspect of a broader category—"conceptions of major figures," which includes parents, friends, etc. We have included some comments on the Russians' perceptions of others under "cognitive modes" below.

10. It is impossible to estimate accurately how many former Soviet citizens had a real chance to choose not to remain under Soviet authority. The best available estimates suggest that at the close of hostilities in Europe in 1945 there were between two and a half and five million former Soviet citizens in territories outside Soviet control or occupation, and of these between 250,000 and 500,000 decided and managed to remain in the West (see Fischer, 1952).

11. After this article was completed we discovered a report based almost entirely on participant observation which yielded conclusions about modal personality patterns among Soviet Russians extra-ordinarily similar to those developed on the basis of our tests and interviews ´see Pfister-Ammende, 1949).

BIBLIOGRAPHY

Bauer, R. 1952. *The New Man in Soviet Psychology.* Cambridge: Harvard University Press.

Bauer, R., Inkeles, A. and Kluckhohn, C. 1953. "How the Soviet System Works." In Fainsod, M. (ed.), *How Russia is Ruled.* Cambridge: Harvard University Press.

———. 1956. *How the Soviet System Works.* Cambridge: Harvard University Press.

Beier, H. and Hanfmann, E. 1956. "Emotional Attitudes of Former Soviet Citizens as Studied by the Technique of Projective Questions," *Journal of Abnormal and Social Psychology,* 53:143–53.

Dicks, H. V. 1952. "Observations on Contemporary Russian Behavior," *Human Relations,* 5:111–74.

Erikson, E. 1950. *Childhood and Society.* New York: Norton.

Fainsod, Merle, (ed.) 1953. *How Russia is Ruled.* Cambridge: Harvard University Press.

Feldmesser, R. 1953. "The Persistence of Status Advantages in Soviet Russia," *American Journal of Sociology,* 59:19–27.

Fischer, G. 1952. *Soviet Opposition to Stalin.* Cambridge: Harvard University Press.

Hanfmann, E. 1957. "Social Perception in Russian Displaced Persons and an American Comparison Group," *Psychiatry*, 20:131–49.

Hanfmann, E. and Beier, H. 1958. "The Mental Health of a Group of Russian Displaced Persons," *American Journal of Orthopsychiatry*, 28:241–55.

Hanfmann, E. and Getzels, J. 1955. "Interpersonal Attitudes of Former Soviet Citizens as Studied by a Semi-Projective Method," *Psychological Monographs*, 69, No. 4.

Inkeles, A. 1950. "Stratification and Social Mobility in the Soviet Union: 1940–1950," *American Sociological Review*, 15:465–79.

Inkeles, A. and Bauer, R. 1959. *The Soviet Citizen*. Cambridge: Harvard University Press.

Inkeles, A. and Levinson, D. J. 1954. "National Character: The Study of Modal Personality and Sociocultural Systems." In Lindzey, G. (ed.), *Handbook of Social Psychology*. Cambridge: Addison-Wesley, II:977–1020.

Murray, H. 1938. *Explorations in Personality*. New York: Oxford University Press.

Pfister-Ammende, M. 1949. "Psychologische Erfahrungen mit Sowjetrussischen Flüchtlingen in der Schweiz." In Pfister-Ammende, M. (ed.), *Die Psychohygiene: Grundlagen und Ziele*. Bern: Hans Huber.

Rosenblatt, D. 1960. "Responses of Former Soviet Citizens to Selected TAT Cards," *Journal of General Psychology*, 63:273–84.

Rossi, A. 1954. "Generational Differences Among Former Soviet Citizens." Unpublished Ph.D. thesis in sociology, Columbia University.

Stalin, J. 1933. *Leninism*. New York: International Publishers, I:95–96.

About the Chapter

Dr. Devereux's chapter analyzes the modal personality concept, one of the most central and widely utilized concepts in the culture and personality field. He distinguishes between psychological and sociological interpretations of the concept. The former deal with the actual motivations that occur in individuals in a particular group, the latter emerge from the sociologist's need to explain uniformities in social behavior by positing some shared motivation. In his discussion of the motivational bases of revolutionary behavior during the Hungarian uprising of 1956, Dr. Devereux suggests that the sociologists' conception of modal personality implies socially relevant motives like "patriotism," "economic interest," and others which stand in an "instrumental" relationship to the actual motives of persons, and serve to channel the diversity of motives into shared behavior patterns, which support social processes. He contends that the modal personality concept, when used in this way, does not require that persons participating in a social process be homogeneous in their motivational dispositions. This position is related to Dr. Spiro's analysis in Chapter 2.

About the Author

GEORGE DEVEREUX is Professor of Research in Ethnopsychiatry, Temple University School of Medicine, Lecturer in Anthropology, Columbia University School of General Studies and a licensed psychologist in the State of New York. He is a graduate of the University of Paris, the University of California, and the Topeka Institute for Psychoanalysis. He did field work among various American Indian tribes, especially the Mohave, and in Papua, New Guinea and Indochina. He was formerly Director of Research of Winter V.A. Hospital, Topeka, Kansas and of the Devereux Schools, Devon, Pa. and taught in the Menninger School of Psychiatry, the Topeka Institute for Psychoanalysis and various universities. In 1959 he was the Géza Róheim Memorial Lecturer. His main field of interest is psychoanalytic anthropology and ethnopsychiatry. His scientific contributions include 6 books and over 150 articles.

Acknowledgments

For permission to use data obtained from a group of recent Hungarian refugees by a multidisciplinary team, the author is indebted to Professors Harold G. Wolff, M.D. and Lawrence E. Hinkle, Jr., M.D., who direct the Study Program in Human Health and Human Ecology at Cornell Medical College, and to the Society for the Investigation of Human Ecology, which supported the study of Hungarian refugees. Many of the data were presented by Drs. Hinkle and Stephenson in the *Second Seminar on the Hungarian Revolution of October 1956* in papers of exemplary psycho-social sophistication. Somewhat different interpretations of the material by certain other social scientists who participated in that seminar induced the author to offer a rebuttal at that time. That rebuttal eventually led to the writing of the present chapter. The papers just mentioned, the supplementary discussions and the author's rebuttal of certain interpretations other than those of Drs. Hinkle and Stephenson were published by the Society for the Investigation of Human Ecology in 1958.

6

Two Types of Modal
Personality Models

GEORGE DEVEREUX

Temple University School of Medicine
and
Columbia University School of General Studies

It is one of the hallmarks of a maturing science that each empirical problem which it solves creates new questions concerning the nature of the science itself. This chapter reappraises the view that the basic construct of culture and personality studies—the socio-psychological conception of the personality—represents a true synthesis of the data and frames of reference of both psychology and social science. This new conceptual model is usually supposed to be a homogeneous, structurally integrated and coherent whole, equally relevant, *in the same way,* for the social scientist and for the psychologist. Logical qualities supposedly characterize all personality models of this type, regardless of variations in their actual form, content or theoretical orientation. Thus, regardless of whether a given (psychoanalytic, Hullian, Tolmanian, etc.) model represents the "modal" personality of Mohaves, of males, of shamans, or of old persons, or the much more concrete and specific "modal" personality of old Mohave male shamans, it is usually supposed to possess all the above mentioned criteria of homogeneity, coherence and dual relevance. Finally, it has been claimed that all such personality models are identical types of logical constructs and belong to the same universe of discourse, in the broad sense in which triangles, squares, pentagons . . . and circles are all polygons belonging to the domain of plane geometry.

This chapter seeks to disprove the belief that all "modal" personality constructs used in culture and personality studies are, in fact, specimens of one and the same category of logical constructs. It will be demonstrated that there are actually at least two ways in which current models of "modal" personalities have been constructed and that each of these two procedures produces a distinctive, *sui generis* model of the "modal" personality. These two models do not differ from each other in form and content only, the way the model of the "Mohave male" may differ from the conjugate model of the "Mohave female," or from the non-conjugate model of the "Hottentot female." Actually these models belong to wholly different conceptual species, having different relevances and demanding to be used in wholly different ways. It is unfortunate that there should—almost inevitably—exist two logically distinct types of models of the "modal" personality. It is infinitely worse that this fact is so systematically ignored, that the two models are treated as interchangeable. Yet, because social scientists and psychologists ask entirely different questions, they must, of necessity, construct different models of the "modal" personality, if they are to find meaningful answers within their own frames of reference.

Those social scientists who are not exponents of the extreme culturological position and take cognizance of the existence of real people, seek to develop the kind of model of "modal" personality which will explain the type of cooperative, or conjugate, or parallel action on the part of many individuals, which permits the unfolding of social and cultural processes. The question such social scientists ask, with various degrees of sophistication, is: "Given all the known facts about society and culture, what characteristics must I *impute* to real people to make their actualization of social and cultural processes understandable?" A typical "modal" personality model evolved in order to answer this question is "the economic man," whom no one ever met in the flesh, for the good and sufficient reason that he does not exist. The logical construction process which culminates in the model of "the economic man" is fundamentally the same as the one which culminated in certain learning theorists' model of the "stat rat," which, even though it does not exist, is a construct or "thought token" enabling one to build one type of logically coherent pattern out of disparate facts related to "learning."

The psychologist who is not too biologically oriented, nor too individual-centered, to ignore society and culture is faced with one of two tasks:

(1) Whenever he observes certain biologically inexplicable con-

gruences between the behavior of two or more individuals, he seeks to develop the kind of model of society and culture which renders these congruences understandable. In so doing he may develop models of society and culture which are quite as esoteric and quite as unsociologistic and unculturalistic as the social scientist's concept of "economic man" is unpsychologistic. He may then, by circular reasoning, explain these psychological uniformities of behavior in terms of a psychologistic model of society and culture, exactly as the naïve social scientist circularly explains socio-cultural uniformities in terms of a sociologistic model of man.

(2) The more sophisticated psychologist, aware of society and culture, will construct a "modal" personality which, by social and cultural means, can be made to fit the prevailing socio-cultural climate and to operate in a manner which implements social and cultural processes. The key characteristic ascribed to this model is socio-cultural teachability, reinforced by a primary orientation to society and culture.

This model of man is definitely psychologistic though its systematic use tends to produce, in the long run, a habitual lack of concern with the non-socio-cultural aspects of the personality. Where the "stat rat" of at least some extreme learning theorists has practically no sensorium and is made up almost entirely of an imaginary sort of "inner motor," which has only the remotest connection with the real neurophysiology of living rats, the "stat human" of the culture-and-personality extremist seems to be all sensorium and no "inner works" or backbone. At this point the extremist, though remaining a psychologist, comes singularly close to the exponent of superorganic or culturalistic extremism.[1] The extreme culturalist position in culture and personality studies is held by the neo-Freudians. Probably because they can do so only by fleeing everything reminding them of the non-socio-cultural segment of man's personality, they have managed to be accepted by many anti-psychological anthropologists and sociologists as more "modern" and more "realistic" than Freud. At this point it seems expedient to turn to a set of carefully documented facts, obtained from a group of some seventy recent Hungarian refugees by a multidisciplinary team which included the present writer.

THE RELATIONSHIP BETWEEN PSYCHOLOGICAL AND SOCIAL ANALYSES OF ACTUAL BEHAVIOR

The type of motivation in terms of which certain historians and political scientists tried to explain the participation of *actual* persons in the 1956 Hungarian Revolution (see Society for the Investigation of Human Ecology, 1958) proved, on careful psychological scrutiny, to have played an almost negligible role in the case of those individuals who actively participated in that struggle. Whenever such a discrepancy between the explanations of two types of behavioral scientists occurs, it is a methodological error—especially at first—to tackle the problem primarily in terms of concrete facts. Such discrepancies are best approached by determining the actual relationship between the divergent frames of reference with which the contending disciplines operate.

In such cases one deals essentially with the vexing problem of the real relationship between psychological–psychiatric (subjective) and socio-cultural-historical-economic-political (collective) explanations of human phenomena. These two sets of disciplines study radically different phenomena. The basic difference between the two subject matters can be clarified most easily by means of an analogy from physical science. (1) The behavior of the individual, when seen as an *individual,* and not in terms of his membership in human society, is understandable only in a specifically psychological frame of reference and in terms of psychological laws *sui generis.* In the same sense, the behavior of the *individual molecule* in a given gas model must be understood in terms of classical mechanics, dealing with reversible phenomena. (2) The behavior of a group, seen as *a group,* and not primarily as an aggregate of discrete individuals, is understandable only in terms of a specific sociologistic frame of reference and in terms of socio-cultural laws *sui generis.* In the same sense, the behavior of the gas model as a whole must be understood in terms of statistical mechanics pertaining to irreversible phenomena (Devereux, 1940).

Somewhere between these two extremes lies a borderline or transitional set of phenomena, whose usual locus is the small group. We may define as "small" any group in which the over-all interaction pattern is about equally determined by, or equally understandable in terms of, the individual makeup of the individuals composing it *and* in terms of the fact that these discrete individuals constitute a group. In such cases it is possible to explain even certain group events equally satisfactorily in exclusively social-collective *and* in exclusively psychological-individual terms. The extent to which this is possible depends primarily on the number of the members. As their number increases, exclusively psychological-individual explanations account for increasingly smaller, and more and more peripheral, portions of the total group behavior, causing the explanations to become increasingly vague. A good physical analogy is the fact that the behavior of two bodies in relative motion to each other can be fully and precisely accounted for in terms of classical mechanics. By contrast, the behavior of three or more bodies can be described only approximately in terms of classical mechanics because the problem of three bodies has never been solved in general terms.

Moreover, such approximations become less and less accurate as the number of bodies in relative motion to each other increases. Hence, at the point where the number of bodies to be studied becomes unmanageably large, it becomes more efficient, economical and accurate to ignore the individual particles and to study instead the system, or aggregate itself, in terms of statistical mechanics. In so doing, one not only shifts one's frame of reference, but even seeks to obtain new and different kinds of results. The relevance of this analogy for an understanding of the difference between the psychological and the social is obvious (Devereux 1940, 1945, 1955, 1958).

Thus, in abstract terms, the question is never: "At what point do individuals and individual phenomena become irrelevant and society and social phenomena all important?"—nor vice versa, of course. The real question is simply this: "At what point is it more economical to use the sociological, rather than the psychological approach?" The same is true, *mutatis mutandis,* in regard to the nature-nurture controversy (Devereux 1945).

Where only individuals and relatively small groups are concerned, the actual outcome of a given process can be equally effectively predicted and equally fully explained either sociologically or psychologically. Thus, it was possible to show (Devereux 1960) that the self-incited (provoked) murder of a Mohave lesbian witch was as absolutely inevitable in terms of Mohave cultural mandates as in terms of that witch's distinctive and unique personality makeup. Moreover, in this case, and in numerous others as well, there is an almost incredibly compendious, perfect and subtle dovetailing of individual and socio-cultural processes: each intrapsychic development mobilizes certain reinforcing cultural mandates and each cultural response mobilizes reinforcing subjective motives and processes. The real objective is not to determine whether the phenomenon is "ultimately" a psychological or a socio-cultural one, but to analyze, as precisely as possible, the dovetailing, interplay and mutual reinforcement (most often through a "feedback") of the psychological and socio-cultural factors involved.

The possibility of adequately predicting and understanding an event in terms of a particular frame of reference, such as psychology, does not mean in the least that the phenomenon is primarily a psychological one and that equally satisfactory explanations and predictions could not have been formulated in socio-cultural terms. Indeed, even though any frame of reference necessarily uses and operates in terms of *partial* abstractions, it can, nonetheless, provide an *operationally* satisfactory and "complete" explanation and prediction of a given phenomenon. A failure to grasp this point is largely responsible for Kroeber's (1948) recurrent objections to alleged attempts to "reduce" anthropology to psychology.

Even more important perhaps is the fact that there appears to obtain a quite genuine complementarity relationship between the individual (psychological) and the socio-cultural (collective) understanding of a given phenomenon (Devereux 1945, 1958). Thus, the more fully I understand John Doe's anger over the arrival of his mother-in-law in socio-cultural terms (autonomy of the U.S. nuclear family, the traditional stereotype of the mother-in-law, etc.) the less I can understand it *simultaneously* in psychological terms (John's irritability, his wife's infantile dependency on her mother, the mother-in-law's meddlesomeness, etc.)—and vice versa, of course. It is logically impossible to think simultaneously in terms of two different frames of reference, especially if, in terms of one of these, the key explanation is: "All mothers-in-law are defined by our culture as nuisances," while in the other system the key explanation is: "Mrs. Roe systematically interferes with her daughter's marriage." Needless to say, the same complementarity relationship also obtains between the sociological and the psychological understanding of phenomena involving large groups and nations. This accounts for many of the exquisite complexities of problems involving "national character" and of many problems in social psychology as well. The difficulty is simply that *consistent* thinking in terms of, for instance, the psychological frame of reference makes it impossible to think, *at the same moment,* also in *consistently* socio-cultural terms.

The social scientist is, thus, literally forced to develop an individual "psychology" to fit his data. In order to understand how a large scale phenomenon can be produced by an inherently heterogeneous collection of individuals, he must assume that these individuals function in accordance with a series of pseudo psychological specifications. This "as if" approach is quite legitimate, but only in regard to that particular set of phenomena,[2] and only as long as one knows that one is dealing with "thought tokens" and "thought experiments." What is *not* legitimate—though it is done day after day—is to go one step further and ascribe or impute to the real and living individual members of that group the specific characteristics ascribed to the explanatory *model* of man. Such a procedure is as scurrilous as though a student of statistical mechanics said: "Since certain gas molecules go from the denser segments of the gas model to the less dense portions thereof, they obviously wish to escape crowding." This is strange reasoning indeed. Yet, it is precisely the type of reasoning used by some historians and political scientists who assume that everyone who rebels and fights against an economically unfair and politically oppressive system has been personally underpaid and harassed. No matter how sophisticated the manner in which such a statement is made, it is still factually incorrect and logically fallacious.

The reverse process—psychologistic sociologizing—is equally illegitimate. Since man is, both actually and by definition, a social being, even the student of the individual must learn to view him as part of a society and as the product of a culture. For example, if one is a Freudian, one must explore and clarify the nexus between the superego, the ego ideal and the patterning of ego functions on the one hand, and the structure of the socio-cultural matrix on the other hand. This is both necessary and legitimate. What is by no means legitimate, however, is the transposition of conceptual models pertaining to the individual to the socio-cultural system as a whole, and the interpretation of the socio-cultural structure and process *purely* in terms of the psychology of the individual, even if he does happen to belong to the society whose structure and processes one "interprets" in this manner. Specifically, and in simplest terms, the Constitution of the United States *is* not and can never *be* the "superego" or the "ego ideal" of American society. Moreover, it can never *function* in that capacity within that—or any other—society, for the good and sufficient reason that society does not have a superego or an ego ideal, any more than the psyche of an individual has a Constitution or a Supreme Court. What can and does happen, is that a particular individual may *incorporate* into his psyche —but only in the form of psychological materials—certain aspects of his society and culture and then *assign* these incorporated psychic representations of outer socio-cultural realities to the sphere of his superego or of his ego ideal. A jurist may subjectively adapt his superego to the Constitution, while a pious Catholic may adapt his to the Creed of the Apostles. Conversely, in times of stress, society may change its formal tenets to fit the average superego needs of the citizen. All this does not make the Constitution a social superego, nor the superego a psychic Constitution.

The social scientist must view his conception of "modal" man as a model valid only in the study of social phenomena, just as the psychologist must view his conception of society and culture as valid only in the study of individual phenomena. In the individual–psychological universe of discourse, society and culture are simply means for the implementation of subjective needs and psychic mechanisms, just as in the collective–sociological universe of discourse individual psychic structures and processes are simply means for the implementation of the collective needs and mechanisms of the socio-cultural system.

A summary analysis of facts and fancies regarding the actual motivation of individual Hungarians—as distinct from the "motivation" of the Hungarian people—who revolted against the system under which brute force on the part of their enemies and timid tergiversation on the part of their friends obliged them to live—will demonstrate with striking clarity the points just made.

MOTIVATION OF THE HUNGARIAN FREEDOM FIGHTER

A tabulation of the conscious motivation of individual Hungarian freedom fighters revealed that many of them had no genuinely personal experiences with cynical exploitation and brute oppression. In fact, quite a few of them were in relatively privileged positions and, externally at least, better off than they might have been under the Horthy regime. Hence, some political scientists held that those fighters who had no *private* grievances of a tangible type—and may even have had much to lose by participating in the revolution—were effectively and subjectively actuated by their indignation over the inherent viciousness of the system and the brazenness of alien rule, or else by national pride and the like. In so interpreting the motivation of these *individuals,* these political scientists actually ascribed to individuals certain characteristics of a sociologistic "modal" personality construct, developed strictly in order to account for collective participation in mass movements and social processes.

It is true, of course, that some of those who had no real personal grievances did, themselves, interpret their conduct in terms of sociologistic and socially respectable motives, such as patriotism, love of freedom and the like. It would, indeed, be quite fallacious to deny that they were in part actuated by such motives, which are essentially components of the sociologistically conceived motivational structure of the sociologist's construct of the "modal" personality.

Unfortunately, this explanation of the active fighting in which these persons had voluntarily engaged, raises more questions than it solves. It leaves unexplained at least the following challenging facts:

(1) Those fighters who did have private and personal grievances and did cite these grievances in explanation of their participation in combat did not, in general, explain their own conduct *also* in terms of patriotism and the like, or at least did not explain it *primarily* and *convincingly* on those terms. This raises the question whether admittedly gallant fighters, who did have personal grievances, were simply unpatriotic and unidealistic individuals, seeking to exact an eye for an eye and a tooth for a tooth. A supplementary question is whether those who, despite unpleasant personal experiences with the Communist system, did *not* fight, were unidealistic, unpatriotic, or cowardly, or else simply pious Christians, who refuse to kill and who leave vengeance to the Lord.

(2) The second, and theoretically more relevant, question is

whether it has not become customary to cite sociologistically conceived motives *only* where *no information* about the individual's subjective motivation is available. In practice, it is precisely this criterion which is used in courts of law to determine the legitimacy of a plea of "not guilty by reason of insanity." A careful scrutiny of what actually happens when such a plea is made, shows that the plea is accepted only if the judge and the jury do *not* seem able to "understand" what could cause a person to commit such a crime. The accused is held to be "not guilty by reason of insanity" if his judges *cannot emphathize* with his *deed, as distinct from his motivation.* Once the court feels that the *deed* itself is understandable in terms of the layman's conception of "common sense" (i.e., sociologistically defined) motives, the plea of insanity is nearly always rejected. Hardly ever is there an attempt to inquire into the accused's *real,* instead of *imputed,* motivation. Yet, only an understanding of the accused's real motives enables one to determine in a valid manner whether or not his seemingly "understandable" deed *actually* had the "sane" motivation *imputed* to it by judge and jury.

The fact is that if the list of non-subjective reasons for the individual fighter's participation in the revolution is supplemented by certain psychiatric insights, derived from data provided by the same informants to the interviewing psychiatrist (Dr. F. Kane) and to the present writer, one suddenly realizes that even these socio-culturally motivated individuals were also motivated in a highly subjective manner, though their motivation may not have been entirely conscious to them, and may have had no direct relationship to the social issues of the 1956 revolution.

The simple fact is that, as a Roman common sense psychologist pointed out long ago: *"Si bis faciunt idem, non est idem"* (If two people do the same thing, it is not necessarily the same thing). Where one man revolts because he had been exploited, another because, twelve years earlier, the Russians had raped his wife, another because he hates all authority, still another may revolt because he wishes to impress his girl friend with his patriotism and valor. All these men may fight with equal ardor, kill an equal number of secret police and Russians, and therefore achieve *militarily and socially identical results. Psychologically, however, the results may not be the same.* Thus the one who thought that he fought from idealism may, in the long run, experience fewer guilt feelings than will the one who sought to destroy a hated father image by killing a secret police captain or the one who, at great personal risk and with conspicuous courage, blew up a Russian tank to impress his girl friend or to reaffirm his membership in a nation noted for its valor.

An interesting case is that of a gentle, well-behaved and well brought up teen age Jewish girl, who, at the risk of her life, carried hand grenades to the active fighters. Except for the routine nationalization of her father's luxury goods store, this girl's family had not been particularly persecuted by the Communists. On the other hand, while she was still quite small, this girl and her family had been cruelly persecuted by the Nazis, and had twice escaped execution at the very last moment. Speaking in terms of so-called common sense (sociologistic) psychology, the last person on earth who had real and "obvious" reasons to risk her life in the revolutionary fighting was this girl. Moreover, given her sweet and gentle disposition, she was the last person one would—using a "common sense" conception of the personality—have expected to engage in violence, be it but to the extent of carrying hand grenades to the fighters.

On closer scrutiny, however, it became obvious that this girl, who had been a helpless child during the Nazi regime, was abreacting, twelve years later, her hatred of oppression and of oppressors. The most telling proof of this is the fact that she merely *carried* grenades to the fighters, but—unlike some other teen age girls—did not lob them personally at the foe, though, in so doing, she would have incurred little additional risk. In other words, she functioned in the revolution simply as a gallant *child,* doing what even a child can do: bring ammunition to adult fighters, as did countless children raised on the American frontier.

Many other examples of unconscious motivations of an authentically subjective nature, hiding behind a conscious façade of sociologistic motivation, could be given. This, however, would represent only a laboring of the obvious.

The real point to be stressed is that *both organized and spontaneous social movements and processes are possible not because all individuals participating in them are identically (and sociologistically) motivated, but because a variety of authentically subjective motives may seek and find an ego syntonic outlet in the same type of collective activity.* This is equally true of spontaneous revolutionary movements and of extreme conformity. Indeed, there are few groups so rent by internecine squabbles as revolutionary cells and hyperconformist organizations. Moreover, just as a revolutionary may fight because he hates father figures, or because he has personal grievances, or else because he wishes to impress his girl friend, so a man may be a hyperconformist from sheer opportunism, from a fear of his own spontaneity, or else because emotionally he still needs his mother's approval.

The way in which the subjective motivations of various individuals find an outlet in the same type of activity, be it revolutionary or conventional, is rather uniform, as far as social effects are concerned. Individual differences in real motivation find a behavioral expression only in differences in the specific details of one's fighting pattern or conformity. Yet, though socially often unimportant, these individual motivational differences may determine intense psychological reactions to the deed which one has performed as a member of a collectivity. Just as the conscious idealist among revolutionaries will, in the long run, probably experience fewer guilt feelings and self punitive urges than the one who killed an anonymous oppressor *instead* of killing his father, so the conformist actuated by a loyalty to the existing system will feel less shame in an hour of lonely self-appraisal than will the cowardly opportunist.

The real theoretical import of the finding that many, highly divergent, types of conscious and unconscious subjective motives can impel people to seek gratification through participation in a given social process is that it *simplifies* rather than *complicates* the possibility of obtaining a *psychological* understanding of the motivational structure of participation. Indeed—taking the Hungarian Revolution of 1956 as our paradigm— were we to assume that all freedom fighters were identically "motivated" (in the sociologistic sense of that term) we would have "solved" the problem of motivation only to be confronted with an even more complex problem. We would have to explain the mystery of a sudden and synchronous mass intensification of one type of motivation or need at a given point in history. At the same time, we would also have to account for its prolonged latency and non-exacerbation from 1944 to 1956. Figuratively speaking, we would have to imagine a single, massive, but subterranean torrent erupting suddenly and inexplicably from the ground, in a single huge explosion. By contrast, if we use the model of multiple psychologistic motivations, all of which can derive a certain amount of gratification from a given collective act, we have to imagine only a very commonplace river, fed by a variety of tiny tributaries coming from various directions.

Hence, it is sufficient to postulate that a large number of differently motivated persons may come to perceive a given historical moment or event as *suitable* for the gratification of their various subjective needs. In the psychological frame of reference, this position enables us to see the Hungarian revolution of October 1956 as a sudden opportunity and means for the actualization and gratification of a variety of private needs, which had been present all along. Moreover, we can visualize various items of "motivation" formulated by some sound sociologists, historians and political scientists—nationalism, class struggle, resistance to oppression, idealism, etc.—as psychologically *instrumental* motives, which render ego syntonic, and not *only* socially acceptable, the acting out of certain needs. Were these needs acted out privately, they would not only be unsanctioned socially, but would also be highly anxiety arousing and productive of intense guilt feelings. Conversely, in the sociologistic frame of reference, this position permits us to view the variety of preexisting and highly individualized needs and motives as the raw material from which a social process, spontaneous or traditional, can crystallize just as a variety of fuels, when thrown in the same furnace, can heat the same boiler.

These considerations do not imply that one must discard, as useless and senseless, the sociologistic motivational structure of a given model of the "modal personality." Indeed, a variety of differently and highly subjectively motivated individuals may find that one and the same process in society at large can provide certain long desired gratifications. If they gratify their needs by participation in this social process, they may be able to render the necessary gratifying acts more ego syntonic than if these acts had to be performed privately. Thus, people go to church for many reasons: to seem respectable; because of piety, and all that piety implies in the unconscious; to show off a new Easter bonnet, and so on. All derive some gratification from this act, even though they are not actuated by a homogeneous set of motives, nor by one massive social motive. Their actual motives, when juxtaposed, form nothing more than a conglomerate, which can be studied only as a conglomerate and not as a motivational torrent, since each qualitatively different motivational "unit" present in that conglomerate will be gratified by the collective act in a different way, and to a different extent.

The difference in the degree of gratification obtainable in this manner is of some importance. One young Hungarian freedom fighter, who fought with real courage and efficiency, would certainly have been a great deal happier had he been able to fight from the deck of a battleship flying the banner of the Holy Virgin, "Patrona Hungariae," not because he was an expert sailor or a religious traditionalist, but for purely subjective reasons. He could think of nothing more glorious than Naval Service (Horthy was an admiral!) unless it was a holy and virginal woman. Yet, this naïve worshipper of the Navy and of virgins fought as well as another, almost delinquent, young worker, who simply hated fathers and father representatives, or as well as still another worker, who was angry over Rakosi's betrayal of the idealistic-socialistic "essence" of communism, or another who had actually suffered persecution. The Russians which each of these men killed were, moreover, equally dead.

In brief, one must sharply differentiate between psychologistic conceptions of motivation and sociologistic conceptions of motivation, both in the construction of models of "modal personality" and in the interpretation of participation in social movements.

In the psychologistic model the motivation is and must be subjective. Hence, the motivational structure of the "modal" personality of a given group must be made up of motives and needs which are systematically stimulated—either through constant and expectable gratification or through systematic frustration—in that society. In the sociologistic model, the motivation must be collective and the motivational structure of the "modal" personality of a given group must be constructed out of the type of "common sense" motives which the social scientist must impute to all members of a given group in order to be able to explain their participation in collective activities: patriotism, economic self-interest, idealism, traditional conformism and the like.

In a sound culture-and-personality theory, the psychologist's conception of the "modal" personality's motivation will be considered as "operant" and the sociologistic conception of the "modal" personality's motivation will be considered as "instrumental." In interpretations, these two sets of motives will be brought into play only consecutively, because one cannot think of the same phenomenon simultaneously both in sociologistic and in psychologistic terms. The common denominator of individual motivations which are statistically frequent in a given society will be *defined* as the true operant mainsprings of social actions. The sociologistic type of motivation obtaining in that culture and society —and closely related to its value system—will be *defined* as the instrumental motivational means for the gratification of the more basic needs.

This theory *does not* undermine the sociologistic interpretation of collective events. It *does* show that the psychologistic definition of the "modal" personality's motivation leads to a science of operant motives, whereas its sociologistic definition forms the basis of a science of instrumental motives, or of "outlets." This view, implies that society and culture provide, by means of something like a feedback mechanism, supplementary motivations which do not modify the initial operant motivation of the personalities but reinforce, trigger and channel them, by making their implementation ego syntonic and by providing the occasion, and often also the means for their implementation and gratification. This explains why a single exasperated but decent man may *not* be able to bring himself to shoot down secretly the Gestapo, MVD or AVO man representing a hated father figure, although he *will* be able to do so if society provides him with the means of defining his act as an ethical and patriotic one. Psychologically, this way of defining the situation may be a simple "rationalization," facilitating the performance of acts leading to gratification. Sociologically, however, this definition of the act represents also its sanctioning. Thereafter the sanctioning itself functions as a *bona fide* motive, but only instrumentally, and only insofar as the *execution* of a subjectively desired act is concerned.

This thesis implies, in turn, that one must sharply differentiate between substantive, subjective and operant motives which are often quite unconscious, and externally provided instrumental motives pertaining to the actualization of behavior permitting need gratification. The psychologizing social scientist must know that his proper universe of discourse, in the psychological frame of reference, is the problem of instrumental motives. The sociologizing psychologist must know that his proper sociological universe of discourse is the actualization of substantive basic needs, representing operant motives, through socially provided means, which, in sociology but not in psychology, can also function as instrumental motives.

CONCLUSION

Any explanation of behavior which uses the conceptual structures known as models of "modal personality" must consist of a series of steps:

(1) The first, psychologistic, step is the listing of the real motives of the actual participants in a given collective activity. These motives may be discovered through interviewing techniques, psychological tests, psychoanalytic procedures and other psychological means.

(2) This list serves as a basis for the construction of a psychologistic model of the modal personality, whose need-and-motivation structure is limited to those needs which are statistically prevalent in, and appear to be closely linked to the structure of a particular society-and-culture.

(3) Next, it must be specified that the needs-and-motivations ascribed to this model of the "modal" personality can be, jointly and severally, gratified in various social or cultural sub-contexts such as participation in rituals, in parties, in revolutions, in counter-revolutions, or in the acceptance of certain mandates of culture, in certain attitudes, and so forth.

(4) Next, a sociologistic model of the modal personality must be constructed, to which are *ascribed* needs-and-motives that explain sociologically—in terms of a social "common sense" psychology related to value systems—the actual participation of individuals in a given social process. This list may include terms like economic interest, patriotism, piety, class consciousness, or conformism.

(5) This list of sociologically meaningful "motives" is then psychologized, by being redefined as "instrumental." These motives then serve to sanction actual individual maneuvers seeking to gratify subjective and genuinely psychologically "operant" needs and motives; they are also means for the actualization of gratification seeking behavior.

Of these five steps only the fifth and last permits the formulation of statements genuinely pertaining to, and relevant in terms of, the culture-and-personality frame of reference.

NOTES

1. It is probably more than a coincidence that the most extreme current exponent of the culturological position took his Master's degree in psychology at a time when the most primitive sort of behaviorism dominated all learning theory and most of American psychology.

2. In order to grasp the significance of this specification, it suffices to imagine what would happen were an economist to decide to fill in existing "gaps" in the present model of "economic man" and wrote a paper on "The sexual and love life of economic man." His essay would be too weird even for a science fiction magazine.

BIBLIOGRAPHY

Devereux, George. 1940. "A Conceptual Scheme of Society," *American Journal of Sociology*, 54:687–706.

———. 1945. "The Logical Foundations of Culture and Personality Studies," *Transactions of the New York Academy of Sciences*, Series II. 7:110–30.

———. 1955. *A Study of Abortion in Primitive Societies*. New York: Julian.

———. 1958. "The Anthropological Roots of Psychoanalysis." In Masserman, J. H. (ed.), *Science and Psychoanalysis, I: Integrative Studies*. New York: Grune and Stratton. 73–84, 171–3.

———. 1960. *Mohave Ethnopsychiatry and Suicide*. Bureau of American Ethnology, Bulletin No. 175. Washington; Government Printing Office.

Kroeber, Alfred L. 1948. *Anthropology*. (New, revised edition.) New York: Harcourt, Brace.

Society for the Investigation of Human Ecology. 1958. Second Seminar on the Hungarian Revolution of October 1956. Forest Hills, L.I., N.Y. Society for the Investigation of Human Ecology, Inc. (Mimeographed). (See papers by Hinkle and by Stephenson and discussion by Devereux.)

About the Chapter

The author of this chapter is a historian who is concerned with the problem of character change in the American Negro in the eighteenth and nineteenth centuries as he was detached from cultural backgrounds in Africa and subjected to slavery in the large plantations of the South. Dr. Elkins compares the Middle Passage and the closed system of slavery in the United States to the Nazi concentration camp and explains why both created a particular kind of character. The analysis focuses on the process of character change that occurs when social requirements are altered. Dr. Elkins suggests that character (or personality) is really a kind of action taken in response to socially defined alternatives. This view differs somewhat from the generally accepted belief that character develops into a more or less hard mold as a result of experiences during the socialization period.

About the Author

STANLEY M. ELKINS studied at Harvard and received his M.A. and Ph.D. degrees in history from Columbia. He is the author of *Slavery: A Problem in American Institutional and Intellectual Life,* and is currently at work on a study of politics and culture in 19th century America. Mr. Elkins is now assistant professor of social sciences at the University of Chicago.

Acknowledgment

Portions of this essay have been incorporated into the author's more extensive study entitled *Slavery: A Problem in American Institutional and Intellectual Life*, published by the University of Chicago Press in 1959.

7

Slavery and Personality

STANLEY ELKINS

University of Chicago

1. PERSONALITY TYPES AND STEREOTYPES.

The study by Gunnar Myrdal of the American Negro, and the great variety of writing on that subject done in the late 1930s and early 1940s under Myrdal's direct or indirect inspiration, left a vast deposit of knowledge. The by-products, on the whole, have been salutary and enlightening. There was one consequence, however, of this intense intellectual involvement with the Negro problem in American life that may not have fully operated in the interests of enlightenment. This by-product was a moral embargo on generalizations about Negro personality types. Since "race" has been so completely and so properly discredited as an explanation for any aspect of human behavior, the application of personality stereotypes—which for the American Negro have meant virtually the same thing as race stereotypes—can hardly have helped falling into similar discredit. None of us believes in race any more. Yet a great many of us have had the disturbing suspicion that in censoring the once-familiar "Sambo" stereotype from all forms of discourse, we have actually been rather furtively sweeping something under the rug. For present-day society, in all its complexity, we may

243

have been doing the right thing. But for a historical reconstruction of Negro personality in slavery times, such a taboo may not be justified.

In this chapter, at any rate, we shall lift the embargo and assume that, as a generalization, the Southerner's description of "Sambo," the antebellum plantation slave, is essentially trustworthy. This picture referred not necessarily to a universal type, but to a dominant plantation type, and well over 50 per cent of the antebellum slaves lived on the large plantations. "Sambo," in Southern lore, was docile but irresponsible, loyal but lazy, humble but addicted to lying and stealing; his behavior was full of infantile silliness and his talk inflated with childish exaggeration. His relationship to his master was one of utter dependence and childlike attachment: it was this *childlike* quality that was the very key to his being. Our strategy here will be not to challenge either the existence of the type, or even the rough accuracy of its description. Rather we shall take that much for granted, and consider instead how to account for the development of such a type over a wide range of the slave population. What, in short, were the conditions, and what were the mechanisms, that could sustain infantilism within the structure of antebellum slavery?

In contrast to the looseness and openness of structure found in the legal and social arrangements of Latin American slavery, the plantation system of the United States was essentially a closed system. The sanctions of authority were virtually self-contained within the plantation unit. Authority, though exercised, by and large, for non-malignant ends, was absolute. The "given," then, for the present purpose, is absolute power in a closed system, and the problem for personality is that of adjustment to such power within such a system.

Two kinds of material will be invoked in an effort to picture the mechanisms whereby this adjustment, whose end-product included infantile features of personality, may have been effected. One is drawn from the theoretical knowledge presently available in social psychology, and the other—in the form of an analogy—is derived from some of the data that have come out of the German concentration camps. Most theory holds that social behavior is regulated in some general way by adjustment to symbols of authority—however diversely "authority" may be defined, either in theory or in culture itself—and that this adjustment is closely related to the very formation of personality. The more diverse those symbols of authority are, the greater is the permissible variety of adjustment to them—and the wider the margin of individuality, consequently, in the development of the self. The question here concerns the wideness or narrowness of that margin on the antebellum plantation.

The other body of material, involving an experience undergone by several million men and women in the concentration camps of our own time, contains certain items of relevance to our problem. The experience was analogous to that of slavery, and was one in which wide-scale instances of infantilization were observed. The material is sufficiently detailed, and sufficiently documented by men who not only took part in the experience itself but who were versed in the use of psychological theory for analyzing it, that the possible advantages of drawing upon these data for purposes of analogy seem to outweigh the risks—the risks being those of not using the material intelligently.

The introduction of this second body of material must to a certain extent govern the theoretical strategy itself. It has been recognized both implicitly and explicitly that the psychic impact and effects of the concentration camp experience were not anticipated in existing theory, and that consequently such theory would require some major supplementation. It might be added, parenthetically, that almost any published discussion of this modern Inferno, no matter how learned, demonstrates how "theory," operating at such a level of shared human experience, tends to shed much of its technical trappings and to take on almost a literary quality. The experience showed, in any event, that infantile personality features could be induced in a relatively short time among large numbers of adult human beings coming from very diverse backgrounds. The particular strain which was thus placed upon prior theory consisted in the need to make room not only for the cultural and environmental sanctions that sustain personality—which Freudian theory already had—but also for a virtually unanticipated problem: actual change in the personality of masses of adults. Hence came a reappraisal and new appreciation of how completely and effectively prior cultural sanctions for behavior and personality could be detached to make way for new and different sanctions, and of how adjustments could be made to a species of authority vastly different from any previously known. One of the revelations for theory, in short, was the process of detachment.

These cues, accordingly, will guide the argument on Negro slavery. Several million people were detached with a peculiar effectiveness from a great variety of cultural backgrounds in Africa—a detachment operating with infinitely more effectiveness upon those brought to North America than on those who came to Latin America. Detachment was achieved partly by the shock experience inherent in the very mode of procurement, but most especially by the type of authority-system to which these people were introduced and to which they had to adjust for physical and psychic survival. The new adjustment to absolute power in a closed system involved infantilization. The detachment was so complete that little trace of prior—and thus alternative—cultural sanctions for behavior and personality remained for the descendants of the first generation. For them, adjustment to clear and omnipresent authority could be more or less automatic—as much so, or as little, as it is for anyone whose adjustment to a social system begins at birth and to whom that system represents normality. We do not know how generally the full adjustment was made during the first generation of fresh slaves from Africa. But we do know—from a modern experience—that such an adjustment was possible: not only within the same generation but within two or three years. It was possible even for a people in a full state of complex civilization—for men and women who were not black and not savages.

2. SHOCK AND DETACHMENT.

Just as no set of characteristics, Sambo-like or otherwise, may possibly be accounted for in terms of "race" or "inborn nature," so must another "explanation" for Negro character, the one which hinges upon survivals of African culture, likewise be eliminated. The slave traders of the eighteenth century were themselves aware that there was no such thing as a particular "African" type; they recognized, as their writings show, a wide diversity in physical, temperamental, and cultural types; and they had to be sensitive to the great variety of customs, social and political arrangements, and languages of the people with whom they had to deal. Slaves were brought to them from many different places. Not only were their own trading stations scattered along an immense stretch of the West African coast, but to each station slave coffles usually were brought from great distances inland, sometimes hundreds of miles. The result, in sheer diversity, does much to undermine any effort to generalize about African cultural types and cultural survivals. Even if we could in fact make out such continuities, they would be so general as to be of very little value in explaining either the individual or social behavior of slaves on our American plantations. The fact is that every African who became a slave—whether light or dark, timid or warlike, primitive or in a high state of culture—underwent an experience whose crude psychic impact must have been staggering, and whose consequences superseded anything that had ever previously happened to him.

The majority of slaves were taken in native wars. This meant that no one—neither persons of high rank nor warriors of prowess—was guaranteed against capture and enslavement. Great numbers were caught in surprise attacks upon their villages. Since the tribes acting as middlemen for the trade had come to depend on regular supplies of captives in order to maintain that function, the distinction between wars and raiding expeditions was rather dim. The first shock, in an experience destined to endure many months and to leave its survivors irrevocably changed, was thus the shock of capture. The second one, the long march to the sea, drew out the nightmare for many weeks. Under the glaring sun, through the steaming jungle, they were driven along like beasts tied together by their necks. Hardship, brutalities, thirst, and near-starvation penetrated the experience of each exhausted man and woman who reached the coast. The next shock—aside from the fresh physical torments which accompanied it—was the sale to the European slavers. After having been crowded into pens near the trading stations and kept there sometimes for days, the slaves would be brought out for examination. Those rejected were abandoned to starvation; the remaining ones—those who had been bought—were branded, given numbers inscribed on leaden tags, and herded on shipboard. The episode that followed—almost too protracted and stupefying to be called a mere "shock"—was the dread Middle Passage, brutalizing to any man, black or white, who was involved in it. The holds, packed with squirming and suffocating humanity, became stinking infernos of filth and pestilence, savagery and death. Stories of the things that happened on the terrible two months' voyage darken the testimony which did much toward ending the British slave trade forever.

The final shock in the process of enslavement came with the Negro's introduction to the West Indies. Bryan Edwards, describing the arrival of a slave ship, writes of how in times of labor scarcity crowds of people would come scrambling aboard, manhandling the slaves and throwing them into panic. The Jamaica legislature eventually "corrected the enormity" by enacting that the sales be held on shore. Seeing the Negroes exposed naked in public, Edwards felt a certain mortification, similar to that felt by the trader Degrandpré at seeing them examined back at the African factories. Yet here they did not seem to care. "They display . . . very few signs of lamentation for their past or of apprehension for their future condition; but . . . commonly express great eagerness to be sold" (Edwards, 1806, p. 340). The "seasoning" process which followed completed the series of steps whereby the African Negro became a slave.

The mortality had been very high. One-third of the numbers first taken, out of a total of perhaps fifteen million, had died on the march and at the trading stations; another third died during the Middle Passage and the seasoning. Since a majority of the African-born slaves who came to the North American plantations did not come directly but were imported through the British West Indies, one may assume that the typical slave underwent an experience something like that just outlined. This was the man—one in three—who was about to enter our "closed system." What would he be like if he survived and adjusted to that?

Actually, a great deal had happened to him already. Much of his past had been annihilated; nearly every prior connection had been severed. The old values, the tribal sanctions, the standards—already unreal—could no longer furnish him guides for conduct, for adjusting to the expectations of a completely new life. Where then was he to look for new standards, new cues? Who would furnish them now? He could now look to none but his master, the one man to whom the system had committed his entire being: the man upon whose will depended his food, his shelter, his sexual connections, whatever moral instruction he might be offered, whatever "success" was possible within the system, his very security—in short, everything.

The thoroughness with which African Negroes coming to America were detached from prior cultural sanctions should thus be partly explainable by the very shock sequence inherent in the technique of procurement. But it took something more than this to produce "Sambo." A comparable experience was also undergone by slaves coming into Latin America; but very little that resembled our "Sambo" tradition ever developed there. So whereas the Middle Passage and all that went with it must have been psychologically numbing, and should certainly be regarded as a long thrust toward the end product, its full fruition depended on the events that followed. The process of detachment was completed by the kind of authority-system into which the slave was introduced and to which he had to adjust—the "closed system" referred to above. At any rate, a test of this detachment and its thoroughness is virtually ready-made. Students of African cultural features among New World Negroes agree that the contrast between North America and Latin America is immense. In Brazil, according to Arthur Ramos, survivals from African religion and other institutional practices are not only encountered everywhere, but such carry-overs are so distinct that they may even be identified with particular tribal groups. Fernando Ortiz, writing of Cuba in 1905, considered the African witchcraft cults flourishing on the island a formidable social problem. One of our own anthropologists, on the other hand, despite much dedicated field work, has been put to great effort to prove that in North American Negro society any African cultural vestiges have survived at all.

3. ADJUSTMENT TO ABSOLUTE POWER IN THE CONCENTRATION CAMP.

The system of the concentration camps was expressly devised in the 1930s by high officials of the German government to function as an instrument of terror. The first groups detained in the camps consisted of prominent enemies of the Nazi regime. Later, when these had mostly been eliminated, it was still felt necessary to institutionalize the system and make it a standing weapon of intimidation—which required a continuing flow of incoming prisoners. The categories of eligible persons were greatly widened to include all real, fancied, or "potential" opposition to the state. Prisoners were often selected on capricious and random grounds. Together they formed a cross-section of society which was virtually complete: criminals, workers, businessmen, professional people, middle-class Jews, even members of the aristocracy. The teeming camps thus held all kinds—not only the scum of the underworld but also countless men and women of culture and refinement. During the war a specialized objective was added, that of exterminating the Jewish populations of subject countries. This required special mass-production methods of which the gas chambers and crematories of Auschwitz-Birkenau were outstanding examples. Yet the basic technique was everywhere and at all times the same: the deliberate infliction of various forms of torture upon the incoming prisoners in such a way as to break their resistance and make way for their degradation as individuals. These brutalities were not merely "permitted" or "encouraged"; they were prescribed.

The concentration camps and everything that took place in them were veiled in the utmost isolation and secrecy. Although a continuing stream of rumors circulated among the population, so repellent was the nature of these stories that in their enormity they transcended the experience of nearly everyone who heard them. In self-protection it was somehow necessary to persuade oneself that they could not really be true. The results, therefore, contained elements of the diabolical. The individual who actually became a prisoner was in most cases devastated with fright and utterly demoralized to discover that what was happening to him was not less, but rather far more terrible than anything he had imagined. The shock sequence of "procurement," therefore, together with the initial phases of the prisoner's introduction to camp life, is not without significance in assessing some of the psychic effects upon those who survived as long-term inmates.

The arrest was typically made at night, preferably late. This was standing Gestapo policy, designed to heighten the element of shock, terror, and unreality surrounding the arrest. After a day or so in the police jail came the next major shock, that of being transported to the camp itself. "This transportation into the camp, and the 'initiation' into it," wrote Bruno Bettelheim (1943, p. 424), an ex-inmate of Dachau and Buchenwald, "is often the first torture which the prisoner has ever experienced and is, as a rule, physically and psychologically the worst torture to which he will ever be exposed." It involved a planned series of brutalities inflicted by guards making repeated rounds through the train over a twelve to thirty-six hour period during which the prisoner was prevented from resting. If transported in cattle cars instead of passenger cars, the prisoners were sealed in, under conditions not dissimilar to those of the Middle Passage. Upon their arrival—if the camp were one in which mass exterminations were carried out—there might be sham ceremonies designed to reassure the exhausted prisoners temporarily. The fresh terrors in the offing would then strike them with redoubled impact. An SS officer might deliver an address, or a band might be playing popular tunes, and it would be in such a setting that the initial "selection" was made. The newcomers would file past an SS doctor who indicated, with a motion of the forefinger, whether they were to go to the left or to the right. To one side went those considered capable of heavy labor; to the other would go wide categories of "undesirables"; those in the latter group were being condemned to the gas chambers. The laborers would undergo the formalities of "registration," full of indignities, which culminated in the marking of each prisoner with a number.

Certain physical and psychological strains of camp life were especially debilitating in the early stages. These should be classed with the introductory shock sequence. There was a state of chronic hunger whose pressures were unusually effective in detaching prior scruples of all kinds; even the sexual instincts no longer functioned in the face of the drive for food. The man who at his pleasure could bestow or withhold food thus wielded, for that reason alone, abnormal power. Another strain at first was the demand for absolute obedience; the slightest deviation brought savage punishments. The prisoner had to ask permission—by no means granted as a matter of course—even to defecate. The power of the SS guard, as the prisoner was hourly reminded, was that of life and death. A more exquisite form of pressure lay in the fact that the prisoner had never a moment of solitude: he no longer had a private existence; it was no longer possible, in any imaginable sense, for him to be an "individual." Another factor having deep disintegrative effects upon the prisoner was the prospect of a limitless future in the camp. In the immediate sense this meant that he could no longer make plans for the future. But there would eventually be a subtler meaning: it made the break with the outside world a *real* break. In time the "real" life would become the life of the camp—the outside world an abstraction. Had it been a limited detention, whose end could be calculated, one's outside relationships—one's roles, one's very "personality"—might temporarily have been laid aside, to be reclaimed more or less intact at the end of the term. Here, however, the prisoner was faced with the apparent impossibility of his old roles or even his old personality ever having any future at all; it became more and more difficult to imagine himself resuming them. A final strain, which must have been particularly acute for the newcomer, was the omnipresent threat of death and the very unpredictable suddenness with which death might strike. Quite aside from the periodic gas-chamber selections, the guards in their sports and caprices were at liberty to kill any prisoner any time.

In the face of all this, one might suppose that the very notion of an "adjustment" would be grotesque. The majority of those who entered the camps never came out again. But our concern here has to be with those who survived—an estimated 700,000 out of nearly eight million. For them, the regime must be considered not as a system of death but as a way of life. These survivors did make an adjustment of some sort to the system; it is they themselves who report it. After the initial shocks, what was the nature of the "normality" that emerged?

A dramatic species of psychic displacement seems to have occurred at the very outset. This experience, described as a kind of "splitting of personality," has been noted by most of the inmates who later wrote of their imprisonment. The very extremity of the initial tortures produced in the prisoner what actually amounted to a sense of detachment. These brutalities went so far beyond his own experience that they became somehow incredible. They seemed to be happening no longer to him, but almost to someone else. "[The author] has no doubt," writes Bruno Bettelheim (1943, p. 431), "that he was able to endure the transportation, and all that followed, because right from the beginning he became convinced that these horrible and degrading experiences somehow did not happen to 'him' as a subject, but only to 'him' as an object." This subject-object "split" appears to have served a double function: not only was it an immediate psychic defense mechanism against shock, but it also acted as the first thrust toward a new adjustment. This splitting-off of a special "self"—a self which endured the tortures but which was not the "real" self—also provided the first glimpse of a new personality which, being not "real," would not need to feel bound by the values which guided the individual in his former life. One part of the prisoner's being was thus, under sharp stress, brought to the crude realization that he must thenceforth be governed by an entire new set of standards in order to survive. ". . . I think it of primary importance," writes Elie Cohen (1953, p. 136), "to take into account that the superego acquired new values in a concentration camp, so much at variance with those which the prisoner bore with him into camp that the latter faded." But then this acquisition of "new values" did not take place immediately; it was not until some time after the most acute period of stress was over that the new, "unreal" self would become at last the "real" one.

"If you survive the first three months you will survive the next three years." Such was the formula transmitted from the old prisoners to the new ones. Its meaning lay in the fact that the first three months would generally determine a prisoner's capacity for survival and adaptation. "Be inconspicuous" was the golden rule. Any show of bravado, any heroics, any kind of resistance condemned a man instantly. There were no rewards for martyrdom: not only did the martyr himself suffer, but mass punishments were wreaked upon his fellow-inmates. To "be inconspicuous" required a special kind of alertness—almost an animal instinct—against the apathy which tended to follow the initial shocks. To give up the struggle for survival was to commit "passive suicide"; a careless mistake meant death. There were those, however, who did come through this phase and who managed an adjustment to the life of the camp. It was the striking constrasts between this group of two- and three-year veterans and the perpetual stream of newcomers which made it possible for men like Bettelheim and Cohen to speak of the "old prisoner" as a specific type.

The most immediate aspect of the old inmates' behavior which struck these observers was its *child-like* quality. "The prisoners," writes Dr. Bettelheim (1943, p. 441), "developed types of behavior which are characteristic of infancy or early youth. Some of these behaviors developed slowly, others were immediately imposed on the prisoners and developed only in intensity as time went on." The inmates' sexual impotence brought about a disappearance of sexuality in their talk; instead, excretory functions occupied them endlessly. They lost many of the customary inhibitions as to soiling their beds and their persons. Their humor was shot with silliness and they giggled like children when one of them would expel wind. Their relationships were highly unstable; they could fight each other savagely one minute and become close friends the next. Dishonesty, lying, and theft among the prisoners themselves became chronic. Benedikt Kautsky (1946, p. 188) observed of his own behavior: "I myself can declare that often I saw myself as I used to be in my school days, when by sly dodges and clever pretexts we avoided being found out, or could 'organize' something." Bruno Bettelheim remarks on the extravagance of the stories told by the prisoners to one another:

They were boastful, telling tales about what they had accomplished in their former lives, or how they succeeded in cheating foremen or guards, and how they sabotaged the work. Like children they felt not at all set back or ashamed when it became known that they had lied about their prowess. (1943, pp. 445–46)

This development of childlike behavior in the old inmates was the counterpart of something even more striking that was happening to them. *"Only very few of the prisoners,"* Cohen says (1953, p. 177), *"escaped a more or less intensive identification with the SS."* As Bettelheim puts it (1943, p. 447): "A prisoner had reached the final stage of adjustment to the camp situation when he had changed his personality so as to accept as his own the values of the Gestapo." To all these men, reduced to complete and childish dependence upon their masters, the SS had actually become a father-symbol. "The SS man was all-powerful in the camp, he was the lord and master of the prisoner's life. As a cruel father he could, without fear of punishment, even kill the prisoner and as a gentle father he could scatter largesse and afford the prisoner his protection." The result, admits Dr. Cohen (1953, pp. 176–77), was "That for all of us the SS was a father image. . . ." The closed system, in short, had become a kind of grotesque patriarchy. Few cases of real resistance were recorded; there was a relative scarcity of purposeful suicides, and—even afterwards—a surprising absence of hatred toward the SS. "It is remarkable," Hottinger noted (1948, p. 32) of the survivors, "how little hatred of their wardens is revealed in their stories."

4. THREE THEORIES OF PERSONALITY.

The immense revelation for psychology in the concentration camp literature has been the discovery of how elements of dramatic personality change could be brought about in masses of individuals. And yet it is not proper that the crude fact of "change" alone should dominate the conceptual image with which one emerges from this problem. "Change" *per se*—change that does not go beyond itself, is productive of nothing; it leaves only destruction, shock, and howling bedlam behind it unless some future basis of stability and order lies waiting to guarantee it and give it reality. So it is with the human psyche, which is apparently capable of making terms with a state other than liberty as we know it. The very dramatic features of the process just described may shatter the nicety of this point.

There is the related danger, moreover, of unduly stressing the individual psychology of the problem at the expense of its social psychology. To minimize these hazards, it may be strategically judicious to maintain a conceptual distinction between two phases of the group experience. The process of detachment from prior standards of behavior and value is one of them, and is doubtless the more striking—but there must be another one. That such detachment can, by extension, involve the whole scope of an individual's culture is an implication for which the vocabulary of individual psychology was caught somewhat unawares. Fluctuations in the state of the individual psyche could formerly be dealt with, or so it seemed, while taking for granted the more or less static nature of social organization, and with a minimum of reference to its features. That such organization might itself become a potent variable was therefore a possibility not highly developed in theory.

The other phase of the experience should be considered as the "stability" side of the problem. It stabilized what the "shock" phase only opened the way for. This phase was essentially a process of adjustment to a standard of social normality—though in this case a drastic *re*-adjustment, and compressed within a very short time. This process, under typical conditions of individual and group existence, is supposed to begin at birth and last a lifetime and be transmitted in many and diffuse ways from generation to generation. Normally, the adjustment is slow and organic. Its numerous aspects extend much beyond psychology and have in the past been treated at great leisure within the rich provinces not only of psychology but of history, sociology, and literature as well. What rearrangement and compression of those provinces may be needed to accommodate a mass experience that not only involved profound individual shock but also required rapid assimilation to a profoundly different form of social organization, can hardly be known. But perhaps a conservative beginning may be made with existing psychological theory.

The theoretical system whose terminology was orthodox for most of the Europeans who have written about the camps was that of Freud. It was necessary for them to do a certain amount of improvising, since the scheme's existing framework provided only the narrowest leeway for dealing with such radical concepts as out-and-out change in personality. This was due to two kinds of limitations which the Freudian vocabulary places upon the notion of the "self." One is that the superego —that part of the self involved in social relationships, social values, expectations of others, and so on—is conceived as only a small and highly refined part of the "total" self. The other is the assumption that the content and character of the superego is laid down in childhood and undergoes relatively little basic alteration thereafter. Yet a Freudian diagnosis of the concentration camp inmate—whose social self, or superego, *did* appear to change and who seemed *basically* changed thereby—is still possible, given these limitations. Elie Cohen's thorough analysis specifically states that "the superego acquired new values in a concentration camp." The old values, according to Dr. Cohen, were first silenced by the shocks which produced "acute depersonalization" (the subject-object split: "It is not the real 'me' who is undergoing this"), and by the powerful drives of hunger and survival. Old values, thus set aside, could be replaced by new ones. It was a process made possible by "infantile regression"—regression to a previous condition of childlike dependency in which parental prohibitions once more became all-powerful and in which parental judgments might once more be internalized. In this way a new "father-image," personified in the SS guard, came into being. That the prisoner's identification with the SS could be so positive is explained by still another mechanism: the principle of "identification with the aggressor." The child's only "defense" in the presence of a cruel, all-powerful father is the psychic defense of identification.

Now one could, still retaining the Freudian language, represent all this in somewhat less cumbersome terms by a slight modification of the metaphor. It could simply be said that under great stress the superego, like a bucket, is violently emptied of content and acquires, in a radically changed setting, new content. It would thus not be necessary to postulate a literal "regression" to childhood. Something of the sort is suggested by Leo Alexander. "The psychiatrist stands in amazement," he writes,

before the thoroughness and completeness with which this perversion of essential superego values was accomplished in adults. . . . it may be that the decisive importance of childhood and youth in the formation of [these] values may have been overrated by psychiatrists in a society in which allegiance to these values in normal adult life was taken too much for granted because of the stability, religiousness, legality, and security of the 19th Century and early 20th Century society. (1948, p. 173)

A second theoretical scheme is better prepared for crisis and more closely geared to social environment than the Freudian adaptation. It may consequently be more suitable for accommodating not only the concentration camp experience but also the more general problem of plantation slave personality. This is the "interpersonal theory" developed by the late Harry Stack Sullivan. One may view this body of work as the response to a peculiarly American set of needs. The system of Freud, so aptly designed for a European society in which stability of institutional and status relationships could always to a large extent be taken for granted, turns out to be less clearly adapted to the culture of the United States. The American psychiatrist has had to deal with individuals in a culture where the diffuse, shifting, and often uncertain quality of such relationships has always been more pronounced than in Europe. He has come to appreciate the extent to which these relationships actually support the individual's psychic balance—the full extent, that is, to which the self is "social" in its nature. Thus a psychology whose terms are flexible enough to permit altering social relationships to make actual differences in character structure would be a psychology especially promising for dealing with our problem.

Sullivan's great contribution was to offer a concept whereby the really critical determinants of personality might be isolated for purposes of observation. Out of the hopelessly immense totality of "influences" which in one way or another go to make up the personality, or "self," Sullivan designated one—the estimations and expectations of others—as the one promising to unlock the most secrets. He then made a second elimination: the majority of "others" in one's existence may, for theoretical purposes, be neglected; what counts is who the significant others are. Here, "significant others" may be understood very crudely to mean those individuals who hold—or seem to hold—the keys to security in one's own personal situation, whatever its nature. As to the psychic processes whereby these "significant others" become an actual part of the personality, it may be said that the very sense of "self" first emerges in connection with anxiety about the attitudes of the most important persons in one's life (initially the mother, father, and their surrogates—persons of more or less absolute authority), and automatic attempts are set in motion to adjust to these attitudes. In this way their approval, their disapproval, their estimates and appraisals, and indeed a whole range of their expectations become internalized, and are reflected in one's very character. Of course as one "grows up," one acquires more and more significant others whose attitudes are diffuse and may indeed compete, and thus "significance," in Sullivan's sense, becomes subtler and less easy to define. The personality exfoliates; it takes on traits of distinction and—as we say—"individuality." The impact of particular significant others is less dramatic than in early life. But the pattern is a continuing one. New significant others do still appear, and theoretically it is conceivable that even in mature life the personality might be visibly affected by the arrival of such a one—supposing that this new significant other were vested with sufficient authority. In any event, there are possibilities for fluidity and actual change inherent in this concept which earlier schemes have lacked.

The purest form of the process is observed in the development of children. This is not so much due to their "immaturity" as such—though their plasticity is great and the imprint of early experience goes deep—but rather because for them there are fewer significant others. For this reason—because the pattern is simpler and more easily controlled—much of Sullivan's attention was devoted to what happens in childhood. Unlike the adult, the child, being drastically limited in the selection of significant others, must operate—reverting to a previous terminology—in a "closed system."

Such are the elements which make for order and balance in the normal self: "significant others," plus "anxiety" in a special sense—conceived with not simply disruptive but also guiding, warning functions. The structure of "interpersonal" theory thus has considerable room in it for conceptions of guided change—change for either beneficent or malevolent ends. One technique for managing such change would of course be the orthodox one of psychoanalysis; another, the actual changing of significant others. Patrick Mullahy, a leading exponent of Sullivan, believes that in group therapy much is possible along the latter lines. A demonic test of the whole hypothesis is available in the concentration camp.

Consider the camp prisoner—not the one who fell by the wayside but the one who survived. Consider the ways in which he was forced to adjust to the one significant other which he now had: the SS guard, who held absolute dominion over every aspect of his life. The very shock of his introduction was perfectly designed to dramatize this fact; he was brutally maltreated ("as by a cruel father"); the slightest resistance would bring instant death. Daily life in the camp, with its fear and tensions, taught over and over the lesson of absolute power. It prepared the personality for a drastic shift in standards. It crushed whatever anxieties might have been drawn from prior standards—such standards had become meaningless. It focused the prisoner's attention constantly on the moods, attitudes, and standards of the only man who mattered. A truly childlike situation was thus created: utter and abject dependency on one, or on a rigidly limited few significant others. All the conditions which in normal life would give the individual leeway—which allowed him to defend himself against a new and hostile significant other, no matter how powerful—were absent in the camp. No competition of significant others was possible; the prisoner's comrades for practical purposes were helpless to assist him. He had no degree of independence, no lines to the outside, in any matter. Everything—every vital concern—focused on the SS: food, warmth, security, freedom from pain, all depended on the omnipotent significant other, all had to be worked out within the closed system. Nowhere was there a shred of privacy; everything one did was subject to SS supervision. The pressure was never absent. It is thus no wonder that the prisoners should become "as children." It is no wonder that their obedience became unquestioning, that they did not revolt, that they could not "hate" their masters. Their masters' attitudes had become *internalized* as a part of their very selves; those attitudes and standards now dominated all others. They had, indeed, been "changed."

There still exists a third conceptual framework within which these phenomena may be considered—the growing field of "role psychology." This psychology is not at all incompatible with interpersonal theory; the two might easily be fitted into the same system. But it might be strategically desirable, for several reasons, to segregate them for purposes of discussion. One such reason is the extraordinary degree to which role psychology shifts the focus of attention upon the individual's cultural and institutional environment rather than upon his "self." At the same time it gives us a manageable concept—that of "role"—for mediating between the two. As a mechanism, the role enables us to isolate the unique contribution of culture and institutions toward maintaining the psychic balance of the individual. In it, we see formalized for the individual a range of choices in models of behavior and expression, each with its particular style, quality, and attributes. The relationship between the "role" and the "self," though not yet clear, is intimate; it is possible at certain levels of inquiry to look upon the individual as the variable and upon the roles extended him as the stable factor. We thus have a potentially durable link between individual psychology and the study of culture. It might even be said, inasmuch as its key term is directly borrowed from the theater, that role psychology offers in workable form the long-awaited connection—apparently missed by Ernest Jones in his "Hamlet" study—between the insights of the classical dramatists and those of the contemporary social theorist. But be that as it may, for the concentration camp situation it provides the most flexible explanation of how the ex-prisoners may have succeeded not only in adjusting to the camp but also in resuming their places in normal life.

A "social role" is definable in its simplest sense as the behavior expected of persons specifically located in specific social groups. Its texture may be interwoven with many subtle qualities, which constitute its style. There is a distinction between "expectations" and "behavior"; the expectations of a role (embodied in the "script") theoretically exist in advance and are defined by the organization, the institution, or by society at large. Behavior—the "performance"—refers to the manner in which the role is played. Another distinction involves roles which are pervasive and those which are intermittent, transitory, and limited. A further concept is that of "role clarity." Some roles are more specifically defined than others; their impact upon performance—and indeed, upon the personality of the performer—depends on the clarity of their definition. And finally, those roles which carry with them the clearest and most automatic rewards and punishments are those which will be, so to speak, best played.

What sorts of things might this explain? It might illuminate the process whereby the child develops his personality in terms not only of the roles which his parents offer him but of those which he "picks up" elsewhere and tries on. It could show how society, in its coercive character, lays down patterns of behavior with which it expects the individual to comply. It suggests the way in which society, now turning its benevolent face to the individual, tenders him alternatives and defines for him the style appropriate to their fulfillment. It provides us with a further term for the definition of personality itself: to some extent we can say that personality is actually made up of the roles which the individual plays. And here, once more assuming "change" to be possible, we have in certain ways the least cumbersome terms for plotting its course.

The application of the model to the concentration camp is simple and obvious. What was expected of the man entering the role of camp prisoner was laid down for him upon arrival: absolute obedience. Expectation and performance, in short, must coincide exactly; the lines were to be read literally; the missing of a single cue meant extinction. The role was pervasive; it vetoed any other role and smashed all prior ones. "Role clarity" was absolute; its definition was burned into the prisoner by every detail of his existence. The role was actually that of the child who had no measure of independence. Its impact upon both performance and personality have already been observed. Its rewards were brutally simple—life rather than death; its punishments were automatic. By the survivors it was, it had to be, a role *well-played*.

Nor was it simple, upon liberation, to shed the role. Many of the inmates, to be sure, did have prior roles which they could resume, former significant others to whom they might reorient themselves, a repressed superego which might once more be resurrected. To this extent they were not "lost souls." But to the extent that their entire personalities, their total selves, had been involved in this experience, to the extent that old arrangements had been disrupted, that society itself had been overturned while they had been away, a "return" was fraught with innumerable obstacles.

The foregoing analysis has shed some light upon the question with which this section began, though the very hideousness of the special kind of slavery may have partially disqualified it as a test for certain features of a far milder and more benevolent form of slavery. Still, one should be able to say, with regard to the individuals who lived as slaves within the respective systems, that just as on one level there is every difference between a wretched childhood and a carefree one, there are limited features which both types share.

Both were closed systems from which all standards based on prior connections had been effectively detached. A working adjustment to either system required a childlike conformity, a limited choice of "significant others." Cruelty *per se* cannot be considered as the primary key to this; of far greater importance was the sheer "closedness" of the system, in which all lines of authority descended from the master, and in which alternative social bases that might have supported alternative standards were systematically suppressed. The individual, consequently, for his very psychic security, had to picture his master in some way as the "good father," even when, as in the concentration camp, it made no sense at all. But why should it not have made sense for many a simple plantation Negro whose master did exhibit, in all the ways that could be expected, the features of the good father who was really "good"? If the concentration camp could produce in two or three years the results that it did, one wonders how much more pervasive must have been those attitudes, expectations, and values which had, certainly, their benevolent side, and which were accepted and transmitted over generations?

From the master's viewpoint, slaves had been defined in law as property, and the master's power over his property must be absolute. But then this property was still human property. These slaves might never be quite as human as *he* was, but still there were certain standards that could be laid down for their behavior: obedience, fidelity, humility, docility, cheerfulness, and so on. Industry and diligence would of course be demanded—but a final element in the master's situation would undoubtedly qualify that expectation. Absolute power for him meant absolute dependency for the slave—the dependency not of the developing child but of the perpetual child. For the master, the role most aptly fitting such a relationship would naturally be that of the father. As a father he could be either harsh or kind, as he chose, but as a *wise* father he would have, we may suspect, a sense of the limits of his situation. He must be ready to cope with *all* the qualities of the child, exasperating as well as ingratiating. He might conceivably have to expect in such a child—besides his loyalty, docility, humility, cheerfulness, and, under supervision, his diligence—such additional qualities as irresponsibility, playfulness, silliness, laziness, and, quite possibly, tendencies to lying and stealing. Should the entire prediction prove accurate, the result would be something resembling "Sambo."

The social and psychological sanctions of role-playing may in the last analysis prove to be the most satisfactory of the several approaches to Sambo, for without doubt, of all the roles in American life that of Sambo was by far the most pervasive. The outlines of the role might be sketched in by crude necessity, but what of the finer shades? The sanctions against overstepping it were bleak enough, but the reward—the sweet applause, as it were, for performing it with sincerity and feeling—that was something to be appreciated on quite another level. The law, untuned to the deeper harmonies, could command the player to be present for the occasion, and the whip might even warn against his missing the grosser cues—but could those things really insure the performance that melted all hearts? Yet there was many and many a performance, and the audiences, whose standards were high, appear to have been for the most part well pleased. They were actually viewing their own masterpiece. Much labor had been lavished upon this *chef d'oeuvre;* the most genial resources of Southern society had been available for the work. Touch after touch had been applied throughout the years, and the result—embodied not in the unfeeling law but in the richest layers of Southern lore—had been the product of an exquisitely rounded collective creativity. And it was indeed—in a sense that somehow transcended the merely ironic—a labor of love. "I love the simple and unadulterated slave, with his geniality, his mirth, his swagger, and his nonsense," wrote Edward Pollard,

> I love to look upon his countenance shining with content and grease; I love to study his affectionate heart; I love to mark that peculiarity in him, which beneath all his buffoonery exhibits him as a creature of the tenderest sensibilities, mingling his joys and his sorrows with those of his master's home. (1859, p. 58)

Love, in short—even on those terms—was surely no inconsequential reward. But what were the terms? The Negro, though a happy child, was to be a child forever. Few Southern writers failed to describe with obvious fondness the bubbling gaiety of a plantation holiday or the perpetual good humor that seemed to mark the Negro character—the good humor of an everlasting childhood.

The role, of course, must have been rather harder for the earliest generations of slaves to learn. "Accommodation," according to John Dollard,

> involves the renunciation of protest or aggression against undesirable conditions of life and the organization of the character so that protest does not appear, but acceptance does. It may come to pass in the end that the unwelcome force is idealized, that one identifies with it and takes it into the personality; it sometimes even happens that what is at first resented and feared is finally loved. (1937, p. 255)

Might the process, on the other hand, be reversed? It is hard to imagine it being reversed overnight. The same role might still be played in the years after slavery—we are told that it was—and yet it was played to more vulgar audiences with cruder standards, who paid infinitely less for what they saw. The lines might be repeated more and more mechanically, with less and less conviction. The incentives to perfection could become hazy and blurred, and the excellent old piece could degenerate over time into low farce. There could come a point, conceivably, with the old zest gone, that it was no longer worth the candle. The day might come at last when it dawned on a man's full waking consciousness that he had really grown up—that he was, after all, only playing a part.

5. MECHANISMS OF RESISTANCE TO ABSOLUTE POWER.

One might say a great deal more than has been said here about mass behavior and mass manifestations of personality, and the picture would still amount to little more than a grotesque cartoon of humanity were not some recognition given to the ineffable difference made in any social system by men and women possessing what is recognized, anywhere and any time, simply as character. With that, one arrives at something too qualitatively fine to come very much within the crude categories of the present discussion. But although it is impossible to generalize with any proper justice about the incidence of "character" in its moral, irreducible, individual sense, it may still be possible to conclude with a note or two on the social conditions, the breadth or narrowness of their compass, within which character can find expression.

One is struck once more, turning to Latin America, by the fact that there one finds no Sambo: more specifically, one finds no social tradition in which slaves were defined, by virtually complete consensus, as children incapable of being trusted with the full privileges of freedom and adulthood. There, the system surely had its brutalities. The slaves arriving from Africa had also undergone the capture, the sale, the Middle Passage. They too had been uprooted from a prior culture, from a life very different from the one in which they now found themselves. There, however, the system was not closed.

Once again the concentration camp, paradoxically enough, can be instructive. A very small minority of the survivors of the camps had undergone an experience in crucial ways different from that of the others, an experience which protected them from the full impact of the closed system. These people, mainly by virtue of wretched little jobs in the camp administration which offered them a minute measure of privilege, were able to carry on "underground" activities. In a practical sense the actual operations of such "undergrounds" as were possible may seem to us unheroic and limited: stealing blankets; "organizing" a few bandages, a little medicine, from the camp hospital; black market arrangements with a guard for a bit of extra food and protection for oneself and one's comrades; the circulation of news; and other such apparently trifling activities. But for the psychological balance of those involved, such activities were vital; they made possible a fundamentally different adjustment to the camp. To a prisoner so engaged, there were others who mattered, who gave real point to his existence. The SS was no longer the *only* one. Conversely, the role of the child was not the only one he played. He could take initiative; he could give as well as receive protection; he did things which had meaning in adult terms. He had, in short, alternative roles. This fact made such a prisoner's transition from his old life to that of the camp less agonizing and destructive; those very prisoners, moreover, appear to have been the ones who could, upon liberation, resume normal lives most easily.

It was just such a difference, indeed, a much greater one, that separated the typical slave in Latin America from the typical slave in the United States. Though he too had experienced the Middle Passage, he was entering a society where alternatives were significantly more diverse than those awaiting his kinsman in North America. Distinct and, at certain points, competing institutions were concerned in some sense with his status. Multiple and often competing "significant others" existed. His master was, of course, clearly the chief one—but not the only one. There could, in fact, be a considerable number: the friar who boarded his ship to examine his conscience; the confessor; the priest who made the rounds and who might report irregularities in treatment to the *procurador;* the zealous Jesuit quick to resent a master's intrusion upon such sacred matters as marriage and worship—a resentment of no small consequence to the master—the local magistrate, with his eye on the king's official protector of slaves, who would find himself in trouble were the laws too widely evaded; the king's informer who received one-third of the fines. For the slave, the result was a certain latitude; the lines did not *all* converge on one man; the slave's personality, accordingly, did not have to focus on a single role. He was, true enough, primarily a slave. Yet he might in fact perform multiple roles. He could be a husband and father—the American slave was legally denied such roles. Open to him also were such activities as artisan, peddler, petty merchant, truck gardener—the law reserved to him the necessary time and a share of the proceeds; such arrangements were against the law for Sambo. He could be a communicant in the church, a member of a religious fraternity—roles guaranteed by the most powerful institution in Latin America. Comparable privileges in the American South depended on a master's pleasure. These roles were all legitimized and protected *outside* the plantation; they offered a diversity of channels for the development of personality. Not only did the individual have multiple roles open to him as a slave, but the very nature of these roles made possible a certain range of aspirations should he some day become free. He could have a fantasy-life not limited to catfish and watermelons; it was within his conception to become a priest, an independent farmer, a successful merchant, a military officer. The slave could actually— to an extent quite unthinkable in the United States—conceive of himself *as a rebel*. Bloody slave revolts—actual wars—took place in Latin America. Nothing on this order occurred in the United States. But even without a rebellion, society here had a network of customary arrangements, rooted in antiquity, which made possible at many points a smooth transition of status from slave to free, and which provided much social space for the exfoliation of individual character.

To the typical slave on the ante-bellum plantation in the United States, society of course offered no such alternatives. But that is hardly to say that something of an "underground"—something rather more, indeed, than an underground—could not exist in Southern slave society.

And there were those in it who hardly fitted the picture of "Sambo."

The American slave system, compared with that of Latin America, was closed and circumscribed. But like all social systems, its arrangements were less perfect in practice than they appeared to be in theory. It was possible for significant numbers of slaves to escape, in varying degrees, the full impact of the system and its coercions upon personality. The house servant, the urban mechanic, the slave who arranged his own employment and paid his master a stipulated sum each week, were all figuratively members of the "underground." Even among those working on large plantations, the skilled craftsman or the responsible slave foreman had a measure of independence not shared by his simpler brethren. Even the single slave family owned by a small farmer had a status much closer to that of house servants than that of a plantation labor gang. For all such people there was a margin of space denied to the majority: the system's authority-structure claimed their bodies but not quite their souls.

It would be out of such groups that an individual as complex and as highly developed as William Johnson, the Natchez barber, might emerge. Johnson's diary reveals a personality that one recognizes instantly as a type—but a type whose values came from a sector of society very different from that which formed Sambo. Johnson is the young man on the make, the ambitious free-enterpriser of American legend. He began life as a slave, was manumitted at the age of eleven, and rose from a poor apprentice barber to become one of the wealthiest and most influential Negroes in ante-bellum Mississippi. He was respected by white and black alike, and counted among his friends some of the leading public men of the state.

It is of great interest to note that the danger of slave revolts—like Communist conspiracies in our own day—was much overrated by touchy Southerners. The revolts that actually did occur were in no instance planned by plantation laborers but rather by Negroes whose qualities of leadership were developed well outside the full coercions of the plantation authority-system. Gabriel, who led the revolt of 1800, was a blacksmith who lived a few miles outside of Richmond; Denmark Vesey, leading spirit of the 1822 plot at Charleston, was a freed Negro artisan who had been born in Africa and served several years aboard a slave trading vessel; and Nat Turner, the Virginia slave who fomented the massacre of 1831, was a literate preacher of recognized intelligence. Of the plots that have been convincingly substantiated, moreover—whether they came to anything or not—the majority originated in urban centers.

For a time during Reconstruction, a Negro elite of sorts did emerge in the South. Many of its members were Northern Negroes; but the

Southern ex-slaves who also comprised it seem in general to have emerged from the categories just indicated. Vernon Wharton, writing of Mississippi, says:

> A large portion of the minor Negro leaders were preachers, lawyers, or teachers from the free states or from Canada. Their education and their independent attitude gained for them immediate favor and leadership. Of the natives who became their rivals, the majority had been urban slaves, blacksmiths, carpenters, clerks, or waiters in hotels and boarding houses; a few of them had been favored body-servants of affluent whites. (1942, p. 164)

The William Johnsons and Denmark Veseys have been accorded, though belatedly, their due honor. They are, indeed, all too easily identified, thanks to the system that enabled them as individuals to be so conspicuous and so exceptional, and as members of a group, so few.

BIBLIOGRAPHY

1791. *An Abstract of the Evidence delivered before a Select Committee of the House of Commons in the Years 1790, and 1791; on the Part of the Petitioners for the Abolition of the Slave Trade.* London.

Alexander, L. 1948. "War Crimes: Their Social-Psychological Aspects," *American Journal of Psychiatry*, 105:170–77.

Aptheker, H. 1943. *American Negro Slave Revolts.* New York: Columbia University Press.

Bettelheim, B. 1943. "Individual and Mass Behavior in Extreme Situations," *Journal of Abnormal and Social Psychology*, 38:417–52.

Bluhm, H. 1948. "How Did They Survive?" *American Journal of Psychotherapy*, 2:3–33.

Bondy, C. 1943. "Problems of Internment Camps," *Journal of Abnormal and Social Psychology*, 38:453–75.

Bosman, W. 1705. *A New and Accurate Description of the Coast of Guinea* . . . . London: J. Knapton.

Cohen, E. 1953. *Human Behavior in the Concentration Camp.* New York: W. W. Norton.

Degrandpré, L. 1801. *Voyage à la Côte Occidentale d'Afrique, fait dans les années 1786 et 1787* . . . . Paris: Dentu.

Dollard, J. 1937. *Caste and Class in a Southern Town.* New Haven: Yale University Press.

Donnan, E. (ed.). 1930 ff. *Documents Illustrative of the History of the Slave Trade to America* (4 vols.). Washington: Carnegie Institution.

Edwards, B. 1806. *The History . . . of the British Colonies in the West Indies* . . . . Vol. 2. Philadelphia: J. Humphreys.

Elkins, S. 1959. *Slavery: A Problem in American Institutional and Intellectual Life.* Chicago: University of Chicago Press.

Elkins, S., and McKitrick, E. 1957. "Institutions and the Law of Slavery," *American Quarterly,* 9:3–21, 159–79.

Falconbridge, A. 1788. *An Account of the Slave Trade on the Coast of Africa.* London: J. Phillips.

Freud, A. 1948. *The Ego and the Mechanisms of Defence.* London: Hogarth Press.

Freud, S. 1947. *The Ego and the Id.* London: Hogarth Press.

Friedman, P. 1948. "The Road Back for the DP's," *Commentary,* 6:502–10.

Gaines, F. 1924. *The Southern Plantation: A Study in the Development and the Accuracy of a Tradition.* New York: Columbia University Press.

Gerth, H., and Mills, C. W. 1953. *Character and Social Structure: The Psychology of Social Institutions.* New York: Harcourt, Brace.

Herskovits, M. 1941. *The Myth of the Negro Past.* New York: Harper & Bros.

Hogan, W. and Davis, A. (eds.). 1951. *William Johnson's Natchez: The Ante-Bellum Diary of a Free Negro.* Baton Rouge: Louisiana State University Press.

Hottinger, A., *et al.* 1948. *Hungerkrankheit, Hungerödem, Hungertuberkulose.* Basel: B. Schwabe.

Kautsky, B. 1946. *Teufel und Verdammte.* Zurich: Buchguilde Gutenberg.

Kennedy, J. 1832. *Swallow Barn.* Philadelphia: Carey & Lea.

Klineberg, O. (ed.). 1944. *Characteristics of the American Negro.* New York: Harper & Bros.

Kogon, Eugen. 1946. *The Theory and Practice of Hell: The German Concentration Camps and the System Behind Them.* New York: Farrar, Straus.

Lengyel, O. 1947. *Five Chimneys: the Story of Auschwitz.* Chicago: University of Chicago Press.

Lingens-Reiner, E. 1948. *Prisoners of Fear.* London: Victor Gollancz.

Matthews, J. 1788. *A Voyage to the River Sierra-Leone . . .* London: B. White.

Mayer, B. 1854. *Captain Canot; or, Twenty Years of an African Slaver . . .* New York: D. Appleton.

Mead, G. 1934. *Mind, Self and Society: From the Standpoint of a Social Behaviorist.* Chicago: University of Chicago Press.

Moore, F. 1738. *Travels into the Inland Parts of Africa . . .* London: Author.

Mullahy, P. 1948. *Oedipus Myth and Complex: A Review of Psychoanalytic Theory.* New York: Hermitage Press.

Murphy, G. 1947. *Personality.* New York: Harper Bros.

Newcomb, T. 1950. *Social Psychology.* New York: Dryden Press.

Ortiz, F. 1906. *Los Negros Brujos.* Madrid: Libreria de F. Fe.

Park, M. 1801. *Travels and Recent Discoveries, in the Interior Districts of Africa, in the Years 1796 and '97.* New York: A. Brodie.

Phillips, U. 1918. *American Negro Slavery.* New York: D. Appleton.

Pierson, D. 1942. *Negroes in Brazil: A Study of Race Contact at Bahia.* Chicago: University of Chicago Press.

Pollard, E. 1859. *Black Diamonds Gathered in the Darkey Homes of the South.* New York: Pudney & Russell.

Ramos, A. 1951. *The Negro in Brazil.* Washington: Associated Publishers.

Rinchon, D. 1929. *La Traite et l'Esclavage des Congolais par les Euro-peëns: Histoire de la Déportation de 13 Millions 25,000 Noirs en Amérique.* Wetteren, Belgium.

Rousset, D. 1947. *The Other Kingdom.* New York: Reynal & Hitchcock.

Smedes, S. 1888. *Memorials of a Southern Planter.* Baltimore: Cushings & Bailey.

Smith, W. 1745. *A New Voyage to Guinea . . .* London: J. Nourse.

Snelgrave, W. 1734. *A New Account of Some Parts of Guinea . . .* London: J., J., & P. Knapton.

Stampp, K. 1956. *The Peculiar Institution: Slavery in the Ante-Bellum South.* New York: A. A. Knopf.

Sullivan, H. 1945. *Conceptions of Modern Psychiatry.* Washington: W. A. White Psychiatric Foundation.

———. 1952. *The Contributions of Harry Stack Sullivan: A Symposium of Interpersonal Theory in Psychiatry and Social Science.* New York: Hermitage Press.

Szalet, L. 1945. *Experiment "E."* New York: Didier.

Tandy, J. 1922. "Pro-Slavery Propaganda in American Fiction of the Fifties," *South Atlantic Quarterly,* 21: 41–59, 170–78.

Tannenbaum, F. 1947. *Slave and Citizen: The Negro in America.* New York: A. A. Knopf.

Wharton, V. 1942. *The Negro in Mississippi, 1865–1890.* Chapel Hill: University of North Carolina Press.

III

METHODOLOGICAL ISSUES IN THE CROSS-CULTURAL STUDY OF PERSONALITY

About the Chapter

From the confusing variety of theoretical conceptualizations of personality processes, Dr. Miller tries to identify categories which are best suited for cross-cultural study. He believes that the interpersonal relationship is the minimal unit of psychological analysis and discusses in detail the problems of describing such relationships. The schema he develops is a skillful blending of sociological, Lewinian, and psychoanalytic concepts.

About the Author

DANIEL R. MILLER is Research Associate at the Institute for Social Research and Professor of Psychology at the University of Michigan. In 1955–56, he was at the Institute for Advanced Study in the Behavioral Sciences. He is co-author with Guy E. Swanson of two books, *The Changing American Parent* and *Inner Conflict and Defense*. The first of these received the Burgess Award in 1960 for the best monograph on the family and socialization in the previous two years.

8

Personality and Social Interaction

DANIEL R. MILLER
University of Michigan

To study personality cross-culturally, one must first have a picture of personality. A specific set of categories is necessary to define testable questions and to classify the empirical data obtained from answering the questions. But which are the best categories for mapping the human personality? The social scientist is likely to feel bedeviled by the many systems described in a standard text on personality. There is no easy way to choose among them; each has its particular assets and liabilities. The selection of a system must be determined by the investigator's problems and the kind of material he is studying. This chapter begins with a list of reasons why social scientists study personality in different societies. There then follows a presentation of concepts that have been helpful in my own empirical investigations of personality. The concepts represent a recasting within an interpersonal context of intrapersonal concepts traditional in psychology. After the interpersonal approach has been outlined, it will be evaluated in the light of the purposes of cross-cultural research.

Criteria for Selecting Concepts

Psychological theories provide a wealth of seemingly fruitful terms. The literature on personality in different societies contains many references to motives, displacement, Oedipus complex, reinforcement, fixation, self-esteem, internalization, anxiety, and many other concepts. But the very variety of concepts is confusing; the theoretical pie has been cut in too many different ways. Some writers take a physiological approach and some focus on personal experience; some devote their attention to perception, some stress learning, and some stress motivation. Some investigate the internal dynamics of an individual and some the behavior of people in groups. There are many other such differences in basic orientation.

It is not possible to integrate the best of the different orientations into one all-embracing system. Thus far, no approach seems inherently superior to the others. It is usually very difficult to decide, therefore, on labels for behavior and on methods of comparing people in different societies. Will an investigator learn more about anxiety if he collects dreams or if he measures psychogalvanic responses; if he administers the Rorschach Test or interviews mothers about weaning practices?

There being no a priori basis for selecting concepts and methods, the most obvious basis is an empirical one: consideration of the ends to which the concepts will be applied. If the investigator intends to compare the personalities of people in different societies, his concepts should satisfy at least three criteria. First, the terms must have comparable meanings in the different societies. The satisfaction of this criterion is no simple matter. While general enough to have cross-cultural meaning, the concepts must also be specific enough to describe concrete behavior in a particular society.

A second criterion is suggested if we ask why one goes to the trouble of traveling to different societies in order to study personality. Why not stay at home? Usually, the investigator is interested in the connections between personality traits and different social structures. He may be asking how personality supports the social system or how certain forms of social organization affect personality. He cannot phrase hypotheses with psychological concepts that apply only to the internal distribution of energy and sociological concepts that are specific to the organization of social groups. To find answers, he needs concepts of personality that he can integrate with categories for describing social structure.

A final criterion for the selection of concepts is suggested by the nature of personality. To be described in a meaningful way, it requires terms that permit the analysis of individual differences.

These, then, are the three criteria for selecting concepts: they should have comparable meanings in different societies; they should permit the phrasing of associations between social structure and personality; they should lend themselves to the analysis of individual differences.

The Interpersonal Relationship

In the short space of one chapter it is not possible to outline a complete system of classification that satisfies the three criteria. It is possible only to indicate the nature of such a system by illustrating a few critical concepts. Underlying the orientation to the selection of concepts is one basic assumption: the minimal unit of psychological analysis is the interpersonal relationship. This relationship is viewed as a system, much as the individual person is viewed as a system in the realm of traditional psychology.

To convey the nature of questions about interaction between two people, it is first necessary to list the primary factors in the system's dynamics. Most obvious are the *dramatis personae,* the two participants. To explain their behavior, the investigator needs information about their dispositions, their values, their defense mechanisms, and the like. To picture their relationship he needs concepts that describe incidents from the point of view of each perceiver. The terms are *self-identity* and *object.* Another integral part of the picture is the *situation.* Are the participants at a cocktail party or at a business meeting? Are they in a kitchen or in an office? The final major source of variance is the nature of the *interaction* between the two participants. Have they been planning a cooperative venture or have they been arguing? Is the relationship an authoritative one or is it a relationship on the level of peers?

In terms of such categories of concepts, one can define not only many traditional problems but one that is basic to many cross-cultural studies. It involves the forces which contribute to the stability and rigidity of an interpersonal system. If the two people are man and wife, we can study the forces, both internal and external, that keep the marriage intact: the fit between the partners' personalities, the maturity of defense mechanisms, the number of mutual satisfactions, the social pressures to maintain the marriage. If the participants are friends, we can analyze the forces that affect the stability of the friendship: the common interests, the extent to which the shared activities gratify reciprocal needs, the sources of friction.

The primary purpose of the ensuing discussion, then, will be to present an interpersonal orientation to theory-building. As will become increasingly evident, this orientation has been influenced considerably by the writings of Cooley (1922) and M. Mead (1935) in sociology, and of Lewin (1939), Parsons, Shils and Murray (1951) in psychology, and of Freud (1949), Klein (1948), Erikson (1954) and Sullivan (1947) in psychoanalysis.

Psychological Space

The concepts to be discussed have been selected with a view to picturing an interpersonal event as it is perceived by the participants. Subjectively many aspects of a situation, and the people in it, are experienced in spatial terms. One thinks in such terms as the distance between people, directions of goals, and deterrance by barriers. It is helpful, therefore, to analyze many aspects of an interpersonal event, by means of concepts developed by Lewin (1939) to describe psychological space.

In spatial terms, an event is experienced as consisting of component *regions*. Regions may represent persons and parts of persons, and physical space between people. Each region has its special structure, defined by component sub-regions, and is delimited by *boundaries*. At such points its qualitative properties begin to change into those of another region. Boundaries may be sharp or vague enough to constitute zones, easily crossed or resistant to communication and movement. In the latter case, boundaries constitute *barriers* between regions. Changes are induced by *forces,* each of which has a point of application, strength, and direction.

In some of the comments on the interpersonal relationship, it will be viewed structurally as consisting of component and interacting regions, and functionally as a system of forces in some sort of equilibrium. The specific regions on which we will concentrate are the situation, the object, and the self-identity. The forces we will consider are the ones that underly reactions of people to each other. In describing dynamics of interpersonal reactions, we will focus on one factor, the defense mechanism, which is of considerable importance in many cross-cultural studies of personality.

1. SITUATION

The interaction between two persons obviously varies with the situation in which they find themselves. A fundamental aspect of the situation is its actual physical characteristics. A locked door can act as a physical barrier; the living room is designed for different functions than the kitchen. But regions need not be defined by physical characteristics and need not even refer to physical places. They may refer to areas in fantasy. Whether a region refers to a real space or a fantasied one, the investigator is interested in its location relative to other regions, its connections with them, its attributes, its amenability to change, the clarity of its boundaries, and their resistance to perception and locomotion.

A situation can also be mapped in terms of the forces that prompt objects to move in various directions, and the *tensions,* or force fields, in particular regions. Tensions tend to create changes, often by prompting an object to move to goals or to other regions or to retreat from sources of potential pain.

To apply such general functional and structural terms, one also needs information about content. Data are required about kinds of forces, goals, and barriers. Some of this information can be gained from a consideration of social structure. To define a situation we begin with the total social system, which is the network of social relationships current in a particular culture. Such a network can be conveniently divided according to at least three different principles, all of which can throw light on the regions in a situation. The most familiar method involves a division into various types of organized social units, like the family, the factory, the church, and the club; and unorganized, but recognized social categories, like men and women, Negroes and whites, white collar workers and manual laborers. The second method classifies the network of relationships in terms of such salient characteristics as economic, political, religious, and educational features. Finally, an organized social unit can ultimately be viewed as a set of social positions. A family, for example, may be divided into the positions of father, mother, husband, wife, son, daughter, brother and sister.

By analyzing a social situation in these three ways, we can usually get a clear picture of the most prominent regions and forces. In an encounter between a saleslady (social position) and a female customer in a department store (social unit), the physical structure of the store, the nature of the saleslady's job, the rules established by the organization, the age, sex, race, and social class of the customer—all these factors may affect the meaning of the situation, which is organized, in great part, to facilitate the distribution of goods and services. The selling situation may be viewed in terms of two regions, the counter acting as a physical and social barrier between them. During working hours the saleslady cannot cross the barrier. She cannot leave her post without seeking a replacement. This rule is reinforced by the presence of superiors, the warnings of peers, and the possible complaints of customers. The tensions in the two regions promote actions leading to the interchange of money for goods and services. The goals of this action are partially interpreted in terms of the meanings and values entailed in the company's structuring of the situation, both physically and psychologically. For a given person, these rudimentary details are rounded out by many others. If the saleslady is very anxious to keep her job, for example, or is very respectful to authorities, she will seldom cross the barrier of the counter and she will experience strong tensions to promote the exchange of goods and services.

2. OBJECTS

Perceptually, the participants in a relationship are most aware of the regions we shall call *objects*. These can be inanimate, but the ones that are most important in most people's lives are animate and human. "Significant others"—parents, siblings, spouses, friends, gods, fellow-employees—provide fulcra about which each person organizes his life. Objects provide the foci of one's deepest needs, one's primary values, and the fundamental goals of the larger community.

Sub-Identities of Objects

Each object can be differentiated into sub-regions with discernible characteristics and interrelationships. To analyze the structure of an object, one must identify its sub-regions, their dimensions and attributes, and their centrality and fluidity.

What are the regions by which a man is known to others? How is he identified by his public? There are two different ways. One refers to his positions in various social units and his various social categories. People think of him in terms of the kind of father or lawyer or man or Catholic or citizen he is. Another basis for picturing him is provided by the identities he developed during earlier stages of his life. People may refer to the self-centered child in him or the infant in him. Some of these earlier identities seem to be organized in terms of people with whom he has identified most strongly. When he does something that reminds us of one of these internalized objects, his father, for instance, we say that his action reflects the father in him.

Together, all the regions by which a man is known constitute his *public identity*. The specific regions into which the total identity is divided are sub-identities. *Sub-identity* is an organized set of attributes representing a particular person: the kind of lawyer he is, the kind of father he is when he manifests the attributes of his internalized father, the kind of child he becomes when he is very fatigued. Like a fingerprint, each pattern of attributes is unique to a particular individual. The sub-identity identifies him and him alone to others in a particular social group. It gives him a continuity of meaning for the others in the group.

Analysis of Sub-Identities: Dimensions and Values

Attributes are actually locations on particular dimensions. A *dimension* is a set of alternative attributes which is conceived as a roughly linear scale. Dimensions are the basic categories for defining the meanings of objects. The particular dimensions and their definitions vary with the social group. In American society, for example, some dimensions of the masculine sub-identity are initiative, physical strength, preference for certain types of dress. Such dimensions are not relevant to masculinity in all societies.

A dimension can contain many attributes or only a few. Attributes on a dimension typically represent only a partially ordered set. They cannot be assigned precise numerical values, so that locations on different dimensions, like degree of maturity and relative status, are not always commensurable.

Social groups assign various values to different locations. The distribution of values for a dimension does not always constitute a linear scale. The values also define thresholds which may divide the dimension into forbidden, acceptable, desirable, and ideal segments. It is desirable for a man to show a lot of initiative and undesirable for him to be passive. It is evil to steal and good to be honest. Sometimes the ideal and the undesirable segments are at opposite extremes of the distribution; sometimes the ideal is in the middle, like Aristotle's golden mean. Then the two extremes tend to include unacceptable attributes.

Types of Sub-Identity

A man can be known to others in terms of the kind of ditch-digger, American, Mason, brother, infantile person, lover, or even pipe smoker, he is. There are obviously many other possible labels. Again we face the issue of content. How does one select a delimited number of sub-identities that is most crucial for explaining the interaction of two people?

A consideration of the nature of attributes suggests one basis for selection. The fact that attributes are experienced as positions on dimensions permits members of a social group to evaluate the relative goodness of two individuals or to compare a man's current attributes with the ones he had previously. This process of invidious comparison is one of the ways in which a social group imposes its will on its individual members. Attributes with considerable significance for the group elicit strong evaluations and often some kind of action. But attributes which do not have much significance for the group's welfare are not evaluated in particularly emotional terms. A banker's career is likely to depend on his business acumen and honesty, but not on his skill as a bridge player or his taste in music. As each member of a group participates in its activities, he learns the common definitions of dimensions, values, and social significance. He uses them to conceptualize the sub-identities of all the members including himself.

Degree of social significance, then, is the primary criterion for deciding on the contents of sub-identities. If we use this criterion, we find that a person's sub-identities are organized primarily with respect to his positions in the social structure, his social categories, and his earlier sub-identities. These, in turn, reflect his former positions and social categories.

Social Positions, Social Categories, and Sub-Identities

Social positions, the basic units of social structure, are defined independently of their occupants. In great part the definitions implement the functions of particular organizations like families or businesses. By occupying positions like father or parishioner, a person becomes subject to the constraints created by the definitions of the positions. He has certain obligations as well as rights. Within particular groups, there are commonly shared standards about the fulfilment of these obligations. There are also standards about different social categories. Standards applicable to the more socially significant dimensions may be enforced by the law and by public pressure. In most cases norms are internalized, so that many define ideals or are enforced by the pressures of conscience.

In relating to a particular member, others in the group perceive him primarily in terms of various social positions and categories. For that reason he becomes known as the person with particular attributes on the dimensions of those positions and categories. He has public sub-identities as a lawyer, a father, a southerner, a man, a Mason, and so forth.

It is important to stress, parenthetically, some similarities and a difference between sub-identities and social positions and categories. At all stages of development, a person has to learn styles of behavior which satisfy his needs and also fulfill his obligations as an occupant of positions in the social structure. Such styles are evaluated as acceptable or ideal; styles which violate his obligations are evaluated as unacceptable or sinful. As a member of the family, the school, the club and other groups, he internalizes their meanings and values. And they define the ways he learns to behave. Hence there is a rough isomorphism between positions and categories, on one hand, and sub-identities on the other.

Another similarity between the social and psychological concepts is crucial for the understanding of human interactions. The concepts are either defined in reciprocal terms or connote reciprocity. Norms to which the occupant of a social position must conform are defined as rights and obligations. A person in a given position has a right to expect he will be treated in a particular way by a person in the reciprocal position. A person in a particular category expects certain kinds of treatment from people in other categories. Similarly, the attributes of a man with a particular sub-identity are established in his relationships with others. By virtue of those attributes he expects certain types of responses from others. All concepts are defined in terms of human interaction.

Although isomorphic and interpersonal, the two types of concepts differ in a fundamental respect. Social positions exist whether or not they are occupied, and are independent of the attributes of particular people. All kinds of people can be fathers or accountants. A sub-identity describes the pattern of psychological characteristics of a particular person in a position or category. His sub-identity refers to the *kind* of father he is: whether he is supportive or conscientious or sadistic or consistent. Some other man occupying the same position might have a very different sub-identity: a different set of attributes on the same dimensions, or even attributes on additional dimensions.

Sub-Identity and Component Sub-Identities

When viewed as a region, each sub-identity contains certain structured components, which are the sub-identities of earlier years. Within him, each man contains such earlier identities as an infant and a little boy and an adolescent. These represent the kind of infant and boy and adolescent he became as a result of the unique relationships he developed with his particular mother and father and brother and teacher and heroes. As an infant, for example, he learned to make passive requests in his relationship with a particular kind of mother—a supportive or a cold or an inconsistent one—so that he became the kind of baby he was. And he internalized his mother—he developed an internal picture of her as the kind of person with whom one relates passively. As an adult, he is sometimes inclined to project this picture to his wife, particularly when things go wrong and he falls back on his passive, infantile self. If he is mature, the earlier sub-identity is integrated with the total structure so that he is passive or demanding at appropriate times, and he rarely resorts to inappropriate infantile expressions.

Spatial Properties of Sub-Identities

In what structural sense can the different sub-identities of an object be considered as separate regions within the total public identity? First they differ in their dimensions and attributes. A man behaves differently when he is expressing the kind of father he is than when he is expressing the kind of husband he is. Some of the attributes of different sub-identities are incompatible. In expressing a childish part of himself, a man may be very greedy; in his more mature identity, he may be generous.

The boundaries of some sub-identities are defined by particular times and regions. A man is an employee at his plant on weekdays, a member of a golfing group on Saturday afternoons, and a teacher of religion in Sunday school. Because of the temporal and spatial separations, the kind of person he is in his golf group might surprise his fellow employees or the children in his Sunday school. Communications among the three sub-identities and their interdependence are affected by their positions in time and space in addition to the differences in their attributes.

Structurally, most objects are surprisingly *fluid:* their attributes are readily changed. Gods, for example, can take the forms of different animate and inanimate objects, can become infinitely small or can encompass everything, including the observer. Of course a man is usually experienced as being less amenable to change—he is usually identified in terms of the confines of his skin, his actions, and, sometimes, his possessions and kin. Yet his attributes, particularly his psychological ones, can vary markedly in the minds of the observers. Even a man's physical attributes can vary to a considerable extent. This variation is extreme when he appears in one of our night dreams or daydreams, or when we are drugged or very fatigued. Even during the waking state, however, our picture of a man can change markedly. After heroic exploits his stature may assume heroic proportions to the onlookers. And he can look "small" if he engages in certain petty, underhanded activities.

3. SELF-IDENTITY

Origins of a Conception of Self

Body Image

Boas (1911) once observed that "the three personal pronouns—I, thou, and he—occur in all human languages," and that "the underlying idea of these pronouns is the clear distinction between the self as speaker, the person or object spoken to, and that spoken of." To be understood, the self, a special kind of object, must be traced back to a body image. Studies of infants during the first year reveal a continual growth of the capacity to discriminate between what is later labelled as self and non-self. The discrimination, which is initially made between the boundaries of one's body and the rest of the world, is based on two kinds of experience. The child learns very early the difference between his sensations when he touches part of his body and when he touches other objects. He arrives at the same division of body and non-body when he compares the things he can and cannot control. He can make his hand move if he wills it, but he cannot make a chair move by an act of will.

Language and Meaning

The concept of self cannot really be described outside the context of the society in which the self is developed. Language provides labels for positions in space and in time, thus enabling a person to think of objects as having an identity. In his social experiences a child learns the necessary labels, the personal and possessive pronouns.

Most important for the present topic, interactions with other people orient a child to the meanings of various facets of self and to the standards for evaluating oneself. Once the standards are internalized they provide the limits for behavior and the incentives necessary for implementing the goals of various social groups. A young child cries for nourishment and soon realizes that his mother wants to provide it. He later learns to think he has a right and that she feels obligated to honor it. Such a definition presumes the interaction of people and the evaluation of the behavior of each.

Social Interaction and the Development of Self-Identity

To picture the conditions under which a self-identity develops, and is continually modified, one need only consider a meeting between two people. At a particular moment, each person reacts to the previous behavior of the other and in anticipation of his next reaction. During the encounter, each person is aware of himself and of the other person. Each evaluates his own behavior and the other's reactions; each gets impressions of the judgments of his behavior by the other, and each reacts to these judgments (Cooley, 1922).

An interaction depends on the participants being members of the same society and having a shared group of meanings and values. Only then can the two people communicate. Only then can either participant anticipate that the other will know the signs of the social positions held by both, and of their different sub-identities. Only then can either participant be confident of obtaining the appropriate behavior from the other; only then can the participants engage in complementary internal and external reactions.

By working out possible responses in his own mind before he makes them, a participant can inhibit impulses that are not consistent with the values of his group and his internalized values, and can substitute more acceptable alternatives. The other person's reactions, both internal and external, prove a test of the adequacy of the resultant action, and elicit new impulses in turn. And so the encounter continues until it terminates.

An individual learns about his identity, then, not only from observing what he is thinking, feeling, and doing, but also from reactions to him by important people in his social group. From the responses of others to his identity, he becomes increasingly aware of it as an object and of the necessity to behave and feel in such ways as to make his identity acceptable to himself and to others. From variations in the responses of others to differences in his behavior, he develops a picture of an ideal self, an acceptable self, and an unacceptable one.

Social interaction conveys to a man not only how people in the community have come to view him, but also how they regard other members. The communication of such pictures among the members in the group contributes to a common frame of reference concerning the meanings, evaluations, and social consequences of actions or other attributes in terms of which identities are defined. The shared definitions of attributes must be learned before a person can evaluate the adequacy with which he fulfills the requirements of different positions. Participation in a group's activities thus ultimately indoctrinates a man into its structure, functions, and rules. A man cannot be regarded as a true member of a group until he develops a public identity within the group, and he becomes concerned with maintaining a self-identity which is compatible with the group's primary goals. The self is then a primary object of value, an object with attributes that must be kept consistent with the requirements of social positions. As Mead (1935) has put it, "Until one can respond to himself as the community responds to him, he does not genuinely belong to the community."

Sub-Identity and Centrality

In much of the literature, the self is viewed as a totality. Such an approach cannot do justice to the complexity of an identity. Since one reacts to one's own identity as an object, one experiences it in the same terms as other objects. It may help the reader to review the terms here, since a considerable number have been presented in a short space. We have been concerned with the analysis of identity as an object of perception. One's public identity is what one stands for in the minds of others. An identity consists of many dimensions, the meanings of which are derived from social experiences. Most of the meanings are shared by members of particular social groups. On interacting with significant people, an individual identifies himself in terms of his social positions and categories. To people in a given social position or category, some subsets of the possible alternative attributes within a dimension are considered undesirable, some are acceptable, and some attractive or even ideal.

Centrality

Self-identity is the picture of oneself built up from the reactions of others and from looking at oneself from others' points of view. A man's evaluation of an attribute and his feelings about the evaluation depend on the *centrality* of the dimension. The degree of centrality is a function of social consequences. The consequences of some attributes can be very great. Certain attributes of the masculine sub-identity provide vivid examples. Nonconsummation of a marriage is considered a justifiable reason for divorce. Attributes contributing to nonconsummation, like lack of sexual desire and impotence, are devalued as effeminate, and seriously lower a man's standing in the eyes of his peers. Similarly, in some societies, a man's skin color or his hereditary background have a considerable bearing on the status of people to whom he has access, the jobs he can hope to obtain, and his level of education. Being in the acceptable or non-acceptable segments of such dimensions can seriously affect a man's public identity. It is not surprising, therefore, that they are among the more *central* dimensions of his self-identity. They are heavily loaded in his self-evaluation.

Fluctuations of one's locations on central dimensions, like sexual potency or occupational skill, produce greater variations in self-esteem than do the same amounts of fluctuation of locations on less central dimension, like skill in bridge or baseball. Evaluations of attributes on central dimensions are likely to be applied to one's total self-identity. A man who fails in his occupation is likely to consider himself a failure; a man who consistently plays a poor game of bridge is more likely to be critical not of himself but of his skill—providing he is not a professional bridge player.

4. INTERACTION

The complex process involving the behavior of two people can be divided into units, which we shall call *reactions*. A reaction is any kind of response to another person. It can be a thought, a glance, a gesture, a statement. Thinking is an internal reaction; it is experienced by oneself but not necessarily communicated to the other person. Communicated reactions, those conveyed to the other person, are the primary vehicle for carrying on interpersonal behavior.

Motives and Action

A need or motivational state is a complicated system of reactions that has significance for interaction and for variations in self-esteem. One judges oneself in terms of the acceptability of one's needs. A need is defined here as a predisposition to engage in any of a group of actions that implement a particular goal state.

The impulse to action can be analyzed in terms of at least four dimensions [1]: the intended act, the object, the affect, and the agent. Elements within each of the dimensions can be ordered from most to least direct with respect to attainment of the goal state. If the goal state is the expression of aggression, physical attack may be the most direct act, an irritating person the most direct object, the self the most direct agent, and rage the most direct affect. But unless direct expression on such central dimensions is provoked, it is evaluated as undesirable in most social groups. To avoid a marked decline in self-esteem, the average person has a tendency to relinquish the most direct forms of expression in favor of other locations on the dimensions of motivational states.

In what terms might the contents of dimensions such as action or objects be analyzed? For purposes of the cross-cultural study of personality, a scheme is needed which is applicable in different societies. There is, unfortunately, no consensus about any of the tentative methods which have been proposed for classifying types of action. Murray (in Parsons and Shils, 1951) has prepared a carefully considered, promising list of actions. Some examples are renunciation, rejection, acquisition, construction, and retention.

Research into the learning process has thrown some light on the organization of dimensions of objects. Empirical work, both clinical and experimental, reveals various dimensions of people, of animals, and of inanimate objects. A person in conflict about an impulse to express a need directly can substitute a less direct dimension for an original one. When all human objects are proscribed, an inanimate one can be substituted by even mature people. And when only some human objects are proscribed, they may be replaced by others that are more acceptable.

Chains of Reactions

A meeting between two people can be viewed as an episode. The events follow a meaningful sequence. There is a beginning and a middle and a termination. At the beginning, each person greets the other and anticipates a greeting in return. Social practice provides other forms of prescribed behavior for the subsequent parts of the episode.

In addition to such socially determined aspects of the sequence, there are others which reflect the sub-identities of the two participants and the nature of the situation. If the relationship is an authoritative one, the episode may start with the dominant person making a demand. The person in the inferior position then engages in an act of compliance or deference, to which the authority responds by signifying his intention— to provide a reward or forego a penalty. If one participant relates passively to the other and is inclined to seek succorance, the two manifest another chain of reactions. The passive one first finds that he has a problem, but avoids any attempts to solve it. Instead he makes implicit or explicit requests of the other, who provides help. Having terminated the emergency, the supportive person obtains satisfaction from signs of adequacy or of gratification.

There exist many other such chains of surprisingly predictable steps. Little information is available about such chains. It is not possible, therefore, to classify them at this time. Some of them are difficult to study because they contain unconscious links. Interactions are difficult to interpret because they usually contain a number of simultaneous or overlapping chains. During the same few minutes, a man and woman in an office may be working to finish a job, flirting with each other, and striving for dominance over each other.

Although hard to analyze, chains of reactions demonstrate some consistent characteristics even on casual observation. Unconscious links, for example, involve repudiated wishes, which are too painful to acknowledge. Consequently, they are not amenable to conscious control. The more unconscious links in a chain, the more slavishly it tends to be followed.

Interactions on the conscious and unconscious levels tend to be complementary. Two people who are consciously involved in a co-operative pursuit may be unconsciously trying to prevent its completion or to hurt each other. Or two people with conscious asexual reactions may have unconscious sexual ones.

Cathexes and Bonds

It is the intra-individual forces which probably contribute the most to the stability of relationships. Forces linking people to each other are not amenable to direct observation. They must be inferred. One such force is the *cathexis* of an object by a sub-identity of the self. A cathexis develops when a particular emotional state has been aroused by some fantasied or actual commerce with an object. One can infer the cathexis from the disposition to re-experience the affect. One is inclined to repeat appropriate acts with the object: to play chess with a friend, to argue with a relative. As forces, cathexes have a point of origin. It is in the sub-region of the self involved in the particular relationship. Cathexes also vary in force, and they have direction. They are aimed at a particular object or type of object. It may be a person, but it can just as easily be a goal, like a university degree. When the object is a person he does not have to be aware of the cathexis; he may even be a creation of fantasy.

Bonds are mutual cathexes. The emotional resultants of a chain of reactions create a bond between two people. As a result, they are inclined to seek opportunities to repeat the shared activities. If they enjoy a trip to the seashore, they look forward to the next holiday when they can make such a trip.

Bonds can entail gratification or pain or both. Examples of the gratifying or positive types come to mind readily: two people love each other, or share a common interest. When pain is involved, it usually provides relief of a more unpleasant condition. A guilty child, for example, may confess a misdeed in order to be spanked. The confession represents an attempt at atonement or a wish to get rid of the fear of inevitable punishment.

Conflict and Sub-Identity

The explanation of the dynamics of interaction requires the consideration of one more concept, that of *defense mechanisms*. Defenses provide one means of resolving conflicts, particularly those between incompatible sub-identities or aspects of a sub-identity. Such conflicts can be very painful if they involve central dimensions.

Values pertaining to the more central dimensions are often difficult to satisfy. The high standards of achievement in certain groups of our society provide a good example, as do the standards for controlling aggression that are imposed on the young child in the middle class. It is often difficult for the child to establish a filial sub-identity which simultaneously satisfies such standards and permits him to gratify his needs.

Once an acceptable identity is established it tends to be maintained tenaciously. It becomes an object of gratification in its own right because it provides a means of relating to others in a socially acceptable manner, and simultaneously gratifying one's needs. But, as we have noted, a boy can persist in his picture of the kind of adequate son he is only as long as it is validated by the reactions of parents and other members of his family. He enters each social situation with certain set anticipations that people will respond in a manner that is appropriate, within limits, to his sub-identity. What if they act as though he is disobedient or disrespectful or destructive—attributes which violate his moral standards? He must then face the contradiction between his self-identity and his public identity.

Some conflicts often involve different sub-identities of the self. In responding to an aggressive action by a competitor, a businessman may be simultaneously prompted to display the initiative characteristic of his occupational identity and the sensitivity and passivity characteristic of his identity as a young child. Or in competing with a relative, the businessman may be prompted to display the overt aggression characteristic of his particular occupational identity and the warmth and sacrifice characteristic of his particular sub-identity as a kinsman.

Both kinds of conflict represent desires for incompatible locations on the same dimension. If a man takes initiative he cannot also make passive appeals. If he makes sacrifices he cannot also regard himself as a tough competitor. Such discrepancies are basic to conflicts involving identity. The selection of either attribute violates the minimal standards for one of the sub-identities, and thus produces a serious lowering of self-esteem.

Defense Mechanisms

To resolve the problem, the man can try to be as realistic as possible about the facts and think about a possible solution. He can change his values for example, or discuss his problem with his relative. If there is no good solution, or if his anxiety becomes too intense, he may have to resort to another kind of problem-solving technique. He modifies his perception of the conflicting attributes.

The concept of defense must be used with caution. Many psychoanalysts describe any kind of behavior that reduces anxiety or any kind of substitute or process of substitution or behavior that might be a substitute for a forbidden impulse as defense. Symptoms and myths and some customs have been described as defenses, which they are in this broad sense.

When a term is applied to so many different kinds of phenomena its meaning becomes imprecise. It seems preferable to use the original concept of defense, a concept that refers to internal processes and not observable behavior (Freud, 1949). Criteria for identifying such processes have been inferred by Miller and Swanson (1960) from clinical practices. One necessary condition for identifying a defense is the inability of a person to give an accurate report of certain anxiety-producing information. A second condition requires that he express the information indirectly in a language he does not understand. The indirect expression may take such forms as slips of the tongue or dreams. A third condition is the initiation of the processes by conflict or some other source of anxiety.

According to this definition, a defense accounts for the misperception of facts. The present criteria reflect the traditional psychoanalytic orientation, one that may have to be broadened. As will be indicated in the next section, some of the same perceptual mechanisms may be found both in defenses and in phenomena involved in accurate social perception.

The nature of a specific defense is inferred from the kind of interpretation and behavior substituted for the original information that induced anxiety. Projection is inferred if a boy gives indirect evidence of a wish to hurt his father, is not conscious of the impulse, but attributes it to his father. If the boy substitutes a dog for his father, the defense is labelled as displacement of the object. If he is inordinately helpful instead of aggressive the mechanism is reversal. If he has attacked his father and now believes that the act was a helpful or friendly one, then the defense is denial.

Symptoms, myths, and customs are not defense mechanisms, but may or may not be the derivatives of blocked impulses. Such behaviors are derivatives if they have been substituted unconsciously for anxiety-provoking information that cannot be reported accurately.

Projection and Introjection

Of particular significance for social interaction are the mechanisms of projection and introjection. The psychological literature contains a number of different conceptions of projection, so that it is necessary to define the one used here. According to the present definition, projection is a displacement of the perceived agent: a person sees an attribute of his own as applying to another person. Such displacement may be viewed as a style of perception, and not necessarily a defensive one. The attribute is not necessarily unacceptable, nor need its perception be distorted in oneself. The perceiver may feel happy and be inclined to exaggerate the happiness of friends. And he does not necessarily feel that he no longer has the attribute after he has used the defense.

As defined here, projective perception is probably a component of the defense mechanism of projection described in the clinical literature. According to that description, an undesirable attribute is disowned and seen or exaggerated in somebody else. A man who is tempted to steal feels he is scrupulously honest, but erroneously suspects others of trying to cheat him. This process seems to involve more than the non-defense version of projection described here. There is also a disowning of the impulse, which is probably accomplished by the mechanism of denial.

Introjection, too, requires clarification, since it need not be a defense, and it is often used interchangeably with identification. We shall view introjection as a perceptual process resulting in the taking to oneself of the attributes of others. Again, such attributes can be either highly valued or devalued. Projection and introjection seem to differ primarily with respect to the direction in which the borrowed attributes are transferred. In the former mechanism, they are shifted from oneself to an object; the process is experienced as putting part of one's sub-identity into the object. In the latter mechanism, the attributes are shifted from the object to oneself. The process is experienced as an internalization of a sub-identity or part of one.

Social Communication and the Splitting of Sub-Identities

A combination of projective and introjective perceptions seems to be a minimal requisite for all interpersonal communication. Klein (1948) has labelled the simultaneous use of the two types of perception as projective identification. Her description of this combination is very similar to Cooley's description of interpersonal behavior. To communicate with someone, we have to know what he is thinking and feeling. First we get information from his statements and his gestures. From this information, we get an impression which we then project to him. Next we put ourselves in his place by means of introjection. We can then visualize what he is thinking and how he is feeling. Then we check the accuracy of this impression in terms of his next comments and acts and our subsequent projections and introjections.

The checking of another's probable reactions is an extremely complex process. It is very easy to err when we judge how he feels in terms of what we would feel if we were in his place when he reacts to us. Temporary confusion about the attributes of self-identity and object are very common. Most normal people use subsequent information to correct their errors. Some neurotic people perpetuate certain kinds of misinterpretations as a means of allaying anxiety. Their perceptions may be interpreted in the light of defensive distortions.

The ways in which a person uses the projective and introjective types of perception also affect the integrity of his sub-identities. Of course, some splitting of the total identity into sub-identities is normal and necessary. The formal, competitive businessman at the office becomes the warm, supportive father at home. He would be in difficulty with his colleagues and with his wife and children if he did not maintain a barrier between the two sub-identities: if he expressed his occupational sub-identity at home and his sub-identity as a father at the office.

Conflict between the ideal and forbidden aspects of a sub-identity, or between incompatible, simultaneous sub-identities sometimes split a sub-identity into the parts that Sullivan has called the "good me" and the "bad me." The splitting is accomplished by projecting the unacceptable part of the sub-identity or the bad introjected object to some real person, who is then perceived as a persecutor. In that event the perception becomes defensive. The bad attributes in one's sub-identity may then be denied and the remainder idealized (Klein, 1948).

Another kind of splitting is accomplished by denying the bad attributes in oneself and explaining them as properties of introjected bad objects. In our society, a man may explain his unwelcome aggression by reporting that he was mistreated in childhood by a cruel parent. Hence the man feels that it is not he but the cruel father in him who is responsible for the aggression. His introjected bad object has been split from the rest of the self. This kind of split is common in Thailand where people assume that they can be inhabited by the spirit of a person who has recently died. A woman who was bathing in a river was possessed by the spirit of a man who had drowned not long before. She spoke in his voice, and talked of past experiences in his life as though she were he. After she was beaten vigorously her body rejected the spirit.[2] One is tempted to guess that this woman was split between her feminine, or good, self and her masculine, or bad, one, that she introjected the man whose death was known to her, and that she denied and projected her feminine self. Hence she was "possessed" by his spirit. Similar processes may be involved in the performances of some religious mediums.

Splitting of sub-identities need not be the result of defensive misperceptions, but can reflect extreme incompatibility in the identities, an incompatibility caused by discontinuities in socialization. Normally a sub-identity of an adult represents an organization of earlier sub-identities. It may not be possible to integrate them if earlier stages of development have been very discontinuous. According to Erikson (1954) sudden changes in the rearing of the Southern Negro make it virtually impossible for him to integrate his sub-identities. In an initial stage, he learns to be a tender, rhythmic, mammy's honey child. Next he becomes the anal compulsive, clean, friendly Uncle Tom. Still later, he develops an identity as a dirty, anal-sadistic, phallic, rapist. Such incompatible early sub-identities cannot be organized as part of the masculine sub-identity of adulthood. By rather primitive defenses the Negro maintains impenetrable boundaries between the different sub-identities, and usually obliterates awareness of all but one of them at any particular time.

Perception of Interrelationships [3]

Events in an interpersonal relationship vary constantly with the perceptions, both conscious and unconscious, of self and other on the part of each participant. The actual sources of information are many, as is indicated in the following diagram.

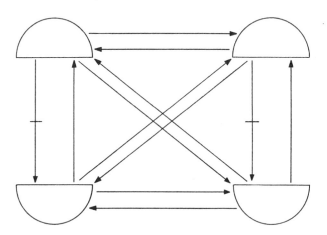

The two semicircles on the left represent one person. The top half is his conscious sub-identity, and the bottom half is his unconscious sub-identity. On the right are two semicircles representing another, interacting person. The arrows represent directions of perception. The two conscious identities have access to each other, as do the two unconscious ones. The conscious part of neither person is aware of his unconscious part, but the obverse is not necessarily true. The conscious part of each participant can also perceive attributes in the other participant of which he is unconscious. And each can respond unconsciously to attributes of which he is conscious in the other participant.

The diagram can be illustrated by some details from a marital relationship. The conscious part of the man is his masculine sex-identity, and the conscious part of the woman is her feminine sex-identity. Unconsciously the man is feminine and the woman masculine. Consciously, the woman can perceive some of her husband's unconscious feminine attributes, just as he can perceive some of her masculine ones. Such perceptions may or may not provide the bases for cathexes or avoidances. The unconscious feminine attributes of the man may enable him to establish a bond with the conscious identity of the woman on the basis of a common interest in cooking. If the man is too feminine, the woman may be repelled.

Bonds and Defense Mechanisms

The presence and absence of bonds is affected in great part by the nature of the mutual defense mechanisms. A man and wife who have become very angry at each other can maintain the relationship if they deny their feelings. But the peace is an uneasy one. It is subject to constant strain by events that contradict the false beliefs of the participants.

A relationship with many more frictions develops if each participant is inclined to project the unconscious, aggressive part of his sub-identity to the other person. While neither individual has to suffer the pangs of guilt, both feel attacked and must defend themselves. Such mutual projection is apparently common among the Dobuans (Fortune, 1932). Yet by itself, projection does not have to cause a weakening of bonds. The stability of a relationship is increased when the aggressive parts of the self are projected to external objects. The Arapesh (Mead, 1935) learn that all friends are good and that most other people are bad. Projections of evil selves to outsiders therefore help to stabilize friendships and to unify the in-group.

The Fit Between Sub-Identities

Almost all the sub-identities of each person in the family tend to become involved in bonds with parallel or complementary sub-identities of the other members. The relationships involve sub-identities developed in earlier years and current ones. Adding to the complexity of bonds between people are split sub-identities and contradictory reactions to objects that have also been split. During his childhood, for example, a man might have developed a good self which co-operated well with a supportive segment of his mother's identity and an evil self which engaged in mutual attack with a non-maternal aspect of her identity. Both of these selves may enter into his current bonds with his wife.

In stable families, many of the bonds between husband and wife are present from the beginning of marriage. The couple also develop other bonds in the course of trying out their relationships with each other, of reliving old bad relationships and finding them improved, and of reorganizing their marriage because of events like the birth of a child.

Even very disturbed people with poorly formed sub-identities and primitive defenses often fit each other astonishingly well. One example is provided by the marriage of a very dominant woman and a man obsessed with his aggression. The woman had been deprived of recognition and love throughout her first twenty years of life by parents who rejected her in favor of her brother. Her husband's sadistic father had been brutal both psychologically and physically and had provoked his son to constant rebellion. In later years, the husband continued the old battle with other men. He was easily overwhelmed by rage, and he sometimes had thoughts, and even committed acts, which caused him considerable guilt. One very strong bond in the marriage was forged by the continuous criticism of the husband by his wife, an act that produced lengthy arguments. Although they were painful, the arguments enabled the woman to reassure herself of her power over a man, and they gave her husband relief of his constant guilt about his homicidal wishes. So strong was the mutual relief provided by the constant conflict between the boyish, aggressive sub-identity of the wife and the raging, guilty, filial sub-identity of the husband that the marriage lasted for many years despite an almost complete lack of common conscious interests, friends, or activities. The couple finally sought professional help because their ten year old son was failing in school and was having accidents in which he hurt himself badly. Both parents had identified with neglectful, cruel fathers and had been taking turns in beating the son. The son got some gratification from these attacks because they relieved his guilt. But they were very painful, and he found he could stop them by hurting himself academically and physically. His resultant inadequacy reassured the mother of her power and reassured the father that the son was not a serious competitor for his wife's love. Temporarily the parents gave the son a respite from attack and granted him some of the attention he craved. Were it not for some of the son's socially handicapping problems, the marriage would probably have continued without professional assistance. Of theoretical interest is the family's stability, a characteristic that would have been difficult to predict from psychological tests of either or even both parents. The stability depended less on the parents' intrapersonal attributes than on an attribute of their interaction: the good fit between unconscious components of the parents' sub-identities.

Stability and Flexibility of Relationships

The issues that have been discussed thus far point to a primary difference between questions raised about intrapersonal and interpersonal events. Interpersonal questions employ the information about individuals, but place it in a special context. Each attribute or defense mechanism or moral standard is interpreted in terms of its contribution to the stability and flexibility of a relationship. If we study honesty, we do not restrict our inquiry to a person's moral standards and his honesty under various circumstances. We also ask how his attributes affect his ability to make bonds with a particular individual in a specific situation.

The possible benefits of viewing attributes in an interpersonal context can be illustrated further by the case of a thirteen-year-old boy who could not read. Tests revealed that his intelligence was at least average. Some light was thrown on his problem by such attributes as his high anxiety with adults, and his inclination to retreat into a world of daydreams when others were talking with him. But the organization of his attributes into a meaningful pattern required further information about his relationships with other members of his family. Some years earlier the boy's parents had become separated, a fact that disturbed him very much. He had made some progress in learning to read, but he lost his skill because he became very anxious and neglected his work. Then his parents patched up their differences. At the time they expressed guilt about having caused the son's symptoms, which they attributed to the broken home. One of their primary reasons for living together again, therefore, was to give him enough security to overcome his problems. From then on, he neglected reading because of the impression that his lack of ability was the one thing that kept his parents together. From his point of view, his symptom maintained the stability of the family.

Factors Promoting Stability and Instability

Some social scientists are inclined to use intrapersonal labels of pathology in describing certain attributes of people in different societies. It is tempting, for example, to describe the Dobuans (Fortune, 1932) and Kwakiutls (Benedict, 1934) as paranoid, the Arapesh (Mead, 1935) and Alorese (DuBois, 1944) as having poor ego structures, and the Balinese (Bateson and Mead, 1942) as schizoid. Such descriptions may be accurate, but in some cases they would be clarified further by information about their positive contributions to interpersonal relationships. It is assumed here that even when "symptoms" are socially handicapping, they are contributing to the stability of some relationships—at least in the eyes of the participants.

Which factors affect the stability relationships between people? Empirical evidence is lacking, but it is possible to speculate with confidence about answers that seem applicable to behavior in different societies. In what follows, the points are phrases in the psychological language of this chapter, and the examples illustrate sources of instability in the marital relationship.

A frequent cause of instability is a poor fit between the sub-identities of participants. The sub-identities may lack congruence because the husband and wife come from different societies or social classes. The resultant differences in the meanings of attributes and values about them interfere with the communication necessary for making bonds. Sometimes a fit is not possible because one of the spouses never developed a particular identity, possibly because of a difficult past, and cannot respond to the complementary identity in the other person.

External factors can also make relationships unstable. A provocative mother-in-law can elicit expressions of early sub-identities and considerable friction between the spouses. Membership in social groups who reject traditional morality weakens the boundaries of the marriage and provides temptations to violate the marital vows thus weakening the marital relationship. A system can be stabilized by some external forces. Examples are rigid external boundaries of the marriage, like the prohibition of divorce among Catholics, and coercive social forces, like the shared belief in some groups that a woman should always obey her husband.

Defense mechanisms provide a third source of fluctuation in stability. A marriage is likely to be stormy if the two people project their hostile, unconscious sub-identities to each other, so that they come to regard each other as attackers; or if either partner acts aggressively and denies the meaning of his act. Frictions can be avoided if the same defenses are applied to other objects or facts: if the husband and wife project their hostilities to an outsider or deny each other's inadequacies. Still more conducive to stability are realistic methods of solving problems or relatively mature defenses like rationalizing one's difficulties.

Poorly formed or immature sub-identities in one or both marital partners can create a further reason for instability. Even if there is a good fit between different sub-identities, the predominant reliance on methods of relating which were serviceable in earlier years produces ambivalent reactions, sudden alternations between different parts of the sub-identity, and splitting of objects, which are seen as either very good or very bad. The more mature the participants, the less they manifest such handicapping reactions, and the more possible it is for them to behave toward each other in a predictable manner.

Ultimately the stability of relationships will probably be viewed in quantitative terms. The positive components will probably include the number and strength of bonds, the number of cathexes, the number and strength of internal and external forces prompting the couple to work together, and the impermeability of the external boundary. The contributors to instability will probably include avoidances caused by various kinds of incompatibilities, splits in the perceptions of sub-identities and objects, the numbers and strengths of internal and external forces prompting the couple to separate, the relative permeability of the boundary, and the presence of attractions beyond the boundary that are greater than the attractions within it.

Factors Affecting the Flexibility of Relationships

Relationships vary not only in stability, but also in degree of flexibility. The more rigid the relationship, the less it can withstand changes in the situation or in the internal forces of either individual.

A common cause of rigid relationships is provided by values which proscribe many forms of behavior. Some couples have such strict moral standards, for example, that they react with guilt to certain impulses which other couples express without qualms. Outlets can also be delimited by the standards of other people. A man thinks twice, for instance, before he acts in ways that friends regard as manifesting actions of questionable taste.

A relationship becomes rigid if a couple maintain considerable psychological distance to overcome the difficulties caused by such problems as poorly fitting sub-identities and incompatible values. The anxiety is allayed by the avoidance of intimacy. On occasions when the marital partners fail to maintain the customary distance, both become anxious.

Rigid measures are also required to stabilize a marriage when there are weak bonds between husband and wife and strong bonds between each spouse and other objects. Such a situation is illustrated by a family in which the father and mother had little in common with each other. The little time they spent together seemed pleasant enough to them, but not particularly absorbing. At home the father had his activities, and the mother hers. The father conducted his activities with his son; the mother conducted hers with her daughter. The bonds between father and son were very strong as were the bonds between mother and daughter. Hence the marriage continued placidly until the children entered adolescence, spent most of their time with their many friends, and virtually abandoned the parents to their own devices.

Stable and rigid marriages can be maintained by means of a number of defense mechanisms. Most conducive to rigidity are denial and displacement of hostility to external scapegoats. Such defenses are not very efficient because the resulting perceptions are often obviously inaccurate. To corroborate them the couple may solicit impressions from people outside the family. A rigid stability may give way to instability if the corroboration is not forthcoming. Isolation and self-attack are more effective in promoting stability, but are also costly. Isolation creates psychological distance. Turning one's aggression inward results in depression, a reaction that can create considerable difficulties in the relationship. Only more mature techniques, like rationalization and rational problem solving, seem to facilitate a fairly flexible relationship.

In general, the stronger the unconscious bonds and the weaker the conscious ones, the more rigid the relationship has to be. The unconscious bonds are the ones that cannot be faced. They may be bonds between sadistic and masochistic components of sub-identity, between the perverted components, or between immature components. If such bonds are stronger than the conscious ones, the couple has to restrict their behavior so as to maintain the unconscious bonds and to avoid becoming aware of their significance. Situations and activities which may expose the meanings of the bonds or weaken them have to be avoided.

A REVIEW

This chapter has been devoted to selection of personality concepts useful in cross-cultural research. At the outset, it was assumed that this could be accomplished most effectively by treating the relationship between two people as the unit for describing personality. The interpersonal situation was divided into four categories: the situation, the object, the self-identity, the interaction.

Functionally, concepts were viewed in perceptual terms. They were analyzed as part of the lifespace, and interpreted in such terms as regions, boundaries, and forces. Objects and self-identity, for example, were regarded as psychological regions which could be divided into subregions, and which could be analyzed in terms of dimensions and attributes. Contents for the concepts were derived from conceptions of social structure and from some of the current conceptions of personality. In the concluding section interaction was described in terms of cathexes, bonds, defense mechanisms, and compatibility between subidentities. Factors affecting the relative stability and flexibility of interpersonal systems were enumerated. A number of examples were given of insights to be gained from viewing some problems in an interpersonal context.

The interpersonal orientation seems to satisfy the criteria for selecting concepts listed at the start of this chapter. The proposed concepts lend themselves to analyses of associations between social structure and personality. The concepts are also general enough to be meaningful in different societies, and are sufficiently linked to common sociological and psychological problems to permit the phrasing of testable problems in a specific society. Finally, the concepts lend themselves to the analysis of individual differences. People can be compared with respect to such characteristics as locations on dimensions, relative strengths of bonds, and predilections for certain defense mechanisms.

NOTES

1. The reasoning behind the selection of these dimensions is discussed by Miller and Swanson (1960).

2. Reported in a personal communication from Eric Miller.

3. The remainder of the chapter was rewritten after I participated with Peter Hildebrand, Herbert Phillipson, and John Sutherland in the planning of a research on marriage. I am grateful to them for their help in clarifying some of the concepts.

BIBLIOGRAPHY

Bateson G. and Mead, Margaret. 1942. *Balinese Character.* New York: Academy of Sciences.

Benedict, Ruth. 1934. *Patterns of Culture.* Boston: Houghton Mifflin Co.

Boas, F. 1911. *The Mind of Primitive Man.* New York: The Macmillan Co.

Cooley, C. H. 1922. *Human Nature and the Social Order.* New York: Charles Scribner and Sons.

Du Bois, Cora. 1944. *The People of Alor.* Minneapolis: University of Minnesota Press.

Erikson, E. H. 1954. "On the Sense of Inner Identity." In Knight, R. P. and Friedman, C. R. (eds.), *Psychoanalytic Psychiatry and Psychology.* New York: International Universities Press.

Fortune, R. 1932. *Sorcerers of Dobu.* London: G. Routledge and Sons.

Freud, S. 1949. *Collected Papers.* London: Hogarth Press.

Klein, Melassie. 1948. *Contributions to Psychoanalysis.* London: Hogarth Press.

Lewin, K. 1939. *The Conceptual Representation and the Measurement of Psychological Forces.* Durham, N. C.: Duke University Press.

Mead, G. H. 1939. *Mind, Self, and Society.* Chicago: University of Chicago Press.

Mead, Margaret. 1935. *Sex and Temperament in Three Primitive Societies.* London: G. Routledge and Sons.

Miller, D. R. and Swanson, G. E. 1960. *Inner Conflict and Defense.* New York: Henry Holt.

Parsons, Talcott and Shils, E. A., *et al.* 1951. *Toward a General Theory of Action.* Cambridge: Harvard University Press.

Sullivan, H. S. 1947. *Conceptions of Modern Psychiatry.* Washington: William Alanson White Foundation.

About the Chapter

A theory of action is an essential frame of reference for understanding what the subject expresses in the personality study situation. This frame of reference requires specification of the motivational component supporting the action as well as the normative component of the situation to which the action is oriented. It is held in this chapter that completion of these two kinds of analyses will reveal the subject's accessibility to study and will make his communications understandable.

About the Author

BERT KAPLAN, the editor of this volume, is Associate Professor of Psychology at the University of Kansas. He received his graduate training in clinical psychology at Harvard and has taught there in the Department of Social Relations and the School of Public Health. He has done field work with the Navaho and Zuni Indians in the Southwest. Together with T.F.A. Plaut he is the author of *Personality in a Communal Society; An Analysis of the Mental Health of the Hutterites.* He is editor of *Primary Records in Culture and Personality* and is presently engaged in research on Navaho psychopathology.

9

Personality Study and Culture

BERT KAPLAN

University of Kansas

This chapter is based on the premise that the optimal approach to personality study varies considerably from one culture to another and that both culture and the modal personality characteristics influence the personality study process. Clinical psychologists have long observed that their techniques work differently with different persons. One subject taking the Rorschach test, for example, may give a full, rich expressive protocol which gives insight into his deepest and most central personality processes while another gives a brief, sparse, stereotyped record which hardly yields any information at all. One of the major problems of the clinical psychologist is the failure of his techniques to yield the hoped-for information in a very substantial number of individual cases. He remedies this principally by varying his tools since experience has shown that very often rich expressive material will be elicited by one method but not by another. (Unfortunately there is a substantial group for whom nothing seems to work very well.) In general one can say that there is undoubtedly a very interesting and important interaction between the personality characteristics of subjects and the methods that should be used to study them. This interaction, about which all too little is known, has an important influence on the success of the study.

During the past four years as editor of the Microcard publication, *Primary Records in Culture and Personality* (1956, 1957), I have examined closely the raw materials of almost seventy-five culture and personality studies. Looking at Rorschachs from thirty societies, for example, or TATs from fifteen societies, the main impression is that the tests work differently in different cultures. While many of the sets of data appear to seem so similar to each other that it is difficult to distinguish them as coming from different groups (see Kaplan, Rickers-Ovsiankina and Joseph 1956) protocols from other cultures are so unique and dissimilar that they can be distinguished at a glance. The Rorschachs may be rich and expressive like those collected from the Hindu groups by G. M. Carstairs (1956), or sparse, stereotyped and defensive like the numerous ones collected from the Ojibwa. They can involve the Pilaga children's responses to details so tiny that we have difficulty in seeing them at all (Henry, 1956) or the vagueness and diffuseness of many of the Melanesian records. The TATs range from the long seventy-five typewritten page records collected from Javanese men by Hildred Geertz (1957) to the two and three sentence stories collected by William Henry from Navaho and Hopi children (1947). The tests obviously are working differently from one culture to another, and in some groups the general result is sparse unexpressive data that is of little use to anyone. I do not believe that this variability necessarily reflects directly any corresponding personality differences or that the reason Hindu Rorschachs are more differentiated than Navaho records is that the former are highly differentiated people and the latter are undifferentiated. Instead the difference appears to be a matter of the approach of the subjects to the test.

Lucien Hanks, Jr.'s TAT study (1957) of Thai agricultural workers from Bang Chan is relevant here. Hanks' subjects almost all told extremely brief stories to a set of specially drawn TAT pictures, with hardly any element of fantasy. Hanks, in speculating on the briefness of the stories, wondered whether the test created anxiety which led to defensive inhibition, or whether the ability to fantasy was undeveloped in his subjects. An examination of the records themselves suggests that the subjects without exception were not telling stories but describing the pictures and saying what seemed to be happening in them. The simplest explanation of their behavior is that they were not trying to produce fantasy. This motivational factor was the crucial one. It seems very possible that the Thais have the capacity for rich imaginative fantasy. The problem is to discover the conditions under which it will be expressed.

One prevalent attitude in work with projective techniques tends to discourage the flexibility and tentativeness necessary in personality study, both in our own society and cross-culturally. This is the view that if results are to be comparable, procedures must be standardized. Standardization, in effect, requires that the same procedures be followed in the same way regardless of what the results are. This is directly counter to my belief that *good* results—in the sense that they reflect personality adequately—depend upon tailoring the procedures to the characteristics of the subject and his culture.

This chapter seeks to analyze the cultural factors relevant to the personality study situation and attempts to provide the rudiments of a general theory dealing with the individual's accessibility to such study. It is hoped that this theoretical orientation will permit some understanding and prediction of the nature of the subject's expression and communication about himself, and the relevance of culture to such expression and communication.

Robert White (1944) has divided personality processes into three categories: those that the subject is aware of and will tell, those that he is aware of and will not tell and those that he is not aware of and thus cannot tell. This division may be modified by adding a fourth category; those the subject is *not* aware of but will tell anyway. The addition recognizes that expression and communication do not depend on the subject's explicit awareness of what he is doing. The fourfold scheme suggests that the two main variables in personality study are the subject's awareness of what is going on and, what is perhaps more important, the subject's motivation with respect to communications about himself.

In general, clinical psychologists have been most interested in the category of expressive behavior in which the subject reveals himself without intending to or knowing that he is doing so. The projective tests have been developed to facilitate this kind of expression which has been regarded as depending upon the subject's lack of attention to the meaning of his behavior. Such expressions have most usually been understood as deriving from the pressure of what the psychoanalyst has called the repetition compulsion and the working through of unconscious personality processes.

In order to understand the social contexts of such expressions of personality processes, we shall make the assumption—which some might hold to be debatable—that they are not a separate category of behavior but that they can be understood in the same terms as other action can. This assumption is fraught with serious consequences since it implies that these expressions are: a) motivated and b) that they are oriented to the subject's understanding of the situation. This means that what the subject expresses can be viewed as being exactly what he wanted to express. Otherwise, he would not lend the support of his motivational energies to the action and without this support no action would be possible. This expression takes place in relation to a social situation. One of the main elements of the social situation is a normative expectation defining what alternatives for action are available and specifying the legitimacy, morality and appropriateness of each alternative. This is a highly simplified version of the sociologist's view of action (see Parsons, 1951).

Action in the personality study situation is almost always action that is taken in relationship to the expectations of another person. For this reason it seems correct to speak of the communicative element in social action. In addition, the self provides an always present observer—an observer who judges action by more rigorous standards than other persons do.

When, therefore, the subject gives a particular response on the Rorschach test we can view this response not simply as something that he sees, a perception for which he has no responsibility, but as a means of saying something to the examiner about himself and at the same time as saying something to the self about himself. In the first context the subject is constituting himself, for the benefit of the other, as a particular kind of person, and in the second context he is constituting himself as a particular kind of person, for his own benefit.[1] In both cases in order to understand the action it is necessary to understand the situation—the attitudes, values, and expectations to which the action is oriented—and the motivations (what the person wants to do) relevant to the situation.

In analyzing personality study in these terms, one should be able to specify the social and cultural elements defining the behavioral alternatives, and the personal or motivational elements supporting particular choices of action. Within this framework it should be possible to understand the action of the subject of a personality study in the same way that all other social action can be understood.

The discussion which follows attempts to spell out some of the sociocultural components of the system of action in the personality study situation. We shall divide our discussion in terms of the two main contexts of such action, the self and the examiner.

THE SELF

Being the subject of a personality study creates the problem necessarily of what one is to tell the examiner. Perhaps equally important, it involves the problem of what one is to tell oneself. Selves do not simply grow or develop; they are made or constructed by the individual. This process of self-building goes on all the time but the personality study is a specially good time for it to happen. The building of the self conception thus is one of the factors which dominate communication. This construction undoubtedly occurs in relationship to normative patterns. It is clear enough that such patterning governs social or interpersonal behavior; it is perhaps less obvious that it orients intrapsychic functioning as well. There is reason to believe, however, that even in actions involving purely personal problems, persons are oriented unconsciously to both latent and explicit definitions of correct and incorrect action. In our society, for example, there is a strong expectation that the person will manage his impulse life in a way that will allow mastery and control but still permit adequate satisfaction. This expectation is reflected in the Freudian conception of a strong ego as being the equivalent of maturity and good health. While this kind of solution may be universally advocated, and is perhaps a condition for existence in a culture, it is none the less a cultural prescription. Ego strength, from this point of view, may be regarded not simply as a characteristic of the person that has developed as a result of particular past experiences, but as a way of experiencing and acting that is consciously or unconsciously selected from a variety of alternatives and can be mainly understood as a consequence of motivational dispositions toward conformity.

A. I. Hallowell (1954) has made a very penetrating analysis of the cultural shaping of conceptions of self. He states:

Just as different peoples entertain various beliefs about the nature of the universe, they likewise differ in their ideas about the nature of the self. And, just as we have discovered that notions about the nature of the beings and powers existent in the universe involve assumptions that are directly relevant to an understanding of the behavior of the individual in a given society, we must likewise assume that the individual's self-image and his interpretation of his own experience cannot be divorced from the concept of the self that is characteristic of his society. For such concepts are the major means by which different cultures promote self-orientation in the kind of meaningful terms that make self-awareness of functional importance in the maintenance of a human social order. In so far as the needs and goals of the individual are at the level of self-awareness, they are structured with reference to the kind of self-image that is consonant with other basic orientations that prepare the self for action in a culturally constituted world. (1955. *Culture and Experience*, p. 76)

One of the most important aspects of the constitution of the self conception is its place as a primary object of value among other objects. Hallowell regards the needs of the person for self enhancement, preservation, defense, and the like as the "keystone of the characteristic motivational structures that we find in man." He suggests that these needs occur in relationship to belief systems and other aspects of culture. One gets the impression that such ego needs vary in their strength from culture to culture although they appear to be universal. Vanity especially is particularly strong in some groups where it is almost the main theme around which the personality is constructed. In the personality study situation the material communicated by the subject is almost certainly governed by the strength and form of these needs.

Hallowell makes the additional point that normative orientations have an important part in the constitution of the self image. He reasons that self awareness is shaped and organized around the dimension of appraisal and that the self therefore is known and experienced in relationship to normative propositions which are frequently phrased in moral imperatives. The outcomes of these self appraisals are the main basis for feelings of self respect and self esteem. The apprehension lest some transgressions of standards be either committed or brought to light is experienced as guilt and anxiety. The particular content of what the self feels guilty or anxious about is a direct consequence of the content of normative orientations.

Since we have held that the building and maintenance of the self conception occurs directly in the personality study situation, it follows that the action of the subject should be seen in relation to the belief systems and values to which the subject is oriented. The subject's relationship to these belief systems or normative propositions however is often complicated. Where it is positive, we can speak of conformative tendencies and see the subject's actions as governed by the norms. However, the relationship to the norms is sometimes negative or ambivalent. In this case, the action or the self conception may be either directly opposite to what is expected or adhere to one of the culturally patterned alternatives for deviance.

The point to be emphasized, however, is that the personality or motivational component of the action, either in constituting the self or in presenting a particular picture to the examiner, generally has to do with the subject's relationship to what is expected, rather than directly to the action itself. Thus if the subject indicates either directly or indirectly that he is lazy, the motivation supporting this action does not have to do only, or even principally, with his passivity and dependence, but with his rejection of the value which holds that he should be energetic and hard working.

What the subject does, according to this view, either in or out of the personality study situation, is not to be explained by motivational processes which lead the subject to seek particular ends or prefer this or that action. Rather it is explained by motivations which have only an indirect relationship to the actions, their direct significance having to do with the subject's relationship to the situation.

This view has certain implications for the understanding of social behavior and for the empirical task of the culture and personality worker. It suggests that socially appropriate behavior is not necessarily a result of motivational processes that are isomorphic to the normative pattern (see the Spiro, Wallace and Devereux chapters in this volume) and which lead the person "to want to do as he has to do" to use Erich Fromm's classic phrase (1941). Instead, such behavior depends on a generalized conformative orientation (see Kaplan, 1957). The motivational or personality support for this orientation involves not the total of the personality processes of the individual but a very specific set of processes. Description of these specific processes may be regarded as the main task of the culture and personality worker. General descriptive studies of the personality characteristics of a particular people must be replaced by selective discovery and analysis of the particular processes that are relevant to the conformity-deviance orientation. David Riesman's, *The Lonely Crowd* (1950) suggests that these bases of conformity are themselves socially shared; they constitute "social character."

Applied to the social action which we have called "the constitution of the self," these considerations provide a formula for dealing with the social influences on the formation of self conceptions themselves and with the social influences on communication about the self to others. They suggest that in the analysis of the normative definition of the social situation of the personality study, and of the subject's orientation to the normative structure and the motivations relevant to this orientation, there lies the key to both the interpretation of the data of the personality study and the understanding of the success or failure of the study. This is, of course, a key which does not short cut by very much the need for detailed individual and cultural analysis. But it should be clear by now that no easy solution to the problem of cross-cultural personality study will be forthcoming.

Before closing our discussion of the "self" and personality study, a variety of other issues may be mentioned briefly. Communication about the self can be seen in the subject's attempt to cope with and solve the variety of problems confronting him and communication will depend upon the nature of the solutions that are attempted. Such solutions or coping measures include the defenses, a category of action that has the greatest consequences for the success or failure of personality studies. The defenses are generally regarded as functioning to inhibit or repress communication about processes that disrupt the orderly construction of the self conception. If, however, they are viewed more positively and more broadly as belonging in that category of action which involves coping with the problem of living, it is apparent that not all defenses are inhibiting in nature and that some are primarily expressive or communicative in nature. Projection, for example, serves the purpose of denial of undesirable impulses. But it is also a solution which involves a considerable degree of expression and communication about the impulse even if this expression is disguised. Other defenses such as intellectualization, displacement and rationalization have similar qualities. On the other hand denial and repression, when successful, prevent impulse expression and inhibit communication. There is much to suggest that choice of defenses is oriented to implicit cultural patterning. Thus middle class values in our society encourage attempts at mastery of problems that are based on active confrontation and working through, rather than withdrawal and inhibition. In cultures where this is so we can expect better results with our personality study procedures than in cultures where it is not.

INTERPERSONAL RELATIONS

Although communicating to someone else about the self is considerably different than making statements about the self when the self is the only observer, the two situations have much in common. Whereas the latter involves the construction of a self conception, the former involves the construction of a social conception in others. Both require purposefulness and planning that do not seem congruent with the apparently spontaneous and often casual interplay that goes on in the personality study. In the projective tests especially, the appearance is maintained that the subject's responses do not have any great significance. He is just saying what he sees, or whatever happens to come into his mind, or telling a made-up story. The subject is encouraged not to think too much about what he is doing, and the examiner generally maintains the fiction that the subject really is not aware of what is going on and is, instead of acting responsibly, relinquishing his capacity to make decisions and placing himself passively in the examiner's hands. It is to be doubted, however, that this is an accurate picture. There is much evidence that the subject exercises considerable selectivity in his communications, even when he is naïve and unsophisticated about personality tests. If nothing else, he exercises the ability not to say anything when what he has to say is dangerous or disturbing.

If the subject is really acting responsibly and purposefully in what he communicates, he must be doing so in relation to the same kinds of standards and expectations we have discussed earlier in this chapter. The appearance he presents to others is related to his conception of how he *should* appear, although there may be a deviant relationship as well as a conformative one. The important point to be emphasized is that the personality study situation is dominated by the prevalent social conceptions of what people are supposed to be like. The subject's productions must be understood in relationship to them. The description and analysis of these social conceptions is perhaps the first step to be undertaken in the interpretation of personality materials in all personality study, cross-cultural or otherwise. In our own society this method is not followed explicitly, in part because psychologists and psychiatrists have not paid enough attention to cultural variables, but also because the relevant belief systems are implicitly recognized and understood and are taken into account unconsciously. In cross-cultural studies these implicit or covert understandings are potential sources of error since they are not easily corrected. There is the danger that they will be carried over to situations where the cultural definitions are quite different.

The actions that psychologists and psychiatrists call defenses are as frequently taken in relationship to the interpersonal situation as they are to the intrapsychic one. Such defenses are generally understood to involve the subject's deceiving himself into believing that he does not have some impulse that he in fact really does have. However, since it is he who is doing the deceiving, it would seem that there must be some sense in which the disguise is not really deceptive and in which the person *is* allowing himself to express indirectly what he would prefer not to acknowledge openly. The defense is really, I believe, not against the impulse or repressed process but against its open and explicit acknowledgment which would have serious consequences for the person's relationships and for the conception of himself that he is trying to present. Thus defensive behavior can be understood as an attempt to maintain a conformative relationship to normative prescriptions both in the intra-psychic and interpersonal spheres.

Our discussion thus far has emphasized the normative factors that govern what a person says about himself. The social patterning of interpersonal relationships also is important, however. Personality study usually occurs in the context of a relationship between two people. Leaving aside the influence of the structuring of the *roles* of examiner and subject, which in our own society define with great clarity the expectations for nurturance and responsibility from the former and respect and compliance from the latter, it seems probable that the much-needed openness of the subject can only occur when the subject feels trust and dependence on the examiner. The subject must *want* to communicate, and his desire must be based on his conception of the nature of the relationship. In our own society the "Wise Elder" theme is so universally understood that subjects in general easily accept and respond to the examiner in these terms. However, we recognize that this supporting relationship can easily be disrupted with a consequent failure of the personality study. In other societies the typical patterns of interpersonal relationships may not encourage openness and free communication. Although very little has been written about variations in the kinds of relatedness that exists in different cultural groups, such differences may be very wide.

Cross-cultural personality study is difficult and complicated and should not be undertaken lightly with inadequate time and resources. Ideally, it should proceed only after some knowledge of typical patterns of relationship has been accumulated so that the investigator can modify his behavior to conform to the subject's conception of an appropriate setting. Practically this is often impossible since the knowledge of such conceptions is one of the aims of the study itself and is not available before it begins. An intensive exploratory study may be necessary to discover what settings and techniques work best. This seems preferable to the usual practice of going ahead with a particular method in a particular way whether or not useful information is being obtained. The idea that the personality characteristics of a people can be studied simply by the administration of a single test like the Rorschach seems to me to be a complete illusion. Such a procedure may yield interesting information; but the information will inevitably be fragmentary and not susceptible to integration into a serious culture and personality study. Also, if these fragments are treated as though they constituted the whole picture, the worker may be led into serious errors.

The present analysis unfortunately has not dealt adequately with the problem of how to discover the best approach to personality study in a particular society. I have merely attempted to provide a theoretical perspective that will point the way to a method of taking cultural factors into account both at the time of data collection and data interpretation.

NOTE

1. This argument owes a good deal to the Existentialist position that action is not to be understood as some by-product of the real characteristics of the person but as being the only means of constituting reality itself. The person, in effect, creates himself by what he does.

BIBLIOGRAPHY

Carstairs, G. M. 1956. "Rorschachs of 40 High Caste Hindus and 10 Moslem Men from Delware, Udaipur, India." In Kaplan, B. (ed.), *Primary Records in Culture and Personality*. Vol. I. Madison, Wisconsin: The Microcard Foundation.

Fromm, E. 1941. *Escape from Freedom*. New York: Farrar, Strauss and Young.

Geertz, H. 1957. "Modified TATs of 33 Javanese Men and Women." In Kaplan, B. (ed.), *Primary Records in Culture and Personality*. Vol. II. Madison, Wisconsin: The Microcard Foundation.

Hallowell, A. I. 1954. "The Self and Its Behavioral Environment." *Explorations.* Vol. II. Reprinted in Hallowell, A. I. 1955, *Culture and Experience.* Philadelphia: University of Pennsylvania Press.

Hanks, L. 1956. "Modified TATs of 47 Thai Men and Women." In Kaplan, B. (ed.), *Primary Records in Culture and Personality.* Vol. I. Madison, Wisconsin: The Microcard Foundation.

Henry, J. 1956. "Rorschachs of 16 Pilaga Children and Adults." In Kaplan, B. (ed.), *Primary Records in Culture and Personality.* Vol. I. Madison, Wisconsin: The Microcard Foundation.

Henry, W. 1947. "The Thematic Apperception Technique in the Study of Culture-Personality Relations," *Genetic Psychology Monographs.* P. 35.

Kaplan, B. (ed.) 1956. *Primary Records in Culture and Personality.* Vol. I. Madison, Wisconsin: The Microcard Foundation.

Kaplan, B. (ed.) 1957. *Primary Records in Culture and Personality.* Vol. II. Madison, Wisconsin: The Microcard Foundation.

Kaplan, B. 1957. "Personality and Social Structure." In Gittler, J. B. (ed.), *Review of Sociology, Analysis of a Decade.* New York: Wiley and Co.

Kaplan, B., Rickers-Ovsiankina, M. and Joseph, A. 1956. "An Attempt to Sort Rorschach Records from Four Cultures," *Journal of Projective Techniques,* 20:2.

Parsons, T. 1951. *The Social System.* Glencoe, Illinois: The Free Press.

Riesman, D. 1950. *The Lonely Crowd.* New Haven: Yale University Press.

White, R. W. 1944. "The Interpretation of Imaginative Productions." In Hunt, J. McV. (ed.), *Personality and Behavior Disorders.* New York: Ronald Press. Pp. 233–39.

About the Chapter

The relationship of linguistics to culture and personality study is both close and incompletely understood. Dr. Hymes surveys the variety of linguistic studies and theories that bear on the field and especially on the problem of cross-cultural personality study. He considers the ways in which personality is expressed and perceived in acts of speech and what the content of language reveals about the personality patterns of those who speak it. The important field of paralinguistics with its focus on the nature of the carriers of meaning and emotion in expression is discussed. This new development is producing a number of insights that are basic to an understanding of the kind of communication that goes on in the personality study situation and especially to an appreciation of the role of cultural factors.

About the Author

DELL H. HYMES is Associate Professor of Anthropology and Linguistics at the University of California, Berkeley. Within the fields of anthropology, linguistics, and folklore, he has contributed articles and reviews to a variety of journals, especially in connection with the description and classification of American Indian languages, problems of method in historical linguistics and anthropology, and the analysis of verbal art. His interest in the role of linguistics in the study of personality developed while he was a Fellow at the Center for Advanced Study in the Behavioral Sciences in 1957–8.

Acknowledgments

The author is indebted to the Center for Advanced Study in the Behavioral Sciences, where this chapter was begun, and to the Laboratory of Social Relations of Harvard University for aid in its completion. For helpful references, comments, and stimulation in many ways, thanks go to several Fellows and Associates of the Center in 1957–8: Ethel Albert, Roger G. Barker, Sol Becker, Ward Goodenough, Neal Gross, David Landes, Sidney Siegel, Milton Singer, Fritz Stern, and John Tukey; to Gordon Allport and Talcott Parsons; and, especially regarding the experimental literature in psychology, to Volney Stefflre.

10

Linguistic Aspects of Cross-Cultural Personality Study

DELL H. HYMES

University of California

INTRODUCTION

In the literature of culture and personality, language is somewhat kin to Mark Twain's weather: many praise it, but few do much about it. Sometimes language does not figure at all in a general treatment of culture and personality. When it does, the discussion usually amounts to two propositions: (a) language is important; (b) linguistic differences are important differences. It may be pointed out how important language is to the socialization of the child, the perception and cognition of adults, the functioning of human society; that linguistic differences may be evidence of differences in personality, among individuals or between cultures; and, sometimes, that linguistic differences may be responsible for differences in personality.

These ideas have long been familiar. George Herbert Mead, for one, stressed the importance of language as the medium through which an individual acquires his personality. Probably intelligent observers have been making such propositions since shortly after the dawn of human society.

313

What such general propositions need is substantive flesh and analytic bones, but little research has been devoted to this. In this chapter I shall try to highlight problems and developments which promise to be of most help for studying personality cross-culturally. I shall begin with the history of interest in personality shown by contemporary linguists, and then discuss the use of linguistic methods by the fieldworker, since this underlies any contribution which linguistic evidence can make. Next I shall take up two broad questions: (1) the signals by which personality is expressed and perceived in acts of speech, and (2) the information which the content of a language may provide about the personality of those who use it. Finally, I shall raise a series of questions about the functions of speech in a society in relation to cultural personality and socialization.

BACKGROUND

Given that language is important to personality, one might expect linguistics, the science of language, to make a considerable contribution to personality study. Yet, there is little in the work of American linguists which bears on personality, and most of this is very recent.

Some thirty years ago the linguistic aspects of personality were posed as a problem by Edward Sapir. In one paper he presented a framework for analyzing speech as a personality trait (1927). In another he stated that "We see and hear and otherwise experience very largely as we do because the language habits of our community predispose certain choices of interpretation" (1929, p. 162). Thus, these papers broached the two broad questions stated in the Introduction: the relation between personality and (1) acts of speech, (2) the content of a language.

Some of Sapir's students investigated these questions. Stanley Newman published several papers on the linguistic aspect of individual personalities (1938, 1939, 1941, 1944), and argued vigorously for the study of individual patterns of verbal expression as part of linguistics (1941, pp. 96, 106). Benjamin Lee Whorf explored the relation of habitual thought and behavior to language (1936, 1941). But otherwise, Sapir's interest was not reflected in the development of linguistics during the ensuing decade or two. When a psychologist, Sanford, reviewed the literature on speech and personality, he had to conclude that "The problems are still more numerous than the facts" (1942, p. 840). There have been two more recent discussions by linguists, one which illustrates pertinent speech phenomena (Herzog, 1949), and one which is broadly discursive (Firth, 1950), but these amount to little substantive advance. Whorf's analyses of semantic patterns were exceptional at the time, and only after his death did his writings become a focus of

American concern with the place of language in culture (Hoijer, 1953; 1954).

Instead, the theoretical interest of American linguists centered during most of the last thirty years on the development of descriptive concepts and methods. Here, as in European centers such as Prague and Copenhagen, a revolution took place in standards for the description of languages. While there are differing schools of descriptive methodology, all share allegiance to some conception of a language as a system, and thus to a fundamental distinction between language and speech. Typically, one refers to the act or process or continuum of speech, but to the structure, pattern, or system of language. Speech is message, language is code. Speech is observable behavior, language a set of habits. In recent years, American linguists have been preoccupied with inferring the constants of the linguistic code from the behavioral variation of speech.

Thus, the major advances were in methodological problems internal to linguistics, and the period was characterized by very narrow definitions of the proper scope of linguistics. Semantics especially tended to be defined as someone else's responsibility. Focus was on the qualitatively different, socially shared basic units of the linguistic code, phonemes and morphemes, and their patterns of occurrence relative to each other. Much of psychological importance in speech and language was neglected. The quantitatively varying attributes of the voice are important in expressing personality, and insofar as the content of language reveals cultural personality, semantics is central. But the former is not part of the linguistic code, and the latter was neglected as not necessary to its formal description. Perhaps the main current of American linguistics in the period need not have been so swept by backwashes of behaviorism and positivism. Still, not only linguistics neglected these broader problems of language. A few years ago Osgood wrote: "In terms of its central relevance to general psychological theory and its potential applicability to complex social problems, no other area of experimental psychology so greatly demands attention as language behavior and in the past has received so little" (1953, p. 727; note also the statement by Spence, in 1957, on the importance of language to the psychology of behavior).

Moreover, the advances in descriptive methods were essential to progress in the study of other aspects of language and of the relation of language to other things. No use of linguistic evidence can be better than the methods by which the evidence is obtained and analyzed. The greater the precision with which the formal units and patterns of a language can be established, the greater the precision with which such things as the linguistic aspects of personality can be investigated.

Sometimes the intensive development of method has been accompanied by a hierophantic air, but this is lessening, and fetishistic concern for methodological purity is giving way to an attitude which has been dubbed "rough justice" (Householder, 1957a), a change which is fortunate for the cooperation of linguists with other scholars.

While descriptive methods continue to be improved, they are adequate, and a growing number of scholars trained in these methods are investigating psychological problems.[1] In general, the interest of linguists has turned more and more to the external relations of their work to other fields, an interest reflected in such terms as "ethno-linguistics" and "psycho-linguistics." While surveys of the linguistic aspects of personality still must draw upon hopes and suggestions more than upon tested conclusions, this situation is changing for the better.

USE OF LINGUISTIC METHODS

There are four ways in which the student of personality in another culture may utilize the descriptive methods which modern linguistics has developed. These methods will facilitate his practical use of a language in field work. If he has to obtain and analyze linguistic data himself, he will need them. If he draws upon the linguistic work of others, he still should have some control of linguistic methods in order to evaluate the work, if it is already done, or to guide it in relevant directions, if it is undertaken as part of his research project. Finally, there is the possibility that linguistic methods may have an application outside language.

Serious students of other ways of life long have realized that no real penetration of a people's psychological makeup is possible without knowledge of their language. Among anthropologists, Franz Boas (who defined ethnology as the study of mental phenomena) wrote that the deeper problems of ethnology could not be approached except through language. Sapir, Lowie, Radin, Kluckhohn, and others have reiterated the point. Kluckhohn's account of the role of language in obtaining autobiographical material is pertinent to all culture and personality research. Stressing linguistic insight as requisite for insight into covert culture, he writes:

I suspect that the meanings which the happenings of his life have for the subject will remain forever opaque to the investigator unless he has obtained entrance to this foreign world of values and significances which are pointed to by the emphases of the native vocabulary, crystallized in its morphological categories, implicit in its semantic differentiations. (1945, p. 112)

Anastasi and Foley (1949, p. 717) make a point about intelligence tests that applies to tests generally: instruments of research that do not involve language are not equivalent to instruments that do, and cannot be substituted for them. They state: "When unfamiliarity with the language makes the application of verbal tests impossible in a given group, the range of processes which can be measured in that group is thereby narrowed."

Kluckhohn points out:

Learning a language, then, is not the only alternative to complete neglect of the language. The direct advantages of *using* a language are to record, to ask set questions, to give stereotyped instructions. *No* language is easy, but substantial progress in the use of *any* language can be made by the field worker who is patient and willing and who has certain minimum skills for going about the task. (1945, p. 113)

For the practical use of another language, descriptive methods are of great value. Every learner must make some analysis, conscious or not, of the other language; linguistic methods make the analysis explicit and precise. For both analyst and user, the goal is a model of the language habits of a group. For the analyst, it is true, it is enough to have the model in his head and notebooks. The user, in addition, must introduce the model into his habits of articulation. The analyst must be able to recognize and accurately record the native speaker's repetitions of utterances; the user must also be able to make the repetitions himself. But for both, the test of success is ability to produce novel utterances which native speakers will accept.

Descriptive analysis is especially helpful in coping with *interference* between the learner's own system of language habits and that of the language to be learned. If the field worker has a descriptive analysis of the units and patterns in his own language and in the one to be used, he can compare the two to make conscious the points where his own language habits are most likely to impede his perception and control of the other set of habits. Interference is clearly critical for the fieldworker sorting out clues to personality in acts of speech. English-speaking fieldworkers are especially likely to be unaware of their complex patterns of stress, pitch, and juncture, and so to misinterpret the emotional import of the use of stress, pitch, and juncture in another language.

For English linguistic habits, Hockett (1958) is the best single guide. The fact that interference in learning can be described precisely and predicted is perhaps the best proof of the vital role that linguistic analysis plays in the practical use of another language. Weinreich (1953, 1957) has made a theoretical analysis of linguistic interference. There is a useful discussion in Gleason (1955, Ch. 18) and a brilliant illustration of phonemic interference in Wolff (1952). Lado (1957) devotes a book to the problems of comparing linguistic systems, and extends the approach to the comparison of cultures. Perhaps the theoretical frame-

works of Weinreich and Lado may shed light also on problems of interference in judging other manifestations of personality.

If the fieldworker goes to a group whose language has been more or
less adequately described, his task is relatively easy, whether he obtains
formal instruction, or is self-taught with the aid of generalized expert
advice. Bloomfield (1942) is an outstanding guide, together with Fries
(1945); there is valuable advice in Nida (1947, 1950, 1956), Pike
(1947), Reyburn (1958) and Swadesh (1937). If the fieldworker has
to undertake his own descriptive analysis, he will need some formal instruction. Roger Brown (1957, 1959) has written lucid introductions to
linguistic concepts, oriented to psychologists. Good, brief, introductions
oriented toward psychologists and anthropologists, respectively, are
those of Miller (1954) and Lounsbury (1953). Introductory texts for
students of linguistics give a more detailed understanding of its operations (Hockett, 1958; Gleason, 1955; Nida, 1949; Pike, 1947); on a
more advanced level, Harris (1951) is a storehouse of analytic procedures.

Whether the fieldworker makes his own analysis, or uses the analyses
of others, it is essential to realize that there are two broad stages to
linguistic description.[2] The first may be loosely called that of the "facts."
In this stage one determines all the phonological and grammatical features that are relevant in each particular linguistic context. In the second
stage, one infers general phonological and grammatical patterns for
the language as a whole. This requires relating the relevant features of
particular contexts to each other, so as to obtain a description that comprises them all in a simple and consistent way. Linguists who agree on
the facts of specific contexts may disagree on the pattern to be inferred.
The disagreement will be due to differences in the criteria of inference
which are given priority, or to different conceptions of the ideal model
for linguistic description.[3]

The non-linguist should know that if a language is described and
handled accurately in the first stage, this will suffice for field research.
Some inference must be made, but it need not be theoretically elegant.
As long as the first stage is clear, others can make other inferences
later, and, moreover, adequate handling of the first stage itself contributes to the science of language, if the data are not otherwise known.
The consumer of linguistic research should know that errors or inadequacies in the first stage will vitiate the results. Disagreements as to the
second stage may spring more from theoretical assumptions than from
the data. For his purposes it may make no difference which of two conflicting interpretations is chosen.

The advances in descriptive analysis have encouraged some linguists to suggest that their methods could be used by others. This hope

has been shared by anthropologists such as Kluckhohn and Levi-Strauss. The nature of the hope has been that linguistic methods might help establish units and patterns in learned behavior outside language.

It is worth noting that language and linguistics figure prominently in discussions of methods for national character study in *The Study of Culture at a Distance* (Mead and Metraux, 1953). Mead and Gorer use them both by way of analogy and as example (pp. 10–11, 13–14, 16, 59, 80–81). This is so much the case, that it is remarkable that neither Mead nor Gorer explicitly suggests the direct transfer of linguistic method to the study of national character.

As Hockett has observed, the difficulty is that we do not know how much the success of linguistic methods depends on what is peculiar to language and how much on what language shares with the rest of culture. All culturally patterned behavior may be as systematic as speech, as Mead asserts (1953, pp. 16–17), but we do not yet know for sure. Probably there is a gradient from the least to the most systematized aspects. It is worth mentioning the principal work along these lines because of its promise. This work is of two sorts, *extensions* of linguistic method and *generalizations* of it.

For personality study, a particularly promising extension concerns gesture, or "body-language." The communicative importance of gesture has long been recognized, together with its cultural basis (LaBarre, 1947). Working with several linguists, Birdwhistell (1952) has sketched an analytic framework for gesture, including a system of notation. If this culminates in the successful descriptive analysis of gesture-systems cross-culturally, it will be a significant contribution to the study of how personality is expressed and perceived.

There are two major examples of the generalization of linguistic methods. Kenneth Pike (1954, 1955, 1956, 1959) seeks to comprehend linguistic and non-linguistic behavior within a single descriptive framework. (The 1956 essay is the best concise exposition of Pike's approach.) Hans Uldall (1957) has published the first part of work done in collaboration with the Danish linguist, Louis Hjelmslev, with whom he developed the school of linguistic thought known as glossematics. Uldall's monograph generalizes a glossematic algebra for all the non-natural sciences, so that its application to language is a special case. It is interesting that a psychologist, Floyd Allport (1955), has developed a concept of structure within which Pike's linguistics-based theory might find a natural place, and that Barker and Wright (1954) discuss their basic concepts and problems, such as "dividing the behaviour stream," in terms remarkably suggestive of linguistic principles. Still, the direct transfer of linguistic ways of handling units and patterns to such areas as culture and personality remains an undemonstrated possibility. It will be some while before we know how much of the attempt to take linguistic methodology beyond language is a "breakthrough," and how much it is the artifact of a climate of opinion. General advocacy of this attempt is found in the writings of Claude Levi-Strauss (see several of the essays in his *Anthropologie structurale,* 1957), Ward Goodenough (1957), George L. Trager (1959), Edward T. Hall (1959), and some other anthropologists. Positive results for problems in social structure have been reported by Goodenough (1951, p. 64) and Levi-Strauss (1957, pp. 37–62, "L'Analyse structurale en linguistique et en anthropologie"). Katherine French (1955) has used linguistic principles like those of Pike to analyze ceremonial patterns on an American Indian reservation, and Marvin Mayers (1959) has applied Pike's approach cogently to the Pocomchi of Mexico. The growing field of ethnoscience has used linguistics-inspired methodology to get at cognitive organization in the areas of kinship, botany, and disease. This could be extended to conceptions of personality and to personal differences in cognitive organization. Applications such as these by people rooted in substantive fields outside linguistics are the crucial test for the broader utility of linguistic methods.

To sum up the central point of this section: linguistic methods are essential for the cross-cultural study of personality. They aid the fieldworker in using the native language; if he is a talented polyglot, they expedite his mastery. Even if the investigator does not use the native language, even if he does not care what the language itself may reveal, it must be controlled so that speech behavior may be observed and recorded. People talk; their talk involves their personalities. Linguistic methods are simply the way an adequate account of what goes on in talking can be rendered.

ACTS OF SPEECH

What are the signals by which personality is expressed and perceived in speech? To judge from a review of literature (Bruner and Tagiuri, 1954) and a recent conference (Tagiuri and Petrullo, 1958), the growing interest in person perception neglects speech. The importance of speech (especially to a theory of personality such as that of Kelly, 1956) is obvious nevertheless.

Sapir (1927) provides a general formulation of the problem, one which is followed by Chao (1953). He proposed two approaches. The first would concern the difference and relation between the individual and social components of speech. This is stressed by Newman (1941) and by Krech and Crutchfield (1948). Sapir observed that speakers are alert for individual speech variations and subtle cues, but are relatively naïve about the specific signals to which they respond. They also often forget that there is a socially-shared pattern in relation to which the individual variations are perceived. Individual expressions of personality in speech can be understood only after the specific signals and the shared patterns have been analyzed.

The second approach would concern different levels of speech. Sapir distinguished five: *voice,* the most fundamental and a form of gesture; *voice dynamics,* including intonation, rhythm, relative continuity, speed, and the musical handling of the voice generally; *pronunciation,* including individual differences in pronunciation, and symbolic associations of sounds; *vocabulary,* that is, individual differences in choice and frequency of morphemes; *style.* Sapir stressed that each level has both a cultural and individual aspect. One level may be used in conflict with another in a given message, so that there could be "a conflict between explicit and implicit communications in the growth of the individual's social experience" (1931, p. 79)—a point Gregory Bateson has recently developed, and that de Groot (1949) has formulated as the "law of the two strata," by which the message of the intonation always takes precedence over that of the words.

The phenomena which Sapir classed under *voice* and *voice dynamics* have been very little understood until recently. Studies had shown that people do judge personality from speech (Pear, 1931; Taylor, 1934; Allport and Cantril, 1934; Wolff, W., 1943; McGehee, 1944; Zucker, 1946). But these studies were more in terms of general impression than in terms of the signals which conveyed the impression. Partly this could not be avoided. Our traditional orthography almost wholly ignores an important group of such signals, so that they are lost when acts of speech are transcribed in ordinary writing. Though part of this group, the complex English systems of pitch, stress, juncture and intonation, form an essential part of the English linguistic code, only recently has linguistics provided an adequate analysis.[4] Very recently, some linguists have begun to analyze what Sapir termed "the linguistically irrelevant habits of speech manipulation which are characteristic of a particular group" (1927, p. 540), that is, ways of using speech which are conventionalized, even though not part of the linguistic code proper. Pittenger and Smith (1957) have addressed an introduction to this pioneering work to psychiatrists, and McQuown (1957) has presented an example of its application to interview material. An extensive publication is to come from one group (Bateson, *et al.*). Meanwhile Trager has published a framework for analyzing the entire group of non-linguistic signals in acts of speech.

Trager distinguishes *voice set* as a background against which are measured *voice qualities* and *vocalizations.* These latter two together are termed *paralanguage*—found in systematic association with language though distinct from it. Voice set involves the physiological and physical peculiarities which identify individuals as members of a population and as persons of a certain sex, age, state of health, and so on. Voice qualities are actual speech events. They are modifications both of language and of vocalizations. The categories of voice quality noted so far are: pitch range, vocal lip control, glottis control, pitch control, articulation control, rhythm control, resonance, tempo. For each of these there are intermittent degrees on a continuum between polar extremes, for instance, for vocal lip control, from heavy rasp or hoarseness to various degrees of openness. Vocalizations are specifiable noises or aspects of noises. There are three kinds: *vocal characterizers, vocal qualifiers,* and *vocal segregates.* The vocal characterizers include laughing and crying, between which giggling, snickering, whimpering and sobbing are considered intermediate; yelling and whispering; moaning and groaning; whining and breaking; belching and yawning; and probably other groups. One "talks through" all these. Vocal qualifiers are three: *intensity, pitch height,* and *extent* (which ranges between drawl and clipping). Vocal segregates comprise such items as English "uh-uh" for negation, "uh-huh" for affirmation, the Japanese hiss, and other actual sounds that do not fit into the ordinary phonological patterns of a language. It is important to note that this classification is based on detailed study of actual speech. Trager suggests a repertoire of symbols for transcribing these paralinguistic phenomena.

The work which Trager synthesizes is still very much in progress. It needs extension to other speech communities outside the English sphere as a check on its adequacy as a transcriptional arsenal.[5] Such extension has already been begun by Trager at Taos Pueblo in New Mexico (Trager, 1960), and the only addition found necessary is one category of voice quality—retracted vs. projected articulation. At present the focus of this work is chiefly on identifying and describing the relevant features. How these features occur relative to each other, how their distribution of occurrences interrelates with such things as situation, role, personality—most of this is yet to be determined. A noteworthy beginning has been made by Danchy, Hockett, and Pittenger, whose fine-grained analysis of the communication system constituted between a patient and a psychiatrist and their interaction during the beginning of their first interview is rich with examples and leads. Besides the Danchy, Hockett, and Pittenger manuscript, recent papers by Bateson (1958), Pittenger (1958), and a manuscript by Hockett are valuable.

At present this work must at the very least alert the student of personality to the significance of paralinguistic phenomena. Much of what would be coded as aggression, nurturance, succorance and the like may be communicated paralinguistically, by what we would conventionally call tone of voice, inflection, innuendo. It should be no surprise if the child's learning of and response to paralinguistic cues is found to play an important part in the process of identification.

The concept of *expressive* devices should be singled out here. As defined by linguists of the Prague School, these may be equivalent to the vocal segregates of the Trager scheme. In a given language, expressive devices are precisely ordinary speech elements which are *not* part of its code, that is, which do not make a difference to the referential meaning of messages. Their expressive function is made possible by this very fact. Thus, there is a phoneme /h/ in the code of some languages, such as English, where *Eat it* is cognitively different from *Heat it*. French has no /h/ phoneme, hence the sound *h* can be used expressively; Gauthier remarks that love is well expressed by "Je t'h'aime," and Flaubert writes "h'enorme" for "enorme" to render emotion.[6]

Expressive devices are important in the speech development of the child, but little is known about them cross-culturally. Intonation seems to appear very early; it is reported to be the first speech element which Czech children acquire to express emotion. Other expressive devices also seem to appear very early: palatalization of consonants is used as a purely expressive device in the first words of Czech children. Though we can single out certain features as expressive *per se,* we must remember that it is also possible to view *all* the features of a speech event as in varying degree expressive of their source. Each feature is selected from among a set of features. Since another feature might have occurred in its place, the selection reflects the sender of the message. Of course, this statement is never literally true, due to the dependence of some features on others. But it serves to single out the importance of not forgetting that in the functioning of speech, as elsewhere, what on one level seems an inherent property is on another level dependent on the point from which we are viewing. An expletive may be colorless through over use, and an intrinsically colorless "no" may be explosive if the preceding utterance has been "Do you take this woman to be your lawful wedded wife?"

New analytic frameworks may prove to be needed for the phenomena which Sapir treated under *pronunciation, vocabulary,* and *style,* but well known methods can be used. It is generally a question of describing the units and patterns of a language and of then studying the relative frequency and contexts of their occurrence. Some linguistic traits, including particular pronunciations and words, may be diagnostic of individuals, of roles, of groups, of situations. This includes the characters in myths, whose personalities and roles are built up wholly by the use of language.[7] Some linguistic traits may differ in the relative frequency of their use by certain people or in certain situations; this is perhaps what Sapir had in mind when he mentioned style, though he may also have intended to indicate some controlling pattern of selection.

All this, then, is a matter of knowing the code and content of a language. One can then tell, for example, whether the use of an *h*-sound is normal functioning of the language, or expresses emotion. Knowing the norms of a speech community, one can tell whether an emotional utterance has a conventional acceptation or reveals a deviant personality. One can know when stereotyped perception of personality is likely to be aroused by the use of particular pronunciations, vocabulary, or styles, which may signal a class, local area, or conventionally recognized type of individual. One can note and follow up regression to an earlier dialect usage or pronunciation under stress, if such occurs. One may be able to detect the subtle interpersonal manipulation of status-controlled levels of vocabulary in languages such as Japanese, Javanese and Ponapean, or the shift between formal and informal styles which occurs in any language. All this entails a control of a language which comes only together with control of the culture as well, but it is essential to any systematic phenomenological approach to personality.

Ideally, linguistics should provide the investigator with complete description of the linguistic and paralinguistic codes in the speech of the people studied and in his own speech. The investigator, or an accompanying linguist, would then be able to specify without interference all those cues which express personality and by which personality is perceived in oral communication. If linguistic research has already adequately studied a language, the fieldworker is enviably prepared. In much of the world this is not the case, but, armed with linguistic methods, or a linguist, the student of personality in another culture may still penetrate the world of meanings borne by the small disturbances of air which are acts of speech.

THE CONTENT OF LANGUAGE

What does the content of language reveal about personality? The psychological import of differences in language has a recurrent fascination, and an honorable tradition in anthropological linguistics from Wilhelm von Humboldt through Brinton, Boas and Sapir to the present day. Most recently, Whorf's gifts for exposition and semantic insight have made his views a reference point. There has been a flurry of studies, ranging from perception of vowel length to conceptual logic and metaphysical presuppositions.

Carroll and Casagrande (1958, p. 20) have put the basic question in these terms:

The linguistic relativity hypothesis is a special case of the culture-personality theory. Substituting terms in Smith, Bruner, and White's precis of culture-personality theory, we may express it this way: Each language creates a special plight to which the individual must adjust. The human plight is in no sense universal save in this fact: that however different the language may be, it has certain common problems with which to deal—time, space, quantity, action, state, etc. But each language handles these problems differently and develops special ways of communicating. These ways of communicating create special needs, special responses, and lead to the development of special modes of thinking.

The alternative to the linguistic relativity hypothesis would be a statement that the behavior of a person is not a function of the language he happens to speak or be speaking, that his modes of categorizing experience and dealing with his world operate independently of language, that language is simply a way of communicating something which is in every way prior to its codification in language.

One will find other statements of this view, ranging from the sweepingly provocative to the gently urbane, in writings of Sapir (1929, 1931b), Whorf (1940a, 1940b, 1941a, 1941b, 1941c), Lee (1938, 1940, 1944, 1949, 1950), Hoijer (1951, 1953, 1954), Brown (1956), and Brown and Lenneberg (1954, 1958).

That language should make a difference follows from many considerations in psychology itself. Carroll terms the hypothesis "essentially a restatement or application of a well-known finding in discrimination learning—that we learn those discriminations which are reinforced; in the present case, linguistic symbols are themselves the cues for the discriminatory responses" (Carroll, 1958, p. 34). Moreover, "the vast majority of signs used in ordinary communication are what we may term *assigns*—their meanings are literally 'assigned' to them via association with other signs rather than via direct association with the objects signified" (Osgood, Suci, Tannenbaum, 1957, p. 8). This view heightens the importance of the patterning of linguistic symbols in a language, as an influence on psychological processes affecting personality, and so does Miller's view of the role of linguistic patterns in the retaining of complex information. Discussing the great disparity between man's limited ability to discriminate sensory stimuli and his great capacity to store information, Miller (1956a, p. 95) suggests that the gap is bridged by successive recodings, "an extremely powerful weapon for increasing the amount of information that we can deal with. In one form or another we use recoding constantly in our daily behavior. In my opinion the most customary kind of recoding that we do all the time is to translate into a verbal code." [8]

We have only the beginnings of research, cross-cultural and otherwise, devoted to demonstrating the nature and extent of the difference that language makes. While many have testified from personal experience, or by selected examples, relatively few have conducted experiments. I shall try to consider this experimental work to show its trend.

Concerning lexical categories of English speakers, Carmichael, Hogan and Walter (1932) showed a generation ago that recall and reproduction of visual shapes depended upon linguistic labels given them by the experimenter. Subsequent work has refined and overwhelmingly supported this proof of the influence of linguistic habit. Hanawalt and Demarest (1939) showed not only the influence in reproduction of visual shapes of labels given by the experimenter, but also brought out the significance of labels the subjects themselves employ. The best demonstration of this latter point is in Herman, Lawless, and Marshall (1957). The results of Prentice (1954) on the relation between language and recognition error were negative, but these must be interpreted in the light of the often overlooked positive results of Tresselet (1948). Bruner, Busiek, and Minturn (1952) obtained positive results with immediate reproduction. Here also should be mentioned the work of Belbin (1950) and J. Brown (1956), and the interesting findings of Norcross (1958).

Recent work by R. W. Brown and Lenneberg (1954) and by Lenneberg and Roberts (1956) found, under certain conditions, that recognition memory for colors depends upon *codability,* that is, the ease with which a sensory experience or concept can be transmitted in the code of a particular language. Under these conditions, the greater the codability, the more speakers of the language agree on the name, and, probably, the shorter the name and the more frequent its use. That experimentally given verbal labels improve recognition memory has been shown by Pyles (1932), Spiker (1956) who summarizes work in this area, and Weir and Stevenson (1959).

Cross-culturally, Lenneberg and Roberts indicate that speakers of English and Zuni differ in their recognition and remembering of colors in ways that are predictable from the codability of the colors in the two languages. Carroll (Carroll and Casagrande, 1958) reports suggestive results using Hopi lexical categories to predict the sorting behavior of Hopi speakers (although the illustrations unfortunately are incorrectly keyed to the text in the published paper). The central importance of lexical categories is considered demonstrated by Soviet psychology (Tikhomirov, 1959, pp. 365–6, citing Pavlov).

Concerning grammatical categories, Brown (1957) found in research of basic importance that English-speaking children take part-of-speech membership of a novel word as a clue to its meaning. Large grammatical classes, such as parts of speech, of course never correlate perfectly with semantic attributes; the class of English nouns cannot be adequately defined as names of persons, places, or things, but only by formal features such as inflection and syntactic position. Still, parts of speech do correlate sufficiently with certain semantic attributes for the relationship to be detected and generalized by speakers of the language (see Flavell, 1958). If languages differ in their major parts-of-speech, then, this may be diagnostic of differences in the cognitive psychologies of those who use them.

Cross-culturally, ethnographic incidents that point to the influence of grammatical categories, especially in Algonquian languages, have been cited by Hallowell (1951, 1958). Casagrande (Carroll and Casagrande, 1958) obtained initially encouraging results using a specific Navaho grammatical category to predict Navaho sorting behavior. This category concerns the classification of objects into several classes according to their shape or form. MacClay (1958) investigated it also, and since his study brings out the problems of such research very well, I shall discuss it in some detail.

MacClay tested sorting behavior of groups speaking Navaho, English, and Pueblo Indian languages, predicting differences in sorting and latency, with what at first seem very discouraging results. He found that subjects indeed sorted in terms of the kinds of classification built into the experiment (by color, form, function or material), but neither of the latency hypotheses was confirmed, and but one of the two sorting hypotheses. Now in every case the latencies for the Navaho and Pueblo groups were much closer to each other than either was to the latency for the English group, which always was notably lower. It is likely that some factor such as previous experience with test situations was at work, and that latency is not a valid measure for the influence of different language habits. Turning to the sorting hypotheses, the more experience a Navaho had had with his language, the more likely he was to sort in terms of its form categories, while the Pueblo group, whose languages lack such categories, showed no such correlation with language experience. The second sorting hypothesis produced surprise. Navahos made more sorts on the basis of form than the Pueblo group, as expected, but English speakers made as many or more such sorts compared to Navaho.

Carroll and Casagrande offer an explanation of such a result. They compared two groups of Navaho children, for one of whom the Navaho language was dominant, for one English, and found a correlation between dominance of Navaho and tendency to match objects by form rather than color or size. But when they compared this to data from white American children, and considered age trends, they came to the view that either of two kinds of experience could increase a child's tendency to match objects on the basis of form: (a) learning a language, like Navaho, which requires him to make certain discriminations of form and material in order to be understood, or (b) practice with toys and other objects which involves the fitting of forms and shapes.

Another problem emerged from MacClay's study. He found from post-experimental interviews that sometimes two of the four objects in a test had the same lexical category in Navaho. The list of objects used suggests other influences may have been operative as well. English speakers might have been classifying by function instead of form at some points, and some of the sets of objects to be sorted contain items that may be lexically linked for English speakers (as "metal," "paper," "cloth," "rubber"). On the other side, it is not reported whether Navaho speakers do indeed use the expected grammatical form of the verb with each pair of test objects whose being sorted together was to reveal the verb form's influence. Like English and other languages, Navaho has no perfect fit between formal classes and semantic patterns; its round-object class of verb stems is notorious for assimilating acculturational items, and most of the test materials were objects common to American culture.

MacClay's study, then, brings out the great complexity of testing the linguistic relativity hypothesis by predicting specific behavioral responses. His results go together with the general trend of others to indicate that language has some influence—for example, the difference between Navaho and Pueblo groups is always in the expected direction—but show how difficult this influence is to measure and specify. Linguistic and non-linguistic experience both may converge on the same behavioral result, and experience with a language may be consistent with alternative responses, since the language may have alternative ways of categorizing a stimulus. Moreover, as Stanley Newman has stressed, predictions from the presence of a feature ignore its frequency of occurrence; MacClay suggests that relative frequency may be the single most significant factor for future experiments.[9] The English statistician Herdan has proposed that *la langue* be conceived as having not only a qualitatively defined structure, but also a set of quantitatively defined probabilities of occurrence. But contemporary structural descriptions of languages do not deal with frequency, and we have no information about it for most languages of the world.

In short, the content of a language may predict non-linguistic behavior, but the relation is not one-to-one; rather, it is many-one and one-many. Simply the known facts of semantic change in languages make clear the interaction between a linguistic code and the other habits of those who use it. Each influences the other, for language is not a closed, but an open system.

Here must be mentioned the Southwest Project in Comparative Psycholinguistics, of which MacClay's work was a part. The field studies were made in the summers of 1955 and 1956 by teams of psychologists and linguists, working with speakers of English, Spanish, Navaho, Zuni, and Hopi. While the bulk of the results have not been published, MacClay's work apparently is representative in that it does not make the clear showing for the great importance of linguistic relativity that some investigators had hoped for. From this failure to find strong positive effects, some students have drawn the negative conclusion that such do not exist (Greenberg, 1959). Such an inference may be plausible, but it has no logical validity. In my opinion, the conclusion to be drawn is the one already indicated: that the meticulous study of the question is complex and difficult. Two summers is not a long time for the testing and developing of instruments in the first experimentally designed field research on the subject. Further research can profit from and build on this pilot venture.

To support my conclusion, let us recapitulate with regard to the content of language as a factor in behavior, and hence personality. That language as such makes no difference would scarcely be seriously argued now, although the view has been stated and is sometimes implied by omissions in research and writing.[10] Against such a view is the massive import of experimental work. To the studies cited, we should add that of Stefflre (1958), which strongly showed the importance of language as a variable in experiments on concept formation, and the studies of Shepard (1956), of Jeffrey (1953), and of Luria and his associates (Luria, 1959a, 1959b; Luria and Yuovich, 1959).[11]

That language is vital in the child's interaction with his world is shown in the field as well as in the laboratory. As part of a cross-cultural study of socialization, two similarly trained men observed the same Okinawan children according to the same procedures. One of the two could understand much of what was said by virtue of his command of Japanese, while the other began without knowledge of the language. When the protocols from the first few months, during which this difference obtained, were scored, one might not have guessed from the results that the two men had been observing children of the same culture.

It might not follow from the generic importance of language that the nature of the particular language makes a difference. Yet the student of linguistic change finds in the results of contact of languages myriad instances of selection and reshaping of perceived phenomena according to a particular language's patterns. The difference that the particular language makes is quite evident to the field worker (see Phillips,

1959–60, and Nadel, 1951, pp. 39–48). And it is on this more obvious or phenomenological level that the student of personality encounters language. Undoubtedly the differences among languages are underlain by universals, by a grounding which in fact makes it possible for the field worker to understand and use a linguistic system other than his own. Undoubtedly also the apparent surface differences may conceal more linguistic universals than we now see; some investigators have gone to extremes in stressing the differences as against the similarities. If work such as that of the Southwest Project quiets those who see little but relativity, well and good. Yet it would be mistaken to see little but similarities instead. The determination of similarities or universals, i.e., the calibration of differences in linguistic background of which Whorf spoke, is something to be achieved rather than assumed. We must recall that Whorf stressed linguistic relativity partly so that it could be transcended. He dramatized the facts of difference among languages, not only for their interest, but also because to be ignorant of them was to be their captive. In my opinion, differences in fact loom larger than uniformities on the level of description and analysis with which the student of another culture must begin. The only sound heuristic advice is to assume differences until proven otherwise.

A final point in this connection is that the sort of linguistic differences which Whorf stressed and which are most important to the study of personality cross-culturally are *habitual* differences (see Whorf, 1941c). It is irrelevant to point out, as some students have done, that human beings probably differ little in what they can potentially perceive and think and do. And it may be misleading to look for differences only in experimental situations which focus on unfamiliar tasks. Each of us might discriminate, for example, many hues and tones and intensities of color, had we the time and interest; but in naming as we run, and in remembering, we fall back on the few conventional labels of ordinary language. That is what the conventions of language are there for, in part. It is in ordinary behavior in its natural habitat that the greatest influence of linguistic habit is to be expected. One can find even better instances than those with which Whorf began his most noted paper on the subject (1941c). Recently a student reported that her roommate had said, "Let's put the radio by the radiator so it will warm up faster."

To sum up, there does not exist an experimentally precise and complete demonstration that differences of language are a major factor in differences in behavior and personality. However, theoretical considerations and a variety of experiences indicate that they are. Such differences do not override the similarities among men due to their common human nature and common natural world, but for the student of personality in another culture, they loom large.

What of the use of language content as evidence for national character, for particular cultural values, world views, or predominant cultural themes, such as motion (Navaho) or preparation (Hopi)? Lenneberg has harshly attacked such interpretations, and they have been cautiously or coolly regarded in some recent conferences (Lenneberg, 1953; Levi-Strauss, *et al.,* 1953; Osgood, 1954; Hoijer, 1954). Two major criticisms are *circularity* and *anachronism*. It is charged that the only evidence is language itself, which is used both to suggest and to prove the presence of values or outlooks. The linguist's analysis of a word, say, in Apache, may break it down into units which have no separate psychological reality for contemporary speakers of Apache; the analysis may be descriptive etymology.[12] Also, the grammatical labels used in the analysis may be artifacts of our linguistic tradition rather than psychological facts for the Apache.

These points are valid criticisms of any attempt to predict non-linguistic behavior or infer psychological reality from language content. To so predict, we go and look, that is, experiment, if we wish to be sure. Instead of regarding language content as a cause, however, we may regard it as the result of past behavior. Though an idiom may have no vitality for speakers now, it must have had when coined. For Apache speakers today, a dripping spring may or may not seem "as water, whiteness moves downward"; for them, the visual metaphor may be dead. For some Apache speaker it was once live, and his coinage was collectively approved. Different semantic patterns must result from cumulative differences in the selective perceptions and cognitions of speech communities over time. As historical products, semantic patterns can be appropriately compared with other historically derived cultural patterns, including those of personality.

Here recent changes in the language are especially important, since they certify the relevance of a semantic trend. In one recent study, Casagrande (1955, p. 24) observes:

> The Comanche characteristically describe many new traits, particularly implements and machines, in dynamic, functional terms rather than static ones of color, size and shape. One is tempted to speculate whether this may be correlated with Comanche personality as described by Kardiner who comments upon, "the emphasis on activity itself," and notes their capacity to deal skillfully, assertively and selfconfidently with the world.

The best fit between language and non-linguistic patterns is to be expected for those areas of learned behavior which are themselves highly structured (see Emeneau, 1941, 1950). There is no question but that particular words and sets of words are often suggestive or illuminating (see Stone, 1954). Hanks (1954) investigates a Blackfoot term for "disregard where respect is normally valued"; "crazy," which has many

North American Indian parallels, has been studied (Casagrande, 1955, p. 24; Olson, 1956, n. 5; Hymes, field notes, for Chinookan). Hallowell (1951, 1958) has good discussions of various Ojibwa words and categories. Detailed investigation of a key term (Oliver, 1949, is a fine example) or of an area of vocabulary which shows special elaboration (Evans-Pritchard, 1940, pp. 41–48; Marsh and Laughlin, 1956; Nida, 1949, 1958)—these should be standard and rewarding fieldwork practices. Casagrande (1948, p. 14) points out: "From the vocabulary (of baby words) itself, one can form some idea of the child's world in a given culture; what objects and affects impinge upon it." For an area of key interest, such as personality, an understanding of the categories held by the people studied is essential; analysis of the terms they use is part of such understanding. Recent discussions of person perception, while calling attention to the importance of people's own categories, also rely very much on English terms for describing emotions and persons (Bruner and Tagiuri, 1954; Tagiuri and Petrullo, 1958, p. *x;* Hastorf, Richardson, and Dornbusch, 1958; Bruner, Shapiro, and Tagiuri, 1958). Full analysis of these terms is essential, both for the understanding of personality among groups of English speakers, and to avoid semantic interference through the use of the terms as translations and tags in the study of personality in other cultures. Allport and Odbert (1936) pioneered in the descriptive study of English names for personality traits. In a notable study, Asch (1946) showed the importance of particular terms such as "hot" and "cold" in people's judgment of personality.[13] Wishner (1960) has explored Asch's distinction between "central" and "peripheral" traits, showing that this distinction depends upon the correlations within particular clusters of traits. His remarks on context, a structural point of view, and the use of antonyms point toward some kinds of problems and methods now being dealt with in anthropology and linguistics. In anthropology there is a renewal of interest in fields of folk-science such as ethnobotany and folk-medicine, using a linguistic approach to the study of native categories (see Conklin, 1955, and Frake, 1961). There also is a renewed attention to semantic description on the part of linguists (see especially Haugen, 1957, and Joos, 1958). This work is especially concerned with the qualitative and hierarchical relations among categories, and the methods devised can be applied to the vocabulary, such as trait-names, which is of importance in personality study. (See also the mention of componential analysis and the semantic differential later in this section.)

The absence of terms is often suggestive. For instance, there is a psychoanalytic interpretation of the absence of an English slang term for the clitoris. Absence of a term for "square" in Zulu helps substantiate findings based on other evidence (Allport and Pettigrew, 1957).

Three points about language categories should be kept particularly in mind. First, an important categorization may be unexpressed linguistically. This is what Goodenough (1951, pp. 61–64) found for some basic Trukese property relationships. Second, the linguistic categorizations studied may be but one way the society has of classifying certain phenomena. If the Trukese grammatical category of possession is taken as a way of expressing property relationships, then Truk is an example. Lounsbury (1956) has shown that a full semantic analysis of Iroquois kinship terminology reveals a simple, coherent system for keeping track of relatives, but one that does not at all match the way relatives are classified for purposes of clan membership. Third, there may be more than one level of linguistic categorization. Conklin (1955) reports four broad color categories in Hanunoo, and Leach (1958) mentions four broad clan categories among the Trobrianders. In each case these are found to be conventional classifications, and a different, much more detailed categorization of colors and sub-clans, respectively is also made.

The student of personality in another culture must conclude that non-linguistic differences will partly depend upon or correlate with differences in language, but there is no simple way of telling how or in what degree from a description of the language by itself. Lexical and grammatical categories can be taken as important guides, especially so the more frequently they are used, but the field worker is likely to have to estimate frequency himself.

As McClelland (1951, p. 152) observes, regarding individual personality, psychologists usually want to use speech or language as evidence of something else. Yet acts of speech and languages embody expressions of personality in their own right. As I shall stress in the final section of this chapter, speech and language are independent and variable in their relation to personality in different cultures. They may or may not fit neatly with other evidence of personality, but it remains true that an account of personality cannot be complete if it omits speech and language.

One important caution is that cultural personality and language may sort differently. The general question—to what kind of cultural unit are personality data to be related—is discussed by Hallowell (1953, pp. 606–607) in relation to languages.

It is a far cry from Whorf's broad and subtle fashions of speaking, which coordinate linguistic data of all sorts, or from a pervasive semantic trend, to the experimental testing of behavioral response to a specific item of lexicon or grammar. What about the specific chunks of language in between? Can linguistics say anything about the implications of these for personality? This is a question of the implications of language typology for cultural personality. The interest might be put this way: Studies with English-speaking subjects have found correlation between various linguistic traits and personality traits, the most cited being between adjective-verb ratio and such traits as anxiety (Balken and Masserman, 1940; Boder, 1940; Sanford, 1942b). Can languages be taken as individuals writ large? If a difference in relative frequency of adjectives and verbs can be significant for an individual personality within a speech-community, could such a difference between speech-communities as wholes be significant? What does it signify if in one language adjectives are a subclass of nouns, but in another a subclass of verbs? I know no reliable investigation of such questions. A great many factors might work to preclude any personality significance for such differences, and the danger of ethnocentric judgment is great. Still, it cannot be assumed that languages differ from each other in these dimensions to no purpose. Some factors of selection and shaping by generations of speakers have been at work. One cannot rule out the possibility that factors which underly the selection and shaping of individual speech patterns may have been collectively pervasive in shaping the patterns of a language.[14]

There is one forthright declaration of a principle running through individual speech, speech disorders, and linguistic codes, which it would be revealing to attempt to measure: Jakobson's definition of the metaphoric and metonymic poles (see Jakobson, 1957, or Jakobson and Halle, 1957). In general, we know very little about language typology. We are far from having adequate frameworks for analyzing language types in purely linguistic terms, let alone for correlating them with culture and personality. A little should be said about phonological, grammatical and lexical type in order to indicate the present situation.

Jespersen once said the phonological pattern of a language reflected psychological characteristics. English is "masculine," contrasting with soft, musical "feminine" languages of Spain, Italy and Hawaii: "You do not expect much vigor or energy in a people speaking such a language." But one might equally well expect speakers of a "masculine" language to be exhausted from the effort of articulating it, and the speakers of soft, musical languages to have energy left for other things. Such speculations have cast a shadow over any attempt to associate personality type with phonological type. Other aspects of the use of sound may still have significance. Martin (1958), exploring Japanese and Korean for keys to national character, notes that

> Korean has perhaps the richest and most extensive sound symbolism in the world; each of over a thousand lexemes occurs not as an isolated item, but as a set of words with systematic variations in shape that correspond to subtle but structured differences in connotation. The Japanese system is feeble by comparison.

Perhaps such a difference in oral behavior (and gratification) is correlated with other differences.

In the nineteenth century there were many classifications of languages
into a limited number of grammatical types, using terms such as isolating,
agglutinating, inflecting, analytic, synthetic, polysynthetic. The classifications were often not logically consistent, often carried untenable evolutionary implications, and did not correlate with anything else. In 1921
Sapir presented a subtle classification of languages into basic conceptual
types, but this approach has not been developed by others. Recently interest in typology has revived among linguists, and broad surveys of
phonological systems have been made, but much is yet to be done for
the grammatical and lexical aspects of language, which are of most interest to personality study.

One thing of obvious interest is how languages handle the category of
person itself. Hallowell (1958, p. 83) has said that "the concept of person, like the concept of self, may be expected to appear as a cultural
universal"; it would seem to be a linguistic universal. Unfortunately,
there has been much speculative writing, but no adequate empirical
study. The one attempt—by Forchheimer in 1953—does provide data
for some hypotheses. All natural languages seem to distinguish three persons in the singular, and between singular and plural in the first person.
These four ("I," "thou," "it," "we") seem to be the universal, minimal
set (Hymes, 1955, p. 298). Brown and Gilman (1959) have made an
extensive study of the intimate second person pronoun in five Indo-
European languages, isolating two dimensions of *power* and *solidarity* to
explain usage and change of usage. These dimensions underly other
types of pronominal usage, as the two third persons of Navaho, or the
inclusive-exclusive distinction in the pronouns of many languages, and
enter into the speech levels of Korean as analyzed by Martin. Sapir
(1915) provides a wealth of examples of "person-implication" in various parts of language, and Haas (1944) formulates the dimensions in
terms of which male and female differences in several languages are
organized. The literature abounds with interesting reports of linguistic
phenomena relevant to the perception, categorization and evaluation
of persons; but such reports are typically not related to a theoretical
perspective. Recently Jakobson has definitively clarified the semantic
nature of the personal pronoun itself, ending a confusion that has pro-
liferated through the literature of linguistics and psychology (1957).
In the same paper he explicates the traditional grammatical categories
of the verb in a way that relates these categories to the concept of person. The inclusion of verbal categories in any study of how languages
differ in their treatment of person is thus made possible. This work, and
that by Haas, Martin, Brown and Gilman, seeking to determine underlying dimensions, is an important step forward.

Here two methodological tools should be mentioned. One is componential analysis, which has been applied to kinship terms by Lounsbury (1956) and Goodenough (1951, 1956), and to personal pronouns by Wonderly (1952). It is a precise way of revealing semantic dimensions not marked by words themselves. As a trivial example, the English kin terms "father, mother; uncle, aunt; son, daughter; grandfather, granddaughter; brother, sister" are differentiated by a semantic component of sex, although gender is not overtly marked in any of them. Many semantic components are not obvious at all, and a careful analysis produces new knowledge.[15] A basic assumption is that the words can be treated as members of a set, or "semantic field." Another tool is the semantic differential, developed by Osgood and others (1957), who devote a chapter in their book to "Semantic Measurement in Personality and Psychotherapy Research." Most results are tentative but very promising. A striking result is the success of the semantic differential with a case of triple personality ("Eve White," "Eve-Black," and "Jane"). Insofar as the differential could reveal the conceptual structure of the three personalities, each was found to be differently organized in its responses to it (Osgood *et al.,* pp. 258–271). The instrument has been tested with Japanese, Koreans, and some American Indian groups. The differential is based on factor analysis of seven-interval scales, whose poles are opposed adjectives such as "fair": "unfair," "strong": "weak," "clean": "dirty." Subjects score concepts such as "myself," "God," "baby," "mother," "Adlai Stevenson," by checking one of the intervals between each adjectival pair. Osgood is especially interested in the potential universality of the main factors that the differential reveals, but the cross-cultural differences are likely to be of even greater interest.[16]

Asch (1958) has called attention to the terms used to describe persons and psychological qualities. He seeks general principles governing the metaphorical extension of physical terms to attributes of personality, but cultural differences in metaphorical pattern are equally striking. Thus, English speakers commonly use animal terms to describe persons ("bearish," "mulish," "pigheaded"), but speakers of Zuni (Newman, 1954) and Wishram Chinook (Hymes, field notes) do not. Such differences in metaphorical pattern are a rich source of insight, especially when one recalls the points made by Kenneth Burke, that every perspective requires a metaphor, implicit or explicit, for its organizational base, and that there is a vast area of reference, such as the supernatural, where metaphor *must* be used.

Ullmann (1952, 1954) has done the most recent work to describe whole languages in semantic terms that would have import for personality. His efforts have the value that they state explicit dimensions on which to contrast languages semantically, but they, like efforts to treat language differences developmentally (Werner and Kaplan, 1956; Kaplan, 1957), suffer from the methodological defect that is shared by most work which relates languages to culture and personality. An intriguing or plausible hypothesis is supported by examples, but the whole of the relevant data is not systematically analyzed. As Weinreich (1955) emphasizes, illustrations are not evidence. Ullman contrasts French and German, a favorite pair for those seeking linguistic evidence of national character differences (e.g., Thorner, 1945), but does not cite negative instances or statistically evaluate them.

In sum, there is no doubt that differences in culture and personality are related to differences in language. There is also little or no satisfactory knowledge of the nature of the relationship. Before such knowledge can be obtained, linguistics must tackle the problems of semantics much more vigorously. It has adequate methods for penetrating the formal structure of a language, but little has been done to develop methods for semantic description.[17] Nor have the concepts required by semantic description received anything like the intensive analysis that has been lavished on the phoneme and morpheme. A number of recent studies have shown requickening interest in such problems, so that there is promise that linguistics will be able to make more of a contribution to that aspect of language most bound up with personality meaning. In the meantime, students of personality in other cultures, if they believe in the relevance of linguistic evidence, and make it part of their research, contribute to linguistics as well as to their own field.

THE FUNCTIONS OF SPEECH

Under this rubric, I want to raise questions about the functions of speech in a society, after a few words about the functions of speech in general. Whereas in the preceding section we considered language more as a "countersign of thought," here we will consider it more as a "mode of action" (see Malinowski, 1923, p. 326).

Many have classified language and speech into various aspects, one of the most popular classifications in American behavioral science being that of Morris (1939) into syntactics, semantics, and pragmatics. For relating the act of speech to personality and culture, Jakobson's classification is much more adequate. He has summarized it in remarks at conferences (1953, 1959). I can only adumbrate it here. As factors in the speech situation, Jakobson recognizes the sender, the receiver, the topic of reference, the code, and the message. All are involved in every communication, but focus on one or another may dominate. As tags for the associated functions, we may use the adjectives "expressive," "persuasive" or "rhetorical" (after Burke, 1951), "referential," "metalinguistic," and "poetic." According to Jakobson, one such function is dominant in each communication; the others are hierarchically arranged below it. In other words, focus on the several factors is hierarchically arranged, either from the viewpoint of the participants or of the analyst. To this classification, I believe that at least the factor of *context* or *scene* should be added (see Burke, 1945). There remain problems of interpretation and application which cannot be analyzed here, except to mention the point made earlier regarding the expressive function. One may either identify certain features as manifestations of a particular function or look at the whole message from the point of view of each function in turn.[18] We may simply note, then, that Jakobson's classification of speech functions keeps a full set of relevant dimensions in mind, and can probably subsume many familiar but more limited concepts, such as Malinowski's "phatic communion" and Piaget's distinction between "egocentric" and "socialized" speech. It is worth pointing out that a sensitive analysis by Burke (1958) largely agrees with the Jakobson formulation.

In what follows, my general conception of the relevant dimensions of speech as a mode of social action is an application of recent theoretical work by Talcott Parsons. I would distinguish four broad aspects of speech activity: the cultural values and evaluations associated with speech activity; the social structure of the contexts of speech activity; the personalities who participate in speech activity (this and the preceding being connected by the speech aspects of roles); and the array of linguistic repertoires and routines available in the society for use in appropriate roles and situations. In Parsonian notation, these four aspects would be dubbed in order L I G A. Since I have but recently developed this conceptual scheme, what follows is not an analytic application of it, but a discursive essay on some of the questions which led to its formulation. I want to call attention to some of the neglected questions about the specific functions of speech. My premise is that speech is vital to personality, and that it varies significantly from society to society in its role as an oral activity and acquired skill. Differences in this regard seem as important as differences in the use of any other learned mode of behavior or of any other sensory modality. Because of space limitations, I shall be skimpy with illustrations, but there are many in the ethnographic literature.

First, cultural differences in the importance and evaluation of speech and language can be taken as something which reflects cultural personality and shapes the personality development of individuals. Speech communities differ in their insistence on skill and precision in speech, certainly as regards the use of their language by outsiders, probably as regards its use among themselves. People differ in their attitude towards speech material of foreign origin. Some refuse to borrow from other languages, some are extremely hospitable to foreign words. In multilingual situations there are differences in identification with the different languages, especially when one language is being replaced or threatened. Swadesh comments: "Obviously we have here a rich area in which to observe the interplay of culture and personality" (Swadesh, 1948, p. 234). Bruner (1956, pp. 617–619) shows the crucial importance of this for the relation between primary group experience and acculturation. Peoples also differ in their conscious interest in the resources of their language and in their exploitation of them. I have mentioned sound symbolism in Korean. The coinage of words by sound symbolism has become a convention in American popular culture, especially in that part, such as comic books, directed ostensibly toward children. (For Russian attitudes see Mead and Metraux, 1953, pp. 166 ff.) Newman has brilliantly contrasted the style of Yokuts, an Indian language of California, to that of English, as austere restraint vs. wild proliferation (Newman, 1940).

Peoples differ in their evaluation of talking, in the kinds of talk and talkers that are conventionally recognized, and in the way talking enters into the definition of statuses and roles. Differences in rewards and expectations will have a selective effect on the development of personalities. Peoples also differ in their criteria for verbal ability.

Second, personality is shaped and reflected by differences in the handling of speech situations. Barker and Wright (1954) have used the methods of psychological ecology to discover what they term the *behavior settings* of a community. By *speech situations* I mean the distribution of acts of speech in relation to behavior settings. Every society defines this relationship in a characteristic way. Most generally, there are some behavior settings in which speech is proscribed, some in which it is prescribed, and some in which it is optional.[19] One must take into account a society's own theory as to who has the power of speech. Supernatural beings, animals, objects may variously be attributed this power. Wherever a society attributes speech, or the power of comprehension, it creates behavior settings in which speech can occur.

The first step in analyzing speech situations would be to discover which behavior settings fall into which general class. The second would be to analyze the contents of the classes. One major factor would be the relative number of settings in each class: societies differ markedly in their toleration of silence (or of talk, depending on the point of view). In what sort of settings is speech proscribed or prescribed? In relation to what persons and roles? Are there settings specifically defined as occasions for speech, such as confession, prayer, praise, oath-taking, therapy, verbal training of children? In our society family table-talk has been studied by Bossard (1948, Ch. VIII, IX). He finds it "a form of family interaction, important in the identification of personality roles and the development of personality traits" (p. 175). In some societies the family is not together at meals; other behavior settings and different persons would be more important for the kind of subtle, indirect verbal conditioning of the child which Bossard describes.

In any society there is a congruence between speech and its setting, whether the setting be defined in terms of time, place, or personnel (e.g., Smith, 1958; Evans-Pritchard, 1948). Some settings not only require speech, but speech about certain topics or the use of certain expressions. From a psychoanalytic viewpoint, Devereux has highlighted cultural differences in the settings in which profanity can occur, the objects toward which it can be addressed, and what its use reveals about character structure (Devereux, 1951). What one cannot talk about, what one must talk about, when, where, and to whom—these differ in ways that involve differences in personality.

The content of speech plays a dual role regarding behavior settings. A situation may define what kind of speech is appropriate. Speech itself may serve to define a situation, and speech manipulation to define ambiguous situations may be an important skill. This dual role of speech involves usages shared by classes, regions, local communities, families, occupants of certain statuses and roles, and even pairs of individuals. On the broadest scale, levels of speech recognized throughout a society are involved (see Bloomfield, 1927). The way these differ from one society to another is itself significant. Thus, "the lack of congruence even between the conventional usage scales for English and French (slang-colloquial-standard vs. *vulgaire-populaire-familier,* etc.) reflects an important difference in the linguistic sociology of the two communities" (Weinreich, 1955b, p. 538).[20]

Some differences in speech behavior seem constant across behavior settings, depending on the persons communicating. An Ainu husband uses his wife's personal name to her, but she may never address him by his. Sapir (1915) and Haas (1944) discuss phenomena of this sort, such as differences in the speech of men and women. Still, the persons involved communicate in certain behavior settings rather than others, so that particular usages become linked to particular situations. Occurrence of these usages elsewhere may refer to such situations, perhaps as a comment on personality, for instance, use of baby-talk to insult an adult.

An important point is made by Sapir:

> Generally speaking, the smaller the circle, and the more complex the understanding already arrived at within it, the more economical can the act of communication afford to become. A single word passed between members of an intimate group, in spite of its apparent vagueness, and ambiguity, may

constitute a far more precise communication than volumes of carefully prepared correspondence interchanged between two governments. (1931, p. 79)

This seems to be the principle underlying effective use of speech surrogates, such as the Mazateco whistle speech or West African drum signals.[21] It also underlies functionally specialized idioms, such as the argot of Ethiopian merchants, or the speech disguise of Tagalog young people (Conklin, 1956, 1959). Friedson (1956) suggests use of the principle as a measure of a speaker's perception of his intimacy with his audience. In general, one would want to know what settings permit conventional or individual economizing in communication.

Behavior settings may differ in the very language or code used. The choice may be for concealment, prestige, or effective communication, and differences will reveal and shape personality. Weinreich (1953) analyzes many of the factors involved.

To function successfully as an adult personality, the child growing into a speech community must acquire a mastery of several sets of rules. He must of course learn the phonological rules, the grammatical rules, the semantic rules, which make an utterance a proper part of the language, and which make possible the vital cultural property of language, the production and understanding of novel utterances. There are the rules of the paralinguistic system, of speech as expressive and persuasive behavior. As Luria (1959a, 1959b) has shown, the child must also learn or grow to associate utterances with actions. Linked perhaps with this kind of "directive" or "adaptive" function of speech is another aspect of speech activity which is also separate from knowing the rules of the linguistic code proper. The successful adult must have mastered some part of the available linguistic routines and repertoires; he must judge not only of possible utterances, but also of their appropriate distribution among roles and behavior settings. He must learn not only how to say, but what to say. With all of this must go the internalization of certain attitudes toward speech activity and his language or languages.

Let us consider now the differences in the role that speech may play in the actual process of socialization, first regarding the onset and rate of language development, then regarding the context of development.

It is clear that children differ in the age at which speaking begins, and in the rate at which they master language. To some extent this is innate, but much depends upon cultural expectation and family situation. Number and relative age of siblings is one factor; only children have been found superior to children-with-siblings, and twins often develop special systems of communication, reducing the need for acquiring the language of adults, while singletons-with-siblings resemble twins more than only-children (Anastasi and Foley, 1949, pp. 337 ff. summarize a number of studies). These results are from studies of North American children, but the cross-cultural implication is clear. Language development in children can be expected to vary with any social, cultural or ecological conditions affecting the makeup of the household.

Most studies of language development are linguistically inadequate, seizing upon external criteria such as number of words and length of utterances, whereas the essential thing is mastery of patterns, which must be studied in terms of a structural analysis of the language (Leopold, 1953–54). Only bare beginnings of such study have been made (Jakobson, 1942; Velten, 1943; Leopold, 1939–1948; Kahane, Kahane, and Saporta, 1958). Still the results discussed by Anastasi and Foley are significant. The importance of the age and rate at which language is achieved is succinctly stated by Bossard: "the acquisition of language is necessary to set into motion the two conditioning factors of social interaction and cultural background which mold the personality of the child" (1948, pp. 177–178). Thus children who differ in the age at which language is acquired must differ in the age at which much of culture is acquired, particularly that whole range of culturally-defined reality which depends on language, such as the supernatural. They will also differ in the part of their first years that is accessible in later life (see Schachtel, 1947). A child who has successfully interacted with its environment without speech for a longer time may be more independent of language's shaping effect in later life.

Societies may differ not only in the age at which children typically acquire speech, but also in the context of its acquisition. For any society, one would want answers to such questions as: When is the child considered capable of understanding speech? Among the Tlingit, for instance, "when the infant is but a few months old the mother talks to him, tells him his moral tales, 'trains' him" (Olson, 1956, p. 681). Is acquisition of speech accompanied by pressure, or treated as something that comes in due course? Are there special word games or speech patterns for teaching children? If there is pressure, at what stage of psychosexual development is the pressure applied? When are other socialization pressures applied, before or after the acquisition of speech? Various writings make clear that pressure, deprivation, and overprotection may variously induce speech defects or the preservation of infantile speech habits (Kluckhohn, 1954, p. 944; Lemert, 1952; Henry and Henry, 1940; Klausner, 1955).

To what extent is a child rewarded by verbal praise, in contrast to material rewards such as candy, or physical affection? To what extent is the child punished by verbal reprimand, as opposed to deprivation, or physical pain? What is the conception of proper speech behavior on the part of the child, relative to particular persons and behavior settings? Are a child's questions about words and meanings welcomed or rebuffed?

Overall, is a child allowed much or little oral gratification through speech? Is a child encouraged, discouraged, or ignored in efforts to find satisfaction in speech play? What is the proportion of speech activity to communication by other means, such as gestures, on the part of the child?

Are there special settings for verbal instruction of children? If there are, how frequent and with what personnel, and about what topics? Is the instruction conventionalized in content, as are proverbs and myths, or only in theme? Is the tone of instruction categorical, as among many American Indian groups, or not, as in West Africa? Is sex involved? There is no sex instruction of the young among the Nupe (Nadel, 1954), but many American Indian children were forced to listen to a mythology rife with sexual incidents.

Does speech enter into the continuities and discontinuities in cultural conditioning (Benedict, 1938)? Every child learns a special version of its language first, usually its family's but that is a minor discontinuity; more significant may be "baby-talk." Is there a specialized "baby-talk"? How elaborated? What is its cultural content? Among American Indians, a Hidatsa mother stated: "We don't like baby talk . . . when they talk, we want them to talk just like us, right from the start" (Voegelin and Robinett, 1954, p. 69, n. 6), whereas the Comanche had an unusually rich, formalized vocabulary of special words used to teach the child to speak between one year and three or four (Casagrande, 1948). Though thought of as simple, baby-talk may be as difficult as the adult language. Herzog (1949, p. 97) says some features of Comanche baby-talk are as difficult to pronounce as corresponding features of the adult vocabulary, and Ferguson (1957) finds some of the most difficult sounds in the language to be among the most frequent in Arabic baby talk. The greatest discontinuity may come in the multilingual situation. Perhaps the most striking case is the Chontal of Zapotec, Mexico, where children are taught Spanish first, learning Chontal when as adolescents they enter the cultural life of the adult community (Waterhouse, 1949). Here an important factor seems parents' desire for children's success in the Spanish-using school. The children actually are forbidden the use of Chontal by their parents, for fear it will impede school progress.

One would expect differences in all these regards to correlate with differences in the functions of speech in the adult society and with the evaluation of speech activity in the adult culture. One could use the methods developed by Whiting and Ford to test hypotheses such as this: does the importance of verbal reward and punishment in socialization correlate with the importance of verbal interaction with the supernatural in adult life? Does late acquisition of speech correlate with an importance of glossolalia ("speaking in tongues") in adult religious life?[22]

To conclude: language is a prerequisite of human society, but beyond this universal function, its significance varies from group to group. Speech is but one mode of communication, and its use involves the choice of one sensory modality as opposed to others. Societies and persons differ in the extent to which they choose this modality, the situations in which they choose it, and their evaluation of it. They differ in the ways speech enters into the definition of situations, conceptions of personality types, the socialization of the child. Its universality should not make us forget that speech activity, like sex and weaning, is a variable for the study of personality cross-culturally.

NOTES

1. Much of the stimulus for this work has come from the Committee on Psychology and Language of the Social Science Research Council.

2. See the discussion of *gathering* and *collation* in Hockett, 1958, Ch. 12.

3. Space does not permit a detailed example, but see Twaddell (1935) and Hockett (1955, section 3232) for discussion of a favorite crux in American descriptive linguistics: the relation of the second consonant in *spill* to the first consonants of *pill* and *bill*.

4. Trager and Smith (1951) is a milestone in this regard; again, Hockett (1958) is the best introduction. Householder (1957b) and Bollinger (1958), and the references they cite, show that a definitive analysis is yet to be stated, but the Trager-Smith system provides an adequate working model.

5. Devereux (1949) has remained one of the very few reports of such phenomena in a non-Western society.

6. Stankiewicz has an excellent manuscript on expressive language, on which I have drawn.

7. See Sapir (1915) and Herzog (1949) for a variety of American Indian examples; see McDavid (1952–53) for social differences in American English.

8. See also, with regard to the role of language, Miller, 1956b, 1956c; Miller, Galanter and Pribram, 1960; and Pavlov, 1957, p. 537.

9. See the review of perceptual studies dealing with word recognition in Allport, 1955.

10. Thus the chapter on "Socialization" in the *Handbook of Social Psychology* (Lindzey, 1954) has a section on "oral behavior" but does not mention speech.

11. Luria and Yuovich, 1959, pp. 11–12 declare: "The study of the child's mental processes as the product of intercommunication with the environment, and the acquisition of common experiences transmitted by speech, has, therefore, become the most important principle of Soviet psychology which informs all research." This follows the statement (p. 11): "By naming objects, and so defining their connections and relations, the adult creates new forms of reflection of reality in the child, incomparably deeper and more complex than those which he would have formed through

individual experience. This whole process of the transmission of knowledge and the formation of concepts, which is the basic way the adult influences the child, constitutes the central process of the child's intellectual development. If this formation of the child's mental activity in the process of education is left out of consideration, it is impossible either to understand or to explain causally any of the facts of child psychology."

12. Pulgram (1954) makes a vigorous attack on the use, without historical perspective, of linguistic evidence for national character.

13. Wishner (1960, p. 96) states that Asch reduced part of the problem of how we know others to manageable proportions, and that "one of Asch's more important contributions was to devise an experimental procedure whereby the general problem is formulated in linguistic terms."

14. Doob (1958, p. 401) finds that from a practical point of view the study of the personality correlates of grammatical style "is by itself not a useful or feasible clinical instrument." One team of investigators (Benton, Hartman, and Sarason, 1955) later found no correlation between the often-cited adjective-verb quotient and manifest anxiety. Yet, as we have indicated, to be important within the total picture of a personality, it is not necessary for a linguistic trait to be highly diagnostic in isolation. Moreover, the right grammatical traits may not have been found. Perhaps a folk-science type of exploratory work is needed to discover if the users of the language themselves notice, distinguish or respond to grammatical aspects of personality expression. These might exist and yet not be the conventional classes that loom large in memories of the schoolroom and in ordinary grammars. Such traits may be more fine-grained. Teachers of composition, despite their frequent misplaced pedantry, work closer to the uses of grammar that may convey personality than do many grammarians. In any event, Doob's judgment is with regard to individual differences. In my view, personality, like style, is a term that can be applied at successive levels of generality. Essentially it indicates differences among the members of a set. Often the set we have in mind is a society or culture and it is individuals who differ. But we can equally well have in mind a set of societies or cultures, and consider the differences in style or personality not within but between them. This is of course the perspective which underlies the relevance for personality of most of the discussion of the content of language in this chapter, and it applies to other sectors of language and speech as well as to grammar.

15. See Wallace and Atkins (1960), on the psychological reality of the components.

16. See reviews by Carroll (1959) and Weinreich (1958) and the exchange between Osgood (1959) and Weinreich (1959).

17. See Hoijer (1954, pp. 98–99), Newman (1954), Garvin (1958), besides those cited already for contributions to this development.

18. On such recurrent problems of "selecting and grouping in attention," see Sinclair (1951).

19. See Woods (1956, pp. 26–29) for examples of culturally prescribed reticence.

20. On levels in non-European communities, see Newman (1955), Martin (1958).

21. See Stern (1957) for a conceptualization and survey of speech surrogates.

22. See May (1956), for a survey of such phenomena as glossolalia.

BIBLIOGRAPHY

Allport, Floyd. 1955. *Theories of Perception and the Concept of Structure.* New York: John Wiley and Sons.

Allport, G. W. and Cantril, H. 1934. "Judging Personality From Voice," *Journal of Social Psychology* 5:37–55.

Allport, G. W. and Odbert, H. E. 1936. "Trait names: A Psycholexical Study," *Psychological Monographs,* 47:1 (whole no. 211).

Allport, G. W. and Pettigrew, Thomas F. 1957. "Cultural Influence on the Perception of Movement: The Trapezoidal Illusion Among Zulu," *Journal of Abnormal and Social Psychology,* 55:104–13.

Anastasi, Anne and Foley, John P., Jr. 1949. *Differential Psychology.* New York: Macmillan.

Asch, Solomon E. 1946. "Forming Impressions of Personality," *Journal of Abnormal and Social Psychology,* 41:285–290.

———. 1958. "The Metaphor: A Psychological Inquiry." In Tagiuri, R. and Petrullo, L. (eds.), *Person Perception and Interpersonal Behavior.* Stanford: Stanford University Press.

Balken, E. R. and Masserman, J. H. 1940. "The Language of Phantasy: III. The Language of the Phantasies of Patients with Conversion Hysteria, Anxiety State, and Obsessive-Compulsive Neuroses," *Journal of Psychology,* 10:75–86.

Barker, Roger G. and Wright, Herbert F. 1954. *Midwest and Its Children.* Evanston: Row, Peterson & Co.

Bateson, Gregory. 1958. "Language and Psycho-Therapy: Frieda Fromm-Reichmann's Last Project," *Psychiatry,* 21:96–100.

Bateson, Gregory; Birdwhistell, Ray L.; Brosin, Henry W.; Hockett, Charles F.; and McQuown, Norman A. "The Natural History of an Interview." Unpublished.

Belbin, E. 1950. "The Influence of Interpolated Recall Upon Recognition," *Quarterly Journal of Experimental Psychology,* 2:163–69.

Benedict, Ruth. 1938. "Continuities and Discontinuities in Cultural Conditioning," *Psychiatry,* 1:161–67.

Benton, A. L.; Hartman, C. H.; and Sarason, L. E. 1955. "Some Correlations Between Speech Behavior and Anxiety Level," *Journal of Abnormal and Social Psychology,* 51:295–97.

Birdwhistell, Ray L. 1952. *Introduction to Kinesics.* Washington, D. C.: U.S. Dept. of State, Foreign Service Institute.

Bloomfield, Leonard. 1927. "Literate and Illiterate Speech," *American Speech,* 2:432–39.

———. 1942. *Outline Guide for the Practical Study of Foreign Languages.* Baltimore: Linguistic Society of America.

Boder, David P. 1940. "The Adjective-Verb Quotient: A Contribution to the Psychology of Language," *Psychological Record*, 3:310–43.

Bollinger, D. L. 1958. "A Theory of Pitch Accent in English," *Word*, 14:109–49.

Bossard, James H. S. 1948. *The Sociology of Child Development*. New York: Harper and Brothers.

Bossard, James H. S.; Boll, E. S.; and Sangor, W. P. 1950. "Some Neglected Areas in Family-Life Study," *Annals of the American Academy of Political and Social Sciences*, 272:68–76.

Brown, J. 1956. "Distortions in Immediate Memory," *Quarterly Journal of Experimental Psychology*, 8:134–39.

Brown, Roger W. 1956. "Language and Categories." Appendix to Bruner, Jerome S.; Goodnow, Jacqueline; Austin, George A. *A Study of Thinking*, 247–312.

———. 1957. "Linguistic Determinism and the Parts of Speech," *Journal of Abnormal and Social Psychology*, 55:1–5.

———. 1959. *Words and Things*. Glencoe, Illinois: The Free Press.

Brown, Roger W. and Lenneberg, Eric H. 1954. "A Study in Language and Cognition," *Journal of Abnormal and Social Psychology*, 49:454–62.

———. 1958. "Studies in Linguistic Relativity." In Maccoby, Eleanor; Newcomb, Theodore M.; Hartley, Eugene L. (eds.), *Readings in Social Psychology*, 3rd ed., pp. 9–18. New York: Henry Holt & Co.

Brown, Roger W. and Gilman, A. 1960. "The Pronouns of Power and Solidarity." In Sebeok, Thomas A. (ed.), *Aspects of Style in Language*. New York: John Wiley.

Bruner, Edward M. 1956. "Primary Group Experience and the Processes of Acculturation," *American Anthropologist*, 58:605–23.

Bruner, J.; Busiek, R. D.; and Minturn, A. L. 1952. "Assimilation in the Immediate Reproduction of Visually Perceived Figures," *Journal of Experimental Psychology*, 44:151–55.

Bruner, Jerome; Shapiro, D.; and Tagiuri, Renato. 1958. "The Meaning of Traits in Isolation and in Combination." In Tagiuri, R. and Petrullo, L. (eds.), *Person Perception and Interpersonal Behavior*, Ch. 18. Stanford: Stanford University Press.

Bruner, Jerome and Tagiuri, Renato. 1954. "The Perception of People." In Lindzey, Gardner (ed.), *Handbook of Social Psychology*, Vol. II, Ch. 17, 634–54. Cambridge: Addison-Wesley Publishing Company, Inc.

Burke, Kenneth. 1945. *A Grammar of Motives*. New York: Prentice-Hall.

———. 1951. *A Rhetoric of Motives*. New York: Prentice-Hall.

———. 1957. "The Poetic Motive," *The Hudson Review*, 11:54–63.

Carmichael, L.; Hogan, P.; and Walter, A. A. 1932. "An Experimental Study of the Effect of Language on the Reproduction of Visually Perceived Form," *Journal of Experimental Psychology*, 15:73–86.

Carroll, John B. (ed.). 1956. *Language, Thought, and Reality: Selected Writings of Benjamin Lee Whorf*. New York: John Wiley & The Technology Press.

————. 1958. "Some Psychological Effects of Language Structure." In Hoch, P. and Zubin, J. (eds.), *Psychopathology of Communication*. New York: Grune and Stratton. Pp. 28–36.

————. 1959. "Review of Osgood, Suci, and Tannenbaum, *The Measurement of Meaning*," *Language* 35:58–77.

Carroll, John B. and Casagrande, Joseph B. 1958. "The Function of Language Classifications in Behavior." In Maccoby, Eleanor; Newcomb, Theodore H.; and Hartley, Eugene L. (eds.), *Readings in Social Psychology*, 3rd ed. New York: Holt, Rinehart and Winston, Inc. Pp. 18–31.

Casagrande, Joseph B. 1948. "Comanche Baby Language," *International Journal of American Linguistics*, 14:11–14.

————. 1955. "Comanche Linguistic Acculturation III," *International Journal of American Linguistics*, 21:8–25.

Chao, Yuan Ren. 1953. "Introduction to Discussion of Speech and Personality." Summarized in Levi-Strauss, C., *et al.* (eds.), *Results of the Conference of Anthropologists and Linguists*, Baltimore: Waverly Press, Inc. P. 33.

Conklin, Harold C. 1955. "Hanunoo Color Categories," *Southwestern Journal of Anthropology*, 11:339–44.

————. 1956. "Tagalog Speech Disguise," *Language*, 32, 136–39.

————. 1959. "Linguistic Play in Its Cultural Setting," *Language*, 35:631–36.

Cooley, C. 1908. "A Study of the Early Use of Self-Words by a Child," *Psychological Review*, 15:339–57.

Danchy, J. S.; Hockett, C. F.; and Pittenger, R. *The First Five Minutes*. Unpublished.

De Groot, A. 1949. "Structural Linguistics and Syntactic Laws," *Word*, 5:1–12.

Deutsch, F. 1959. "Correlations of Verbal and Nonverbal Communication in Interviews Elicited by Associative Anamnesis," *Psychosomatic Medicine*, 21:123–30.

Devereux, George. 1949. "Mohave Voice and Speech Mannerisms," *Word*, 5:268–72.

————. 1951. "Mohave Indian Verbal and Motor Profanity." In Róheim, Géza (ed.), *Psychoanalysis and the Social Sciences*. New York: International Universities Press. Vol. 3, pp. 99–127.

Doob, L. 1958. "Behavior and Grammatical Style," *Journal of Abnormal and Social Psychology*, 56: 398–400.

Eldred, S. H. and Price, D. P. 1958. "A Linguistic Evaluation of Feeling States in Psychotherapy," *Psychiatry*, 21: 115–22.

Emeneau, Murray B. 1941. "Language and Social Forms: A Study of Toda Kinship Terms and Dual Descent." In Spier, Leslie; Hallowell, A. Irving;

and Newman, Stanley S. (eds.), *Language, Culture, and Personality: Essays in Memory of Edward Sapir*. Menasha. Pp. 158–79.

――――. 1950. "Language and Non-Linguistic Patterns," *Language*, 26: 199–209.

Evans-Pritchard, E. E. 1940. *The Nuer*. Oxford: Clarendon Press.

――――. 1948. "Nuer Modes of Address," *The Uganda Journal*, 12:166–171.

Ferguson, Charles A. 1956. "Arabic Baby Talk." In *For Roman Jakobson*. s'Gravenhague: Mouton & Co. Pp. 121–28.

Firth, J. R. 1950. "Personality and Language in Society," *Sociological Review*. Ledbury. Vol. 42, sect. II, pp. 8–14.

Flavell, John. 1958. "A Test of the Whorfian Hypothesis," *Psychological Reports*, 4:455–62.

Forchheimer, Paul. 1953. *The Category of Person in Language*. Berlin: de Gruyter and Company.

Frake, Charles O. 1961. "Sickness in Subanun Society," *American Anthropologists*. (In press).

French, Katherine Story. 1955. *Culture Segments and Variation in Contemporary Social Ceremonialism on the Warm Springs Reservation, Oregon*. Columbia University dissertation.

Friedson, Eliot. 1956. "The Varieties of Individual Speech," *Quarterly Journal of Speech*, 42:355–62.

Fries, Charles C. 1945. "On Learning a Foreign Language as an Adult." In *Teaching and Learning English as a Foreign Language*. Ch. I. ("University of Michigan Publications, English Language Institute," No. 1.) Ann Arbor.

Garvin, Paul L. 1949. "Standard Average European and Czech." *Studia Linguistica*. Lund and Copenhagen. Vol. 3, No. II, pp. 65–85.

Gleason, Henry A., Jr. 1955. *An Introduction to Descriptive Linguistics*. New York: Henry Holt & Co.

Goldman-Eisler, F. 1958. "Speech Analysis and Mental Processes," *Language and Speech*, 1:59–75.

Goodenough, Ward H. 1951. *Property, Kin, and Community on Truk*. ("Yale University Publications in Anthropology," No. 46.) New Haven.

――――. 1956. "Componential Analysis and the Study of Meaning," *Language*, 32:195–216.

――――. 1957. "Cultural Anthropology and Linguistics." In Garvin, Paul L. (ed.), *Report of the Seventh Annual Round Table Meeting on Linguistics and Language Study*. Washington, D.C.: Georgetown University, Monograph Series on Languages and Linguistics, No. 9. Pp. 167–73.

Gottschalk, Louis; Kluckhohn, Clyde; and Angell, Robert. 1945. *The Use of Personal Documents in History, Anthropology, and Sociology*. ("Social Science Research Council Bulletin," 53.) New York.

Greenberg, J. 1959. "Current Trends in Linguistics," *Science*, October 30; 130:1115 ff.

Haas, Mary H. 1944. "Men's and Women's Speech in Koasati," *Language*, 29:142–49.

Hall, Edward T. 1959. *The Silent Language*. New York: Doubleday.

Hallowell, A. Irving. 1937. "Introduction: Handbook of Psychological Leads for Ethnological Field Workers." Washington, D.C.: National Research Council, Division of Anthropology and Psychology, Committee on Personality in Relation to Culture.

———. 1951. "Cultural Factors in the Structuralization of Perception." In Rohrer, J. H., and Sherif, M. (eds.), *Social Psychology at the Crossroads*, New York: Harper & Bros. Pp. 164–95.

———. 1953. "Culture, Personality, and Society." In Kroeber, A. L. (ed.), *Anthropology Today*. Chicago: University of Chicago Press. Pp. 597–620.

———. 1958. "Ojibwa Metaphysics of Being and the Perception of Persons." In Tagiuri, R. and Petrullo, L. (eds.), *Person Perception and Interpersonal Behavior*. Stanford: Stanford University Press. Pp. 63–85.

Hanawelt, N. G. and Demarest, I. H. 1939. "The Effect of Verbal Suggestion in the Recall Period Upon the Reproduction of Visually Perceived Forms," *Journal of Experimental Psychology*, 25:159–74.

Hanks, L. M., Jr. 1954. "A Psychological Exploration in the Blackfoot Language," *International Journal of American Linguistics*, 20:195–205.

Harris, Zellig S. 1951. *Methods in Structural Linguistics*. Chicago: University of Chicago Press.

Hastorf, Albert H.; Richardson, Stephen A.; and Dornbusch, Sanford M. 1958. "The Problem of Relevance in the Study of Person Perception." In Tagiuri, R. and Petrullo, L. (eds.), *Person Perception and Interpersonal Behavior*. Stanford: Stanford University Press. Pp. 54–62.

Haugen, Einar. 1957. "The Semantics of Icelandic Orientation," *Word*, 13:447–60.

Henry, Jules. 1936. "The Linguistic Expression of Emotion," *American Anthropologist*, 38:250–56.

Henry, Jules and Zenia. 1950. "Speech Disturbances in Pilaga Children," *American Journal of Orthopsychiatry*, 10:362–9.

Hermann, D. T.; Lawless, R. H.; and Marshall, R. W. 1957. "Variables in the Effect of Language on the Reproduction of Visually Perceived Forms," *Perceptual and Motor Skills*, 7:171–286.

Hertzler, J. O. 1953. "Toward a Sociology of Language," *Social Forces*, 32:109–19.

Herzog, George. 1949. "Linguistic Approaches to Personality." In Sargent, S. Stansfeld and Smith, Marian W. (eds.), *Culture and Personality*. New York: Wenner-Gren Foundation for Anthropological Research. Pp. 93–102.

Hoch, P. and Zubin, J. (eds.). 1958. *Psychopathology of Communication*. New York: Grune and Stratton.

Hockett, Charles F. 1955. *A Manual of Phonology*. ("Indiana University Publications in Anthropology and Linguistics," Memoir 11 of the *International Journal of American Linguistics*).

————. 1958. *A Course in Modern Linguistics*. New York: Macmillan.

————. "Ethnolinguistic Implications of Recent Studies in Linguistics and Psychiatry." To appear in the *Georgetown University Monograph Series on Languages and Linguistics.*

Hoijer, Harry. 1951. "Cultural Implications of Some Navaho Linguistic Categories," *Language,* 27:111–20.

————. 1953. "The Relation of Language to Culture." In Kroeber, A. L. (ed.), *Anthropology Today*. Chicago: University of Chicago Press. Pp. 554–73.

————, (ed.). 1954. *Language in Culture*. (Redfield, Robert and Singer, Milton, (eds.), "Comparative Studies of Cultures and Civilizations," No. 3; "Memoirs of the American Anthropological Association," No. 79.)

Householder, Fred W., Jr. 1957a. "Rough Justice in Linguistics." In Garvin, Paul L. (ed.), *Report on the Seventh Annual Round Table Meeting on Linguistics and Language Study*. Washington: Georgetown University Press. Pp. 153–60.

————. 1957b. "Accent, Juncture, Intonation and My Grandfather's Reader," *Word,* 13:234–45.

Hymes, D. H. 1955. "Review of Forchheimer, Paul, *The Category of Person in Language,*" *International Journal of American Linguistics,* 21:294–300.

————. 1960. "Discussion of the Symposium on Translation Between Language and Culture," *Anthropological Linguistics,* 2:81–85.

Jakobson, Roman. 1941. *Kindersprache, Aphasie und Allgemeine Lautgesetze.* ("Sprakvetenskaplija Sallskapets i Uppsala Forhandlinger," 1940–1942). Uppsala.

————. 1953. "Chapter Two." In Levi-Strauss, Claude, *et al.* (eds.), *Results of the Conference of Anthropologists and Linguists*. Baltimore: Waverly Press, Inc. Pp. 11–21.

————. 1957. *Shifters, Verbal Categories, and the Russian Verb*. Harvard University: Russian Language Project.

————. 1960. "Results of the Conference from the Viewpoint of Linguistics." In Sebeok, Thomas A. (ed.), *Aspects of Style in Language*. New York: John Wiley.

Jakobson, Roman and Halle, Morris. 1957. *Fundamentals of Language.* s'Gravenhague: Mouton & Co.

Jeffrey, W. E. 1953. "The Effects of Verbal and Non-Verbal Responses in Mediating an Instrumental Act," *Journal of Experimental Psychology,* 45:327–33.

Joos, Martin. 1958. "Semology: A Linguistic Theory of Meaning," *Studies in Linguistics,* 13:53–70.

Kahane, Henry; Kahane, Rene; and Saporta, Sol. 1958. *Development of Verbal Categories in Child Language*. ("Publication Nine of the Indiana University Research Center in Anthropology, Folklore, and Linguistics," *International Journal of American Linguistics,* Vol. 24, No. 4, Part II.)

Kaplan, Bernard. 1957. "On the Phenomena of 'Opposite Speech,' " *Journal of Abnormal and Social Psychology,* 55:389–93.

Kelly, George. 1956. *The Psychology of Personal Constructs.* New York: W. W. Norton.

Klausner, Samuel Z. 1955. "Phonetics, Personality, and Status in Israel," *Word,* 11:209–15.

Kluckhohn, Clyde. 1945. "The Personal Document in Anthropological Science." In Gottschalk, L.; Kluckhohn, C.; and Angell, R., *The Use of Personal Documents in History, Anthropology and Sociology.* New York: Social Science Research Council Bull. 53. Pp. 79–173.

———. 1954. "Culture and Behavior." In Lindzey, Gardner (ed.), *Handbook of Social Psychology,* Vol. II. Cambridge: Addison-Wesley Publishing Company, Inc. Pp. 921–76.

Krech, David and Crutchfield, Richard S. 1948. *Theory and Problems of Social Psychology.* New York: McGraw-Hill.

La Barre, Weston. 1947. "The Cultural Basis of Emotions and Gestures," *Journal of Personality,* 16:49–68.

Lado, Robert. 1957. *Linguistics Across Cultures.* Ann Arbor: University of Michigan Press.

Leach, E. M. 1958. "Concerning Trobriand Clans and the Kinship Category 'Tabu.' " In Goody, Jack (ed.), *The Developmental Cycle in Domestic Groups* ("Cambridge Papers in Social Anthropology," No. 1). Pp. 120–45.

Lee, Dorothy D. 1938. "Conceptual Implications of an Indian Language," *Philosophy of Science,* 5:89–102.

———. 1940. "A Primitive System of Values," *Philosophy of Science,* 7: 355–79.

———. 1944. "Linguistic Reflection of Wintu Thought," *International Journal of American Linguistics,* 10:181–87.

———. 1949. "Being and Value in a Primitive Culture," *The Journal of Philosophy,* 46:401–15.

———. 1950a. "Notes on the Conception of the Self Among the Wintu Indians," *Journal of Abnormal and Social Psychology,* 45:538–43.

———. 1950b. "Lineal and Non-Lineal Codifications of Reality," *Psychosomatic Medicine,* 12:89–97.

Lenneberg, Eric H. 1953. "Cognition and Ethnolinguistics," *Language,* 29: 463–71.

Lenneberg, Eric H. and Roberts, John M. 1956. *The Language of Experience: A Study in Methodology.* ("Indiana University Publications in Anthropology and Linguistics," Memoir 13 of the *International Journal of American Linguistics.*)

Leopold, Werner. 1939–1949. *Speech Development of a Bilingual Child.* · 4 vols. Evanston: Northwestern University Studies.

———. 1953–54. "Patterning in Children's Language Learning," *Language Learning,* 5:1–14.

Levi-Strauss, Claude. 1957. *Anthropologie structurale*. Paris: Plon.

Levi-Strauss, Claude; Jakobson, Roman; Voegelin, C. F.; and Sebeok, Thomas A. 1953. *Results of the Conference of Anthropologists and Linguists*. ("Indiana University Publications in Anthropology and Linguistics," Memoir 8 of the *International Journal of American Linguistics*.) Baltimore: Waverly Press, Inc.

Lounsbury, Floyd. 1953. "Field Methods and Techniques in Linguistics." In Kroeber, A. L. (ed.), *Anthropology Today*. Chicago: University of Chicago Press. Pp. 401–16.

————. 1956. "Semantic Analysis of the Pawnee Kinship Usage," *Language*, 32:158–94.

Luria, A. R. 1959a. "The Directive Function of Speech, I," *Word*, 15:341–52.

————. 1959b. "The Directive Function of Speech, II," *Word*, 15:453–64.

Luria, A. R. and Yuovich, F. Ia. 1959. *Speech and the Development of Mental Processes in the Child*. Translated by J. Simon. London: Staples Press.

Maccoby, Eleanor; Newcomb, Theodore M.; and Hartley, Eugene L. 1958. *Readings in Social Psychology*, 3rd ed. New York: Henry Holt.

MacClay, Howard, 1958. "An Experimental Study of Language and Non-Linguistic Behavior," *Southwestern Journal of Anthropology*, 14:220–29.

MacClay, H. and Osgood, C. E. 1959. "Hesitation Phenomena in Spontaneous English Speech," *Word*, 15:19–44.

Malinowski, Bronislaw. 1923. "Meaning in Primitive Languages." Appendix A in Ogden, C. K. and Richards, I. A., *The Meaning of Meaning*. London: Kegan Paul.

Mandelbaum, David (ed.). 1949. *Selected Writings of Edward Sapir*. Berkeley and Los Angeles: University of California Press.

Marsh, Gordon H. and Laughlin, William S. 1956. "Human Anatomical Knowledge Among the Aleutian Islanders," *Southwestern Journal of Anthropology*, 12:38–78.

Martin, Samuel E. 1958. "Speech Levels and Social Structure in Japan and Korea." Paper given at Association for Asian Studies Meeting, New York.

May, L. Carlyle. 1956. "A Survey of Glossolalia and Related Phenomena in Non-Christian Religions," *American Anthropologist*, 58:75–96.

Mayers, Marvin. 1959. "Religious Activity Among the Pocomchi of Guatemala." Paper read at the annual meeting, American Anthropological Association, Mexico City.

McCarthy, Dorothea. 1943. "Language Development in the Preschool Child." In Barker, Roger G.; Kounin, Jacob S.; and Wright, Herbert F. (eds.). *Child Behavior and Development*. New York: McGraw-Hill. Pp. 107–28.

McClelland, David C. 1951. *Personality*. New York: The Dryden Press.

McDavid, Raven I., Jr. 1952–53. "Some Social Differences in Pronunciation," *Language Learning*, 4:102–16.

McGehee, F. 1944. "An Experimental Study of Voice Recognition," *Journal of General Psychology*, 31:53–65.

McQuown, Norman A. 1957. "Linguistic Transcription and Specification of Psychiatric Interview Material," *Psychiatry*, 20:79–86.

Mead, Margaret and Metraux, Rhoda (eds.). 1953. *The Study of Culture at a Distance*. Chicago: The University of Chicago Press.

Miller, George A. 1951. *Language and Communication*. New York: Mc-Graw-Hill.

―――. 1954. "Psycholinguistics." In Lindzey, Gardner (ed.), *Handbook of Social Psychology*, Vol. II, Cambridge: Addison-Wesley Publishing Company, Inc. Ch. 19, pp. 693–708.

―――. 1956. "The Magical Number Seven, Plus or Minus Two: Some Limits on Our Capacity for Processing Information," *The Psychological Review*, 63:81–97.

Miller, G. A.; Galanter, E.; and Pribram, K. 1960. *Plans and the Structure of Behavior*. New York: Henry Holt.

Morris, Charles W. 1939. *Foundations of the Theory of Signs*. ("International Encyclopedia of Unified Science," Vol. 1, No. 2,) Chicago.

Nadel, S. F. 1951. *The Foundations of Social Anthropology*. Glencoe, Illinois: The Free Press.

―――. 1954. "Morality and Language Among the Nupe," *Man*, 54:55–57.

Newman, Stanley S. 1939. "Personal Symbolism in Language Patterns," *Psychiatry*, 2:177–82.

―――. 1940. "Linguistic Aspects of Yokuts Style." In Gayton, Ann and Newman, Stanley S., *Yokuts and Western Mono Myths*. ("University of California Publications, Anthropological Records." 5,) Berkeley. Pp. 4–8.

―――. 1941. "Behavior Patterns in Linguistic Structure: A Case Study." In Spier, Leslie; Hallowell, A. Irving; and Newman, Stanley S. (eds.), *Language, Culture, and Personality: Essays in Memory of Edward Sapir*. Menasha. Pp. 94–106.

―――. 1944. "Cultural and Psychological Features in English Intonation," *Transactions of the New York Academy of Science*, 7:45–54.

―――. 1954. "Semantic Problems in Grammatical Systems and Lexemes: A Search for Method." In Hoijer, Harry (ed.), *Language in Culture*. Chicago: University of Chicago Press. Pp. 82–91.

―――. 1955. "Vocabulary Levels: Zuni Sacred and Slang Usage," *Southwestern Journal of Anthropology*, 11:345–54.

Newman, Stanley S. and Mather, Vera G. 1938. "Analysis of Spoken Language of Patients with Affective Disorders," *American Journal of Psychiatry*, 94:913–42.

Nida, Eugene A. 1947. "Field Methods in Descriptive Linguistics," *International Journal of American Linguistics*, 13:138–46.

―――. 1949. *Morphology: The Descriptive Analysis of Words*, 2nd ed. Ann Arbor: University of Michigan Publications in Linguistics II.

————. 1950. *Learning a Foreign Language: A Handbook for Missionaries.* New York: Committee on Missionary Personnel of the Foreign Missions Conference of North America.

————. 1956. "Selective Listening," *Language Learning,* 6:17–23.

————. 1958. "Analysis of Meaning and Dictionary Making," *International Journal of American Linguistics,* 24:269–72.

Norbeck, Edward and Norbeck, Margaret. 1956. "Child Training in a Japanese Fishing Community." In Haring, Douglas G. (ed.), *Personal Character and Cultural Milieu,* 3rd ed. Syracuse: Syracuse University Press. Pp. 651–73.

Norcross, K. J. 1958. "Effects on Discrimination Performance of Similarity of Previously Acquired Stimulus Names," *Journal of Experimental Psychology,* 56:305–09.

Oliver, D. L. 1949. *Human Relations and Language in a Papuan-Speaking Tribe of Southern Bougainville, Solomon Islands.* ("Peabody Museum Papers," vol. 29.) Cambridge.

Olson, Ronald L. 1956. "Channeling of Character in Tlingit Society." In Haring, Douglas G. (ed.), *Personal Character and Cultural Milieu,* 3rd ed. Syracuse: Syracuse University Press. Pp. 675–87.

Osgood, Charles E. 1953. *Method and Theory in Experimental Psychology.* New York: Oxford University Press.

————. (ed.). 1954. *Psycholinguistics, A Survey of Theory and Research Problems.* ("Indiana University Publications in Anthropology and Linguistics," Memoir 10 of the *International Journal of American Linguistics.*) Baltimore: Waverly Press.

————. 1959. "Semantic Space Revisited," *Word,* 15:192–99.

Osgood, Charles E.; Suci, George J.; and Tannenbaum, Percy H. 1957. *The Measurement of Meaning.* Urbana: University of Illinois Press.

Pavlov, I. 1957. *Experimental Psychology and Other Essays.* New York: Philosophical Library. (Same as *Selected Works.* Moscow: Foreign Languages Publishing House, 1955).

Pear, T. H. 1931. *Voice and Personality.* London: Chapman and Hall.

Phillips, Herbert B. 1959–1960. "Problems of Translation and Meaning in Fieldwork," *Human Organization,* 18:184–92.

Pike, Kenneth L. 1947. *Phonemics.* Ann Arbor: University of Michigan Publications in Linguistics, III.

————. 1954, 1955, 1959. *Language in Relation to a Unified Theory of the Structure of Human Behavior.* Parts I, II, III, preliminary edition. Glendale: Summer Institute of Linguistics.

————. 1956. "Towards a Theory of the Structure of Human Behavior." In *Estudios Antropológicos publicados en homenaje al doctor Manuel Gamio,* Mexico, D. F. Pp. 659–71.

Pittenger, R. E. 1958. "Linguistic Analysis of Tone of Voice in Communication of Affect," *Psychiatric Research Reports,* 8:41–54.

Pittenger, R. E. and Smith, Henry Lee, Jr. 1957. "A Basis for Some Contributions of Linguistics to Psychiatry," *Psychiatry,* 20:61–78.

Prentice, W. C. H. 1954. "Visual Recognition of Verbally Labeled Figures," *American Journal of Psychology,* 67:315–20.

Pulgram, Ernst. 1954. "Language and National Character," *Quarterly Journal of Speech,* 40:393–400.

Pyles, M. E. 1932. "Verbalization as a Factor in Learning," *Child Development,* pp. 108–13.

Reichard, Gladys. 1949. "The Character of the Navaho Verb Stem," *Word,* 5:55–76.

Reyburn, William O. 1958. "Don't Learn That Language," *Practical Anthropology,* 5:151–78.

Riess, Bernard F. 1946. "Genetic Changes in Semantic Conditioning," *Journal of Experimental Psychology,* 36:143–52.

Sanford, Fillmore H. 1942a. "Speech and Personality," *Psychological Bulletin,* 39:811–45.

———. 1942b. "Speech and Personality: a Comparative Case Study," *Character and Personality,* 10:169–98.

Sapir, Edward. 1915. *Abnormal Types of Speech in Nootka.* (Canada, Geological Survey, Memoir 62, Anthropological Series No. 5.) Ottawa: Government Printing Bureau.

———. 1927. "Speech as a Personality Trait," *American Journal of Sociology,* 32:892–905.

———. 1929. "The Status of Linguistics as a Science," *Language,* 5:207–14.

———. 1931a. "Communication," *Encyclopedia of the Social Sciences,* 4:78–81. New York: Macmillan.

———. 1931b. "Conceptual Categories in Primitive Languages," *Science,* 74:578.

Schachtel, E. G. 1947. "On Memory and Childhood Amnesia," *Psychiatry,* 10:1–26.

Sebeok, Thomas A. (ed.). 1960. *Aspects of Style in Language.* New York: John Wiley.

Shepard, W. O. 1956. "The Effect of Verbal Training on Initial Generalization Tendencies," *Child Development,* 25:311–16.

Sinclair, Angus. 1951. *The Conditions of Knowing.* London: Kegan, Routledge, Paul.

Smith, M. G. 1957. "The Social Functions and Meaning of Hausa Praise-Singing," *Africa,* 27:26–44.

Spence, K. W. 1957. "The Empirical Basis and Theoretic Structure of Psychology," *Philosophy of Science,* 24:97–108.

Spiker, C. C. 1956. "Experiments with Children on the Hypotheses of Acquired Distinctiveness and Equivalence of Cues," *Child Development,* 27:253–63.

Stankiewicz, Edward. "Expressive Language." Unpublished.

Stefflre, Volney. 1958. *An Investigation of the Role of Language in E. Heidbreder's Experiments on Concept-Formation.* Reed College dissertation.

Stern, Theodore. 1957. "Drum and Whistle 'Languages': An Analysis of Speech Surrogates," *American Anthropologist,* 59:487–506.

Stone, Leo. 1954. "On the Principal Obscene Word of the English Language," *International Journal of Psycho-Analysis,* 35:30–56.

Swadesh, Morris. 1937. "A Method for Phonetic Accuracy and Speed," *American Anthropologist,* 39:728–32.

———. 1948. "Sociologic Notes on Obsolescent Languages," *International Journal of American Linguistics,* 14:226–35.

Tagiuri, Renato and Petrullo, Luigi (eds.). 1958. *Person Perception and Interpersonal Behavior.* Stanford: Stanford University Press.

Taylor, H. C. 1934. "Social Agreement in Personality Traits as Judged from Speech," *Journal of Social Psychology,* 5:244–48.

Thorner, I. 1945. "German Words, German Personality, and Protestantism," *Psychiatry,* 8:403–17.

Tikhomivov, O. K. 1959. "Review of B. F. Skinner, Verbal Behavior," *Word,* 15:362–66.

Trager, G. L. 1958. "Paralinguistics: A First Approximation," *Studies in Linguistics,* 13:1–12.

———. 1959. "The Systematization of the Whorf Hypothesis," *Anthropological Linguistics,* 1:31–35.

———. 1960. "Taos III: Paralanguage," *Anthropological Linguistics,* 2:24–30.

Trager, G. L. and Smith, Henry Lee, Jr. 1951. *An Outline of English Structure.* (Studies in Linguistics, Occasional Papers 3.) Norman, Oklahoma: Battenburg Press.

Tresselet, N. E. 1948. "The Influence of Suggestion on the Recognition of Visually Perceived Forms," *Journal of General Psychology,* 39:259–71.

Twaddell, W. Freeman. 1935. *On Defining the Phoneme.* (Language Monographs, No. 16). Baltimore: Linguistic Society of America.

Uldall, Hans. 1957. *Outline of Glossematics,* Part I. (Travaux du Cercle Linguistique de Copenhague, Vol. X₁). Copenhagen: Nordisk Sprogog Kulturførlag.

Ullmann, Stephen. 1952. *Précis de semantique française.* (Bibliotheca romanica, Series prima: Manualia et commentationes, No. 9.) Berne: Editions A. Francke S. A.

———. 1953. "Descriptive Semantics and Linguistic Typology," *Word,* 9: 225–40.

Velten, H. V. 1943. "The Growth of Phonemic and Lexical Patterns in Infant Language," *Language,* 19:281–92.

Voegelin, C. F. and Robinett, Florence M. 1954. " 'Mother Language' in Hidatsa," *International Journal of American Linguistics*, 20:65–70.

Wallace, Anthony F. C. and Atkins, John. 1960. "The Meaning of Kinship Terms," *American Anthropologist*, 62:58–80.

Waterhouse, Viola. 1949. "Learning a Second Language First," *International Journal of American Linguistics*, 15:106–09.

Weinreich, Uriel. 1953. *Languages in Contact.* (Publications of the Linguistic Circle of New York, 2.) New York.

———. 1955. "Review of Ullmann, *Précis de semantique française*," *Language*, 31:537–43.

———. 1957. "On the Description of Phonic Interference," *Word*, 13:1–11.

———. 1958. "Travels Through Semantic Space," *Word*, 14:346–66.

———. 1959. "A Rejoinder," *Word*, 15:200–01.

Weir, M. W. and Stevenson, H. W. 1959. "The Effect of Verbalization in Children's Learning As a Function of Chronological Age," *Child Development*, 30:143–49.

Wells, Rulon. 1957. "A Mathematical Approach to Meaning," *Cahiers Ferdinand de Saussure*, 15:117–37.

Werner, Heinz and Kaplan, Bernard. 1956. "The Developmental Approach to Cognition," *American Anthropologist*, 58:866–80.

Whorf, Benjamin Lee. 1936. "A Linguistic Consideration of Thinking in Primitive Communities." In Carroll, John B. (ed.), *Language, Thought, and Reality: Selected Writings of Benjamin Lee Whorf.* New York: John Wiley & Sons, Inc. and the Technology Press, 1956. Pp. 65–86.

———. 1940a. "Gestalt Techniques of Stem Composition in Shawnee." *Prehistory Research Series*, I, No. 9. Indianapolis: Indiana Historical Society. Pp. 393–406.

———. 1940b. "Science and Linguistics," *Technology Review* (M. I. T.), 42:229–31, 247–48.

———. 1941a. "Linguistics as an Exact Science," *Technology Review* (M. I. T.), 43:61–63, 80–83.

———. 1941b. "Languages and Logic," *Technology Review* (M. I. T.), 43:250–252, 266–268, 272.

———. 1941c. "The Relation of Habitual Thought and Behavior to Language." In Spier, Leslie; Hallowell, A. Irving; and Newman, S. (eds.), *Language, Culture, and Personality: Essays in Memory of Edward Sapir.* Menasha. Pp. 75–93.

Wishner, Julian. 1960. "Reanalysis of 'Impressions of Personality,' " *Psychological Review*, 67:96–112.

Wolff, Hans. 1952. "Phonemic Structure and the Teaching of Pronunciation," *Language Learning*, 4:92–101.

Wolff, W. 1943. *The Expression of Personality.* New York: Harper & Brothers.

Wonderly, William L. 1952. "Semantic Components in Kechua Person Morphemes," *Language,* 28:366–76.

Woods, Sister Frances Jerome. 1956. *Cultural Values of American Ethnic Groups.* New York: Harper & Brothers.

Zucker, L. 1946. "Psychological Aspects of Speech Melody," *Journal of Social Psychology,* 5:37–55.

About the Chapter

Art, folklore and literature are aspects of culture that tell us much about modal personality processes. On the one hand, they are institutions of socialization, having the function of communicating key values and attitudes, and on the other, they reflect key personality processes in a kind of culturally sanctioned fantasy. In addition, they often seem interpretable in the same terms that projective techniques are, although one must decide to what or to whom the interpretations refer.

The present chapter is divided into two parts. The first part presents an interpretation of the social and personal significance of artistic productions and suggests how the analysis of art can contribute to an understanding of personality processes. The second part is an account of the literature of psychological interpretation of art and folklore. In this literature, which is one of the most fascinating parts of the culture and personality field, we find a meeting place in which anthropology, psychology, psychoanalysis, art and literary criticism are all concerned with the same phenomena.

About the Authors

GEORGE DEVEREUX's bibliographical note appears at the beginning of Chapter 6.

WESTON LA BARRE, educated at Princeton and Yale, is Professor of Anthropology at Duke University, and has also taught at Rutgers, New York University, Wisconsin, Northwestern, North Carolina, and Minnesota. He has been Sterling Fellow of Yale, an SSRC post-doctoral fellow, and Guggenheim Fellow; in 1958 he received the Róheim Award. In area an Americanist, in interests he is a student of culture-and-personality, psychoanalytically-oriented anthropology, native narcotics, and primitive religion and art. He is the author of books on Peyote, the Aymara, and *The Human Animal*.

11

Art and Mythology

PART I: A GENERAL THEORY

GEORGE DEVEREUX, *Temple University School of Medicine*

PART II: THE PRESENT STATE OF THE PROBLEM

WESTON LA BARRE, *Duke University*

I. A GENERAL THEORY *

The study of the relevance of art for the investigation of problems of culture and personality is severely handicapped by the inadequacy of basic studies which seek to clarify:

(1) The nature of art,
(2) The socio-cultural function of art,
(3) The psychological function of art.

The entire field is so poorly understood that Freud himself "threw in the towel" in a study devoted to Leonardo da Vinci, and declared that the explanation of the nature of genius is, for the time being, beyond the powers of psychoanalysis (Freud 1910, 1930). With a few exceptions, the relevant studies on art compare unfavorably with the conceptual tautness and methodological rigorousness of psychoanalytic and/or culture and personality investigations of science, such as Sachs' (1942) essay on the delay of the machine age. Last but not least, both cultural and psychological studies of the most essential of all arts—music—are, on the whole, more disappointing and also much less numerous than are similar studies devoted to the other arts.

* This portion of the chapter by George Devereux is the second (1959) Géza Róheim Memorial Award Lecture.

361

Art versus Expressive Behavior

The first distinction to be made in clarifying the nature of art pertains to the difference between art and expressive behavior, including quasi-artistic projective tests. If mere "expressiveness" and/or "projecting" were the criteria whereby one determines whether a given product is art or something else, then the bellowing of an agitated catatonic—the almost uninhibited expression of a hypothalamic storm—would be the most genuine of all arts. Conversely, were style and other conventions the true criteria of art, then classroom exercises in strict counterpoint would represent the summit of artistic behavior.

Definition of Art

Ideally, the dynamic criterion of art is the straining of pure affect against pure (culturally structured) discipline, and the incidental evolving of new rules which permit the less and less roundabout manifestation of more and more affect and also of hitherto artistically unusable affect segments within an expanded, but internally even more coherent, discipline. The discipline itself—the rules of the game—is the means whereby society determines whether a given expressive act represents art or something else, and also whether the product in question is good, mediocre or bad art. The relevance of the first of these functions of the "discipline" is best highlighted by the fact that folk and primitive arts have only recently been recognized as genuine art, though artistic objects of that type have existed long before they were recognized as art.

The arbitrariness of the rules whereby an item is adjudged to be good art is revealed by the fact that Beethoven's *Violin Concerto* was derisively called a "concerto for tympani" because—most "improperly" —the first *solo* instrument heard is the tympanum. Hanslick ironically called Liszt's *First Piano Concerto* a "Triangle Concerto," because Liszt conspicuously used that instrument as part of the percussion section. Even the kind and the amount of affect demanded or allowable is culturally regulated. An early critic called Beethoven's *Violin Concerto* "vulgar." The intellectually brilliant and musically impeccable "romantic" music criticism of Schumann and of Berlioz used, side by side with purely musical considerations, also the quality and intensity of affect as a yardstick of musical excellence. Today's music criticism is as conscious of affect as Schumann's was, but appraises affect negatively. It considers an emotional deep freeze—and a "well aereted" score—the acme of excellence, and demands a spuriously baroque music for spuriously baroque organization men. This, by the way, may explain why those who also seek affect in music sometimes take refuge in the hypothalamic orgies of modern jazz, so as to sate the affect hunger left unstilled by listening to tinny filaments of sound emitted by poorly balanced chamber orchestras.

It is implicit in the preceding considerations that art is basically a medium of communication, and conforms to certain rules which represent the grammar and syntax of a kind of meta-language. This finding raises further questions as to the legitimacy of treating "Draw a man" or "TAT" tests as art forms. It is my view that, insofar as such tests represent art, they are communications directed at an audience of one—the tester. Moreover, the testee's communication is couched in a "language" whose grammar and vocabulary the tester must decipher, the way Champollion deciphered the Rosetta stone. Indeed, in test productions a kind of Alice in Wonderland system holds sway: Things mean only what the test subject unconsciously intends them to mean. This point is important enough to warrant a brief discussion of "tests and art."

A number of tests exist in which the subject is called upon to create "art" or else to respond to "art"; the first type being represented by Draw-a-Man and related tests, the second by the TAT and perhaps also the Rorschach tests. It is my thesis that these tests do not really meet the basic criteria which differentiate art from other activities.

(1) The subject's behavior is primarily expressive rather than an act of communication. Insofar as he communicates at all, he has an audience of one: the tester. Moreover, the validity—qua test—of the subject's productions decreases as his orientation to the tester increases and as his productions become communication rather than expression.

(2) In optimum cases—in the testing sense—the production is pure expressive behavior, which is then transformed by the tester into a communication—or, more specifically, into information. The tester is, thus, *not* functioning like a person addressed in normal communication. In the case of the latter, the communicator makes an effort to couch his communication in terms understandable to his interlocutor. He uses a language known to the latter, an audible intensity of voice production, etc. What "noise" there is, is largely filtered out and is meant to be filtered out. Moreover, both the speaker and the listener usually agree on what is information and what is noise. The opposite is true in testing: What, to the subject, is information which he communicates, may be largely "noise" to the tester, and what may seem "noise" to the testee may represent information for the tester. Moreover, the "grammar" of that portion of the testee's communication which is of interest to the tester must be reconstructed by the tester himself. It is not a "given," except empirically, in the sense in which certain Rorschach responses have been empirically found to "mean" the presence of a certain trait.

Practically none of the considerations discussed in this section are applicable to genuine art, whose language is, by definition conventional.

Whether this convention demands that the human figure remain more or less undistorted, or that it be distorted according to certain rules; whether it demands—as early non-unison music theory did—nothing but parallel fifths, or whether it taboos parallel fifths—all this is irrelevant. What is relevant, is that there is a kind of convention, and that this convention must be viewed in a historical perspective, as an elaboration of, or as a reaction against, the rules of an earlier period. The taboo on parallel fifths outlaws the basic rules of an earlier practice and at least some of the objectives of modern "neo-classical" music are those of the romantics turned upside down (Barzun 1950).

The culturally standardized "discipline" of art is therefore of prime concern to the student of culture and personality. The rules of artistic communication, of which this discipline is made up, must be understood as cultural conventions. The anthropologist must study the grammar, the syntax and even the chosen vocabulary of art. He must trace changes in the ratio between consonances and dissonances, between "noble" and "four letter" words, etc. Moreover, he must realize that the intrusion of four letter words into the artist's vocabulary did not expand the verbal palette of literature. The genuine expressive gain represented by these crude terms was balanced by an impoverishment of the palette in such words as "noble," "elevated," "sublime," and the like, dear to romantics. The student of culture may neither approve nor lament this change. Rather must he stress that the evolution of every style represents a patterned enrichment in one direction and impoverishment in another direction, both as regards the building blocks at the artist's disposal, and the range of affects deemed artistically acceptable by society. This impoverishment, balanced by enrichment, is never random and is—as Kroeber (1957) apparently did not fully realize—the very essence of style. Indeed, "let us have a roll in the hay" and "we shall walk hand in hand under the starry sky" mean the same thing behavioristically . . . and, now and then, even emotionally, alas. What concerns the student of culture is simply this: Which of these two utterances is accepted as artistic (and authentic) by a given society, at a given point in history?

At this juncture we must realize that, insofar as a style represents both an enrichment and an impoverishment, insofar as style is a method of selection, it inevitably implies a *distortion*. In relatively unsophisticated art, the distortion affects primarily the substantive content of the statement or utterance: the sculptor may shorten the legs of the human figure; the novelist may populate his human scene with ideally pure women and double dyed villains; the composer of a canon may discard an inspired passage which comes to his mind, because it would disrupt the orderly development of a strict canon; the writer of a sonnet may remold an image in order to submit to the rhyme pattern and may short circuit his chain of thought in order not to exceed 14 lines. In some cases the artist's physical material (medium) itself imposes distortions upon the utterance: the fragility of marble and its inability to stand much stress calls for a far more compact structure than does bronze. Hence, in some marble statuary certain elements are included solely in order to support the weight of a jutting body or limb. A truly great artist—like the sculptor of Laocoön—makes these structural additions seem indispensable and integral parts of his utterance, so that it is felt to be "communication" rather than "noise." The lesser artist asks us to *ignore* the presence of an inexplicable truncated pillar under the belly of a rearing horse.

In a Beethoven piano sonata the high treble imitation of a motif, first played at a middle level, is changed because, in Beethoven's times, the piano keyboard did not extend as far up as it does at present. Hence, many modern pianists play that passage not the way Beethoven actually wrote it, but the way he *would have* written it, had he had a modern, extended keyboard piano at his disposal. In some instances certain earlier material or performer limitations of the artistic utterance are consciously exploited by the modern artist to produce striking effects. The Hungarian peasant singer, whose untrained voice has a smaller range than has that of a concert singer and who, moreover, does not know enough about music to transpose a song so that its range will not exceed the range of his voice, sometimes replaces a step of a second downward, which is too low for him, with a leap of a seventh upward. This "clumsiness" of peasant singers was transmuted into an artistic device by Bartók. Examples of such octave displacements in Bartók's violin sonatas are given by Stevens (1953), who cogently remarks: "This device is not resorted to indiscriminately; in the First Sonata it gives the distinctive shape to the waltz-like second member of the principal thematic complex, and is thereafter used, with very few exceptions, only for reference to that member." An image inspired by the rhyme pattern is a comparable phenomenon, revealing the creative side of technique.

In over-sophisticated art the medium itself is subjected to distortion. Such manipulations range from maximal but spurious nondistortion, as in "trompe l'oeil" paintings, to Liszt's passion for experimenting with out-of-tune pianos,[1] to Joyce's schizophrenoid experiments with language and to those of some modern poets with punctuation. The latter maneuver reaches a pathetic climax of absurdity in a semi-pornographic French novel, in which a sexual act between a woman and an ape is "described"—for nearly a whole page—exclusively by means of punctuation marks, somewhat as follows: ".!..!!...?!!!??!, etc."

We shall return later on to the problem of balance between substantive utterance and style-and-technique. For the moment it suffices to stress that the artist himself is as keenly aware of the social-cultural rules governing *artistic* distortion as the writer of parodies and pastiches . . . and sometimes experiences the boundaries set by society as confining. It is said that the leading Victorian purveyor of ethereal guff, Lord Tennyson, wrote obscene poetry for private consumption. To the indignation of his contemporaries, Heine often concluded a lofty poem on a jarring note of derision—conspicuously in the exquisite poem: "Jesus walks on the waters." Prokofieff "steps on the throat" of his own melodies, which usually start in a lyrical vein and end in a sneer. Beethoven composed an impressively and unmistakeably Beethovenesque—and also musically inferior—rondo "in anger over a mislaid penny." An aging or ailing artist, whose best work had a distinctively personal style, often ends up by simply imitating himself, long after he has run out of inner tensions leading to authentic utterances. Thus did the dying Chopin "chopinize" in some parts of his very last works.

Needless to say, the culturally prescribed distortion (style) glaringly reflects the tensions and problems of the artist's milieu. Given the unquestionable technical expertness of the African sculptor, his distortion of the human figure is not due to a technical inability to represent reality —in the sense in which pre-Renaissance painters distorted space because of their ignorance of the laws of perspective. The African, Melanesian, Maori, Marquesan, Kwakiutl, Aztec, Maya or Inca artist distorted his figures intentionally and in accordance with cultural rules governing artistic utterances. Moreover, as regards certain African, Melanesian and medieval gargoyle carving artists, their nightmare vision of the human body—reflected in its artistic distortion—is closely related to what I, for one, view as their nightmare vision of the universe and of life. This process is, of course, paralleled also on the individual level. There is reason to believe that the painter Bosch was psychotic, which explains his—at that time no longer culturally demanded—gargoyle like distortions of the human body. The case of Toulouse-Lautrec is even more instructive. Dysplastic as a result of having been thrown by a horse, Toulouse-Lautrec—perhaps through the mechanism known as "identification with the enemy" (Anna Freud 1946)—sneeringly distorted the human body, but created almost ideally perfect horses. This convergence between culturally required and individually determined distortions raises, of course, the question to what extent the gargoyle carver obeyed a cultural mandate and to what extent he expressed in his carving of distorted bodies also his private nightmare vision of human flesh. Perhaps the most practical way of solving the problem is to say that in great art the cultural and the idiosyncratic converge, in so-called academic art the cultural holds the center of the stage, while in freak art—comparable to a frankfurter drowned in oceans of mustard—the idiosyncratic overshadows all other considerations.

Closely related to the problem of whether or not a certain distortion is artistic, is the problem of its *conventional* "plausibility"—a matter already touched upon elsewhere (Devereux 1948). It should be stressed from the start that the plausibility of a work of art is distinct from the plausibility of reality.[2] The Greeks found centaurs quite plausible in mythology; one suspects, however, that, had they met one in their backyard, they would have found the centaur as implausible as did the physiologist Du Bois-Reymond, who protested against mammals with three pairs of limbs. For the medieval Catholic the existence of angels was a dogma—but he would have been as startled by the appearance of his guardian angel as was Maurice d'Esparvieu in Anatole France's *La révolte des anges* and he would have found the angel as implausible as La Barre (1954) does on anatomical grounds. The discrepancy between artistic and real life plausibility is the key theme of *Don Quixote*. In brief, when writing poetry, the poet may experience as plausible a Belovèd with stars for eyes, bunches of grapes for hair, pearls for teeth and coral for lips—but, to paraphrase Dorothy Parker, "men seldom crave kisses from pearl-toothed Misses," or from ladies with abrasive lips of real coral.

One major obstacle to cross-cultural esthetic experiences is precisely the difference between the artistic plausibility concept of the artist's culture and that of the art-consumer's culture. The profusion of amok scenes in the Malay prose epic *Hikayat Hang Tuah* fits the Malay's concept of artistic plausibility, but not that of Bostonians, or of Mohave Indians. Only in a society acutely conscious of sibling rivalry would the theme of the cannibal baby strike a responsive chord. Even the choice of a "proper" theme is related to matters of plausibility. Using Róheim's (1941) insightful distinction, we may say that some societies prefer narratives about fathers (myth) at one time, but may come to prefer, later on, stories about sons (folk tales); the *Odyssey* appears to have had a—now lost—sequel, in the form of a *Telemacheia*.

In brief, art is a stylized (distorted) communication, recognizable as art by artist and connoisseur alike.[3] In fact, it is recognizable as such by everyone except U.S. customs and postal authorities and by the Watch and Ward Society. Indeed, in one of the defensive essays which protectively surround his sickening novel, *Lolita,* Nabokov rightly stresses that true pornography *must* be inartistic if it is to achieve its aim. In brief, an invitation to make love can be crude insolence or lofty art, depending on whether or not its wording fits the rules of the game. That which is, or was, a scandalous dissonance on the downbeat, is viewed as subtle and correct art when it occurs on the upbeat—due exception being made for dissonances on the downbeat in syncopation, and in related devices. Moreover, these exceptions are highly significant for an understanding of one's adherence to formal rules as a means of alibiing the content of one's utterance: Theories of art always hobble behind practice, painfully thinking up new and devious ways of justifying unusual, but effective and meaningful, modes of communication—witness some truly singular theoretical "explanations" of revolutionary musical practices. One is forcibly reminded here of the perhaps apocryphal story that the French Academy hastened to give its seal of approval to the Empress Josephine's solecism, who once said *l'harricot* instead of *le harricot*.

It is clear, then, that style—the hallmark of artistic quality—plays the role of an alibi. The aesthetical value of the experience bribes the superego just as humor bribes it in wit (Freud, 1905). However, society lays down definite rules as to what may be perceived as artistic, exactly as it lays down rules for what may be considered funny. It also appraises the social tolerability of an utterance in terms of the intensity of the artistic-aesthetic quality of the product—exactly as a modern lady may say that she is willing to listen to a naughty story if it is *really* funny. Cross-cultural differences in ways of alibiing improper utterances by means of art or humor explain why one sometimes fails to see that an alien artistic product is art, or that a foreign joke is funny. In fact, as regards the cross-cultural understanding of humor, we are no better off today than we were some 35 years ago, when Kroeber (1925) first pointed out this gap in our information.

Society's Stake in Art

Every society—even the acultural small town of the Middle West—is concerned with art, be it but negatively, as was Plato, who proposed to banish poets from his Republic. The plain fact is that art—like the grocery store—exists because it meets a social need not gratified by other cultural activities. The safety valve function of art was perceived most clearly perhaps by Cardinal Mazarin who, on hearing that songs were sung against an unpopular new tax, said in his inimitable Franco-Italian jargon: *Ils cantent, ils pagaront* ("they sing [and therefore] they will pay"). This epigram both minimizes the effectiveness of art as a means of social action and maximizes its effectiveness as a harmless safety valve. It also dispels some of our illusions about governmental *respect* for a free press (or art), because, where the press is truly influential, it is always quickly made unfree. The American press and the American artist are free only because they have either muzzled themselves— or else have nothing upsetting to say.

In addition to viewing art as a harmless safety valve, society and the artist alike consider the artistic utterance as *unrepudiable* in regard to *form,* but *repudiable* as to *content*. A Sedang Moi girl who, together with others, took advantage of my daily walks, to gather forest produce under the protection of my gun, once improvised a little song to tell me that they were tired and wished to go home. Asked why she did not tell me this in ordinary language, she replied that to do so would have been rude. Apparently, by expressing her wish in the form of a song, she left me free to decide whether to hear it only as a bit of vocal music, or to take cognizance also of its conceptual content. A talented young friend of mine—uncertain as to how his communication would be received were it made in prose—first declared his love to the girl of his choice in a rather good poem, whose content he could always repudiate by saying: "It is just a poem; it is not a declaration of love." At the other extreme of repudiability, a neurotic young boy spoke only "Donald Duck language" (squawk speech), until granted permission to voice his hatreds (to squawk) in plain language—whereupon he became quite fluently abusive in perfectly normal English. In his case there was a naked communication of affect which was, however, not clothed in ordinary speech capable of conveying the conceptual equivalent of his anger (curses) (Devereux, 1956a).

In brief, art can function as a social safety valve precisely because, like wit, it is a compromise and is, moreover, repudiable as to intent and content. It permits the artist to say—and the consumer to hear (or to see)—the forbidden, provided only that:

(1) The utterance is formulated in a manner which a given society chooses to call "art,"

(2) The actual content of the utterance is officially defined as subordinate to its form, and

(3) The utterance is understood to be repudiable.

"Let us roll in the hay" differs from: "Oh come with me and be my love" only in that the second of these statements, by submitting to the conventions of Victorian art, provides itself with a social alibi. The utterance is thereby turned from an idiosyncratic into a conventional, from a non-repudiable into a repudiable, from a straightforward into an ambiguous, from a private into a public, and from a personal into an impersonal statement.[4]

This statement can be further clarified by contrasting private acts with ritual ones. The announcement: "Miss Jones and I plan to sleep together" is scandalous because it is an improperly publicized private utterance. The announcement: "I take thee to be my wedded wife," followed by "and the twain shall become one flesh," is sacred, because it is ritualized (= stylized), and *de-individualized*. The term "de-individualized" is of prime importance in this context. Miss Jones, invited to participate in a "roll in the hay," perceives the pointedly personal nature of the invitation, as does everyone else. By contrast, "Oh come with me and be my love" has a broader scope and validity—any and every girl may respond to it with affect . . . as millions of girls have responded to "I take thee to be my lawful, wedded wife," which has echoed down the corridors of history as an impersonal, collective, ritual utterance. The point I seek to make is that practically all rites are conventionalized acts of sacrilege. This is strikingly demonstrated by the fact that the only *real* (ritualized) Mohave *wedding* is that of persons who—being cousins—should not marry at all, since their extramarital cohabitation is unequivocally defined as incestuous (Devereux, 1960). These data suggest that art is socially explosive because it presumes to deal *privately* with matters so sacred (= dangerous) that they are usually handled only by the group as a whole, ritually or legally. This, in turn, explains why society insists on socializing and on regulating art. (*Index librorum prohibitorum,* Comstock Act, etc.)

Art is even closely related to etiquette, in that it prescribes polite ways for saying impolite things; it provides ways for expressing the inexpressible. The Victorian lady would never have said "legs"—she may even have concealed the improperly suggestive legs of the piano under little skirts—but she did utter the term "limbs" (= legs) quite "brazenly." The word "trousers" was certainly taboo for her—but the acceptable term "inexpressibles" did provide her with a proper means for expressing the inexpressible.

Style—as the means whereby art comes into being—is, thus, best seen as a grammar and rhetoric of circumlocutions—and never more so than in the crudest "earthy" works, in which an innocent "spade" is circuitously referred to as a "bloody shovel."

Art and Taboos

Having demonstrated that art provides a safety valve for the expression of that which is tabooed, we must next seek to define the tabooed subjects which find expression in art. These subjects belong to three main layers:

(1) The generally human taboos: Incest, in-group murder, etc.

(2) The culture specific taboos: Sex in puritanical society, avariciousness in Mohave society, cowardice in Plains Indian society, etc.

(3) The idiosyncratically (neurotically) tabooed: Repressed wishes, etc. It is hardly necessary to add that the nature of idiosyncratically tabooed wishes depends to an appreciable extent also upon the dictates of the individual's cultural milieu (Devereux, 1956b).

Each and every one of these taboos must, to a certain extent, find expression in a work of art. Where the idiosyncratically tabooed factor is minimal, the work of art lacks flavor and individuality.[5] Where the culturally tabooed substance is minimal, the wine has no "body." It is timeless but also lifeless; it is not metacultural but simply rootless. By observing no particular code of plausibility, it has no plausibility at all. Where the universally human tabooed material is infinitesimal, the work of art is simply "arty-crafty." It is wine without alcoholic content.

In brief, one unmistakeable hallmark of all great art—of art whose validity and appeal transcend time, space and cultural barriers—is that, in real masterpieces, these three sets of tabooed materials are perfectly expressed, by means of a complex and balanced interlocking of all three of these elements. Such art has transcultural and diachronic validity. It appeals powerfully to Philadelphian, Roman, Parisian, Chinese and Hottentot alike—though without doubt Aeschylus meant something else to the ancient Athenian than to the modern New Yorker, and what it did mean to the Athenian is probably lost without retrieve. Thus, the Sedang Moi, who love music, rapidly came to prefer Mozart's C-major "Dissonant" (K. 465) Quartet to 1933 jazz songs, even though they were at first fascinated by the human voice emerging from a talking machine, simply because Mozart was more "basic" and more universally human than were the 1933 equivalents of "Purple People Eater."

There are, of course, appreciable barriers to cross-cultural artistic communication, comparable to the barriers which prevent even a highly acculturated honorary Mohave like myself from understanding just what is so funny about the Mohave way of referring to a visit to one's in-laws as "I am going to wash the hips of my relatives." The sense of alienness in the face of the artistic products of other people, and even of a past period, can have four major sources:

(1) The alienness of the latent subject matter, which is determined by the consumer's non-repression of that which the artist's culture (or neurosis) does repress. Thus, the sexually uninhibited Mohave found the plots of *Tristan* and of *Romeo and Juliet* ridiculous and even disgusting. They simply could not see why there was so much fuss about these lovers being united, in or out of wedlock. In other cases the sense of alienness is due to the excessive specificity of the artist's private taboo system. This extreme specificity also explains why the utterances of neurotic minor poets are so perishable, are so easily "dated" and have so limited an appeal.

(2) The alienness of plausibility conventions (see above).

(3) The alienness of artistic conventions. In such cases the non-responsiveness of the consumer betokens extreme cultural rigidity. Thus, according to Rhodokanakes (1948), when Rabindranath Tagore visited Athens, he gave the Parthenon a passing glance and then ignored it, apparently because the artistic convention incarnated in that temple was not

perceived by him as "artistic," perhaps because Indian art is florid rather than lean, and multiplies detail instead of emphasizing structure.[6] In exactly the same sense, the Western visitor seldom senses the "exquisite courtesy" of the act of greeting a friend in parts of West Africa by spitting into his hand, nor is he properly moved when a Bantu affectionately calls him "my ox."

(4) As we saw, techniques are conventionalized means for producing items susceptible of being recognized as art by society and by culture. An adequate technique permits one to express that which one would have to repress, if one lacked technical excellence. In this sense, then, technique (= artistry) is legal tender for bribing the superego, on the personal level, and for bribing the guardians of society's morals, on the cultural level. However, since this "legal tender" varies from society to society, the occidental mind usually refuses to be bribed with Indian artistic rupees, perceives some Hindu religious sculptures only as obscene representations of coitus, unredeemed by any trace of artistic quality, in the occidental sense of that term. Hence Westerner's react *only* to the tabooed utterance itself.[7] The same happens also when the conservative consumer of art is faced with a hypermodern work, whose new artistic technique is not accepted by his superego as a bribe offered in legal tender. This explains the anger and disgust wherewith modern works are usually rejected by the artist's contemporaries.

Dynamically speaking, the anthropologist studying art functions as a genuine student of culture and personality when he investigates:

(1) The types of tabooed materials which society views as the "proper" subject matter of art—and thereby comes to understand, e.g., why the Mohave have practically no love poetry, while we, alas, have too much—and much too bad—poetry of that sort.

(2) The rules of the game for expressing tabooed impulses—the subterfuges which enable one to be crude and yet be rated as a poet.

(3) The technical skills needed for complying with the rules of the artistic game: The amount of musical training one needs in order to allow oneself to become publicly flatulent by writing a brilliantly scored staccato passage for brass instruments, and especially the tuba. The amount of plastic skill needed to enable one to erect a symbolic phallus in public and to persuade the people to call it an obelisk, or to paint a nude and have her accepted as Golden Aphrodite and not as a barroom nude.

(4) Changes in the content of the ethnic unconscious (Devereux, 1956b) and in the rules for turning the forbidden into art.

This manner of investigating art is clearly cultural in scope and yet provides massive information about the psychological climate of the culture: about its nuclear areas of conflict and typical defenses.

The Ugly

Mathematicians, since the time of Abel (Bell, 1937), are familiar with the technique of "inverting the problem" which is refractory to ordinary approaches: It consists in taking as one's point of departure that which one actually seeks to prove and then working back from that point to the premises. A comparable approach can be effectively used also in scrutinizing the problem of beauty in terms of ugliness.

It is generally felt that artistic technique transmutes truth into beauty, or adds the quality of beauty to that which has the quality of felt (inner) or objective (outer) truth. Unfortunately, no one appears to ask why truth should have to be beautified, or the lily gilded. The only reasonable answer to this question is that only painful or upsetting truth needs to be "varnished." This means that the beauty of an utterance is, in itself, *prima facie* evidence of the upsetting quality of the substance of that utterance.

An illuminating sidelight is shed on this problem by Freud's hypothesis that man's original olfactory interest in the genitalia was gradually replaced by a repression of this interest in its original form and the displacement of that interest (in terms of beauty) to the rest of the body. Freud saw this repression and displacement as a consequence of man's assumption of an erect posture. However, I feel that the erect posture could not have come into being without a *previous* repression of the humanoid's compelling olfactory interest in the genitalia. Be that as it may, Maslow (1939, 1940), in demonstrating that the capacity to perceive the genitalia as beautiful is highly correlated with sexual dominance, indirectly highlighted also the fact that most people cannot perceive the genitalia as beautiful.

The problem of ugliness in art is therefore of prime importance. An item professing to be art, can be apprehended as "ugly" in two highly distinct senses:

(1) The substance of the utterance itself may be too little disguised for the taste of the times, as in the so-called "ashcan school of painting," and the like. In such instances, even though the public makes a predominantly ethical or "moral" judgment, the product itself is rejected as *art*. Thus, the courts often rule that a given work is too obscene to cover its scandalous nakedness with what meager scraps of artistry it does contain. The work is said to be "ugly" = *not* art.

(2) The means whereby the artist seeks to smuggle his utterance past the inner—and also past the social—censor, the manner in which he is "art-ing," may be at variance with social and superego standards, which test the artist's "artistic" alibi as carefully as that of the criminal. A work

with a deviant alibi is said to be "ugly," to = *bad* art, even where the substantive utterance itself is insipid enough, as it is in many of Stravinsky's later works.

These two meanings of the term "ugly" radically differ from each other and pointedly highlight the focus of the entire problem of beauty in art. On the whole, a work is accepted as (primarily) artistic if it satisfies the following criteria:

(1) The artist first experiences a mood capable of *contaminating* his audience; this mood is the conscious repercussion of an unconscious wish or impulse also present in others and must be accompanied by unconscious fantasies (visual, auditory, etc.) which, while at variance with those of his audience ("originality"), are susceptible of being re-translated by the audience into private images and moods referrable to the same specific wish (communicability). He allows these images or fantasies to erupt into his conscious (Kris, 1952) and then reorganizes them by means of a technique of art acceptable to the superego as a bribe, tendered in legal currency. Moreover, the final—and now "artistic"—utterance is such that it is still able to communicate a mood in all its intensity; otherwise stated, it still "contaminates" the audience with the artist's initial mood. Hence, figuratively speaking, the poet must not strive to be a logician; he must seek to give the impression that he is a musician. He achieves this goal by using seemingly conceptual communication as a means for achieving genuine affective contamination.

(2) The consumer is able to empathize with the artist's mood; his unconscious wishes and impulses resemble those of the artist. Moreover, he is able to bribe his own superego with the artistic currency placed at his disposal by the artist himself, and yet is able to retranslate the formal conceptual communication (imagery, or "wisdom") of the work into its unconscious referrents: A mood and the unconscious wish or impulse underlying that mood. This is genuine "brainwashing," of the Spence, Klein and Smith (1959) type.

The artist's creative process unfolds in the following characteristic sequence: Conscious mood, reflecting the mobilization of an unconscious wish, and also of unconscious fantasies pertaining to that wish. Eruption of the unconscious fantasies into the conscious in the form of imagery, melody, "ideas," and so forth (Kris, 1952). Reworking of this intruding material by means of an artistic technique, which the artist's superego is willing to accept as a bribe, but which not only does not destroy the material's capacity to induce a comparable mood in the audience, but even heightens it by making it ego syntonic, and does not distort or "purify" the imagery to the point where it can no longer be re-translated by the audience into the basic wish to which it pertains. Kubie's (1958) researches suggest that this blending of unconscious substance with conscious technique takes place in the preconscious.

It is extremely important to realize—as Kris (1952) pointed out—that the wishes in question are always pregenital and never genital ones. Now, it is a basic characteristic of pregenital wishes that they involve only a minimum of object libido, if any, and seldom have truly interpersonal dimensions. It appears to be the essence of artistic creativity that it manages to sublimate these basically autistic wishes in such a manner that they become object directed and endowed with the object-libidinal qualities of genital wishes. This process represents, to my mind, the very essence of sublimation. Novel as this view is, it fully dovetails with the more and more often voiced view (Menninger, 1942, etc.) that only pregenital impulses are capable of being sublimated, while genitality is not, since it is, in itself, a completely mature and reality adequate psychological position.[8]

Returning to the problem of the art "consumer," his task consists in:

(1) Learning to bribe his superego with the artistic currency placed at his disposal (music and art appreciation courses), and

(2) Referring back the artist's "distortion" of the underlying unconscious wish to a similar wish in his (the consumer's) unconscious. In a way, the consumer must learn to *un*-distort the artist's distortion of that wish; his astigmatism must, so to speak, compensate for that of the artist. Needless to say, no consumer's personal astigmatism *exactly* compensates for that of the "distorting" artist, which explains why an artistic item means different things to different consumers and also why it means different things to the same consumer at different times, even though he perceives the artist's distortion as aesthetically satisfying at all times. This, as I see it, is the psychoanalytic meaning of Copland's (1939) cogent remark, that a great work of art is inexhaustible, and means something different every time one hears it. We may well add that this inexhaustibility also implies that, in great art, the underlying wish is a very basic and intense one.

A concrete example may help us to pin down this idea more definitely. It is well known that the genuine "statue" of a Greek deity was not the artistic marble displayed in the public portion of the temple; it was the crude and inartistic hewn log, kept in a sacred and reserved precinct. We might almost say that, in classical Greece, the aesthetic statue was a public statement about a secret log statue, and comparable to an allusion to esoteric matters in a lay poem. In the public statue beauty replaced sacredness as alibi and connotation. This, in turn, implies that there can be no *bona fide* art which is not separated from esoteric utterances; from religion and from profanity alike. It was non-idolatry which permitted occidental church statuary to achieve the status of art; where there is idolatry, the evolution of religious statuary into art inevitably marks the decline of religion and also the loss of the statue's religious relevance and content.

Signalling Methods

It is seldom recognized that the artist habitually uses certain formal devices for signalling that his product is "art," which carries the "imprimatur" of the superego. A very simple example of this is the traditional way of beginning a tale: "Once upon a time" in England, "Cric—crac" in Haiti, and the like. A symphony does not start like a jazz tune. A pornographic novel does not open with the lyrical description of a landscape. In other instances, such as in brilliantly foreshortened figures, in five-part fugues, etc., technical virtuosity is used as a signal that "This is art; I am art-ing." An, alas, very common device of signalling that "This is serious art," is to be simply dull, just as the device of countless footnotes and references and an even greater dullness often seek to signal: "This is scholarship." Such signalling devices are often used even where the actual content is quite trivial and are resorted to—interestingly enough—also in many so-called "revolutionary" works. As regards the latter, a moment of thought will show that so-called *musique concrète* is, in many ways, an urbanized bastard descendant of the bird call passages in Beethoven's *Pastoral Symphony* and of many lesser works of a similarly imitative nature. In fact, even a certain type of ugliness—of content or of execution—can be used at various points in the history of culture as a token of "artistry." A good example of this are contrapuntal monstrosities for 24 voices—or so the composer tells us—which are not only devoid of beauty, but cannot even be perceived by the ear (as distinct from the eye) as having even half a dozen voices, let alone 24. Yet art—incomprehensibly—claims such works as its own, but barely grants second class citizenship to certain genuinely remarkable jazz compositions, because the latter distort the basic (erotic-aggressive) utterance either inadequately, or else by technically and stylistically unconventional means, which are inacceptable to the "square" superego as a "bribe."

The Medium

Art is communication which works *directly* through the medium of the senses. However, it is noteworthy that, even though fine cooking and perfumery are sometimes referred to as "arts," in essence all real art involves only sound and sight, or is—like the dance—in some manner subordinated to, or correlated with, sound or sight. Poetry speaks to us through images and through "music"; dance always associates itself with music and makes it appeal to the eye, being a plastic art in motion. It is my thesis that a sphere of the senses can become a medium for art only if it is not (phylogenetically and ontogenetically) so archaic and organismally so "basic" as to obstruct the path of sublimation. This explains why pure bodily sensations—be they kinesthetic, coenesthetic or tactile—as well as the olfactory and gustatory sensations, are not media suitable for the *sublimated* expression and communication of basic impulses. Moreover, all of these sense spheres are mobilized already *in utero*. Of the remaining two senses, hearing and seeing, hearing can also be stimulated already *in utero,* but is both phylogenetically and ontogenetically less archaic than are all other senses, sight always excepted. Apparently hearing is activated just late enough and is just dinstinct enough from the most archaic and basic senses to permit a degree of sublimation. By contrast, the sensations of the more archaic sense organs are so intense that they are best coped with by repression, rather than by sublimation. At the same time, hearing is close enough to archaic intra-uterine experiences to possess an affect mobilizing power which exceeds that of the only other sublimable sense-sphere. This may explain why no art has had to impose upon itself a technical straight jacket comparable in intensity, complexity and plain obsessive irrationality to that of music.[9] Sight, being mobilized only after birth is, of all senses, the one most closely related to reality testing (Devereux, 1949). It is therefore less hallucinatorily evocative than is hearing. This explains, in turn, why the rules of painting are less rigid than those of counterpoint.

This is a good time for a minor aside, to justify my having called music the art par excellence, apart from the fact that hearing is already stimulated *in utero*. In no other art is creativeness hedged about by so many "rules" bordering on obsessive ritual and having no aesthetic validity whatsoever. There is hardly a student of counterpoint who did not hear his teacher say: "Beautiful—musical—but against the rules." In no other art do truly great creative artists, as distinct from hacks, write technical exercises for the executant (Liszt's *Études*), or displays of purely contrapuntal virtuosity (Bach's *Kunst der Fuge*), or ukases sanctioning the use of a particular tool (Bach's *Well Tempered Clavichord*) *and* manage to persuade the multitude to *accept it* as "art." I hold that the obsessiveness of music rituals (theory)—the elaborateness of the conditions under which a musical utterance is accepted as art—is *prima facie* evidence that music utters most directly the most basic of forbidden impulses. Hence, in no other art is the conflict between utterance and means of utterance so constantly in the fore of artistic preoccupations.

The Contract Between Artist and Consumer

Turning from the psychological problem of art in culture to the relationship between producer and consumer, several basic points must be discussed.

We can best distinguish between artist and consumer by recognizing the existence of a binding contract between the two. Both parties agree that the artist shall be permitted to make an objectionable public confession, provided that his confession has a built-in escape clause,[10] implying the repudiability of the basic utterance. Only if there is such a built-in repudiability, can the consumer—and the executant artist as well—accept the creative artist's utterance and make it, in a way, his own, without guilt over being an accessory to a crime. The situation is strictly comparable to the "conspiracy" between "virtue" and "vice," which permits the sale of certain pharmaceutical items with the "understanding" that they are sold, purchased and used "for the prevention of disease only." An extraordinary example of such a "built-in escape clause" is the intentionally vague mystico-religious (= erotic) correspondence between Julian Sorel and the Maréchale de Fervacques, in Stendhal's *The Red and the Black*. In some instances the consumer can even turn the tables on the artist and exploit to the utmost the "escape clause" provided by the artist himself: The previously mentioned young poet, who declared his love in fine verses, was shocked when, on pressing for tangible tokens of his Belovèd's affection, the latter—a cynical scalp-hunter—replied with wide-eyed "innocence": "But I thought these were simply lyrical poems!" In other instances repudiability is achieved by hiring poets to write letters and poems to one's Belovèd, as did the aging Henri IV of France, when, while courting his niece-by-marriage, the Princesse de Condé, he asked his court poet to throw the mantle of romance over his senile infatuation. Still another way of exploiting repudiability may consist in humming love-lyrics into the ear of one's dancing partner. This technique of approach leaves the partner free to accept the humming of the "official text" as a purely "artistic" activity, and not as a proposal.

A point of equal importance is the intrusion of artistic material into the unconscious, which has been noted by Freud (1913) and, later on, by Lóránd (1935, 1937), both of whom studied the appearance of fairy tale material in dreams. Fairy tales do, of course, express tabooed impulses, identical with those of the dreamer himself. The real problem is, however, that this material appears in dream in a *borrowed* (culturalized) guise and *not* in a purely subjective wording. I hold that the appearance in dream of artistic day residues—of fairy tales, or of something read the night before—is a kind of intrapsychic alibiing. "Not I but my culture (as represented by its artists) has such wishes" [11] is combined with "Well, I may have such wishes, but they are at least culture-syntonic and artistic." (Devereux, 1956b, 1957). It is, thus, a particularly ego-syntonic type of dream work to use pre-stylized, and artistically culturized material in dream, as a means for the construction of the manifest dream content. As stated elsewhere (Devereux, 1956b), from the consumer's point of view, folklore, art and the like provide "cold storage" for those of the non-creative man's impulses which he cannot quite handle by means of *subjective* defenses. Whenever he responds to this material, and even incorporates it into his dreams, the consumer achieves two ends:

(1) He can pretend that the impulse itself is a borrowed, ego-alien one, in the very precise sense in which a sadistically obstructionistic bureaucrat will "sincerely" say: "I'd like to help you, but Article 27, paragraph 2, forbids me to do so," and

(2) He can "borrow" the impulse *complete with* the sanctioned (artistic) defenses against (or compromises with) it, which society itself officially recognizes as adequate, presentable and housebroken. This parallels the maneuver of a half-breed Indian (Devereux, 1956b), who managed to voice his private oedipal hatred of his father quite openly, by couching it in terms which were "respectable" in at least parts of American culture: "A lousy Indian (= father) has no business to cohabit with a pure white woman (= mother)."

The thrill of the consumer is vicarious, or, more precisely, is imagined to be vicarious. When listening to a poem of intense eroticism, when entranced by the sensuous loveliness of a Rodin statue, he can forever bribe his superego with the alibi: "In the first place, this is not my doing, but that of Baudelaire or Rodin, and, in the second place, mine is an artistic, and not a lecherous, experience." This alibi is akin to that of the sex obsessed members of anti-obscenity societies, except that the second part of *their* alibi is: "This is the condemnation of lechery and not its enjoyment."

The Greatness of Art

The last problem to be discussed is the one which psychoanalysis has not yet solved and which caused Freud to declare that genius is not explicable. I believe that Freud threw in the towel prematurely, since it is self evident that there is, indeed, both a cultural and an intrapsychic distinction between the experiences of a musical person who listens to Berlioz' *Romeo and Juliet* love scene and those of a member of an Orwellian "Junior Anti-Sex League." This difference is not only explicable, specifiable and meaningful, but is also pertinent to the understanding of genius.

The basic issue is the crucial distinction between the artist's perception of his utterance as subject matter and of his utterance as "artistic." We already saw that even his "improper" subject matter is closely related to his culture, in that culture determines what, beside universally taboo items, is to be repressed. It would be hard to imagine a contemporary

U.S. poet achieving fame by singing the praises of property, though near-artistic defenses of property were common enough when the rising middle classes struggled to displace the feudal lords as the prime economic force in society. Horatio Alger is today a topic of art only for literary Piltdown Men—as phony as the "original" one. The great artist achieves a complex and organic blending between the three layers of his subject matter—the universally human repressed impulses, the culturally (and historically) repressed ones, and the privately (idiosyncratically, neurotically) repressed ones. This blending may be massive and monolithic as in Aeschylus, or it may be subtly contrapuntal as in Shakespeare. But a blending—presumably preconscious (Kubie, 1958)—there must be and flaws in this blend are flaws in the latent subject matter.

The artist's perception of the rules of his game and his alibi maneuvers, which turn his "obscenity," "rebellion," or "blasphemy" into art, are also significant. In the case of some artists, there is so wholesale an acceptance of the rules that their manipulation becomes an end in itself. Both genius and cobbler can take this road, witness Bach's *Art of the Fugue* and Kaikhosru Sorabji's even more recondite contrapuntal obsessions. There can also be a wholesale rejection of one *type* of rule, and its replacement with *another* set of *equally binding* rules. Schoenberg got rid of one set of rules, only to invent a perhaps even more obsessive set of rituals, the twelve-tone system. Innovators of technique alone are very much like the famous "rebel without a cause" (Lindner, 1944), in that they unify their works not by means of a logico-affective internal continuity, as did Shakespeare or Berlioz, but by external technical devices.

Hence, apart from the problem of having to interlock three sets of tabooed wishes, the artist must also possess supreme skill in "skating on thin ice." Indeed, the better the skater, the thinner can be the ice (of rules of art) on which he can skate. In other words, the better an artist masters his craft, the nearer he is able to come to expressing, *without loss of affect,* the tabooed. Moreover, by covering it with the thinnest—and most exquisitely wrought—veneer of artistic convention, which suffices to make his utterance both culture and ego syntonic, he often actually heightens the intensity of its experienced affect. But veneer there must be, differentiating the love scene in Berlioz' *Romeo and Juliet* from a rutting bull elephant's "musht"—endocrine actuated—trumpeting.

The artist is, thus, constantly confronted with the choice between:

(1) Skating on ice so thin that it will break and cause the forbidden utterance to erupt from behind the stylistic alibi, and

(2) Freezing his real utterance over with a crust of ("artistic") ice so thick as to cause the elemental utterance, and the affect pertaining to it, to be lost . . . thereby turning the boiling lake into a refrigerated

indoor rink, where figure-skating—pattern making on the ice—becomes the real goal.

Here, too, there are major cultural and historical differences to be noted. There is, at one end, the volcanic eruptiveness of "romantic" art, and, at the other end, the icy technical virtuosity of "neoclassical" watchmakers. Personally, I feel that in the greatest of great art the lake is truly boiling, but erupts in a beautifully patterned column, or, if the lake is frozen over with technique, the ice is paper thin, of exquisite purity and incised with magnificent figure skating patterns. Whether the experience of beauty is the product of a controlled eruption: of a boiling lake foaming up like the water-spouts of Versailles, or of a creative control: of the incising of patterns on paper thin ice, the basic artistic experience is the same. *There is a sense of the imminent closeness of danger,* the feeling that at any moment the controls may lapse and the love song turn into a rutting bull elephant's elemental and quite unartistic proboscidian fanfare. In this frame of reference, the experience of beauty is a product of *the sense of imminent instinctual danger controlled down to the finest hairline.* As Hanns Sachs (1942) wisely said, the problem of beauty is to *endure* it, rather than to *understand* it.

Two major aspects of art are relevant in this context:

(I.) *Art is socially creative and cohesive.* This, of course, is a descriptive and empirical statement and not an explicatory one. Nonetheless, it must be borne in mind that:

(1) Art is a sublimation and not an ordinary defense. As such, it has three major characteristics:

  (a) It is, unlike other defenses, strengthened and not weakened by psychoanalysis (Jokl, 1950).
  (b) It liberates energies and is not, like the defenses, parasitical on them.
  (c) It is primarily in the service of the ego and not of the instincts (as in lechery or blind hate) or of the superego (as in a self-appointed guardianship of public virtue).

(2) The impulses and wishes perpetuated by art are the same as those which actuate the normal, the neurotic, the compulsive rebel and the inhibited Puritan. However, these impulses are neither distorted, nor negated, nor are they permitted to erupt in the form of a brute, almost subcortical discharge. They are disciplined without being negated. They are not dissipated, but are discharged in such a manner that there occurs a kind of "feedback" which automatically increases:

  (a) The ability to mobilize and to discharge affect, and
  (b) The technical proficiency of achieving a *disciplined* discharge.

These latter two findings are, in general, characteristic of all sublimations, as listed above, and especially fit criterion 1b. Moreover, the technique of the discharge implies creative outgoing communication, receptivity, and *object relations*—three processes which presuppose, and are uniquely characteristic of, maturity. Great art is always art *directed at an audience;* though, in the case of great innovators, it is often directed at an as yet non-existent audience. The socially evolved and provided technique is recognized as of external origin, is assigned a place in the preconscious and is internalized adequately, but without its ever becoming a panicky compulsion. The new techniques one originates are, moreover, intended to have trans-personal validity.[12]

This observation explains also the constant evolution of art and, moreover, does so in terms which presuppose the thesis already discussed, that all great art is inexhaustible. It is one of the basic characteristics of all great art—be it a Mozart quartet which I happen to hear today for the fiftieth time, or a Bartók quartet whose beauty is, because of its novelty, only partly accessible to me on first listening to it—that it gives one simultaneously an uncanny sense of *déjà entendu* or *déjà vu* and a complete and startling sense of something utterly new. It is increasingly recognized in psychologically sophisticated critical circles that all major themes are eternal. This is but another way of saying that the number of wishes important and intense enough to require or deserve artistic "distortion" is limited. Each such wish is a perpetual challenge, which each period meets to its own partial satisfaction, and yet in a manner which leaves the problem unsolved for all future generations. Each new twist of plot or melody, each new artistic manipulation, each re-statement of the human figure, represents, on the one hand, a new attempt to solve an ageless problem and a partial repudiation of previous solutions. At the same time, a new attempt of turning a tabooed wish into art is also a protest against the kind of boredom which past and hackneyed solutions induce in us. A further major cause of artistic revolutions is the fact that, due to culture-historically determined changes in the composition of the unconscious and of the conscious of successive historical periods (Devereux, 1956b), past solutions no longer fit the present psychic constellation of the new artists and their audiences and therefore fail to provide an adequate defense against, or compromise with, the unconscious wish. Once the problem is formulated in this manner, it does not matter in the least whether the eighteenth century solution of such emotional conflicts repelled Victorians because of its coldly hedonistic sensuality, or whether the Victorian solution strikes us as inadequate because of the amount of repression it demands from us. All that matters is that the single true cause of changes in art is the eternal nature of the eternally ungratified and therefore eternally challenging wishes underlying it.

(II.) *Art demands an integration of the personality.* In the best cases there is, on the one hand, a complete interlocking of the three forms of humanly, culturally and subjectively tabooed impulses, and on the other hand, a meshing of these "topics" with ego-syntonic and highly organized means of expression (ritual or style of art), without loss of affect, the whole being directed at an audience, which implies object libido. In this sense, then, *art is the perfect medium for the most highly individualized contribution man can make to culture,* and the cultural element—the factor which proclaims a given product as "art"—is: Style, which presupposes technique. In fact, in one sense at least, style is *behaviorally* the pattern of techniques.

Technique may, thus, be thought of as that which differentiates a brute, elemental but static utterance from dynamic art. Its real function is revealed by a remark I sometimes make to adolescent analysands wantonly rebelling against not overly obnoxious social rules:

"Your bones admittedly limit the flexibility of the arm. They are, in a way, like constricting rules. But if your arm had no bones whatsoever, you could not use it at all."

Conclusions

In terms of communication theory, art is a message in which the basic information is overlaid by a special kind of (pseudo) "noise," which is actually a kind of meta-language, conveying supplementary information ("beauty") and which, like a contrapuntal voice, comments and highlights the *cantus firmus* of the basic utterance.

In terms of psychoanalytic theory, art—like love—deepens and broadens the psychic scope of the instincts, by placing at their disposal the immense resources of the ego.

In terms of the theory of culture, art is the means whereby a healthy society manages to put to a constructive use man's seemingly least socializable impulses, and even to augment their ultimate intensity, by placing at their disposal the vast resources of culture, thereby making them both expressible and culturally productive.

It is therefore probable that, in the long run, the psychoanalytically oriented culture and personality study of art will become one of the most effective means for the study of man in society.

NOTES

1. In this respect—as in many others—Liszt was a precursor of the most modern music of our times, such as Cage's pieces for "prepared" pianos.

2. The fact that this view is directly related to the subsequent discussion of the repudiability of art was pointed out to me by Miss Elizabeth de Szinyei Merse.

3. The specific nature of this communication will be discussed further below.

4. The ambiguousness of art is determined by the doubt as to whether its center of gravity—and/or objective—is its offensive content or its acceptable form. This, by the way, may explain why the substantive content of technically revolutionary works is often so timorous and insipid: The melodies of Stravinsky are often appallingly static and impoverished and the plot of *Finnegan's Wake* would disgrace Elynor Glyn.

5. It is conceivable that difficulties in attributing an early Italian painting to artist A, rather than to artist B, may be partly due to the minimal subjective involvement of these artists, who had just begun to emerge from the anonymous craft art of the medieval Church craftsman. However, it may also be due in part to our lack of subjective empathy with the individuality of the artists of that remote period, in the sense in which "all Chinamen look alike to us." This, in turn, suggests that the study of depth psychology is an indispensable part of the art historian's equipment (Kris, 1952), as is the study of culture and personality.

6. Of course, had Tagore visited Athens in classical times, when the Parthenon was not yet a skeleton of lean beauty, but was painted and loaded down with ornaments as gaudy as those of an Italian village church, he might have responded differently. It is well to recall that the lean beauty of classical Greek art, as we see it today, required the cooperation of time, which peeled off the paint, and the aesthetic dedication of pillaging Roman legionaries, who mercifully stole the chryselephantine gingerbread. What Greek statues really looked like in the heydays of Greece, is shown by a marble miniature reproduction of a statue of Athena; the headgear worn by this surviving miniature beggars description and outdoes in garishness anything that ever adorned even Carmen Miranda's locks.

7. In the same sense, a person is said to have a peculiar sense of humor, not appreciated by others, if his "private currency" for bribing his superego with "wit" is not accepted as "wit" by the superego of his listener. In such cases, his check "bounces."

8. In terms of this scheme, cheaply sentimental "art" (?) peddles mere affect, detached from any kind of basic utterance, which is totally lacking in such works. The genuine utterance is destroyed and replaced by a phoney and derivative pseudo-utterance.

9. The fantastic rigors of early poetical rules may—apart from their mnemonic function—reflect attempts to curb the magico-evocative, irrational and autistic potentialities of language. The liberation of the poet from this linguistic-poetic straight jacket may have resulted from the increasing use of language for the communication of rational information.

10. Compare the Oriental preamble: "Majesty, may I speak and live?"

11. The titillating spuriousness of this pretense is revealed by the naïve public's need to "hiss the villain," though the actor is clearly only a mouthpiece.

12. Although I do not happen to like Schoenberg, I recognize that he did evolve his technique in a *teachable* form, and with the *intention* of teaching it. All this does presuppose object libido.

BIBLIOGRAPHY

Barzun, Jacques. 1950. *Berlioz and the Romantic Century*, 2 vols. Boston: Atlantic–Little, Brown.

Bell, E. T. 1937. *Men of Mathematics*. New York: Simon and Schuster.

Copland, Aaron. 1939. *What to Listen For in Music*. New York: McGraw-Hill.

Devereux, George. 1948. "Mohave Coyote Tales," *Journal of American Folklore*, 61:233–55.

———. 1949. "A Note on Nyctophobia and Peripheral Vision," *Bulletin of the Menninger Clinic*, 13:85–93.

———. 1956a. *Therapeutic Education*. New York: Harper.

———. 1956b. "Normal and Abnormal." In Anthropological Society of Washington (ed.), *Some Uses of Anthropology, Theoretical and Applied*. Washington, D.C. Anthropological Society of Washington.

———. 1957. "Psychoanalysis as Anthropological Field Work," *Transactions of the New York Academy of Sciences*, Series II. 19:457–72.

———. 1960. "Mohave Ethnopsychiatry and Suicide," *Bureau of American Ethnology, Bulletin*. No. 175, 1960.

Freud, Anna. 1946. *The Ego and the Mechanisms of Defense*. New York: International Universities Press.

Freud, Sigmund. 1905. "Wit and Its Relation to the Unconscious." In *The Basic Writings of Sigmund Freud*. New York: Modern Library, 1938.

———. 1910. *Leonardo da Vinci*. New York: Dodd, Mead, 1932.

———. 1913. "The Occurrence in Dreams of Material from Fairy Tales." In *Collected Papers*, IV. London: Hogarth, 1925.

———. 1930. "Ansprache im Frankfurter Goethe Haus." In *Gesammelte Werke*, XIV. London: Imago Publishing Co., 1948.

Jokl, R. H. 1950. "Psychic Determinism and Preservation of Sublimation in Classical Psychoanalytic Procedure," *Bulletin of the Menninger Clinic*, 14:207–19.

Kris, Ernst. 1952. *Psychoanalytic Explorations of Art*. New York: International Universities Press.

Kroeber, A. L. 1925. "Introduction." In Parsons, E. C., *American Indian Life*. New York: Viking.

———. 1957. *Style and Civilization*. Ithaca, N.Y.: Cornell University Press.

Kubie, L. S. 1958. *Neurotic Distortion of the Creative Process*. Lawrence: University of Kansas Press.

La Barre, Weston. 1954. *The Human Animal*. Chicago: University of Chicago Press.

Lindner, R. M. 1944. *Rebel Without a Cause*. New York: Grune and Stratton.

Lóránd Sándor. 1935. "Fairy Tales and Neurosis," *Psychoanalytic Quarterly*, 4:234–43.

———. 1937. "Fairy Tales, Lilliputian Dreams and Neurosis," *American Journal of Orthopsychiatry*, 7:456–64.

Maslow, A. H. 1939. "Dominance Feeling, Personality and Social Behavior in Women," *Journal of Social Psychology*, 10:3–39.

————. 1940. "A Test for Dominance Feeling (Self-Esteem) in Women," *Journal of Social Psychology*, 12:255–70.

Menninger, K. A. and J. L. 1942. *Love Against Hate*. New York: Harcourt, Brace.

Rhodokanakes, K. P. (also Rhodochanachi, C. P.) 1948. *Athens and the Greek Miracle*. London: Routledge, Kegan Paul.

Róheim, Géza. 1941. "Myth and Folk-Tale," *American Imago*, 2:266–79.

Sachs, Hanns. 1942. *The Creative Unconscious*. Cambridge, Mass.: Sci-Art.

Spence, D. P., Klein, G. S. and Smith, G. J. W. 1959. "Subliminal Effect of Verbal Stimuli," *Journal of Abnormal and Social Psychology*. Vol. 59, no. 2.

Stevens, Halsey. 1953. *The Life and Music of Béla Bartók*. New York: Oxford University Press.

II. THE PRESENT STATE OF THE PROBLEM *

The cross-cultural use of culture and personality insights into art and mythology is a subject which must be interpreted somewhat broadly, if we are to assemble any considerable number of studies for our attention. In part this is due to a general neglect of art and literature by anthropologists in recent decades, in part to the limited number of competent culture-and-personality students who have interested themselves in these subjects. This is not to say that substantive collections of good materials have not been made. We have those of Wingert, D'Harnoncourt, Segy, Muensterberg, and others in native art, and collections of native myths by many anthropologists and linguists. What have been lacking, rather, have been theoretical studies, or empirical works testing our hypotheses, or even significant studies on the level of the single tribe.

Modern clinical psychologists, meanwhile, have been thoroughly aware of the significance of art as a projective index of the psychology of a people. Theodora Abel, for example, used free designs of limited scope as a personality index, applying these to the study of normal controls, Navaho subjects, Balinese, and paranoid schizophrenics. Her conclusions, which no doubt need cross-cultural sophistication for their interpretation, are that the Balinese test very similarly to paranoid schizophrenics in our society. Anastasi and Foley analyzed spontaneous drawings by children of different cultures, including American Indians. As might be expected, they found quite varied subject-matters, influenced (they believed) by geographic, climatic and environmental factors; the horse, for example, was a common Plains Indian subject among boys; and the interest in people versus animals varied from society to society. Paget studied "Some Drawings of Men and Women made by Children of Certain Non-European Races"; Schubert investigated the "Drawings of Orotchen Children and Young People"; and Taylor has contributed "A Note on the Cultural Determination of Free Drawing."

Of plastic art forms, "The Thematic Apperception Technique in the Study of Culture-Personality Relations" has been much used, both in its original and in modified forms (though less so than the Rorschach perhaps), as summarized by W. E. Henry in the above-titled paper. In the general area of art forms and projective techniques, George Devereux was the first to use finger-painting as a projective technique. Wayne Dennis investigated the performance of Hopi children on the Goodenough

* This portion of the chapter, by Weston La Barre, is a bibliographical essay, supplemented by an extensive bibliography. At the author's express request, many of the usual editorial changes have not been made.

387

"Draw-a-Man Test" and interpreted these in the light of projective psychology; Havighurst, Gunther and Pratt investigated the "Draw-a-Man" test and the influence of cultural environment in the performance of Indian children. Honigmann and Carrera reported on the cross-cultural use of Machover's Figure Drawing Test as applied to Indians and Eskimos. The McAdory Art Test was applied to Navaho Indian children by Steggerda, who also gave the Form Discrimination Test to groups of Navaho, Negro, and white children. Baudouin, within a Jungian framework, used the Chinese Taoist "double-comma" as a kind of TAT or Rorschach stimulus in his search for the "collective unconscious" of various persons. All these studies, however, are significant primarily as projective techniques for clinical psychologists, and for cultural anthropologists they are at best mere methodological devices for the study of larger problems.

Psychoanalysts have written a formidable number of studies of western writers and literature, but only a few on art. Characteristic of studies on art are Freud on the Moses of Michelangelo; and Ferenczi, Freud, and Coriat on the symbolism of the Medusa-head. L. B. Boyer wrote a psychiatric study of sculpture and depression in a case study of a modernistic sculptress with a depressive personality. Likewise, the anthropologist Seligman has contributed clinical notes on three celebrated Chinese artists, Kuo Hsi, a "mildly obsessional" painter of the 11th century A.D.; Mi Fei, a Sung artist and "obsessional neurotic"; and Pien Tsai of the 7th century who suffered a trauma and fatal dysphagia.

One of the rare persons with a triple competence as analyst, anthropologist, and distinguished collector of primitive art is Warner Muensterberger, who has written on "The Roots of Primitive Art" and has published on African sculptures, many of them from his own collection. Among classic American anthropologists of his generation, only Clark Wissler, trained as a psychologist, seems to have been interested in the psychological implications of primitive art. The Boas volume on *Primitive Art* remains the best comparative ethnography of art on anthropological lines, although Weltfish has written a Marxian interpretation of art.

One of the very few cross-cultural studies of art that would satisfy the modern culture-and-personality specialist is the brilliant paper by Anthony F. C. Wallace, modestly titled *A Possible Technique for Recognizing Psychological Characteristics of the Ancient Maya from an Analysis of their Art.* Working on the basis of his general familiarity with the categories used by Rorschach, Machover, Elkisch, and Schmidl-Waehner, Dr. Wallace studied the Maya codices and formulated a "structuralized personality portrait" of the ancient Maya with considerable clarity and articulateness:

The typical Maya male of the period of the three codices appears to have been a somewhat introverted person who sought the clarification of his problems in ideation rather than in social interaction; he had, however, little real insight into the sources of his anxieties; he was blandly egocentric. This does not mean, however, that he was a solitary boor; on the contrary, he was distinctly sociable, but in a superficial way—he was a type who would like being "alone in a crowd." He made a sincere effort to appear outgoing and friendly, and he was able to support a mechanical and ritualized social facade, but he felt little need for relating himself to others emotionally.

The Maya was an ambitious, creative individual with considerable initiative. In view of his introversiveness and the slightness of super-ego (conscience) development, these ambitions were essentially egocentric rather than attached to the fortunes of church or state, city or tribe.

At heart the Maya conceived other people as hostile to himself. This anticipation of the hostility of others was probably the outgrowth of unsatisfactory relationships with the mother. The almost fetishistic emphasis on the breasts as the criterion of female sexuality suggests a fixation of libido at an oral level. This undoubtedly has profound implications for economic, social, and religious institutions.

In response to this stereotype of the social world as inherently frustrating, the Maya nourished his own aggressive impulses. He felt hostile towards people. This aggression, however, he normally suppressed rather rigidly, presenting to the world a preoccupied, restrained, almost constricted social facade. If and when the social facade broke down, however, there were no defenses in depth against the underlying aggressive tendencies; behavior, then, was likely to become disorganized and irrationally destructive. One thing which no doubt helped to bleed off some of this aggression was the lack of inhibitions about the exercise of phallic aggression in sexual relations.

The egocentricity of historic Maya character (if, as is likely, it was old and well established) may have had something to do with the brittleness of Maya society. The unexplained breakup of the Old Empire, and the instability of the New Empire, may have been grounded in the incapacity of the Maya themselves to really "get together" in any but a formal, conventional way.

Wallace's "personality portrait" is reported at length for several reasons: first, as an example of the exactness with which statements can be made with this technique; second, it should remind the layman of the necessity for his learning the discipline of projective techniques before he is in a position either to assess or to criticize its results; and third, because of the vistas of potential ethnographic meaning which are opened by this method in the hands of an expert. Notable in Wallace's paper are the repeated confirmations of his analysis by other sources. William Davidson collected thirty-six Rorschach protocols on modern Maya Indian males which were interpreted by Otto Billig of the Duke University School of Medicine. Billig's results strikingly validate Wallace's analysis; and furthermore these "blind" projective analyses are themselves further validated by Bishop Landa's description of the post-Conquest Maya. The technical details of Billig's Rorschachs and of Wallace's analysis (in his Appendix) are too long to be quoted here; but the attention of qualified students is invited to these remarkable materials.

Other provocative and thought-arousing articles are that by Heilbronner on the stylistic treatment of the sexes in the art of various periods of the Palaeolithic period, and that by Kohen on the featureless Levantine Stone Age fertility figurines as the Oedipal mother of the nightmare. Both should perhaps be read in connection with an equally suggestive study by Rattray Taylor of institutionalized sex modalities in history. With an almost schizoid sensitivity to body-image language, Doris Webster has also written a veritably Schilderesque study of the *Origin of the Signs of the Zodiac.* The psychoanalyst Ernst Kris has summarized some psychiatric *Approaches to Art;* Franz Alexander has given us a psychoanalytic view of modern art; while Reitman has written a book on *Insanity, Art, and Culture.* There are a number of works of varying competence on primitive art—few approach the sensitivity of Lisle March Phillipps' classic descriptions in *The Works of Man*—by Adam, Bunzel, Christensen, Hooper and Burland, Kühn, and Mukerjee, as well as superb studies of special subjects like West African sculpture by Kjersmeier, Gaffé, Griaule, Portier and Poncetton, Rasmussen, Sadler, Schweeger, Segy, Sweeny, Sydow, Trowell, and Wingert. But, on the whole, psychiatrically and anthropologically adequate studies of primitive art are very much for the future. The surface of the great possibilities has scarcely yet been scratched.

With respect to mythology and primitive literature in general, the situation is far more encouraging. Psychoanalysts very early perceived the relevance of mythology to their own studies. Notable are the classic works of Abraham on *Dreams and Myths,* Rank on *The Myth of the Birth of the Hero, Das Inzestmotiv in Dichtung und Sage, Die Nacktheit in Sage und Dichtung,* and *Psychoanalytische Beiträge zur Mythenforschung,* as well as Ernest Jones on "The Symbolic Significance of Salt in Folklore and Superstition," and Riklin on "Wishfulfillment and Symbolism in Fairy Tales." Freud gave major credit to Riklin, Abraham, Rank, Jones, Storfer, and Jung for such studies of folklore and myth; but Freud himself also wrote two analytic papers on "The Occurrence in Dreams of Materials from Fairy-Tales" and "The Theme of the Three Caskets." Ferenczi, Lorand, and Mather have continued the study of motifs in fairy-tales; a typical paper is that by Desmonds on "Jack and the Beanstalk." Rank had been a classical scholar before he became interested in psychiatry, and several students have continued the interest in classic myths, Berenice Engle writing on Attis, Lemnos, Melampus, and the Amazons; Siegfried Bernfeld on Tantalus and Sisyphos; and George Devereux variously on Oedipus and Laius, Penelope's character and a counter-oedipal episode in the *Iliad.* Pan Codellas has shown how even modern Greek folklore preserves distorted, superstitious cause-and-effect explanations of endemic anthrax among flocks; La Barre, using ethnobotanical folklore has sought to show how folk descriptions of the behavior of peyote current among tribes in the southern Plains and Southwest actually record accurate observations, when read in terms of local tribal symbolisms. On a larger scale, Edith Weigert-Vowinckel has written a superb study of *The Cult and Mythology of the Magna Mater* which must impress both anthropologists and analysts with its soundness and fine scholarship. In a similar study of the Great Mother Goddess, Arthur Brenner has investigated puberty rites and the Covenant of Abraham in particular; and Zelig has described analytically "Two Episodes in the Life of Jacob." In similar vein, Theodor Reik has written illuminatingly on couvade, puberty rites, Kol Nidre, and the Shofar.

A number of anthropologists have used folkloristic materials to obtain psychological insights cross-culturally. M. K. Opler and F. Obayashi, for example, have shown how psychological tensions at the Tule WRA camp were expressed in folk-poetry of *senryu* form. Lucille Charles and J. J. Honigmann both have described the function of ritual clowns; Devereux has analyzed the psychological significance of Mohave coyote stories; and recently Melville and Frances Herskovits have published an important work on *Dahomean Narrative,* which they discuss from the viewpoints of the Freudian Oedipus formulation, the Jungian archetype, the Cambridge myth-from-ritual school, Lord Raglan's anti-historicism, and Malinowski's functionalism. La Barre has examined the content of the normal unconscious mind when the superego is liquidated in alcohol in his content-analysis of limericks collected at two major Eastern universities, in a study of *The Psychopathology of Drinking Songs.* The same author has essayed an anthropological appraisal of obscenity, as also has Honigmann. Kluckhohn, among other anthropologists, has written an important paper on *Myths and Rituals, a General Theory,* which should be required reading for all students of the subject.

The authors mentioned in the previous paragraph have all been more or less directly influenced by psychoanalysis. But the same awareness of the value of mythology in studying psychological and ethnographic problems was early evident in the mainstream of American anthropology. Boas, for example, wrote both on "Psychological Problems in Anthropology" and on "Kwakiutl Culture as Reflected in Mythology," expressing therein opinions which have since become standard in the profession. Among students of British background who have used folklore for psychological purposes a minimal list would include Hocart, Rivers, C. G. and B. Z. Seligmann, Glover, Bartlett, Jones, Bateson, Gorer, Fortune, Darlington, and Beaglehole. Americans would first of all include Sapir. Linton, Benedict, Kroeber, Mead, Goldenweiser, Radin, Dollard, Kluckhohn and Hallowell. In addition to these, the following have also shown in their publications an interest in the psychological content of folkloristic materials: Ashley Montagu, R. F. Barton, C. Dubois, W. Dyk, C. S. Ford, J. Gillin, A. Joseph, J. Henry, W. W. Hill, G. B. Johnson, O. Klineberg, R. Landes, S. Mekeel, M. E. Opler, M. K. Opler, L. Simmons, L. Thompson, and R. Underhill—to use only those named in the well-known anti-psychological ukase of the archaeologist Betty Meggers. The major fault of her list is its non-inclusiveness, for one would have expected to find in it, for example, J. Belo, R. Bunzel, J. M. Cooper, A. H. Gayton, E. Goldfrank, E. A. Hoebel, A. H. and D. C. Leighton, A. Lesser, S. Newman, E. C. Parsons, H. Powdermaker, M. Siegel, F. G. Speck, S. Tax, C. and E. Voegelin, J. W. M. Whiting, Erikson, Tomašič, and A. Métraux. A. Métraux has, in fact, made a standard statement which is worthy of quotation:

> Folklore, if properly handled, constitutes the most valuable document not only to understand the many nuances of the culture, but also to grasp the general psychological pattern of those who share it. Even such patternized and widely scattered stories as those of the Trickster can be flavored so as to stress the fundamental values of the society . . . The general psychological trend of a society can survive in the form of traditional tales.

Perhaps it is fair to say that most modern anthropologists are now aware of the projective significance of folklore and mythology, especially since the work of Linton and Kardiner. Nevertheless, it should not be forgotten that earlier workers, such as Paul Radin on the Trickster, had this same essential insight into mythology as projective material and index to the rest of the culture. Likewise, though largely unattended-to by other anthropologists, the late Géza Róheim wrote a veritable library of psychological interpretations of folklore, whether primitive, European, Hebrew, or classical Greek and Roman.

A representative sampling—though not an exhaustive summary—of the types of current interest may be shown in the following list of papers. Margot Astrov has written on the concept of motion as the psychological leitmotif in Navaho life and literature; Bartlett has analyzed symbolism in folklore in general. La Barre made observations on the *ethos* of the Aymara in connection with their known history, as evidenced in a content analysis of Aymara folktales. Esther Goldfrank has written on "The Impact of Situation and Personality on Four Hopi Emergence Myths," and Melville Jacobs has made "Psychological Inferences from a Chinook Myth." Margaret Lantis has described Nunivak Eskimo personality as revealed in their mythology; Puckett has depicted the Negro character as revealed in their folklore. M. C. Randle has elicited psychological types from Iroquois folktales; and Thorner has minutely studied certain German words, German personality, and Protestantism. Indeed, the modern fieldworker's psychological sophistication has reached the point of Wallace's recognizing a type of psychoanalytic theory among the Seventeenth Century Iroquois!

The list could be made almost indefinitely long. Abou Zeid has shown that the telling of folktales is one type of disguised satisfaction of repressed desires in Egypt; and his fellow-countryman, M. M. El-Sayyad, has made an interesting approach to folk-psychology through a study of Egyptian folk-songs. M. E. Opler has argued that the symbolism of the snake in Japanese folklore is quite opposite from that to be expected in western society, though La Barre has pointed out the possibility of different conclusions, on the basis of Opler's own cited materials. For the rest, Fortune, Reed, Jones, and Hambly have well discussed the widespread phallic significance of snakes in folklore generally. Karlson has written a paper on "Psychoanalysis and Mythology"; and Marett a book, on *Psychology and Folklore*. One of Róheim's most extended works on the subject is *The Eternal Ones of the Dream: A Psychoanalytic Interpretation of Australian Myth and Ritual;* his article, on "Psycho-Analysis and the Folk-Tale" is a useful summarizing of his method and theory. La Barre has written a summary of studies in "Folklore and Psychology," and Cox a paper on "The Place of Mythology in the Study of Culture."

Folk festivals have received attention in Tarachow's "Totem Feast in Modern Dress," Sterba's paper on Hallowe'en, and L. and S. Fraiberg's "Hallowe'en: Ritual and Myth." Desmonde has examined another folk celebration in "The Bull Fight as a Religious Ritual" which Jack Conrad has studied anthropologically at greater length. Desmonde has also written on "The Origin of Money in the Animal Sacrifice," on "The Eternal Fire as a Symbol of the State," and on "Psycho-Analysis and Legal Origins." Sterba has also analyzed a Dutch celebration of a festival. John Dollard has reported on a tension-reducing American Negro game, the "Dozens," which he observed in Mississippi.

There seems no logical reason why we should exclude studies of modern folklore from our present survey. Marie Bonaparte has written on the widespread "Myth of the Corpse in the Car," on "The Legend of the Unfathomable Waters," and on "Saint Christopher, Patron Saint of the Motor-Car Drivers." Sterba has analyzed the World War II phenomenon, "Kilroy was Here." Moellenhoff has written "Remarks on the Popularity of Mickey Mouse," and Grotjahn on "Ferdinand the Bull." Grotjahn, in fact, has collected into a book a number of his essays on Mickey Mouse, Ferdinand the Bull, popular jokes (in particular the Jewish joke), the daily "comics," Alice in Wonderland, amusement parks, and the folklore of television. La Barre has analyzed the projective content of responses to the popular cartoons of William Steig. Esman has described the history and cultural meaning of an American folk art in "Jazz, A

Study in Cultural Conflict." With respect to another popular amusement, the movies, Gregory Bateson has analyzed a Nazi film in his "Cultural and Thematic Analysis of Fictional Films." A longer research is reported in the book by Wolfenstein and Leites on *The Movies, A Psychological Study.* The usefulness of such psychological approaches in general has been summarized in a paper by La Barre.

BIBLIOGRAPHY

Abel, Theodora M. 1938. "Free Designs of Limited Scope as a Personality Index: A Comparison of Schizophrenics with Normal, Subnormal and Primitive Culture Groups," *Character and Personality,* 7:50–62.

Abou Zeid, A. 1946. "La psychanalyse des mythes," *Egyptian Journal of Psychology,* 2:233–51.

Abraham, K. 1913. *Dreams and Myths.* Nervous and Mental Disease Monograph Series, No. 15.

Adam, L. 1940 (revised and enlarged edition, 1949). *Primitive Art.* Pelican.

Alexander, Franz. 1957. "The Psychoanalyst Looks at Contemporary Art." In Phillips, W., *Art and Psychoanalysis.* New York: Criterion Books.

Anastasi, A. and Foley, J. P. 1936. "An Analysis of Spontaneous Drawings by Children in Different Cultures," *Journal of Applied Psychology,* 20:689–726.

———. 1938. "A Study of Animal Drawings by Indian Children of the North Pacific Coast," *Journal of Social Psychology,* 9:363–74.

Astrov, Margot. 1950. "The Conception of Motion as the Psychological Leitmotif of Navaho Life and Literature," *Journal of American Folklore,* 63:45–56.

Bartlett, F. C. 1924. "Symbolism in Folklore," *Seventh International Congress of Psychology.* Cambridge, 278–89.

Basler, Roy P. 1948. *Sex, Symbolism and Psychology in Literature.* New Brunswick: Rutgers University Press.

Bateson, G. 1943. "Cultural and Thematic Analysis of Fictional Films," *Transactions of the New York Academy of Sciences II,* 5:72–78.

Baudoin, C. 1946. "Les Symboles Fixes, Centres d'énergie, Introduction à une Étude Experimentale de l'"inconscient Collectif,'" *Revue de Psychologie Des Peuples,* 1:211–24.

Bernfeld, S. C. 1928. *Sisyphos, oder ueber die Grenzen der Erziehung.* Internationaler Psychoanalytischer Verlag, Vienna.

———. 1931. "Die Tantalus-situation," *American Imago,* 17.

———. 1951. "Freud and Archaeology," *American Imago,* 8:107–28.

Boas, Franz. 1910. "Psychological Problems in Anthropology," *American Journal of Psychology,* 21:371–84.

———. 1935. "Kwakiutl Culture as Reflected in Mythology," *Memoirs American Folklore Society,* 28.

———. 1957. *Primitive Art.* New York: Dover.

Bonaparte, M. 1941. "The Myth of the Corpse in the Car," *American Imago,* 2:105–26.

———. 1946. "The Legend of the Unfathomable Waters," *American Imago,* 4:20–31.

———. 1947. "Saint Christopher, Patron Saint of the Motor-Car Drivers," *American Imago,* 5:49–77.

Boyer, L. B. 1950. "Sculpture and Depression, A Psychiatric Study of the Life and Productions of a Depressed Sculptress," *American Journal of Psychiatry,* 106:606–15.

Brenner, A. B. 1950. "The Great Mother Goddess: Puberty Initiation Rites and the Covenant of Abraham," *Psychoanalytic Review,* 37:320–40.

Bunzel, R. 1929. "The Pueblo Potter, A Study of Creative Imagination in Primitive Art." *Columbia University Contributions to Anthropology,* 8.

———. 1938. "Primitive Art." In Boas, F. (ed.), *General Anthropology,* New York: D. C. Heath, pp. 535–88.

Charles, L. C. 1945. "The Clown's Function," *Journal of American Folklore,* 28:25–34.

Christensen, E. O. 1955. *Primitive Art.* New York: Crowell.

Codellas, P. 1945. "Modern Greek Folklore: The Smerdaki," *Journal of American Folklore,* 58:236–44.

Conrad, Jack. 1957. *The Horn and the Sword.* New York: Dutton.

Coriat, I. H. 1941. "A Note on the Medusa Symbolism," *American Imago,* 2.

Cornford, F. M. 1922. "The Unconscious Element in Literature and Philosophy," *Proceedings of the Classical Association.*

Cox, H. L. 1948. "The Place of Mythology in the Study of Culture," *American Imago,* 5:83–94.

Davis, R. G. 1957. "Art and Anxiety." In William Phillips (ed.) *Art and Psychoanalysis,* New York: Criterion Books, pp. 440–53.

Dennis, W. 1942. "The Performance of Hopi Children on the Goodenough Draw-a-Man Test," *Journal of Comparative Psychology,* 34:341–48.

Desmonde, W. 1951. "Jack and the Beanstalk," *American Imago,* 8:287–88.

———. 1952. "The Bull Fight as a Religious Ritual," *American Imago,* 9:173–95.

———. 1953. "The Eternal Fire as a Symbol of the State," *Journal of the Hillside Hospital,* 2:143–47.

———. 1953. "Psycho-Analysis and Legal Origins," *International Journal of Psycho-Analysis,* 34:1–11.

———. 1957. "The Origin of Money in Animal Sacrifice," *Journal of the Hillside Hospital,* 6:7–23.

Devereux, G. 1953. "Why Oedipus Killed Laius: A Note on the Complementary Oedipus Complex," *International Journal of Psychoanalysis,* 34:132–41.

Devereux, G. 1955. "A Counter-Oedipal Episode in Homer's Iliad," *Bulletin of the Philadelphia Association for Psychoanalysis,* 4:90–97.

———. 1957. "Penelope's Character," *Psychoanalytic Quarterly,* 26:378–86.

Dollard, J. 1939. "The Dozens: Dialectic of Insult," *American Imago,* 1:3–25.

El-Sayyad, M. M. 1945. "The Psychology of the Egyptian People from Folksongs," *Egyptian Journal of Psychology,* 1:151–71.

Engle, B. S. 1936. "Attis, A Study of Castration," *Psychoanalytic Review,* 23:363–72.

———. 1942a. "The Amazons in Ancient Greece," *Psychoanalytic Quarterly,* 11:512–44.

———. 1942b. "Malampus and Freud," *Psychoanalytic Quarterly,* 11:83–86.

———. 1945. "Lemnos, Island of Women," *Psychoanalytic Review,* 32:353–58.

Esman, A. H. 1951. "Jazz, A Study in Cultural Conflict," *American Imago,* 8:219–26.

Ferenczi, S. 1926. "The Symbolism of the Medusa's Head," *Further Contributions to Psychoanalysis,* London: Hogarth.

———. 1928. "Gulliver Phantasies," *International Journal of Psychoanalysis,* 9:283–300.

Fortune, R. F. 1926. "The Symbolism of the Serpent," *International Journal of Psychoanalysis,* 7:237–43.

Fraiberg, L. & S. 1950. "Hallowe'en: Ritual and Myth," *American Imago,* 7:289–328.

Freud, S. 1924. "Obsessive Acts and Religious Practices," *Collected Papers II.* London: Hogarth. Pp. 25–35.

———. 1924. *Psychoanalytische Studien an Werken der Dichtung und Kunst.* Leipzig: Internationaler Psychoanalytischer Verlag.

———. 1925. "The Relation of the Poet to Daydreaming," *Collected Papers IV.* London: Hogarth. Pp. 173–83.

———. 1934. "The Moses of Michelangelo," *Collected Papers IV.* London: Hogarth. Pp. 257–87.

———. 1934. "The Occurrence in Dreams of Material from Fairy-Tales," *Collected Papers IV.* London: Hogarth. Pp. 236–43.

———. 1934. "The Theme of the Three Caskets," *Collected Papers IV.* London: Hogarth. Pp. 244–56.

———. 1938. *Totem and Taboo.* Modern Library, 807–930.

———. 1939. *Moses and Monotheism.* New York: Alfred A. Knopf, Inc.

———. 1941. "Medusa's Head," *International Journal of Psychoanalysis,* 22.

———. 1943. *The Future of an Illusion.* The International Psycho-Analytical Library, No. 15.

Gaffe, R. 1945. *La Sculpture au Congo Belge.* Paris and Bruxelles: Editions du cercle d'art.

Goldfrank, E. S. 1948. "The Impact of Situation and Personality on Four Hopi Emergence Myths," *Southwestern Journal of Anthropology*, 4: 241–62.

Griaule, M. 1950. *Folk Art of Black Africa*. New York: Tudor Publication Co.

Grotjahn, M. 1940. "Ferdinand the Bull," *American Imago*, 1:33–41.

———. 1957. *Beyond Laughter*. New York: McGraw-Hill.

Gutheil, E. A. 1935. "Musical Day Dreams," *Psychoanalytic Review*, 22: 424–31.

Haldar, R. 1935. "Art and the Unconscious," *Indian Journal of Psychology*, 10:191–95.

Hambly, W. D. 1929. "The Serpent in African Belief," *American Anthropologist*, 31:655–66.

Harrison, J. E. 1921. *Epilegomena to the Study of Greek Religion*. Cambridge: The University Press.

Hassell, J. C. 1919. "The Serpent as Symbol," *Psychoanalytic Review*, 4:296–305.

Havighurst, R. J., Gunther, M. K. and Pratt, I. E. 1946. "Environment and the Draw-a-Man Test: the Performance of Indian Children," *Journal of Abnormal and Social Psychology*, 41:50–63.

Heilbronner, P. 1938. "Some Remarks on the Treatment of the Sexes in Palaeolithic Art," *International Journal of Psychoanalysis*, 19:441.

Henry, W. E. 1947. "The Thematic Apperception Technique in the Study of Culture-Personality Relations," *Genetic Psychology Monographs*, 35:3–135.

Herskovits, M. J. & F. S. 1958. *Dahomean Narrative: A Cross-Cultural Analysis*. Evanston: Northwestern University Press.

Honigmann, J. J. and Carrera, R. N. 1942. "An Interpretation of the Socio-Psychological Functions of the Ritual Clown," *Character and Personality*, 10:220–26.

———. 1944. "A Cultural Theory of Obscenity," *Journal of Criminal Psychopathology*, 5:715–33.

———. 1957. "Cross-Cultural Use of Machover's Figure Drawing Test," *American Anthropologist*, 59:650–54.

Hooper, J. T. and Burland, C. A. 1954. *The Art of Primitive Peoples*. London: Fountain Press.

Jacobs, Melville. 1951. "Psychological Inferences from a Chinook Myth." Paper delivered at the Annual Meeting of the American Anthropological Association.

Jones, E. 1923. "The Symbolic Significance of Salt in Folklore and Superstition." Chapter four in *Essays in Applied Psychoanalysis*. London and Vienna: The International Psycho-analytical Press.

———. 1926. "Snake Symbolism in Dreams," *Psyche*, 24.

Jones, E. 1933. "Psychoanalysis and the Psychology of Religion," in Lorand, S. (ed.). *Psychoanalysis Today.* New York: Covici, Friede.

Kardiner, A. 1939. *The Individual and His Society.* New York: Columbia University Press.

———. 1945. *The Psychological Frontiers of Society.* New York: Columbia University Press.

———. 1945. "The Concept of Basic Personality Structure as an Operational Tool in the Social Sciences." In Linton, R. (ed.). *The Science of Man in the World Crisis.* New York: Columbia University Press.

Karlson, K. J. 1914. "Psychoanalysis and Mythology," *Journal of Religious Psychology,* 7:137–213.

Kjersmeier, C. 1935–38. *Centres de Style de la Sculpture Nègre Africaine.* Paris: A. Morancé.

Klein, M. 1929. "Infantile Anxiety-Situations Reflected in a Work of Art and in the Creative Impulse," *International Journal of Psychoanalysis,* 10: 436–43.

Kluckhohn, C. 1942. "Myths and Rituals, A General Theory," *Harvard Theological Review,* 35:45–79.

Kohen, M. 1946. "The Venus of Willendorf," *American Imago,* 3:49–60.

Kris, E. 1944. "Approaches to Art," in Lorand, S. (ed.). *Psychoanalysis Today,* New York: International Universities Press. Pp. 354–70.

Kuhn, H. 1923. *Die Kunst der Primitiven.* München: Delphin-Verlag.

La Barre, W. 1939. "The Psychopathology of Drinking Songs," *Psychiatry,* 2:203–12.

———. 1947. "Kiowa Folk Sciences," *Journal of American Folklore,* 60: 105–14.

———. 1948. "Folklore and Psychology," *Journal of American Folklore,* 61:382–90.

———. 1949. "The Apperception of Attitudes," *American Imago,* 6:3–43.

———. 1950. "Aymara Folktales," *International Journal of American Linguistics,* 16:40–45.

———. 1952. "A Classified Bibliography of the Literature on Personality as Viewed by Dynamic Psychology," mimeographed, pp. 19–23.

———. 1954. *The Human Animal.* Chicago: University of Chicago.

———. 1955. "Obscenity: An Anthropological Appraisal," *Law and Contemporary Problems,* 20:533–43.

———. 1958. "The Influence of Freud on Anthropology," *American Imago,* 15:275–328, footnotes 22 and 23, 307–08.

Lantis, M. 1953. "Nunivak Eskimo Personality as Revealed in the Mythology," *Anthropological Papers of the University of Alaska,* vol. II, no. 1. Pp. 109–174.

Lewis, C. S. 1942. "Psycho-analysis and Literary Criticism," in *Essays and Studies by Members of the English Association,* 27:7–21. Oxford.

Lorand, S. 1937. "Fairy Tales, Lilliputian Dreams, and Neurosis," *American Journal of Orthopsychiatry*, 7:456–64.

Lowenfeld, H. 1957. "Psychic Trauma and Productive Experience in the Artist." In William Phillips (ed.), *Art and Psychoanalysis*, New York: Criterion Books.

Marett, R. R. 1920. *Psychology and Folklore*. London: Methuen and Co., Ltd.

Mather, J. 1933. "The Unconscious Significance of Fairyland," *Australian Journal of Psychology and Philosophy*, 11:258–74; 16–32.

Meggers, B. J. 1946. "Recent Trends in American Ethnology," *American Anthropologist*, 48:176–214.

Métraux, A. 1946. "The Ethnographic Approach," *Journal of American Folklore*, 59:504–06.

Moellenhoff, F. 1940. "Remarks on the Popularity of Mickey Mouse," *American Imago*, 1:19–32.

Muensterberger, W. 1951. "Roots of Primitive Art." In *Psychoanalysis and Culture Essays in Honor of Géza Róheim*. New York: International Universities Press.

———. 1955. *Sculpture of Primitive Man*. London: Thames & Hudson.

Mukerjee, Radhakumal. 1948. *The Social Function of Art*. New York: Philosophical Library.

Opler, M. K. & Obayashi, F. 1945. "Senryu Poetry as Folk and Community Expression," *Journal of American Folklore*, 58:1–11.

———. 1945. "Japanese Folk Belief Concerning the Snake," *Southwestern Journal of Anthropology*, 1:249–59.

Paget, G. 1932. "Some Drawings of Men and Women made by Children of Certain Non-European Races," *Journal of the Royal Anthropological Institute* [of Great Britain and Ireland], 62:127–144.

Phillipps, L. M. 1951. *The Works of Man*. New York: Philosophical Library.

Portier, A. and Poncetton, F. 1930. *Les Arts Sauvages-Afrique*. Paris: A. Morancé.

Puckett, N. N. 1934. "Negro Character as Revealed in Folk Lore," *Publications of the American Sociological Society*, 28:12–23.

Radin, P. 1956. *The Trickster: A Study in American Indian Mythology*. London: Routledge and Paul.

Randle, M. C. 1952. "Psychological Types from Iroquois Folktales," *Journal of American Folklore*, 65:13–21.

Rank, Q. 1912. *Das Inzestmotiv in Dichtung und Sage*. Vienna: Franz Deutiche.

———. 1913. *The Myth of the Birth of the Hero*. New York: Nervous & Mental Disease Monograph Series, No. 18.

———. 1913. "Die Nacktheit in Sage und Dichtung," *American Imago*, 2.

———. 1919. *Psychoanalytische Beiträge zur Mythenforschung*. Vienna: Internationaler Psychoanalytischer Verlag.

Rasmussen, R. 1951. *Art Nègre, ou le Salut par les Sauvages*. Paris: Presses du libre français.

Reed, R. 1922. "Serpent as Phallic Symbol," *Psychoanalytic Review*, 9: 91–92.

Reik, T. 1940. *Ritual: Psychoanalytic Studies*. New York: International Universities Press.

————. 1951. *Dogma and Compulsion*. New York: International Universities Press.

Reitman, F. 1954. *Insanity, Art and Culture*. New York: Philosophical Library.

Riklin, F. 1915. *Wishfulfillment and Symbolism in Fairy Tales*. Nervous and Mental Disease Monograph Series, No. 21.

Róheim, Géza. 1912. *Drachen und Drachenkämpfer*. Berlin.

————. 1912. "Survivals of Shamanistic Cure in a Nursery Rhyme," *Ethnographia*, 23:360–62.

————. 1913. "Zwei Gruppen von Igelsagen," *Zeitschrift des Deutscher Verein für Volkskunde*, 23:404–14.

————. 1915. "Killing the Divine King," *Man*, 15:26–28.

————. 1917. "Spiegelzauber," *American Imago*, 5:63–120.

————. 1918. "Nefanda Carmina," *Ethnographia*, 29:271–76.

————. 1919. "Allerseelen im Volksbrauch und Volksglauben," *Pester Lloyd*, 11:4–6.

————. 1920. "Zur Psychologie des Bundesriten," *American Imago*, 6:397–99.

————. 1921. "Ethnologie und Völkerpsychologie," *Bericht über die Fortschritte der Psychoanalyse*, 1914–1919. Pp. 164–94.

————. 1922. "Psycho-Analysis and the Folk-Tale," *International Journal of Psycho-Analysis*, 3:180–86.

————. 1922. "The Significance of Stepping Over," *International Journal of Psycho-Analysis*, 3:320–26.

————. 1922. "Stone-Shrine and Tomb: Ethnological Remarks on Totemism and Culture Stages in Australia," *International Journal of Psycho-Analysis*, 3:121–27.

————. 1923. "Heiliges Geld in Melanesien," *Internationale Zeitschrift für Psychoanalyse*, 9:384–401.

————. 1923. "The Passage of the Red Sea," *Man*, 23:152–55.

————. 1923. "Passover and Initiation," *Man*, 23:178.

————. 1924. *Elementargedanke, Wanderungstheorie und das Unbewusste*. Budapest: Pester Lloyd.

————. 1924. "Die Sedna Sage," *American Imago*, 10:159–77.

————. 1925. "Arunta and Marind-Anim," *Anthropologica Hungarica*, 1:1–11.

———. 1925. *Australian Totemism.* London: G. Allen & Unwin, Ltd.

———. 1925. "Cuchulainn and the Origin of Totemism," *Man*, 25:85–88.

———. 1925. "The Pointing Bone," *Journal of the Royal Anthropological Institute*, 45:90–114.

———. 1926. "Hungarian Calendar Customs," *Journal of the Royal Anthropological Institute*, 56:361–84.

———. 1926. "Die Völkerpsychologie und die Psychologie der Völker," *American Imago*, 12:273–91.

———. 1926. "Die Wilde Jagd," *American Imago*, 12:465–77.

———. 1927. *Mondmythologie und Mondreligion.* Vienna, & *American Imago*, 13:442–537.

———. 1928. "Mother Earth and the Children of the Sun," *Jubilee Congress of the Folk-Lore Society.* London, 1930, pp. 238–64.

———. 1929. "Dying Gods and Puberty Ceremonies," *Journal of the Royal Anthropological Institute*, 59:181–97.

———. 1930. *Animism, Magic and the Divine King.* London: K. Paul, Trench, Trubner & Co.

———. 1930. "Zur Deutung der Zwergsagen," *Internationale Zeitschrift für Psychoanalyse*, 16:95–105.

———. 1932. "Animism and Religion," *Psychoanalytic Quarterly*, 1:59–113.

———. 1937. "Death and Mourning Ceremonies at Normanby Island," *Man*, 37:59–60.

———. 1939. "The Covenant of Abraham," *International Journal of Psycho-Analysis*, 20:452–59.

———. 1939. "Racial Differences in the Neurosis and Psychosis," *Psychiatry*, 2:375–90.

———. 1940. "The Dragon and the Hero," *American Imago*, 1 (2), 40–69; 1 (3), 61–94.

———. 1940. "The Garden of Eden," *Psychoanalytic Review*, 27:1–26; 177–99.

———. 1940. "Magic and Theft in European Folk-Lore." *Journal of Criminal Psychopathology*, 2:54–61.

———. 1941. "Myth and Folk-Tale," *American Imago*, 2:266–79.

———. 1942. "Transition Rites," *Psychoanalytic Quarterly*, 11:336–74.

———. 1943. "Children's Games and Rhymes in Duau (Normanby Island)," *American Anthropologist*, 45:99–119.

———. 1945. "Aphrodite, Or the Woman with the Penis," *Psychoanalytic Quarterly*, 14:350–90.

———. 1945. *The Eternal Ones of the Dream.* New York: International Universities Press.

———. 1945. "War, Crime and the Covenant," *Journal of Clinical Psychopathology, Monograph Series* No. 1.

Róheim, Géza. 1946. "Charon and the Obolos," *Psychiatric Quarterly Supplement*, 20:160–96.

————. 1946. "Saint Agatha and the Tuesday Woman," *International Journal of Psycho-Analysis*, 27:119–126.

————. 1946. "Teiresias and Other Seers," *Psychoanalytic Review*, 33:314–34.

————. 1947. "The Story of the Light That Disappeared," *Samiksa*, 1:51–85.

————. 1948. "The Bear in the Haunted Mill," *American Imago*, 5:70–82.

————. 1948. "The Divine Child," *Journal of Criminal Psychopathology*, 9:309–23.

————. 1948. "The Song of the Sirens," *Psychiatric Quarterly*, 22:18–44.

————. 1948. "The Thread of Life," *Psychoanalytic Quarterly*, 17:471–86.

————. 1948. "Witches of Normanby Island," *Oceania*, 18:279–308.

————. 1949. "The Symbolism of Subincision," *American Imago*, 6:321–28.

————. 1950. "Fire in the Dragon," *American Imago*, 7:3–11.

————. 1950. "The Oedipus Complex, Magic and Culture," *Psychoanalysis and the Social Sciences*, 2:173–228.

————. 1950. "Totemism in Normanby Island," *Mankind*, 5:189–95.

————. 1951. "Hungarian Shamanism," *Psychoanalysis and the Social Sciences*, 3:131–69.

————. 1951. "Mythology of Arnhem Land," *American Imago*, 8.

Rosenzweig, E. M. 1941. "Surrealism as Symptom," *American Imago*, 2:286–95.

Sadler, M. E. (ed.). 1935. *Arts of West Africa*. Oxford University Press.

Schubert, A. 1930. "Drawings of Orotchen Children and Young People," *Journal of Genetic Psychology*, 37:232–44.

Schweeger, A. 1948. *Afrikanische Bronzen*. Wien: Wolfram.

Segy, L. 1952. *African Sculpture Speaks*. New York: Wyn.

Seligman, C. G. 1940. "A Note on Neurosis in Three Celebrated Chinese Painters," *Character and Personality*, 9:49–50.

Steggerda, M. 1936. "The McAdory Art Test Applied to Navaho Indian Children," *Journal of Comparative Psychology*, 22:283–85.

————. 1941. "Form Discrimination Test as Given to Navajo, Negro and White School Children," *Human Biology*, 13:239–46.

Sterba, R. 1941. "A Dutch Celebration of a Festival," *American Imago*, 2:205–208.

————. 1948. "On Hallowe'en," *American Imago*, 5:213–24.

————. 1948. "Kilroy was Here," *American Imago*, 5:173–91.

Sweeney, J. J. 1935. *African Negro Art*. New York: Museum of Modern Art.

Sydow, Eckart. 1954. *Afrikanische Plastik*. New York: Wittenborn.

Tarachow, S. 1948. "Totem Feast in Modern Dress," *American Imago*, 5.

Taylor, G. R. 1954. *Sex in History*. New York: Vanguard.

Taylor, W. S. 1944. "A Note on the Cultural Determination of Free Drawing," *Character and Personality,* 13:30–36.

Thorner, I. 1945. "German Words, German Personality and Protestantism," *Psychiatry,* 8:403–17.

Trilling, L. 1957. "Art and Neurosis." In Phillips, W. *Art and Psychoanalysis.* New York: Criterion Books.

Trowell, M. 1954. *Classical African Sculpture*. New York: Praeger.

Wallace, A. F. C. 1950. "A Possible Technique for Recognizing Psychological Characteristics of the Ancient Maya from an Analysis of their Art," *American Imago,* 7:239–58.

———. 1958. "Dreams and Wishes of the Soul: A Type of Psychoanalytic Theory among the Seventeenth Century Iroquois," *American Anthropologist,* 60:234–48.

Webster, D. 1940. "Origin of the Signs of the Zodiac," *American Imago,* 1:31–47.

Weigert-Vowinckel, E. 1937. "The Cult and Mythology of the Magna Mater," *Psychiatry,* 1:347–78.

Weltfish, G. 1953. *Origins of Art*. Indianapolis: Bobbs-Merrill.

Wilson, E. 1957. "Philoctetes: The Wound and the Bow." In Phillips, W. *Art and Psychoanalysis.* New York: Criterion Books.

Wissler, Clark. 1906. "A Psycho-Physical Element in Primitive Art." In *Boas, Anniversary Volume,* 189–92.

Wolfenstein, M. and Leites, N. 1950. *The Movies, A Psychological Study.* Glencoe, Illinois: Free Press.

Zelig, D. F. 1952. "Two Episodes in the Life of Jacob," *American Imago,* 10:181–203.

About the Chapter

It may seem paradoxical that one of the best ways to understand normal personality processes in a culture is to study the ways that people become mentally ill. Normality and abnormality, rather than being poles apart, are very intimately related. Each may be thought of as being in large part defined by the other. If modal personality processes are understood as constituting the kind of normality that is fostered by the group, prevalent patterns of mental illness can be understood as reflecting that which is specially disruptive or troublesome to social systems. Dr. Kennedy suggests that these patterns vary considerably from group to group and may also be culturally shaped. An awareness of trouble spots within the social system may lead to an appreciation of the implicit and covert patterns that are difficult for the field worker to discover, just as we frequently find that the themes in the overt mental life of mentally ill persons often exist in covert fashion in normal persons. Dr. Kennedy's paper discusses fourteen issues that are pertinent to the cross-cultural study of mental illness.

About the Author

DONALD A. KENNEDY is Research Fellow in the Training Program for Social Scientists in Medicine at Harvard University. He is also Assistant Social Anthropologist at McLean Hospital, a Division of the Massachusetts General Hospital. Dr. Kennedy received his graduate training in the Department of Sociology and Anthropology at Cornell University where he was associated with the Stirling County Study and the Cornell Project on Culture and Applied Science at the field station in the American Southwest.

Acknowledgments

This study has been carried out as part of the Cornell Program in Social Psychiatry. Financial support has been provided by the Ford Foundation, by a pre-doctoral fellowship from the National Institutes of Health, and by the Harvard Training Program for Social Scientists in Medicine. The author wishes to express his appreciation to Alexander H. Leighton for his enduring interest and active support of this research, and to Bert Kaplan for his editorial assistance. The members of the Training Program for Social Scientists in Medicine at the Department of Social Relations, Harvard University, gave valuable aid through discussion and critical commentary of the ideas expressed in this chapter.

12

Key Issues in the Cross-Cultural
Study of Mental Disorders

DONALD A. KENNEDY

Harvard University

Introduction

Within recent years there has been a quickening of interest in studies of mental illness in the community and family habitats where symptoms first emerge. Sociologists, psychologists, and anthropologists have joined with psychiatrists to study problems such as the distribution of psychiatric cases in the general population and identification of etiological factors in the sociocultural environment. The work of Eaton and Weil (1955); the Leightons (1955, 1956, 1959); and of Hollingshead and Redlich (1958) are examples of such studies. But these studies have, for the most part, been conducted within the framework of the dominant Anglo-American culture of the United States and Canada. Cultural contrast has been limited to *subcultural* variations to be found in comparing ethnic groups, social classes, and family types.

With the emergence of the new field of social psychiatry (Leighton, Clausen, and Wilson, 1957) and the re-awakening of interest in cross-cultural method (Whiting, 1954), we find ourselves at the start of a series of empirical investigations aimed at the cross-cultural study of mental disorders. Studies now in the active planning stage include Bert

Kaplan's comparative study of forms of psychopathology among the Navaho and Zuni, and Alexander Leighton's extension of work begun in Nova Scotia and New York City to include a community of non-literate peoples outside the Anglo-American cultural tradition.

As part of the preliminary planning for the latter project, I conducted two pilot studies among the Navaho Indians of the American Southwest and undertook library research to identify key issues to be faced by a program of empirical research in this subject area (Kennedy, 1959). Out of this survey of the literature and testing of methods of approach under actual field conditions, I formulated a series of problems that I felt to be essential for consideration during the "first-round" of research.

For purposes of presentation, I have grouped these issues according to their intrinsic interest to the psychiatrist *or* to the anthropologist. Although both kinds of specialist will participate in a cross-cultural study in the field, there will be a tendency for the psychiatrist to focus attention upon certain issues of primary interest to psychiatric medicine and for the anthropologist to place an emphasis on problems of more traditional interest to his field. This is not to discount the contributions of each specialty to the goals of the team effort, but to suggest that both professions may find important topics to explore from their respective vantage points. The fourteen issues to be presented are grouped into three major classes: those of primary interest to the psychiatrist; those of interest to psychiatry and anthropology in about equal measure; and those of primary interest to cultural anthropology.

FROM THE VANTAGE POINT OF SOCIAL PSYCHIATRY

Epidemiology: the Location and Counting of Psychiatric Cases

Epidemiology is the study of the distribution of disease in human populations. It is, in a sense, the investigative branch of the public health field. The basic method is to locate populations with high rates of illness and those with low rates, and then to search for factors which may be responsible for these differences. The methods are fairly simple in conception. They have led to considerable success in understanding and controlling germ diseases such as yellow fever, typhus, and tuberculosis as well as such illnesses as beri beri and sickle cell anemia. It has been only in very recent years, however, that attempts have been made to extend this approach to the study of psychiatric disorders (Milbank, 1950; Gruenberg, 1954). Recent research that has used this approach includes the work of Eaton and Weil among the Hutterites, the field study of the Leightons in Nova Scotia, the project initiated by Thomas Rennie in New York City, and the investigations of Hollingshead and Redlich in New Haven.

Information gained through epidemiological research is of value on several accounts. First, there is the possibility of locating previously undetected factors of etiology and contagion. Second, basic administrative information is acquired which indicates how to allocate psychiatric facilities and personnel so as to make optimum use of limited resources and to improve service to those parts of the community that require the most assistance. Third, even without a thorough understanding of the etiology involved, it may be possible to predict and take preventive action. Knowledge of indicators of change in the community may make it possible to pragmatically forecast an increase in incidence of disease. If rapid change in migration rate or extensive acculturation occurs in a community, then we may be able to predict an increase in mental disorders in the population even though we do not understand just how this comes about.

In a cross-cultural approach, the basic epidemiological question to be asked is: What difference, if any, is there in actual prevalence and incidence rates for psychiatric illness between large, industrial, urban societies and small, rural, tribal societies? The Eaton and Weil study was directed to this question, but it is necessary to extend their work into a non-literate group where the cultural contrast is even greater than that exhibited by the Hutterites.

In order to collect data to answer this question, we must not only solve extremely difficult definitional problems as to what constitutes "a psychiatric case," "psychiatric symptoms," and "degrees of impairment"; we also must utilize a single method of assessment in two groups of sharply contrasting racial and cultural makeup. And once the transcultural standards have been devised, a further difficulty remains in implementing the diagnostic procedures themselves. Since the services of a psychiatrist are a rare commodity—especially in the epidemiological and research field —it will assist the research endeavor if questionnaire and interview survey techniques can be adapted to this assessment task. As will be reported in a forthcoming book, the Leightons have attempted to test questionnaire results against clinical evaluations made by a team of psychiatrists in their Stirling County Study (Macmillan, 1957). It is to be hoped that techniques will be devised to substitute for lengthy clinical interviews, so that non-psychiatrists may be trained to conduct the evaluations in the future.

There remains one further complication. The epidemiological question at stake here is one of determining *actual* rates of prevalence and incidence rather than *treated,* or known rates. In the past, most reports of rates of mental illness have been estimates based upon hospital admission figures and similar kinds of data collected by service agencies. An investigation of actual rates requires, (1) a random sampling of the total population, and (2) an assessment of whether the selected individuals exhibit evidence of mental disorders. The study of Hollingshead and Redlich (1958) is based upon *treated* prevalence rates; the work of the Leightons (D. C. Leighton, 1956) is based upon *actual* or true prevalence rates.

In summary then, epidemiological research provides us with basic background information about the types and rates of mental illness in the natural surroundings of the community. Against this baseline we can conduct specialized studies in order to more rigorously attack problems of etiology or to plan programs of improved medical service.

Situations of Stress in the Sociocultural Environment

In order to locate etiological features of the sociocultural environment it is first necessary to identify events and kinds of interpersonal interaction which cause anxiety, tension, and stress for members of the cultural group under study. A set of standard categories must be developed for the classification of situations and the location and measurement of indications of stressful reaction or strain in the participants.

The concept of "situation" is crucial to this approach. Although a number of social scientists have used this idea in their work, few attempts have been made to provide a standard classification scheme for observing and categorizing "situations" as such. An important exception to this is the work of Henry A. Murray (1938) in the field of personality theory. By his use of the concept of "press" he has given serious attention to the problem of classifying the environment that operates on any individual at a given time. In more recent years there have been other attempts. Ruesch and Prestwood (1950) have provided a descriptive set of approximately forty social situations. Their discussion emphasizes sociological factors more than personality variables, as is the case with Murray's scheme. In a recent book, Timothy Leary (1957) presents a classification system for collecting data on interactions. This system may prove valuable in describing key features of the social environment in the interactional sphere. But more work must be done in methodology if the study of "pathogenic situations" in the social environment is to be pursued on the level of small groups and interpersonal relations.

In a more theoretical vein, the work of Hans Selye (1956) on biological stress may be useful to the study of pathogenic situations on a psychosocial level of analysis. Although Selye's set of "stressors" is limited to physical and biochemical types of agents, there is little doubt that his general line of reasoning might be extended to sociocultural factors as well. His discovery of the General Adaptation Syndrome, which is triggered by a wide variety of stressful agents operating on the organism, gives a biological background for the kinds of problems we are exploring in a psychological and sociocultural frame of reference. There is also the work of Parsons and his students, which has centered attention on the stresses and strains inherent in the role systems and social structures of a society (Barrabee, 1951; Sutton, 1956; Field, 1957). Analysis in terms of role conflict and ideological conflict has often yielded new insights into social events where dysfunction and friction are most evident. Leighton's (1959b) work in the area of conflict in "systems of sentiments" falls within the scope of this orientation as well.

To sum up, it appears that in the study of a small, tribal village it should be possible to collect data on role conflict and interpersonal influence that are difficult to elicit in a society with a multiplicity of occupations, a high level of literacy, and a well-developed system of mass media of communication. In a non-literate society, where the only channels of communication are through face-to-face contact and the system of social situations is fairly rudimentary, it seems feasible to press beyond the gross variables of *social disorganization* and *social class* to learn how specific features of the sociocultural environment operate so as to induce or modify the emergence of psychopathology.

The Clarification of Concepts

This problem has both theoretical and methodological facets. What kinds of clarifications are necessary when the terms "illness," "health," and "symptom" are applied to mental disorders? For the practicing physician this is a needless worry; but for the field worker engaged in epidemiological research it becomes a critical problem. Further difficulties arise when an attempt is made to relate these concepts to the ideas of "deviance" and "conformity" as used by the social scientist. As the term "illness" is further extended from the biological sphere into psychological and sociocultural realms, the problem of explication becomes particularly acute. And yet interest grows in the possibility of applying these basic ideas to events in the sociocultural domain. Temple Burling at Cornell University has long been concerned with what he calls "the clinical treatment of group problems"; Caudill (1958) and others have reported cases of "collective disturbances" in mental hospitals; and Leighton (1959b) has written of "disorganized communities and neighborhoods" in a manner indicating the strong influence of health and illness concepts from the field of medicine.

On an empirical level, questions arise as to how different groups and actors in various social roles look at the definition of mental illness and related events such as crime. In our own society, the lawyer and the judge often do not share the viewpoint of the psychiatrist, the social worker, or the minister in regards to these concepts. Even within the medical and psychiatric professions it is difficult to find a consensus on the boundary points for various syndromes. And as Leighton points out, this is seldom a concern for the therapist, who has only to treat the already diagnosed individual referred to him. Unlike the epidemiologist, the clinician does not roam the streets of the town looking for "cases."

When approaching the study of mental illness in a culture radically different from our own, the question of viewpoint and definition becomes indeed challenging. Non-literate peoples share few of the perceptions and assumptions of western medicine as to diagnostic categories, etiologic agents, and therapeutic methods (Winslow, 1944, Chapters I–III). Their systems of thought emphasize supernatural causes and most of their techniques of treatment utilize magical means (Whiting and Child, 1953, pp. 122–123). Even in the attempt to match patterns of symptoms, the physician and the medicine man may find it difficult to agree (Kennedy, 1959, p. 73). As Ladd (1957, p. 223) has noted in his study of Navaho thinking, there is a preference for classifying diseases, not according to patterns of symptom, but according to presumed cause. And these presumed causes range from contact with ghosts, witches, or certain animals, to improper conduct at a ceremonial, or experiencing a physical trauma such as falling off a horse (Wyman, 1957, pp. 16–18; Kluckhohn and Leighton, 1946, p. 132). Because of these differences of perception and definition to be anticipated in a study of mental illness among a non-literate group, concepts of a high order of abstraction should be avoided in working with native informants. The data need to be collected in the form of a number of concrete and detailed case examples derived from the experience of the informant.

The last point directs our attention to the need for a field approach which will study the distribution of personality patterns in a community while at the same time searching for people who show signs of psychiatric symptoms. Kaplan and Plaut (1956) have pioneered this approach in their work on patterns of personality and psychopathology among the Hutterites. This approach counterbalances the exclusive concern with pathology that marks epidemiological research and tends to point up the intimate relationship between normal and abnormal personality process (Parsons and Bales, 1955, p. 243). In a similar vein, Leighton *et al.* (1957) have made a strong plea for a return to descriptive psychiatry in an era when etiology and treatment receive so much attention in psychiatry. All of these suggestions are applicable to the planning of field studies among non-literates where the informants are not facile in working long chains of abstract reasoning of the type that dominates the communication process of psychiatrists trained in western medicine.

As a number of authors have pointed out (Suchman *et al.,* 1955) the methodological problems of equivalence of concept are exceedingly difficult in cross-cultural studies. But they must be dealt with in some pragmatic way in order to conduct empirical studies on a comparative basis. As a minimum, it is necessary to describe a set of criteria and explicit boundary conditions which can be applied, for general classification purposes, on a transcultural basis. A variety of criteria have been suggested and Redlich (1957) provides a survey and discussion of current trends of thinking. Much more attention to this subject is required, however, as empirical studies are started in groups of contrasting culture.

The concept of "positive mental health" needs further study and clarification as well. Any program of prevention and education in the field of mental illness and mental health requires a set of explicit standards and positive goals. And the mental health movement in this country has reached the stage where a large number of individuals and agencies are urgently requesting such a set of criteria (Jahoda, 1958). In research on a cross-cultural dimension it is necessary to expand our horizons from a nearly exclusive interest in abnormality to a careful study of normal and even optimal personality functioning (Maslow, 1954, pp. 199–234).

In summary then, there are a number of problems of conceptual clarification that require attention during empirical study of mental disorders in societies other than our own. These conceptual difficulties appear to stem from: (1) attempts to extend epidemiological method founded on the study of infectious disease to the area of mental illness morbidity; (2) application of concepts of illness and health to non-biological levels in the study of psychodynamics, group and sociocultural process; (3) attempts to integrate the conceptual frameworks of behavioral science and medicine when studying events such as "mental disorders," "sociopathic behavior," and "deviance;" (4) extrapolating from concepts of illness and disease process to outline positive concepts of mental health; (5) initiation of cross-cultural comparisons in populations which do not share the perceptions of western medicine as to diagnostic categories, etiological agents, and methods of treatment.

Possible Discovery of New Forms of Psychopathology

How ethnocentric is the present classification of psychiatric disorders developed by western psychiatry? Over the past thirty years, anthropologists have reported a number of unusual forms of extreme behavior of possible interest to social psychiatry. Kluckhohn (1954, pp. 943–947) and Linton (1956) have discussed some of the more striking examples of this abnormal behavior reported among non-literate tribes. I shall mention briefly only a few of their examples for purposes of illustration and commentary.

Witchcraft has been reported on quite extensively. For our purposes there are two things of particular interest in the subject. First, among such groups as the Navaho, there seems to be a close association between accusations of witchcraft and implications of "craziness." Second, there is the distinct possibility that witches who are killed are the psychiatric cases of the village being "treated" for this affliction in a peculiarly abrupt manner. Thus the study of witchcraft falls within the purview of a cross-cultural search for new forms of pathology.

Magical death, or *voodoo death,* represents another extreme behavior of interest to the psychiatrist. Cannon (1942) offered a tentative explanation of these cases of "psychic death" in terms of psychosomatic reaction to extreme fear. But any set of beliefs that can operate to produce such results seems worthy of first-hand study by competent psychiatrists. Psychic death may, then, become a candidate for inclusion in the category of "psychophysiological disorders."

The *windigo psychosis* which occurred among the Chippewa and Cree tribes of Canada during historic times is another unusual form of psychological state that usually results in death for the victim. Here the individual, under conditions of extreme deprivation and isolation during winter months, would cannibalize his own family until tracked down and killed (Linton, 1956, pp. 65–67). This is one of the most startling examples of psychosis to be found among non-literate peoples. But it remains to be seen whether we can locate any cases of this type in the world today.

Running amok among the men of the Malays has a similar suicidal result. The individual would "run amok," killing anyone in his path. The hysteric nature of this reaction is fairly certain, because the condition disappeared shortly after the Dutch authorities insisted that the "patient" be caught alive and confined to several years at hard labor instead of being killed (Linton, 1956, p. 116). This is another historical example that gives no clues as to whether similar cases may be found today in that part of the world.

In a more recent study, Kaplan and Plaut (1956) point to a specific form of depression frequently encountered among the Hutterites called "anfectung." In this type of depression, members of this highly religious community become convinced that they have sinned and succumbed to the intentions of the devil. The imposition of basic beliefs of Hutterite society upon the content of the depression is strikingly evident.

Some of these unusual forms of behavior are quite understandable in terms of cultural variation in the content of the symptoms. For example, certain types of "snake sickness" among the Navaho appear to be hysteria with a content determined by Navaho taboos about contact with snakes (Kennedy, 1959, p. 145). But there remains the possibility that we may find a syndrome or a new subtype that will require a modification of our system of diagnostic categories (American Psychiatric Association, 1952).

It will be interesting to see if cross-cultural studies extend the range of variation within any given category of mental disorder to the point where we find new relationships between clinical types and etiologic agents. At the very least, a search for new forms may assist western psychiatry in enlarging its perspective on nosology and pointing up some implicit assumptions that operate as organizing principles in the present system of classification. Further, if we do find new forms of psychosis, neurosis, or psychophysiological reaction, it may be possible to determine the relative importance of biological and sociocultural factors which control the patterning of their specific form.

Before leaving this topic it should be mentioned that the cases cited in the literature are of only limited value to the psychiatrist doing research in cross-cultural psychiatry. In any serious quest for new forms of psychopathology, the psychiatrist must find actual clinical cases in order to conduct his investigations. Library research can only suggest where he might look for unusual forms; it cannot provide the ample detail and accurate description necessary for clinical assessment and verification.

A Testing Ground for Psychiatric Theories

A major contribution of anthropology to the study of human behavior has been to emphasize the cultural variability to be found in the living patterns of mankind. Observations and assumptions about the "nature of human nature" have been made many times during the development of European civilization. Some of these beliefs about invariant universals have been brought seriously into question by studies in groups of contrasting culture. The several thousands of cultures in the world provide a natural laboratory in which various hypotheses may be tested. Malinowski's work (1927) on the Freudian theory of the *Oedipus complex* provides an example of this kind of test in the cross-cultural laboratory.

In his studies of the Trobriand Islanders, Malinowski came to the conclusion that the *Oedipus complex* did not exist in that society. Linton (1956, p. 99) proposed an alternate explanation by indicating that the oedipal relationship probably involves the mother's brother instead of the biological father, for it is the mother's brother who provides the male discipline for the child. According to Linton's interpretation, Freud's assumption about the biological nature of the parent-child relationship should be modified to emphasize the social roles of parental figures who interact with the child during the enculturation process.

With this work of Malinowski and Linton in mind, it seems reasonable to propose that psychiatrists make it an explicit practice to test specific theories and hypotheses in a clinic located among a non-literate group of contrasting racial and cultural characteristics. This stratagem could provide a rapid testing of ideas about etiology and therapy for a wide range of disorders. Both psychodynamic and biological theories could be studied in such a setting. The geographical isolation, small numbers of people, differences in racial stock, and strict marriage rules to be found in many tribal societies would provide an opportunity to check ideas about hereditary factors in the etiology of certain mental disorders. In a research-oriented clinic located in a non-literate group, psychiatrists might avail themselves of a number of racial and cultural contrasts so as to gain precious leverage on some of the perplexing problems that face them in understanding the causes and cures of mental illness.

FROM THE VANTAGE POINT OF PSYCHIATRY AND CULTURAL ANTHROPOLOGY

The Indigenous Viewpoint toward Psychopathology

Psychiatrists and anthropologists share a common interest in understanding the subjective viewpoint of the people they study. To practice psychiatry it is necessary to learn about the beliefs and perceptions of the patient; to do field work of the classic ethnographic type it is necessary to report the world view of the non-literate group under investigation.

Consequently, any study of psychopathology in a non-literate society must include a description of the relevant native vocabulary and beliefs. What are the indigenous categories of mental illness? What are the assumptions as to cause and effective cure? Where are their boundaries on the events that *we classify* as mental illness and criminal behavior? What kinds of action and subjective experience do they label "illness," and institute treatment to correct? Under what conditions is one of their group exempted from normal role obligations and defined as "sick"?

To give some idea of the kinds of beliefs likely to be encountered in such a study, I shall present a few of the Navaho beliefs on the etiology of mental illness, to illustrate the differences from our western views (Kennedy, 1959, pp. 160–162). As with other forms of sickness, the Navaho believe that mental disorders result from violations of taboo, contact with witches, and the suffering of physical trauma. You can become crazy if you marry a woman who is not a Navaho, or if you stir food with an arrow, or leave the poker pointing into the fire, or if you gamble too much.

A child will be born mentally deficient if the father completes the making of a buffalo-tail rattle during his wife's pregnancy; if the dog eats the afterbirth; or if the father sees a bear. If a man falls from his horse and is knocked unconscious, he may become mentally deranged. If a person beats a witch, he will become crazy; fainting and epileptic seizures are principal symptoms of victims of witchcraft. And violations of the incest taboo invariably result in insanity for one or both of the participants.

Of all the factors mentioned above, violation of the incest taboo assumes a central position in Navaho discussion of the cause of mental illness. Insanity is the supernatural punishment for incestuous relationships. Here is very strong reinforcement for the prohibition in Navaho culture against marriage within either the clan of the mother or the father. And as Kluckhohn and Leighton (1946, p. 64) report, violations of this prohibition are very rare indeed.

Insanity is also connected with witchcraft. Since witches are assumed to engage in incest and other forms of repulsive and forbidden behavior, any person suspected of witchcraft is likely to be considered mentally ill. An ordinary person can become mentally ill from accidental contact with a witch, or from witchcraft intentionally directed at him as its victim. As previously mentioned, epileptic seizures and fainting spells are considered the result of witchcraft. In Navaho mythology this connection between incest, insanity, and witchcraft is maintained as a recurrent theme (Kluckhohn and Leighton, 1946, p. 136).

Thus we find a crucial connection between the condition of mental disorder and two activities which the Navaho consider the most serious of crimes—incest and witchcraft. Navahos fear insanity because it is the supernatural punishment for violation of the most serious taboos in their society. For this reason we can appreciate the reluctance of Navaho informants to freely discuss with outsiders the subject of mental illness.

Comparison of this set of etiological beliefs with those of western psychiatry reveals several contrasts. Navahos place heavy emphasis upon supernatural entities to explain cause and effect; psychiatrists postulate only natural entities of empirical science. Navahos hold the patient responsible for his present state of illness if he violated one or several taboos; western medicine exempts the patient from such personal responsibility for his diseased condition. The Navaho patient is exempted from responsibility through becoming a target of witchcraft; the western physician believes it is impossible for such magical action to occur at a distance. On the patterning of symptoms, the Navaho pay little attention to the Aristotelian "law of the excluded middle" (Kluckhohn, 1949, p. 368) and find it difficult to describe an invariant relationship between a given cluster of symptoms and one set of postulated etiological agents; the western doctor assumes this requirement of pattern invariance in his diagnostic work as well as in his search for causative agents of disease.

As may be seen in this brief account, there are many features that make it difficult to elicit and to crystallize an indigenous pattern of belief and then to formulate it in a way that assists comparison with the belief systems of western psychiatry. Although the difficulties appear to be considerable, the possibilities for future study look especially challenging for both the research psychiatrist and the field anthropologist.

Personality Development: Normal and Abnormal

While the study of mental illness encompasses the entire life-arc of the individual, most theories of etiology in psychiatry have placed special emphasis upon the earliest phases of personality development and the socialization process. As a result of this emphasis, we will need a detailed description of the child rearing patterns of non-literate societies selected for study. How do the parents treat the child? How are rewards and punishments administered? How are the universal problems of weaning, toilet training, sex play, aggression, and dependency handled? Where are the points of conflict and strain? Where do the emotional vulnerabilities and ego strengths get their start?

Normal and abnormal personality development apparently are intermingled and must be studied within a single conceptual framework. In a recent publication (Parsons and Bales, 1955, pp. 243–257), Parsons and Olds have given a general outline of how this may be accomplished. They feel that there are no separate mechanisms for the emergence of normal and pathological patterns; there are only differences as to conditions on a given set of parameters. This theoretical approach must be given serious attention by investigators entering the field in a cross-cultural project that includes the study of personality development.

In accordance with this view of the phenomenological relatedness of normal and abnormal process, indications of unusual psychological health should be studied at the same time a search is conducted for psychiatric symptoms. This is in keeping with the approach of Kaplan and Plaut (1956) whose research design called for a mapping of the distribution of personality patterns within the Hutterite community without initial regard for evaluations in terms of mental illness or mental health.

During a study of child development we also have the opportunity to check on the concept of basic personality structure. Is there a modal type of personality which is molded by a standard set of socialization practices, and which the adult members of the society use as a guide to their judgments of deviant behavior and psychiatric disorder? In their definitions of deviancy and abnormality, what standards do they use? Is it inability to perform certain minimal role behaviors, or is it malfunction of personality in a wider and more general sense?

But whatever theoretical orientation is taken, it will be necessary to study personality development in the early years of life, as well as the patterns of influence exerted by adults as part of the process of enculturation. There is little likelihood that a cross-cultural study of mental disorders can avoid the cross-cultural study of personality development in a very real and important sense.

The Natural History of Variant Behavior

In addition to the longitudinal study of personality development, the natural history of the growth of psychopathology and other forms of deviance must be described. Working backward from the extreme forms of deviance where the culprit is clearly identified and the most severe sanctions have been imposed, we must ask what the earlier incipient stages were like when this person was described as simply "a difficult person," or "an eccentric who was hard to get along with." We must learn to identify variant behavior at early points in its career so as to better understand the forces that bring it into being and cast it in a specific form.

A study in time depth should also reveal important features of the interplay between emergent forms of variant behavior and the changing definitions placed upon that behavior by individuals in the immediate social environment. Here we might learn how significant persons who are in daily interaction with the potential deviant define his actions and accommodate themselves to his problematic acts before finally resorting to a request for aid from formal authorities such as the medicine man, the police, or the white doctor.

As Schwartz (1957) has pointed out, there are various perspectives on problematic behavior held by incumbents of different social roles related to the potential deviant. The wife of the mental patient does not define her husband's behavior in the same way the psychiatrist does. Furthermore, these definitions shift during the natural history of deviance as the people in complementary roles attempt to maintain a normality frame of reference in the face of a mounting series of normative violations that affect an ever-increasing range of people. These shifts and discrepancies in the definition of variant actions play an important part in generating a career for the potential deviant. You might say his future is very much in the "hands of the images" formed of him in the minds of the people who surround him in the social environment.

Reactions of Society to the Mental Patient

In the research on mental disorders and social environment completed to date, there has been an emphasis upon only one direction of the coupling—that between the features of the environment which cause or precipitate the emergence and patterning of psychiatric symptoms in specific individuals. The suggestion made by Leighton, Clausen, and Wilson (1957, pp. 10–11) is that future research should include study of the modes of societal reaction to illness—that the other side of the transaction be examined.

The first question to be answered in such a study is whether the deviant individual is revered, ignored, or condemned by those who surround him. Many societies condone or even worship forms of exceptional behavior which we would classify as deviant or pathological. An individual who has hallucinations may be placed in a position of power and influence in a culture where the dominant belief system is supernatural in character and truth by revelation is esteemed. The expression of a psychiatric symptom may be prerequisite to the assumption of certain roles in the society, as was the case with the vision quest among aspirants to warrior status in the Plains Indian cultures. In order to clarify the impact of deviant action on the social environment, we must understand the subjective definitions placed on various forms of psychiatric symptoms by both the society at large and the dominant institutions or agencies administering the sanctions. A study of this subject raises many problems about the complex relationship between social role and personality configuration in primitive society (Devereux, 1956).

The second research question relates to the position of the deviant person within the power structure of the society in which he lives. Persons suffering from psychiatric disorders who serve as gatekeepers and leaders can influence the morale of large groups of people, and can actually change the course of events in cooperative ventures. This is especially true in huge, urban, industrial societies such as our own where interdependency is well advanced throughout the system (Leighton, *et al.,* 1957, pp. 10–11).

A further problem of interest lies in the connection between manifestations of specific forms of deviance and changes in the types of sanction applied. The case of "running amok" among the Malays may serve as an illustration of this point. Linton (1956, p. 116) reports that this form of deviance disappeared shortly after the Dutch authorities insisted that "amok runners" be captured alive and sentenced to several years at hard labor instead of being killed as had been the previous practice.

There also seems to be a changing fashionability of psychiatric syndromes from one historic period to the next. Hysterical syndromes were common among women in Europe and America at the turn of the century; now they are seldom seen at all. During World War I, the most frequent psychoneurotic complaints concerned the heart; in World War II, the most frequent symptom was general anxiety. It would be of value to explore this question further to see if the change in symptom pattern is accompanied by a shift in societal reaction or informal sanction.

Some forms of mental disorder pose a unique and critical threat to society in terms of their fundamental connection with the motivational structure and basic system of interpersonal expectations. In the United States the majority response is to attach a grave stigma to most forms of mental illness and to confine individuals suffering from these conditions, thus effectively isolating them from the rest of the community. In Navaho society, some individuals who are defined as "crazy" are believed to have committed the worst of crimes, while others who are mentally deficient are treated with great tolerance and given every consideration. It will be of interest to learn if the subject of mental illness is treated in similar manner in other cultures of the world.

Mental Disorders and the Problem of Levels of Analysis

This is an issue having to do with conceptual frameworks rather than substantive problems. The phenomena of mental disorders involve several levels of analysis that have been traditionally the domain of different groups of specialists working in relative isolation from one another. Some forms of mental disorder are ascribed to organic brain damage, others are more directly linked with unusual experiences in the patient's sensorium, while still others are connected with quite specific behaviors that conflict with important expectations of people in the patient's immediate environment. In the realm of treatment, striking results have been obtained by using such diverse techniques as tranquilizing drugs and psychotherapy.

All of these factors suggest that the time is propitious for a truly multidisciplinary approach to the study of mental disorders. If significant progress is to be made in this field, we must concern ourselves with working within a framework that includes levels of analysis ranging from the study of protein structure and hormonal process, to the nature of the sociocultural environment.

As mentioned earlier, there are hereditary as well as environmental factors to be tested in a cross-cultural study. And there is the distinct possibility that new forms of herbal treatment will be discovered that will benefit the modern field of psychopharmacology. The key question is: what frame of reference is necessary in order to include all pertinent levels of analysis in planning a cross-cultural study of mental disorders?

FROM THE VANTAGE POINT OF CULTURAL ANTHROPOLOGY

Acculturation and Mental Illness

As demonstrated in the surveys of Keesing (1953) and Siegel (1955), one of the active fields of interest in anthropology today is that of culture change. In most instances, the research concern within this field has been with the process of acculturation where non-literate tribes acquire the characteristics of the dominant society in their immediate environment. But whether the stimulus for change comes from inside or outside the culture, it seems fairly certain that culture change may create conditions of anomie and conflicting orientation (Hughes, 1957) within a community, to the point where personalities are affected in an adverse manner.

In a recent publication, Leighton (1959a) presents the hypothesis that rapid and extensive acculturation does, indeed, affect the state of mental health in a population. He provides a convincing discussion of how rapid acculturation can create social disorganization, and how this process—if it is long sustained—can, in turn, lead to an increase in the number of psychiatric disorders in the group.

A thorough exploration of the coupling between personality disturbance and changing cultural systems should be included as part of a cross-cultural study of mental disorders. It will be necessary, of course, to locate a community that has not yet become involved in acculturation in order to compare the prevalence of disorders in that group with populations undergoing rapid transition from one way of life to another. As a practical point, the participation of psychiatrists in making personality assessments in the field may facilitate the description of changes occurring in individuals who are at various stages in the acculturation sequence (Vogt, 1951, pp. 85–89).

With a large number of non-literate peoples poised on the edge of extensive and accelerated acculturation, the study of a possible link between culture change and psychopathology is timely from both theoretical and applied points of view. As we become more aware of the dynamics of culture and personality, we are able to consciously control and administer a greater range of aspects of our sociocultural environment. And with an increasing amount of governmental participation in the process of culture change in under-developed areas of the world, it may be feasible to implement suggestive results as they flow from empirical studies of the type outlined above. The practical application of findings thus, in turn, may create a form of natural experiment to foster theoretical enlightenment.

Cultural Universals and the Study of Mental Disorders

Within recent years a number of anthropologists have engaged in extended cross-cultural studies in several substantive areas. The works of Murdock (1949) on kinship, or Horton (1943) on alcoholism, and of Whiting and Child (1953) on socialization, are some of the better known examples. At the same time, other authors have attempted to construct a set of cultural universals that would serve as invariant points of analysis both in describing individual cultures and in doing comparative studies (Kluckhohn, 1953). It is quite conceivable that cross-cultural studies in the field of mental health will contribute to the substantive, theoretical, and methodological facets of this current trend.

As I see it, there are several reasons for connecting a cross-cultural study of mental illness with the search for universal categories of culture. First, it appears that illness is a universal experience for man in all cultures. Thus we have a solid anchor point for doing studies about a specific kind of event that is likely to occur in any culture we may visit. Second, as Kluckhohn (1953, p. 509) has pointed out, the successful comparative studies of the past were those that focussed attention upon events closely tied to basic physical and biological features of man's experience. A study of mental illness will keep us linked closely to a biological base so as to increase our likelihood of success on this account alone. Third, while mental disorders are closely associated with biological processes, they branch over into areas of personality and social structure in ways that completely organic diseases do not. They form a convenient bridge to problems of deviance, social control, cultural values, and a number of other important aspects of culture and society. Fourth, a focus upon comparable prevalence rates of illness, and upon a search for etiological factors in the social environment, will require that careful attention be paid to locating non-culture-bound units of description and analysis. If "social disorganization" is an etiological factor in the environment, then we must have criteria that work in any village or town, no matter what the cultural context.

For these reasons cultural anthropologists engaged in the cross-cultural study outlined above may link themselves with both the general reawakening of interest in comparative method and with the search for a uniform set of cultural universals.

National Character and Studies of Modal Personality

As Inkeles and Levinson (1954) have described the current research scene, there is much discussion in the literature of the concepts of "national character" and "modal personality." But a major criticism is levied by these authors against the empirical studies that have been reported. None of the investigations have included a clinical assessment of individual personalities drawn on the basis of a random sample from a national or tribal population.

In the epidemiological studies being planned in the mental health field there will exist just such a random sample of individuals. Why not study the personality patterns of these subjects for the purpose of locating basic personality types for the tribal population, at the same time a search is made for indications of psychiatric disorder? Kaplan and Plaut (1956) have, in fact, tried to advance this kind of combined approach in their small-scale study of the Hutterites. It would be necessary to make only small modifications in the research design of an epidemiological study in order to provide basic empirical data to check on the existence of this hypothetical entity, "modal personality."

On the other hand, the concept of basic personality structure is important to the study of mental disorders in a non-literate society. A study of deviance and psychopathology requires an understanding of the standards of comparison used by the natives in evaluating each other's behavior and performance. The actual distribution of personality types provides an important criterion against which the native compares deviant acts and personality disturbances. In this way the study of mental disorders may test the usefulness of the concept of basic personality structure in a particularly exacting and empirical way.

Mental Illness as Deviance

A study of mental illness among a non-literate group gives the anthropologist ample opportunity to examine important facets of the process of deviance and social control. Of all the types of deviance that can elicit strong and organized negative sanctions, mental illness is one of the best. Thus, through a study of community reactions to psychopathology we may locate techniques for maintaining social order, as well as map the range of variant behavior to which they are normally applied.

But there are additional reasons for combining the study of mental illness with an examination of patterns of deviance. First, an argument can be made for the practical necessity of extending our search to this wider context on the grounds that the native informant must be allowed to place his pattern of conceptualization on the events in his own way. We must extend *our* frame of reference so as to include all events which the native may possibly wish to define as examples of pathology. For example, the informant may wish to define as "illness" certain events that we define as "crime." Second, the social scientist operates with a theoretical orientation that differs in some ways from the orientation of the psychiatrist trained in medicine. A number of social scientists view mental illness as a sub-class within the field of deviance or social pathology (Lemert, 1951). And since many mental disorders occupy a unique position in standing athwart the psychosocial as well as biological levels of analysis, there is some justification in viewing them as similar to such events as crime, cult activity, and nativistic movements instead of adhering strictly to the categories of the diagnostic manual of the American Psychiatric Association.

There is the further point that cultural anthropologists have become interested in sub-cultural variation within the primitive groups that they have traditionally described in terms of ideal type. With the work of Roberts (1951) on small group differences among the Navaho and the publication of life histories of deviant persons such as Sun Chief (Simmons, 1942), there is an indication of a trend where variant patterns will become more carefully studied and delineated in future field research. For these reasons variant actions will quite likely fall within the scope of study of a field anthropologist working on problems in the mental health area.

BIBLIOGRAPHY

American Psychiatric Association. 1952. *Diagnostic and Statistical Manual: Mental Disorders*. Washington: American Psychiatric Association Mental Hospital Service.

Barrabee, P. 1951. A Study of a Mental Hospital: the Effect of its Social Structure on its Functions. Unpublished Ph.D. dissertation, Department of Social Relations, Harvard University, Cambridge, Mass.

Cannon, W. 1942. "Voodoo Death," *American Anthropologist*, 44:169–81.

Caudill, W. 1958. *The Psychiatric Hospital as a Small Society*. Cambridge: Harvard University Press.

Devereux, G. 1956. "Normal and Abnormal: the Key Problem of Psychiatric Anthropology." In J. Casagrande and T. Gladwin (eds.), *Some Uses of Anthropology: Theoretical and Applied*. Washington: The Anthropological Society of Washington.

Eaton, J., and Weil, R. 1955. *Culture and Mental Disorders*. Glencoe, Illinois: The Free Press.

Field, M. 1957. *Doctor and Patient in Soviet Russia*. Cambridge: Harvard University Press.

Gruenberg, E. 1954. "The Epidemiology of Mental Disease," *Scientific American*, March, pp. 38–42.

Hollingshead, A., and Redlich, F. 1958. *Social Class and Mental Illness*. New York: John Wiley and Sons.

Horton, D. 1943. "The Functions of Alcohol in Primitive Societies: a Cross-Cultural Study," *Quarterly Journal of Studies on Alcohol*, 4:292–303.

Hughes, C. 1957. "Reference Group Concepts in the Study of a Changing Eskimo Culture." In *Cultural Stability and Culture Change* (Proceedings of the 1957 Annual Spring Meeting of the American Ethnological Society). Ithaca, New York, pp. 7–14.

Inkeles, A., and Levinson, D. 1954. "National Character: The Study of Modal Personality and Sociocultural Systems." In G. Lindzey (ed.), *Handbook of Social Psychology*, Vol. II. Cambridge: Addison-Wesley.

Jahoda, M. 1958. *Current Concepts of Positive Mental Health*. New York: Basic Books.

Kaplan, B., and Plaut, T. 1956. *Personality in a Communal Society: an Analysis of the Mental Health of the Hutterites*. University of Kansas Social Science Studies, Lawrence, Kansas.

Keesing, F. 1953. *Culture Change*. Stanford University Press.

Kennedy, D. 1959. Explorations in the Cross-Cultural Study of Mental Disorders. Unpublished Ph.D. dissertation, Cornell University. (Ann Arbor: University Microfilms Inc., L.C. card No. Mic 59–2468)

Kluckhohn, C. 1949. "The Philosophy of the Navaho Indians." In F. Northrop (ed.), *Ideological Differences and World Order*. New Haven: Yale University Press.

———. 1953. "Universal Categories of Culture." In A. Kroeber (ed.), *Anthropology Today*. Chicago: University of Chicago Press.

———. 1954. "Culture and Behavior." In G. Lindzey (ed.), *Handbook of Social Psychology*. Cambridge: Addison-Wesley.

Kluckhohn, C., and Leighton, D. 1946. *The Navaho*. Cambridge: Harvard University Press.

Ladd, J. 1957. *The Structure of a Moral Code*. Cambridge: Harvard University Press.

Leary, T. 1956. *Interpersonal Diagnosis of Personality*. New York: Ronald Press.

Leighton, A. 1955. "Psychiatric Disorder and Social Environment: an Outline for a Frame of Reference," *Psychiatry*, 18:367–83.

———. 1959a. "Mental Illness and Acculturation." In I. Gladston (ed.), *Medicine and Anthropology*. New York: International Universities Press.

———. 1959b. *My Name is Legion*. New York: Basic Books, Inc.

Leighton, A., Clausen, J., and Wilson, R. (eds.). 1957. *Explorations in Social Psychiatry*. New York: Basic Books.

Leighton, D. 1956. "The Distribution of Psychiatric Symptoms in a Small Town," *American Journal of Psychiatry*, 112:716–23.

Lemert, E. 1951. *Social Pathology*. New York: McGraw-Hill.

Linton, R. 1956. *Culture and Mental Disorders*. Springfield, Illinois: Charles C. Thomas.

Macmillan, A. 1957. "The Health Opinion Survey: Technique for Estimating Prevalence of Psychoneurotic and Related Types of Disorder in Communities." *Psychological Reports*, 3:325–39, Monograph Supplement 7.

Malinowski, B. 1927. *Sex and Repression in Savage Society*. New York: Harcourt, Brace.

Maslow, A. 1954. *Motivation and Personality*. New York: Harper & Brothers.

Milbank Memorial Fund. 1950. *Epidemiology of Mental Disorders*. New York: Milbank Memorial Fund.

Murdock, G. 1949. *Social Structure*. New York: Macmillan.

Murray, H. 1938. *Explorations in Personality*. New York: Oxford University Press.

Parsons, T., and Bales, R. 1955. *Family, Socialization and Interaction Process*. Glencoe, Illinois: The Free Press.

Redlich, F. 1957. "The Concept of Health in Psychiatry." In Leighton, A., Clausen, J., and Wilson, R. (eds.), *Explorations in Social Psychiatry*. New York: Basic Books.

Roberts, J. 1951. *Three Navaho Households: a Comparative Study of Small Group Culture.* ("Papers of the Peabody Museum, Harvard University," Vol. XL, No. 1) Cambridge.

Ruesch, J., and Prestwood, A. 1950. "Interaction Processes and Personal Codification," *Journal of Personality,* 18:391–430.

Schwartz, C. 1957. "Perspectives on Deviance—Wives' Definitions of Their Husbands' Mental Illness," *Psychiatry,* 20:275–291.

Selye, H. 1956. *The Stress of Life.* New York: McGraw-Hill.

Siegel, B. (ed.). 1955. *Acculturation: Critical Abstracts, North America.* (Stanford Anthropological Series, No. 2) Stanford University Press.

Simmons, L. (ed.). 1942. *Sun Chief: the Autobiography of a Hopi Indian.* New Haven: Yale University Press.

Suchman, E., Williams, R., and Fink, R. 1955. "The Comparative Method in Social Research." Unpublished manuscript, Dept. of Sociology and Anthropology, Cornell University, Ithaca, New York.

Sutton, F. 1956. *The American Business Creed.* Cambridge: Harvard University Press.

Vogt, E. 1951. *Navaho Veterans: a Study of Changing Values.* ("Papers of the Peabody Museum, Harvard University," Vol. XLI, No. 1) Cambridge.

Whiting, J. 1954. "The Cross-Cultural Method." In G. Lindzey (ed.), *Handbook of Social Psychology.* Cambridge: Addison-Wesley.

Whiting, J. and Child, I. 1953. *Child Training and Personality.* New Haven: Yale University Press.

Winslow, C. 1944. *The Conquest of Epidemic Disease.* Princeton: Princeton University Press.

Wyman, L. (ed.). 1957. *Beautyway: a Navaho Ceremonial.* (Bollingen Series LIII) New York: Pantheon Books.

About the Chapter

How do the characteristics of the people being studied influence the way they should be approached? In this chapter, Dr. Lerner gives an account of the difficulties and problems that arose in interviewing Frenchmen and interprets these problems in terms of French national character. He describes the characteristics upon which successful interviewing was based to cope with French defensive attitudes. The lesson clearly emerging from this chapter is that personality study must proceed with great flexibility and that procedures must be modified and reformulated as more is learned about one's subjects.

About the Author

DANIEL LERNER is Ford Professor of Sociology and International Communication at the Center for International Studies of the Massachusetts Institute of Technology. He was the Research Director and founder of the Institute d'Etudes Européennes in Paris and has taught at Columbia, Stanford and the Sorbonne. He is the author of 14 books including *The Passing of Traditional Society: Modernizing the Middle East; The Human Meaning of the Social Sciences; Evidence and Inference;* and with H. D. Lasswell *The Policy Sciences.* He has been awarded the Palmes Académiques.

Acknowledgment

This chapter has adapted material previously published in "Interviewing Frenchmen," *American Journal of Sociology,* September, 1956, and in "The Hard-Headed Frenchman," *Encounter,* March, 1957.

13

An American Researcher in Paris: Interviewing Frenchmen

DANIEL LERNER

Massachusetts Institute of Technology

When a Frenchman answers the telephone, he says: *"j'écoute"* (I am *listening*). In this way he takes up a position of defence against the unknown interlocutor at the other end of the line. To the greeting on the street, *Comment va?* (How goes?), one is likely to receive the ironic reply, *On se défend* (One defends oneself). In this slightly mocking fashion, with their special gift for self-conscious clarity, the French take note of a profound trait of their national character. The defensiveness of this posture startles an American used to the open style of saying "hello!" to every anonymous telephone ring and "fine!" to every casual "Hi?"

Defensive remarks greeted me when I arrived in September 1954 to start interviewing Frenchmen of the "elite classes," as part of a larger sociological study. What could one learn from such interviews? Besides, how could it be done? There was universal doubt about the value and the feasibility of the enterprise. The French, I was told, would never talk to a stranger with no other claim to their confidence than that of being an interviewer. Two years later, we had in fact managed to complete over fifteen hundred long interviews with Frenchmen of very high standing. Respondents included, in round figures, five hundred top businessmen,

427

three hundred political leaders (including all but two of the post-war prime ministers and foreign ministers), a hundred high civil servants representing *les grand corps de l'État,* a hundred senior military men, a hundred clerical and lay spokesmen of the church, and a hundred officials of labor, farmer and other pressure groups.

The trick was to get them started; but, once started, how they talked! The average length of the fifteen hundred interviews was over two hours, and a substantial number of them ran toward eight hours. (The same interview schedule, in England, averaged a bit over one hour and the questions were fully answered.) Frequently the interviewer was requested to return, after a single session lasting two or three hours, by respondents eager to have their full say in an interview that resembled an interior dialogue uttered aloud. The essential is that, once engaged, the Frenchman talked volubly. But, to engage him, one had to scale the defensive wall— as the French put it, *franchir le mur.*

"Les Formules de Politesse"

Our first approaches to interviewing were modest, tentative, apologetic. Trial-and-error, hit-and-miss (what the French love to call *"l'empirisme anglo-saxon"*) finally produced a workable formula. To each prospective respondent, the interviewer explained that his Institute had undertaken a study of attitudes among the elite. As Frenchmen do not respond readily to questionnaires, he continued, we were seeking the counsel of specially qualified persons. "Would you be so kind as to review with us the questionnaire we propose to use and give us the benefit of your criticisms? In responding yourself, you could explain which questions a Frenchman would be likely to resist and why; which questions would draw ambiguous or evasive responses that could not be properly interpreted; and which questions could be altered in such a way as to require reflective rather than merely stereotyped answers."

By casting the interviewee in the role of expert consultant, we gave him the opportunity to indulge in a favourite indoor sport—generalising about Frenchmen. This exercise suggested procedures that were, in fact, used in subsequent interviewing. More important, it provided us with a comprehensive set of French images of the French. How Frenchmen see each other—this became the starting-point of our inquiry on how they see the world around them.

Their comments clarified, for example, the psycho-cultural role of French conventions of courtesy. The highly elaborated set of *formules de politesse* is an elegant way of maintaining proper distance between individuals. By comparison with the American desire for quick intimacy, for promptly reaching a first-name basis, there is a general appreciation in France of the reserved person. This is the mark of a person *bien élevé,* raised with a proper sense of right conduct. A rule that governs personal relations in France is: *"Il faut garder ses distances"* (One must keep his distance). It is generally believed that a person is likely to suffer if, *par manque de reserve* (lack of personal reserve), he exposes himself to the will and way of others. French distance-maintaining mechanisms make it easier to ritualise all sorts of relationships that elsewhere are met by improvisations.

There is an established code of behavior in most matters of daily routine. French gastronomy is a case. *La cuisine française* is widely recognised as a high order of artistic achievement, but its ritual characteristics are less widely noted. Frenchmen tend to be rigid in all matters associated with feeding. There is practically no variation in *les heures de repas* (eating hours) of any region. There is little deviation as to which type of wine goes with which food, and few venture from established rules in order to "try something different." Even the conception of a well-composed meal (*repas bien composé*) is a distinctly Gallic idea with certain fixed features. A young French writer, returning from a summer vacation in the U.S.A., where he was outraged by many native practices, gives priority to the utter shock (*bouleversement*) he suffered from the American habit of non-scheduled snacks—*"les repas pris à n'importe quelle heure et n'importe comment"* (meals taken no matter when and how).

The case is more dramatic with respect to Chinese cuisine, which many non-French gastronomes regard as the only serious rival to the French if not its superior. But the notion of eating according to another logic than the linear progression from the spicy appetizer (*pour ouvrir l'appétit*) through fish, flesh, salad, cheese, fruit, sweet, coffee, seems to Frenchmen curious and *invraisemblable* (improbable). The Chinese logic, if anything more complex and refined, of arranging taste sensations in cyclical fashion appears to them as being merely comic: *"Figurez-vous, ils vous servent un entremêt, tout d'un coupe, après quelques poissons variés et puis ils terminent le repas avec le soupe! C'est drôle, hein?"* (Imagine, they serve you a sweet, suddenly, after a variety of fish dishes, and then they end the meal with soup. Droll, eh?)

"Le Refus de s'engager"

The French desire for an environment arranged in a stable fashion, with familiar routines defined by recognisable limits, manifests itself also on questions of public consequence. Typical expressions of distaste for innovation are *"Pas de surprise!"* (no surprises) and *"Pas d'aventure!"* (no adventures). This systematic French distrust of whatever is new and strange underlies a variety of otherwise inexplicable phenomena.

Take the notorious case of French politics. During many years, the government suffered from a sustained incapacity to act decisively. Characteristically, the French themselves quickly found *le mot juste* (the correct term) to describe this situation: *l'immobilisme.* Political immobility became pervasive when France was confronted by a new and strange set of demands. The major test was the European Defense Community, which asked nothing less than that Frenchmen henceforth conceive their political identity in terms of being Europeans. There were better reasons for hesitation than many foreigners recognise. But to prolong the issue over four years before they finally rejected an idea they had themselves created was peculiarly characteristic of French politics. Perhaps its sublime expression was the declaration of M. Antoine Pinay, former prime minister and minister of foreign affairs: *"Je suis autant que personne partisan du mouvement, mais j'entends qu'il ne débouche pas sur l'aventure."* (As much as anyone I favor action, but I don't intend action to expose us to adventure.)[1]

France has become a land in which "surprise" and "adventure" are pejorative words. Every approach from "the outside" must be regarded with suspicion by a person in his right mind. The prudent posture, when confronted by any new and strange proposition, is defence: *"On veut m'avoir"* (they want to do me out of something). The safest way to defend one's self, naturally, is a refusal to participate at all (*"je ne marche pas"*), thereby avoiding the risk of *l'aventure.* And the danger of adventure, among people whose defensive shell often protects a wistful interior, is that one would be disappointed. It seems especially important to avoid *déception* (the peculiar French word for disappointment). The famous French scepticism is, at bottom, a defensive measure for avoiding future deprivation by maintaining deliberately low expectations.

Underlying this view of political action is a more general ontological perspective that has been worked into the French sensibility. Frenchmen commonly perceive the environment as more detached and remote from themselves than do, say, Anglo-Americans. The external world possesses for them rather definite characteristics, including a capacity for action which is independent of the will of particular human beings. Ordinary French conversation produces an array of phrases which expresses this idea. One speaks often, for example, of *"la force des choses"* (the power of circumstances), a notion rarely heard in America—where it is regarded as defeatist rather than realist—and hardly more often in Britain. Another way of referring to the external world as possessing a reality independent of human effort is the phrase *"les choses sont ce qu'elles sont."* ("Things are as they are" implies for a Frenchman that it is useless to try to change them.) [2]

This perspective tends to disengage the individual from great public issues. Politics becomes a random series of events about which one can do little. The Anglo-American idea that policy is a sequence of decisions by which one seeks to alter events before they become the *données* (data) of the next public crisis—this idea seems to very many Frenchmen pretentious and rather tiresome. The young express this sentiment by making *je m'en-foutisme* (privatization) into an ideology; their elders are content with the celebrated Gallic shrug whereby passive indifference connotes superior intelligence. Either way, this attenuates political life by a widespread *refus de s'engager* (refusal to get involved), which limits personal interaction with *la chose publique.*

A consequence of the *refus de s'engager* is the relative scarcity of voluntary organisations in France as compared with the massive American proliferation of channels whereby individuals engage themselves in public enterprise. The absence of active civic participation is evident in all social classes in France. There are very few "clubs" of the sort developed by the upper social groups in Britain. Among the middle class there are few parallels of Rotary, Kiwanis, and Lions. Certainly, such institutions as the Parent-Teachers' Association, the League of Women Voters, and the Association of University Women play only a feeble role among a people whose women remain firmly rooted in their primordial sexual role. Among the working class only the labor union has made any headway. Still, it hardly touches the French worker in his daily life—offering him neither educational opportunities, recreational facilities, consumers' co-operatives, nor social diversions. All classes of Britons are likely to be shocked by the absence of an effective Society for the Prevention of Cruelty to Animals. The participant life languishes because the Frenchman is repelled by "groupism": he guards his inner privacy, the mastery of his individuality (*maîtrise de soi*), by a resolute *méfiance* (distrust) toward others.

This is part of the fixed self-image of Frenchman as *réalistes,* which finds varied expression in the phrases used to praise one's compatriots. The French are "hard-headed" (*réfractaires*); they do not get taken in (*pas d'illusions*). Or, as one of our "consultants" phrased it, *"les français n'aiment pas se raconter des histoires"* (the French do not like to kid themselves). Realism is associated intimately with another self-ascribed trait: scepticism. A person who holds optimistic views on practically any subject is sure to suffer a hard blow (*prendre un coup dur*). In popular parlance the man who buys the Brooklyn Bridge is a "soft fruit" (*une poire*). He gets universal derision with little of the underlying sympathy Americans retain for the "sucker." For the Frenchman, *une vache à lait* (milch cow) is strictly *un pauvre type* (boob) and *"tant pis pour lui!"* (too bad for him!). After all, *"il faut savoir se défendre!"* (one must know how to defend oneself!).

And so *la chose publique* yields pride of place to the austere demands of privatization. By rejecting involvements in the public arena, *le soi* (the self) guards its privileged status as a *territoire sacré*. The flow of public discourse in France profoundly respects the sanctity of the ego. Even in technical psychology, the vocabulary used for describing the "self-system" and its manifold operations is underdeveloped. Privacy among Frenchmen is less the product of mutual respect than a code of self-defense.

"In the Soup"

Once the restraints of privacy have been loosened, an interviewer must deal with the special French conventions of cognition. The metaphysics which endows the external world with active attributes of its own also creates new problems of question-formulation for a foreigner accustomed to more empirical habits of thought. In our earliest interviews I was baffled by the recurrent request from respondents to state "precisely" various questions that seemed to me already precise. It required much conversation and reflection before I realised that, for the French, precision has a quite different and special meaning, a literally Cartesian meaning. What makes questions "precise" for Frenchmen is their capacity to frame the object of reference in a specific context (*bien délimité, dans un cadre qui lui est propre*). The object of reference, to be clear, must be perceived as discrete—with external boundaries sharply defined (*"circonscrire l'objet"* in the conventional vocabulary of French philosophy).

French insistence upon a discrete, disengaged object of reference underscores their revulsion against relationships without clearly perceived boundaries. The language abounds in pejorative expressions to express this horror of inadequate distance between subject and object. Such phrases as *dans le jus, dans le sirop, dans la soupe,* convey vividly the image that fluidity (*des idées floues*) is the enemy of clarity because liquids exhibit no boundaries. Other expressions of distaste for "fuzziness" are *dans le cirage, dans la vaseline, dans le coton* (wax, vaseline, cotton wadding), where the soft and shapeless mass without defined margins represents the antonym of clarity and precision.

The limits which such a posture impose upon the interview are illustrated by a respondent who served us as "consultant." Director of an important national research organisation, with long experience in survey work, this man seemed perfect for our purpose. Indeed, he gave us many practical suggestions for question-wording, which helped us to avoid the vague and achieve the "precise." At first, different questions scattered through our interview schedule, however, made this man throw up his hands in utter contempt and despair. "You will never get any Frenchman to answer questions like these," he declared, without explaining why. These were the questions:

1. If you were *président du conseil* (prime minister), what would be the main lines of your policy?
2. If you had to live in another country, which one would you choose?
3. If you had your life to live over again, what sort of life would you want?
4. Who are the most enviable people in the world? Why?
5. What functions do you think you could fill in a Communist France?

What these questions have in common—reflection suggested and experience confirmed—is that they ask the interviewee to imagine himself in a situation other than his real one (i.e. they are "role-playing" questions). Such an idea is regarded as frivolous, not worth the attention of Frenchmen, who are, after all, *"des gens sérieux"* (sober people). These questions were bound to provoke resistance among people who consider as their strongest traits realism, scepticism, and mistrust. And indeed they did, many interviewees regarding them as merely silly: *"de la blague!"* *"de la fantaisie pure!"* (a bad joke! pure fantasy!).

An instructive study could be made of the diverse ways in which people of different nations respond to role-playing questions of this sort. Our British interviewees, for instance, responded to precisely these questions with only minor incident. In general, such questions are handled with greater facility by people who are habituated to ready ego-involvement with the new and strange. Such people, having a less rigid conception of themselves and their proper conduct in the world, show a more supple capacity for rearranging their self-image upon short notice. A clear difference in the capacity to empathize, to play roles, emerged from interviews conducted in the Middle East several years ago. There it was possible to identify the Traditionalists by their total incapacity to answer such questions as "What would you do if you were president of Egypt?" By contrast, the Moderns seemed to experience no difficulty whatsoever when asked what they would do as editor of a newspaper, or as leader of their country, or if they had to live in another country.

There is a vast psychic difference between the illiterate and untutored traditionalism of the Middle Eastern peasant and the traditionalism which prevails among the contemporary elite of France. The Frenchman has acquired his traditionalism as an intellectual discipline and as part of an explicit psychic code. He is taught from childhood an articulate conception of *le bonheur* and a system of appropriate behavior designed to maximize his satisfactions. Whereas the Arab peasant usually has no sense of possible alternatives to his traditional ways but simply "does what comes naturally," the Frenchman has a very sophisticated rationale for his conduct. He not only is quite aware of other ways of behaving but can, and usually does, tell you with the greatest clarity why his way is better than any other.

The personality associated with traditionalism takes a quite different turn, then, among the French. It explains why Frenchmen often accuse Americans, who used to think of themselves as the world's greatest individualists, of a *manque d'individualisme*. For contemporary Americans, individualism implies non-conformity; expressing one's self means doing something just a little differently from the other fellow. For Frenchmen, individualism lives quite comfortably with a massive conformism. Their underlying principle is not to do some things a little differently, but rather not to do very many things at all. In French eyes the American loses individuality by identifying himself too readily with other persons, by associating himself too intensely with public causes, and by joining too many organisations. The Frenchman guards his individuality by maintaining *le soi* inviolate from the impingements of the public arena.

Politics and Police

We gained *entrée,* in due course, to spokesmen of those social groups which constitute the political Centre and Right—businessmen, high civil servants, military leaders, even chiefs of the non-Communist trade unions. But we made little headway on the Left, a sector of the political continuum which is inadequately interpreted even in France and which reaches far beyond the Communist Party and fellow-travellers.

There exists in France a pervasive political sentiment called *gauchisme*. It is a sentiment because it entails no specific judgments on specific issues but expresses rather a diffuse general hostility to the powers-that-be and things-as-they-are. One approximation of a psychological definition of this sentiment was sketched by Albert Camus in *L'homme révolté,* with reference to "the alienated intellectual." The special importance of *gauchisme* in France is its sociological diffusion. Types of Frenchmen have been affected by chronic oppositionism who, in other countries, are conservative or have no clearly defined political sentiment at all (e.g. army officers, civil servants, rich businessmen). A systematic sociology of the diffusion of *gauchisme* in France would do much to explain the French incapacity to act decisively on critical public issues during the last two decades.

It was among these *gauchisants* that our inquiry encountered the most widespread suspicion and resistance. We had decided, early in the game, that complete candor on the sponsorship of our study was essential. Our interviewers had been instructed to respond, when questioned, that the inquiry was jointly sponsored by French and American universities and that an American professor was a member of the scientific committee directing the study. The impact of this disclosure upon French *gauchisants* was strong enough to draw caustic remarks, to limit responsiveness, and, in some cases, to distort substance. Some *gauchisant* respondents framed their remarks primarily to cause anguish to the American professor—a performance more frequent among those who took their *gauchisme* rather lightly.

More committed Leftists not only refused to answer at all, but in some cases went further. We were reported to the weekly journal *L'Express,* a leading mouthpiece of *gauchisme,* and for most of a week were haunted by a young reporter determined to denounce and expose our enterprise. Several hours of explaining carefully our interview schedule, our sampling procedure, and our modes of analysis failed to persuade the sleuth that it would be impossible for us to derive information useful to the police, French or American. It was perfectly clear to the reporter that there must be some hidden trick; once I was an American, the enterprise was necessarily a maneuver of the Right and, *ipso facto,* despicable.

The extreme *gauchisant* went even further. In two regions we were denounced to the departmental *préfet.* Our interviewers there reported that, unless we could clear matters with the *préfet,* their usefulness would be at an end. In Paris we were subjected to two visits by agents of the DST (*Défense de la Sécurité du Territoire,* the French FBI). These persons scrutinized very carefully our intentions, procedures, and, most particularly, our affiliations in France. We were able to surmount those inquiries, only because our committee of sponsors (*comité de patronage*) was composed of Frenchmen of impeccable standing.

Les Anglais: A Projective Test

We learned from these interviews, among other things, that how the French see other nations is now a function of how they see themselves. This sector of French sentiment has a special piquancy with respect to the British. With no other people do the French lead as complex and many-layered a psychic life as with their neighbours across the Channel. For penetration of the French fantasy world, *les Anglais* make a splendid projective test.

We can deal better with current French judgments of others when we recall André Siegfried's theorem that French culture had been "completed" by the 18th century. Indeed, one can usefully classify Frenchmen today in terms of their reckoning with the marvellous XVIII*ème.* There are those who are still for it (and sometimes in it); those who flaunt the XIX*ème's* reaction against it—the *bons esprits* who, in the phrase of Marcel Aymé, "still assign a high revolutionary coefficient to masturbation"; those who have reacted against XIX*ème's* reaction against it (the, so to speak, anti-anti-XVIII*èmes*). Here and there, one encounters someone who is in and of the XX*ème*. In some ways he seems hardly French any more!

These historic levels reverberated, like geologic layers in a tremor, when our interviewers asked Frenchmen how they felt about *les Anglais.* The ancient orders—military and clerical—emitted the sonorous peals of classic Anglophobia. No happenings *circa* A.D. 1960 dim, for the true Gallic Anglophobe, the vivacious souvenirs of Jeanne d'Arc and Waterloo. Compiègne still symbolises *perfide Albion* and not a few among our respondents still used, as a summary expression, some variant of the ancient formula *"l'argent anglais et les poitrines françaises."* (Military alliance between the two countries is said to consist of "English money and French lives.")

Recent events not only fail to alter this undertow of Anglophobia, but are themselves transformed by its force. Thus, one 70-year-old retired cavalry colonel attributes current French ills mainly to British design—the interbellum failures of French policy; the defeat of 1940 "caused" by British evacuation at Dunkerque; the undermining of European unity by British non-participation in EDC; even the tragedy at Dien Bien Phu (where British desire to safeguard Burma, he alleges, prevented U.S. use of the napalm bombs that would have gained the French victory). Doubtless he is today explaining why the sad situation in Algeria is due to the British. Enveloped in his antique reverie, this Old Soldier—who interlards trenchant critiques of others with such dicta as *"L'Etat doit être fondé sur la fidelité, la discipline et l'honneur!"*— still considers the principal obstacle to French glory to be *les Anglais.*

The classic Anglophobia, while still vibrant in the subsoil of French emotion, no longer is a prescriptive item in the national doctrine to which every Frenchman good and true must subscribe. The evidence of our interviews suggests, indeed, that Anglophobia of all types has declined in frequency and intensity. A perfectly upright Frenchman can nowadays ignore the old chestnut of British perfidy and say: *"Les Anglais ont une grande loyauté dans l'execution des contrats particuliers."* (The English are honorable in the performance of private commitments.) This revision of diehard dogma occurs mainly among people who have scaled down ancient French pretensions to an appropriate up-to-date level of national aspiration. The relationship, in a word, is this: as appraisals of French power decline so evaluations of British virtue rise.

Frenchmen are certainly not enamoured of their other principal allies —Americans and Germans. By contrast, *les Anglais* come to seem utterly admirable to many Frenchmen. Interesting variations occur when the Anglo-French relationship is cross-tabulated with French sentiments toward these others. It is rare, for example, that one should look with equal favor upon both Germans and Englishmen. To look with equal disfavor upon both is less rare and forms the basic syndrome of French xenophobia, since these are still the two most salient national entities in the conventional French image of the world. To the Germanophile—and he constitutes a species of Frenchman more numerous than is ordinarily supposed—the English usually figure as rivalrous and even diabolical, the principal component of disarray in a world that might otherwise be molded into an orderly image of heart's desire. Such a person is much more likely than most of his compatriots to reveal a highly authoritarian set of preferences, including, if he is a relentless ideologue, the peculiarly French variety of matter-of-fact racism. He is likely, on current issues, to despise the Arabs (for whom his main adjectives are *sâle, bête,* and *brutal*) and to blame French decline in North Africa upon British lack of imperial backbone in dealing with the colonial peoples.

Conversely, the Germanophobe—when he is not comprehensively xenophobic—is more likely to tend toward Anglophilia. For him *les Anglais,* at least, have the virtue of sharing his antipathy for the Germans (by contrast with the Americans, say, whose idolatry of productivity and efficiency supposedly blind them to more fundamental traits of human character). Depending upon the intensity of his Germanophobia, such a Frenchman's Anglophilia may carry him to extreme postures of filiopietism towards *les Anglais.* If there is intense anxiety in his feeling against Germany—and paranoid symptoms are not infrequent among such respondents—then his attitude toward the English is likely to exhibit the ambivalent adoration usually reserved for Big Brother.

These extremist syndromes of Germanophilia-cum-Anglophobia and Germanophobia-cum-Anglophilia are most clearly defined, of course, at the limits of the French spectrum of attitudes. While they surely resonate in the breasts of many ordinary Frenchmen, they are most revealing as expressions of political psychopathology in a nation whose historic self-imagery makes a poor fit to the current reality of forced choices presented, largely, by its partners.

"Private Faces in Public Places"

More subtle, in this context, are the discriminations which Frenchmen make between their major pair of partners—the English and the Americans. For a majority of Frenchmen the direction of sentiment is unilateral: they "like" both or "dislike" both with approximately equal vigor. But two substantial clusters of deviant cases appear among our respondents. One group dislikes the English and likes the Americans.

These appear to be largely the same authoritarian types who like the Germans. They are also relatively more discontented with *"l'état actuel des choses"* in France. They find in common among the Germans and Americans the admirable traits of diligence, organization, efficiency. These traits satisfy a compulsive craving for orderliness—traits whose absence they deplore in France and whose failure to triumph in the world they attribute to the wily and unpredictable *Britanniques* (the epithet which usually replaces *les Anglais* in this context).

The other deviant group dislikes the Americans and likes the English. The underlying sentiment here appears to stem from a sense of shared greatness gone, a wistful affection for the lifeways evolved during the centuries when Frenchmen and Englishmen disputed between themselves for supremacy in the familiar arena of Europe (and the game overseas was merely an extension of the continental play). These older lifeways are felt to be a more suitable *règle de jeu* than the stark code, known as the Cold War, which defines right conduct for the powerful primitives (U.S./U.S.S.R.) now disputing mastery of the great globe itself.

This preoccupation with the aesthetic surface of life starts from a net affirmation of W. H. Auden's dictum that

> private faces in public places
> are nicer and wiser
> than public faces in private places.

It expresses itself in the frequent selection, for special admiration, of personal deportment among the English as compared with the Americans or the Russians—since the two giants are usually perceived by such respondents as more alike than different. The preference for a private style of life is manifested also in their evaluation of public behavior. There is a wistful conviction, among these Frenchmen, that the English have somehow managed better than others to adapt their admirable traditions to *la force des choses* in the world today.

The tensions generated by the current need to reconstrue one's Self in terms of Others imposes a new set of demands upon French culture and personality. In meeting these demands, the French pay a heavy psychic cost. It may be, as some have averred, only the rentier's horrified and belated discovery that his vested values have declined and he has been living off capital. But current French psychopathology as the outcome of a XVIII*ème* culture that was too "complete" may aid diagnosis without advancing therapy. Granted that France no longer is what it was, its future will be shaped by the modes that prevail among Frenchmen of perceiving what it is. For the classic self-image no longer works. Gone are the days when Frenchmen could see their civilization as a perfect whole (*un tout*), and rank all others peoples simply by the direction and degree of their deviation from this perfect model. Nowadays, Frenchmen are obliged to judge themselves afresh when they judge others. This is a far more complex psychocultural task.

Some Notes on Method

Interviewing Frenchmen thus involves a number of special problems derived from the national character, reinforced by behavioral codes and social institutions, and made acute by current political conditions. Making initial contact is complicated by the distance-maintaining mechanisms imbedded in the French code of courtesy. The *formules de politesse* serve as index and agent of French distrust of the strange, their identification of security with privacy. Most refusals were based squarely upon the feeling that such an interview was an unwarranted intrusion into their personal affairs. Few said simply "No!" Rather more evaded a flat refusal by having their secretaries phone to postpone the rendezvous indefinitely as a less rude rejection. But, of those who explained instead of evading their refusal, many said: "This is not my concern!" "My opinions would not interest you!" "I do not know your Institute!" "Could you have Monsieur X [a member of our committee known to him] phone me to explain your purpose and introduce you?" To scale the defensive wall was not at all, among Frenchmen, a routine matter.

Once received, however, the interviewer figured as a person rather than a faceless machine for recording a one-way flow of short answers. Quite often, before granting a rendezvous, the interviewee specified that, if this was merely *"un Gallup"* (i.e., Yes-No contact poll), he was not interested. He would, however, be willing to *discuss* some of the important questions that concerned us. In such discussions the interviewer figured as a respected specialist. His own opinions on the questions, and on the respondent's expressed views, were often solicited. This was partly a gesture of courtesy but mainly an expression of the profound preference for the dialogue in French discourse.

The impact of the interviewer as a person was especially dramatic among Leftists, who are perhaps more richly endowed with the manipulative inclinations of the propagandist. Quite often a *gauchisant* who began by refusing an interview sponsored by "the Americans," and berating the French interviewer for using his talents under such auspices, would be drawn into heated discussion of the specific questions. After several hours of such dialogue, which furnished some extremely rich data, he might conclude by inviting the interviewer to have a drink—over which, if a relentless ideologue, he might advise the interviewer to quit this job and take more respectable employment.

The insistence upon a highly participant interviewer—one who relieved the respondent's anxieties about "exposing" himself to a strange person—gradually reshaped the basic format of our interview. In the early phase, a particularly gifted and versatile member of the interviewing team had tried out a variety of roles, ranging, as he put it, from the *lampiste* ("poor slob") to the *gavroche* ("dead-end kid"). His experiments indicated that the preferred role was that of the competent specialist, who, maintaining a posture of self-respect, exhibited the expectation that he would accord and receive respect from others. It was less effective, for example, to say, "Please answer my questions or I will lose my job," than to say, "I am obliged to ask you a number of questions, but you are obliged to answer only those that interest you." The latter formula seemed to define the relationship between subject and object— the distance between interviewer and interviewee—in a manner liberating to respondents worried about "engaging" themselves in a strange situation that might lead to *déception*.

As we moved from pretesting into the main phase of interviewing, the highly structured questionnaire with which we began became a minimally-directive dialogue in the format of a free-flowing conversation. This transformation of the schedule reduced the utility of precoding and other mechanical devices for assuring uniform reporting. Instead, we used more personal procedures for testing interviewer reliability— mainly, brief daily meetings between the research director and each interviewer, and a weekly three-hour meeting attended by all interviewers. At each session detailed discussion of the new interviews gradually produced clarity and consensus on the permissible range of variation in wording questions and recording responses.

The consistency developed thereby was demonstrated in the subsequent coding phase, when extremely high rates of speed and reliability were obtained by the former interviewers acting as coders. While lacking the elegant simplicity of objective procedures, the method of continuous personal consultation among interviewers solved empirically some thorny problems of open-ended interviewing in a sample survey. These problems are threefold: (1) Since respondents are not obliged to choose one precisely-worded answer (precoded) to a precisely-worded question, strict comparability of responses is reduced; (2) As comparability is reduced, so the analytic code must be expanded to take account of all significant variations in the responses; (3) As the code is expanded, so reliability among coders tends to be reduced (since increases of choices normally increase chances of errors).

Daily review of each interview between the interviewer and research director, supplemented by weekly reviews of the full week's work among all interviewers, enabled us to solve problems of comparability as they arose. The interviewers presented every significant variation of question and response that occurred in their conversations. Each variation was thrashed out until a clear agreement on its interpretation (coding) was understood and accepted by all interviewers. Naturally, such a crude empirical procedure depends greatly upon the quality and quantity of the personnel. It is the research director's taxing job to review each interview, detect significant variations and arbitrate differences of interpretation among interviewers. The interviewers must be few in number, high in quality, and steadfast in performance.

Our team consisted of six "hard core" interviewers, who stayed with the project from start to end. Only a few others were taken on, at peak periods or for special purposes, and each of these worked directly alongside a member of the "hard core." In a larger team, the demands of continuous intercommunication might easily become excessive. Each interviewer must be intelligent enough to recognize the essential matter in each of his responses, to detect the significant variations among them, to discriminate the comparable and non-comparable components exhibited by the verbal variations. Finally, the interviewers must be steadfast, since the method hinges on establishing very high consensus (virtual unanimity) among the team. Comparability can be steadily increased only as the interviewers reach clear and common understandings on how to deal with varied responses. Hence, any defection from the "hard core" increases the time and cost of obtaining comparable responses and reliable codes—since the whole team marks time while any new member is brought into the consensus.

Even under favorable circumstances, as in the present study, the method lacks the satisfying certifications conferred by more objective procedures. It is impossible to determine precisely how many significant variations of response have been undetected or misinterpreted (consensus can be formed on an erroneous interpretation). Yet, the "hard core" of this team was able to obtain reliability scores averaging around .90 in coding each other's interview records at high speed during the final stages of the project. This indicates that the method *can* gain the richer data obtained in open-ended interviews without paying the excessive costs of ambiguity, non-comparability, and unreliability in their analysis.

The initial conditions of our study imposed the method upon us by the unassailable argument of *faute de mieux*. Our exploratory pretest showed that highly structured, fully precoded interviews would get us nowhere—or, at least, nowhere we wanted to go. They would save us time, money, and uncertainty, but they would not produce the data we wanted. Since these initial conditions involved nothing less than French culture and personality, as characterized in the preceding pages, they were not amenable to rapid rearrangement for the purposes of our study. Having to do the best we could, we did. The method evolved merits consideration by scholars concerned with studying personality cross-culturally.

A postscript on the sequel may be worth noting. Our interviewing program, begun in 1954, was executed in periodic "waves" over the next five years. By the spring of 1959, when we re-interviewed a panel of 100 French respondents who had been interrogated one or more times in preceding years, we felt able to use a structured, precoded questionnaire in a contact-poll type of interview. On this "wave" we encountered less rejection or evasion of our questions—fewer "don't knows" and "no opinions"—than in any preceding year. This fact raises important questions. Had these particular respondents become habituated to interviews by their previous experience with us—either accepting more readily invasion of their privacy by interviewers or ceasing to regard our interviewers as strangers? Or had some transformation of French behavioral conventions—manifestations of the deeper characteristics of traditional French culture and personality—occurred in the short space of five years? Neither hunch carries *prima facie* conviction with it. Our analysis, at present, indicates that a satisfactory account of the data will have to contain elements of both explanations. Whatever the new psychocultural mixture in France, it is clearly not the mixture as before. But this is a different story to be told on another occasion.

NOTES

1. A detailed case study of EDC is presented in Daniel Lerner and Raymond Aron, 1956, *La Querelle de la CED* (Paris: Armand Colin). The American title is *France Defeats EDC* (New York: Praeger, 1957).

2. Professor Laurence Wylie's excellent study *Village in the Vaucluse* (1957) shows how this metaphysic is built into French perspectives from their earliest school years: "Children are not encouraged to formulate principles independently on the basis of an examination of concrete cases. They are given the impression that principles exist autonomously. They are always there: immutable and constant. One can only learn to recognize them, and accept them. The same is true of concrete facts and circumstances. They exist, real and inalterable. Nothing can be done to change them. One has only to recognize and accept them." (p. 73)

BIBLIOGRAPHY

Lerner, D. and Aron, R. 1956. *La Querelle de la CED*. Paris: Armand Colin. The American title is *France Defeats EDC*. New York: Praeger, 1957.

Wylie, L. 1957. *Village in the Vaucluse*. Cambridge: Harvard University Press.

IV

PROBLEMS OF CROSS-CULTURAL RESEARCH

About the Chapter

What kind of variables can be compared cross-culturally? Dr. Sears addresses himself to the classification of the nature of variables that have enough conceptual equivalence so that they are truly transcultural. In other words, these variables can be measured directly by similar operations in different societies and the measurements compared. A distinction is made between the instrumental acts that are indices of the motivational state and the hypothetical goal responses of the motive, or end state, to which the action is directed. Dr. Sears suggests that the former will vary considerably from one culture to another and that it is not often feasible to try to compare them. However, the goal responses, which are descriptive of the motivational systems themselves, are often universal and can be regarded as transculturally usable variables. Differences in such variables can be related to diverse "background" or cultural factors.

About the Author

ROBERT R. SEARS is Executive Head of the Department of Psychology at Stanford University. He received his Ph.D. in Psychology at Yale University in 1932, and later was a member of the research group in the Institute of Human Relations that published *Frustration and Aggression*. He was Professor of Child Psychology and Director of the Child Welfare Research Station at the State University of Iowa from 1942 to 1949, when he went to Harvard as Director of the Laboratory of Human Development. His main research interests have been in psychodynamics and parent-child relationships, a field that has led to a number of collaborative studies with anthropological colleagues. A past president of the American Psychological Association, Dr. Sears is also the author of *A Survey of Objective Studies of Psychoanalytic Concepts,* and a co-author of *Patterns of Child Rearing* (1957).

Acknowledgment

This chapter is based on a paper presented at the Conference on Cross-Cultural Research on Personality Development, sponsored by the Committee on Personality Development of the Social Science Research Council, at Kansas City, May 20–22, 1955.

14

Transcultural Variables and
Conceptual Equivalence

ROBERT R. SEARS
Stanford University

Transcultural variables are variables that can be measured in all cultures. They are universal properties of man or of his environment. By no means all the variables used in American researches on personality have this quality. For example, value dimensions such as those measured by the Allport-Vernon scale, or occupational interests as defined by the Strong inventory, are probably local to Western culture. These kinds of culture-bound variables may be of considerable value either for engineering purposes or for actual theory construction, but only within their own culture area. For cross-cultural research which is designed to develop personality theory that will be universally applicable, variables are required that can be measured everywhere.

The Purposes of Cross-Cultural Research

The reasons for this rest on the two functions of cross-cultural research. One of these functions is to provide a population sample, for testing hypotheses, that offers greater extremes on relevant variables, and broader variation among irrelevant variables, than can be obtained within a single culture. Cross-cultural research done with these aims in mind normally makes use of the modal behavior of a reasonably homogeneous culture group (the primary sampling unit, or PSU) as the unit. This procedure contrasts with ordinary research methods on personality in which the modal behavior of an individual person is the unit. The works of Murdock (1949) and of Whiting and Child (1953) offer examples.

The second function is to provide appropriate conditions for the systematic variation of factors that cannot be varied within a single culture. If some cultural characteristic such as "authoritarian government" or "sororal polygyny" is believed to have interacting effects on the variables between which relational principles are being sought, then the testing of the hypotheses must be done in different cultures that can provide for such interaction. This is sometimes spoken of, rather inexactly, as "varying the background factors."

Whichever purpose is the basis for a given cross-cultural research venture, the variables used must be transcultural. They must be measurable in whatever culture is chosen, whether the culture be a unit of the sample population or a source of systematic variation of an interaction variable.

Conceptual Equivalence and Operational Definitions

The first requirement for testing any hypothesis, or for discovering any empirical relationship, is to have two or more variables which can be precisely defined. These definitions must be in sufficiently operational terms that actual measurements can be made of the variables. These are obvious rules for any investigative procedure, and they could go without saying except for the fact that they create a special problem in cross-cultural research, the problem of *conceptual equivalence*.

In most natural science research and even in much behavioral science research, crucial variables are defined by reference to a direct operation of measurement. A given variable is represented by a single operation. Thus a principle that states the relationship between (X) duration of dark adaptation and (Y) visual threshold in the human eye is a statement about the relationship between two exactly specified measurement operations, one based on amount of time under conditions of non-illumination, and the other on a precise psychophysical measurement of responses to light stimuli of different intensities. In the field of personality, however, the variables with which we seem usually to concern ourselves are once removed from a perceptually unique measurement operation. They are constructs that subsume several kinds of instigating situations or actions. For example, the behavior concept of *aggression* cannot be measured by any single operation; it may be defined in terms of the relative number of homicides in a society, the frequency of insults, the intensities of physical injuries as judged by some *a priori* scale, or any one of a dozen other kinds of action. Likewise, an antecedent variable like frustration may be measured by reference to interference with a host of different action systems.

There is nothing intrinsically wrong with using each of these many separate "aggression" or "frustration" items as a single variable, except that to do so would be inefficient. For the sake of economy, it is desirable that we have as few behavior variables as will conveniently provide adequate predictability of the entire scope of behavior that we consider a suitable subject matter for science. From the standpoint of measurement, on the other hand, single behavior items that permit single measurement operations provide the greatest precision in the statement of relationships.

A solution to this dilemma can sometimes be found in a compromise. For example, in the problem of dark adaptation, mentioned above, there are three different psychophysical methods for measuring visual threshold. Any one of these can be used for determining a general principle that states the relation between time of adaptation and visual threshold. They all give the same principle. The actual threshold values obtained will vary, of course, depending on the method. All three measures are indices of a more general concept, *viz.,* visual threshold. Another way of saying the same thing is that there are three interchangeable operational definitions of this concept. The compromise between economical, but unmeasurable, "globality" of concepts, and uneconomical, but measurable, operationism lies in the discovery of the exact relationships between the various indices of a given concept. When indices are interchangeable, and provide the same $X \rightarrow Y$ principles, they display *conceptual equivalence.*

There is one difficulty to be kept in mind, however. When we are dealing with spontaneous behavior, i.e., actions that are elicited by the natural environment and the person's internal sources of instigation, we find that there is sometimes systematic interaction between the items of behavior that we believe should be used as indices. In the case of aggression, for example, overt and displaced aggression have a very complex non-linear relationship that prevents us from using one kind as an index interchangeable with the other. There may be other instances, as in the defense mechanisms, in which two behaviors seemingly comparable as "anxiety reducers" are actually alternatives. This means that $X \rightarrow X$ and $Y \rightarrow Y$ relationships must be examined carefully before $X \rightarrow Y$ relationships are sought.

This problem is hard enough to solve when one is working with a single construct like *aggression* in a single and quite homogeneous culture group. Over the last two decades, considerable labor has been expended in the study of just what behavior items are conceptually equivalent within the aggression system. So far, at least, one can say that most of this research effort has not seriously questioned whether aggression itself is a useful and desirable concept within the American culture. But that is about as far as one can go. Research has not yet provided more than a minimal start toward a study of the actual equivalence and functional interactions of different types of aggressive action (Berkowitz, 1958).

From a cross-cultural standpoint, a more primitive question must be raised. Is *aggression* itself a good behavior concept? Is this a unitary kind of behavior that exists in the behavior repertories of all peoples, regardless of the cultures in which they are reared?

Transcultural Determinants

To the extent that there are universal characteristics of people as biological organisms and universal characteristics of environment, to that extent there are likely to be transcultural properties of behavior. In other words, we presume that when a given kind of organism has to interact with a given kind of environment, all organisms having the same general property will develop behavior repertories that can be conceptualized in the same way. This reasoning rests explicitly on the assumption that not only are there universal biological qualities in man, but that the basic characteristics of the learning process, including the acquisition of motives, are universal, too.

Biologically, there are a number of universals in man. Some of these can be specified by reference to what are commonly called the primary drives, while others are referrable to common structural characteristics. Primary drives relate mainly to the biological integrity of the individual. For his own maintenance, man must eat, drink water, eliminate waste products, maintain a certain range of body temperature, avoid damaging injury to his body wall, sleep and rest, exercise his muscles, and breathe air. If the species survives, obviously most men engage in sexual activity also.

Structurally and functionally there are other universal qualities which are of importance. Man is a warm-blooded mammal, hairless over most of his body; he is ground living, with neither wings nor tail nor strong arms to take him into the air or into tree tops; he is omnivorous, but with neither the digestive system of a ruminant nor the teeth and claws of carnivora; he is big brained, lacks a good smell sense but has excellent vision and audition; he has a capacity for the use of spoken language. Perhaps as important as anything is the fact that he has an organismic growth rate that requires several years of direct physical care of the young by mature animals.

It is difficult to specify the universalities in the human environment. There are two aspects of it that need separation. First is the physical or nonhuman environment. One could point to such facts as that food never grows on man's body itself, but always must be sought by hunting or fishing or climbing or agriculture. The same is true of water, in the sense that it exists on the earth's surface independently of the biological organisms that also exist there. There are few places in which man can live without at least occasional activity related to maintaining body temperature within its proper limits. There are many dangerous objects that can injure him. There are cliffs to trip him, lightning to fell him, the dangers of fire, falling objects, sharp pointed objects, wild beasts and smothering caves; and there are poisonous snakes, fruits, fish and springs.

The second aspect of the environment is the human. The same universal qualities that establish universal behavior repertories also create environmental universals for other men. Every human being lives in a world in which there are others who are also seeking food and water, others who become fatigued and sleep, others who become enraged and destructive because of pain or injury, and so on. The basic biological and physical environmental universals create certain universal qualities in man, and since there are always many men as part of the environment, these learned behavioral qualities also become universal parts of the environment. There are, in other words, what might be called *derivative* or *secondary* universals.

It seems evident that there are two broad general classifications of transcultural variables, one monadic and the other dyadic. Monadic variables are those that are constructed in the individual's behavior repertory by experiences that do not involve any regularized interaction with other people. Some such variables may be characteristic of the person as a biological organism (i.e., they are unlearned), while others may be a function of inevitable universal experiences.

Dyadic variables are those that depend upon universal interactions with other persons. They involve mutual expectancies and mutual reinforcements. There are obviously some dyadic variables related to behavior that is initially established in the individual by his interaction with one or perhaps two other people (e.g., dependency in relationship to the mother, or competition among peers), and eventually become behavioral properties of the person more or less independent of any one other individual but related to his functioning as a member of a social system. This would be the case, for example, with such a concept as *aggression anxiety* or *inhibition of aggression*.

Another distinction to keep in mind is that between antecedent and consequent variables. The *conditions* for establishing transcultural behavioral variables belong in the category of antecedents. In man, with his potentialities for learning new motives and expectancies, these antecedents create transcultural consequent variables. These may play the logical role, in some instances, of intervening variables, as is the case with "anticipation of success or failure." Such a concept may then be used, for all practical purposes, as an antecedent of action. In other cases, the consequent variable produced by these universal antecedents is an abstraction of some action quality. Aggression or competition or status-striving are examples.

These abstractions point up the problem of conceptual equivalence. Take aggression as an example. A distinction must be made between the instrumental acts that are indices of aggression (e.g., hitting, insulting, nonco-operating) and the hypothetical "goal response" of the aggression motive (perceiving another person's reactions to injury). It is the latter that one would expect to find transculturally. The aggressor's instrumental activities that serve to hurt someone else—and thus enable him to perceive reactions to injury in his victim—will differ from one culture to another. The form of an insult, for instance, depends on the values held by the insulted one. Or to take another example: automobile racing and football can be instrumental activities for competition only if the society has automobiles and knows how to play football.

It seems doubtful that there are very many transcultural variables at the level of description of the instrumental act. Societies differ too much both in their structure and in the natural resources they have available to permit identity of instrumental actions across cultural lines. Of course, there are a few instrumental acts that are almost inevitably transcultural. Such aggressions as hitting, kicking, stabbing and biting probably create pain responses in others (the *Beta* persons in dyadic relationships) no matter what culture is involved. But such universal instrumental acts appear to be rare.

At the goal response level of description, however, the actions are essentially descriptive of what the motivational system is. The actions are defined in terms of the Environmental Events they tend to produce. In other words, securing the unsharable goal, perceiving nurturant orientation, and perceiving pain responses refer to the Environmental Events that are brought about by motivated actions. The details of the actions that bring about such Environmental Events will differ radically from culture to culture, but the events themselves should be identical.

These action "abstractions" are only one type of variable that may be transcultural. Since it is possible that the methods of discovering useful variables may be different, depending on the kind involved, it is worth listing what seem to be different types. There are various ways in which one can conceptualize action or learning, and the following terms are representative of but one (Sears, 1951).

1. *Environmental Events.* As indicated above, these are the occurrences in the environment that a motivated action system seeks to produce. It is assumed that the person, Alpha, develops an *expectancy* of such events, through the process of motive acquisition, and that their occurrence is the necessary condition for his gratification. They are often a form of behavior in another person, Beta. They can be defined at either a phenomenal or a genotypic level. Presumably only the latter would be transcultural.

2. *Goal responses (or action abstractions).* These are the hypothetical actions that occur in Alpha when the appropriate Environmental Events occur. They are "consummatory" responses. In the case of acquired motives, they may prove to be useless concepts, since in fact all we ever know about, or can observe, are the Environmental Events and the instrumental acts that produce them.

3. *Instrumental acts.* Underlying the phenomenal multiplicity of behavior that produces Environmental Events, there are genotypic qualities that are likely to be transcultural. That is, "aggressive" acts are designed to produce a pain response in Beta. In many instances, the form of aggression will not be transcultural, but the genotypic quality of "aggression" will be.

4. *Learning situations.* These have been discussed above.

5. *Action instigators.* Once an action system has been formed, there must be instigators to set it off. These can presumably be transcultural.

6. *Intervening mechanisms of response.* Such processes as displacement, retroactive inhibition, repression, projection, etc., are essentially statements of complex relations between antecedents and consequents. They appear to have the logical status of intervening variables, and are among the general laws of learning and action that are here presumed to be universal. Their identification transculturally will doubtless involve the same problems as those related to antecedents and consequents, plus the additional one of determining, for each culture, the special dimensions of stimulus similarity unique to the culture.

Motivational Systems

At present we know little about what motivational systems may prove to be transcultural. Three examples that seem likely candidates are aggression, dependency and competition. Brief descriptions will indicate why.

Aggression

Aggression may be defined as a goal response to instigation to injure an organism or an organism-surrogate. While a rage response appears to be a native characteristic of mammals, elicitable by various types of frustration even in early infancy, the peculiar quality of aggression involves perception of pain responses in another person. One hypothesis to account for its development requires that it would occur in all human beings. This reasoning rests on the fact that all people can feel pain, and respond to it by expressive movements that are perceivable by a child. One of the commonest reactions to pain is an attempt to remove its source. When this source is another person who is making demands on one, this attempt is likely to be in the form of a compliance with those demands. In other words, the young child can secure compliance from his mother or older siblings by hurting them, and because their signs of pain reaction are associated with the gratification of his needs, he develops a secondary motivational system for which the goal response is perceiving another person's signs of being hurt. (For a more extended discussion, see Sears, Maccoby and Levin, 1957.)

The problem of securing transculturally usable indices of aggression is probably not too serious. What is required is that we be able to identify the Environmental Event (pain responses) for all cultures. With overt physical aggression, this is simple, for the signs of pain are themselves of a universal reflex character. More subtle forms of aggression, such as insults and techniques of injuring someone's ego or pride, may be more difficult to equate cross-culturally. The defensive character of people's responses to these more subtle forms of injury tends to hide direct indications of pain. To identify aggression of this kind, then, it may be necessary to examine what transcultural motives there are in people that can provide for pain when they are frustrated. For example, if it turns out that we can deduce the universal existence of such a motive as pride, we will need only to discover, for each culture, of what things any individual is ordinarily proud. The behavior of someone else that interferes with a person's pride in these things can then be identified as a form of aggression.

Dependency

The dependency drive can be defined as instigation to be oriented toward and cared for by another person. Since man has such a long period of physical dependency, he has a tremendous number of reinforcements of maternal orientation toward him, accompanied by primary drive gratification. As a consequence, it may be assumed that this orientation, and other signs of caretaking behavior, become the appropriate Environmental Events for the gratification of a secondary drive of dependency. Again, as with aggression, the manifestations will vary from one culture to another, depending in this case upon the characteristic forms of caretaking that have been applied to the child in early childhood. Behavior connected with food offerings is probably important. There seems to be no alternative to simple empirical investigation of different cultures in order to discover the commonest forms of orientation toward the child and of the latter's techniques for securing such orientation. The techniques that will work for him will differ from culture to culture.

Competition

The competition drive may be defined as instigation to secure an unsharable goal. There seems no doubt that competitive behavior is a transcultural variable. In the very nature of family living the attention and help of the mother or other major caretaker is to some degree unsharable among the various people who want it. As a consequence, children from a fairly early age are forced to seek such goals in the presence of similar striving from other persons (competitors). To the extent that such competitive efforts are successful for a particular youngster, to that extent he should develop a competition drive which would lead him to respond to almost any goal as an unsharable one. The qualities of competition, then, would enter into his behavior in connection with attempting to secure the goal.

Criteria of Conceptual Equivalence

Since action categories such as aggression, dependency and competition describe the reference events in which we are ultimately interested, attention should be given to discovering which ones are transcultural.

The criteria for determining conceptual equivalence of responses are not at all clear. However, the problem is probably no worse at the cross-cultural level than at the inter-individual. For example, one might ask what criteria there are for defining both a street fight and the telling of malicious gossip as indices of aggression. We seem to accept this identity on some intuitive basis and without critical examination of the criteria involved. Equally, we have to this point accepted reasonably obvious similarities cross-culturally, doubtless on the same intuitive basis. Actually, of course, intuition is merely a word to indicate that our reasoning and observations on this matter have been unsystematic. If we are to go beyond the few concepts which many students of behavior have been examining and working with for many years, however, these criteria must be formalized. Perhaps it will help get us started if we try to analyze the implicit criteria we have been using in the past.

1. *Is there a universal learning situation?* In the case of aggression and dependency, at least, we appear always to have rested the case for conceptual equivalence, in part, on the fact that we could imagine the transcultural existence of the learning conditions. For aggression, this was the capacity of Beta to feel pain and to comply with directions for future behavior when she did. Alpha was presumed to have the capacity for producing pain stimulation. For dependency, the learning situation

was the long period of physical dependency in infancy, together with Alpha's presumed capacity for developing a strong object cathexis.

To use this criterion, we must be able to specify in detail what the exact antecedents of any given response are. Have we any present evidence that mothers *do* comply with children's demands when these are accompanied by pain-inducing acts? *Does* such (presumed) compliance occur in association with grimaces of a standard and oft-repeated kind? *Are* these (presumed) grimaces uniquely indicative of the occurrence of pain stimulation?

2. *Can the appropriate Environmental Event be identified?* Since this Event is the "goal" of the action which is being studied, it must be recognizable. For aggression it has been defined as Beta's expression of pain-response. For dependency, it is nurturant orientation from the adult caretaker.

3. *Are there discoverable instrumental acts that produce these Environmental Events?* These acts will differ, of course, from person to person and from culture to culture. However, the measurement of the action category depends upon our finding quantifiable forms of behavior that are regularly used for producing the specified Environmental Events. The relation between such actions is a major unknown even in our own culture. Some appear to be alternatives to one another, as is the case with positive and negative attention-getting in young children. Others appear to be positively related, as are the frequencies (under some circumstances) of overt and fantasy aggression.

It seems likely that a great deal of work needs doing on the mechanisms of development of instrumental activity before we can go far with this criterion. The mechanisms of projection and displacement, for example, suggest that sheer correlational studies of consequent-consequent measures are covering up elaborate mechanisms that relate these responses to one another in regular but very complex ways.

4. *Are the same antecedent-consequent relations demonstrable in all cultures?* The methodological implications of this criterion are both vast and expensive. If the first criterion (universal learning situations) is met, and if the assumption is valid that the laws of learning and action laws are universal, this criterion would automatically be met. However, there is good reason to examine it separately, for we find it difficult to be satisfactorily rigorous about any of these matters as yet. A good many psychologists have assumed that the frustration-aggression relationship is universal, but Gregory Bateson (1941) has expressed doubt that this holds true in Bali.

There would be some value in knowing whether certain of the other relationships that we find in American culture are as valid elsewhere. This can be done by replication of experiments. But at this point, the reasoning turns back to the original problem itself, for one of the purposes of cross-cultural research is simply this—to discover whether certain antecedent-consequent relations are universal!

BIBLIOGRAPHY

Bateson, G. 1941. "The Frustration-Aggression Hypothesis and Culture," *Psychological Review,* 48:350–55.

Berkowitz, L. 1958. "The Expression and Reduction of Hostility," *Psychological Bulletin,* 55:257–83.

Murdock, G. P. 1949. *Social Structure.* New York: Macmillan.

Sears, R. R. 1951. "A Theoretical Framework for Personality and Social Behavior," *American Psychologist,* 6:476–83.

Sears, R. R., Maccoby, E. E., and Levin, H. 1957. *Patterns of Child Rearing.* Evanston, Ill.: Row, Peterson and Company.

Whiting, J. W. M. and Child, I. 1953. *Child Training and Personality: A Cross-Cultural Study.* New Haven: Yale University Press.

About the Chapter

The concept of psychological ecology, developing out of Lewinian psychology, refers to the psychologically relevant aspects of environment. The problem of comparing the ecological conditions in which children develop in two small towns, one in Kansas, the other in Yorkshire, England, is discussed in this chapter. The Barkers are specially concerned with a difficulty dealt with in Dr. Sears's chapter, the isolation of measurable units that are equivalent across cultures. They contend that children and adults may be adequate subjects for study if one is concerned with personality; but they are not proper subjects when one is concerned with the sources of personality. The Barkers proceed as natural scientists, attempting to discover the "natural" units that occur in social phenomena. They isolate what they have termed the "behavior setting" which they believe is equivalent and comparable from culture to culture, principally because it occurs at the same level of analysis.

About the Authors

ROGER BARKER is Professor of Psychology at the University of Kansas. He has taught previously at Harvard, the University of Illinois, Stanford and Clark. He is a former President of the Society for Research in Child Development and was a Fellow at the Ford Foundation Center for Advanced Study in the Behavioral Sciences. He is the co-author of *Child Behavior and Development; Frustration and Regression; Adjustment to Physical Handicap and Illness; One Boy's Day;* and *Midwest and Its Children.*

LOUISE BARKER had her graduate training in biology at Stanford. She has taught extensively at all levels from pre-school to university and has been a field worker in research in psychological ecology in Kansas since 1947. She is the co-author of a number of publications in this field.

Acknowledgments

The work reported in this chapter was supported by grants from the Carnegie Corporation of New York and the National Institute of Mental Health. The chapter was written during Roger Barker's tenure of a fellowship at The Center for Advanced Study in the Behavioral Sciences.

15

Behavior Units for the Comparative
Study of Cultures

ROGER G. BARKER and LOUISE SHEDD BARKER

University of Kansas

This chapter is based upon our experiences in studying the psychological ecology of children in the United States and Great Britain. It deals with a central problem of all cross-cultural investigation of behavior and its circumstances, namely, the identification and description of units of behavior. This problem is central if we are to achieve quantification. For quantification we must have stable units to count, and we must be able to identify across cultures the units which belong to the same class. If we are to make much progress in mathematizing culture, we must in addition be able to place units in order according to the degree to which they possess particular properties. We will go further if we can determine not only the order, but also the amount of these differences in the properties of behavior units.

The specific context within which our ideas of culture units have developed is a study of the child behavior systems of Midwest, Kansas, and Yoredale, Yorkshire. The exposition and illustration of these ideas will follow rather closely their development in the course of this investigation.

The term *child behavior system* is used here to refer to intact patterns of children's behavior-and-situation. It designates the whole of the children's regimens of Midwest and Yoredale rather than particular phases of these regimens, such as the discipline, the feeding, or the play of children. It denotes the behavior and situation of children generally rather than of particular children. It refers to children *in situ* rather than as excised parts of functioning systems. And it points to the causal connections between the parts of the system rather than to a description of the surface arrangements. The overworked word *system* is used here in much the same way it is commonly employed in the term *transportation system*. In both cases it means a stable structural and dynamic arrangement among separate entities, but without reference, necessarily, to particular entities, i.e., to particular vehicles and children. A concrete example may better identify the phenomenon with which we have dealt than any abstract description we are able to make at the present time. It is important that the reader understand what has shaped our thinking.

Everyone familiar with the life of America and Britain knows the national differences which exist in methods of moving persons and materials within and between communities. The British transportation system is characterized relative to the American system by, for example, more walking, more vigorous walking, heavier shoes, more carrying of things in baskets and bags, the greater use of walking sticks, more bicycling, lesser use of automobiles, smaller automobiles, better bus service, slower auto speeds, shorter trips, more winding paths and roads, cheaper bus fares, AA men who salute, narrower roads, both finer and poorer vehicles. The strength of the pressures within this system toward conformity are great. When we were in Britain for the first time, this was an issue upon which we thought we would not compromise. We planned to cling unobtrusively but obdurately to our American ways on this one minor matter. But we were defeated by the system before we began. We *had* to get a small car. An American car was impossibly expensive, too awfully conspicuous, and plainly dangerous on the narrow roads of North England.

With our party of seven in a Ford Consul, the five-minute trip to the hotel had the flavor of a sporting adventure, as the British like motoring to be. We parked with relief in front of the hotel. What a pleasure to have plenty of parking space, right on the street! But not so. "No night parking without parking lights," the Police Constable told us five minutes after lighting-up time. The garage was five blocks away. So within fifteen minutes of arriving, one of us was walking vigorously through the half mist–half snow, resolved to get some heavy shoes the first thing in the morning to ward off chilblains, and also a walking stick to help cope with the cobbles. The system had won a complete victory.

Some of the sources of power of the British transportation system and some modes of its application can be seen almost directly: the physical arrangements, the rules with their authority symbols and figures, the coerciveness of the on-going pattern of behavior (e.g., the inexorable line of traffic bearing down upon you as you happily start out on the right side of the road). Everything one sees both from within and without the system points to some generality in the psychological context of persons within the British locomotion system, and some commonality in the pattern of physical forces, such as winding roads which enforce slower driving speeds. Here, then, is a concrete example of a behavior system as we are using the term.

While the precise loci and materials of our study were the child behavior systems of a town of eastern Kansas and one of North Yorkshire, our aim was far wider. It was, in fact, to examine the American and the British child behavior systems. And this aim created the basic issue we have raised here: what are psychologically significant and scientifically adequate parts of a culture, in this case the culture of the United States and the culture of Great Britain? We could not escape this problem; for it was clear from the beginning that despite our interest in the wholeness and generality of the living conditions and behavior of American and British children, we could not deal scientifically with the American and British child behavior systems "in general." We had in some way to divide them into parts; we had to deal with concrete, denotable behavior and situations.

CHILDREN AS UNITS

We considered doing this by using a sample of particular children representative of the ages, social classes, sexes, schools, communities, economic levels, parental vocations, etc., of children in the United States and Great Britain. But it soon became clear that there were insuperable difficulties along this path. Some were technical difficulties. The sampling requirement of independence applies in this kind of research to situations as well as to subjects. One has to obtain data from the separate communities, schools, Sunday schools, Scout troops, friends, etc., associated with each child in the sample. One therefore has to multiply the number of subjects in his sample by a factor of 10, 20, maybe 50 to obtain an estimate of the number of his information sources. Even 50 subjects grows into a formidable forest of sources: 500, 1,000, 2,000. This was, for us, an impossible task.

An even greater difficulty with the usual sampling method is the fact that it does not focus upon the phenomenon with which we were concerned, namely the *system*. Samples representing the children of the United States and Great Britain are related to the functioning child behavior system in which we were interested in much the same way that the performances of individual baseball and cricket players are related to the rules of baseball and cricket. To write the rules of baseball from the statistics of individual players' performances is an impossible task. The restriction one suffers if one focuses upon individual children when studying a child behavior system is dramatically revealed by the fact that what children do *not* do (which others in the culture do do) can be as revealing of the child behavior system as what children *do* do. It is as significant for understanding the Yoredale child behavior system to know that children do *not* attend the plays of the Dramatic Society as that they *do* go to the cinema, and this fact is missed if one looks only at the children. One would not simplify the games of baseball and cricket for a novice, and make the positions of pitcher and bowler, for example, more intelligible to him by having him watch these players exclusively, through a tube or similar device. Isolating these players from the rest of the game would in fact greatly interfere with comprehending the overall structural and dynamic characteristics of intact baseball and cricket and the places of pitcher and bowler within these "systems."

Finally, and most importantly, concepts which are adequate to deal with the behavior of individual children within cultures are not adequate to deal with child behavior systems. A game analogy is appropriate here, too. Personality theory can hope to explain the behavior of a pitcher who blows up in a tight place and the different behavior of one who calmly pitches his way out of a difficulty. But personality theory cannot explain why Joe Smith is inactive, even appears listless most of the time when he plays center field, and is a ceaseless dynamo of energy at quarterback. Some of the differences in the behavior of American and British children are undoubtedly due to the same kinds of factors as those behind Joe Smith's behavior transformation between baseball and football.

It may be, of course, that prolonged exposure to the forces which bear upon a center fielder or a quarterback, an American child or a British child, bring about irreversible changes so that the person no longer behaves "appropriately" when exposed to the forces of the different position or culture. In this case personality changes have occurred, and the concepts of personality theory apply. However, it is well to keep in mind that the first step in this permanent transformation is, in all known cases, a reversible accommodation of an individual's behavior to the demands of the system. It is the final, irreversible resultant, which we call a personality change, that requires concepts of a different order. This is exemplified in physical systems. A broken (severed) beam has a permanent property (two-ness) which is entirely different from the forces which cause it, and from its initial reversible accommodation to these forces, i.e., resistance and change of shape. In this study we are interested primarily in the forces within the child behavior systems of Midwest and Yoredale, and in the original accommodation of children's behavior to these forces, rather than in their irreversible resultants.

For these practical, methodological and conceptual reasons we found individual children *as they enter a usual sampling design* to be inadequate units for the study of the child behavior systems of Midwest and Yoredale. This does not mean, of course, that individual children are not adequate subjects for some purposes in cross-cultural studies, e.g., if one is concerned with the personality which a culture produces and not with its precise cultural sources. And it does not question the aim of finally explicating the behavior of individual children.

TOWNS AS UNITS

We selected for our study material two whole towns. We carefully chose these towns to eliminate community differences with which we did not wish to be concerned. Both are non-industrial, rural trading centers; Midwest is a "Saturday night" town and Yoredale a market town. Both are local government centers; Midwest is a county seat and Yoredale is the seat of a rural district council. Both are within a similar size range; Midwest has a population of 715 people, including 128 children under 12 years of age, and Yoredale has 1,300 citizens with 245 children under 12 years of age. The towns are similarly situated with respect to cities; Midwest is 20, 35 and 45 miles, respectively, from cities of 20,000, 100,000 and 800,000 population, and Yoredale is 17, 30 and 45 miles from cities of 15,000, 100,000 and 700,000 population. Both are inland towns located almost equidistant from each country's borders. The people of both Midwest and Yoredale are overwhelmingly from family lines whose historical roots are in northern Europe; in Midwest there are, however, 37 Negroes. Both towns are naturally bounded regions separated from the surrounding farming areas by greater population density, and by different prevailing patterns of behavior. Neither town is isolated in a cultural backwater; both have open channels of communication with the larger culture via roads, telephones, radio, television, newspapers and mail. Neither Midwest nor Yoredale is obviously atypical within its culture; both are vigorous, thriving communities.

A technical advantage of working in two towns such as these is that the investigator deals with a manageable number of situations and sources of information; with one Scout troop, two schools, and three Sunday schools in each town. Furthermore, he is able to see the children *in situ*. All of each child's interpersonal and community connections are intact and functioning, leaving the child behavior systems of

Midwest and Yoredale whole and undisturbed, ready to be observed, analyzed and understood if one is able to do so.

The disadvantage of this approach is obvious, too. What does Midwest and what does Yoredale represent? Do they represent anything but themselves? Are they the United States and Great Britain? It is inevitable, we think, that Midwest and Yoredale do represent much that is peculiarly American and British in the rearing of children. However, only more data can say if this is true. In the absence of such data, the following are pertinent.

1. In case Midwest and Yoredale do represent only themselves, and have no larger significance for the United States and Great Britain, still *if* they differ with respect to their child behavior systems, they afford the opportunity of studying the operation and effects at least of these two systems. If, in addition, the towns turn out to exhibit important aspects of the whole American and British systems, the significance of the study is increased; without this, its significance is not entirely lost.

2. Although we are not able to secure replicating data from a number of American and British towns, we can secure evidence regarding the wider occurrence of particular, critical features of the Midwest and Yoredale systems. For practical reasons, complete replication is seldom possible in this kind of work, but critical, limited observations in different locales can accomplish most of the purposes of replication. There is unfortunately not space in this chapter to present this evidence.

The decision to use the whole towns of Midwest and Yoredale as our study material meant, in effect, that we considered these towns to be adequate parts of the American and British culture, and the largest units necessary for our purpose. We shall not further discuss this decision here but we shall consider the same issue in another context.

TESSERAE AS UNITS

For the very same reasons that we could not deal with American and British child behavior systems in general, we could not deal with the Midwest and Yoredale systems in general either. We had to begin with concrete units of these local systems. Again the issue was raised: What are psychologically significant and scientifically adequate parts of the behavior systems of Midwest and Yoredale, and, equally important, what are *equivalent* parts of these systems and what are the degrees of difference between non-equivalent parts?

It was suggested that we mark off arbitrary systemic units suitable for our particular scientific purposes. By means of grids with time and space axes a sample of the complex happenings which constitute the

Midwest and Yoredale systems could be secured. We could determine what happens on street corner number 17 at 4:23–4:28 P.M. on 16 July and in schoolroom number 9 at 9:29–9:34 A.M. on 6 May 1955. Would not a detailed schedule of this sort provide a sufficiently complete picture of the Midwest and Yoredale child behavior systems? It is certainly true that Midwest and Yoredale can be divided into an infinite number of parts, and that scientific *tesserae* are common, well-tested ways of sampling aggregations of related phenomena. A beaker of pond water, a quadrate of the earth's surface, a ten-minute moving picture of a beehive, and a five-minute observation on a playground provide in some respects less fragmentary pieces of functioning systems than individual, isolated amoeba, plants, bees, or children. They provide *some* of the normal contexts within which the individuals live.

Unfortunately such *tesserae* are even less adequate samples of systems than are individuals. An individual has a basic integrity; it is a self-limited unit. It is, on one level, an intact functioning part of a system; it creates and is created by the system in which it lives; it is a subsystem of the system. Its boundaries, its shape, its size, its internal system provide *some* indication of its place within the system and hence of the nature of the system. One knows that the system provides a place for it to fit. But the beaker, the quadrate, the ten-minute film and the five-minute observation are true fragments with a randomly imposed relation to the intact system. A *tessera* is created by the investigator because he is ignorant of the system.

It was here that we obtained help from the older sciences. We noted that all of them are concerned with the natural structure, the self-bounded particles, of their material on *all* levels of inclusiveness. Atoms do not detract from the reality or importance of molecules, or nuclei from cells, or hail stones from hail storms—or vice versa. A central problem of science is the interrelationships between natural particles at different levels of inclusiveness. We noted that many sciences have devised special, nondestructive techniques for the purpose of revealing structure. Here we find X-ray analysis, and electrical, magnetic and resonance techniques. A primary concern of geographers, geologists, geophysicists, oceanographers is, precisely, with the naturally occurring, unrearranged structure of the earth's surface, from quartz crystals to the planet earth. The problem of what are the "natural" units of the material of a science, i.e., units uninfluenced by the investigator, is fundamental for every science.

This was exactly the problem we faced; we wished to describe the behavior systems of Midwest and Yoredale uninfluenced by our methods, and not coerced by the assumed primacy of entities on one level, i.e., the level of the individual person. We wished, indeed, to do as other sciences have done: to look at the natural units of our material at different levels of inclusiveness and to study the interrelations of these levels. We have done this in Midwest and Yoredale on two levels, on the level of behavior settings and the level of individual persons within behavior settings.

BEHAVIOR SETTINGS AS UNITS

Behavior settings have been described in detail in the book *Midwest and Its Children* (Barker, R. G. and Wright, H. F., 1955). There is space here only to identify them concisely and to mention some of their

MIDWEST

Variety Name	Particular Name	Hours/Yr.
Streets & Sidewalks	Variously Named Streets	77,544
Grocery Stores	Kane's Grocery	24,780
Drug Stores	Clifford's Drug Store	20,855
Restaurants	Gwyn Cafe	17,000
Restaurants	Pearl Cafe	16,821
Banks	Midwest State Bank	14,719
School Classes	7th Grade	14,705
Department Stores	Cabell's Department Store	13,911
Drug Stores	Denton's Drug Store	13,871
Post Office	Midwest Post Office	13,602

YOREDALE

Variety Name	Particular Name	Hours/Yr.
Streets & Sidewalks	Variously Named Streets	300,000
Markets	Yoredale Market Day	44,000
Railroad Station	Yoredale RR Station	29,585
Milk Depot	Express Dairy	28,830
Cinemas	Supreme Cinema	28,704
Garages	Marble's Garage	27,565
School Classes	Upper Juniors	26,694
Builders	Church, Builder and Funeral Director	26,325
School Classes	Lower Juniors	26,082
Cinemas	Castle Cinema	22,880

characteristics which have special significance for the present discussion.

When a mother writes, "There is a baseball game in progress on the playground across the street," she does not refer to any individual's behavior, but to the behavior of children *en masse*. The same is true of a newspaper item which reports, "The annual fete held in the St. Ambrose Church garden was a great success."

These are behavior settings and laymen mention them as frequently as they do individual persons (Barker, R. G. and Wright, H. F., 1955, p. 7). They name them with both variety and particular names. The chart on page 464 lists the ten behavior settings of Midwest and Yoredale in which the residents of the towns spend the greatest amount of time, together with the person-hours spent per year in each setting.

When we examine these behavior phenomena, we find that they have some common features.

1. Each setting involves a characteristic pattern of behavior which is relatively independent of the presence of any particular person. The setting Presbyterian Church Worship Service is the same setting week after week with a relatively invariant patterning of its behavior even though the actors regularly change. A behavior setting is an extra-individual behavior entity; it is a standing pattern of behavior.

2. Behavior settings have a soma, a non-behavioral framework, of surrounding and internal structures and objects with which behavior is transacted. The walls, doors, shelves, groceries, cash register, etc., and their spatial arrangement are parts of the setting Kane's Grocery Store. The soma tends to stabilize the position, shape, and pattern of behavior settings.

3. Each setting has a boundary; a person knows when he is inside and when outside a setting. This boundary may be marked by a physical partition, as with Kane's Grocery Store; but there may be no fence or wall, as with Market Day. Two essentials of a behavior setting boundary are: 1) At the boundary there occurs a sudden, perceptible change in the standing behavior pattern. 2) The boundary is self-generated; it is a product of the system; it is not imposed by the investigator either purposefully or by chance, either directly or indirectly. A behavior setting is a self-bounded behavior entity.

4. The patterning of the behavior in settings is not usually uniform or iterative, but polymorphic. In the case of the setting School Class, Upper Juniors, the pattern of the pupils' behavior and that of the teacher clearly form two different figures within the total behavior pattern of the setting.

5. There are forces within settings which are usually highly coercive upon individuals to behave in accordance with the accepted behavior pattern of the setting.

6. There are forces which extend beyond the boundaries of a setting and act upon individuals to demand or encourage their entrance or to impede or prohibit it, often in a very selective way. These forces can be, in Lewin's terms, both "own" or "foreign" forces; i.e., a person may enter a setting because he wants to or because he is required to (Lewin, 1938). Sometimes both operate simultaneously. We have called the forces toward a setting, both the own and the foreign, the *claim* of the

setting upon the person; the forces away we have called the *resistance* of the setting for the person. The setting School Class, 7th Grade has an almost irresistible claim upon Midwest's twelve-year-olds. Supreme Cinema has a lesser, though still a strong claim on Yoredale children of a wider age range.

7. There are definite minima with respect to the manpower requirements for the viability of a setting; a single person is rarely enough. A setting of the variety School Class requires at least two people, a teacher and a pupil. A sand-lot baseball game of two members is a very weak setting, although we have seen it occur in this attenuated form in Midwest, i.e., a batter-catcher and a pitcher-fieldman. Three persons improve the vigor of this setting greatly.

Above the minimum manpower requirement of each setting there is usually a gradient in the claim of the setting upon persons which *decreases* as the occupancy of the setting increases, and at some point the claim often changes to resistance.

When the claim gradient of a setting is at its highest point, the pressure upon persons to enter the setting is maximal, and the selectivity of the setting for particular kinds of persons is minimal.

8. Within behavior settings there is usually a hierarchy of positions with respect to the extent of influence and responsibility over the behavior pattern of the setting. In the setting School Class, Lower Juniors, for example, the position of teacher has more power and responsibility than the position of pupil.

9. There are intra-setting claim gradients in connection with positions of power and responsibility. The claim of each position upon the occupants of a setting is a positive function of the power and responsibility of the position and an inverse function of the number of eligible occupants. This is common knowledge. It is generally recognized that the presidency or other position of highest power and responsibility in a setting has the first claim upon the membership, i.e., the strongest pressure is brought to bear upon the "right" person to fill this position. Furthermore, most people know that if they join a small church, lodge, or class they will be under more pressure to take an active and responsible role in it than if they join large settings of these sorts.

The special significance of intra-setting claim gradients in the present connection is this: the smaller the number of occupants of settings, the greater the proportion of these occupants who must serve in positions of power and responsibility.

10. The behavioral parts of a setting are highly interdependent; the activity of the teacher and that of the pupils, for example, are completely dependent one upon the other; there is high internal unity.

11. Behavior settings are interdependent with other settings. Occur-

rences in the setting Cabell's Department Store can have a direct effect on the setting Midwest State Bank; e.g., a sale in Cabell's causes funds to be transferred at the bank. However, occurrences in one department of Cabell's store usually have a greater effect upon other departments within the store than the store has upon the bank. In other words, the internal interdependence of settings is greater than their external interdependence. This internal and external interdependence of settings is crucial. It is this which makes it possible to identify behavior settings with a defined degree of internal unity and of separation from other settings. We know with precision that the behavior setting School Class, 7th Grade is equivalent in degree of internal and external relatedness to the setting Post Office and that the latter in Midwest is equivalent to Supreme Cinema in Yoredale. This is the essential feature of behavior settings which makes them natural units of the Midwest and Yoredale systems and suitable for the first important step in quantification: comparison by counting equivalent parts.

Because the list of settings which we have identified reads, for the most part, like a commonsense directory of a town's businesses, organization meetings, school classes, and so forth, it is sometimes overlooked that their identification involves highly technical operations and precise ratings of interdependence.[1] The symbol K-21 designates the precise quantitative criterion which we have used to establish the limits of behavior settings. This was selected so that the settings would fall within the usual range of laymen's discrimination. Nevertheless, the criteria for their identification are not lay criteria (Barker, R. G. and Wright, H. F. 1955, pp. 50–56 and 491–495).

This raises the question whether behavior settings are, in fact, natural units. How can this be when their size is influenced by an arbitrarily chosen criterion? This issue is discussed in *Midwest and Its Children.* Here we shall only refer to an analogy. How many rooms has a house? The answer to this depends upon how bounded an area has to be, to be defined as a room. What about areas separated by doorways without doors, by double doors, by archways, by different floor levels, by railings, by counters, by curtains? One is free to define as he wishes the degree of boundedness of a room. But when this degree is established, the number of rooms in a house is determined by the structure of the house, not by the investigator. Furthermore, as the criterion of boundedness changes, the number of rooms does *not* change as a monotonic function of the change in degree of boundedness; it changes in a saltatory way. Finally, there is a finite minimum and a finite maximum number of rooms in any house, independent of the criterion of boundedness used.

12. Similarity of parts has no place in the identification of a behavior setting; interdependence is the sole criterion. However, settings identi-

fied on the basis of degree of interdependence have greater or less similarity of behavior pattern and soma. This provides a basis for the meaningful classification of settings into varieties. This is a taxonomic problem.[2] Here, too, one has some freedom as to the degree of similarity he requires for establishing a variety; but once this limit is set, nature determines the number of varieties. The degree of similarity that we have adopted for the S-30 variety of behavior setting (the variety used here) is, essentially, the lowest degree of similarity which still allows for the transposition of standing behavior patterns between the somas of members of the variety without disturbing in crucial ways the functioning of the setting. Thus, the Pearl Cafe and the Gwyn Cafe in Midwest could change loci without appreciably disturbing the functioning of either. They belong to the same variety. Such an exchange would not be possible for the Gwyn Cafe and the Midwest Post Office. They belong to different varieties of settings.

This rating is crucial in intercultural studies for it is the basis for establishing the equivalence of settings in different cultures. By means of it we have answered the important question: Do the same varieties of settings exist in Midwest and Yoredale?

13. Behavior settings are comprehensive; they blanket the entire town. No behavior occurs in Midwest or Yoredale outside the boundaries of a behavior setting.

In addition to these structural and dynamic characteristics of behavior settings, they have many other behavioral and somatic properties useful in studying the functioning systems of towns.

These characteristics of behavior settings are in the nature of primitive hypotheses; they are, more properly, prototheories. Most of them are very close to the facts to which they refer. Thus, the *claim* of settings over people is so clear that in some cases it has a market value. A thriving store sells for more than the value of its soma (its building and its inventory); its claim over its employees, its suppliers, and its customers will often bring much more than its physical assets. These prototheories are not the product of a more inclusive set of theories; they stand alone at the present time. However, they pass some of the tests of useful theories: they point to some new knowledge and they bring some new order among otherwise discrete facts. Furthermore, most of these characteristics of behavior settings are widely possessed by other natural particles of scientific material, both animate and inanimate. Gerard has named entities with these properties *orgs,* and has pointed to their occurrence at many levels of phenomena (Gerard, 1957).

It will be obvious to the reader that towns, too, possess all the properties of behavior settings, but with lesser internal unity. They, too, are bounded, *extra-individual,* behavior entities within the context of a nation, or regional culture. Persons on the other hand, are bounded *individual* entities. We have, in fact, in this study identified natural behavior units on four levels in a series from more to less inclusive, and *pari passu*, with less to more internal interdependence; namely,

Nation:	United States	Great Britain
Town:	Midwest	Yoredale
Behavior Setting:	Settings of Midwest	Settings of Yoredale
Person:	Individual Residents of Midwest	Individual Residents of Yoredale

We have focused our attention upon the behavior setting level of this series and upon some functional relations between settings and the behavior of individuals.

EXEMPLIFYING DATA

Representative enumerative data concerning behavior settings and persons will now be presented for Midwest and Yoredale, and some of their consequences for the child behavior systems of the two towns will be discussed. The behavior setting data refer to one category of settings only, Community Behavior Settings. These are all of the settings of a town *except* those which occur within homes; they are the town's public settings. Private, family behavior settings are not included. In the discussion which follows we shall use the terms *setting, behavior setting,* and *community behavior setting* interchangeably to indicate what are, technically, K-21 Community Behavior Settings.

The numbers of parts of Midwest and Yoredale on the levels of behavior settings and persons are:

	Number of Settings	*Number of Persons*
Midwest	579	715
Yoredale	494	1300
Ratio: MW/YD	1.18	0.55

Midwest has more settings and fewer persons than Yoredale. The average Midwest setting has 47% as many occupants as the average Yoredale setting. The same relationship holds for the children of the towns when we consider only the settings which children actually inhabit. According to the theory of behavior setting claim gradients, Midwest behavior settings bring stronger pressures on citizens to enter and participate in them than do Yoredale settings. We would therefore expect Midwesterners to spend more time in behavior settings than Yoredale citizens and we would expect the occupants of Midwest settings to be less rigidly selected with respect to age, sex, and other individual characteristics.

Data respecting time spent by various age groups in behavior settings are as follows (mean hours per person per week spent in behavior settings by children, adolescents, and adults and aged persons):

	Children (under 12 years)	Adolescents (12 to 17 yrs. 11 mo.)	Adults & Aged (18 yrs. & over)
Midwest	20.5	53.7	23.6
Yoredale	19.8	41.9	22.3

At each age level, Midwest citizens spend, on the average, more time in community behavior settings than do Yoredale citizens. Over all ages, Midwesterners spend 25.2 hours per week in the town's settings and Yoredale citizens 23.0 hours. The greatest occupancy of behavior settings occurs in adolescence in both towns; this is also the age when the difference between the towns is greatest.

Here are data on the selectivity of behavior settings (percent of behavior settings unsegregated for age, sex, social class):

	Age	Sex	Social Class
Midwest	52	86	92
Yoredale	23	83	76

More of Midwest's than of Yoredale's settings are unsegregated: they are inhabited by persons of all ages, both sexes, and all social classes. The lesser segregation on the basis of age is especially marked in Midwest.

According to the theory of intra-setting claim gradients, Midwest's behavior settings place greater pressure upon their fewer inhabitants to assume positions of responsibility and functional importance than is true of Yoredale settings. The data show that the average Midwesterner in the course of a year fills 7.1 responsible positions in behavior settings; the average Yoredale citizen fills 2.3 similarly responsible positions. Data for separate age groups follow (mean number of responsible positions filled by children, adolescents, and adults and aged persons):

	Children	Adolescents	Adults & Aged
Midwest	8.4	16.6	5.9
Yoredale	2.7	4.7	2.0

At all ages the average Midwesterner is more than three times as frequently in responsible positions within settings as the average resident of Yoredale. The relationships between the age groups with respect to average number of responsibilities is surprisingly similar; in both towns, the order of the ages in terms of increasing number of responsibilities is: adults and aged, children, adolescents. It should not be overlooked that adults and aged *as a class,* because of their larger total numbers, perform the greater total number of important jobs in both Midwest and Yoredale.

We can summarize these findings in two general statements: (1) People are functionally more important in Midwest than in Yoredale; and (2) differences between people are functionally less important in Midwest than in Yoredale. We shall briefly assess and exemplify the evidence for these statements and then point out some of their consequences for the behavior of individual children within the Midwest and Yoredale systems.

IMPORTANCE OF PEOPLE IN MIDWEST AND YOREDALE

The average citizen of Midwest is busier in essential jobs in community behavior settings (as secretary, president, teacher, soloist, clerk, trustee, etc.) and does a larger share of the town's public work than is true of Yoredale citizens. People, including children and adolescents, are in greater demand and in shorter supply. Midwest has fewer replacements; the average person is functionally more important.

Children are not exceptions. Sixty-four (11%) of Midwest's settings would have to shut up shop for lack of *operating* personnel if children and adolescents were removed from the town; 14 (3%) of Yoredale's settings would have to close under these circumstances. Another 64 of Midwest's settings would be greatly inconvenienced in their functioning by the withdrawal of their child and adolescent functionaries; this is true of 29 Yoredale settings. In all, 22% of Midwest's and 9% of Yoredale's behavior settings are dependent to an important degree upon children and adolescents for their operation. This does not include those settings in which children and adolescents constitute the bulk of the membership or audience, but are not essential operators, such as school and Sunday school classes, playgrounds, and children's choir practice. It includes only those settings where children and adolescents fill positions of power and responsibility.

The setting *Midwest Weekly* is an example. The editor of the paper, who is also a member of the school board, occasionally asks the school principal to release one of his schoolboy part-time employees for an afternoon to help meet a printing deadline. This setting depends for its successful functioning upon adolescent press and linotype operators. Whole varieties of Midwest's settings are similarly dependent. Of Midwest's 23 sports settings, 83% are completely dependent upon child and adolescent contestants; this is true of 25% of Yoredale's 16 sports settings. Of Midwest's 27 plays, concerts and programs, 85% involve child and adolescent actors almost completely; this is true of 12% of Yoredale's 34 plays, concerts and programs. All of Midwest's paper routes and half of Yoredale's are carried by children and adolescents.

This feature of the Midwest and Yoredale systems creates quite different conditions of relevance for the social perceptions, values, and skills of individual citizens.

First, there is a cognitive difference. The importance of all kinds of people, including children, is clearly visible in Midwest. The children of Midwest do not have to be told of their importance; they, themselves, can see directly the current value of children in the operation of the town. This is much less true in Yoredale. We have seen that the children of Yoredale are, in fact, only half as important, functionally, as the children of Midwest. Their visible importance is even lower, because the settings in which they have an essential part are more obscure. For example, they are essential in the setting Schoolboy Cricket Games, but this setting has very few spectators; the adult team draws the audience. The equivalent setting in Midwest, Highschool Football Games, has no adult competitor; it is the one which attracts the crowds.

Second, a set of motivational differences is engendered by the two systems. The more frequent responsible participation of Midwest children and adolescents in community behavior settings inevitably provides them with more frequent personal and vicarious achievement satisfactions and elicits for them more frequent approval, both individually and as members of valued groups. It also confronts Midwest children with more frequent difficulties and possibilities of failure. Any system in which these positive and negative experiences occur with greater frequency and before a wider audience can be expected to produce greater feelings of self-esteem and social status and, also, more self-analysis and personal uncertainty for the persons involved. Midwesterners believe that these are necessary ingredients of a child-rearing system. They think this is the way character is formed, and that the earlier a person learns to "take it"— the difficulties, the failures, the decisions, and the tension as well as the achievements and satisfactions—in real life situations, the better for him. They call the behavior produced by these experiences social maturity, a term with positive meaning to them; Yoredale citizens are likely to call it precocity, a negative word to them.

In Yoredale, on the other hand, children are prepared for *future* participation and responsibility in prominent community behavior settings. This preparation is thought to occur best in special settings removed from the main areas of adult living where most of the difficulties and achievements are somewhat shielded from public notice. A system in which critical positive and negative experiences are less frequent and less widely visible can be expected to generate less self-regard and social status, and also less self-analysis and uncertainty. Yoredale believes that slow preparation is best for children. They call the product wholesome behavior; Midwesterners are likely to use the adjective immature.

Third, rather specific behavior and value differences are produced by these systems. A system in which many behavior settings compete via pressures and rewards for the participation of a limited number of children and adolescents places a premium on versatile, adaptable, and responsible behavior. In the Midwest system the all-around person, the adjustable person, the person who is willing to do his part even when he cannot do it very well, has a higher value than in the Yoredale system. It is these versatile, willing people who make the Midwest system function, and they reap much approval and many satisfactions within the town's behavior settings.

There is another side to this coin. Of two behavior systems with different numbers of participants, the one with the fewer participants has either to be content with achievements on a pass level in settings where manhours are required for excellence, or it must be content with fewer settings. Midwest makes the former choice. It openly and explicitly values participation, responsibility, willingness and adaptability more highly than level of performance. It believes it is better for children, and for the town, to have a school band *and* a chorus whose performances are only adequate than to have a band *or* a chorus drilled to excellence. Yoredale, on the other hand, can and in some settings does spend its manhours to achieve a higher level of performance than is possible in Midwest. We do not have data to determine whether this is true for Yoredale settings generally. We do know that in some settings Yoredale does not make efficient use of its greater manpower, and that in others it does not use its extra manpower. The latter is the case with school settings, for example.

Yoredale does not lavish manpower on its schools; classes are 35% larger than in Midwest. Neither does it focus the efforts of the children on school subjects. The school days are, almost to the minute, the same length in both towns, and the numbers of school days in the year are nearly identical. The Yoredale curriculum includes more of the so-called fringe subjects such as needlework and woodwork than the Midwest curriculum. Yoredale brings more manhours of effort into education in two places; it starts its children to school at 5 years of age instead of 6, and it sends 20 of its 101 adolescents out of the town to public or private grammar schools where the teaching manpower is greater. However, Yoredale does use manhours effectively on sports and dramatics, and the level of achievement in them is much higher than in Midwest.

The lower maximal level of functioning in Midwest behavior settings has an important secondary consequence, and one which helps to make the Midwest system internally consistent. It is this: although Midwest settings make greater claims on children for participation and responsibility and give them more satisfactions, some behavior setting claims are tempered by the lower levels of performance which are tolerated. If this were not so, such widespread participation and responsibility would not be possible for the children of Midwest. This is a difference between the towns to which citizens are very sensitive. When we told Yoredale citizens of this feature of the Midwest system, they spoke with disapproval of the juvenilization of Midwest life. Midwesterners, in turn, judged the adults of Yoredale to be selfish and insensitive to the welfare of children. Participation by children and adolescents is not the primary source of instances of a lower, maximal level of functioning of Midwest settings; but the presence of children and adolescents in important positions does not usually act to increase the level of operation of settings.

DIFFERENCES BETWEEN PEOPLE IN MIDWEST AND YOREDALE

The second general difference between the towns which is revealed by the data on differentiation, participation, and segregation is this: the differences between people are functionally less important in Midwest than in Yoredale. Because of their greater claim upon participants, Midwest settings are less selective, and people of all ages, sexes, and social classes associate more often on a functionally equivalent level in Midwest than in Yoredale.

The greater egalitarianism of the different age groups in Midwest is especially marked. Seventy-four (13%) of Midwest's behavior settings explicitly exclude children under 12 years of age; this is true of 141 (29%) of Yoredale's settings. In 200 (35%) of Midwest's settings children or adolescents share responsible positions with adults; this occurs in 123 (25%) of Yoredale's settings. Two hundred and sixty-nine (47%) of Midwest's settings have only adults (no children, adolescents, or aged persons) in responsible positions; this is true of 317 (66%) of Yoredale's settings.

The greater joint responsible participation of children, adolescents, and adults in the settings of Midwest reduces the difference in the functional value of these classes of people, and contributes, without doubt, to the greater self-esteem and social status of Midwest children. This often leads to a familiar, often first-naming, kind of relationship between the children and adults which is in sharp contrast to the greater separation and distance in Yoredale. The reduction of functional differences between people in Midwest contributes, also, as we have mentioned, to lowering the maximal level of behavior setting operation in Midwest. Thus Midwest's summer band concerts are produced by the town's band whose members range in age from 10 to 45 years. These concerts are on a different level from those in Yoredale's Market Square which are provided by professional and semiprofessional military bands from training camps in the area.

These differences in the behavior systems of Midwest and Yoredale appear to be required by the differentiation of the towns on the levels of behavior settings and persons. But this does not tell us why Midwest's 715 people maintain 579 settings and why Yoredale's 1300 people maintain only 494 settings. Settings are not imposed by outside authorities to any restrictive degree; 360 of Midwest's and 257 of Yoredale's settings are of endogenous origin and maintenance, and could be abandoned with no opposition from outside the town. Midwest could easily reduce the number of its settings to Yoredale's 494, or even to 272, making them proportional to the towns' populations. And no authority prevents Yoredale citizens from creating 85 new settings, or even 475. These are the levels of behavior setting differentiation which the citizens of the towns find congenial. However, after the behavior setting systems are established, they coerce individual persons, particularly children. A series of circular processes is initiated: of individuals creating congenial settings, and then being coerced by their own creations to behave appropriately. Finally some of this appropriate behavior becomes fixed and irreversible. When this occurs, the system is not only maintained by the continual shaping of the behavior of new entries, particularly of new-born children, by the systemic influences we have described (and others too), but change in the system is internally resisted by the personalities the system has created.

Here, then, is an instance of the usefulness of the extra-individual behavior entities we have called behavior settings in the comparative study of cultures. It will be obvious that settings have many other characteristics in addition to degree of differentiation. We have studied such attributes of settings in Midwest and Yoredale as the number of varieties (Midwest has fewer varieties than Yoredale), the amount of time spent in different varieties of settings by citizens of different ages, sexes, and social classes, and the degree of occurrence in settings of such behavior as emotional expressiveness, large muscle actions, social interaction; aesthetic behavior. The standing behavior patterns of settings are as rich and variable, and as measurable as is the behavior of individual persons.

NOTES

1. The interested student should study carefully the basis of judging the limits of behavior settings as set forth in *Midwest and Its Children.*
2. Our solution to it is described in *Midwest and Its Children* where a precise method of rating the degree of similarity of any two settings is given.

BIBLIOGRAPHY

Barker, R. G. and Wright, H. F. 1955. *Midwest and Its Children*. Evanston, Ill., Row, Peterson and Co.

Gerard, R. W. 1957. "Units and Concepts of Biology," *Science*, 125:429–33.

Lewin, K. 1938. *The Conceptual Representation and Measurement of Psychological Forces*. Durham, N.C., Duke University Press.

About the Chapter

This chapter illustrates how methodologically rigorous techniques can measure psychological changes associated with acculturation in a changing American Indian group. The Rorschach test is used, to define precisely and statistically the modal processes of both Menomini men and women and of each of the acculturative groups. This enables the authors to locate the psycho-cultural center of gravity of both men and women and to specify the nature of psychological continuum in acculturation. The Spindlers' study is a fine example of the application of experimental design in the culture and personality field.

About the Authors

GEORGE A. SPINDLER has been Associate Professor of Anthropology and Education at Stanford University since 1950. LOUISE SPINDLER is a research associate in the Department of Anthropology at Stanford. They have collaborated on most of their field work and much of their writing on the Menomini Indians of Wisconsin, whom they have studied intermittently since 1948, and on the Blood Indians of Alberta, Canada, whom they have studied during recent summers. Together they have published numerous articles on the Menomini and on general processes in culture changes. In their collaboration Louise Spindler has taken major responsibility for collection and analysis of data on the women, and George Spindler on the men.

16

A Modal Personality Technique in the
Study of Menomini Acculturation

LOUISE SPINDLER and GEORGE SPINDLER

Stanford University

This chapter describes the exploratory application of a technique of analysis to data collected in a comprehensive study of acculturation of the Menomini Indians of Wisconsin. The study as a whole has been concerned particularly with the relationships between psychological and sociocultural dimensions of acculturation.[1]

The modal personality technique discussed here, applied to Rorschach data, was developed first by Wallace (1952) for his study of the Tuscarora. It was used in our study of the Menomini for different purposes. In explaining what we did and why we did it, we will first describe certain aspects of the treatment of our data before we applied the modal personality technique and indicate some problems left unsolved by this treatment. Then we will describe the application of the technique to these same data, and show how it shed light on these problems and generated new questions. We will indicate some first steps toward solution of these problems.

We do not mean to imply that the technique, presented and applied as it is here, is a "final answer" to the knotty problems of treating with modalities in Rorschach data. There are many unresolved statistical as well as logical problems. But the method used is offered as a promising new approach to the analysis of trends and patterns in the psychological concomitants of acculturation.

Initial Treatment of the Data

We studied the male Menomini first. We drew a sample of 68 adult men, all one half or more Menomini, and did a limited case study of each one. The data collected included a Rorschach for each, an interview of an hour to several hours in length, information on 24 sociocultural items (such as house type, knowledge and use of native language, use of native medicine, income, occupation, participation in groups, etc.), and observational data on the subject's interaction with others in his household and in other groups. We also collected nine short autobiographies from men selected on the basis of typicality in their particular acculturative level (and later, fifteen from women), and we participated and observed in the normal round of community activities intermittently over a period of seven years (G. Spindler, 1955).

We subjected much of our data to quantitative statistical treatment. It was necessary to define our variables sharply if we wanted to get information on the co-variance of psychological and sociocultural process. Our first problem was to properly place each subject in an acculturative sequence. We did this by first dividing our sample into acculturative categories on the basis of religious identification and participation. The categories thus constituted were then validated by application of a measure of association (tetrachoric r) to each sociocultural index (occupation, etc.). This application proved that we had a progressive continuum of acculturation, with the groups as posited, ranging from least to most acculturated, and from lowest to highest socio-economic status in terms of western values. We then applied a measure of differentiation (chi-square) to determine whether or not the groups as posited were significantly different from each other in respect to the same indices. There was overlap of course, since these acculturative groups participate in the same community, but all were differentiated in certain important items. The range of acculturation thus posited and confirmed in its sociocultural dimensions is graphically described in figure 1.

With our sociocultural variable "pinned down," the problem became one of discovering what significant differences were exhibited by our subjects in respect to personality structure. We applied quantitative measures to our Rorschach data, and used autobiographic, interview, and observational data for a more qualitative interpretation of the relationships between psychological and sociocultural process. Chi square and "exact probability" techniques were applied to the Rorschach scores of each socioculturally defined group, in comparison with every other one. This necessitated treating each score, such as "human movement" (M), form (F), etc., and each ratio (such as M:sum color), separately. The differences thus revealed among the various sociocultural groups of males were numerous, highly significant statistically, and "made sense" with

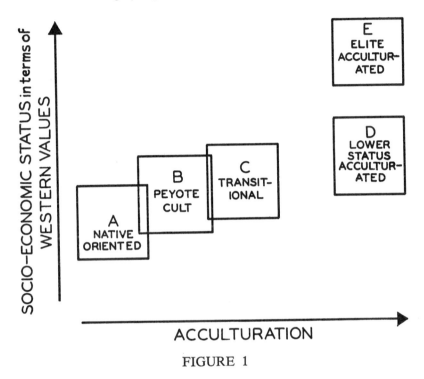

FIGURE 1

respect to relationships between psychological and sociocultural process. A discussion of these differences is not necessary to our purposes at the moment.

Extending the Sample to Include the Women

In the middle period of our field work we began collecting data from a similar sample of women (61 cases), many of them married to men in our sample, or in the same household. But we did not analyze the data from this part of the sample until after the work with the men was finished (L. Spindler, 1956). We proceeded to apply the same techniques that had worked so well with the male sample. The sociocultural data created no serious problems, because the female sample fell into the same groupings as the male. But the Rorschach data did not. We went through the same laborious process of applying chi-square and exact probability measures of differences in the distribution of separate Rorschach scores, in all possible comparisons between sociocultural defined groups of females. But little was revealed by way of either statistically or logically consistent differences. Apparently the females were a sample of a universe that was not responding to the same forces as the males. Or they were responding to the same forces, but differently.

This led us to perform a massive test of over-all differences between all males and all females without regard for separate sociocultural groupings. The chi-square technique thus applied did reveal certain significant differences that were internally consistent in terms of psychological hypotheses.[2]

Unanswered Questions

The analysis up to this point left us with many unanswered questions, some of which were partially answered for the male sample. We knew little about the differences that might exist in the complex relationship of psychological and sociocultural processes in the female sample in comparison to the males. Some of the questions occurred to us after we had devised a new approach to the problem. Others were apparent by the time we had finished with the analysis described above. We will discuss three of them.

The first question has to do with homogeneity. We had ample proof that both our males and females were highly differentiated socioculturally, as graphically displayed in figure 1. We therefore had a socioculturally heterogeneous sample for both sexes. But to what extent were these socioculturally differentiated samples psychologically homogeneous? And were the females more psychologically homogeneous than the males—despite the sociocultural differentiations exhibited in common by both sexes?

The second question has to do with continuity. If we start with a native-oriented baseline in a synchronic acculturative sequence, we would expect to find some continuity of psychological structure irrespective of overt sociocultural adaptation. Hallowell's work has indicated that there was a high degree of personality persistence throughout his several levels of acculturation among the Ojibwa in Canada and Wisconsin (1951). And other workers have described parallel persistences in their studies (Mekeel, 1936; Thompson, 1948), though they did not use the same data in the same way.

The third question has to do with location of modal psychological adaptations in the acculturative sequence. We have termed this the "psycho-cultural center of gravity" (henceforth p.c.g.). What we mean by this can be expressed in a question: What part of the acculturative continuum (see figure 1) represents most adequately the typical psychological adaptations characteristic of a whole sample? If the least acculturated (native-oriented) group is most representative, then our sample is psychologically more conservative than would be the case if one of the acculturated groups ("D" or "E") was. And since we already knew that our males and females were adapting differently, we wanted to find out whether the p.c.g. was different for males than for females.

These three questions are interrelated, and constitute the main points of departure in our further analysis. Before we answer these specific questions we will describe the modal personality technique and the Rorschach profiles it revealed as most characteristic of the Menomini men, and women, separately.

The Modal Personality Technique

Details of the procedure of constructing modal personality profiles may be found in Wallace's monograph (1952). The most important reason for using the technique is that the personality structure (as revealed by the Rorschach) is not fractionated. The technique permits expression of a configuration of interrelated psychological characteristics. This configuration is most directly expressed, in Rorschach analysis, in the psychogram, a bar graph of scores representing the thirteen most important determinants of perception (see Fig. 2) such as human movement (M), animal movement (FM), form in outline (F), form-controlled shading (Fc), form-controlled color (FC), color predominant (CF), and so on in usages standardized in the Klopfer system of scoring responses (1956). A psychogram of this kind, summarizing the total number of scored responses given by a subject in each determinant category, can be constructed for any individual protocol. It can also be done for a group of protocols, using expressions of central tendency such as means.

The difficulty with using means as measures of central tendency for a group of protocols is that the distributions of most Rorschach scores are highly skewed (most people give 1 or 2 "M's" for example, but some give a few, or many more), and the extreme scores bias the mean out of proportion to their significance. Other objections of this kind apply also to the raw mode, and the median. In addition, for our purposes, what is wanted is an expression of range around each measure of central tendency that will include the Rorschach records of all those individuals that are enough alike as to be psychologically indistinguishable, so that this "class" of individuals can be located wherever they may be in the acculturative continuum.

The procedure of construction of modal personality types, in the form of modal Rorschach psychograms, with expressions of acceptable range, is as follows. First, the crude mode was found for each score (of which there are 21) for all males and all females separately. Then a function of the standard error of measurement for Rorschach scores, based on an estimated reliability for the Rorschach test of 0.800 (Wallace, 1952, p. 65), was used to set limits on either side of these crude modes.[3] This operation defined the "modal range" for each score. All scores falling in the modal range are considered indistinguishable from each other. Therefore all individual Rorschach protocols whose scores fall within the modal ranges for all 21 scores were regarded as belonging to a "modal" class. One such modal class was found for the females, and one for the males. The scores of all the individual protocols in each modal class were then averaged, so that a modal psychogram for the men, and for the women, could be drawn. The results are expressed in Figure 2, and will be discussed later.

Modal Menomini

The modal psychograms for Menomini males and females are presented in Figure 2 below. Our first application of the new information gained by construction of these modal types will be concerned with the psychological differences between males and females they may be presumed to represent.

It is apparent that the modal psychogram for the males is quite different than that for the females. The "m," "k," "Fk," and "c" determinants are represented in the former and absent in the latter and the "FC"/ "CF" ratios are reversed. These determinants express inanimate movement (m), "squeezed down," two-dimensional percepts of what are ordinarily three-dimensional concepts (k), diffuse, vague percepts (K), vista percepts (FK), and use of achromatic color (C'). The CF dominance over FC in the male psychogram indicates that there is less control by form perception (F) over color perception (C) than is the case with the modal women. These determinants together, as usually interpreted, combine to produce a picture of disturbance, diffuse anxiety, and decrease in emotional and intellectual controls among the modal males that is not represented among the females. It is therefore indicated that males have a more difficult time adapting to the conditions existing in the reservation community than do the women.[4]

These are the same indices that differentiated the males and females in our previously described overall test of differences between all males and all females. This suggests that the differentiation springs from the modal personality characteristics for the two sexes respectively. Otherwise we might as well assume that the differences revealed by the massive statistical test were the result of inconsistent distributions of single scores. This is important to us because it contributes to our understanding of the regularity of the psychological processes of adaptation taking place in our population.

This kind of interpretation of the psychological meaning of Rorschach scores will be questioned by many. A discussion of the complex problems of validity and reliability of the Rorschach would lead us too far, here. But there is a large mass of published literature on the subject (Ainsworth, 1956). Whatever the ultimate status of the Rorschach, we need to be even more wary of over-interpreting, in our cross-cultural usage, than users of the technique in our own society. For that reason, in most of what follows we have applied the Rorschach technique in such a way

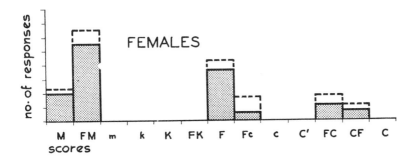

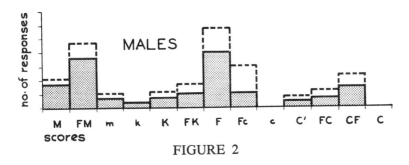

FIGURE 2

that conventional interpretations concerning the meaning of scores are unnecessary. The way we do this should become clear as we proceed.

The Three Questions Discussed

We can now discuss the questions about homogeneity, continuity, and the location of the p.c.g. A tentative answer to the first question appears when we see that 12 percent of the males and 25 percent of the females in the whole sample are included in the modal class represented for each sex by the psychograms in figure 2. Our sample is socioculturally heterogeneous, and in a general way, this is accompanied by psychological heterogeneity as well. There are many more cases left out of the modal class for each sex than are included within it. More interesting to us is the fact that the women are apparently more homogeneous psychologically than the men, despite the fact that socioculturally they are differentiated in the same way and degree as the men.[5]

The questions concerning continuity and the p.c.g. must be discussed together since they are closely interrelated. The p.c.g. can be located by

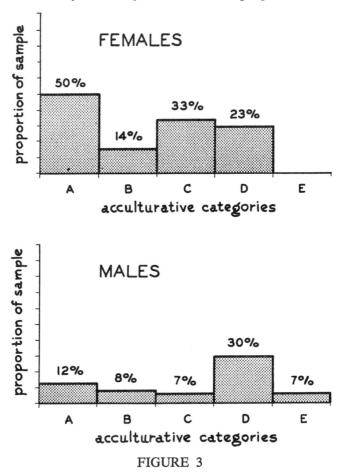

FIGURE 3

several different procedures. The simplest one is to compare the modal psychogram for each sex to the "typical" psychogram of each sociocultural category. The construction of typical psychograms for each category requires a separate operation (see G. Spindler 1955, pp. 169–70). The modal male psychogram for the whole Menomini sample is most like that of the transitional category, and that of the females is most like that of the native-oriented category. This location of the p.c.g. by inspection is a simple but forthright procedure that suggests that Menomini females tend typically to be psychologically more conservative than do the males. It also suggests that the males typically tend to be neither acculturated nor native-oriented, psychologically speaking, but suspended in between the two more culturally coherent stages of acculturation.

Another way of locating the p.c.g. is to find the proportion of each acculturative category that is composed of members of the modal class for males and for females on which the modal psychogram for each sex is based. The chart above (Figure 3) presents this information in graphic form. Table 1 gives the data upon which the chart is based.

TABLE 1

DISTRIBUTION OF MODAL PERSONALITY TYPE IN
ACCULTURATIVE CATEGORIES

Category	No. Protocols	No. Modal Class	Modal as Per Cent of Category
		MALES	
A	17	2	12
B	13	1	8
C	15	1	7
D	10	3	30
E	13	1	7
Totals	68	8	
		FEMALES	
A	8	4	50
B	7	1	14
C	12	4	33.3
D	26	6	23
E	8	0	0
Totals	61	15	

The percentages of each acculturative category composed of modal class representatives are noted. The percentages do not, of course, total 100%, since they are proportions of different total numbers. For example, the native-oriented female category (A) numbers 8 women, 4 of whom are in the modal class, "C" numbers 12 women, 4 of whom are in the modal class, and "D" totals 26 women, 6 of whom are in the modal class.

This procedure affords us information on both the p.c.g. and continuity. The p.c.g. for the women is still the native-oriented group, since that group contributes the highest proportion of its number to the modal personality type.[6] The hypothesis of psychological conservatism for the women is given some support. It is also important, however, that all female acculturative categories, excepting that of the elite acculturated and Peyote Cult group, contribute substantially to the modal class. The Peyote Cult group contributes only one case. This highlights the nature of this group, which we have termed a "systematic deviation" in the context of Menomini acculturation. Disregarding the Peyote group as a special case, the female native-oriented psychological structure exhibits continuity throughout the acculturative continuum until the elite acculturated position is reached. Elite Menomini women represent a clear departure in terms of modal psychological adaptation within the Menomini acculturative continuum.

The information conveyed by the distributional chart (Figure 3) for the males gives us some further support for the interpretation of the results of location of the p.c.g. by inspection. The p.c.g. is even further along the acculturative continuum than the inspection procedure indicated—in the lower status acculturated category. The psycho-cultural position of the males, as indicated by this procedure, is therefore practically the reverse of that for the females. The *modal tendency* in psychological adaptation for the Menomini males is towards full acculturation. For the females it is towards a least acculturated status. As we would expect, the distributional chart also conveys the information that each acculturative category contributes in some degree to the male modal class. Apparently there is continuity here also, but in lesser degree, and the continuity is not in terms of a native-oriented psychological structure or cultural position. The continuity that does exist for males is apparently a result of acculturation rather than nativistic persistences.

The People in the Modal Classes

This application of the modal personality technique calls for us to turn to the actual people composing the modal class for each sex and ask what characteristics they exhibit with respect to the norms of their groups. This provides both another approach to the location of the p.c.g. and a qualitative sense of the relationships we are examining. We can only indicate the direction such an analysis would take. We will discuss the women first.[7]

The members of the modal class for the whole sample that are in the native-oriented group of women are typical members of their group. They all exhibit a full complement of nativistic cultural retentions, and self-consciously try to raise their children as Indians.

The one modal class woman in the Peyote Cult group was born as a Peyotist but retains strong social and cultural ties with the native-oriented group. She is thus deviant in the context of the cult, though typical in terms of modal psychological characteristics for the women as a whole.

The transitional women in the modal class lack any clear-cut group identifications. Although all of the women in the transitional group were placed in the group through the use of the same criteria as were used in placing the males, the term "marginal native-oriented" would describe more accurately their psychological and cultural adaptations. For, unlike the males, the women in the transitional category all express traditional Menomini values in their behaviors. Further, the modal cases found here are not psychologically deviant within their group as far as Rorschach scores indicate since most of the women in the transitional acculturative category either fall within the modal class or exhibit all but one scoring criterion of this class. This underlines the psychological conservatism of this group, since the modal pattern is identifiable as native-oriented.

The lower status acculturated women who are in the modal class, with one exception, self-consciously chose to interact and identify with older relatives who had experience with the traditional Menomini culture, even though these modal women themselves have had no direct experience in groups or patterns representative of Menomini culture. They are deviant in their group, since the majority of lower status acculturated women are second or third generation Catholics who, at the verbal level at least, exhibit values not unlike those of middle class white women, and do not exhibit the Rorschach pattern of the female modal class.

There are no modal class women in the elite acculturated group. This category is composed of women striving self-consciously for acceptance on middle class white terms. They represent a marked, deviant minority in the acculturative continuum for women, together with the non-modal women from the lower status acculturated category.

The males in the modal class express in varying degrees, in both their Rorschach records and in other behaviors (such as brawling, drunkenness, apathy, and criminality) the disorganization in cognitive and emotional controls and in social adjustment that are aspects of what may be termed a transitional syndrome in Menomini acculturation. There are three partial exceptions to this statement. They are men who exhibit highly constricted personality structures that presumably represent the result of social withdrawal and psychological defense against threat. This latter structure may be considered a permutation of the first.

These modal class males represent the central tendency of psychological adaptation in the male acculturative continuum. They are all, however, deviant in some degree within their particular acculturative categories, as would be expected because the male categories are so sharply differentiated from each other. Each represents an intra-category homogeneity of psychological adaptation that differentiates it from each other category—with the exception of the transitionals who are psychologically more heterogeneous.

The information revealed by the procedure adds support to the inferences concerning the location of the p.c.g., and concerning continuity. The p.c.g. for the women is native-oriented. This native-oriented pattern in Rorschach scores and in other behavioral characteristics is retained in comparatively high degree through the acculturative continuum (disregarding the Peyote group as a special case) until the acculturated departure, representing a small minority, takes place. For the males, the picture is quite different. The male p.c.g. in terms of individual cases is transitional-disorganized. The conditions of acculturation permit the maintenance of psychological continuity for women in conservative terms, but require the men to adapt differentially, depending upon which part of the social structure and acculturation continuum they represent.

Concluding Statement

The application of the modal personality technique has made it possible to ask and provide tentative answers to questions that our previous treatment of the data did not permit. It is of particular importance that this application requires minimal acceptance of standard interpretations concerning the meaning of Rorschach scores. The application depends primarily upon the analysis of concentrations and dispersions of a complex of behavioral indices of psychological process.

The psychological process that we presume to sample most directly with the Rorschach is perception. We believe that the tool permits expression of a wider range of percept organization in problem-solving response than do most other psychological techniques that are usable cross-culturally. It does so with an adequate degree of reliability for research concerned with group trends. We presume that perception and culture are linked together. But the perceptual structure in the individual —formed out of both his past and present experience in a culturally patterned environment—may or may not co-vary with the more manifest aspects of his adaptation to the conditions of acculturation exemplified by his house, his occupation, his clothes, or even the language he speaks. The application of the modal "personality" technique, using Rorschach data, makes it possible to advance systematic inquiry into this covariance.

NOTES

1. Those interested in other phases of the study can read further in the authors' publications on the Menomini, listed in the bibliography.

2. A brief discussion of them may be found in L. and G. Spindler, 1958.

3. Different Rorschach scores exhibit different reliability, ranging considerably below, and somewhat above, 0.800. The use of a high estimated reliability merely means that the modal range around each raw mode will be smaller than if we used a lower estimated reliability. Therefore the criteria for what is to be included in the modal class will be more rigorous.

4. Discussion of these relationships may be found in L. and G. Spindler, 1958.

5. Many users of statistics will object to using the proportionate size of

the modal class as a suitable index of homogeneity. The objection is that a metric concept—standard error—is applied in this technique to scores where equal intervals between scores cannot be assumed. The ins and outs of the problem cannot be pursued here, but the reader is forewarned. The fact that the male acculturative groups were distinguished Rorschach-wise in many scores in the initial treatment of data and the females were not is congruent with the hypothesis of greater homogeneity for the latter.

6. A chi-square test applied to the distribution of the modal class throughout all of the various acculturative groups will not show a statistically significant differentiation. Since we use Rorschach scores from the whole sample, from all persons in every acculturative group, to define a modal class, we would not expect the distribution of modal cases to distinguish the groups from each other in an overall test of differentiation. What we are looking for is the *modal tendency* for our cases to concentrate in one part of the continuum. When this is discovered, the information can be put together with other observations designed to locate the p.c.g. The consistency of this information then leads us to make an inference. This inference, taking the form of a partially supported hypothesis, then gives us a new starting point for analysis of the acculturative process.

7. See L. Spindler, 1956, for greater elaboration.

BIBLIOGRAPHY

Ainsworth, Mary D. 1954. "Validity and Reliability." In Bruno Klopfer, et al., *Developments in the Rorschach Technique*, Vol. I: Technique and Theory. New York: World Book Co.

Hallowell, A. Irving. 1951. "The Use of Projective Techniques in the Study of the Sociopsychological Aspects of Acculturation," *Journal of Projective Techniques*, 15:27–44.

Mekeel, H. Scudder. 1936. *The Economy of a Modern Teton Dakota Community*. Yale University Publications in Anthropology, No. 6. New Haven: Yale University Press.

Spindler, George D. 1952. "Personality and Peyotism in Menomini Indian Acculturation," *Psychiatry*, 15:151–59.

———. 1955. *Sociocultural and Psychological Processes in Menomini Acculturation*. University of California Publications in Culture and Society, 5. Berkeley and Los Angeles, University of California Press.

Spindler, (Mary) Louise. 1956. *Women and Culture Change:* A Case Study of the Menomini Indians. Unpublished Ph.D. dissertation, Stanford University.

Spindler, Louise and George. 1958. "Male and Female Adaptations in Culture Change," *American Anthropologist*, 60:217–33.

Thompson, Laura. 1948. "Attitudes and Acculturation," *American Anthropologist*, 50:200–15.

Wallace, Anthony F. C. 1952. *The Modal Personality Structure of the Tuscarora Indians*. Bureau of American Ethnology, Bulletin 150. Washington D.C., Government Printing Office.

About the Chapter

This chapter presents what is best described as a program of research. The authors and their collaborators assert that the problem they are studying—the social and personality changes related to the development of industrialization in a Maori community in New Zealand—requires many years of intensive work and can be approached from different vantage points. Since the task is so large, even when only the personality part of it is tackled, large scale resources have been mobilized in the form of a team of as many as eleven workers who have coordinated their research efforts into an integrated pattern. This integration is specially notable since most research programs consist of a miscellaneous group of tenuously connected projects. The Rakau program is divided into several different phases and makes use of a number of different kinds of research methodology, each appropriate to the needs of the program at the time. Exploratory studies, descriptions of the sociocultural system, developmental studies, rigorous testing of hypotheses by objective measures, and theoretical analyses are all brought to bear on the problem. This is a departure from the usual procedure of depending on one or at most two of these approaches.

About the Authors

ERNEST BEAGLEHOLE is Professor and Head of the Department of Psychology in the Victoria University of Wellington. He was trained in London and at Yale and has done extensive field work among Hopi and in the South Seas. His interests in social psychology have lead through personality and culture studies with Sapir to his present theoretical interest in ethnopsychology and practical concern with international proposals for ameliorating the lot of unprivileged indigenes in Latin America and elsewhere.

JAMES ERNEST RITCHIE is lecturer in the Department of Psychology in the Victoria University of Wellington. He received his Ph.D. at the University of New Zealand in 1960 and has participated in the Maori (Rakau) Research project since 1953. His field work among New Zealand Maori has been combined with interest in personality studies and race relations. At present he is exploring the role of values in the theory of personal and social change. His publications include *Basic Personality in Rakau* and (with others) *Personality and Physique: A Rorschach Study of Maori and Europeans*.

Acknowledgments

This research was originally reported in the *Journal of the Polynesian Society*, 1958, 67:132–154. It is here represented in an altered form by kind permission of the Editor of the *Journal*. The research of which this publication is one report was made possible by funds granted by the Carnegie Corporation of New York to the University of New Zealand. The statements made and the views expressed herein are the authors', and not necessarily those of the Carnegie Corporation.

17

Basic Personality in a New Zealand Maori Community

ERNEST BEAGLEHOLE and JAMES E. RITCHIE

Victoria University
Wellington, New Zealand

The Rakau Maori studies initially were focused rather narrowly on the problem of understanding what kinds of social and personal change industrialization would bring to the lives of a group of Maoris living in a dominantly rural farming area when the stage was being set for large-scale forest exploitation and the development of a paper-pulp industry.[1] Subsequently it became evident that with the resources at hand, understanding of this problem could only be achieved after many years of intensive work. What was done at first, therefore, was a fairly comprehensive study in the field of Maori culture and personality, by a team of five investigators using customary anthropological field methods and projective personality tests as data collecting techniques. This chapter summarizes some of the background and preliminary conclusions of this comprehensive study.

Research has been carried out primarily in the Maori community we have called Rakau. We have used this name for our community for two reasons. The first is that it seems reasonable in much social science research to secure anonymity for the community that is being put under the scientists' scrutiny. Such anonymity is desirable not necessarily because scientists are likely to stir up forgotten scandals, but simply because the members of any modern community are entitled to a little privacy in the way they carry on their lives, irrespective of the fact that for one reason or another they have been chosen, often unknowingly, as the subjects of intensive study. Secondly, we think that the greatest need today in contemporary Maori social studies is to analyze the processes of social change in a relatively few, well-chosen communities each one of which can stand as roughly typical for a number of communities, all of which are facing the same social problems or are stabilized at approximately the same point on an acculturation gradient. The exact characterization of "type" is of no immediate relevance. We think in general that there may be a number of different "genotypical" communities with reference to which actual or "phenotypical" communities may be evaluated. Thus Rakau is conceived of as one such genotype. The community that one of us earlier labelled Kowhai might be thought of as another. How many there are in New Zealand today we do not know. But basic to this thinking is the hypothesis that for every recognizable Maori community, there exists a distinct variety of Maori culture.

Rakau then is a Maori community comprising 70 families (340 persons) organized around three maraes. Originally it was a semi-isolated rural community, its way of life centred on sheep farming and a land development scheme, its location on the fringe of a conservative core of small "hinterland" Maori groups rendering it rather backward compared with the mainstream of Maori life. Rakau is surrounded by huge areas of exotic forests. With the decision to exploit these forests commercially, Rakau suddenly became the centre for the development of a large scale logging industry. The Maori people in the district almost overnight became enclaves in an area peopled by Pakeha workers, including a number of Canadian emigrant lumber workers. A new town was laid out and built. New jobs were now available for Maori workers. The inevitable pub (liquor store) appeared like magic. What was hitherto an almost forgotten community, dreaming away its life in the inconsequential events of everyday routine, rather poor in economic terms, rather backward technologically, became in the course of a year or so the central headquarters for a busy new industry.

This is the change that came to Rakau, phrased in rather a dramatic fashion. The scientific problem, as we saw it in 1954 after a rapid initial survey, was to lay bare the social structure of this Maori community as a preliminary to further study of the actual processes of social change that must inevitably accompany the new economic way of life with the opportunities and challenges that it offered the Maori people in the area.

It might be well at this point to mention a quite fundamental decision that had to be made before the investigations could take shape. The social change we were interested in understanding could presumably have been studied purely in terms of social structure and functioning. That is, we could have conceived the Maori community on the model of a social system, subjected to social forces whose effects we might hope our model would be adequate enough to explain in a structural fashion. Our data and our explanatory tools would then have been limited to the customary data of the social anthropologist (kinship data, role analysis, authority structures and the like) and to the conceptual baggage which seemed relevant or plausible in contemporary social science theory. Alternatively we could think of our problem as involving persons and personality systems in addition to social structures. Then social change would be conceived as being mediated through the interaction of personality system on social system. Changes in social structure would inevitably involve changes in personality structure, in the beliefs and values on which choice is based. In so doing our data and our concepts would be themselves changed. Thus we would have to devise methods for collecting information about personality structure and function, about persons interacting in small groups, about how personality develops in the Maori child from birth to maturity, about the way persons come to occupy and change particular statuses and roles, about the beliefs people hold about themselves and their world. Finally our concepts would have to be broad enough to shape themselves as reasonable ways of organizing and comprehending such data.

Both of us are psychologists by professional training, though well aware of anthropological research—ethnopsychologists, to use a yet barely accepted nomenclature. It was inevitable therefore, that we should make a decision that has led us fairly deeply into the analysis of Maori basic personality as one important prerequisite for the study of social changes.

Nothing need be said about the concept of basic personality at this point except that it is useful to explain the phenomenon of psychologic screening. Apparently, some selective factor operates in the processes of social change whereby only something of what is presented to a group as new is chosen for incorporation into a group's culture. This selection or screening is carried out partly on the basis of what a people feels is congruent with its implicit basic personality structure. As we conceive it, this structure consists of the organization of motives, emotions, sentiments and values (or whatever is thought, according to one psychological theory or another, to be the raw material of human nature) into a system which is shared, through common behaviour and expectation, by the majority of the members of a group.

RESEARCH DESIGN

If we assume that the concept of basic personality type is useful in the ordering of socio-psychological data the problem arises: What shall be our starting point (exploration)? What methods shall be used (assessment)? What formulations shall be applied to the data (formulation)? How shall the formulations be tested and amplified (amplification and integration)? What is the relevance of the formulations for further research (testing)? The terms in parenthesis indicate the phases of our design. They are summarily set out in the table depicting Rakau Research Design. We may usefully comment briefly on each phase.

The elaboration of the first phase of our design began with the suggestions as to the nature of Maori basic personality put forward some years ago in a study of another type-Maori community, Kowhai (Beaglehole and Beaglehole, 1946). Building on these suggestions and using descriptive categories applied to materials assembled from qualitative observations and interviews with a wide variety of informants, it proved possible to develop a picture of Maori personality that seemed to fit the facts and to explain Maori behaviour (Ritchie, 1956a, pp. 34–87). Phase two, three and four involved an assessment of this qualitative description through successive stages of the experimental use of a number of psychological measuring devices. The emphasis here has been on a double assessment: of the descriptive material and of the various tests themselves. Most of the tests have been "projective" tests. They are tests for structuring an interview situation with relatively unstructural material (to talk in a paradox) in such fashion that the informant, whether young or old, inevitably responds with data that can later be analyzed qualitatively and quantitatively to give insight into his personality structure.

In point of fact it does not seem very rewarding to distinguish sharply between tests and interviews as opposed or different methods of social science research. The test situation is simply a special kind of interviewing which uncovers material that can be analyzed qualitatively or treated statistically and which can be theoretically secured a second or third time by equally trained interviewers using the same test procedure. The material, thus, meets one methodological requirement of scientific investigation. In controversies that have from time to time filled many pages of the anthropological journals (Henry 1955; Henry and Spiro 1953) we tend to see more value in the position of those who argue in favour of the use of tests than in those who uphold the unique value of the interview method.

There is one proviso, however, that must be added to the judgment just

RAKAU RESEARCH DESIGN

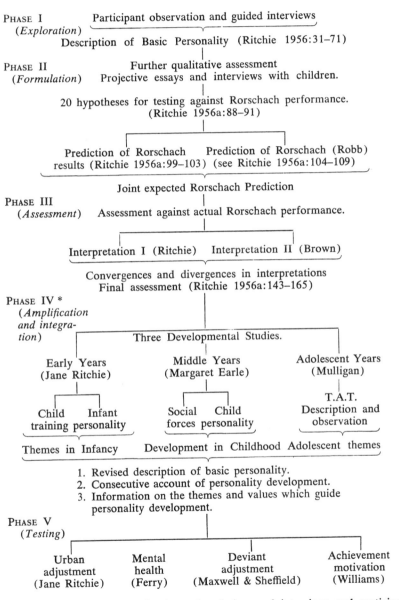

PHASE I
(*Exploration*)   Participant observation and guided interviews

Description of Basic Personality (Ritchie 1956:31–71)

PHASE II   Further qualitative assessment
(*Formulation*)   Projective essays and interviews with children.

20 hypotheses for testing against Rorschach performance.
(Ritchie 1956a:88–91)

Prediction of Rorschach   Prediction of Rorschach (Robb)
results (Ritchie 1956a:99–103) (see Ritchie 1956a:104–109)

Joint expected Rorschach Prediction

PHASE III
(*Assessment*)   Assessment against actual Rorschach performance.

Interpretation I (Ritchie)   Interpretation II (Brown)

Convergences and divergences in interpretations
Final assessment (Ritchie 1956a:143–165)

PHASE IV *
(*Amplification
and integra-
tion*)   Three Developmental Studies.

Early Years   Middle Years   Adolescent Years
(Jane Ritchie)   (Margaret Earle)   (Mulligan)

                                                T.A.T.
Child   Infant   Social   Child   Description and
training personality forces personality   observation

Themes in Infancy   Development in Childhood Adolescent themes

1. Revised description of basic personality.
2. Consecutive account of personality development.
3. Information on the themes and values which guide
   personality development.

PHASE V
(*Testing*)

Urban   Mental   Deviant   Achievement
adjustment   health   adjustment   motivation
(Jane Ritchie) (Ferry)   (Maxwell & Sheffield)   (Williams)

* These studies have variously used techniques of interviews and participant observation, doll and plasticine play, other projective tests and sociometric analysis.

given. Quantitative analysis of projective tests results depends upon a prior evaluation of "scoring" of what the informant has said in response to the test situation. Since projective tests have been used most frequently (though far from exclusively) with western European subjects (English, American etc.), the scoring categories emphasise the significance of responses as real or valid for western European culture. How far these same scoring categories are equally significant as indices of equivalent behaviour in non-western peoples is at present an open question. This point is particularly relevant in phase two of our design where the Rorschach ink-blot test was used. Some recent work in a research project that has been running parallel to the Rakau project suggests the need for considerable caution in the analysis of Rorschach test material. It also proposes a method—the psychologist's "factor analysis"—whereby such an analysis may be made more scientifically valid (Adcock and Ritchie, 1958; Adcock *et al.*, 1957, 1958). Incidentally, one conclusion of this parallel research has been to suggest that a dominant characteristic of Maori intellectual functioning is what might be termed "extreme limitation of the role of imagination and fantasy in Maori cognitive organization." This characteristic is shared with at least one other Polynesian group, Aitutaki, for which there are comparable data (Beaglehole, 1957, pp. 219–223). It is far from fanciful to state that "imagination-deficiency" may have as many repercussions for Maori success in secondary and advanced education as would vitamin deficiency for the proper and healthy metabolic functioning of the body.

To return to our research design. Phase three has consisted of a more precise formulation of Maori basic personality through the checking of qualitative formulation against the results of Rorschach testing. A new procedure has been introduced here which has added considerably to the validity of the final characterization. This procedure has consisted in (a) deriving two independent probable Rorschach basic personality patterns from the qualitative data and (b) checking these probable patterns by two independent evaluations of the actual Rorschach responses. As a result of this checking and cross-checking it is reasonable to assume that the interim formulation of Rakau basic personality is sufficiently valid to provide the starting point for amplification and cross-checking by other methods and techniques.

This interim formulation is phrased in, and therefore defined by, some 20 themes or hypotheses about the way in which the Rakau Maori tends to respond to other people (Ritchie, 1956a, pp. 88–91). Seven examples of these themes, taken at random from the list, are the following:

The early years of Maori life are characterized by parental indulgence which predisposes the personality towards patterns of direct satisfaction.

This pattern is sharply interrupted by a discontinuance of close parental care and attention.

Fear of the threat of further rejection remains as a permanent character trait.

The personality has strong needs for affection resulting from the early deprivation.

As the person moves towards others, patterns of mild extraversion are adopted to increase the person's social stimulus value without risking involvement.

As the expression of sexuality without involvement is demanded, its expression is physical and direct without phantasy or need for repression.

Preoccupation with management of personal orientation and expression rather than attempts to understand the objective world; the self and its relations with other selves is valued rather than goods, material forms or distractions.

So phrased the themes may appear rather dessicated and unenlightening. It is true to say therefore that a rather large effort of imagination is required to visualize the interpretation of these themes in the behaviour of actual persons. Nonetheless, these themes have provided very useful signposts in the organization of data collected about Rakau children of all ages.

An example may be of more use here than pages of description: In 1954, on the basis of the observational records alone, it was suggested that the warmth and social spontaneity so characteristic of Maori group life probably derived from the early experiences of Maori life, reinforced by later social patterns in childhood and in adolescence. In particular, the process we have called rejection seemed relevant. By this process we mean the early experience, in or about the second year, of separation from the absorbed attention of the mother. Rejection is the result of successive annual, or near annual, births, of certain beliefs about child development and a low level of household technology and labour resources. It does not mean that the mother is consciously hostile towards the child or that she wishes it ill. Nor does it mean that she does not value the child nor that she is purposely neglectful. She simply has not the time and believes that the development of walking with its consequent increased mobility is a sign of intrinsic independence in the child. She believes the child is now ready to do without her assistance and that there is no longer any great need for his every whim to be immediately gratified. From the child's point of view it is likely that this process appears far harsher than the mother intends. We have argued that this process sets the child questing for the affection which he once so liberally enjoyed and which is now relatively hard to gain. Other things being equal, this would result in a person who strives to achieve, and for some it does. But, for most, the peer group culture of the middle-years child exerts its own influence to lower standards of aspiration and reduce the need for material or status rewards. The peer group comes to take the place of the home as the source of warm relationships.

Thus the rejection crisis in Rakau Maori development passes away leaving its stamp upon the person's eventual personality. We expressed the results of this process in the fourth theme cited above. In order to test the effects of this probable rejection crisis, a hypothetical question was asked: If this statement were true what kind of data would one expect to find in Rorschach test records collected from a group of such people? An attempt was made to answer this question using, for convenience, the technical jargon of the Rorschach test. It could, however, not be answered with any great degree of confidence by one person alone. Hence an independent and similar prediction was made, by another investigator, Dr. J. H. Robb. With the greater degree of confidence thus gained, two opinions being better than one, the predictions were combined and put to test against the actual Rorschach performance of seventy-eight Rakau individuals drawn from the one hundred and thirty of the population between the ages of six and twenty-one years. These records had been collected in the summer of 1954 following the first observational phase. A second check on the combined predictions was independently made by Dr. L. B. Brown. The final theme-statement was regarded as of high probability and a reasonably true expression of one aspect of the motivation of people in Rakau. So much then for the formulation stage (phase 3).

The original pattern of social relations which we sought to describe, the social ease, the laughter, the search for responsiveness in others, is however, only one side of the picture. It applies both to well-established relationships with others and to ephemeral or chance contacts. The observational record also suggested another kind of motivation operating where long-term relationships involving personal commitment were concerned. People in Rakau seemed trusting, as indeed they often are, but unwilling to put this trust to test. Trust is quickly given but quickly withdrawn in the face of apparent threat. The people appeared responsive to the stimulus of social recreation, but not to the arduous monotonies of the kind of work needed in tribal committee activities. They made friends easily, but dropped them often; they had frequent altercations in which each party moved, socially, away from the necessity of keeping up the relationship; friendship would often be rejoined when a warm social opportunity was offered. Rakau people seemed, on balance, rather defensive about entering into long-term, lasting and firm involvements with others. Even in marriage, as Metge has noted for quite a different Maori group, there was a feeling of impermanence in the relationship involved (Metge, 1957, p. 168). We felt this characteristic aspect of Maori behaviour might be related to the rejection process in early childhood. The relationship was stated thus:

> The personality exhibits a protective defence against further rejection by adopting patterns of non-involvement with situations or persons (Ritchie, 1956a, p. 89).

The statement is rather abstract and does not have much of the ring of social reality about it. In three further studies, therefore, one task was to elaborate and amplify this generalization and to see more of the developmental processes involved. These studies reveal the working-through of early experience as the child grows to maturity.

In her report on the first five years of Rakau child development, Jane Ritchie examines the rejection process itself (Ritchie, Jane, 1957, pp. 83–99). She interviewed twenty-four mothers from the forty indigenous families which could be assumed to be still increasing in size. Thus, she saw at least once, and often four or five times, sixty percent of the child-bearing women of Rakau. An extract from the report clearly shows how lavish and permissive is the parental love before rejection:

> When the baby becomes a toddler he starts gradually to wean himself from the mother's continuing care. So long as he is still the baby of the family he is still the undisputed focus of her attention, but he will venture out into the yard with his siblings. If visitors come, the older children are nearly always sent outside to play. The toddler will be treated with leniency. He is allowed to play on the floor of the kitchen with a stick, or his father will hold him on his knee while he talks. If he wants a cake from the table, it will be given to him, while the other children have to wait until after the visitors have eaten. On one occasion a two year old baby girl had been playing with the egg beater. No reproach was made, but when her brother picked it up the mother reprimanded him. If the baby reaches out for the visitor's tobacco, the mother will give him her packet to play with. The little girl mentioned above was even allowed to smoke cigarettes by her indulgent parents. They thought she looked so cute with her cigarette, but none of her siblings was indulged in this way.

Evidence of rejection comes from the interviews:

> This then, is how the break comes: the toddler is tolerated, fed and put to sleep, but with the advent of the new baby, the amount of fondling that comes his way is very scanty compared to what he used to receive when he was the baby. The toddler does get some cuddling, but it is when the baby is asleep, or being nursed by someone else.
>
> If the mother is feeding the baby and the toddler is hungry, then he must wait until the baby is fed. If a big sister is home, then she may take pity on him and give him a piece of bread to keep him quiet. When the older children are sent outside while parents talk to visitors, the toddler will be allowed to stay inside as long as he is quiet, but if he starts to cry an older sibling will be called in to take him outside. The baby, meantime, is being nursed by the mother. (*Ibid.,* pp. 79–81.)

Additional evidence in support of the personality theme is found in the way Rakau children play with dolls and plastic material.

A process not previously noted was illuminated by Jane Ritchie's study, namely, that rejection by the parent of the child is followed by counter-rejection. That is, the child tends to have feelings of hostility towards those who have rejected him but whom he still regards as the source of affection. To the psychologically unsophisticated this process may seem extraordinary, but a similar kind of phenomenon, usually termed ambivalence, is not unfamiliar in the life of any child and has found general recognition in psychological theory and research. In addition, counter-rejection appears as hostility towards the younger child who supplants the toddler in the focus of maternal attention. Independence, of a kind, follows from this complicated interaction of rejection and counter-rejection.

To show the nature of this independence it may be best again to quote directly from Jane Ritchie's report:

Counter-rejection is surely the "natural" reaction to emotional rejection by parents. Though in the long run the rejection of others leads to personal isolation and feelings of hate, its short-term expression brings immediate, though temporary, satisfaction. Counter-rejection is assertive and thus seeks to deny the social diffuseness of the mother's attitudes. Its content implies not the ego-picture "I am good" but the ego-picture "I am better than he whom I reject" and this can be validated by compliant activity which establishes my "betterness." Independence is an early response to the adult environment and follows rejection because the other alternative, dependence, is utterly impossible. (*Ibid.*, pp. 155–156.)

This process seems to explain further how the child seeks to maintain surface social warmth and yet keep relatively isolated from involvement with, and dependence on, other people. Thus, older children, as they grow through the middle years and adolescence to adulthood, should be implicitly working out this pattern and the personality conflicts it engenders. Let us now look briefly at the middle years study (Earle, 1958) and the report on adolescence (Mulligan, 1957).

The chief feature of social relations between children of the ages five to twelve years in Rakau is the amorphous groups in which they work and play. Loosely structured, these groups are activity groups. They are organised around some common task, and the positions which children hold in them are related chiefly to their abilities with reference to the task in hand (Ritchie, 1956a, pp. 39–54). There are no "leaders" whose role carries over from group to group, but rather leaders for this and leaders for that. Margaret Earle illustrates this point in her data from sociometry. With this technique one is able to build up for a small group a diagram which illustrates networks of friendship and of antipathy.

In this network there are widespread rejections. In addition, Margaret

Earle records nine kinds of pressures and tensions in child-parent relationships which produce these rejections, noting such patterns as inconsistent rewards and punishments, arbitrary punishment, the parents' general preference to have the children somewhere else rather than around or with them. Almost universally children see themselves as subordinates to the harsh requirements of work in the home. These tensions and pressures, which come from the children's own reports as recorded in interviews, are repeated in sibling relations, in peer-group relations as well as in response to parents.

Turning to the projective test data for children of these ages we find that the children's apperception test shows that by the time they have reached this age group the children have entered a world of their own that is other than and apart from the world of adults. Their physical environment is different since they play away from home a good deal. Their emotional climate is different since they regard their parents as indifferent to their activities and feel excluded from the adult world. There is continuity with the phase of later infancy—a growth of independence which has both its positive and its negative aspects. Amongst the former is the egalitarianism which the peer group engenders, a happy "working-together" on immediate tasks. Amongst the less socially desirable features is the underlying unwillingness to become involved. Childhood groups lack the permanent acceptance of roles and statuses which may be necessary for long-term achievement. Though the adult world may be, on occasions, ready to include middle-years children in its activities, the children themselves maintain a relative isolation or discontinuity with adult activities.

We have followed this feature of Rakau development through to the threshold of adolescence. We have seen a growing separation of parents and children. The twelve year old still has a long way to go to adulthood and much to learn. Let us now look at how the Rakau parent manages the final stages of socialization. What happens in adolescence?

The chief feature of Mulligan's report centres on the growth of awareness in the child that the adult role awaits him and, from the other point of view, the efforts of parents to prepare the child for this role. The childhood groups are now seen by the individual to be less satisfying. They cannot provide the secure source of affection which the adolescent seeks. Such groups "are seen to provide little consolation and security . . . they are objects towards which aggression may be expressed and from which aggression directed towards oneself may be expected in return" (Mulligan, 1957, p. 65). The conflict between the need for affection and the desire for non-involvement was again seen when Mulligan classified the personal interactions in the Thematic Apperception Test records he collected. He found 81 cases of stories involving peer group interaction.

Of these, sixty-three involved hostile actions moving against the group or defensive actions moving away from others. Only eighteen cases showed people moving towards each other in friendly interaction. It seems that Jane Ritchie's theme of counter-rejection has begun again to operate strongly in adolescence as the individual strives for adult status. The home becomes more important and emotional ties with parents become stronger. However, parents now make adult demands of the adolescent. Since such demands amount to involvement, the adolescent tends to resist or reject them.

Such demands conflict with the independence which the young Rakau boy or girl has learned so well from the experiences of the peer group period. Mulligan sums up their self-view thus: "that which I find to be within myself, though acceptable to me, is not acceptable to others. Therefore, in order not to lose all that I cherish (security, self-esteem) I must be careful to display only those things which others deem desirable (*ibid.,* p. 95). Thus a strong social façade is built and maintained to increase apparent compliance but to retain non-involvement. The youth of Rakau are useful to the community to which they belong, but reject the control of that group over their activities. Until marriage forces some commitment this pattern persists. And even after marriage the commitment rests uneasily on young men who tend to find their entertainments outside the family, in places where they are less involved.

It will now be evident that the hypotheses concerning affections—needs and the need for non-involvement have far reaching implications. The hypotheses are empirical since they generalize about a wide range of facts. They are not experimental since they cannot be tested with precision and rigour. They are in fact convenient ways of abstracting central features of Rakau personality development and focussing attention on continuities within it.

We have suggested the kind of material which bears directly on two traits abstracted from the original description and have selected two on which there is very substantial agreement. But in the last three studies mentioned differences of focus appear. Jane Ritchie stresses the rejection component, Margaret Earle the parent-child insecurity, the inconsistency of rewards and punishments, and the demand that the child works within the house to relieve the mother's tasks. Mulligan stresses the decline of the group as a satisfying surrogate for family security when the group members find themselves unwilling to accept the hostility of other group members.

Not all these different foci were present in Ritchie's original record. It should now be possible to take that record and to incorporate in it these details. All of them seem capable of integration into an internally consistent picture. Some parts of the original presentation, it must be con-

ASSESSMENT OF BASIC PERSONALITY HYPOTHESES *

	Hypotheses	Rorschach	T.A.T.	Childhood Themes	Middle-years CAT
I.	Early Indulgence	Confirmed	Not assessed	Confirmed	Highly likely
II.	Traumatic Rejection	Confirmed (Q)	Not assessed	Confirmed	Highly likely
III.	Threat Orientation	Confirmed (Q)	Confirmed	Plausible	Confirmed
IV.	Love Needs	Confirmed	Confirmed	Confirmed	Confirmed
V.	Non-involvement	Confirmed	Confirmed	Confirmed	Confirmed
VI.	Anxiety	Confirmed (Q)	Confirmed	Confirmed	Confirmed
VII.	Mild Extraversion	Rejected	Not assessed	Plausible	Rejected (Q)
VIII.	Aggression	Confirmed (Q)	Confirmed	Confirmed (Q)	Confirmed
IX.	Hostility	Confirmed (Q)	Confirmed	Confirmed (Q)	Confirmed
X.	Resolution of Unexpressed Affect	Confirmed (Q)	Rejected	Plausible	Rejected
XI.	Sexuality	Confirmed	Confirmed	Plausible	Probable
XII.	Achievement	Confirmed (Q)	Rejected	Rejected	Rejected
XIII.	Conformity	Confirmed	Confirmed	Confirmed	Confirmed
XIV.	Passivity	Confirmed (Q)	Confirmed	Confirmed	Confirmed
XV.	Intellectual Limitation	Confirmed	Not assessed	Confirmed	Confirmed
XVI.	Perceptual Limitation	Confirmed	Not assessed	Confirmed	Confirmed
XVII.	Practicalness	Confirmed	Not assessed	Confirmed	Confirmed
XVIII.	Control	Confirmed	Confirmed	Confirmed	Confirmed
XIX.	Orientation	Confirmed	Confirmed	Confirmed	Confirmed
XX.	Sex Differences	Confirmed (Q)	Not assessed	Confirmed	Confirmed (Q)

* The symbol Q stands for *qualified* confirmation or rejection. Reference should be made to the original data for an explanation of the kind and weighting of the qualification.

fessed, show over-emphasis in the light of later studies. Such a confession, however, is no more than a statement of the way in which most scientific generalizations have to be re-cast in order to comprehend facts discovered later.

Perhaps the chief point of all this is that the Rakau person finds in his own social group and in its ongoing life an adjustment that works. He remains happy and healthy. He is active and content so long as the kinds of support which he requires to keep personal threat at bay remain themselves secure. His security depends on the social pathways which his culture opens for him and in this sense his world is known, prescribed and safe. He takes on the mask which his culture expects of, and offers to, him.

When change comes, as come it must, he will react to such change in terms of a personality defined by this known social way. Should this change become dysfunctional and disturbing to any marked degree, he will react in ways consonant with what he expects from the world around him. Such expectation is based on past experience. The speed and the success of technological development will depend, in a very real way, on how far changes fit Rakau personality, and how far the Rakau person can learn new responses that will enable him to manage the dislocations that will inevitably result from the personal and social conflicts engendered by those aspects of technological development which do not fit in with his personality.

So much for an actual instance of how the phase called amplification has operated in the research design. The results of all the amplification to date are summarized in the preceding table which has been taken from Margaret Earle's study of children in the middle years (Earle, 1958, pp. 102–103).

From this Table it is evident that the original twenty statements about basic personality in Rakau have, apart from four cases, been generally supported. We do not claim that this support amounts to absolute proof, whatever that might mean. All that is implied is that a number of lines of empirical study converge at these points. This convergence suggests that a greater measure of confidence can be placed in the statements than would have been possible without the confirming research. There are gaps since some statements could only be inferred, not given additional testing. There is much qualification of the original formulations because the original statements were not always phrased in precise enough terms. A physiologist, for example, observing the regularities in the distribution of bodily organs, might say that the body in general is bilaterally symmetrical. But with reference to any specific organ, say heart or liver, this statement would require qualification. The same kind of qualification has happened with, for example, our original hypothesis regarding differences in role anxiety between the sexes in Rakau and, doubtless for the same reasons, with other hypotheses also.

In brief, the revised form of the original statement can be summarized as follows: The early years of the child's life in Rakau are indulgent and permissive until the arrival of the next child brings about a break with parental indulgence. From then on, the child becomes increasingly independent of parental control, but increasingly dependent on substitute gratifications. Early on, the peer group comes to provide such gratification but the threat of rejection is never eliminated. This leads to caution, a lack of real trust and the expectation of further rejection. Defences against this situation come to operate, chief amongst which is non-achievement in Maori social situations; recourse to practical rather than abstract tasks; a belief in the ultimate validity of self-evaluations and counter-rejection which expresses itself chiefly through attacking achievers by gossip or by interpreting their actions as ego-centric rather than altruistic. Strong affection-needs persist, giving warmth and vitality to spontaneous social life, but non-involvement limits such spontaneity. Thus, much of the social activity of Rakau is minimumly related to the ends and goals of activity but maximumly related to keeping up an idealised pattern of social relations. No one is really much concerned with how much a man gets done, but everyone is tremendously concerned with how he behaves in relation to others. Social life is like a pond which is continually ruffled by personal disturbances caused, paradoxically enough, by the desire to keep the surface unruffled! The idealised patterns of social relations (e.g. people should work together, old men know best, kinsfolk should exhibit unquestioned solidarity) work out well enough in emergencies. But they are undermined in ordinary social intercourse by the anxiety, aggression, vague hostility and defence-needs which form the major preoccupation of Rakau personality. The pride, the craggy independence, the attempts at assuming mastery which often reveal themselves in Rakau relations with those in authority, are in fact a rejection of authority. But they do not reduce the need for dependence. We have here the profoundest key to the complex functioning of Rakau's social life.

At this point it might well be asked: what is the significance of all these statements about basic personality for the school-teacher, the social worker, the welfare officer, the administrator, all of whom may be intimately concerned with helping Rakau and other Maoris make the best of the business of living? From one point of view, this question is an acid test of any piece of psychological or social science research because it forces any investigator to ask himself what his research is all about. Without in any way accepting the idea that research must always be good for something practical or that knowledge has significance only as a guide to action, an outline answer to the question of the practical man could be attempted even at this stage.

The practical value will, of course, be of a different kind and degree for different purposes. Thus the primary school-teacher, particularly the infant-room specialist, will find that while the general principles of child development everywhere apply, she might well ponder on the special features of Rakau personality for the light that they may shed on her charges and their needs. Intelligence may appear lower, for example, than is really the case (Ritchie, 1957). The probation officer might be directed to consider the group relations of his clients in terms of the processes we have studied. He might keep in mind the positive self-valuations of later adolescence and consider their meaning for the inner and outer control of behaviour. The administrator could be advised to remember that when he deals with a Maori group or with Maoris he deals not only with people of a different culture but with individuals whose personality is constructed on a different plan, with different emphases and needs from his own. He might be warned not to dismiss the behaviour of Maoris as irrelevant to his decisions because he can apparently characterize such behaviour as indicating stubbornness, fickleness, irresponsibility, ignorance or indifference. The Rakau personality, with its inner balances and its adjustment methods, is no less desirable than the anxiety-loaded personality of the West—nor, for that matter, is it any more desirable. It is merely different. But unless this difference is accepted, recognised and used as a guide in planning social action, the baffled and bewildered administrator may find his most idealistically conceived and genuinely intended programmes for social betterment disintegrating by contact with the hard facts of misunderstanding, distrust, and rejection. Educational change in Rakau has been hampered by just this kind of process (Ritchie, 1956b).

For the employer, the labour manager, the personnel officer, it is more difficult to suggest practical application. He daily sees before him a stream of people who come to him for work. Let us take a composite Maori work record and see if, using the knowledge our research has accumulated, we can suggest how a labour foreman might handle the work problems our imaginary person creates. Our case is merely an example of a labour problem but it may show how essential is an understanding of Maori personality in guiding Maori workers. We begin the case with a profile of a Maori man we call Joe. We will then recount some of the minor crises of Joe's work history and suggest how these might be understood.

Joe is twenty-seven, father of five children to whom he says he is attached. He has left his home area to work for higher wages at a nearby development project in order, he says, to put his children through school and prepare for their further education. He has no special skills but is agreeable and willing, can drive and "knows a bit about engines." His 1927 Dodge is a running tribute to his skill as he uses the car regularly to go home weekends and does his own repairs. Joe has a brother and two uncles on the same job. He has no particular hobbies (except football in the winter), enjoys a drink with a few friends when he feels like it, goes hunting occasionally, but otherwise, just sits talking, playing cards or sleeping in his off hours. In general, Joe on first interview seemed a good prospect. He had his family to motivate his work, relations to give him some friendly contacts and support, few expensive habits or tastes and enough intelligence and skill to be trainable. Joe was therefore accepted for employment as a full time worker on the project. He was put to work with his brother on an outdoor job which allowed the two of them to work as a team.

In the second week there was a violent argument between Joe and his brother, leading to blows. Joe was changed to another job. Following that weekend he arrived a day late for work. The same thing happened the third weekend. Joe explained that he had insufficient time to go home and see his family in the two-day weekends. His boss gave him permission to work a four-day week provided he made up the hours of the fifth day by overtime work.

Six weeks later Joe was reported drunk in a hotel during his Monday off work. He continued drinking into the night, causing a disturbance in the workers' residential camp and interfering with the very necessary sleep of other workers. He was warned but no other action was taken.

By now Joe was developing signs of restlessness. He was also showing a growing skill which the company thought worthy of further development. He was therefore placed in a training job in which he was given special instruction. Three weeks later Joe asked to be put back to his old job; he had been doing well at the new one but did not like it. The management agreed but, disappointed in Joe, they gave no further leniency when, two weeks later, he was caught pilfering. He would then have been dismissed had he not left of his own accord for another job nearby.

This specimen work record is not necessarily a normal Maori record. It is, in fact, a composite of several cases. Yet, on the other hand, it is not so abnormal that it cannot be used for our purpose. Each of Joe's seemingly erratic actions takes place within the context of a Maori social and personality pattern. An understanding of his actions can come only from understanding the nature of the pattern.

The employment officer placed Joe with his brother because, he says, "Maoris always like to work with their relations." A good enough generalisation on cultural grounds but Maori brothers often show thinly masked hostility for each other. Joe and his brother got along well most of the time, but sometimes old rivalry broke through. This is not to say that all Maori brothers ought not to be allowed to work together but only to suggest that one ought not to expect cordial Maori kinship relations without fair evidence of them nor to be surprised if Maori kinsmen prefer to work separately and not together in the same team or work gang.

Of course Joe wanted to see his family. His employer was a humane and understanding man who made arrangements for him to do so. In short weekends Joe saw too little of his family, but in three-day weekends, complemented by a weekly drudge of overtime, he felt he was seeing too much of his family and too little of his friends. The spending spree, "shouting" his friends to a party was a gesture to them, a validation of wider social relationships than just those of the family, not an irresponsible action. Three-day visits home on alternate weekends would have been far better for Joe with the Monday's lost time made up over the fortnight rather than the week.

Joe's rejection of the training job was the bitterest blow to a management which felt it had been generosity itself. But Joe was following out the dictates of his own personal economy of security. Being trained meant promotion at the cost of solidarity with his work mates. It implied stepping outside the security of his work group to achieve a proto-pakeha (European) form of superiority. There is no easy way out of this dilemma for any Maori. Joe might have come to realise that his new training job would not necessarily and immediately have meant superior status: that would only come with time. He could have been helped to work through the social problem during this period. Furthermore, Joe could have been counselled so that he kept his high job status limited to the factory environment. The thing Joe feared, namely his fellow workers' scorn for one who seeks to better himself by assuming status over his fellows, need not have conflicted with the cultural sanctions concerning social status outside the factory. There is a conflict here, but not an uncommon nor insoluble one.

Whether Joe's stealing from the firm resulted from resentment against the company because of the conflict situation in which it had placed him, or whether it was a means of giving the company cause to remove him from that situation, is difficult to say. Perhaps Joe simply stole for material gain or his actions may have been due to a conflict in social situations; perhaps in his own locality his actions would not have been labelled as stealing. Whatever the real explanation (and this may include something of each alternative) Joe avoided the necessity of having to seek rehabilitation in the company's favour, withdrew in the face of threat in order to preserve his self-esteem and began anew, somewhere else. Joe may go on shifting from one job to another until someone, somewhere, is able to understand his personal and culturally phrased problems, and accept the fact that sympathetic counselling might assist Joe towards adopting a more settled life in which most, if not all, of his personality needs are met.

We are not Joe's apologists making a list of socio-psychological excuses that he is too unsophisticated to make for himself. The important point to keep in mind is that Joe actually sees people, jobs and events in this way; so seen, they constitute his reality. He may not be able to verbalise all the relevant attitudes, purposes and sentiments; but they are not therefore less real or less relevant. It is possible to give each of the events a cultural interpretation: the argument with his brother may be related to Maori status ranks within the family; the return home to cultural sanctions, and so on. The whole sequence might be related to disjunctions in the passage from one culture to another. We have chosen to put the facts into a psychological framework, because the other, the cultural, is more obvious, more easily apprehended and less neglected. Both the cultural and the psychological meaning of Joe's actions, however, are part of the total sequence of events and their meaning for him, trying to live in a New Zealand world that spans two cultures and includes at least two different and distinct basic personality types.

Our example, shows, we hope, how useful it may be to use this kind of socio-psychological thinking when one considers events which occur in culture contact situations. After all such situations are not the result of the clash of two abstractions, two cultures, but are problems of the relationships between people. These people may represent, as carriers, two different systems of belief and value. But, primarily, people meet as people not as cultural representatives.

CROSS-TESTING OF RAKAU HYPOTHESES

Five additional pieces of research may now be mentioned. Though not strictly part of the Rakau project as originally conceived, these pieces have grown organically out of the basic research approach. They can therefore be looked upon in some respects as a cross-testing of some of the major hypotheses of the Rakau approach to contemporary Maori life.

The first piece of research is an attempt to study some of the patterns of psychological adjustment of Maori families as these families come to live and work in a large New Zealand city. Jane Ritchie, the investigator, is interested in disentangling some of the variables that affect urban adjustment: age, sex, religion, length of stay in city, type of occupation, personality tensions and the like. She is also interested in exploring the effect of Maoris living on the one hand in an "occluded" Maori community which is left each day for work elsewhere as compared with living dispersed among pakeha (European) neighbours. Arguments have been advanced showing irrefutably that one or the other kind of living produces better urban adjustment. The only conclusion from this kind of armchair social science is that no-one really knows the significance for Maori urban adaptation of different types of social grouping.

One point is worth mentioning in this context. For all the research so far described there has been little use of that "sacred cow" of the socio-psychological investigator, the so-called control group. Partly this omission is due to the fact that in its spirit the research has been following on its anthropological side the traditional approach of the anthropologist which might be described in its modern form as the functional penetration of the small community and the analysis of the relation of this small community to the larger whole of which it is part. The psychological side of the research has grown from an interest in defining primarily the way in which a contemporary Maori thinks, feels and acts, not so much the way in which his personality compares with that of the contemporary New Zealand pakeha. Furthermore, a meaningful control group for Rakau, since we think of it genotypically, would be virtually impossible to find. The pakehas in the same area differ in socio-economic status from the Maori and are immigrants from other parts of New Zealand. Other country areas do not include the concentrations of labourers that one finds at Rakau. City labouring families conversely would not show the operation of the community variable.

Furthermore we have not felt that control of a customary kind is necessary. Our job has been to describe Rakau and to this end we have concentrated our resources. Some outside comparisons have helped us in this task. Jane Ritchie has compared her child-rearing data with Pukapukan and classical Maori models. Margaret Earle used Navaho material to compare with one of her tests and contrasted her middle-years developmental model with the results of American, Japanese, Hopi and Egyptian studies.

Phrased in another way, our apparent lack of controls is due to the fact that we are trying to describe the basic personality of one community which we think of virtually as a sub-culture of New Zealand society. We have, of course, labelled this sub-culture "Maori." We have been tempted to do this because all our informants think of themselves and call themselves Maori. When there is need to question the validity of our informants' own self-designation, then and only then will control studies and control groups be methodologically necessary.

In the meantime, a more important methodological problem has seemed to be that of determining objectively how Maori our Maori informants really are. Following a research lead given by Spindler (1955, pp. 6, 110, 118) it has proved fruitful to visualize an acculturation gradient moving diagramatically from aboriginal Maori culture at one end of the continuum to contemporary New Zealand culture at the other. On this gradient one tries to place the different Maori groups with which the research has dealt according to a summation index which comprehends a number of different "locations" based on a variety of social and economic sub-indices. As an aid to location, what has been called somewhat grandly a Maori Background Data Schedule has been elaborated. This schedule has been tested in Rakau itself and adapted versions are being tried for all the additional pieces of research. An item analysis and a factor analysis, both of which appear to offer new insights, are being carried out. Althought the schedule still requires a good deal of refining it appears to be operating in such fashion as to make significant distinctions between Maoris who are highly acculturated and those closer to a vague core of "Maoriness" in their way of life (Williams, 1960). Incidentally, one major conceptual advantage of thinking about an acculturation gradient is that it enables one to avoid characterizing data with reference to the social disorganization of the Maori. One thinks, more positively so to speak, of processes of social and personal change which are resulting, as one compares from one time-point to the next, in new and different attempts to adjust to an ever-changing cultural present. Few, if any, of these processes and these attempts appear to be dysfunctional, though in the long run some of them may lead some Maoris into blind alleys. A good deal of sympathetic help of the social welfare type may be required to lead these groups back again to the open road of freer social and personal adjustment.

That there are these blind alleys is shown by very high contemporary Maori crime rates. Two additional pieces of research are therefore exploring some of the implications of our conception of basic Maori (Rakau) personality structure for a greater understanding of the incidence and quality of crime in young Maori offenders. As a very rough initial hypothesis, here we are inclined to think of Maori personality as being deficient in super-ego strength. Metaphorically, it is held together more by the collective shell or social mask of Maori ego-structure than by a well-articulated moral skeleton of internalized moral norms. When this collective shell begins to crack as the result of the pressures of personal and social change, a person has recourse either to forms of mental disorder (psycho-neurosis or psychosis) or to characteristic forms of crime, or to excessive alcohol-consumption—most of them forms of inadequate ego functioning. Two investigators therefore, have been studying the culture of younger Maori criminal offenders, Sheffield (1958) being chiefly concerned with theft offences by males, and Maxwell with female offenders of all categories. Earlier studies of Maori mental disorder (Beaglehole, 1939a and 1939b) are being brought up to date by Jacqueline Ferry.

It is generally held—and the judgment receives some support from statistical evidence—that present day Maori culture, attenuated as it is, offers such measure of support that the incidence of mental disorder is reduced in the Maori to a degree far below that of the New Zealand pakeha. Just how good the evidence is remains to be seen after a careful re-examination of available facts and figures. On the one hand, one is now accustomed to assume that every society exacts its overhead charge —the cost of running a given social group—and that this charge can hardly fall below a minimum amount. Recent work on the Hutterites would suggest that even under conditions of social life favourable to the development of mental health this minimum overhead is not inconsiderable (Eaton and Weil, 1955; Kaplan and Plaut, 1956). On the other hand, it is possible that personalities organized on the collective shell principle (strong tribal and group loyalties) are less vulnerable to mental disorder than those built round internalized moral skeletons. Equally however, it is possible that crime and alcoholism form the psychological equivalent to mental disorder: they represent primarily a failure of adjustive behaviour whereas mental disorder can be viewed as a breakdown of the normal controls over perceptions. In the one case there is too little inner control, in the other case too much, but in both cases the overhead of the business of living is not noticeably different in amount. Whether this hypothesis of equivalent overhead charges stands up to the testing by empirical data remains to be seen after the three précis of research just described have been completed.

Finally mention needs to be made of research directed at the educational achievements of young Maoris attending two New Zealand teacher training colleges. Independently of the Rakau projects, Professor David P. Ausubel of the University of Illinois Bureau of Educational Research and Fulbright Research Professor at the Victoria University of Wellington, has been studying the educational progress of young Maori adolescents in two selected secondary schools (Ausubel 1957, 1960). His theoretical framework has points of similarity and of difference with that of the Rakau work. The Rakau-inspired project of John Williams starts with the assumption that Rakau basic personality does not have built into it those controls which are necessary if a young person is to defer immediate impulse-gratification in favour of long-range goals. Such impulse-control can only be effective if the collective shell has strong structure—if, that is, the ardours and endurances of higher education are at all stages and phases fully supported and rewarded in young people by ongoing Maori culture. It can be effective with a broken shell only with those Maori young people whose personality structure is organized more on a pakeha than on a Maori model. That the Maori student of higher education may have difficulties with his work because of an *average* lower mental functioning is not improbable according to recent psychological investigations (Adcock *et al.,* 1954). That his difficulties will be increased by an inability, unsupported by strong group controls, to stick to his studies year after weary year, is highly likely. Therefore, in his investigation John Williams is not only seeking to find out how Maori are his Maori subjects, but what is the specific nature of their achievement motive as such and how this motive interlocks with the general structure of their personalities. His results, it is hoped, when read in conjunction with those of Dr. Ausubel, will have some relevance for policies of Maori higher and professional education (Williams, 1960; Ausubel 1960).

CONCLUSION

The studies discussed in the preceding section are not programmatic only. Most of them are at the point of completion. Looking at the Rakau project as a whole it seems fair to say that what has been done and reported represents something significant in scope and method. There have been assembled for instance more projective personality and other test data than have yet been reported for any other single non-western community. Six different research workers have worked on the community materials, an additional five have made the cross-testing surveys. One might at times have wished that it were possible to develop more methodological rigour in some of the studies. On the one hand, however, it will be obvious that "whole-pattern" research of the community or personality type must always lack the extreme sophistication and precision of the model for physical or laboratory research. On the other hand it is expected that the completed cross-testing studies will at least bear comparison with other contemporary socio-psychological research both in New Zealand and elsewhere. As with the proverbial pudding, however, the proof of these statements must ultimately lie with the Maori and pakeha consumers, not with the recipe-makers nor with the scientific cooks.

NOTE

1. Some field work results have been published in a preliminary form: Ritchie, 1956; Ritchie, 1957; Earle, 1958; Mulligan, 1957.

BIBLIOGRAPHY

Adcock, C. J., McCreary, J. R., Ritchie, J. E., Somerset, H. C. A. 1954. "An Analysis of Maori Scores on the Wechsler Bellevue," *Australian Journal of Psychology,* 6:16–29.

————, *et al.* 1957. "Personality and Physique: A Rorschach Study with Maori and Pakeha Subjects," *Australian Journal of Psychology,* 9:158–89.

Adcock, C. J., *et al.* 1958. *Personality and Physique: A Rorschach Study of Maori and Europeans.* Victoria University of Wellington Publications in Psychology No. 12. Wellington, New Zealand, Department of Psychology, Victoria University.

————, and Ritchie, J. E. 1958. "Intercultural Use of Rorschach," *American Anthropologist,* 60:881–92.

Ausubel, D. P. 1957. *A Comparative Study of Aspirational Traits Among Maori and European Adolescents in New Zealand:* Preliminary Prospectus. Bureau of Educational Research University of Illinois: Department of Psychology, The Victoria University of Wellington (cyclostyled).

————. 1960. *Maori Youth.* Victoria University of Wellington, Publication in Psychology No. 14. Wellington, New Zealand, Department of Psychology, Victoria University of Wellington.

Beaglehole, Ernest. 1939a. "Culture and Psychosis in New Zealand," *Journal of the Polynesian Society,* 44:144–55.

————. 1939b. "Psychic Stress in a Tongan Village," *Proceedings, 6th Pacific Science Congress,* 4:43–52.

————. 1957. *Social Change in the South Pacific.* London, Allen and Unwin.

————, and Beaglehole, P. 1946. *Some Modern Maoris.* Wellington, New Zealand, Council for Educational Research.

Earle, Margaret Jane. 1958. *Rakau Children from Six to Thirteen Years.* Victoria University of Wellington Publications in Psychology No. 11. (Monographs on Maori Social Life and Personality, No. 4.) Wellington, New Zealand, Department of Psychology, Victoria University.

Eaton, J. W. and Weil, R. J. 1955. *Culture and Mental Disorders.* Glencoe, Illinois, Free Press.

Henry, J., *et al.* 1955. "Symposium: Projective Testing in Ethnography," *American Anthropologist,* 57:245–70.

Henry, J., and Spiro, Melford E. 1953. "Psychological Techniques: Projective Tests in Field-work." In Kroeber, A. L. (ed.), *Anthropology Today.* Chicago, University of Chicago Press.

Kaplan, B., and Plaut, T. F. A. 1956. *Personality in a Communal Society.* Kansas, University of Kansas Press.

Metge, Joan. 1957. "Marriage in Modern Maori Society," *Man,* 57: Article 212.

Mulligan, D. G. 1957. *Maori Adolescence in Rakau.* Victoria University of Wellington Publications in Psychology No. 9. (Monographs on Maori Social Life and Personality No. 2.) Wellington, New Zealand, Department of Psychology, Victoria University.

Ritchie, J. E., 1956a. *Basic Personality in Rakau.* Victoria University of Wellington Publications in Psychology No. 8. (Monographs on Maori Social Life and Personality No. 1.) Wellington, New Zealand, Department of Psychology, Victoria University.

————. 1956b. "Human Problems and Educational Change in a Maori Community," *Journal of the Polynesian Society,* 65:13–34.

———. 1957. "Some Observations on Maori and Pakeha Intelligence Test Performance," *Journal of the Polynesian Society,* 66:351–56.

Ritchie, Jane. 1957. *Childhood in Rakau: The First Five Years of Life.* Victoria University of Wellington, Publications in Psychology No. 10. (Monographs on Maori Social Life and Personality No. 3.) Wellington, New Zealand, Department of Psychology, Victoria University of Wellington.

Sheffield, M. C. 1958. *Maori Crime.* Unpublished thesis. The Library, Victoria University of Wellington.

Spindler, George D. 1955. *Sociocultural and Psychological Processes in Menomini Acculturation.* University of California Publications in Culture and Society. Berkeley, California, University of California Press.

Williams, J. S. 1960. *Maori Achievement Motivation.* Victoria University of Wellington, Publications in Psychology No. 13 (Monographs on Maori Social Life and Personality No. 5). Wellington, New Zealand, Department of Psychology, Victoria University of Wellington.

About the Chapter

This case study focuses on the field problems of personality study in a highly literate Western society, in contrast to the emphasis on the study of smaller non-literate cultures which prevails in this volume. Dr. Rabin was chiefly interested in the ego and personality development of children and describes the main features of Kibbutz child rearing practices. He analyzes the special problems that were created by the particular cultural context in which he worked.

About the Author

ALBERT I. RABIN is Professor of Psychology and Director of the Psychological Clinic at Michigan State University with which he has been affiliated since 1948. He is a fellow of the American Psychological Association, American Association for the Advancement of Science and a diplomate of the American Board in Professional Psychology (Clinical). Dr. Rabin is author of numerous articles and chapters in several books. He is currently working on a book which deals with personality development in Kibbutz-reared children and adults. He is an active researcher in the field of projective techniques and is specially concerned with the effects of early childhood experience on later development and with the problem of time perception and time perspective.

18

Personality Study in Israeli Kibbutzim

ALBERT I. RABIN
Michigan State University

The cultural anthropologist has traditionally conducted his field work among non-literate societies and among so-called "primitive" peoples. These groups or peoples almost invariably were homogeneous in their culture and closely associated with specific geographical areas. Their practices and modes of behavior most often reflected age-old traditions which were deeply rooted. These traditions, in a sense, shaped their lives for centuries, perhaps longer, since in most instances recorded history was unavailable.

The methods of the cultural anthropologist were varied and diffuse. Herskovits (1948, p. 79) described his work as follows:

> To carry on his field work, he goes to the people he has elected to study, listening to their conversation, visiting their homes, attending their rites, observing their customary behavior, questioning them about their traditions as he probes their way of life to attain a rounded view of their culture or to analyze some special aspect of it. In this he is the ethnographer, the collector of data, which, in its wider ethnological significance, he will later, on his return from the field, analyze, and relate to other materials.

The problems to be studied, the hypotheses to be tested rarely were formulated prior to the undertaking of the field work itself. There was not a "pin-pointing" of problems and issues but a "shot-gun" approach in data collecting. However, the masses of data obtained frequently yielded generalizations and conceptualizations of broad application, depending upon the theoretical sophistication and ingenuity of those applying the analysis. Controlled observations and standardized testing procedures were generally not employed.

Our study of personality development in the Kibbutz differed from the traditional cultural anthropologist's field work characterized above. Some of the more significant differences are set forth in the following paragraphs.

Present Investigation

The setting of our investigation possessed the following uncommon features:

1. A highly literate (non-primitive) society, primarily of European origin was the subject of study.

2. The Kibbutz constitutes a society within a society; it is a culture whose physical units are not rooted in a particular geographical locale, but are scattered throughout the whole country.

3. The unique aspects of the particular "culture" are of comparatively recent origins, consciously and artificially fostered and nurtured. Traditions are few and conscious programs, ideals and strivings are many.

4. Kibbutz culture was not entirely *terra incognita*. Available published information (Infeld, 1944; Irvine, 1952) as well as familiarity through an earlier visit to Israel and to some Kibbutzim made it possible for me to confine my investigation to certain boundaries and seek answers to a number of specific questions (Rabin, 1954, 1957, 1957b, 1958a, 1958b, 1959a, 1959b, 1960). The focus, therefore, was not upon a description of a "whole culture," but on studying the relationship between certain variables and a comparison of similar relationships in our own society.

5. Finally, a number of methods of controlled observation and testing (primarily projective) techniques were decided upon beforehand. Their application and adaptability to the anticipated conditions were carefully considered.

Modern Israel

When the State of Israel was established in 1948, the vast majority of its inhabitants consisted of immigrants from Eastern and Western European countries. A sizable percentage of these immigrants belonged to the "intelligentsia" who, for a variety of ideological, traditional-religious and economic reasons, left the countries of their origin in order to establish a new society in Palestine. In addition, there had been an exodus of many people of the lower classes (small tradespeople and laborers). The unique characteristics of the immigrants, coupled with the traditional Jewish respect for learning and the concomitant high level of literacy among them, made this newly formed society the most literate in the Middle East. As a matter of fact, the level of literacy compared favorably with most European countries. Since 1948, the new waves of immigration have doubled the country's population, but have threatened its status of high literacy. Most of the new immigrants are "Eastern" immigrants among whom the percentage of illiteracy is fairly high. There is conscious and heroic effort to raise their level of literacy with the utmost speed and thus prevent a marked cleavage and to hasten complete cultural integration.

Many are the cultural influences that the early immigrants have imported into Israel from countries such as Russia, Germany, Poland and Hungary. These influences were subsequently augmented by the more recent waves of cultural imports from Morocco, Tunis, Iraq, Egypt, and elsewhere. There is no homogeneous culture in Israel, but a combination and conglomeration of many cultures. There are no common traditions of long standing, with the possible exception of those referring to the distant past, prior to and immediately following the inception of the Christian era. To study present day Israeli society would be not to study a culture, but to study the dynamics of interaction and gradual integration of numerous cultures. One would need to describe the "state of flux" and many different types of processes of acculturation.

The Kibbutz Subculture

Within the boundaries of the present Israeli society there are more than two hundred villages with a communal economy which are called Kibbutzim. There is no territorial unity or geographical identity to this group of settlements whose population constitutes somewhat less than five per cent of the total population of the country. The Kibbutzim are scattered all over the map of Israel, from the northern Syrian frontier to the south toward the Red Sea and Egypt. Although the Kibbutzim are not located in any particular region in the country, as are many subcultural groups in other societies, there is considerable unity among them since they differ from the rest of the country in their economic structure, social organization and family relationships. Every Kibbutz is a member of one of three major federations. These federations are affiliated with three major political parties; they centralize considerably and supervise the activities and the conduct of affairs of each member-Kibbutz. Thus, although an individual Kibbutz may be geographically isolated from other Kibbutzim and be located closely to villages which are not communal and in which "rugged individualism" is the rule, psychologically, culturally, and economically it is a member of a larger federation, a part of a larger movement which is the more encompassing social unit, the total subculture itself.

Unlike most cultures or sub-cultural segments within larger societies which formed organically and developed for many years without conscious design, the Kibbutz movement grew from deliberate attempts to alter and reform early twentieth century European social organization. The Kibbutz was created as a result of a movement of rebellion by groups of educated young men and women from Eastern Europe. By going to Palestine, they rebelled against the society which treated them as second and third class citizens. By forming economic communes, they rebelled against economic and social injustice. They rebelled against the miserable urban life by returning to nature, to the soil. Finally, they rebelled against their own families, the inequality between the sexes, the absolute authority of the family patriarch, and many other perceived injustices. Thus, there emerged an idea and an ideal of life in Palestine. It combined a traditional Jewish nationalism with socialism, Marx with Tolstoi; respect for tradition but rebellion against one's own family and its structure. From all this emerged the concept of the Kibbutz—a new form of community life.

Although the first Kibbutzim were established during the first decade of the present century, the bulk of them came into existence during the second quarter of the twentieth century. The vast majority of the founders of most of the Kibbutzim are still living, either within the villages they helped to establish or in the more conventional cities or towns where some of the disenchanted ones established themselves. There are many ex-members of Kibbutzim in Israel. Many tried Kibbutz life, but few held out and remained devoted to the original Kibbutz ideology. Thus, when one comes to a Kibbutz, he may encounter several generations of Kibbutz members—some of the original founders and other old timers (the "Vatikim") and still other, younger groups of adults who have come on successive waves of European immigration. More recently, of course, there is a growing number of adults who have been born and raised under Kibbutz conditions. This new generation knows no other life but in the Kibbutz. For them it is not a conscious effort or a realization of a dream and an ideal.

Until 1948, the influence of the Kibbutzim upon the entire people was considerably out of proportion to the number of their members. The Kibbutz society constituted a sort of elite which was respected and admired by the rest of the country's population. Their highly intelligent, courageous, self-sacrificing and militarily adept membership commanded considerable respect at all levels of the social structure. With the doubling of the population in less than ten years, and with the bulk of the immigrants, coming from non-European countries, being unacquainted with the Kibbutz and its origins, the relative size of Kibbutz society was reduced and its old influence has dwindled. Yet, its political and moral effect on the country is still marked despite its relative diminution. The threat of being overwhelmed by the "outside" is, however, not inconsiderable.

Design and Method

As a highly literate society the Kibbutzim have described in great detail, in print, many of their planned and executed social changes, economic, democratic and educational programs. In addition, a number of visitors-observers have published their impressions of the Kibbutzim (Irvine, 1952; Caplan, 1954). Therefore, I set for myself the specific task of assessing a number of aspects of personality development of groups of children at several age levels and comparing them with like-age groups of children who were reared under the conditions of ordinary Western society family structure.

Some of the main features of the child-rearing practices in the Kibbutz are as follows:

1. Separation of mother and infant, shortly after birth, upon their return from the hospital.

2. Placement of the infant with a peer group in the "infant house" under the supervision of a nurse—a biologically unrelated "mother surrogate."

3. The nurse as the main socializing agent in relation to the infant-child.

4. Continuous residence of the child in a peer-group setting until maturity with simultaneous maintenance of relationships with the biological family through daily visits with the parents and biological siblings.

The plan was to study ego and personality development of the children at three age levels: at the age of one year, ten years, and seventeen-eighteen years. The study of the children themselves presented no particular problems. The observation of the infants involved no verbal communication with them, and the examination of the children and adolescents could be easily accomplished by translating the instructions and presented materials (such as sentence completion) into the language used by the subjects (Hebrew). However, the access to the children and additional information concerning them (such as histories) are controlled by the adults. Negotiation with the adults, obtaining their cooperation in the investigation and getting information from them regarding their children or charges, constituted major steps in the study of Kibbutz children.

As our study was designed somewhat along nomothetic lines and since we wanted to expand the generalizability of our findings, we did not confine ourselves to *one* Kibbutz, but attempted to obtain data from a representative sample—from *several* Kibbutzim. Considerable effort would have been involved in making contacts with the leaders and educators of each individual Kibbutz selected, to find out whether they had children who would meet our age specifications in the particular Kibbutz and whether permission would be granted and cooperation given to examine the children. The more efficient route was to approach the educational leaders of the two Kibbutz *federations* considered for our study. The third federation was not included because of frequent departures from the established Kibbutz child-rearing practices.

The Leadership

We mentioned above that there is a good deal of centralization—political, economic, educational, etc.—in the activities of the Kibbutzim, lodged in central bodies appointed by the federation. The central educational committee of the federation has much of the current information about the school systems of the member Kibbutzim. Members of the committee also have a great deal of influence on the affairs of the individual educational programs which are administered by the local committees, elected by the local Kibbutz members. The central committee is also in constant contact with the local committees and keeps its hand on the educational pulse of the Kibbutzim under its jurisdiction. The cooperation of such a central body, therefore, would be important and a great contribution to the efficiency of a research program involving Kibbutz children. Hence, the first important step is contact and discussion with these educational leaders of the federation.

A number of attitudes on the part of this leadership, but characteristic of many other Kibbutz members, need to be borne in mind.

1. Since the Kibbutz was deliberately and consciously established and since most of its adults were reared under radically different circumstances outside the Kibbutz, there is a keen awareness of the uniqueness and experimental nature of their mode of life. There is a self-consciousness about it that comes from the knowledge of the difficulties involved and from the commitment of a lifetime to it.

2. Along with the clear awareness of the experimental and "different" nature of Kibbutz life, there is, of course, great sensitivity to criticism of it. This sensitivity is also due to awareness of a number of problems in Kibbutz child-rearing which remain unsolved (such as enuresis and night terrors among the children). There is a readiness to listen to "experts" and to make some modifications in the child-rearing procedures providing they do not change the over-all framework and the major principles. For example, several years ago one of the Kibbutz leaders in the field of education sought the advice of Anna Freud, in several sessions,

regarding a research program for the Kibbutz movement. More recently, upon receiving an advance copy of a paper, to be read at the meetings of the American Orthopsychiatric Association in which some criticism of infant-rearing during the first year of life was implied (Rabin, 1958a), a reform program was immediately undertaken (Golan, 1957).

Such modifications in procedures employed in child-rearing make the task of the investigator more complex. He must be aware of the changes that took place in the Kibbutzim under study, their temporal sequence, and their relation to the ages of the children studied.

3. Related to the sensitivity just described, the attitude of many of the leaders is one of vigilance. Being a highly literate group they are aware of every utterance made about the Kibbutz on the world cultural arena. They are ready to defend their system and, probably with some justification, point out the parochialism and ethnocentrism of many Western psychiatrists, psychologists and social scientists who because of their theoretical investment must find the flaws in Kibbutz child-rearing practices and must "prove" it harmful and inadequate. For example, child rearing in the Kibbutz has been criticized as follows (Kardiner, 1954, p. 161):

> What is the actual picture that we find? The human unit is egocentric and envious, with little capacity for affective relationship, a good deal of mistrust and a good deal of mutual contempt. One of the best evidences for the latter is the fact that a very high percentage of the marriages take place outside the Kibbutzim; that they are exogamous.

Quite apart from the merits, accuracy and correctness of the conclusions reached in the passage quoted above, is the issue of supporting *evidence*. This quotation is not presented side by side with the pertinent proof but appears as a mere expression of opinion. Thus the criticism reinforces the suspicion of Western science and scientists on the part of Kibbutz members. It reinforces a healthy skepticism of Western methods and an even more profound doubt regarding their overall intentions. Such occasions enhance a growing reluctance on the part of Kibbutz people to allow outsiders to enter the Kibbutz and gather data which will be ultimately interpreted by someone else, other than the interviewer. This other person may be sitting in New York and may not bother even with firsthand contact with the objects of his pronouncements.

The investigator who wishes to study closely any phase of Kibbutz life must counteract this "sophisticated suspicion" and sensitization to criticism. I pointed out that my objectives in studying the effects of child-rearing practices in the Kibbutz on later personality development were not to find out whether the Kibbutz methods are "right" or "wrong," or whether the product is "good" or "bad." The goal of the investigation, was to find out how different (if at all) the Kibbutz children are from other children and whether such differences may be accounted for by the differences in the rearing methods.

Kibbutz Rank and File

After the investigator has convinced the leadership on the points mentioned above, and also that he is, if not sympathetic, at least not antagonistic to the Kibbutz ideology, he is ready to enter the Kibbutzim which he has chosen jointly with the central educational committee. Here he begins to encounter the rank and file of the membership—the parents, nurses and teachers. His "introduction" into the Kibbutz by the central committee facilitates matters considerably; he gets in touch with the persons who are most relevant to the needs of the investigation. Yet some fairly common attitudes on the part of the rank and file are not to be ignored.

1. Many Kibbutz members, perhaps because of some ambivalence about their membership in the communal settlement, are antagonistic, suspicious and derisive in their attitude toward "outsiders." There is a good deal of defensive reaction. At best, there is tolerance of the outsider, not without a touch of superior condescension. The Kibbutz member has a consciousness of his status, probably more exalted in the past than at present, as a pioneer, a reformer and a member of the vanguard of society.

2. Politics and ideology, which are substantially left of center in most of the Kibbutzim, add in some instances to the suspiciousness (and contempt?) directed at an outsider who is also a member of a capitalist society—an American. The majority of Kibbutz membership is in favor of Israel's neutralism in the East-West political alignment; it is against complete commitment to the Western alliances.

3. In common with many Europeans and Israelis, Kibbutz members admire American technology, but not its scholarship, literature, science, and especially social science. They have not modified the old notions regarding the superficiality of American cultural life, the injustices of American society (still based on readings of Upton Sinclair, Steinbeck's *Grapes of Wrath*, etc.) and the "gimmick" aspects of its education and its scientific endeavor.

These attitudes do not constitute an exhaustive list, but may be considered dominant and of major importance. Despite these general trends, there was genuine friendliness on the part of many members, "cooperation" at the request of the central committee on the part of some, and an ignoring attitude on the part of still others. The degree of personal threat symbolized by the outsider and the defensiveness related to it, combined with the relative strength of the anti-capitalist, anti-American ideology, determined in a large measure the overall attitude of each individual member with whom I came in contact. Of course, the individual personal factors are not to be ignored altogether and lend a unique twist to the stereotyped aspects of the attitude.

The Children

The interaction between the investigator and the subjects of the study, the Kibbutz children at the several age levels, presents some interesting problems as well. Of course, there are wide individual differences, but some limited generalizations may be permitted.

Many of the Kibbutz infants (one-year-olds) were examined individually without the "moral support" of an adult-nurse or parent being present. Such arrangements are rare with infants in the ordinary family setting. The Kibbutz infant seems to be used to, and acquainted with, a wider circle of adults. The appearance of still another adult, although a stranger, does not threaten or frighten him ordinarily.

This relative feeling of security with strangers and trusting attitude toward them becomes particularly marked with the older children—the ten-year-olds. As soon as the investigator was introduced to the group by the teacher (sometimes even without formal introduction) the children flocked around him, pelted him with personal questions and exhibited a direct, friendly and unreserved interest. Many of them sought the physical proximity of the investigator and were particularly pleased at being interviewed by him individually. These conditions, of course, reduced constriction and stimulated considerable productivity in response to the projective devices employed. This type of interaction may be contrasted with the greater bashfulness and more reserved attitude of the control, non-Kibbutz children.

The adolescents, however, presented a picture resembling more closely that of the adults described above. They were rather reserved, almost reticent, somewhat suspicious and highly controlled. Kibbutz upbringing, throughout, but particularly during adolescence, emphasizes self-control, postponement of gratification, especially in the sexual area, and devotion to ideals and common objectives. During adolescence, greater mobilization of the defenses (control mechanisms) becomes imperative. The more generalized self-control and possibly some ethnocentric attitudes due to ideological indoctrination, make the contacts with an outsider a bit strained and result in somewhat more limited productivity and communication.

The Investigator's Conflict

Last, but not least, is the state of ambivalence and conflict of the observer-investigator in the Kibbutz setting. Many of the characteristics of Kibbutz members, such as idealism, perseverance, industriousness and devotion to duty, are valued highly in Western culture. The principles of economic justice and equality which are fundamental to Kibbutz ideology also have their persuasive aspects. All these combine to facilitate a degree of identification of the investigator with the Kibbutz, its values, ideals and, even, its members. This identification may color his observations, dull his objectivity and criticism, cause him to perceive selectively and unconsciously exhibit a bias *in favor* of the Kibbutz and its practices.

In a perceptive and penetrating paper that deals with some of these issues, Eva Rosenfeld (1957, p. 2) pointed out that:

. . . some situations are conducive to certain unique conflicts; also, scientists are often drawn to certain areas of investigation because they are particularly sensitive—both attracted and vulnerable—to those particular conflicts.

The conflicts referred to are those aroused in the scientist whose results and observations may question the values of the Kibbutz and its practices. While he has learned to appreciate many aspects of its ideology and the idealism of its members, there are unconscious conflicts which may be accompanied by feelings of guilt and anxiety and a sense of betrayal due to identification with the Kibbutz enterprise.

BIBLIOGRAPHY

Caplan, G. 1954. "Clinical Observations on the Emotional Life of Children in the Communal Settlements in Israel." In Senn, Milton J. E. (ed.), *Problems of Infancy and Childhood*. New York: The Josiah Macy Jr. Foundation.

Golan, S. 1957. Problems of Child-rearing in a Kibbutz Society. Paper read at the Annual Meetings of the American Orthopsychiatric Association in Chicago, March 1957.

Herskovits, Melville, Jr. 1948. *Man and His Works*. New York: Alfred A. Knopf.

Infeld, Henrik F. 1944. *Cooperative Living in Palestine*. New York: The Dryden Press.

Irvine, Elizabeth R. 1952. "Observations on the Aims and Methods of Child-rearing in Communal Settlements in Israel," *Social Relations*, 247–75.

Kardiner, A. 1954. "Social Stress and Deprivation." In Gladston, Iago (ed.), *Beyond the Germ Theory*. New York: A New York Academy of Medicine Book.

Rabin, A. I. 1954. Proposal of an Investigation of Child-rearing Practices in the Kibbutz and their Effects on Personality Development. Unpublished manuscript.

———. 1957a. "The Israeli Kibbutz (Collective Settlement) as a 'Laboratory' for Testing Psychodynamic Hypotheses," *The Psychological Record*, 7:111–15.

———. 1957b. "Personality Maturity of Kibbutz (Israeli Collective Settlement) and Non-Kibbutz Children as Reflected in the Rorschach," *Journal of Projective Techniques,* 21:148–53.

———. 1958a. "Infants and Children under Conditions of Intermittent Mothering in the Kibbutz (Israeli Collective Settlement)," *American Journal of Orthopsychiatry,* 28:577–84.

———. 1958b. "Some Psychosexual Differences between Kibbutz and Non-Kibbutz Israeli Boys," *Journal of Projective Techniques,* 22:328–32.

———. 1959a. "Kibbutz Children—Research Findings to Date," *Children,* 5:179–84.

———. 1959b. "Attitudes of Kibbutz Children to Family and Parents," *American Journal of Orthopsychiatry,* 29:172–79.

———. 1960. Kibbutz Adolescents. Paper read at the Annual Meetings of the American Orthopsychiatric Association in Chicago, February, 1960.

Rosenfeld, Eva. 1957. The American Social-Scientist in Israel: A Case Study in Role Conflict. Paper read at the Annual Meetings of the American Orthopsychiatric Association in Chicago, March 1957.

V

APPROACHES TO CROSS-CULTURAL PERSONALITY STUDY

About the Chapter

It is perhaps not too much to say that most of our knowledge of personality processes has been gained from psychiatric and psychoanalytic work with patients. These settings have provided both the opportunity and the motivation for frequent, serious, intensive and prolonged interviewing of a kind hardly possible with normal persons. Psychiatric interviewing can play an important role in cross-cultural studies. With his special skills and interests and his therapeutic orientation, the psychiatrist has access to a type of communication unavailable to others. The role of being of help to someone else is specially apt to create trust and intimacy in the subject or patient.

Dr. Carstairs' chapter is concerned with the complications created in psychiatric interviewing and in the relations between psychiatrist and patient when the two come from different cultural backgrounds. His observations apply, to a considerable extent, to the whole problem of cross-cultural study.

About the Author

G. MORRIS CARSTAIRS, psychiatrist and social anthropologist, studied under Evans-Pritchard, Mead and Fortes before carrying out field work in three villages of Rajasthan, India—reported in his book *The Twice-Born*. He is the author of chapters in *The Patient and the Mental Hospital; Health Culture and the Community; Culture and Mental Health; Medical Surveys and Clinical Trials;* and *Modern Trends in Occupational Health.* Since 1954 he has been engaged in research in social psychiatry. He is currently Director, Psychiatric Survey Research Unit, Medical Research Council, University College Hospital, London.

19

Cross-Cultural Psychiatric Interviewing

G. MORRIS CARSTAIRS
Medical Research Council, London

At the risk of being pedantic, it may be as well to begin by defining what one means by "psychiatric"—a term which is readily confused with "psychoanalytic" or "psychological." A psychiatrist differs from a psychologist in that his basic training is in general medicine, to which he has added further years of study and practice in medical psychology. He has taken the Hippocratic oath which binds him to exert himself to help the sick and to avoid doing anything which might harm them. He has, in fact, a therapeutic bias which sometimes renders him suspect to the rigorously "scientific" psychologist.

The psychoanalyst may also have had medical training. He certainly shares the psychiatrist's involvement in therapy, but with this difference: he is convinced that the key to his patient's problems is to be found in the patient's emotional life, as revealed by the psychoanalytic techniques of free association, dream analysis and analysis of the transference. The contrast between the approach of the psychoanalyst and that of the psychiatrist can be seen in their first interview with a patient. The former asks very few, if any, leading questions; he prefers to leave it to the patient to talk about whatever first comes into his mind, believing that once the patient has learned to talk quite freely, holding nothing back, the things that matter most to him will reveal themselves. The analyst usually refrains on principle from giving his patient a physical examination; should a frank illness occur during the analysis, he will advise his patient to consult another doctor for treatment. The psychiatrist, on the other hand, begins by making a physical examination and by taking a detailed medical and social history. He thus indicates his theoretical bias in favour of the multiple aetiology of mental and emotional disorders. For him, the key to the problem may lie in the patient's physical constitution, in his material and social environment or in his personal history—or in all three. In an interview with a patient from a culture other than his own, a psychiatrist will begin by finding out as much as he can about the patient's background, whereas an analyst may prefer to await the elucidation of cultural differences as they appear in the course of the patient's associations.

The psychiatrist is, of course, not alone in claiming that any one of a multitude of influences may be relevant to the understanding of a particular individual. With different professional emphases, similar claims have been advanced by anthropologists, sociologists and social psychologists—and even by poets. (*"Quidquid agunt homines"* wrote Juvenal nearly nineteen hundred years ago: "All that men are engaged in, their wishes, fears, anger, pleasures, joys and varied pursuits, form the farrago of my book.") The psychiatrist differs, however, in making the medical and psychological examination of the individual his principal mode of investigation.

Cross-cultural psychiatric interviewing may take place in two types of circumstances: (a) where the interview occurs in the psychiatrist's own culture-setting with which the patient is not wholly familiar, or (b) where the psychiatrist is the foreigner, interviewing the patient in the latter's home country. Interviews in these two settings present quite different problems.

INTERVIEWING IN THE PSYCHIATRIST'S CULTURE-SETTING

I have deliberately chosen the general term "culture-setting" in order to include in this category not only cases in which patients from overseas seek the advice of a Western psychiatrist, but also other cases in which the interview is conducted in a setting and in a manner which conforms to the psychiatrist's value system but not necessarily to that of the interviewee. This can happen, for example, when pupils of Westernized colleges in Singapore or Honolulu, Bombay, Abadan or Hong Kong seek counselling advice from their student health service; it happens much more frequently when the psychiatrist practising in a clinic is confronted by a patient who belongs to his own race, but comes from a different social class with different (and often quite unfamiliar) values to those of the psychiatrist.

In all of these situations, certain obstacles to mutual understanding arise. When the psychiatrist and his patient belong to different ethnic groups, the first obstacle is that of language. The interview will almost invariably be conducted in English, because the client is expected to know it in order to carry on his studies, or his business; in fact he will take pride in his command of English and feel hurt if it is suggested that it is imperfect. Tactfully handled, this barrier can readily be overcome because the interviewee also wants to perfect his English. The psychiatrist's task is to help him to express himself clearly, without putting words into his mouth.

The next obstacle is a more complicated one. It lies in the subject's tendency to assert a greater familiarity with Western ways than he has in fact yet acquired. Here the psychiatrist has to be particularly alert in his perceptions and circumspect in what he says, because of the danger of injuring the patient's self-esteem by revealing that the patient is ignorant of some aspects of Western life. If this source of confusion is disregarded, there is great scope for mutual "parataxic distortion," to use the late Harry Stack Sullivan's term. This can be avoided, to some extent, if the psychiatrist knows some of the details of his patient's experiences during his upbringing among his own people, and the expectations which colour the patient's encounters with the West.

Both of these impediments to communication can, however, be turned to advantage because they are both related to accomplishments which the patient keenly desires to acquire. Often the presenting symptom itself will be associated with anxiety over examinations, or over personal relationships with his teachers or Western acquaintances, or over his inability to fit in naturally in such unfamiliar surroundings.

It is often illuminating to view these problems not so much as neurotic illness but rather as akin to the emotional disturbances of adolescence, which also centre largely upon personal insecurity and role identification. To deal with them successfully the psychiatrist has to make a considerable effort of imagination. He must visualize even the minor every-day aspects of Western daily living as if they were strange and challenging. He has, above all, to establish a rapport with his patient of such a quality that the latter can admit to perplexity over quite simple, naïve problems, which he would be ashamed to discuss in normal conversation. The psychiatrist must avoid the tendency to connive with the patient in excluding these seemingly trivial problems from consideration.

An example of this type of situation arose recently in my practice, in London. A young Indian law student was referred to me as a case of anxiety neurosis in an immature personality with clearly unresolved oedipal conflicts. The referring agency was a clinic with a predominantly psychoanalytic orientation. It was not difficult to confirm their diagnosis. The young man had been driving himself with obsessional insistence to study his textbooks day and night, only to find that he did not seem to take in their contents, and failed examination after examination. He felt self-reproachful and guilty towards his parents who had sent him here at considerable expense to study. He was also depressed at his failure to strike up friendships with young English people on his infrequent incursions into society. In the course of a few interviews it became apparent that he was in fact studying law only in deference to his father's wishes; his own preference was for technical training in radio or photography. Formal testing showed that, in spite of his unexceptionable command of polite conversation, his English vocabulary was in fact severely limited, whereas his manual dexterity and abstract problem-solving were of a high order. Heartened by this discovery, he plucked up the courage to abandon his law studies and to persuade his father that his natural gifts lay in another direction. This was not accomplished without anxiety, but it had the result of relieving the young man of most of his depressive obsessional symptoms.

The key problems in consultations of this kind are usually concerned with difficulties of adjustment to the unfamiliar culture. Sometimes these, in turn, are symptomatic of a deeper conflict. Some years ago I was consulted by an Oxford student, the son of a celebrated Pakistani authority on the Mohammedan religion. This young man was intellectually brilliant. In his philosophical studies he found himself increasingly drawn towards a humanistic agnosticism; but at the same time he found that his co-religionists persisted in regarding him as the paradigm of the strict orthodoxy from which they themselves had lapsed. At last he asserted his independence, shaved his beard and moustache and announced that he would no longer abstain from eating pork and drinking wine. This proved to be much more than an intellectual decision. Having successfully confronted his fellow-students with his apostasy, he fell victim to an acute anxiety neurosis. Treatment of the neurosis led back to his early ambivalent relationship with his father, long before points of philosophical doctrine began to weigh upon his consciousness.

This case serves to show that sometimes the deeper problems of our overseas patients fall into a familiar pattern, especially when patients come from a patriarchal culture with a strongly developed super-ego, as did this young man. More often, however, it can be misleading to conclude that a patient who presents an apparently classical psychopathology can be treated on orthodox psychoanalytic lines. In the drama in which the growing child is at once the audience and a central character not only does the cast alter in different societies, but the phantasies which the actors re-enact are also sometimes profoundly singular. Generally, it must be considered inadvisable to attempt formal psychoanalytic therapy with a patient of an alien culture unless it is one which bears a very close affinity to that of the analyst. As Dr. Krapf (1955) has shown, when a multilingual patient is analysed, there always comes a point at which he relapses into his mother tongue in order to express primitive emotions and to recreate infantile gratifications: it is essential that the analyst should be able to keep in contact with him at this crucial time.

Multilingual analysis has in fact been very frequently practised in the Western world, if only because so many of the early analysts were originally Viennese but came to work in England or America. Their ability to work in a different country underlines the essential similarity of middle-class culture in the countries of Western Europe and the Americas. In spite of the multiplicity of languages and of the several emphases of national character, it is probable that this similarity of experience and values is greater than would be found between members of the middle class and of the working class in any one of these countries. This was one of the first reactions to Freudian theory of the Polish anthropologist Bronislaw Malinowski (1927), who wrote: "My personal knowledge of the life, customs and psychology of Eastern European peasants has allowed me to ascertain deep differences between the illiterate and the educated classes of the same society as regards the mental attitude of parents to children and vice versa."

Freud himself was not unaware of the cultural gulf between the working classes of Vienna and the middle-class patients upon whose treatment his psychological theory was built. Ernest Jones (1953, Vol. I, p. 208) has published a letter written by Freud to his fiancée in 1883 in which Freud commented on the very different upbringing and way of life which must be experienced by members of the working classes. He wrote: "I will not follow these thoughts further, but one might show how 'das Volk' judges, believes, hopes and works quite otherwise than we do. There is a psychology of the common man which is somewhat different from ours."

Strangely enough, neither Freud nor any of his followers ever returned to this theme. The profound differences in culture values and in personality formation in members of the industrial working classes have never been adequately explored. But there is no lack of evidence to confirm that they exist. In a study of parental behaviour patterns in families with a schizophrenic patient, and in matched control families in an American town, Kohn and Clausen (1956) found that the differences between middle-class and lower-class family norms were no less striking than the differences which they found between families which had, or had not, a schizophrenic member. They concluded:

> One fact we feel is abundantly clear: comparisons of parent-child relationships of schizophrenics and normals cannot ignore the factor of social class, as has so often been done in the past. Those studies which compared schizophrenics, largely from lower social status levels, with normal middle class students or with groups of professionals, have quite possibly documented a social class difference in maternal dominance rather than a disease-specific difference. Only if such differences are found between schizophrenics and normals drawn from the same class levels will we have real reason to assume that more intensive research in this area will be fruitful in terms of etiology.

More recently, Hollingshead and Redlich (1958) have driven this point home. Their survey of patients undergoing psychiatric treatment in New Haven has shown that even in a subsidised clinic, where the economic factor was controlled, patients from the two lowest social-class groups were seldom offered psychotherapy and, when offered it, were unable to profit from it. Nineteen out of twenty patients from Social Class V who were offered psychotherapy broke off their attendance at the clinic before the initial interviews of the intake procedure were completed. The authors found that the principal obstacle to psychotherapy in these cases was the mutual incomprehension, leading often to mutual hostility, between the working-class patient and the middle-class psychiatrist.

Such a profound failure of communication can only be aggravated where both ethnic and social-class differences separate the patient and the therapist. Yet even here, although the classical procedure of psychoanalytic treatment may be impossible, it by no means follows that psychotherapy must be abandoned in favour of organic treatment. On the contrary, if the limitations of the treatment situation are accepted, much can be achieved through individual and group psychotherapy directed towards helping the patient to improve his social role performance. Marvin Opler (1956, 1957) has developed the concept of "cultural push" to describe a process of group therapy for members of ethnic minorities. Patients are encouraged to begin by comparing notes, in a group of diverse backgrounds, upon their several traditional modes of family and social relationships. Here, it is no disadvantage if the therapist is unfamiliar with the patient's culture, so long as he shows himself interested, accepting, and willing to learn. This paves the way for the discussion of the difficulties which the immigrant has encountered in his new environment. "Cultural push" could clearly be used to advantage with groups of students from various countries. Just as the attentive analyst learns to map out his patient's psychopathology, so the therapist in such a group will be in a position to note those points of friction which reveal the significant divergences between his patients' culture and his own.

It may well prove that a similar modification of the customary two-person interview, with its aim of heightening the patient's awareness of his own deeper motivation, will bridge the gap between the psychiatrist and his working-class patients. These patients are unaccustomed to self-analysis, and believe themselves to be confronted with practical problems of daily living, not with abstruse emotional conflicts. In a number of mental hospitals and treatment centres new forms of group therapy have been developed, in which the emphasis is placed upon patients' current practical difficulties. Here the psychiatrist may play a relatively self-effacing role, as in Maxwell Jones' (1952) Social Rehabilitation Unit. Or he may first establish contact with his patients through shared activities, as in the remarkable examples of group therapy with seemingly inaccessible chronic schizophrenics reported independently from Glasgow (Freeman, Cameron and McGhie, 1958) and from the Wayne County General Hospital and Infirmary, Eloise, Michigan (Beard, Goertzel and Pearce, 1958). These are all pioneer ventures, in which the psychiatrists are learning what really matters to these hitherto neglected patients. As in the other examples, quoted above, of interviewing patients with whose culture the psychiatrist is unfamiliar: the first task is to establish a good rapport. The patient must be reassured that he is not simply helpless and inferior but that his problems deserve serious consideration, and that in discussing them he can actually teach the psychiatrist— as well as his fellow-patients—something which they want to learn.

INTERVIEWING IN THE SUBJECT'S CULTURE-SETTING

Psychiatrists have long been curious about the mentality of non-Western peoples. Their knowledge of these alien cultures has necessarily remained largely second-hand, mediated through the reports of travellers and anthropologists. But as early as 1898 William McDougall carried out psychological tests with natives of New Guinea as his share in the work of the Cambridge expedition to the Torres Straits (McDougall, 1912). In 1904 Kraeplin investigated patients in the mental hospitals in Java, collecting observations which found a place in the later editions of his textbook (Kraeplin, 1909). The first psychiatrist, however, who carried out prolonged field studies was the brilliant Cambridge scholar, W. H. R. Rivers, who achieved distinction in turn as a neurologist, as a psychiatrist and as an anthropologist. Men of such abundant talents are rare, and Rivers has had no equal. But both before and since his day interest in primitive mentality has been quickened by the spread of psychoanalytic theory. Freud himself was keenly interested in the applications of his theory to the interpretation of primitive myth, ritual and taboo. But, although widely read in ethnology, he remained strictly an armchair anthropologist. The pioneer of anthropological fieldwork by a trained psychoanalyst was of course Géza Róheim, who devoted two years to field studies in Somaliland, Central Australia, and New Guinea, concluding with a two-month visit to the Yuma Indians in Arizona (Róheim, 1932). At about the same time the analyst O. A. R. Berkeley-Hill (1933) published material interpreting Hindu religious beliefs and practices on the basis of his first-hand experience in India.

In more recent years, the work of Kardiner and Linton (1939, 1954) and of Erik Erikson (1943, 1950) stimulated a number of anthropologists to turn to psychoanalytic theory for the analysis of their data, often working in collaboration with psychiatrists for this purpose (e.g., Du Bois, 1945; Gorer and Rickman, 1952). When the Leightons carried out their studies of the Navaho (Leighton, A. H. and D., 1944), they were probably unique in their combination of experience and training in anthropology and psychiatry. Among their successors can be included Stainbrook (1952), the present writer (Carstairs, 1957), and Kilton Stewart (1955). The following discussion of interviewing informants in their own culture-setting has been influenced by all of these authors, but illustrations will be drawn for the most part from my own field experience in India.

As in the former type of cross-cultural interview, the first problem to be considered is that of language; and here lies a fundamental difference in technique. When the informant is interviewed in his native setting, it is essential that this should be done either in his native language or in a lingua franca which he uses in his normal experience. If this is not done, there is an almost insuperable barrier to establishing a good rapport. With every sentence which he has to formulate in an unfamiliar speech, the informant is reminded that his interlocutor is a stranger, an outsider. Some workers have relied upon well-trained interpreters to overcome this difficulty. There is no doubt that an intelligent interpreter can be taught to become highly competent in the conduct of interviews. But his presence inevitably interferes with the establishment of rapport. No one who has had practice with both methods can doubt that the additional time and effort spent in learning to converse in the informant's language is time well spent. This presupposes a certain gift for languages without which no one should attempt cross-cultural work. It does not necessarily demand either a scholarly or a comprehensive knowledge of the language in question. Provided that the interviewer can command a flow of conversational small-talk, he can begin interviews while still learning the language. Often he will find that by asking for clarification of an obscure word or concept, a new light is thrown on his informant's attitudes.

It was mentioned above that in his own country the psychiatrist must beware of attributing to.his patient a greater knowledge of Western ways than he really has. In the field, the situation is reversed. Now it is the informant who tends to assume that the interviewer knows more than he really does about the surrounding culture. In normal social intercourse there is an assumption of common knowledge in the use of gesture, symbol and metaphor. The interviewer, however, must strike a balance between showing familiarity with the conventions of everyday speech (which puts his subject at his ease) and prematurely thinking that he has mastered the local conversational signal-system. For example, when the writer first settled down for some months' stay in an Indian village, he found that men from the surrounding countryside who came to consult him about their illnesses invariably opened the consultation by offering him their wrist for him to take their pulse. Only after some weeks did he realise that they assumed that he, like their own village healers, could tell by the tremors of their tendons whether a witch, a demon or an evil spell was at work in their bodies. The gesture was the same, but its implications were quite different.

The interviewer can, however, turn his ignorance to advantage by insisting that hints and allusions be made quite explicit. As a stranger he has licence to ask questions with a frankness which might be resented in one of the informant's own community. It is important that he should avoid, so far as he can, being cast in the role of an important and knowledgeable person. At whatever cost to his self-esteem, he should try instead to present himself as someone who genuinely seeks help from his informants and is willing to offer some tangible help in return.

Naturally, it is difficult for illiterate country folk to understand exactly what the psychiatrist is up to. But they are keenly appreciative of medical treatment, especially if its effect is quickly and dramatically evident, and are willing to humour the visitor's requests in return for his assistance. The more educated the informants, the more prone they are to ascribing ulterior motives to their visitor. Thus, in the first village in which I worked, it took four months before the womenfolk of the village overcame their initial shyness. Later they were able to discuss this freely, as in the following extract from an interview with Dhapu, the wife of Nol Singh, and her son, Panna Singh:

DHAPU: "When you came, we were all afraid of you." (laughs)

PANNA SINGH: "I remember when you first came, I saw you coming. I was afraid and ran round the back way to avoid you."

DHAPU: "The women were very much afraid of you."

G.M.C.: "Why?"

DHAPU: "They said, 'Why has he come?' "

PANNA SINGH: "Mal Singh said, 'We shouldn't let him stay here, he'll kill us all. He will call up airplanes and have us all killed.' "

DHAPU: "The women hadn't seen anyone like you before and so they

were afraid. They said, 'We don't know what work he's come to do.'
. . . Then, when you came to live in the village, they gossiped
about you, saying, 'What is he?' and 'Why did he come here into
this hungry country?—What sort of trick is this?' But Nol Singh was
never afraid because he had seen lots of white men, so he understood about you very well."

Nol Singh had once served for a time in the Indian army, and he
made sense of my activities by explaining that I was really a medical officer on a "course"; when I had learned to talk their language with real
fluency I would return to my regiment and receive an increase of pay.

This attribution of a recognisable role served a useful purpose,
silencing the wild assertions of the blacksmith in the neighbouring village who said that fifty thousand Europeans had appeared in villages all
over India taking notes, and that this presaged the reconquering of the
nation by Britain, or Russia, or America.

But if Nol Singh's intervention was helpful, others were less so. During
the early weeks of my stay in this village, a father brought his heavily
veiled daughter for advice about her mysteriously recurring pain and
weakness, which was always at its worst when she went to live in her
husband's village. In this interview the father studiously evaded any
discussion of the relationship between the girl and her husband. Clearly
he did not think it proper to mention such private matters before the
Doctor Sahib. Later in the evening, in the company of one or two distant
kinsfolk belonging to the village, the full story came out of how she had
been married off in childhood and then violated prematurely by her
husband.

This interview was typical of many, in that the informant took heart
and spoke much more freely when he met the psychiatrist not alone, but
supported (as so often in everyday life) by representatives of his extended family. The first principle of good psychiatric interviewing is to
encourage the informant's free flow of communication. Mention has
been made of language, and of the need to identify the interviewer as a
sympathetic (perhaps rather helpless) and non-threatening figure. With
unsophisticated informants the need to take continuous notes is a serious
impediment to free communication. As one informant put it: "Won't
you take these notebooks and some government official will see them?"
Again, appealing to a neighbour sitting within earshot: "It's just that he
writes down all our names, so we suspect that someone may get to see
them." In this village the writing down of names at once conjured up
memories of interminable lawsuits and, less obviously, the practice of
sorcery which often entailed writing the victim's name.

It has to be remembered that in some cultures not only is the act of
writing suspect, but there may be a taboo upon saying certain things

aloud. For example, in the village of Sujarupa everyone believed in witchcraft. In the course of some months, several informants let it be understood that there was a particularly malevolent witch in this village. No one dared to name her directly because a witch knows at once, and takes . revenge, if her name is betrayed. It was a small boy, carried away by indignation at her latest supposed act of child-murder, who finally indicated by gestures that the witch was no other than my nearest neighbour, an old woman of some eminence who nearly always spent her afternoon working and gossiping with other grandmothers in seeming friendship. Once she had been denounced and beaten in an attempt to save a sick child's life. She herself talked readily about witchcraft in the next village, but denied that any witch lived here. At the very end of my stay, during a cordial farewell interview, I brought up this subject again and asked Dakhu why some perfectly respectable and worthy people such as she herself were sometimes maligned as witches. This was going too far. Dakhu was astonished, hurt, offended and then furious. She devoted several hours to shouting abuse and curses, with so vigorous a display of malice that her reputation became quite understandable.

A year later, news reached me that Dakhu had again been accused of practising death-dealing witchcraft, and beaten with sticks. This time she had died of her wounds and the village was split into two warring factions as a result. I was summoned from the village, a day's rail journey away, where I was now living, and both sides appealed to me to act as peacemaker in this feud.

This incident brings home the ethical problem of the interviewer's responsibility for the consequences of his interview. True, Dakhu was already secretly hated and feared, and had already once been defied. Still, one could not help wondering whether her outburst against the white visitor (who had by that time been adopted into two of the village families as a "dharm-bhai" or blood-brother) might not have contributed to her fate. Things which are hinted at, but which remain unspoken, excite the interviewer's interest because in field inquiry, just as in individual psychotherapy, these concealed topics are likely to be of emotional significance to the subject. But one has to try to anticipate the harmful consequences, if any, of bringing them into the open. Fortunately, crises as serious as this rarely occur. I found that by living in the village and participating in all that went on, I was able to share in a succession of other crises, such as the sickness and death of a child, the attack by a panther on someone's flock of goats, the financial negotiations for an engagement ceremony. My knowledge of these successive crises gave added meaning to my informants' conversation, and to their dreams.

In psychoanalytic technique, analyst and patient meet only during the hour of consultation. In this, as in many other respects, the interview in the field is quite different. As Róheim found, the primitive informants show great curiosity about their interviewer. It is necessary to keep in touch with their concept of what he is, and to take steps to modify this concept if it should prove destructive to good rapport. At various times, in three Indian villages, I learned that I was regarded as a spy from Pakistan, a black market inspector, a sorcerer, a holy man and once (in a grateful patient's hyperbole) as an incarnation of Lord Krishna.

Other differences between analytic technique in the consulting room and in the field are the frequent presence of other persons besides the informant being interviewed, and the inadvisability of confronting the informant with an interpretation of his unconscious thought-processes. Róheim discovered that when he offered his informants interpretations of sexual and aggressive themes, they usually reacted by breaking off the interview. He reflected sadly: "But our savage informant is not making efforts to tell the painful truth and cannot therefore be compared to the patient in analysis" (Róheim, 1932, p. 21). In spite of these limitations, Róheim believed that the task of the psychoanalytically trained field-worker was to give added depth to the descriptive account of the social anthropologist by demonstrating "the latent wish-fulfilment formula in each specific type of social organization." This could be done by dream analysis of the individual, observations of the sexual life, play-analysis with children and the interpretation of a people's myths, ceremonies and customs.

Róheim has emphasized the primary importance of dream analysis as a means of penetrating the informant's ego-defences: "When the analyst begins to loom conspicuous in the open or in the latent contents of the informant's dreams, he may be sure that he has got a transference and by analysing the dream he will be able to understand the exact nature of that transference" (Róheim, 1932, p. 9). Róheim does not, however, mention one important obstacle to dream analysis, namely the stereotyped attitudes towards dreams and their interpretation which prevail in many cultures and which add their own standardised "secondary elaboration" to the content of the dream as it is told by the informant.

I encountered this difficulty among certain Hindu sub-castes. In 1950, prior to my second tour of fieldwork, I was urged by the distinguished Jungian author of *Stone Men of Malekula* (Layard, 1942) to see if I could confirm the latter's hypothesis that certain specific archetypal symbols would be found in the dreams of lepers. During the following year, in the North Indian village of Deoli, the opportunity to do so presented itself when I found a middle-aged leper living in retirement in the outskirts of the village. Unfortunately, this man, although friendly and co-operative in other respects, insisted that dreaming was something only children and simpletons indulged in and firmly repressed the memory of his own dreams if he had any. Others in the village were not so reticent, although it was characteristic of the older men that they tended to give their interpretation of them and to omit the vulgar details. The young men, on the other hand, recounted dreams which both reflected and illuminated their current conflicts over sexuality and hostility; and it was in discussing one of these dreams that I was given a valuable insight into my Hindu informants' attitude towards aggression. This dream showed (and later direct observation confirmed the point) that a Hindu pictures a quarrel as typically a drama with three actors, two contestants and a peacemaker; and it is not the protagonists but the peacemaker who is seen as the victor in the dispute.

Over-eagerness in interpretation is a weakness to which the interviewer, as well as the informant, can become prone. This applies not only to informants' dreams but also to the appraisal of their neurotic traits and traumatic experiences. Here, a period of "masterly inactivity" is called for. Often it will be found that syndromes which are apparently abnormal —such as extreme concern over the state of the bowels, or over an imaginary spermatorrhoea—are evidence not so much of individual as of shared neurotic traits. These, of course, are not perceived as abnormal by other members of the community. It is only after a gradual process of feeling one's way into the accepted values and expectations of the group that one learns to recognise behaviour which *they* regard as abnormal.

I fell into just such a trap at the outset of my third field study, in a jungle village inhabited by primitive Bhil tribespeople (Carstairs, 1954). I entered this village after having spent eleven months studying a community of high-caste Hindus, one of whose most salient characteristics was the recurrence of crises of paranoid distrust. In talking with Bhil informants, it seemed at first that their outlook was even more paranoid. A constant refrain in their interviews was the threat of attack from neighbouring villages, of fights, of abduction of one's wife. But before long I came to realise that this was no preoccupation with a phantasied danger. In these villages theft and aggression were extremely common. Hardly a week went by without the sounding of the war-drum to announce a raid. It was not morbid anxiety but a firm grasp of reality which made these Bhils sleep lightly round their open fires with a weapon always ready at hand.

This jungle tribe also gave me my first experience of interviewing members of a group in whom both sexual repression and patriarchal authority counted for little. In striking contrast to the attitude of the Hindus, in whom submission to the father-figure is strongly over-determined, was the following passage from an interview with Bhumtia, an adolescent warrior: "When you grow up a little, your father tells you to work—sow corn, plough, graze the goats. If you don't work well, he beats you. He's often beaten me but when I'm big I'll fight him. Then, I'll hit my mother and my father and big brothers; then they'll be afraid to beat me any more." His elder brother Chinio had already grown to maturity and announced his independence by besting his father in a fight. Greater familiarity with these Bhils taught me that the constantly recurring episodes of violence in their daily experience were not to be interpreted as necessarily traumatic events. On the contrary, controlled aggression appeared to be one of their preferred modes of communicating with each other, playing quite a part also in their love affairs.

In all psychiatric interviewing there becomes apparent an antithesis between emotional problems which are idiosyncratic to the individual and conflict situations which are inherent in his membership of his culture. Therapeutic interviews, whether with patients of one's own or of a different culture, tend to focus upon the former type of problem, with a view to helping the patient to do something about it. Psychiatric interviewing in the field, however, is concerned less with individual than with shared experiences of emotional stress.

It would make a neatly symmetrical conclusion to this one chapter if one could say that the same bias could be observed in interviews carried out across the social-class barrier in our own cultures. But this is not quite true. Psychiatric interviewing has been carried out in the separate sub-culture of the working class in a number of different contexts. Pioneers of industrial psychiatry like Elton Mayo (1946) and May Smith and Millais Culpin (1930) carried out interviews with working people in their work setting. These interviews were designed to elicit not only facts but also their feelings about their job. In later years members of the Tavistock Institute of Human Relations (Wilson, 1952; Jacques, 1951) developed the technique of introducing a psychodynamically trained therapist as a participating member of worker-management groups which discuss current problems as they arise. His role is to identify the covert emotional resistances which sometimes lie behind apparent differences of opinion about factual matters. Open-ended, "trouble-seeking" interviews and participant observation are also used nowadays in the course of sociological surveys which are filling in the gaps in our knowledge of the life and value-systems of sub-sections of our own complex communities, whether in "Street-Corner Society" (Whyte, 1943), in "Crestwood Heights" (Seeley *et al.*, 1956) or in Bethnal Green (Young and Wilmot, 1957), or in enquiries directed to specifically psychiatric problems, such as the attitude of different sections of the community to mentally ill patients in their midst (Cumming and Cumming, 1957; John Clausen *et al.*, 1955; Freeman and Simmons, 1958; Brown, Carstairs and Topping, 1958).

It is characteristic of all of these studies that, although aimed at mapping out group problems and points of social tension, they also incidentally revealed many cases who needed fairly immediate personal help as well. It appears that, when the psychiatric interviewer enters into the territory of his working-class informant, he meets much less hostility and a greater readiness to accept help than appears to be the case when the same subject is sent, perhaps unwillingly, to the psychiatrist's office. One has to recognise that the psychiatric interview is a technique which is potentially quite disturbing. In the working-class home, as in the witch-haunted village, it may bring into the forefront conflicts and threats which have long been kept in abeyance. This is the basis for the well-tried psychiatric principle: No research without therapy.

BIBLIOGRAPHY

Beard, J. H. and Goertzel, Victor. 1958. "The Use of Activity Group Therapy with the Chronically Regressed Schizophrenic," *American Group Psychotherapy Journal.* (In press.)

Berkeley-Hill, O. A. R. 1933. *Collected Papers.* Calcutta: Calcutta Book Co.

Brown, G. W., Carstairs, G. M. and Topping, Gillian G. 1958. "Post-Hospital Adjustment of Chronic Mental Patients," *Lancet,* 2, 685–89.

Carstairs, G. M. 1954. "The Bhils of Kotra Bhomat," *Eastern Anthropologist,* 7:169.

———. 1957. *The Twice-Born: A Study of a Community of High-Caste Hindus.* London: Hogarth Press. (1958, Indianapolis: Indiana University Press.)

Clausen, John (ed.). 1955. "The Impact of Mental Illness on the Family," *Journal of Social Issues,* 11:6–11.

Culpin, Millais S., and Smith, May. 1930. *The Nervous Temperament.* Industrial Health Research Board Report Series No. 61. London: H.M.S.O.

Cumming, John and Elaine. 1957. *Closed Ranks: An Experiment in Mental Health Education.* Cambridge: Harvard University Press for the Commonwealth Fund.

Du Bois, Cora. 1944. *The People of Alor.* Minneapolis: Minnesota University Press.

Erikson, Erik H. 1943. *Observations on the Yurok: Childhood and World Image.* Berkeley: University of California Press.

———. 1950. *Childhood and Society.* New York: Norton.

Freeman, H. E. and Simmons, O. G. 1958. "Mental Patients in the Community: Family Settings and Performance Levels." *American Sociological Review,* 23:147–54.

Freeman, T., Cameron, J. L. and McGhie, A. 1958. *Chronic Schizophrenia.* London: Tavistock Press.

Gorer, G. and Rickman, J. 1949. *The People of Great Russia.* London: Cresset Press.

Hollingshead, August B. and Redlich, Fred. H. 1958. *Social Class and Mental Illness.* New York: Wiley; London: Chapman and Hall.

Jacques, Elliot. 1951. *The Changing Culture of a Factory*. London: Tavistock Press.

Jones, Ernest. 1953. *Sigmund Freud: Life and Work*. London: Hogarth Press. Vol. I.

Jones, Maxwell S. 1952. *Social Psychiatry*. London: Tavistock Press; published in U.S.A. with the title *The Therapeutic Community*. New York: Basic Books.

Kardiner, A. 1939. *The Individual and His Society*. New York: Columbia University Press.

————, *et al.* 1954. *The Psychological Frontiers of Society*. New York: Columbia University Press.

Kohn, Melvin L., and Clausen, John C. 1956. "Parental Authority Behavior and Schizophrenia," *American Journal of Orthopsychiatry*, 26:297–313.

Kraeplin, E. 1909. *Psychiatrie*. (8th ed.). Leipzig: Barth.

Krapf, Edward E. 1955. "The Choice of Language in Polyglot Analysis," *Psychoanalytic Quarterly*, 24:343–57.

Layard, J. 1942. *Stone Men of Malekula*. London: Chatto and Windus.

Leighton, Alexander H. and Dorothea. 1944. *The Navaho Door*. Cambridge: Harvard University Press.

McDougall, William and Hose, C. 1912. *The Pagan Tribes of Borneo*. London: Macmillan.

Malinowski, Bronislav. 1927. *Sex and Repression in Savage Society*. London: Kegan Paul.

Mayo, Elton. 1946. *The Human Problems of an Industrial Civilisation*. Macmillan Co. for Harvard University.

Opler, Marvin K. 1956. *Culture, Psychiatry and Human Values*. Springfield, Illinois: C. C. Thomas.

————. 1957. "Group Psychotherapy: Individual and Cultural Dynamics in a Group Process," *American Journal of Psychiatry*, 114:433–38.

Róheim, Géza. 1932. "Psycho-analysis of Primitive Cultural Types," *International Journal of Psycho-analysis*, 13:1–224.

Seeley, John R., *et al.* 1956. *Crestwood Heights*. Toronto: University Press.

Stainbrook, Edward. 1952. "Some Characteristics of the Psychopathology of Schizophrenic Behaviour in Bahian Society," *American Journal of Psychiatry*, 109:330–35.

Stewart, Kilton. 1955. *Pygmies and Dream Giants*. London: Gollancz.

Whyte, William F. 1943. *Street Corner Society*. Chicago: University of Chicago Press.

Wilson, A. T. M. 1951. "Some Aspects of Social Press," *Journal of Social Issues*, Suppl. No. 5.

Young, Michael and Wilmot, Peter. 1957. *Family and Kinship in East London*. London: Routledge and Kegan Paul.

About the Chapter

Dreaming is perhaps the most personal of all action. In many cultures dreams are the most available of all depth personality data although it should be recognized that they may also be the most difficult to interpret. Dorothy Eggan, while recognizing the dream's function of expressing the forbidden impulse life of the unconscious, emphasizes the ego aspects of dreaming and treats dreaming in the same terms as other types of action. This leads her to an emphasis on the manifest content of dreams rather than on their latent and symbolic meanings. In the now classic set of Hopi dream materials that she has collected and worked with, there emerges a clear picture of Hopi reality, of its traditional values and morals, plus an understanding of the dreamer's relationship to these cultural processes. This conception of the dream leads us to see in it a much more comprehensive reflection of the mental life than does the psychoanalytic position which views it almost entirely as expressing one aspect of the person, namely the id impulses.

About the Author

DOROTHY EGGAN is a Fellow of the American Anthropological Association and a member of the Council of the American Folklore Society. She has engaged in field research among the Hopi Indians, and other groups, in cooperation with her husband, since 1938, and has been particularly interested in the relevance of dreams for research on both personality and culture. Her first major paper was on "The Problem of Hopi Adjustment" in the *American Anthropologist,* Vol. 45, 1943 (reprinted in C. Kluckhohn and H. A. Murray, *Personality in Nature, Society and Culture.* Another recent paper is "Instruction and Affect in Hopi Cultural Continuity" in the *Southwestern Journal of Anthropology,* Vol. 12, 1956.

Acknowledgments

The author would like to thank Fred Eggan, Bert Kaplan, David and Evelyn Riesman, David Schneider, Milton Singer, Melford Spiro, and Montague Ullman, M.D. for reading this chapter in various drafts and making comments or suggestions. In addition Leon Saul, M.D. and Edith Sheppard, M.D., as well as David Schneider and Marie Reay, have kindly allowed quotation from manuscripts or personal communications.

20

Dream Analysis

DOROTHY EGGAN

In the last decade a major synthesizing effort in the social sciences has focused attention on the interrelations of culture and personality. Murphy (1947), Kluckhohn and Murray (1948, Chapters I and II), Asch (1952) and several others have provided clear discussions of the problems involved, and a framework within which specific information about the individual and his culture can be more precisely collected and examined. But conspicuous by its absence in most of these, is any effort to harness the immense potential of the dream—that most profoundly subjective of all personality productions—to further these ends.

The difficulty in dealing with dreams in a scientific manner is, of course, the bogy man which has stopped us all. It is the specter responsible for what Murphy (1947, p. 416) has called "one of the greatest instances of myopia in contemporary psychology": the neglect in personality studies of the television qualities of the nightlife of the mind. For in the early stages of a fusion between two pioneering fields it is difficult to draw the line between scientific vigilance and too great caution. This is particularly true in the study of personality and culture. Both involve finding the "right point of entrance" to a maze of concentric "circular and interactive processes" (Kluckhohn, 1954, p. 696), and both subsequently present the problem of unambiguous definition and description which will be meaningful cross-culturally and in inter-disciplinary research.

Can we then show evidence which will justify the addition of another "intangible," a perceptual experience during sleep, to this somewhat chaotic tangle of circular processes and elusive concepts? Can the study of dreams be of use in "attaining broader and more precise generalizations," in "formulating more precise conceptualizations," and in "posing fruitful hypotheses for further empirical research?" (Kluckhohn, 1945, p. 147). In other words, can we fit them into the present attempt to refine and integrate the techniques and objectives of personality research? Few scholars would deny the *relevance* of dreams in personality studies; in fact, Kroeber (1952, p. 324) in reference to his Walapai studies, says: "I had the impression that the dreams revealed more personality than the life histories . . . a dream is bound to be personal, while a life history can be heavily depersonalized." And Murphy (1947, p. 415) fortifies my own bias when he speaks of the "private world" of dreams, and says: "When it is discovered, when its richness, strength, and individuality are studied as objects of value for science . . . there will be a psychology of personality more worthy of the name."

The study of dreams has of course played a major role in the development of psychoanalysis. But in recent years there has been a renewed interest in the use of dreams in other contexts, particularly in the use of manifest dream content in personality research involving nonpatient subjects in our own society. The answer to the question of whether dreams can be used *cross-culturally* lies in part in the degree to which dreams can be considered both a projection of the personality and a reflection of the culture. On these points there is much affirmative evidence, both experimental and ethnographic. In fact, the most convincing indication that we should shift our thinking from depth analyses of dreams as a therapeutic device *only,* to a consideration of the amplified manifest content of dreams as an instrument to be used for a better understanding of the interactions between culture and personality, comes from non-Western cultures. In many of these societies great psychological wisdom is frequently shown in their beliefs regarding illness, dreaming and catharsis (see Herskovits, 1934; Hallowell, 1941; LaBarre, 1947; Eggan, 1949). Dreams are not only remembered and told, but are an active force in cultural conditioning and personality expression.

Sophisticated intuitions among non-Western peoples regarding the nature of the dreaming process, and in handling emotions connected with it, are reported in Lincoln's (1935) comprehensive survey of primitive dreams from Australia, Melanesia, Polynesia, Africa and the Americas. Beliefs varied widely of course; among the Yuma and Mohave Indians, for instance, dream experiences influenced most waking activities. The

Huron Indians believed that dreams were a revelation of the secret and hidden wishes of the soul, while the Trobriand Islanders reversed this belief and thought that magically induced dreams could *produce* a wish in the dreamer, and thus influence his waking conduct. The Naga of Assam dismissed much of the manifest content and looked for symbols. Other groups, such as the Hopi and Navaho Indians, treated the manifest content at face value, interpreting it loosely, depending upon the dreamer's emotional and physical reaction on awakening. Among the Hopi a bad dream was so serious an experience that a relative had to be immediately awakened to hear it, after which the dreamer went outside to spit four times and thus further purge his emotions. The Navaho treated a bad dream as they did any illness, by religious ceremony and native medicine. And Firth (1934) shows how the Tikopia escape the emotional consequences of their dreams by blaming them on spirits who dupe sleepers, so that the dreamers feel no sense of moral responsibility for their dream behavior.

One of the most dramatic examples of native discernment regarding dreams is reported by Marie Reay (1957) for the Kuma of New Guinea. In this society all adult males in the patrilineal line are forced into close and constant cooperation in order to survive. But they spontaneously expressed their resentment of this cooperation, saying that they "would like to act like wild pigs," and grab whatever they wanted by physical violence, if they did not have to obey rules which enabled them to live in groups. Witchcraft among them is "the only real crime and the grossest of evils —a danger which may strike at the community, or a poison which may seep into it, through the traitorous agency of one of its members," and their term for dreams, *wur kum banz,* is very revealing. *Wur* is sleep, *kum* is witchcraft, and *banz* is honey. Thus their phrase for dreams is freely translated "sweet witchcraft while you sleep," and all adult males regularly reported three nightmarish dreams in which the honeycoating has fallen off. One of these is the dream of eating pork, which for the Kuma is

a prized and rare delicacy. . . . Pigs are so valued for ritual presentation to other groups that a man can rarely claim a whole pig for eating without apportioning the meat to particular clansmen. . . . He can privately eat any animal he has stolen from a neighboring group . . . but in the event of discovery, this does nothing to enhance the reputation of a man who has to stoop to pig stealing. It is not surprising that one often hears a Kuma say that he has dreamed of eating pork. But we cannot predict, from the waking culture, what his fellows' response will be.

In this dream the dreamer "eats some pork and enjoys it, but people tell him . . . that it is not pork, but human flesh that he has eaten. The dreamer is afraid, but he has already eaten the meat and he can do nothing to alter that fact. He wakes when he can no longer bear the fear and remorse his dream action has caused him." The Kuma are aware that the practice of cannibalism exists in far places but they attribute cannibalism to witches. "People are only accused of witchcraft if they are in some way traitors to their clan. A suggestion that a person has tasted human flesh is tantamount to alleging that he has acted in the most despicable and unnatural way possible by betraying his clan." Thus, while the waking desire to "act like wild pigs" is often artificially sweetened in, for instance, hunting dreams, in this frequent dream of eating pork, which begins as a simple wish fulfillment dream, the "coating" deceives neither the dreamer (who awakens in shame and fright) nor his dream companions, and the tribe clearly recognizes the social psychological implications of such dreams by calling all dreams "sugar coated evil."

Whether different societies regard dreams as "sugar coated evil," or a direct message from their Gods, it is evident that culturally induced preoccupation with the dreaming process, in response to varying cultural concepts, can operate in one direction as a sanction for witchcraft, murder and cannibalism (Lincoln, 1935, p. 84), and in the opposite direction to maintain group unity and individual equilibrium (Devereux, 1951, p. 85; Eggan, 1955; Wallace, 1958). Hallowell (1955, pp. 96, 99), commenting on the self and its behavioral environment, says:

> One common type of past experience that may become particularly important when integrated with certain concepts of the nature of the self is dreaming. Once we recognize the fact that self-awareness is a generic human trait, that a self-related experience of the past depends upon a memory process (recall) and that the human individual is at the same time exposed to some culturally constituted self-image, there is nothing psychologically abstruse about the incorporation of dream experience into the category of self-related experiences. . . . It would be possible to demonstrate from other dream material how the horizon of self-related experience is enormously broadened through the integration of this kind of experience with that of waking life.

Erikson (1956, pp. 57, 70) has recently developed and clarified his concepts of ego-synthesis—"a multiplicity of successive and tentative identifications" with individuals, group ideals and goals—and ego-identity—an "identity of something in the individual's core with an essential aspect of the group's inner coherence." It can hardly be denied that a universal necessity in any society is the attainment, by ego-synthesis, and the maintenance through ego-identity, of individual mental equilibrium. And the dream process, influenced by cultural beliefs, frequently gives a clear picture of a culturally constituted self-image "walking a tight-rope" toward the mental equilibrium of ego-identity balanced by a "pole" of culturally shared dream experiences.

In the dream, then, we have a *universal* process as confirmed by recent studies of Dement and Kleitman (1958), a process which is adaptive with respect to the individual and functional with respect to the group. It seems clear that a maturing science of personality and culture cannot afford to relegate phenomena of this magnitude to a minor role despite the scientific hazards involved in working out ways to include them.

In fact, personality as well as cultural comparisons can "best proceed from the invariant points of reference supplied by the biological, psychological and sociosituational 'givens' of human life" (see Kluckhohn, 1953, p. 521). The dream, however intangible it may seem to the dreamer or to the hearer, is deeply and sensitively rooted in each of these three "givens." Like a seismograph built into the human organism it records multidimensional responses to the need drives in each of them. But it is precisely the dilemma inherent in the complexity of such a record which has made psychologists and anthropologists alike wary of an attempt to use dreams in comparative personality research. To use these responses exactly as they were reported by most dreamers in our society seemed an impossible task. Moreover, Freudian dream theory and interpretative techniques had so firm a grip on the minds of most researchers that it was virtually impossible to think in terms of the use of manifest content only. For, as Riesman (1951, p. 130) has said in another context, "psychoanalytic terminology can in itself become a defense mechanism, a blockage" in the path of independent thought. A researcher who wished to use dreams, therefore, had either to independently formulate and test new hypotheses through the time-consuming collection and examination of large numbers of dreams, or resort to a technique of "symbolic" interpretation of various elements in the manifest content of dreams. The latter procedure, when removed from the framework of a complex and integrated body of Freudian psychological theory, or variants of it (and particularly in the absence of associations which connected the symbols with their source), did not seem promising in cross-cultural personality research.

The question of caution with regard to dream interpretation through "universal" symbolism was raised by Freud himself and by most psychoanalysts since. However, when confronted with a collection of non-Western dreams one is tempted to ignore this advice. It is far easier to equate "bear" with "father" and/or with "mother's brother" and stop there, than to take one's informant back through labored associations to that traumatic day when he was playing alone by a stream and was suddenly confronted by a bear. From that point, there *may* be a bridge, through more associations, to equally traumatic male authority in his childhood, and to the fact that he resented herding sheep for his mother's brother yesterday. But if these bridges cannot be found, may an anthropologist *assume* they are there, and thus interpret the dream? Freud

(1938, pp. 371, 375) has said that every symbol "may possess many and varied meanings," and has warned against "overestimating the importance of symbols in dreams." Later he said more strongly (1949, p. 135): "It is no part of our task to perform tricks nor is that method of interpretation which is based on a knowledge of symbolism one which can replace or even compare with that of free association. It is complementary to the latter, and the results are only useful when applied in connection with the latter." French, in his comprehensive work on the *Integration of Behavior* (1952), where he gives a clear exposition of modern psychoanalytic method and techniques, not only points out (p. 92, fn.) that "the uncritical use of such [universal] symbol interpretation can lead to very untrustworthy conclusions," but also says (p. 34) that "psychoanalytic theories owe their existence to our interpretative method. If our interpretations start with these same theories, then we shall be merely reading back our preconceptions into the facts."

The use of Freudian analysis of dreams and particularly the "universal" symbolic interpretation of dream elements by anthropologists will not be emphasized in this chapter for two reasons: first, because there are serious difficulties in the application of these techniques cross-culturally, and second because the method itself and the work of those who have thus applied it are widely known. Lincoln (1935) discusses dreams from many cultures and gives both a summary of Freudian ethnological work with dreams and an excellent bibliography on dreams to that date. Róheim (1932; 1949), a militant pioneer in the use of psychoanalytic interpretations of customs and dreams in non-Western cultures, provided much valuable field data but his "unquestioning acceptance of Freudian terminology, coupled with his undisguisedly emotional strictures" (Herskovits, 1934, p. 76, fn.) regarding the whole question of dream interpretation, introduces a doubt in the reader's mind about the objectivity of both his field work and his analysis of it. In this connection Kroeber (1952, p. 308) pays tribute to Freud's many contributions to anthropological science but comments on the "all or none" attitude of Róheim and others and characterizes certain of Róheim's statements as "arbitrarily dogmatic."

Devereux (1951, pp. 85, 90–91) uses the same theoretical background with more flexibility in his report on the use of dreams with a "Wolf" Indian during therapeutic counseling. He considers the manifest content of dreams to be important in itself, and says that the dreams are themselves a major psychic defense encouraged by "Wolf" culture for purposes of ego defense and ego gratification. Thus "Wolf" dreams, like Hopi dreams, "work" toward equilibrium.

More convincing to many researchers, however, than psychoanalytic analysis of individual dreams from other cultures is the use of Freudian psychological theory applied to a body of dream data (Opler, 1942; Devereux, 1957). Wallace (1958, p. 234) clearly illustrates a "primitive" people (the Iroquois) actively using in the seventeenth century "a theory of the mind similar in many essentials to that expressed by Sigmund Freud and his intellectual heirs in Western European cultural tradition of two centuries later."

However, the application in non-Western cultures of basic Freudian techniques in the analysis of individual dreams—if the results are to be scientifically significant—demands verification by the psychoanalyses of individuals in these cultures. This in turn requires:

1. A psychoanalyst in the field situation (not merely a researcher who has been psychoanalyzed as many of us have been);

2. Either a psychoanalyst who is also an anthropologist, or a team including a psychoanalyst and an anthropologist;

3. A long period of residence in the field; and

4. Enough psychoanalyses of individuals from various cultures so that results can be adequately evaluated.

Even if these requirements are met, the questions of ambiguity and objectivity will remain in many minds. For the essence of psychoanalysis is that it is a unique experience. In it the subject is directed to turn his thoughts inward and backward toward his earliest memories in contradistinction to society's normal demand that they be turned outward and forward. Furthermore, the phenomenon of transference, the subject's tendency to transfer to the analyst ambivalent emotions felt for individuals in his past, must be used to manipulate his emotional reactions into useful sublimations. Friedemann (1957, p. 363) writing of representative and typical dreams says: "My own point of departure is the psychoanalytic situation itself. . . . The crux of my hypothesis is that there is a more or less constant affinity between the unconscious and emotional factors stirred up in the analytic situation, on the one hand, and the manifest dream content, on the other." It is difficult in such a situation (as in the examination of dreams under hypnosis) to rule out the possibility of some degree of uniformity in the dreams of analysands in response to the analytic situation itself. Would a Hopi Indian, or a white Chicagoan, or a Kuma of New Guinea, reporting his dreams to his analyst record the same number and kind of dreams during the same period of time if he were not under analysis? This question can never be answered. Is it possible for any psychoanalyst (who is both a product of Western pressures and education, and of this convincing but highly specialized segment of experience which is psychoanalysis) to work on a depth analysis of dreams with an informant from another society and maintain complete scientific detachment toward the problem of universal processes and symbolism in dreams? Having had the experience of psychoanalysis, and having worked on Hopi dreams, I am acutely aware of the problems involved.

For the present then, it seems clear that in spite of much subject matter in non-Western dream collections which seems to lend itself to Freudian symbolic interpretation, we cannot justify "borrowing" these interpretations from psychoanalytic theory without confirmation of them through the use of psychoanalytic techniques with the dreamers. And "psychoanalytic techniques" cannot be translated simply as "including the dreamer's *comments* on his dreams." The process of "free association" as used by psychoanalysts is a complicated and time consuming procedure which cannot be undertaken by most cross-cultural personality researchers. Moreover, the risk to certain informants can be very grave if this process is attempted by inadequately trained investigators since partially resolved repressed conflicts, which should be handled only by a skilled therapist, may thereby become seriously activated. If then, dreams are a universal phenomenon which affords a kaleidoscopic picture both of an individual's culture and his reaction to it, and if psychoanalytic techniques are inexpedient for use by the majority of personality researchers, must we conclude that all of this potential information must remain useless except to therapists?

Fortunately, the last decade has brought significant reappraisal and advance in the examination of the dreaming process in its biological, psychological, and sociosituational aspects. Dement and Kleitman (1957, p. 685) have demonstrated through EEG experiments "a much greater amount of dreaming than was heretofore realized, both in the invariability of its presence from night to night and its frequency and duration in a single night." Ullman (1956; 1958), in referring to these and other physiological experiments, examines the adaptive function of the dream with respect to different *levels* of consciousness rather than as a phenomenon of the unconscious, an important distinction if one wishes to use manifest dream content.

Wolff (1952, p. 2) considers "dream patterns rather than dream elements," and says:

> My interpretation of dreams is based upon a dream *synthesis* instead of a dream *analysis*. The unity in the expression of our organism, the synthesis which we experience in our perception and our thinking, the psychosomatic unity which we observe in the findings of modern medicine and psychotherapy, are also presumed to be present in the dream, the language of the unconscious.

Wolff (pp. 305–307) also cites the "equilibrium" which is achieved by the dream (see Devereux, 1951; Eggan, 1952) and considers the dream a "mirror" of man's conscience. From this point of view, dream analysis has important implications in determining individual "value systems."

French has modified and amplified classical Freudian dream interpretation in several important directions. He calls attention to the ego's function of "reality testing in dreams" (1937a; 1937b) and suggests that every distortion of reality in dreams will be followed by a tendency to correct the distortion in subsequent material, a concept which is exceptionally useful cross-culturally, particularly when applied to a dream series (see Eggan, 1949; Devereux, 1951; Schneider and Sharp, n.d.). Later he describes (1954, p. 4) the "close-knit logical . . . cognitive structure" of dreams as they relate to each other in a series of dreams and to the cognitive patterns which guide the individual's behavior. The student of dreams, whether or not he is psychoanalytically oriented, will find much guidance in French's work.

Also encouraging for those who are interested in the use of dreams in cross-cultural personality research is the growing sophistication and precision in the use of manifest content. "Even in the camp of the strict Freudians there has been a tendency of late toward greater flexibility in evaluating the manifest dream content and the role of the ego and superego in dreams" (Friedemann, 1957, p. 363).[1] This remark refers to a panel discussion (reported by Rangell, 1956) held at the American Psychoanalytic Association meeting, where Leon Saul described the experimental evaluation of the dynamics of a dream from manifest content alone. The dream was presented to several raters who had no other information about it. The conclusions deduced by this group were later confirmed in detail by material subsequently obtained by the patient's therapist. Saul further suggested that what is lacking in associations to one dream can often be provided by the examination of manifest content in a series of dreams. During the discussion Franz Alexander commented favorably on the methodological significance of Saul's experiments in arriving at the true gestalt of the dream. There is no implication in the discussion that associations to manifest content are not useful in therapy. But it does point up the fact that manifest content alone has important possibilities which a number of researchers have begun to investigate systematically.

Noting a striking difference in the manifest dream content of hypertensive patients compared with normotensives, Saul and Sheppard, both psychoanalysts, report (1956, p. 501) an attempt to develop a quantitative method for evaluating emotional forces in manifest dream content:

A preliminary hostility scale has been derived from a content analysis of 500 manifest dreams obtained from 200 subjects presenting wide variation in personality structure. In using the scale one divides the dream into its "conceptual elements" similar to the independent clause, and matches each element against a six-point scale for intensity of hostility. . . . Seventy-eight dreams of 17 hypertensive and 16 normotensive subjects were scored according to the hostility scale by three unbiased judges. [These judges did not know the purposes of the study but they were trained in the use of the scale through typed instructions for its use, and were then asked to follow the prescribed procedure on ten sample dreams.] It was found that the scale was reliable and that it discriminated between hypertensive and normotensive subjects used in this study.

Although inferences from the study are limited by the presence of several uncontrolled variables, the results are encouraging. Scales for the estimation of other emotional forces are being constructed and are being applied to dreams and other psychological material. It is felt that a quantitative method for the estimation of emotional forces should cast light on certain theoretical problems and later prove of practical use.

Continuing their experimentation with quantitative measures applied to dreams and early memories, Sheppard (1958) reported on a systematic study

made of the dreams and earliest memories of college students in an effort to determine how these mental products relate to the dreams and earliest memories obtained from patients with frank neurotic and psychotic symptoms, and further to develop quantitative methods which will elucidate the activities of the ego in these processes.

An ego rating system was constructed from observations on ego functions in the dreams, earliest memories and associative material of neurotic, psychotic, and organically ill patients. (The functions of the ego in dreams were classified in the following twelve categories: Source of Impulse, Expression of Impulse, Object of Impulse, Completion of Impulse, Outcome of Impulse, Reality of Setting, Body Image, Age of Characters, Logic of Dream Story, Relationships, Bodily Functions and Evaluation of Characters. In each category four sub-groups describe degrees of "distancing" of the ego from awareness of its motivations.)

To test the rating system, dreams and earliest memories of the following groups were scored: (1) college students in an anthropology class writing down their dreams and earliest memories on two separate occasions at the request of an investigator (psychologist) previously unknown to them; (2) college students in a psychology class writing down their dreams and earliest memories at the request of their psychology instructor; (3) hospitalized psychotic patients relating their dreams and earliest memories to a psychiatrist previously unknown to them, and (4) psychotic patients relating their dreams and earliest memories to a psychiatrist who is their psychotherapist.

The dreams and earliest memories were rated on the ego rating system in order to evaluate: (1) occurrence of a consistent dream pattern and early memory pattern for each subject on separate occasions several months apart; (2) differences in material offered to an outside interviewer met for the first time, or a teacher or doctor with whom the subjects were in continuing relationship; (3) the nature of any differences in the first and subsequent collections; and (4) the relationships between a subject's dreams and his earliest memories.

When applied by two judges to the dreams of 28 psychotic and 30 non-psychotic subjects, the scores of the ego rating system differentiated between the two groups to a statistically significant degree. By contrast, two psychiatrists and two psychologists unfamiliar with the rating system were unable to distinguish between the two groups. The ego rating system of evaluating dreams appears to be promising enough to justify further testing, refining, and application to other psychological data.[2]

Since these projects were set up by researchers who are thoroughly experienced in handling dreams, and with commendable caution regarding problems involved in evaluation of normal versus non-normal dreaming, degree of personal relationship between investigator and informant, and testing by judges not involved in the formulation of the original hypotheses, these quantification projects may well serve as models for other research based on manifest dream content.

One of the most extensive coordinated projects on manifest dream content is that of Hall and his associates which began at Western Reserve University in 1947. A report of experiments in this project is given in a paper by Hall which reviews current trends in dream research and provides an extensive bibliography on dreams. In this report (1956, p. 243) he says:

> The impetus for these [Western Reserve] studies was the development of a dream series method (Hall, 1947a) of analyzing manifest dream narratives which could be used to investigate the personality dynamics of non-patient populations. The dream series method is considered to be another projective technique for investigating personality. The objectives of the Western Reserve program of research are set forth in the following outline form:
>
> I. The collection of a large number of dream series, using a standard form, from males and females of various ages (Hall, 1953a). The collection also includes a large number of single dreams as well as dream series.
>
> II. The formulation of a general theoretical framework for comprehending the psychological significance of dream series (Hall, 1953b; 1953c).
>
> III. The development of methods for analyzing, categorizing, and quantification of manifest content of dream series (Hall, 1947b; 1948).
>
> IV. The investigation of various aspects of personality using the foregoing methods and theory.

Continuing his report (p. 244) on experiments with this collection of dreams, Hall describes several papers which are available only as unpublished theses at Western Reserve. In one of these Reis compared 25 various aspects of personality ratings—psychosexual development, family relationships and emotional adjustment—obtained from an examination of the dreams alone and of the dreams plus associations to them. "The general conclusion drawn from the findings was that substantial agreement on most of the ratings between dream series with and without free associations does exist," and that "free associations are not necessary for personality assessment involving the type of variables that are derived from psychoanalytic theory," although Reis points out that associations may be necessary in psychotherapy (see Saul, p. 559 above).

Several studies in this series plus one by Gordon (1953) which compared dreams as projective phenomena with projective test material are also discussed by Hall (1956, pp. 246–247). These studies indicate that dreams express more socially unacceptable material than TATs do. This suggests that both dreams and projective tests should be used in personality studies. All of these studies employed a variety of scoring and rating techniques by independent judges. While the collection of dreams used was from subjects with a Western cultural background, they provide important inferential leads for work on manifest dreams in other cultures.

It is obvious that comprehensive experimentation in cross-cultural analysis of manifest dream content is a prerequisite for using dreams in a cross-cultural analysis of individual personality. In this connection cooperation between collectors of dream data and other researchers who are interested in using dreams is vital. Admittedly it is difficult to work with a body of data collected by someone else. But this will have to be done both because we need to experiment with many dreams from many cultures in order to formulate and test hypotheses and techniques, and because we shall have to minimize the danger of the researcher's projection of his own personality into the analysis of others' dreams. In an important pioneering experiment in 1941, Schneider used dreams collected by Sharp from the Yir Yoront in Northern Australia in a statistical analysis of four content areas in manifest dream content. In a recent revision of this work Schneider states that he is "interested in the relationship between the culture and the dreams of members of that society." He assumes "with Freud that dreams are determined and not random; that dreams are in large part a function of the personality of the dreamer; that although the whole of any given personality is by no means simply stated in toto from a cultural mould, the culture plays a role in shaping personality." Further assumptions are that the actor's "definition of the situation"—his image of objects, of relationships, and of his own and others' roles—is one (but only one) of the determinants of his waking life behavior, and that *"the manifest content of dreams expresses the actor's definition of the situation* (italics added)." Culture is defined as a "system of shared norms or patterns of waking life behavior."

In this study of Yir Yoront dreams (Schneider and Sharp, n.d.), analysis is limited to four items with which peoples in many nonliterate cultures are concerned, but which each culture tends to treat differently: (1) white culture; (2) copulation; (3) aggression; and (4) death. The data are organized and examined in several ways. First, the whole pattern of self-other relations of a dream is analyzed. Second, a group of dreams are taken as a collection of acts which are related to other acts and are thus fragmented and analyzed statistically. Third, after this is done, a selected group of dreams (for instance dreams involving relations with whites) is analyzed, i.e., each dream as a unit is regarded as an integrated pattern of "self-other" relations. And fourth, a combination of some of these techniques is tried—specific acts are treated statistically and the dreams are then grouped by their dominant themes, a group being used as a homogeneous unit, and the abstracted main theme is analyzed and used in comparison with other main themes.

Many significant patterns emerged from this treatment of the four selected content areas. For instance:

In dreams of sexual intercourse, the sexual act was not usually completed without some interruption, however slight. When the partners to the act were plotted with respect to their kinship relations, it was seen that the magnitude of the interruptions correlated with the *strength of the incest prohibition*. When the partners occupied positions where sexual relations were most strongly tabued, the act was attempted but due to interruption was not completed; while dreams of those in positions where sexual relations were least strongly prohibited involved only minor interruptions. Interestingly enough, in this collection of men's dreams, the women were consistently pictured as the source of the interruption.

The women were pictured as deficient sexual partners in an assortment of ways, which implied either that the women were carriers and enforcers of the prohibition against incest, or an ambivalence toward women in general, or both. The waking life tendency to brag of sexual prowess was also realistically corrected in dreams.

When all dreams involving acts of aggression were reviewed, similar regularities clearly emerged. Thus acts of aggression are directed against the dreamer more than twice as frequently as those committed by the dreamer. If the aggressor and aggressed are plotted with respect to their relationships, members of the outgroups, mother's brother and elder brother commit more than two-thirds of all acts of aggression.

In this society ego marries mother's brother's daughter, and avoidance, respect and gifts are involved in the relationship. Ego must also respect elder brother, and the "demands" in this relationship differ in degree rather than in kind from the one above. Brothers compete for the same women. Thus in waking life, overt aggression is prohibited, but hostility is quite probably present. Very rarely does a younger brother or sister's son aggress in dreams. Seventy-one percent of aggression is within the kin group, twenty-three percent between ego and outsiders and five percent is undetermined. Here one sees clearly the self-view of the dreamers as non-aggressive, as well as their evaluation of others as aggressors, neither of which attitudes would be expressed in waking life.

"Among the interesting patterns in death dreams is a regularly recurrent theme of [immediate] resurrection, an idea which does not occur in waking life. E.g., I am killed; I 'stand alive.' Moreover, others die permanently but the dreamer 'stands alive.' " In a tribe where men of necessity live dangerously, fear of death must not be admitted, but evidently it must be dealt with.

Dreams dealing with whites and white culture fall into three rather simple groups. In one group of dreams, whites and white culture situations are pictured as affectively positive and desired, in another, affectively neutral but confusing and unpredictable; and a third—a single dream—shows whites and white culture situations as affectively negative and rejected by the dreamer.

Unfortunately space prohibits a further discussion of the many interesting patterns and suggestions for comparative research which emerge from this stimulating manuscript. It uses manifest dream content data with a realistic appraisal of what can be done with the kind of dream collections which are normally made by anthropologists. Few can devote more than a small fraction of their time in the field to recording dreams, even where conditions for dream collecting are favorable, and the Yir Yoront were not particularly interested in dreams. Like Aberle's (1951) sophisticated psychosocial analysis of a published Hopi life history, it indicates what precise definition and procedures can produce with the "intangible" material found in life histories or dreams, even—or perhaps particularly—when using data from another researcher's collection and with his cooperation.

A recent paper by Dittman and Moore (1957) also uses dreams from a non-Western culture. The authors were examining disturbance in dreams as related to peyotism among the Navaho. Their paper is recommended as another precise and useful formulation of procedure which could be extended to include many facets of personality, and for use in other cultures.

My own work with Hopi Indian dreams grew out of long friendship with several Hopi and intimate association with their extended families. The persistence of Hopi culture and an abundance of English-speaking informants, combined with Hopi interest in dreams, offered an exceptional opportunity to investigate the interrelations of personality and culture through dreams, and in a direction which would be of value in a study of social and cultural change on which Fred Eggan was working.

Since assumptions which provide the incentive for any research inevitably influence the collection and examination of material, these will be briefly stated:

1. Dreams were regarded as a universal phenomenon, both because (a) the biological processes in human mental activity were assumed to be universal; and (b) dreams have been reported both historically and currently from all over the world.

2. In spite of their resemblance to psychoses—a point well documented in psychiatric literature—dreams were believed to be neither an

irrational nor an isolated form of mental activity, but a characteristic arrangement of such activity concerned chiefly with problems, both universal and personal.

3. Ethnological evidence indicates that there are pan-human qualities in man, among them ambivalence toward death and a capacity for emotional involvement with others, which are more invariant than variant. But cultural provision for different ways of adjustment to universal problems does alter many visible facets of personality, and quite probably weights many elements of it toward culturally valued norms. In that case, manifest dream content would reflect both cultural stresses and cultural supports.

4. The idiosyncratic component in dreams is, as Schneider has said, "the dreamer's definition of the situation," and this definition reveals important aspects of the dreamer's personality.

5. But since each of us hides, not only from others but from ourselves, behind a screen of culture, an important part of pan-humanness is precisely the inability of any person in waking life to make objectively "correct" observations either about himself or his culture; manifest dream statements frequently give a more accurate picture.

For example, death is a universal problem, but ritual murder is not; though ritual murder is a cultural provision in certain societies (Aztec) to which individuals in the society must make an adjustment. Would ritual murder, either in reality or dream be similarly perceived and described by an Aztec and a Quaker? In waking life it obviously would not; their definition of that situation would then differ to the extent that the ego system's waking activity presented an organized, socially acceptable front to society, and a socially constructed self-image to the individual. But if in sleep the ego system's waking activity has been largely replaced by "reality testing" (see French, p. 559 above) *vis à vis* the organism's own uncertainties—and assuming the pan-human qualities mentioned above—Aztec and Quaker dreams might reveal more similarities between the personalities in these cultures than waking statements would indicate.

The assumptions stated above may be summarized thus: dream forms are the expression of *unique* sequences of *personal* events, which are perceived through a *cultural screen,* but they are the result of underlying processes that represent constants in human experience (see Herskovits, 1948, p. 619). Thus dreams, and the associations introduced in the telling of them, are facets of a projective process, and subjective materials are experienced as images and events and thus reported. The dreamer responds to his own mind's image of the culturally perceived world as it is, or as he wishes or fears it to be.

The first question formulated then, was: could a dynamic interaction between the manifest content of Hopi dreams and the culture of the dreamers be demonstrated? Second, would the idiosyncratic elements in their dreams give us important, and perhaps otherwise unobtainable, information regarding differences in Hopi personalities? Third, could Hopi personalities be compared and contrasted with those of Navaho or white Americans through dreams?

To answer these questions, the first necessity was a large collection of dreams and relevant material, including the "meaning" of dreams to the Hopi themselves. The problems involved in dream collection and the subsequent use of undisguised personal data in publications will, of course, vary from tribe to tribe and from person to person in the tribe. Among the Hopi, dream collection was at first comparatively easy. Later, resentment by their tribesmen of those who were employed as "informants" made them reluctant to work with any investigator. In writing of the Saulteux, Hallowell (1948, p. 343) says that "emphasis placed upon dreams and the interpretation of them in relation to conduct obviously enhances the role of fantasy in the inner life." But the fact that they could not tell their dreams except under special conditions would presumably make dream collection among the Saulteux more difficult. DuBois (1944, pp. 45, 46, and 192), who collected dreams in connection with life histories of Alorese, reports that while recording was facilitated by tribal attention to dreams, she rarely heard the first version, since dreamers regularly aroused a household in the night to relate their dreams. This habit increases the possibility of "cultural standardization" (see Kluckhohn, 1945, p. 106) through previous discussion of the dream.

Linguistic barriers are always a serious hazard unless the group—or the investigator—is truly bi-lingual. But this problem is no more serious with dreams than in projective testing. One factor, which at first disturbed me in my work with Hopi dreams, was the impossibility of interviewing each subject immediately after each dream. This fact, at first regarded as a handicap, now seems to have had certain advantages, for the entire body of Hopi dream material suggests that the theme of a dream is seldom finished in one arrangement. Had the interviews followed each dream they might have influenced successive dreams and thus affected the spontaneous amplification of a theme. In this connection, Freud (1938, pp. 477–479) indicates that, for a variety of reasons, dreams of former years are often more easily interpreted than current ones.

Finally, the importance of all of these problems will vary somewhat with the intended use of the material. If the collection is intended, as ours was, primarily for use in the experimental formulation of hypotheses, the above issues are less vital than when the aim is theory validation.

Many factors combined to facilitate dream collection among the Hopi.

First, a rich personal fantasy life was encouraged among them by group preoccupation with fantasy. The Hopi "educational" system (Eggan, 1956), in which the whole tribe participated, was characterized by emotional intensity, and important aspects of it centered around folklore, colorful religious rituals involving mythology, and dream recitals. A second factor was that among the Hopi overt emotions were strongly controlled by an urgent necessity for group cooperation, and affectual relations between any two individuals were subordinated to the more important demands of group loyalties. In this situation there were not only strong sanctions against talking about oneself, but trusted confidants were rare. The recital of one's dreams, or stories about occasional journeys away from the reservation, was one of the few ways in which a Hopi could abandon his self-effacing role and become the center of attention, an exceedingly important compensation in a somewhat constricted emotional environment, and in a definitely unfavorable physical world. And third, of great importance in recording Hopi dreams was the already mentioned fact that a bad dream required immediate confession and action, while a good dream had to be remembered but not told until it "came true." In this suggestive atmosphere the Hopi tended to dream much, to remember their dreams, and to welcome my interest in hearing them, so that the project was begun simply by talking with friends about dreams as we went about daily tasks together.

After a few weeks of exploring the subject with any and every Hopi with whom we talked, about fifty subjects were tried out, including three who would also be used as interpreters in the few situations where interpreters were needed. These three were chosen with care from among a trusted category of relatives for a specific informant, and had been well known to the recorder for a year or more, as had most of the informants in the project. The original group selected soon narrowed to twenty, although random dreams or meanings brought in by visitors were usually accepted. The informants were each asked to talk about what dreams in general might mean, where they came from, and to add anything they could think of to say about dreams. They were then asked to comment on each item of a previously prepared dream "meaning" list, and to suggest other meanings if they could. This list had been prepared from incidents and objects (dreaming of catching game before a hunt, of beetles, rainbows, snakes, yucca) which included all those previously mentioned by Hopi in our general discussion of dreams, and many others which we knew were important to them. To these were added a few items found in the scanty literature about Hopi dreams, as well as various Freudian symbols (flying, falling, box, tooth, etc.). The list was used in five villages on two mesas for several months; from it we hoped to find elements which might represent consistent dream symbols throughout the tribe.

But the survey indicated that the Hopi did not have a well-developed, culturally interpreted body of dream lore. Although many referents seemed to be invested with an almost universal Hopi definition, an informant most frequently explained such an element in his *own dreams* in terms of his physical and emotional state upon awakening.[3]

Each of the informants was given a notebook and asked to record his dreams if he could write at all legibly. It was felt that the dreams would thus be more accurately recorded and amplified, even though reading the script was difficult. If the dreamer could not write (and about two-thirds could not), the recorder or, in a few cases an interpreter, wrote for him. All dreamers were encouraged to carry associations to their dreams as far as they were able, but we were careful not to ask leading questions. Occasionally we would ask, "Who was this person in the dream?" or jog a lazy talker with "Can you say any more about this dream?" Or we might ask for associations to words in the dreams, but we made every effort to avoid influencing spontaneous recital of the dream, or the dreamer's comments on it.

Only two informants [4] became at all competent in the process of free association, except as associations were included by elaboration in the first report of the dream. One advantage in having the dreams recorded by the dreamer is the tendency for associations to be written down as part of the dream. For the most part giving associations to dream content, either directly to the whole dream or to words abstracted from the dream, was labored, and the dreamers became so embarrassed over trying to give them that it seemed unwise to press the matter beyond what was offered spontaneously. However, most informants would volunteer incidents from which the dream might have sprung. In addition each dreamer was asked to evaluate the dreams as good, bad, or indifferent and to indicate his physical and emotional state on awakening after each dream.

In a group such as the Hopi, where dreams are frequently elaborated into "dream stories," the recorded version is often a long and complicated fantasy production, part dream and part associations to it. In any case, the complexity of dream forms, even at the manifest level, clearly demands a flexible and systematic organization of materials into comparable units, and an arrangement which will call attention to the correlation of items in successive dreams. It was found that the data were more easily examined, and that further problems were more clearly indicated, when each dream was arranged on a chart. One such chart, which I began in 1939, now presents 254 out of 310 dreams from one Hopi (Eggan, 1952). On it each dream is numbered in the order in which it was recorded, and all of the manifest elements in the dream are distributed in horizontal columns across the page. Primarily these categories were empirically derived from the data themselves and they are still being extended as the examination progresses. One typical category is *Security Reinforcement*. This is subdivided into the following elements: 1. Support of whites; 2. The dreamer's own acts of personal strength, wisdom or bravery; 3. Help from a Guardian Spirit or other culture hero; 4. Help from influential Hopi. Another category reports seven different elements of persecution and conflict (e.g., verbal attacks by other Hopi, abuse by whites, etc.); other columns record physical hazards, sexual, supernatural and religious elements, and people and activities of importance in the dreamer's life, among many other items.

In addition to this kind of category, there is a column which records the dreamer's own awakening physical and emotional reaction to each dream, e.g., laughing, crying, ears ringing, sweating, trembling, indifference, elation or depression. The reporting of these reactions is of value in correcting the recorder's own personal or cultural bias when evaluating the affectual charge of the dream. A column which indicates a repeated theme calls attention to the tendency of dreams to work on specific problems over months or years. Reading across the chart, therefore, one finds, (a) a fairly comprehensive summary of the manifest elements of any one dream; (b) its affectual impact; and (c) its factual contents. Reading *down* the chart, each item is seen in relation to a similar one in other dreams, so that the massing of items becomes self-evident, and a historical perspective on an individual's dream life is provided.

A glance at this dreamer's chart shows a consistent picture through the years of 305 elements of discomfort, such as persecution, conflict, or physical or moral danger, in the 254 dreams. But the chart also quickly makes evident a total of 260 elements of security support in the same dreams, and one sees immediately that most of these are culturally derived. We find, for instance, that in one-third of the dreams from this informant he uses specific folklore characters or themes, many times combining several of these, and most of them are directed toward at least a temporary resolution of his personal problems (Eggan, 1955).

Thus, in his attempt to fashion dream elements into what he calls his "dream stories," this man uses the process of association to the original core of the dream. This brings into focus conflict situations and inappropriate behavior which is often spontaneously recognized and abandoned. But often, in the absence of an acceptable reality solution, we find an interesting interaction between the problem solving quality in tribal myths and in his dreams. Through the fusion of personal and tribal fantasy he is able to deal with anxiety in a somewhat impersonal manner, a device which gives him a reassuring sense of identity with his people, even during periods of conflict with them.

We can locate on the chart a number of dreams which involve ceremonial incontinence, and fear provoking "guilt" is clearly depicted in these. In others, which are concerned with the dreamer's inadequacies as a runner or hunter, "shame" is likewise clearly present. This suggests that by illustrating (see p. 563 above) the dreamers' very conscious awareness of the moral code and world view of the culture (Singer, 1953, p. 68), important information on shame and guilt in non-Western cultures may be found. For as Kaplan has said (1957, p. 97), "Motivations toward conformity and acquiescence to legitimate authority (moral orientation) are among the chief points of contact between the social structure and the personality." And dreams, by calling the dreamers' attention to violations of the moral code, not only tend to push him toward cultural conformity, but also tend to indicate to an investigator the degree to which the informant has made the cultural code his own (see M. Spiro's paper in this volume).

From such a chart one sees clearly the consistency of individual patterns of dreaming over periods of months and years, as well as the clearly indicated cultural uniformity in the dreams. In one series of thirteen dreams, which occurred over a period of five years, and which were scattered among the 238 dreams this man had then recorded for me, a seemingly unrelated cast of characters were manipulated puppet-wise, until the context finally made clear an amazing and un-Hopi-like bit of the dreamer's behavior, which had continued during the entire five years. The manifest content of these dreams, and the dreamer's associations to the content, developed a theme which brought into sharp focus one instance among many of the discrepancy between the reality situation and the dreamer's own conception of his relations with a number of people (Eggan, 1949).

The chart does not constitute, in itself, an "analysis" of any dream. It merely illustrates a technique for the arrangement of manifest dream data which enables analysis of materials to proceed more effectively. When handling a large body of data, composed of various units which are frequently closely related to others but which are widely separated from them both by time and numbers, it is obviously difficult to discover and to hold in mind relationships between various components without the aid of some such mechanical arrangement. Yet it is precisely these *patterns* in dreaming—and this tendency to correct previous distortions in successive dreams—which are most useful to any researcher who works with dreams.

It is also evident that only a beginning has been made in "answering" the questions which were addressed to the Hopi data.[5] The examination of these materials has not been completed. We have, however, found many suggestions which will aid us in the further examination of these dreams and other dream collections:

1. An interaction exists between manifest dream content and the culture. Thus Hopi deities, who threaten or aid the dreamer, have become more "real" in the culture through the telling of dreams.

2. The "balance" between psychic discomfort and security support, and the continuity of this dreamer's preoccupation with certain problems of courage, interpersonal relations and sexual security, among others, clearly reveal how consistent a picture of personality is drawn by dreams over a period of years.

3. The data with respect to Hopi personality in general are as yet less clear, both because we do not have a comparable sample (362 dreams recorded over a period of 20 years) from each of our dreamers, and because less attention has been given to this portion of the material. It has seemed more expedient to form working hypotheses from an adequate sample from one dreamer, and allow these to guide the examination of the rest of the data. While this dreamer cannot be considered a "typical" Hopi, neither can he be considered unique. We have reason to assume that both the individual and cultural mechanisms which shape his dreams were at work in varying degrees and over various personal problems among all of these older Hopi who shared a remarkably integrated body of culture and very similar goals. In fact, in these dreams, Hopi attitudes as "part of a mutually shared field" are so clearly pictured and so subtly reinforced that one can see in them the "center of the person's social relations and . . . the heart of the dynamics of the group process" (Asch, 1952, p. 577).

Finally, we shall consider the use of dreams in personality research from the standpoint of the questions "Where are we now?" and "Where are we going?" We are, I think, at a crossroads. We can continue to contribute "working hypotheses" which can be (and usually are) carefully examined for the society in question through the worker's own data. This road will doubtless, through the publications of many scholars, and by a process of successive approximations, eventually yield results which will win for dreams a logical place in developing theories relating to the functioning of personalities in specific societies. We are familiar with this crab-wise advance of science. But if we choose this direction, libraries on "personality in culture" will continue to resemble a movie studio's cutting room floor—for both dreams and personalities are notably difficult to "photograph."

Or we can substitute the word "analysis" for "interpretation" (which has the misleading connotation that an "ultimate meaning" can be assigned to a dream), and make a *cooperative* attack on the *analysis of manifest dream content* in cross-cultural study of personality, first by an honest effort to eliminate faulty communication through shared precise definitions, and second by a trial exchange of hypotheses and data, profiting by models provided in the cooperative research outlined above. Specifically:

1. We need to test—on dreams from non-Western cultures—every promising lead in the reports reviewed here and elsewhere, remembering that although any hypothesis is expendable, the eclectic information imbedded in dreams is not.

2. We need organized groups of students working together who, after agreement on definitions and hypotheses for that specific project, will then independently examine a collection of non-Western dreams and compare the results. This research would be invaluable both from the standpoint of evaluating the potential of the dream in cross-cultural studies of personality and in assessing the degree to which the investigators were able to avoid projection of their own personalities and cultural biases onto the dreams examined. (We hope to have 1 and 2 done on our Hopi collection.)

3. We need more dream collections from non-Western cultures.

Finally, regardless of the ultimate correctness or depth of personality content which is evaluated in any of the studies described in this chapter, it seems clear that we have made important progress in using dreams in personality research. If the Saul-Sheppard-Hurvich, and the Hall–Western Reserve projects were duplicated in Universities in Japan, India, the Philippines and Hawaii, where students from many sub-cultures are in the process of adaption to Western influences, we would be able to make more precise statements with regard to the use of dreams in cross-cultural personality study in literate groups. And if we examined dream collections from less sophisticated non-Western groups, using the Schneider-Sharp content categories, the disturbance-peyotism formulations of Dittman and Moore, and the myth-dream interaction and dream series approach suggested in the Hopi study, as well as other promising leads found in many dream research reports, dream analysis would quickly occupy an important role in the cross-cultural examination of personality.

That there are serious problems in dream research is recognized in *every* paper cited above. *All* emphasize the "tentative" nature of their work. Clearly there are also problems in cross-disciplinary, or even in intra-disciplinary, use of one body of data. Even if definitional questions are eliminated there remains the necessity for workers—at this stage of developmental experimentation at any rate—to acquire an adequate background in the cultural and social environment of the dreamers. Lacking a knowledge of Hopi mythology, for instance, one could miss the significance of the Mother of Wild Game, or of the Water Serpent, in Hopi dreams. But there will rarely be a collection of dreams where either the literature on the tribe or the collector cannot provide this information.

There is also the question of sampling, and of verification (Honigmann, 1954, p. 157). But these issues arise in any form of investigation. Ideally, the sample should not only be statistically representative for the group, but should be taken over a long enough period of time to rule out unusual influences—an epidemic of smallpox or an unusually good crop. Realistically, however, as Gillin says (1954, p. 261) "we must recognize that at a certain stage of many a scientific exploration or inquiry [the ideal] condition cannot be met . . . ." Unrealistic demands—overemphasis on hazards rather than possibilities—and careless methodology can be equally fatal to scientific advancement. Actually, the vital prerequisite for arranging the jig-saw pieces found in dreams into a useful map of personality exists in the cautious attitude of the investigators mentioned toward the techniques they describe. The outlines of the map, however, are beginning to emerge and these will become more distinct through cooperative work on the arrangement. When the map finally blends the "topography" of psychiatric wisdom with regional details contributed by anthropology, and is drawn with the precise techniques of psychology, we shall have made progress toward that "psychology of personality more worthy of the name."

NOTES

1. Friedemann (1957, p. 364, references in text) also points out that "Jung had already raised the objection that while associations may lead to complexes, there is no guarantee that these complexes really caused the dream. Even Schultz-Hencke's elaborate classification of dream associations does not lead us much further. French goes so far as to hold free associations responsible for the so-called chaotic nature of the unconscious. But the severest critic of the method is Gutheil who believes that in many cases, far from giving us guidance, it only leads us astray."

2. Summarized from a personal communication from Sheppard, and from the abstract of a paper by Sheppard, Saul and Hurvich, presented by Sheppard to a panel on dreams at the 1958 meeting of the American Psychiatric Association.

3. The aim in the project was to get a cross-section of dream lore, and subsequently of dreams, from conservative old Hopi as background material for a longer and more detailed study of a few Hopis' dreams. All Hopi in the project had reached maturity before 1939. It must be remembered that "Hopi" here or in my other publications refers to this section of the tribe, rather than its younger and more acculturated members.

4. In fairness to the informants, projective processes—in the sense of objectifying what is essentially subjective material—were explained to them. One informant quickly learned from associations to her own dreams just

how plain a story dreams did tell, and subsequently she and all of her family refused to let us use their dreams, thereby subtracting more than a hundred dreams from the collection. But most of the informants demanded only that I conceal their identities, and were not concerned with what the dreams would tell me. Even this demand, however, imposes serious handicaps on about half of the material. In a small community, where families are regularly large, how does one use subjective data effectively and still conceal the identity of a family who lost all of their six children in an epidemic of measles? Even stating relationships (a man with no mother's brothers, another with no brothers and five sisters) might identify the informants to anyone in the Hopi country.

5. Data collected now consist of more than 650 dreams and a variety of related material. Of these, 362 are from Talayesva, the Sun Chief, whose autobiography was published (Simmons, ed.) in 1942. Talayesva has been recording his dreams for me since 1938. The rest of the dreams (around 300) were recorded during the first two years of the project, primarily from six women and seven men, except for occasional dreams which are always accepted when they are offered; 190 of these are now available in Kaplan, (ed.), 1957, *Primary Records in Culture and Personality*, Vol. II. The rest will be available in following volumes, and it is hoped, that in spite of the necessity to disguise identities, they will be useful to other students who are interested in dreams.

BIBLIOGRAPHY

Aberle, D. 1951. "The Psychosocial Analysis of a Hopi Life-History," *Comparative Psychology Monographs*, Vol. 21, No. 1. Berkeley & Los Angeles: University of California Press.

Asch, S. 1952. *Social Psychology*. New York: Prentice-Hall, Inc.

Dement, W. and Kleitman, N. 1957. "Cyclic Variations in EEG During Sleep and Their Relation to Eye Movements, Body Motility, and Dreaming," *Electroencephalography and Clinical Neurophysiology*, 9:673–90.

Devereux, G. 1951. *Reality and Dream, Psychotherapy of a Plains Indian*. New York: International Universities Press.

———. 1957. "Dream Learning and Individual Ritual Differences," *American Anthropologist*, 59:1036–45.

Dittman, A. T. and Moore, H. C. 1957. "Disturbance in Dreams as Related to Peyotism among the Navaho," *American Anthropologist*, 59:642–49.

Du Bois, C. 1944. *The People of Alor*. Minneapolis: the University of Minnesota Press.

Eggan, D. 1949. "The Significance of Dreams for Anthropological Research," *American Anthropologist*, 51:177–98.

———. 1952. "The Manifest Content of Dreams: a Challenge to Social Science," *American Anthropologist*, 54:469–85.

———. 1955. "The Personal Use of Myth in Dreams." In Sebeok, T. (ed.), "Myth: a Symposium," *Journal of American Folklore*, 68:67–75.

————. 1956. "Instruction and Affect in Hopi Cultural Continuity," *Southwestern Journal of Anthropology*, 12:347–70.

————. 1957. "Hopi Dreams and a Life History Sketch." In Kaplan, B. (ed.), *Primary Records in Culture and Personality*, Vol. 2, No. 16, 1–147. Madison: The Microcard Foundation.

Erikson, E. 1956. "The Problem of Ego Identity," *Journal of the American Psychoanalytic Association*, 4:56–121.

Firth, R. 1934. "The Meaning of Dreams in Tikopia." In Evans-Pritchard, E. E.; Firth, R.; Malinowski, B.; and Schapera, I., (eds.). *Essays Presented to C. G. Seligman*. London: Kegan Paul, Trench, Trubner and Co. Ltd. Pp. 63–74.

French, T. 1937a. "Reality and the Unconscious," *Psychoanalytic Quarterly*, 6:23–61.

————. 1937b. "Reality Testing in Dreams," *Psychoanalytic Quarterly*, 6:62–77.

————. 1952. *The Integration of Behavior. Vol. I: Basic Postulates.* Chicago: The University of Chicago Press.

————. 1954. *The Integration of Behavior, Vol. II: The Integrative Process in Dreams.* Chicago: University of Chicago Press.

Freud, S. 1938. *The Basic Writings of Sigmund Freud.* New York: Random House.

————. 1949. *A General Introduction to Psychoanalysis.* New York: Garden City Publishing Company.

Friedemann, M. 1957. "Representative and Typical Dreams with Emphasis on the Masculinity-Femininity Problem," *The Psychoanalytic Review*, 44:363–389.

Gillin, J. (ed.). 1954. *For a Science of Social Man.* New York: The Macmillan Company.

Gordon, H. 1953. "A Comparative Study of Dreams and Responses to the Thematic Apperception Test: I. A Need-press Analysis," *Journal of Personality*, 22:234–53.

Hall, C. 1947a. "Diagnosing Personality by the Analysis of Dreams," *Journal of Abnormal and Social Psychology*, 42:68–79.

————. 1947b. "Three Methods of Analyzing Dreams," *American Psychologist*, 2:425.

————. 1948. "Frequencies in Certain Categories of Manifest Content and Their Stability in a Long Dream Series," *American Psychologist*, 3:274.

————. 1953a. *The Meaning of Dreams.* New York: Harper Brothers.

————. 1953b. "A Cognitive Theory of Dream Symbols," *Journal of General Psychology*, 48:169–86.

————. 1953c. "A Cognitive Theory of Dreams," *Journal of General Psychology*, 49:273–82.

Hall, C. 1956. "Current Trends in Research on Dreams." In Brower, D. and Abt, L. E. (eds.), *Progress in Clinical Psychology.* New York: Grune and Stratton.

Hallowell, A. I. 1941. "The Social Function of Anxiety in a Primitive Society," *American Sociological Review,* 7:869–81.

———. 1948. "Acculturation Processes and Personality Changes as Indicated by the Rorschach Technique." In Kluckhohn, C. and Murray, H. (eds.), *Personality in Nature, Society, and Culture,* 340–46. New York: Alfred A. Knopf. (Reprinted from *Rorschach Exchange,* Vol. 6, 1942.)

———. 1955. "The Self and Its Behavioral Environment." In *Culture and Experience.* Philadelphia: University of Pennsylvania Press. (Reprinted from *Explorations, II,* 1954.)

Herskovits, M. 1934. "Freudian Mechanisms in Primitive Negro Psychology." In Evans-Pritchard, E. E.; Firth, R.; Malinowski, B.; and Schapera, I. (eds.), *Essays Presented to C. G. Seligman,* 75–84. London: Kegan Paul, Trench, Trubner and Co. Ltd.

———. 1948. *Man and His Works.* New York: A. A. Knopf.

Honigmann, J. 1954. *Culture and Personality.* New York: Harper and Brothers.

Kaplan, B. 1957. "Personality and Social Structure." In Gittler, J. B. *Review of Sociology: Analysis of a Decade.* New York: Wiley and Sons. Pp. 87–126.

Kluckhohn, C. 1945. "The Personal Document in Anthropological Science." In *The Use of Personal Documents in History, Anthropology and Sociology,* Bulletin 53, pp. 79–173, Social Science Research Council, New York.

———. 1953. "Universal Categories of Culture." In Kroeber, A. L. (Chairman), *Anthropology Today,* 507–23. Chicago: The University of Chicago Press.

———. 1954. "Southwestern Studies of Culture and Personality," *American Anthropologist,* 56:685–97.

Kluckhohn, C. and Murray, H. (eds.). 1948. *Personality in Nature, Society, and Culture.* New York: Alfred A. Knopf.

Kroeber, A. 1952. "A Southwestern Personality Type." In *The Nature of Culture,* pp. 323–26. Chicago: The University of Chicago Press. (First published in 1947.)

———. 1952. "Totem and Taboo in Retrospect." In *The Nature of Culture,* pp. 306–09. Chicago: The University of Chicago Press. (First published in 1939.)

La Barre, W. 1947. "Primitive Psychotherapy: Peyotism and Confession," *Journal of Abnormal and Social Psychology,* 42:294–309.

Lincoln, J. 1935. *The Dream in Primitive Cultures.* Baltimore: The Williams and Wilkins Company.

Murphy, G. 1947. *Personality; a Biosocial Approach to Origins and Structure.* New York and London: Harper Brothers.

Opler, M. K. 1942. "Psychoanalytic Techniques in Social Analysis," *Journal of Social Psychology*, 15:91–127.

Rangell, E. 1956. "Dream Symposium," *Journal of the American Psychoanalytic Association*, 4:122–37.

Reay, M. 1957. "Sweet Witchcraft." Paper presented at the Ninth Pacific Science Congress, Bangkok, November.

Riesman, D. 1951. "Some Problems of a Course in Culture and Personality," *The Journal of General Education*, 5:122–36.

Róheim, G. 1932. "Psychoanalysis of Primitive Culture Types," *International Journal of Psychoanalysis*. Parts I and II. Jan.–April.

———. 1949. "Technique of Dream Analysis and Field Work in Anthropology," *Psychoanalytic Quarterly*, 18:471–79.

Saul, L. and Sheppard, E. 1956. "An Attempt to Quantify Emotional Forces Using Manifest Dreams; a Preliminary Study," *Journal of the American Psychoanalytic Association*, 4:486–502.

Schneider, D. and Sharp, R. L. n.d. "Yir Yoront Dreams." Manuscript.

Sheppard, E. 1958. *See* Sheppard, E., Saul, L. and Hurvich, M., 1958.

Sheppard, E., Saul, L. and Hurvich, M. 1958. "Quantitative Measures Applied to Dreams and Early Memories," Abstract of paper presented at the 1958 meeting of the American Psychiatric Association.

Simmons, L. (ed.) 1942. *Sun Chief: The Autobiography of a Hopi Indian.* New Haven: Yale University Press.

Singer, M. 1953. "Shame Cultures and Guilt Cultures." In Piers, G. and Singer, M. *Shame and Guilt: a Psychoanalytic and a Cultural Study.* Springfield, Illinois: Charles C. Thomas.

Ullman, M. 1956. "Physiological Determinants of the Dream Process," *The Journal of Nervous and Mental Diseases*, 124:45–48.

———. 1958. "Dreams and Arousal," *American Journal of Psychotherapy*, 12:222–42.

Wallace, A. 1958. "Dreams and the Wishes of the Soul: a Type of Psychoanalytic Theory among the Seventeenth Century Iroquois," *American Anthropologist*, 60:234–48.

Wolff, W. 1952. *The Dream, Mirror of Conscience.* New York: Grune and Stratton.

About the Chapter

This case presents a Cree Indian dream together with associations and describes the way it was analyzed. Dr. Honigmann deals primarily with the manifest content of the dream and shows how it expresses some major themes both in the life of the subject and in the Attawapiskat Cree as a group. The problem of validity of the interpretation is also discussed.

About the Author

JOHN HONIGMANN is Professor of Anthropology at the University of North Carolina and Research Professor in the Institute for Research in Social Science. He was elected a member of Sigma Xi and a fellow of the American Anthropological Association. In 1958 he received a Fulbright Research Grant for work in Pakistan. His major publications are *Culture and Ethos of Kaska Society*, the textbook *Culture and Personality*, and *The World of Man*.

21

The Interpretation of Dreams in Anthropological Field Work: A Case Study

JOHN J. HONIGMANN

University of North Carolina

This case study illustrates how dreams can be used to secure or support interpretations of socially standardized personality—"social" personality [1]—and indicates one method of anthropological dream interpretation. What follows is divided into three parts: (1) a section presenting a dream together with associations—translated from the Cree text in which it was recorded—as well as a brief sketch of the dreamer and his life situation; (2) a section containing clues to the individual and social personality furnished by the dream together with an appraisal of the reasonableness of these clues at the current stage of research into the culture concerned, and (3) critical remarks about the technique illustrated. Unfortunately, without a comprehensive knowledge of the particular culture which is involved, the reader may not be able to comprehend fully all the references in the dream nor the use made of them in interpretation. It is well to state quite clearly that the general procedure followed in this analysis falls a good way short of any strict application of scientific method. But, then, much in anthropology is essentially humanistic and yet manages to serve well for certain purposes.

I

In collecting dreams among the Attawapiskat Indians, who live on the west coast of James Bay, Ontario, as growing competence in language permitted, I followed, whenever possible, recording of a dream with a request for associations. Because the Indians traditionally classify dreams as good or bad portents, informants were requested to categorize their dreams in one of those rubrics. To obtain associations it was usual to present various elements in a particular dream to a cooperative subject with the request that he explain them further, indicate where he had encountered the referents previously, or how he regards them. I used these devices in an attempt to secure additional information to use in arriving at a plausible interpretation of the dream. The dream is given below and is followed in the next paragraph by associations.

[What did you dream when it was night?] I forget. Ah! I dreamed of a very big white bear, just like a house, very big. We were not able to kill it, I dreamed. With three guns and shells, he can't hit it, I dreamed. It is too big. They are extremely afraid, I dreamed. We are not able to kill it because it is night, I dreamed. And while walking, always we are afraid, I dreamed. The children cry in my house, I dream. Very much they are afraid, and I too, very much I am afraid, I dreamed.

Not a good dream. [Why do people dream of big animals like bears? What do people say?] People say no good. Just like when somebody divines with supernatural aid (*tapiskutc maniituukew*). I don't believe this, me. Nobody killed the bear in this dream. I had a gun. Four shells I shoot from the gun. I cannot kill. After four times I give Xavier the gun. Three times he shoot. Then it is seven altogether. We cannot kill. Then Louis Anwastin took the gun and shot twice. Nine times in all. We cannot kill. [What kind of a man is Louis (i.e., the subject's Wi Br)?] Good man. Very smart. He is always working—every day. This morning he made sled with iron runners. Mud on the runners is not good during the spring, he says, because the days are too warm. Last week, Friday, he made another sled. He gave it to me. Next week, Monday, he will go to the Ekwan River, far up. And I too will go with my wife. I made a mistake. It is not four weeks that I will stay here to work with you. I am afraid because I have no things, no flour, tea, nothing. I have no rabbitskin blanket. And no moccasins for shoes. . . . My father will go up the Lawaacii River but not his wife (i.e., the dreamer's stepmother). He will go Monday. I will not go up the Lawaacii because my father reports that there are not any muskrat there and not many squirrels or rabbits.

At this point I felt I possessed enough information relevant to the dream to risk a provisional interpretation. I noted in my field notebook that the dream might constitute an expression of anxiety about sex, for it occurred the evening after the informant had revealed his distaste for sex. But another interpretation suggested by the associations was that the dream constituted an expression of worry concerning the subject's ability to provide for his family. Nothing further was done to interpret this particular dream until nine years later, in the fall of 1957–58, when work began on the present chapter. In the interim I had analyzed other field notes from Attawapiskat and had made two return visits to that place, one lasting nearly three months [2] (see Honigmann, 1958).

Field notes contain about a dozen other dreams of this informant, whom we shall call Bob Stone. He was an exceptional Attawapiskat Cree Indian, if only because he sought out the anthropologist regularly to spend time with him. Twenty-nine years old, he was the son of a nearly 80 year old man who had married a second time. Bob was himself married to the attractive daughter of Xavier Anwastin (the girl was his Mo Si So Wi Si Da, but that fact has little if any cultural significance). They had one child, a girl. Supporting the family was hard going, even though Bob lived with his father-in-law. It is useless to talk of the informant's class position in this egalitarian fur-trapping community. It is much more important to keep in mind that he was a young married man who had earned $400 two years back but reported his income for the previous winter to have been only $70. Now he was short of food. The dream took place in March after a winter that had been marked by an exceptionally poor fur catch for everyone. The Indians, after having been in the trading-post settlement since Christmas were getting ready to leave for the bush again, this time to trap for muskrat and to kill whatever game the environment provided. Bob had a choice of visiting either of two trap lines: his father's or his father-in-law's. Because these lay in quite opposite directions he could not exploit both within a short time. He decided it would be more profitable to spend the spring hunt with his father-in-law together with his wife's brother. Field notes indicate that he did not leave on the following Monday as, in associations, he had declared it was his intention. The Hudson's Bay Company manager, aware that Bob's fall debt remained partly unpaid, refused to advance him enough food against the probable outcome of the muskrat hunt to allow Bob to take the risk of a three-week journey with wife and child. Of course, he faced even bleaker prospects if he remained in the post. However he applied to the government-appointed chief for standard relief rations. His application was granted and he received relief. This augmented what the Company advanced and, despite still being concerned about an inadequate supply of ammunition, Bob quit the post on March 21 for the Ekwan River. The story has a happy ending. He returned on May 3 with $165 worth of fur. With those earnings he settled his debts.

II

The dream manifestly is laden with anxiety. Indications are that Bob is an anxious man and abundant confirmatory evidence exists in interview data. For example, on March 13 he spoke to the anthropologist about the fear he had once felt on a winter moose hunt after he had lost his matches and had eaten nothing for two days. On this and other occasions his fear had expressed itself violently—with palpitation and trembling. As a child he had dreaded being in the bush alone and at the age of 13 was traumatized by the sight of two horned moose swimming in the river on which he was traveling with his parents. We are, however, less interested in Bob qua individual than in the Attawapiskat Indian generically conceived. Hence we note the possibility, actually confirmed by other data such as life histories, interviews, and simple observation of overt behavior, that Attawapiskat males possess a high level of generalized anxiety.

Of what is Bob anxious and to what extent can the sources of his anxiety be generalized to help construct a picture of Attawapiskat social personality? The existing theory of dreams, poorly validated for Euroamerican society and much less so for exotic communities, suggests that fear-inspiring, large animals represent impulses—especially sexual impulses—which the dreamer dreads. Such an interpretation once suited the facts in another northern forest community where I worked with Kaska Indians. Will it fit the facts about these Cree Indians? Field notes definitely confirm that Bob is conflicted about sex. For example, speaking of copulation on March 16 he had said: "I also do not like it." He thought it was not "nice" and said "My wife alone likes it." He reported having once been shocked enough to reveal to adults a childhood friend's exhibitionistic masturbation. Also he had reported to parents sex play on the part of two young children, his Wi Fa Br Da and Wi Si. Hence there is strong likelihood that sex anxiety is a part of the latent content of the dream. Because our research interest is primarily centered on elucidating social personality, this interpretation may be generalized tentatively to apply to any Attawapiskat male. That is, it will be kept in mind to be tested against other data. The psychologically sophisticated reader will appreciate that, since dreams are over-determined, this interpretation is not denied by other meanings derived from the same content.

There is abundant evidence that Bob, more immediately and quite consciously, is anxious about his family's food supply. The associations are preoccupied with this anxiety. Here, then, is another plausible interpretation of the dream. It is an interpretation which we generalize with greater certainty because field notes are replete with data that reveal the Attawapiskat Indians' anxiety about food. Bob is clearly in desperate straits in a community that has little tolerance of dependence or sponging —though it permits channelizing dependence toward Euroamericans like missionaries, government representatives, and traders (see Honigmann, 1957). A man who works hard can count on winning approval. In the dream, however, Bob is ineffectual as a hunter but so are his father-in-law and brother-in-law. Yet, Bob in association consciously recognizes his Wi Br as a hard worker. It would seem that Bob, when he compares himself to Louis, feels inadequate as a provider, though he denies this in the dream. It has been observed in other contexts that Attawapiskat Indians are quite sensitive about how they measure up to expected standards and feel touchy about their social image, particularly with respect to work performance.

It is possible that the large animal, the white bear, may be a parental symbol or parent-surrogate symbol, perhaps Bob's Wi Fa, a man whose opinion Bob values. Xavier is also likely to be critical about the precarious situation in which Bob, his wife, and child are living. Were we to generalize this interpretation it could be confirmed only if our field notes turn up congruent structural expectations about the Wi Fa's role.

Interpretations ceased at this point because it was felt that the most plausible significance of the dream had now been uncovered and that further, more esoteric, interpretations would be exceedingly difficult to test with available data.

III

The interpretative procedure which has been described remains essentially logical instead of experimental. The analyst looked to the dream for clues to the subject's motivational states. These states, it was theorized, would be symbolized in the manifest dream content. The extraction of such clues depends on hunches about what the symbols mean. Sometimes hunches derive from psychoanalytic dream theory. Sometimes the hunches are directly based on associations. For example, associations in this instance are full of Bob's anxiety about his precarious economic position and about his ability to risk going on the spring hunt. These elements suggest that the dream is also motivated by concern over his ability to act as a satisfactory provider.

It is difficult to explain why I felt that the most plausible significance had been uncovered at the point where analysis ceased. Perhaps the extent to which dream content is used by a particular analyst varies in the first place with the value he puts on dreams as a source of information. Then, too, the theoretical orientation of the analyst (e.g., his readiness to employ psychoanalytic and other systems of interpretation) probably constitutes a significant factor. I was reluctant, at this time, in exploring the dream's latent content to accept any conclusion which could not be tested immediately against other data or which would be difficult to match in fairly direct fashion against supporting data. I preferred that supporting data come from some source other than dreams. Interpretation of Rorschach and TAT protocols from Attawapiskat remains uncompleted at this time In other words, currently I mistrust too elaborate dream interpretations of motivation which cannot unequivocally be tested for reasonableness alongside non-dream data.[3]

How do we know that any interpretation is true? Truth in this kind of analysis and considered in the light of our present knowledge regarding personality dynamics is a matter of being able to find a congruent fit between a particular interpretation and some other facts of the dreamer's life situation. On the level of social personality an interpretation is accepted as plausible (perhaps a better word than "true") when it accords with other data at hand. These procedures mean adherence to logical rather than experimental truth, to an evidential rather than experimental method.

An obvious limitation of dreams as a source of personality information lies in the fact that they are generally interpreted in the light of known facts about a person or culture. Interpretations are checked to make them congruent with other elements of the cultural or personality system being studied. The dreams, therefore, are not a truly independent source of data with which to validate other data.

For me dreams are merely one source of information to draw upon in studying a socially standardized system of personality. The structure of a culture, or of a system of social personality, emerges only after many data from a variety of sources have been fitted together into a reasonably congruent and coherent system. The very mass of data with which the field worker normally deals distracts him from basing too much on any one source. His understanding comes from assessing one set of insights in the light of other data. The procedure of dream interpretation illustrated in this paper is useful to the extent that it contributes, along with other techniques, to one's understanding of a people or culture.

NOTES

1. The term "social personality" seems preferable to "modal personality." The procedure in culture and personality research is rarely statistical and therefore does not often bring out modal trends in personality. Rather, anthropological research in personality generally produces *ideal* types of personality.

2. A preliminary report, *Foodways in a Muskeg Community: Anthropological Report on the Attawapiskat Indians Presented to the National Committee for Community Health Studies* (manuscript, 1948) is available on Microfilm through the Wilson Library of the University of North Carolina.

3. For another, somewhat more adventurous, approach to social personality see Honigmann, 1949.

BIBLIOGRAPHY

Honigmann, J. J. 1949. *Culture and Ethos of Kaska Society.* Yale University Publications in Anthropology, 40:249–356.

———. 1957. "Interpersonal Relations and Ideology in a Northern Canadian Community," *Social Forces,* 35:365–70.

———. 1958. "Attawapiskat—Blend of Traditions." *Anthropologica,* 6: 57–67.

About the Chapter

Projective tests have come to have a salient role in the culture and personality area. While their usefulness is widely conceded, there is a considerable amount of controversy about the wisdom of depending on them as the chief tool for the description of personality. Dr. Henry discusses the uses of projective techniques in cross-cultural research and describes a variety of problems that confront the user and interpreter.

About the Author

WILLIAM E. HENRY is Professor of Psychology and Human Development at the University of Chicago. He was formerly the chairman of the Committee on Human Development at Chicago and is a recent president of the Society for Projective Techniques. Among his major publications are *Warriors Without Weapons* (with Gordon Macgregor and Royal Hassrick), "The Thematic Apperception Technique in the Study of Culture-Personality Relations," and *The Analysis of Fantasy*. His interests center around the interrelations of cultural and social factors and personality development. His work has included the analysis of projective technique data in both contemporary modern and non-literate societies.

22

Projective Tests in Cross-Cultural Research

WILLIAM E. HENRY

University of Chicago

In recent years the projective techniques have had a marked surge of popularity among students of culture. As anthropology has concerned itself increasingly with the relevance of the individual to his culture, or has been concerned with essentially psychological concepts about aggregates of persons, students of culture have looked to the psychologist—or at least to psychological concepts and methods—for the key to their revised scientific interest. Similarly bothered by the culture-bound nature of their techniques and data, many psychologists have seen the collection of projective technique data from other societies as their entry into the mysteries of exotic cultures. This entry provided them with some comparative framework, previously available only with laborious and time-consuming field work with methods and a discipline generally unfamiliar to them.

No comprehensive evaluation can yet be made of the wedding of the projective instrument to the anthropological datum. In fact, a more apt analogy would refer only to a courtship, since the wedding has hardly been consummated, nor has either partner really made up his mind about the other. Certainly, as the courtship has progressed, the psychologist has begun to wonder whether the data provided by the anthropologist as a means of testing the psychologist's hypotheses are indeed appropriate to the task. The anthropologist, on the other hand, is discovering that the projective instruments, and the psychologists who accompany them, are not without history or previous experience as had been thought. The "previous experience" of the standard objective tests, typically of the intelligence test form, has been abundantly clear both to the psychologist and the anthropologist. In sum, this experience has meant norms determined by data from a single culture: it has meant test items which, regardless of normative problems, are in themselves bound to the culture of their origin; it has meant the use of a method of conceptualizing responses which if not specific to our own culture has at least seemed "strange" when applied to non-literate societies.

The projective techniques seemed the answer to these many problems, if only because of the psychologist's insistence that there were "no right or wrong answers" to the questions posed by these new tests. The joker of course soon appeared: while for the subject, there may be no particular specific answer that is right or wrong, nonetheless for the interpreter, there are right and wrong categories into which the answers could and were fitted. Somewhat prematurely, I believe, skepticism was aroused. Was the picture developed of the "other" society merely a distorted image of our own? For the psychologist, this skepticism can be more appropriately attributed to the general question of validity—an issue of great importance which has not even been solved for the direct clinical use of these instruments in our own natural habitat. If there is no assurance, in essence, that the instrument predicts the correct thing about our neighbors, patients, and local subjects, how can one be at all sure that it tells anything of value about a group whose social habits and ways of living are strange?

For the anthropologist, concerned to a lesser degree with this same problem, the central issues seem to take a different form. For him, it is more a question of whether or not to trust another profession's "magic." For him, the anthropologist's own "magic," his personal eye-witness observation seems more reliable and somehow less potentially biased. That the anthropologist, long trained in field work in which the human eye was the basic instrument, should be asked to "check" (i.e., validate) his skilled observations against either an impersonal instrument, or even worse, the instrument plus a psychologist (sitting in New York or Chicago or at best spending a quick few weeks in the field) seemed indeed an insult. When results sometimes did not seem to agree, or, more usual and equally important, when the concepts used by the psychologist appeared either strange to the anthropologist or degrading to his native informants, an entirely justifiable degree of skepticism arose.

For the psychologist, on the other hand, the instruments often were more "real" than the field operations. The analyses made from them sounded reasonable to him—based of course on his own similar use of comparable data and comparable concepts on local subjects. He was no more disturbed by the application of his habitual concepts to another society than when they were applied to his own. Out of the various contemporary uses of the psychological instruments have come a series of issues which point up the problem more precisely and which may give some guide to future use of psychological tests in cross-cultural work.

Have we been asking questions that are too broad for meaningful answers?

The early, and to some extent, the present use of tests in other societies has been based primarily on an exploratory motive. We have asked in essence, does this technique "work?" By "work" we have generally meant, can the test be administered so as to secure responses which, upon inspection, appear to be sufficiently similar to the responses of local subjects to permit the application of our usual methods of analysis. Part and parcel of this question has been the equally gross question: What is personality like in the culture in question? This latter question has often been quite implicit, and therefore has not been subject to the kind of criticism and cautions which it would have received had it been explicitly phrased. Thus issues of sub-group variations within the culture, problems of sampling (often covered on a total sample of community basis), and above all issues of theoretical constructs in terms of which the question might be answered, all of these and others have been given minimal consideration.

It seems essential now to move systematically to the phrasing of more explicitly stated, and considerably more specific questions. It does not matter whether these questions are made more specific and pointed in terms of general personality issues important primarily to the psychologist, or in terms of the anthropologist's interest in the relation of selected personality attributes to various aspects of culture. What does matter is that significant specific theoretical issues are phrased and that the use of the psychological test is made dependent upon its relevance to the hypotheses formulated.

There are various approaches to the analysis of the projective record. The approach predominantly used so far has been based upon the "single case" concept, in which the facts of the single case are analyzed as they would be in the culture of the psychological interpreter. The terms appropriate to general personality tend to be used, whether one deals with a single individual or with a group of cases. These personality concepts are largely determined by the scoring categories of the test, as in the case of the Rorschach, or by the preferred personality descriptive terms of the interpreter, as in the case of the TAT. Seldom are these terms specifically appropriate to the culture of the individual subject and they are rarely specifically utilized to throw light upon the hypotheses and general theoretical propositions at issue in the research. In part this reflects the fact that such investigations frequently have not been theoretically oriented and are in fact merely looking for "what can be found." For these kinds of fishing expeditions, the projective instruments provide a tempting degree of ambiguity. Such studies should not be entirely disparaged by the term "fishing expeditions" since they are often extremely profitable and may go considerably farther in defining transculturalities than may at first appear.

It does seem appropriate, however, to put the projective techniques to a second general use in which the terms and in fact the design of the instruments themselves are made specific to the hypotheses under investigation. While the first general use of the projective instruments asks very gross questions and tempts the investigator to explore all the nuances and dynamics, the second general use to which these instruments should be put, does not call upon all the possible nuances at all. It would in fact utilize only very specific and limited aspects of the record—only those that had been defined as relevant to some hypothesis under investigation. Thus limited aspects of either the Rorschach or the TAT may be so used. Similarly quite limited and specifically designed projective instruments can be constructed whose structure and purpose are determined not by an effort to cover the range of personality, but by the specific personality issues at stake in a research.

To what extent should we rely upon projective test data alone?

It is a commonplace of both clinical practice and research in our own culture that the results of test analyses seldom stand alone. The psychologist's picture of the entire functioning person is derived from a number of sources of data other than the test. Thus, a psychiatrist's interview, a social worker's interview and observations, comments of parents, teachers, probation workers and other relevant persons seem necessary to complete a picture of a single individual. In many instances biological assays and medical or neurological examinations are of importance. To presume, therefore, that not merely a single individual of another society, but aggregates of persons, may be described and related to theoretical issues upon the basis of test data alone seems entirely unreasonable. Certainly, direct field observations, as well as social structure, beliefs and myths analysis are of utmost relevance, not merely to the understanding of the culture from the anthropologist's point of view, but also for the proper interpretation of the test responses themselves.

In this connection the issue of the "blind interpretation" should perhaps be raised. There are many eloquent denials of the value of the blind analysis. The philosophy within which such denials seem to me appropriate, is the "single case" concept in which a maximum of nuances and subtleties is looked for and in which issues of validity and independent verification do not arise. In most studies in other cultures, and in the ordinary clinic, the blind analysis has a real place. We are by no means on such firm ground that when an attribute presumed present and openly discussed is subsequently found to be "true" in the projective analysis, we can unqualifiedly call it validation. We take great care in other areas of research to assure ourselves independence of judgment on two separate scales, subsequently to be compared for relationships. Certainly at least comparable precautions should be attempted in the area of that minimally validated psychological technique, the projective instrument. Once conclusions within any conceptual framework are determined independently, they should not necessarily remain so. This is the point at which the standard clinic procedure is valuable. In this procedure each source of data is presented, discussed, and integrated with other data. Assuming some degree of independence of estimate, such comparisons and contrasts will be highly useful. They will permit raising issues of verification and proposing various correspondences and interrelationships of data. This kind of attempted independence of initial estimate followed by a study of comparisons and contrasts is appropriate to either the single case approach or, when only limited aspects of the projective data are used, it may serve as one test of a specific hypothesis.

To what extent is the projective analysis a "check" on field observations?

This issue is clearly related to the one discussed above. In essence, the projective test data are a "check" upon anthropological field data in the same sense that the field data are a "check" on the projective data. Both systems constitute different approaches to the same basic datum, the individual or group under study, and some type of systematic interrelationship of these two sets of data should certainly appear. It should not be assumed, however, that one set is more "real" or "basic" than the other. A distinguished anthropologist was once accused of being merely a "summer tourist" in some observations he made about another society. Certainly, one should keep in mind the possibility that the view obtained by the projective instrument is comparable to the tourist's glimpse from the train window. We should seek to elaborate our views of another society both with an eye to extending our own knowledge of that society as well as to defining the nature of the glimpse provided by our instruments.

As in the clinical use of these instruments in our own society, we may assume in cross-cultural studies that the data from interview and observation are not of the same sort as the projective data; rather they tend to be complementary in some fashion. It may well be that similar data can be derived from certain interviews as well as from Rorschach or TAT but, generally, this is not so. Either we do not ask the same questions from interview data or, more frequently, the interview itself was so structured as to make question-asking impossible. The projective data may be viewed as generally dealing with feelings, attitudes, and emotional tendencies, sometimes consciously recognized and sometimes not. The observational and interview data, on the other hand are primarily in the area of overt behavior, general behavioral tendencies, observable events, personal retrospection and expressed conscious opinion.

To what extent have we been utilizing relevant constructs in our analyses of the test responses of subjects from other societies?

This question is as vital for studies of our own society as it is for the study of other societies. The psychologist has often been accused of seeing all other societies as deviant in one way or another, an accusation which he can neither deny nor ignore. The problem stems in part from the very terminology of test analysis, which unquestionably has the air of pathology. The terms commonly used for the description of personality bear the strong flavor of the original home of the projective tests— the clinic, the hospital, the disturbed and the deviant. It is no solution to claim that these terms do not necessarily imply pathology or that certain amounts of these "pathological" states are "normal." Rather, it seems imperative to concentrate further upon the study of the normal and the culturally-conventional and to emphasize, both in our studies and in our theory making, the ego sustaining functions. This may necessitate a re-evaluation of our concepts of maturity and adjustment, a re-evaluation greatly aided by the comparative framework of cross-cultural study.

Furthermore, it is significant to what extent the tests generally used on such studies are so designed that their systems of analyses are specific to the test. Both the test and its dominant method of analysis may be culture-bound, although this need not necessarily be the case. Tests are most likely to be culture-bound when responses can only be analyzed in one set system. The question is whether or not the concepts utilized in the analysis of the test (and of course the scored properties of the response which stand for these concepts) are appropriate to our own society or others. The answer depends on the extent to which these concepts permit descriptions of individuals or groups, or substantiation of hypotheses which can be validated by other means.

A third issue involves the question of whether we have by-passed the problem of norms. We have indeed been aware of the issue, but our solutions to it are by no means adequate. When a test has a scoring system based on reasonably objective norms the problem is somewhat clearer.

Here at least we can compare our score-averages in differing groups and at least know against what standard we are judging the scores from the second culture.

Thus one may compare groups who appear deviant in terms of our regular American norms against persons appearing deviant in terms of norms established exclusively on the basis of records from the community being studied, with those who appear deviant on the basis of a combination of those sets of norms, and again with those persons who appear deviant on some behavioral, non-test criteria. Comparisons among these various groups would help considerably in determining to what extent our own ethnocentrism influences our interpretations. Tests which provide a sort of behavior-sample, such as the TAT, rather than a to-be-scored-response, appear on the surface to suffer least from our limited knowledge of the meaning of norms. In terms of interpersonal relationships the kind of analysis possible from such behavior-samples is not unduly distorted by normative-interpretative tendencies. It should not be forgotten, however, that in this case some sort of "normative" notions exist within the background of experience of the interpreter.

The real hazard of the issue of norms, however, is the implicit one of "associated conditions." This involves not merely the notion that a certain percent of F on the Rorschach test, for example, is deviant for our society (and hence may be for another), and not merely the interpretive assumption that such scores relate to preoccupations with order, system, rules and regulations. There is also the next link in this chain of associations, the link which proposes that this state is very likely "constricted" or pathogenic in some fashion. It could be made clear that high F may indeed always be sensibly interpreted in terms of order and system, but that its specific personality meaning—its reference to constriction or its pathological quality—is specific to our own society. In that case we might become less prone to think of everybody else as pathological. When these associated assumptions are examined with care and brought into the open, it may appear more profitable to think of high F as reflective of "concern with order and system" and not as diagnostic of neurotic constriction. This would permit us to examine the possibility that the specific cultural meaning of the personality attribute might vary greatly. What in our society is pathological constriction may be in another an extreme, but non-pathological, enthusiasm for etiquette and symmetry, an attribute which could lend great ego-support to individuals and a formal continuity to the culture.

Should every anthropologist have (or be) his own psychologist?

In the exploratory phases of an area such as cross-cultural research, and in a stage in which the concepts of the anthropologist and those of the psychologist do not readily blend or are not equally familiar to each group, there is considerable merit in the anthropologist treating the psychologist as a visiting consultant, and vice versa. This is a kind of situation in which the local general practitioner might call in the appropriate specialist and say to him "what does it look like to you?" If the specialist responds "super-ego," then the general practitioner feels he has advanced somewhat and at least has a new string to his bow. The reverse situation in which the anthropologist serves as the consultant specialist is growing in frequency.

In either of these cases, the problem of course is that the issues at stake for the one group may not be clear to the other. Hence the terms in which the response of the specialist is presented may be irrelevant, meaningless or even misleading. The analyses of the psychologist, handled in this way, may be quite "interesting," informative, and even genuinely useful to some problem the psychologist in question has in mind. The results thus may be important to those persons who already think in the same way the psychologist does. This is not of maximum usefulness to the anthropologist, however, who is interested in bringing some new ideas and new techniques to bear upon the problems which he defines differently from the psychologist.

Two further developments may bring improvement. The first fundamental goal is to increase the base of training for both the psychologist and the anthropologist—a kind of major and minor field situation. This should result in increased breadth of theoretical foundation and an increased ability for the single individual to himself utilize the techniques and concepts of the other field. During the stage now in progress, in which this kind of amalgamation of problem and method is going on, a second general approach seems worthwhile. The anthropologist must become his own psychologist; the anthropologist and the psychologist must ask each other a few questions and not be satisfied unless the answers make sense.

Many of the techniques traditionally used by the psychologist might well be tried out by the anthropologist and analyzed in the anthropologist's terms. It is appropriate for the anthropologist to "learn Rorschach" but unless he also "learns psychodynamics" he is apt just to be a bad psychologist. Short of going through the training of the psychologist, many extremely pertinent and useful analyses can probably be made of projective techniques in ways not traditional in psychology, but created by the anthropologist—created by him to answer the questions he has in mind and not those the psychologist told him he ought to ask. There is a strong tendency, admittedly, and sometimes for good reasons, encouraged by the psychologists, to treat the psychologist's weapons as magic. Thus it is felt that the Rorschach will remain fast to the rock and not come to life for anyone without a certificate. This is undoubtedly true, for the individual case analyses in which the ramifications of the subtleties are of great importance. Techniques which are more of the behavior-sample type (TAT, modified picture tests, sentence completion, draw-a-person) may be of more use. Of the TAT, for example, we do not need to ask questions of highly technical issues of personality structure. We can ask equally important questions dealing, for instance, with the kinds of emotions and behavior attributed to males or females. Rather than asking, "is this individual's aggression reactive," we can ask, "what situations of aggression arise (in these records as opposed to those records) and what solutions are proposed for them?" These kinds of analyses are entirely appropriate and do not require the particular technical training of the psychologist. In fact, they may be more appropriate to the questions the anthropologist wants to answer.

Profitable work can be expected from close collaboration between the psychologist and anthropologist in which the psychologist is obliged to observe and participate in field work and to relate his observations to his test. Conversely, the anthropologist might design and give a few tests, try to observe the things that the psychologist says should be observed, and similarly relate his observations to the tests. Above all, the psychologist and the anthropologist should know what the other thinks he is observing. Each group is fond of calling its observations "objective," as though somehow there is something "natural" about observing and as though each was trying only to "get the facts." It is clear, however, that each has a set of assumptions—seldom stated—and that each observes and records in terms of those assumptions.

In sum, it may be pointed out that we should not assume that these tests are entirely fitting and appropriate, valid and adequately reliable in our own culture and that the only question is whether or not they "work" in another. Rather, all of these problems of culture-boundness and validity, appropriateness of constructs, and integration of sources of data, require careful scrutiny and continued exploration. This applies both to their use here and elsewhere. The fact that a culture is distant and exotic does not make the facts of its values and beliefs, its social organization, its institutions and myths any more important. The necessity for the integration of test analyses and cultural data is as great within our own society as when the tests are utilized elsewhere. The simultaneous exploration of these issues in a cross-cultural context will greatly assist our understanding of these instruments and their potential contribution. Above all, we need a theory of the meaning of the behavior involved in projective tests—a theory which is itself transcultural.

In the projective tests we may have a camera with only one lens setting with which we must take what we get, not knowing how far the camera was from the subject nor what the circumstances of lighting were at the time of exposure. The answer to these questions and to the others posed above can come only with time and experience. Benefit from experience can be enhanced by:

More work in closer collaboration with the field workers;

More analyses of tests in the light of the behavioral situation in which the responses were gathered;

Systematic efforts to relate our analyses of tests to the analyses of field data within the same conceptual areas;

Serious effort on the psychologist's part to re-align his framework of analysis to deal with essentially normal and ego supporting processes;

More studies in smaller, tighter social settings in which the variance of social factors is better known;

More use of projective instruments to test specifically stated hypotheses, framed either by general personality theory or anthropological theory, which are testable by the data of the field worker's observations.

One may maintain enthusiasm for the use of such instruments in cross-cultural work, because we expect benefits for use of such tests in our own society and others and for our theories of human personality. But it is clear that such benefits will come only with closer collaboration and more precisely phrased questions asked of our data. The psychologist must temper his temptation to luxuriate in the role of astounding his colleagues with his interpretations and settle down to the task of exploring the validity of these interpretations and of the concepts which he uses in phrasing them.

About the Chapter

This chapter presents a theoretical analysis of one of the most difficult of all problems in cross-cultural personality study, the interpretation of affective symbolism across cultures. It also provides a series of case studies on the analysis of the symbolic content of Rorschach responses in three societies. A vivid picture of the complexity of Rorschach analysis emerges that shows how the clinical psychologist's sensitive approach attempts to master the test.

Dr. De Vos believes that emotional symbolism is a form of communication making use of the same intellectual processes that language in general does. The affect laden symbolism that is found in dreams, in art or in the projective tests refers to deep, unconscious, and highly personal experiences which cannot be spoken of explicitly and publicly but which nevertheless are often shared or are common to all members of a particular group. The symbol refers to this common experience obliquely or indirectly, but nevertheless is utilized in the cause of unity and communication with others. The four case studies provide dozens of examples of analyses of Rorschach symbolism, each supported by an understanding of both the cultural and personal context in which they are given. Dr. De Vos demonstrates that, given this kind of knowledge, the approach to Rorschach responses used in our own society can be applied in others as well. The cases come from Arab, Japanese and Slavey Indian subjects.

About the Author

GEORGE A. DE VOS is Associate Professor in the School of Social Welfare, Associate Research Psychologist in the Institute of Human Development and Research Associate of the Center for Japanese Studies at the University of California, Berkeley. He is specializing in the development of psychological methods useful in the fields of culture and personality and socialization. He has participated in studies of acculturation in Japanese-Americans. With Japanese social scientists he has conducted studies of the change in urban and rural modal personality in Japan, studies of delinquency in Japan as well as with American ethnic minorities. He has done analyses of Algerian and Slavey Indian personality materials. He was trained in both anthropology and psychology at the University of Chicago and has been Chief Psychologist at Elgin State Hospital and Supervisor of Diagnostic Testing in the Psychological Clinic at the University of Michigan.

23

Symbolic Analysis in the Cross-Cultural Study of Personality

GEORGE DE VOS

University of California

THE DUAL FACE OF SYMBOLIC REPRESENTATIONS

Man has become a culture-bearing animal because he is capable of symbolic thought. Within the wide variations of culture developed in the evolution of mankind there have come into being an awesome diversity of concepts and beliefs through which man seeks to communicate his experience of the outer world and of his inner psychological states. To encompass the complexities of his experience man resorts to symbolic means of representation. As "collective representations," to use Emile Durkheim's (1933) term, they are necessary to man's continuity in culture. They are imbedded in forms of art, enacted in religious rituals, embodied in myths and cosmologies.

Anthropologists such as Frazer (1894) and Durkheim (1915) at first used an evolutionary approach to systems of thought assessed for their symbolic referents. They sought to trace specific myths and rituals in a social-historical sense back to man's evolutionary infancy. Later Radcliffe-Brown, (1922) adhering to Durkheim's (1933) basic sociological frame of analysis, analyzed functions of ritual, myth, and other collectively held symbolic representations in terms of social structure. In developing a sociologically-oriented functionalist school around the analysis of symbolic material, others have followed Radcliffe-Brown's insistence that society and its social structure, in both a synchronic and diachronic dimension, is the only principal unifying concept. The individual and his development are unimportant.

This approach was criticized by Malinowski and by later functionalists. They saw man's collective symbols not solely as representations of outer social reality, but in addition, as commonly held symbols that in many instances are deeply expressive of inner affective states that cannot be directly related to social structure per se. This alternative functionalist approach to symbolic analysis is related to the frame of reference taken by adherents to psychoanalytic psychology. Both are concerned with man's ontogenetic maturational development within a social group. An attempt was made to include certain biological maturational variables involved in individual socialization as well as the social determinants affecting the development of symbolic expression.

Psychoanalytic psychology, as applied to the field of culture and personality, has made us deeply aware of possible vicissitudes occurring in the normal processes of development of thought. The inchoate forms of thought, termed "primary processes," characteristic of infantile maturational stages, are transmuted through social living within the primary family and community into "secondary processes" shared by the group as a whole. Nevertheless, adult thought content of any group still includes vestiges of the primitive forms of logic in the scientific, magical, and religiously-based beliefs and concepts peculiar to the particular society and its history.

The socialization of thought consists of transforming associative processes with their primary symbols from the spontaneous affectively-guided relationships, described aptly by Piaget (1930) as "ego-centric" and "syncretic" in nature, into processes of consciously-guided communication characterized by objectivity, reciprocity, and mutuality. In short, thought becomes permeable to social experience and to external laws of logic whatever their imperfections are in any particular society.

It follows, therefore, that with the development and evolution of human ego control the capacity to symbolize itself comes under the direction of objectively-organized ego functions. The most obvious aspect of this development in control is found in language. The origin of language is enshrouded in that dim time where outwardly expressed signs of affective states somehow became consciously controlled and ordered into discriminant verbal symbols. Language, even in its simplest form, is a symbol. Therefore, symbols are used first of all to indicate something which is not visually present in the situation. For example, I can communicate to you the idea that I have burned my finger by fire using the word (symbol) "fire" and pointing to the burn on my finger (*not* symbol). You understand even though fire is not physically present. This is the simplest basic use of symbols.[1] Usage of symbolic words to communicate ideas of a complex nature is a more sophisticated stage of this simple basic use of symbols.

The word symbol as used in this chapter is broadly defined to include unconscious representations. Durkheim's "collective representations" as described by him definitely include symbols. As they are described by him, they are certainly not totally conscious portrayals, since their actual function in referring to the social solidarity, for example, is mostly unconscious to the users of these collective representations.

Some scholars attempt to understand man as a symbolizing animal solely in terms of his development of verbal communication either as an inner language or a mode of external communication. The artist would never make such a mistake. Those working in the plastic or graphic arts seek consciously to control and to represent outwardly in visual or dramatic form, inner perceptions of which the person is deeply aware but which have no ready verbal referent. One may speculate that inner experiences are perhaps communicated symbolically to the mind prior to their expression in outer communication. Inner affective states are usually experienced in other modalities than the solely verbal one. Visual images are most probably prior. But since such images are less subject to abstraction in communication, they tend to remain more inchoate or primitive, or, in Freudian terms, more subject to "primary process associations" and less subject to ego controls. We tend to dream more in visual images, although it is not uncommon to make use of verbal condensations in dreams as well.

What is termed "symbolic analysis" by either the sociologically or the psychologically-oriented social scientist is usually *not* the analysis of graphic or verbal symbols used consciously. Rather, attention is usually focused on what is *inadvertently* expressed as a "by-product" either in religious beliefs and rituals, dreams, or even ordinary conversation, or, as we will consider in some detail in this chapter, in such projective tests as the Rorschach. The social scientist intends to analyze symbolic expressions as they are related to underlying social or psychological processes, and as these expressions are conceptually understood by the scientific analyst within his own frame of reference. These expressions are not necessarily self-consciously understood by the bearers of the culture or personality structure examined. To make this distinction between inadvertent and conscious use of symbols clear, let us very briefly consider some of the functions of a symbol in both its cognitive and its affective-expressive aspects.

Some Sociological and Psychological Functions of Symbolic Communication.

One important function of any symbol used consciously or not is to state something that cannot be stated directly in a factual communication. For example:

1. Symbols are used for *precise conceptual economy* in communication when concepts are of a complex nature. If a set of abstract symbols is mutually understood, communication is more rapid and economical. This is the disciplined, objective use of symbols found in greatest development in such fields as mathematics.

2. Symbols are used less precisely to convey *concepts* that are felt to be *too complex for comprehension,* but when some communication is necessary. Man is still prone to symbolize even when he feels something is conceptually beyond his power to comprehend fully. He often feels himself in some relation to certain invisible realities. It is then necessary to represent what is ill-understood or what cannot be directly comprehended by some verbal term, graphic design, or expressive gesture. The concept of "god" and religious terms and rituals in their cognitive aspects have such a symbolic function. Representations of this nature were the basis of the approach developed by Durkheim (1915) in his analysis of cultural behavior. The cabalists of the middle ages developed a very complex system of "incomprehensible" symbols as a means of "comprehending" reality. Zen Buddhism seeks truth or enlightenment reached only through a sudden comprehension. Obscure symbolic conundrums with manifest incongruity are used to stimulate the seeker into sudden realization.

3. Symbols can be used to *convey complex emotional states.* What is to be communicated not only may be a complex cognition, but also may be a complex feeling. Usually both cognitive and affective elements are present in symbols, but in certain instances emphasis is more on one or on the other. When man becomes conscious of himself, he becomes conscious of the complexity of his emotional nature as well. He attempts to communicate this complexity to others. Such communication, to be effective, demands means other than direct cognitive communication, since the goal is often to arouse like states in others. Art, drama, literature, especially in such forms as lyric poetry, depend upon artistic ability in symbolic expressive media to produce in the audience certain emotional states which allow them to comprehend at least affectively, if not cognitively, the intent of the artist. The French symbolic poets, such as Verlaine, for example, despaired of communicating general truths or the "inner cosmos," except by means of indirect, vaguely apprehended, affect-laden symbolic statements. Religious rituals, similarly, function to

create in their participants certain states of affect related to what has deep meaning for a group as a whole, as well as for its individual members. Great drama, as well as simple folk tales, depends on an undercurrent of symbolic meanings to produce its emotional impact as well as to convey cognitive significance.

Both sociological and psychological interpretations of such cultural expressions are possible. It is often the artful, mostly unconscious use of primary process associations with psycho-sexual developmental referents *common to members of a particular group* that cause these artistic creations to be treasured and preserved. Conversely, in a Durkheimian sense they also bear "meanings" of great value to the social life of the group whether consciously or unconsciously understood.

4. Symbols in a broadly psychoanalytic sense are inadvertently used as *projections of inner states*. In this form of symbolic expression the desire to communicate may be entirely lacking on a conscious level. The very manner in which an individual perceives an object, answers a question, recounts an event, or tells a spontaneous story is of symbolic significance to the trained observer of behavior. This is the form of symbolism handled in projective tests. To the casual glance such expressive material is not symbolic. Yet it often performs another very important function of a symbol, namely to express indirectly what cannot be directly expressed due to the presence of negative sanctions.

Symbolizing is sometimes used consciously by dissident groups within a culture whose values or behavior are opposed by the majority whose will is enforced by punitive means. Analogously, the individual often expresses affect symbolically so as not to arouse the censorship of his own ego, which acts as an internalized representative of socially held values. For the individual, as for the group, some feelings or thoughts are unconscionable in direct naked form, yet are of such importance that they seek some form of communication. Feelings or thoughts of this nature can be represented only in some indirect form. They may be disguised from direct view by being put in a form which is seemingly non-symbolic or supposedly consciously and acceptably symbolic of something else shared by those in communication. Dramas such as Hamlet, therefore, can have a double meaning. First there is the overt problem faced by Hamlet and its solution, which fulfill the necessary requisites of noble tragic drama according to Aristotelian aesthetics and, second, as analyzed by Ernest Jones, there is the basic oedipal theme shared by members of a western audience witnessing the play.

While it is a far cry from the analysis of Hamlet to the analysis of the symbolic meaning of single Rorschach responses, both are related to inherent expressive symbolizing functions of man's intellect. No matter in what culture, man cannot help but symbolize more than he intends to do.

He never can completely escape primary affective associations in his thought processes, regardless of what energy is expended to remain objective. Each night man must, albeit sometimes reluctantly, return to the past and to the primitive when he returns to sleep and rest. In so doing, his mind reverts to less disciplined patterns. Somatic and affective states guide the residues of associations through regressive modes requiring less energy for direction. So, too, even in the waking state man cannot always escape the influence of strong emotions. His hard-won objective controls can give way under the sway of uncontrollable feelings that color total perception. Less overtly, some of these patterns of emotion, especially as involved in primary relationships, are constantly coloring the world for any particular individual. The perception is influenced by past experience in an affective as well as cognitive sense. The degree of strength and the nature of these affective states differ radically between individuals and groups.[2] By use of standardized techniques eliciting responses to standard stimuli, these patterns of differences are subject to comparison and analysis. In this chapter by way of illustration we shall consider results obtained through the use of the Rorschach as it is applied to several cultural groups.

SYMBOLIC ANALYSIS USING THE RORSCHACH IN CROSS-CULTURAL RESEARCH

It is curious to note that one of the least exploited aspects of the Rorschach test when applied to cross-cultural research is its potential value for a standard analysis of the content of Rorschach responses as related to affective symbolism in various cultures. This neglect is basically a reflection of the relative lack of systematic attention to content found in Rorschach work generally.

Content has not been treated quantitatively to the degree that other aspects of the test have. There are a number of reasons for this lack of quantification in the area of content analysis. First and foremost is the fact that Herman Rorschach himself set the direction of interest in the use of his test toward the understanding of the *structure* of personality and its relation to perception. In establishing the validity of his test he was concerned most with the relatively inflexible modes of perception found in characteristic personality traits, especially those signifying pathological aberrations. He devoted most of his attention, therefore, to establishing norms with respect to the formal nature of the blots; i.e., use of form, color, shading, and other determinants in the "structure" of a response, and noting specifically the structural modes of perception selective as to location, size and complexity of the responses given. The unstructured nature of the blots in respect to *symbolic* stimulus value received no systematic attention. No method for testing quantitative differences in content symbolism was developed.

This lack of quantification of content in terms of its affective or symbolic referents created a serious problem in attempting to use the test with varying cultural groups. Sometimes the most meaningful differences are found in the use of affect-laden content rather than in the formal determinants traditionally scored.

In order to overcome this problem in my own work (De Vos, 1954; 1955), I developed a systematic, quantifiable, notational system which permits a statistically reliable scoring of each Rorschach response for its "affective inference" in addition to the customary scoring now in use (De Vos, 1952). Overall indexes of hostility, anxiety, body preoccupation, dependency, positive content, as well as content seemingly neutral in affective tone can be tabulated and compared statistically between individuals and groups.

Relation of the Scoring System for Symbolic Analysis of Content to Psychoanalytic Theory

The system of scoring used in the studies presented in this chapter is highly dependent on psychoanalytic theory for its rationale. It is not devoted solely to the recording of the affective tone of Rorschach responses. It is concerned also with the nature of content symbolism as it directs attention to the relative strength of libidinal vectors attached to the various stages of psychosexual development.

The various factors involved in analyzing content symbolism according to this system are as follows: (a) the nature of the underlying affective tone of specific content—is it generally positive or negative? To what degree is it balanced in one direction or another? A second factor is (b) the psychosexual developmental level of response—what does the content suggest in terms of various libidinal developmental stages? Is there a fixation on or regression to earlier stages of psychosexual development? Content often suggests in some manner the amount of energy or interest directed toward oral, anal, or phallic pregenital developmental stages. Hence a third factor concerns (c) the degree and nature of the socialization of the ego as a mediator between outer presses and inner needs—what is the nature of the socialization and sublimation of libidinal interests? Are libidinal concerns expressed in a more or less direct manner in the content? What ego defenses are used to handle impulses as well as affects? Are repression, denial, projection, displacement used? Are the affects used diffuse in nature or localized? A fourth factor involves (d) the attitudinal stance or "set" taken toward outside objects—is the affective relationship to objects structured in active or passive terms? Are outside objects related to in terms of dependent needs or in terms of active interests? The fifth factor relates to (e) the nature of the object cathexis involved in affective drives—is cathexis basically of outer objects or of self? Does the content suggest positively or destructively toned narcissism? To what extent is the narcissism of a primitive or secondarily socialized variety? Is object cathexis essentially constructive or destructive in nature?

These five analytic factors are used to classify responses within the scoring system. Complexity results from the many combinations of these factors involved in responses and differences in their relative pertinence to the particular responses. Most responses showing any kind of affective determination are located between the polarities of content suggesting (a) positive, (b) mature, (c) sublimated, (d) active, (e) object-oriented characteristics on the one hand and content suggesting (a′) destructive, (b′) primitive or aggressive, (c′) non-socialized or defensive, (d′) passive, (e′) narcissistic characteristics.

CHANGES IN AFFECTIVE SYMBOLISM IN ACCULTURATIVE AND OTHER STRESSFUL SITUATIONS

Study of affective symbolism with the present system has been and is being applied to a number of divergent cultural groups. It has not only produced results discriminating groups of different cultures, but it has also been notably successful in tapping differences seemingly due to the effects of acculturation on groups from similar cultural backgrounds. To illustrate the use of the system with groups on a quantitative basis some illustrative material involving acculturation of Japanese and of Algerian Arabs will be examined.[3]

Arabs compared with Japanese on overall Rorschach configurations are very different in many respects. However, within groups of Japanese or Arabs living in an acculturative situation similar trends are found in respect to the increased production of certain responses suggestive of the internalization of stress. When we compare men living within their traditional cultural environment with individuals of similar background living as members of a minority group within a Western cultural setting, specific forms of body content material and specific forms of hostile symbolism show significant increase. Table 1 demonstrates significantly, for example, more body preoccupation content in the immigrant Japanese-Americans and in the urbanized, gallicized Casbah-area Arabs than in comparable rural samples, respectively. Arabs living in the Casbah, coming from the same village as Arabs tested in an oasis setting, reach a level of body preoccupation content in approximately 10 per cent of their total responses, in contrast to the 2 per cent of similar content found in the oasis group. These responses are concerned with both bone and flesh anatomy, disease, sexual or anal anatomical percepts or organs.

TABLE 1

INCREASE IN HOSTILITY AND BODY PREOCCUPATION CONTENT IN ACCULTURATING MINORITY GROUPS

(Men Only)

	N	Hsm*	Hhad*	Hsm + Hhad	% cases Hsm + Hhad	Mean H%	Mean B%	Mean Pos%	Hostility N	Hostility %	Body Pre. N	Body Pre. %	H &/ or B.P. N	H &/ or B.P. %
AMERICAN														
Normal	30	2	3	4	13	9.2	5.4	16.1	5	17	5	17	9	30
Neurotic	15	4	3	5	33	15.1	10.3	11.3	5	33	5	33	8	53
Schizophrenic	15	3	4	5	33	10.9	15.9	7.3	5	33	10	67	11	73
Negro ‡	24	21	—	—	88	—	10.2	—	—	—	—	—	—	—
JAPANESE IN AMERICA§														
Issei	25	9	1	10	40	12.2	14.6	17.6	8	32	9	36	14	56
Kibei	15	5	2	7	47	13.1	10.5	17.3	9	58	8	53	12	80
Nisei	30	12	3	14	47	10.7	12.7	18.3	9	33	12	40	18	60
JAPANESE IN JAPAN														
Urban	61	28	6	29	49	10.0	4.0	15.2	17	29	12	20	24	40
Rural	31	7	4	8	23	9.0	4.7	13.3	7	23	6	19	11	32
ARABS IN ALGERIA														
Urban Casbah	28	7	9	13	46	10.6	10.7	9.4	7	25	6	21	12	42
Rural Oasis	20	4	4	6	30	6.8	2.6	13.1	3	15	1	5	3	15
Total	64	17	19	27	—	8.5	5.7	10.7	10	16	7	11	15	23

The rightmost group of columns is headed: **N + % cases significantly high †**, subdivided into Hostility (N, %), Body Pre. (N, %), and H &/ or B.P. (N, %).

* Hsm are sadomasochist responses usually involving tissue mutilation; Hhad includes responses in which body parts are missing or distorted (De Vos, 1952).

† Significantly high defined at 1 S.D. above total American normal. Sample (Mean Hostility 9.4 + 7.1 S.D.; Body Preoccupation 4.1 + 4.9 S.D.)

‡ The Goldfarb sample reported in Kardiner and Ovesey, *The Mark of Oppression* (1951), includes both men and women.

§ Issei—immigrant Japanese; Nisei—American-born Japanese; Kibei—American-born Japanese who spent at least 5 years during childhood in Japan.

The Issei immigrant generation have an even higher percentage of anatomical responses, close to 15 per cent of their total responses being so characterized. The American-born Japanese Nisei men also have a very high level of body preoccupation (12 per cent). The samples of acculturating individuals of Japanese background in the United States are significantly higher in body preoccupation than either rural (4.7 per cent) or urban (4.0 per cent) samples of Japanese men obtained in Japan. It is noteworthy that the Japanese samples obtained in Japan show levels of body preoccupation similar to those found for the American normal control group (5.4 per cent).[4]

These results suggest that there may be a turning in of hostility and/or an emotional withdrawal from difficult object relationships within a social context into an unhealthy self-preoccupation. Similar Rorschach results emphasizing the prevalence of anatomical responses were reported by Abel and Hsu in respect to acculturating Chinese males (Abel and Hsu, 1949).

This sort of interpretation can be extended to other groups showing the psychological effects of social stress other than that specific to acculturation. The American Negro as a group is prone to primary family and secondary social experiences related to minority status that can only be thought of indirectly as related to an acculturation concept. Yet Goldfarb (1951), in a recent study reporting a sample of Negro Rorschachs, found very high amounts of anatomical material. The mean percentage of anatomy reported by him was also approximately 10% of the total responses given.

In the general category of hostility material, Table 1 shows that in the Arab Casbah group there is a general increase in hostile content compared with an Oasis group, although not to a degree sufficient for statistical significance. The American Japanese groups are also only slightly higher in hostile content than those found in Japan. However, if one examines specifically the number of responses in the various groups listed under the hostility sub-categories of sado-masochism and body distortion (suggestive of castration anxiety), one finds that the urban Arab and Japanese groups are significantly higher. These findings are related to Goldfarb's report on American Negro records that 21 of the 24 individuals tested in his sample had some sort of content suggesting mutilation of the body.

Again, the differential appearance of this specific content in certain cultural groups may result from stress experienced continually by people who live in a specific stressful situation, as well as from specific psychosexual developmental experiences. It is the more emotionally constrictive Arab and Japanese rural groups (whose rigidity scores are the highest) who show the lowest amount of hostile symbolism. In the case of the Arab groups almost all of those tested left the oasis after age 14. Therefore, the differences in the content of the responses for the city dwellers cannot be directly attributed to the early developmental years. These results suggest the necessity for further exploration of the concept of intrapsychic stress as related to adult life experiences. It is noteworthy in this context that the Japanese urban male sample, taken in Japan, gave a very heavy incidence of mutilation responses in the age groups between 35 and 50; 22 of 28 individuals of this age period in the urban group made such responses in contrast to the younger and older groups. These ages include most of the individuals who have been exposed to severe war experiences.

A Rorschach study of stress in Air Force men participating in bombing raids over Germany (Alexander and Ax, 1950) might be cited in support of the concept that environmental tension experienced as an adult is related to the reflection of intrapsychic stress in the Rorschach. It reveals that those individuals who showed the greatest psychological disorganization in coping with the chronic stress of participating in bombing raids were specifically those who produced a great deal of sado-masochistic concern with mutilation in the content of their Rorschach responses. These sado-masochistic responses, however, tended to disappear after the individual had recuperated from the tensions of combat work.

Comparing the specific sado-masochistic material in the Arabs and Japanese, certain notable differences were observed. Japanese-Americans, in a number of instances, talked of crushed lungs or operations. These responses could be related to concern over health. For example, tuberculosis—which is prevalent among Japanese—is a very strong cultural concern both in Japan and among acculturating Japanese-Americans. But the specific concern over health is often structured in sado-masochistic terms. In the Arabs the mutilation responses were more apt to be concerned with the tearing or penetration of the body as the result of a violent, aggressive act. Very often the mutilation was directly perceived as related to the sexual organs of men or women. These responses in Arabs seem to be a reflection of specific continuing difficulties resulting from culturally-patterned relationships between the sexes in Arab culture.

The question arises at this point whether symbolic material of this nature or of any other sort can actually be interpreted as meaning the same thing as far as personality structure is concerned for Arabs or Japanese as it would for Americans. It might be argued that certain statistical differences in supposedly symbolic content material have much more to do with culturally-conditioned differences in perception than with underlying affective states.

If we take the Arab materials in regard to human content as an example, such an argument would point out that human movement responses are relatively lacking in the Arab records generally. Would it not hold that cloaked human figures, for example, are not as easily discernible as are humans in Western garb whose limbs are emphasized? Moreover, the human form receives little representation in Arab art generally. There are some who would hold that it is against the Koran to represent the figure. Likewise, the Arabs are prone to give a number of vista responses that cluster enough on certain cards to reach the level of being popular for the group. Could such results not be related to the habit of scanning the almost-always present desert horizon? Seeing figures in hiding and emphasis on trees with specific attention paid to the relative denseness of the leaves can be readily seen as related to conditions of desert life.

Granting some cultural influence in making certain percepts more prepotent than others, one can still point out the relative prevalence of these responses in *certain* individuals in comparison with others. Also, these responses, when given, form part of a consistent pattern in individual cases with other elements which are not suggestive of cultural prepotency, as pointed out in some of the individual cases considered below. Moreover, the fact that certain ways of handling the blot are fairly common to groups as a whole does not necessitate the conclusion that the traits suggested are any less important in considering individual cases. The Arabs, for example, give many animal responses, although animals are no more portrayed in art than are humans. There is, likewise, no reason culturally why the human head should be any more apparent on Card III than the entire body. Yet a number of Arab records see human details or individuals at a distance—neglecting the more commonly seen humans for what would be considered more pathological material if found in American clinical records. The tendency to see genii or mythological afreet, or to see humans only in antagonistic situations when they are perceived, is not without psychological significance. The manner in which the human form or other content material is handled or avoided is consistently suggestive of difficulties in human rapport general to the Arab group as a whole. In the study described above, close work by the Rorschach analyst with the anthropologist, who knew the individuals concerned, allowed Rorschach inferences to be checked against actual impressions of personalities based on observation. This collaboration brought out the usefulness of the Rorschach in the individual cases.

In reference to the striking difference between acculturated and non-acculturated groups in the prevalence of anatomical mutilation material, it becomes obvious that groups in the acculturation situation stress the anatomical and mutilation content, rather than groups tested in a traditional cultural setting. One cannot argue that the meaning of these responses is necessarily more benign or more readily perceived due to a lack of cultural repressions or other hypothetical cultural influences. For it is precisely the individuals in the stressful situation that are prone to this sort of perception, rather than those living in traditional settings.

THE RELATIONSHIP OF CONTENT SYMBOLISM TO SPECIFIC CULTURAL BELIEFS AND PRACTICES

Not only does the Rorschach content symbolism show significant variation between groups; but the test, when used in conjunction with detailed observational ethnographic field material, is also directly applicable to the understanding of within-group differences in other cultures. Horace Miner organized his study of Arab acculturation so that, in working together with a psychological specialist, he was able to analyze the direct relationship of content symbolism to specific cultural beliefs and practices as they show change in the acculturative situation. Miner and I found a very striking relationship in the Algerian Arabs between strong belief in and use of religious charms, and appearance or lack of appearance of specific Rorschach symbolic content. Rorschach variables were also significantly related to other supernatural beliefs, opinions concerning seclusion practices of women, and punishment of children.

Arabs living in the Casbah who were high on quantitative measures of rigidity and maladjustment [5] and who no longer strongly believed in the efficacy of Koranic charms included all those who were significantly high in the production of body preoccupation responses (we defined "significantly high" arbitrarily as one standard deviation above the mean of the American normal groups). These individuals with high hostility ratings in no case included an individual who believed strongly in the efficacy of charms. On the other hand, those who were significantly high in hostility content were much lower in scores of overall rigidity and, in a number of cases, also lower in maladjustment scores. Looking at it the other way, none of the individuals in the urban sample of Arabs who maintained a strong belief in charms scored significantly high in either body preoccupation or hostility symbolism. These results, as well as others of a similar nature suggest that the appearance of stress patterns of reaction in response to the vicissitudes of the French-Arab acculturative situation is related to the loss of previous beliefs which, had they been kept, might have acted as an effective intrapsychic buffer.

Three basic alternative reactions seem to be present in the urbanized Arab. First, there is a pattern of intrapsychic adjustment in terms of a traditional belief system which allows for the release and expression of affect without undue internalized conflict. In this system of beliefs there is some discharge value which possibly lowers internal tension. In a sense this is a socially-acceptable working projective system. Another of the patterns involves more internally located psychic tensions, which in turn result in a somewhat passive social withdrawal. There is a turning in on the body with a narcissistic withdrawal of affect from free, outer expression. This kind of person seems to "take it out on himself." Such Arabs invariably maintain a rigid personality defense structure (see Table 2).

TABLE 2

RELATION OF BELIEF IN CHARMS TO MEASURES OF
RIGIDITY AND PERCEPTUAL THEMA SUGGESTING
HOSTILITY AND BODY PREOCCUPATION

Casbah Arabs N = 28	Rigidity*		Body Preoccupation		Hostility		B and/ or H — high
	50+	low	10+†	low	17+†	low	
BELIEF IN CHARMS							
Strong	5	2	0	7	0	7	0
Slight	5	3	3	5	3	5	5
No Belief	5	8	3	10	4	9	7
							B or H high
RIGIDITY							
High			6	9	1	14	6
Low			0	13	6	7	6

*50+ on Fisher's Rigidity score roughly over 1 S.D. above American Normative mean 27.7 + 15.3.
† 1 S.D. above normal American mean.

A third pattern appears among those who maintain less rigid defenses. These individuals reveal, by their production of various forms of hostile images such as biting animals, volcanic explosions, depreciatory attitudes suggested by clowns and depreciated Negroes, sado-masochistic and body distortion responses, that they are continually coping with inner hostile impulses that are seeking outer expression. Very often a solution to this problem is sought by projecting the hostile feelings outward onto the environment. Their own hostile reaction to the environment is thus seen stimulated by outside hostile forces. This projection of hostility, therefore, tends to be related to paranoid-like mechanisms in those who would take a more active stance toward their environment.[6]

Further cross-cultural comparisons between groups with respect to content symbolism promise to be a most fruitful pursuit in the study of culture and personality. Such research with a number of different cultures will make possible a comparison of modal variations in affecting loadings in personality as well as of variations in the ego mechanisms used to cope with disturbing inner affective states.

ANALYSIS OF CONTENT SYMBOLISM OF INDIVIDUAL RORSCHACH RECORDS IN CROSS-CULTURAL STUDY

In addition to ascertaining statistical differences between groups or within groups related to a particular culture, it is often profitable to study single individual cases that exhibit particular modes of behavior which may or may not be frequent in the culture at large. Such clinical type analysis reveals the presence of similar psychological mechanisms underlying differences in cultural expression from group to group. The following cases, taken from Arab, Japanese, and Slavey societies, illustrate this cross-cultural clinical use of the Rorschach.[7]

Ahmed, A Man who Can Live in Two Worlds

Thirty-eight years old, tall, and somewhat more heavy-set than the average Arab, Ahmed is a handsome man except for an eyelid partially destroyed by an infection. His white turban and flowing robes are kept scrupulously clean, his nails well tended, and his face close-shaven every Friday. He lives in a house in the oasis adjacent to that of his parents and one of his brothers. His father had two wives in polygamous marriage. Ahmed's mother was the second wife and he is the youngest of her twelve children.

Ahmed states that his one wife is all he desires. He says he gets along well with her and has no liking for the inevitable quarreling which polygamy produces. Primarily, though, Ahmed does not want the additional children another marriage would entail. Only one of his offspring is a daughter, and he concedes that one more girl would be desirable. His attitude toward women generally is conservative. He contends that he has confidence in their morality, but he is very restrictive concerning the movements of his wife, not even permitting her to visit his garden.

As a child Ahmed attended the local French school. The boy was a bright scholar, completing six years' training and earning his *certificat d'étude,* a rare accomplishment. He was even recommended for a scholarship for advanced study, although he did not receive it. In addition,

Ahmed had a year's Koranic training, from which he derived maximal benefit. Not only did he memorize a quarter of the Koran, but also he became remarkably literate in Arabic. At seventeen Ahmed went to France, where he worked for two years in a metallurgical factory in Lyons. While there he dressed as a Frenchman, but on returning to the oasis he assumed Arab clothes except for sweater, shirt, socks, and bedroom slippers, which are not uncommon "street wear." His wristwatch remains the most obvious symbol of French contact. The effects of his acculturation are, however, much more marked than this.

He has been an outstanding innovator in the community. Both economically and politically he has benefited from his dual cultural role. In addition to managing his large garden, irrigated with water from a gasoline-driven pump, he runs the characteristic small store his father started and also operates the local post office. He serves as president of the elected town council and seems to be quite conscious of his bi-cultural role. He is aware of both its advantages and disadvantages in different situations.

Ahmed's poised and composed attitude toward both French and Arabs is so controlled that he never seems entirely relaxed. The only real indication of inner strain, however, is his habit of cracking his knuckles. He appears to be a very pliable individual, accepting suggestions with no show of insecurity or threat. Even in a situation of mutual exchange of confidences, he is careful never to express hostility, acting in a completely non-authoritarian manner. He is in marked contrast to the generally more ebullient Arabs, who are more apt to express hostility openly. Ahmed, however, is not prudish and will speak freely on any topic other than his wife and his own feelings.

In spite of his close association with the anthropologist and his readiness to converse, Ahmed never invited him to his home, as other Arabs did. Much contact took place at Ahmed's store. Here his generosity toward others was apparent. Ahmed's affective behavior is generally reserved, except with his youngest son, who is three and who lives with a sister-in-law.

Ahmed shows himself to be quite sensitive to sensory stimulation. He loves his gardens and will put rose petals in his nostrils to savor them long and fully. In this sensitivity he is not unique among the perfume-loving Arabs. But he is unusual in that, during the hot, thirsty days of Ramadan, he immerses himself in a pool in his garden and will gargle the fresh, cool water. In so doing, he remains within the letter of Koranic religious proscriptions, but he maximizes his comfort. His supernatural beliefs adhere to Islamic dogma, but he does not hold the elaborate beliefs about dream interpretation, the evil eye, and genii, which characterize others in the oasis.

Although the Rorschach picture of Ahmed is generally in accord with the behavioral impression, it also reveals some surprising internal stresses. He is a very flexible person compared with most Arabs. Oriented outwardly rather than in on himself, Ahmed shows extremely good outer control, very unusual in Arab records, and can be pleasantly compliant whenever necessary. Positive affect is expressed in 15 per cent of his responses, close to the mean for an American normal group. Symbolically, these responses show an aesthetic approach emphasizing clothing and ornamentation as well as the beauty of nature.

A strong achievement orientation is indicated by the high response total and by the emphasis on complex, well integrated whole responses found throughout, including the more difficult color cards. As is true for the Arabs generally, he is not systematic or methodical, but shows his intelligence best when stimulated affectively in a positive way.

What seems lacking, as is true for many Arabs, is a mature inner life. His inner satisfaction still seems basically bound to childish or infantile motives. In Ahmed's case these wishes are strongly held back and repressed. The Rorschach suggests, therefore, that Ahmed's capacity to relate well socially does not carry over into deeper, more meaningful responsiveness as far as basic inner attitudes are concerned. In his deeper relationships he may have no inner peace. There are strong sado-masochistic tendencies related to an unresolved authority threat. Attention to anal material in certain responses is suggestive of strong latent homosexual submissiveness. In no quantitative score, however, is strong maladjustment suggested. He remains within the low range on Fisher's (1950) overall measure and is very low in comparison with the Arab group generally.

The nature of his human content and an obsessive preoccupation with butterflies suffering various forms of destruction give the record an unhappy tone, full of concern with sado-masochistic mutilation, until his mood shifts to a pleasurable one on the last three cards. Card I starts with depressive content—"An animal carcass." Also seen is a person without a head. There is some preoccupation with the bones of the legs protruding without any feet. He decides they must be made of stone, because if they were flesh, they would become bloated and would rot. On Card III the usual humans are perceived as skeletons. On Card IV he produces his only human movement. On the tower of a mosque seen at the distance are two marabouts, described as arguing. Card VII is a poorly perceived body of a person. The center of Card IX is a woman dressed in a long gown revealing the form of her breasts.

The theme of butterfly percepts is interesting to follow from card to card, for Ahmed sees butterflies on almost every card. They are not seen perseveratively but rather in a different context and expressing different underlying affect from card to card. He unconsciously uses the butterfly percept to express symbolically various fears and pleasures. One has the impression that he believes himself to be like a butterfly, basically rather soft and defenseless. To defend himself he has developed firm outer controls. His harder, outer social roles are represented by such shelled animals as snails and tortoises. On Card II the butterfly makes its first appearance "ready to eat," lighting on a thumb. The remains of the butterfly are found "torn in several pieces" on Card III. On Card IV there is the stomach of a butterfly that has been "burned by a candle." On Card V a butterfly appears without elaboration and carries no special meaning. Only the head of a butterfly appears on Card VI, followed by the mouth of a grasshopper. The butterfly has big wings on Card VII. Under the stimulation of color on Card VIII two butterflies are seen stuck together by their "back ends," clinging to a tree and copulating "to make little ones." The butterfly again appears on Card IX but in a neutral tone. On Card X there are two butterflies. One response is the "back end" of a butterfly and the other a butterfly in pretty colors.

This preoccupation with oral, anal, and genital sexuality centering around butterflies suggests a period of experience in childhood or youth when Ahmed felt weak and vulnerable but nevertheless sought gratification as a favored and beloved child. He was probably considered attractive and was indulged. Later in life he developed more mature outer controls and no longer resorts to the earlier passive techniques of gaining attention and indulgence. But passive narcissistic feelings, as well as feelings of vulnerability to attack because of his passivity, still remain as strong but hidden currents underneath the surface poise and maturity.

It is noteworthy that his particular personality development suits him for a bi-cultural role. In addition to his obvious intelligence, his poise, flexibility, and underlying "permeability" to others in social situations make him easily acceptable. It is doubtful that many individuals can maintain such a delicate balance between the French and Arabs without arousing animosity in one or the other or even both groups.

Ahmed's Rorschach

Card I: (1) An animal carcass (that's the tail; these marks which are generally found on the back of the animal. He's dead because he has no head. D4).
(2) A bird (W).
(3) Resembles a relief of a mountain (upper half—blot seen in vista).
(4) Resembles a person (there's the neck without a head. There are the hands, the feet, which are pulled off. Similar to the bones of the foot. The bones—where the bones of the foot penetrate through the flesh. It should have a thickness. It would be rotten if it were a real body. D4).

Card II: (1) A butterfly ready to eat (D5).

(2) A thumb. The front's here; the back's there. (It's not attached to the butterfly. The butterfly is poised on it to eat something. It resembles a thumb. You can see well the emplacement of the nail. The butterfly is poised on it. It penetrates underneath.)

Card III: (1) A tie (a cravat. It has a butterfly tie and it has a knot.).

(2) The skeleton of a man (the head, the holes of the eyes, the nose, and the mouth. D1).

(3) The remains of the butterfly (it's torn up in several pieces; the wings are gone; the body remains; all the rest is gone. W).

Card IV: (1) A fish (a sea fish that has a kind of horn. It's soft because those things are a little elevated. W).

(2) The stomach of a butterfly (it's a butterfly that has been burned by something—a candle or something—and all that remains there is the stomach. D).

(3) A plant (it's planted there and it grows. The leaves and shoots. This part is the old leaves. W).

(4) An edifice. Two people are arguing (a construction like a minaret and two people arguing in the tower on top—very small. Dd in D1 upside down as tower).

(5) A kind of toad (there are the feet, the tail, the head. W).

Card V: (1) A bat (W).

(2) A bird (there are really differences with the head of the bat, in that the bat has no beak. W).

(3) A butterfly (W).

(4) A head of leaf lettuce (with rough edges. W).

Card VI: (1) A flying insect (head and wings; the wings are open. D3).

(2) A tortoise (the feet come out this way, tail, that's the shell. W).

(3) The head of a butterfly (moustache seen from behind and above. D7).

(4) The mouth of a grasshopper (it has a long thing, a tail; the mouth seen from below. D7).

(5) A sparkplug (these are the points. D7).

Card VII: (1) A butterfly with big wings (D2).

(2) The feet of a frog or a toad (DS2 + 5).

(3) A person with feet and hands (DS2 + 5).

(4) Smoke (goes up into the sky like that by layers. It rises from there as it forms. W).

Card VIII: (1) A real butterfly (D2).

(2) A tree or something on which two animals are climbing; a lion on each side (D1 + D4, the lion may be clinging to the side).

(3) A decorative lamp of a house (the lamp that one has in rich houses decorated in these ways. You put electricity or even candles in it and you hang it up from there. W).

(4) The body of a butterfly. It's made as if those two butterflies are stuck to one another by their back ends, tails, to make little ones (D6 + D7).

(5) A tree on which animals are clinging (identical with response 2).

Card IX: (1) The back end of a dungbeetle (it's colored. It comes out at night and goes on the walls, it's black. It can be red or yellow. It depends upon the plants where it's found. DS8).

(2) The body of a person (stomach, a belt here, shoulders, the sleeve.

This resembles a dress, looks like a woman shown with a dress, a silk dress, you can see the breast on either side. DS).

(3) The back part of a butterfly (all the green, the body sticking out here. D1).

(4) Two deer heads (head, eyes, and horns. D2).

(5) A flower (color and the form of petals. D6).

Card X: (1) A painting, a design (in colors. W).

(2) The scorpion-stingers (has a spine which curves in that form in the back. D and D8).

(3) The wing-like bones of a person's skeleton (pelvic bones. D6).

(4) A bird (has a bill. D7).

(5) Tree trunks (a false-pistachio. The twisting, it's not straight. D9).

(6) The back end of a butterfly (has two horns on the back. D7).

(7) Snail shells (tail is here. This is the opening of the body. The rolls on the shell are indicated by these lines. D13).

(8) A bouquet of flowers, a little pot of plants (a pot of glass with a design here. W).

(9) The form of a butterfly (the head and the form. Ws).

Abderrahman, A Retired Soldier

A non-commissioned officer during the latter part of his career, Abderrahman had fifteen years' service with French native troops in Algeria. Now forty-nine, he has been employed as a night-watchman in Algiers. Clean, dressed in European clothes aside from his fez, Abderrahman speaks good French, which he says he learned to read and write on his own. His only formal schooling consists of three years of Koranic training. After leaving the Army, he received a diploma from an institute of physical education. His army service fell between the two wars. Retiring from the *Tirailleurs* with a modest pension, Abderrahman married and divorced one wife before seeking his present mate from a nomad group.

Abderrahman has a wealth of opinion concerning supernatural beliefs. His respect for modern medical techniques explains his contempt of traditional Arab practices, such as the use of charms. Insisting that a person's welfare depends upon his own character, he claims that few *talebs* are possessed of real supernatural power enabling them to help others. Although he is not afraid of the evil eye, he says that some people do have supernatural power and are naturally aggressive; they possess the evil eye as the natural result of damming up all this power and aggressiveness. As for *afreet,* "Solomon purified the world of them. Hitler and Stalin are human *afreet* and Stalin is the biggest *afreet* alive."

When questioned about *sahharin* (those who make love magic) Abderrahman admits he believes that such individuals can make love potions, which he considers harmful. The materials now used have been introduced by the French to weaken the people. These substances attack the stomach and lungs, whereas the ingredients used in the old days were harmless. Abderrahman first blames the French and then, inconsistently, attacks the *sahharin* themselves. "A *sahhara* takes a person's nail-clippings or hair and puts them in a potion which makes the victim sick. Fingernails are dirty. Even if you touch your eyes with dirty hands, you get eye diseases." He knows from old Arab books that the Arab drugs reinforced sexual powers, whereas the present ones just weaken a man. The authorities, however, close their eyes to this, as they do to the drug traffic. Jewish women have acted as intermediaries in the introduction of the new drugs, because they can speak Arabic. He reiterates that through these practices European control is continued. His first wife tried to use this kind of magic on him, debilitating him so that he was powerless to sleep with other women. It was then that he studied the subject. He learned of two old Arab practices. A woman will love a man a great deal if he massages his penis with honey before intercourse. Or, if a man washes his hands well and then gives a drink to a woman, it will make her love him. When questioned as to whether he follows these customs, Abderrahman says, "No. If a woman doesn't like me, I don't bother with her." Finally he took his first wife home to her parents, intending to teach her a lesson and then to take her back in three or four months. She took his marriage papers with her, as well as other papers in his name, so he divorced her.

His bitterness toward the French appears frequently. For instance, he blames them for the decline of Arab astrology. They have limited the study of this science, although they use it themselves, as witnessed by the observatories they have built. His hostility is again evident when he discusses tattooing. He is careful to hide a tattooed female head of Western design on his arm, saying that he detests tattooing, introduced by early Catholics in North Africa prior to the Arab invasion. As a matter of fact, many of the indigenous Berbers who did tattoo were Catholic, but the emphasis on the religion of the French is significant. Abderrahman says that the French are responsible for the present lack of respect for women. Since the French occupation, if women are molested in the streets, the authorities will do nothing. If a woman is picked up as a prostitute, the police just let her go. He maintains that the Arabs do not want to keep their women shut up in the house but are forced to do so in order to protect them. Actually, he has permitted his daughters to attend school, accompanied to and from class by their mother. When an older daughter, then sixteen, was returning from school one day with her mother, she was accosted by some men, one of whom threatened the women with a knife. Only the screaming of the women frightened the men away; the police did not even appear.

Abderrahman is distrustful of the purpose of the Rorschach testing as described, seeing the anthropologist's work as some sort of political inquiry. He believes the ink-blots are deliberately constructed drawings.

While in itself this suspicion is not diagnostic of paranoid pathology, it fits in with the nature of his record. He indicates, at the end, that he had a definite approach in mind in giving the responses; namely, to present the "real spirit of Arab mentality." In one sense he does this by presenting in extreme form certain types of thought found scattered with less intensity throughout many of the records. The responses of this anti-French soldier, if given in a psychiatric setting, could only be described as diagnostic of paranoid ideation, with grandiose overtones, in an extremely intelligent individual.

Looking at the record one notes throughout various forms of illogical and projective type thinking (Rapaport, 1945). For example: (1) Throughout the cards there is the use of grandiose, fabulized symbolism of world forces in conflict or great evils, threatening to overpower and destroy. The red and the black of the cards are used to represent various abstractions of such things as "greed" or "evil." (2) The affect attributed to the cards is overbalanced and extreme in nature. Attention is focused on the "feeling" in the cards. Form is not used much as a determinant except to start a chain of fabulized associative elaborations. (3) The language is "queer" and body parts are "vitalized" in an unusual way. For example, on Card IV, "It's a person—completely savage— *all that comes out of him* is savage. It's a devil." . . . "The arms *go out from the body but come back to it*. They are not free. The top part is a covering of some kind. Black legs come out below. The covering represents the normal, but the thing isn't normal. It is set on a pillar instead of on its legs—savage—bad." (4) Continual attention to coverings, invisibility, hiding, and guarded passages, such as the fortified Suez Canal on Card VII, are found mostly in individuals of an extremely suspicious, paranoid nature. (5) The fear of penetration, which appears in milder form in many of the other Arab records, takes on a more malignant tone here. The feeling is represented almost independent of concrete content. For example, on Card VI, "It is something which opens a breach in all the rest and remains superior to all the rest." "It splits open all that was in the previous cards. This black represents the arrow which made the breach and turned part of the black into white. The black is evil that has become somewhat white and conserved its strength. It is strong, because it is on top and has more arrows." (Here one can note the indirect sexual symbolism.) (6) Card VIII brings out an extreme form of illogical juxtaposition of elements technically described as a "fabulized combination" or as "confabulation." The language, again, is peculiar. *"Now you show me green flags* (indicating the deliberate purpose of the examiner). Above them is a headdress of green. The red is the liver. The red animals put their feet on the headdress, the flag, and the liver. The liver is just for them to put their feet on. The paw on the headdress is black. *You aren't doing this for a book."* (This implication that the anthropologist's work is political is a clear projection from his own percept to the intentions of the tester.) "The flag, headdress, and liver are all symbols of one people." On the actual percept the subject comments, "It looks like a lung," but he continues to use the word "liver." "Liver" is similar to our "heart" in symbolic content in the thinking of the Arabs. By deliberately symbolizing his response, the subject rationalizes and thereby shows a need to maintain a surface logic. Such capacity helps explain how he can continue to function without some breakdown that would manifest the nature of his paranoia in a more overtly non-adaptive manner.

The above is sufficient to indicate to the clinically experienced person the unequivocally paranoid-ideation of this record. Is it fair to consider this record paranoid in the context of Arab culture, especially since the behavioral material presents an individual who seems to have made an acceptable, responsible adjustment to French military service and who now has comparatively moderate economic security working as a watchman?

Considering the evidence available, this material may well be interpreted as one would interpret the Rorschach of an American as far as its dynamic meaning is concerned. What is not as easily determined from such a record (as is equally true for American records) is the nature of the positive ego forces which maintain this person in spite of paranoid structuring. The definition and diagnosis of paranoid pathology is difficult to define in psychiatric interviews with Americans in some instances. If the paranoid delusion coincides with enough of outer reality to make it plausible to others, the person can maintain himself very well without drawing undue attention to himself. It is only when the stresses of life exacerbate a situation that a latent paranoid structure reveals itself by the increasing implausibility of a persecutory system or a compensatory grandiosity.

There is nothing at present to indicate that Abderrahman is under any undue strain which would cause him to manifest such implausible ideation to the degree that he would become socially malfunctioning. Yet, if we examine the report of his divorce from his first wife for weakening his sexual power through magic, we find a story with definite paranoid elements. It is noteworthy that it is the weakening of his sexual ability that is projected to outside malevolent forces. His culture in this instance helps disguise the pathology of his story, because the belief system of the relatively uneducated Arabs supports such ideation. In his case he gives a somewhat naturalistic explanation in terms of "drugs." Likewise, his hatred of the French and Jews and his blaming them for many of the evils of his own society are not uncommon for the Arabs. We must, however, point out that structurally Abderrahman's ego is using mechanisms of projection whatever the license he receives from his culture.

Abderrahman's Rorschach (Abbreviated Summary)

Card I: (1) Two invisible men arguing (they are invisible because they are covered by these things. W).

Card II: (1) Communists separate themselves from all danger. They infiltrate throughout the world. (W).

Card III: (1) Two men holding the world. They are all red, black fellows— evil people. They are both cut in half (W).

Card IV: (1) A person—savage. It's a devil. The arms go out from the body but go back into it. The top is a covering of some sort (W).

Card V: (1) Something unseen which destroys all the greed of the previous cards. (In the center is a bird which is going through the other parts and encompassing it. W).

Card VI: (1) Something opens a breach in all the rest. (It splits open all of it. W).

Card VII: (1) A geographic thing with a passage very narrow and guarded, like the Suez or Panama Canal (WS).

Card VIII: (1) Green flags (D5).
(2) A headdress of green (D4).
(3) The liver (D2).
(4) Red animals, the paws in the black (D1). (He then combines these responses saying, "The flag, headdress, and liver are all symbols of one people.")

Card IX: (1) The continuation of the other (refers to Card VIII, continues his symbolization).
(2) Geographic design (W).

Card X: (1) A design—a crown—with it perhaps one gains control of the world.
(2) A big pillar in the crown.
(3) The red succeeds in becoming the greatest (confabulation of all parts to a concept of control). The red will be eaten by the green until empty.

Takao, A Japanese Villager with an Ulcer

The ready applicability of Rorschach interpretation of symbolic content to clinical cases cross-culturally was well demonstrated for me in my observations in a Japanese neuropsychiatric clinic. Rather than discussing a case taken from clinic files, however, it may be more dramatic to show the relevancy of the test cross-culturally by comparing the record of a villager with a known ulcer with recent clinical findings on American ulcer-prone and ulcer patients.

At 46, Takao is a leading figure in his village's political activities. He has been responsible for the introduction of dairying as a side occupation in his particular village. He has recently also served as village head. He sees himself consciously as a leader. Looking at the opinion scales, interviews, and Thematic Apperception and Problem Situation projective tests given him, one gains the impression that he is a man who is concerned with traditional Japanese values of family, household lineage, and community responsibility. The terminology used in some of his answers is suggestive of identification with Samurai traditions. We have found in studying village attitudes that his particular village indeed does trace its origins to a Samurai family.

Takao's appearance suggests a certain boyishness. He has regular, almost delicate features, although he comports himself in a somewhat assertive, direct fashion. There is a slight aura of physical weakness about him but no obvious signs of physical defect. An interview by one of the Japanese psychiatrists during intensive interviews in this village brought out the fact that a few years ago he had developed an ulcer of the stomach and has not felt well since. At present he is bothered with hepatitis and complains of attacks of fever, headaches, and stiff shoulders—a widespread Japanese complaint. He spends considerable time in bed.

Takao has completed a course of education in an agricultural middle school. As oldest child in the main lineage of his family, he assumed the succession of the household after his father's death. His aged mother continues to live with him in the family home. He was married at the age of 24 by means of a professional go-between. The marriage is a successful one by Japanese standards, although only one of Takao's seven children is a boy. Though exhibiting the tactfulness of the dutiful wife, Sachiko takes considerable initiative, not only in the family but in the farming activities as well. She organizes the daily chores and maintains the farm in spite of Takao's sporadic participation and frequent resort to bedrest. His 12-year old son is the favorite. A somewhat unusual closeness to an adolescent daughter was noted by the visiting members of the research team who reported that he was seen lying under the same *futon* (bedding) with her, a fairly uncommon occurrence in a Japanese household.

Takao's Rorschach

Card I: (1) Well, does this not seem to be a bat? (A bat sticks fast to something such as a wall and spreads out his wings. W). [Dcl.]
(2) It looks like a moth. (Because this is the same with a bat. And this here indicates him spreading out his wings. W). [N.]
Card II: (1) These look like two puppies side by side (These look like heads and they are facing each other. They lift up their forefeet like this. D1 + D1). [Dch.]
(2) Although I turned the card to this direction (upside down) these still look like two puppies. (These are the same. These two quarrel and bleed. D1 + D1). [HhDch.]
Card III: (1) What is this? Skeletons scattered about. (Skeletons are lying here scattered about. This is a head, shoulder, feet. Skeletons and stones too are scattered about the earth. D1). [AglBbAdeh.]

(2) (upside down) These look like somebody dancing in the dark at night (on the upside down they raise their hands like this and dance. These two persons are back to back. D1). [Prec.]

Card IV: (1) This looks like an animal. Here is his eye. This looks like a small seafish in the sea. (For a small seafish, this is too short. These are its eyes. Say a lobster or something like that. This is something that cannot be determined clearly. The animal is swimming forcibly in the water, raising his head. W). [N.]

Card V: (1) This looks like a butterfly (The butterfly raises his wings and is rubbing them together forcibly. W). [N.]

Card VI: (1) This looks like an emblem. Like the Order of the Golden Kite. (A kite stands up here; this looks like the Order of the Golden Kite [The Golden Kite is a military order bestowed by the Emperor for distinguished work].). [Daut.]

Card VII: (1) This looks like a horse or animal that bends backward. (This raises forefeet and bends backward. D1). [N.]

Card VIII: (1) The young ones of an animal face each other and climb up. (They stick fast to something and climb up. D1). [DchDclPst.]

Card IX: (1) I don't understand. These look like animals. These are eyes. They are back to back. (These look like eyes, two animals. Here are heads, and a back is inner side and a stomach is outer, I think so. D1). [N.]

Card X: (1) It seems to me that this looks like small animals in a sewer ditch swarming about. (I don't know; like bugs in a ditch. They are not clear; they are small. W). [Adis.]

Summary of Affect

(Total Responses: 13)

Hostility	4%	Dependency	32%
Hh., .5		Dcl., 1, .3;	
		Dch., 1, .5, .4; Daut., 1	
Anxiety	14%		
Agl., .4; Adeh., .3;		Positive Feeling	10%
Adis., 1		Prec., 1; Pst., .3	
Bodily Preoccupation	2%	Neutral, 5	38%
Bb., .3			
Total Unpleasant	20%	Total	80%

The most outstanding content feature of Takao's record is its dependency symbolism. Although this is a rather sparse record, the content provided is nevertheless highly consonant with the type of material obtained from American ulcer patients. Interestingly enough, the record also resembles that of individuals with a high pepsinogen level in the blood, a condition which has been demonstrated to be closely indicative of predisposition to ulcer (Weiner, *et al.*, 1957). Thaler, the psychologist in the interdisciplinary study just cited, used De Vos's scoring system for affective symbolism (see pp. 605–06) to show that it is possible to differentiate on a statistical basis high secretors of pepsinogen from low secretors on specific Rorschach content criteria. In a second study similar statistical differentiation was possible between actual ulcer cases and control groups with other psychosomatic bodily disturbances (Thaler, 1957).

There seems to be some relationship between physiological propensity, unresolved psychological conflict, and social pressures which contribute to the formation of an ulcer. In Takao's case the nature of the symbolism is in line with the formulation of Alexander (1934) and others (Kapp, *et al.*, 1947; Minsky and Desai, 1955; Streitfeld, 1957), who see as a common feature of ulcer patients a conflict related to the persistence of a strong infantile wish to be loved and cared for on the one hand, and, on the other hand, the repudiation of these wishes by the adult ego in terms of outer circumstances.

Table 3 demonstrates how Takao's Rorschach and Figure Drawing material coincides with ulcer-prone individuals on 11 of 15 criteria. To elucidate: The most outstanding feature of Takao's record is its dependency symbolism (see criteria 7). Takao gives 3 responses which show a childish immaturity in underlying self-perception. Responses in which the young of animals are specifically seen where most individuals do not so specify are scored childish dependent. Card II, right side up, is seen by him as "two puppies." Upside down it is again two puppies; however, this time they are seen as quarreling and bleeding. Card VIII is the "young ones of animals who face each other." In the inquiry they "stick fast to something and climb up." "Sticking fast" appears also on the bat percept Card I. Although the bat would normally be considered a normal response, the elaboration "sticking fast" is unusual and can be scored. Clinging, hanging, or leaning responses suggest a dependent clinging. Another form of dependent symbolism in Takao's record is found on Card VI, on which he perceived "The Order of the Golden Kite." This is a military order given by the Emperor for distinguished service. By definition any seals, emblems, crests, or even bearded patriarchs are related to an implied authoritarian personality structure with a need for a dependent relationship on higher authority. Such an individual may or may not himself in turn be assertive to those he perceives as subordinate. There is, however, an incomplete identification with the authoritarian role and a dependent quality remains. This sort of response is usually found in an individual who has an essentially masculine identification rather than a feminine one (see criteria 15, Table 3. Takao does not give any feminine figures in his protocol).

The overall percentage of 31% dependency content in Takao's record is extremely high in comparison with usual norms for dependency content and suggests the intensity of the unresolved dependent needs in

Takao's personality. In actual cases of ulcer, the dependency score often tends to be high in this manner. Unlike some individuals in the ulcer-prone group, Takao does not produce much in the way of anxious symbolism (see criteria 2, Table 3). The Japanese village group as a whole is extremely low in the production of indicators of free anxiety in the con-

TABLE 3

RORSCHACH (AND FIGURE DRAWING) CRITERIA DISTINGUISHING SUBJECTS WITH HIGH PEPSINOGEN SECRETION (ULCER-PRONE SUBJECTS) FROM THOSE WITH LOW CONCENTRATION IN COMPARISON WITH TAKAO'S RORSCHACH RECORD *

(De Vos Scoring)	Responses: Cut-off score	High Secretors N = 63	Low Secretors N = 57	Takao
Rorschach Content Criteria				
1. Per cent hostile responses	25%+	13	27	(4%) †
2. Openly symbolized anxiety (Athr. Adif. Adef)	3+	27	14	(2)
3. Sado-masochistic (Hsm)	present	11	20	no †
4. Anxious face details (Aobs)	present	1	8	no †
5. Fantastic forms (Afant)	present	1	10	no †
6. Over-all per cent unpleasant (H + A + Body Preoc.)	40%+	30	39	(19.5%) †
7. Dependent Responses (Daut + Dch)	present	37	21	(4) †
8. Oral symbolism (Hor. Dor. Por. Mor.)	31%+	35	19	no
9. Neutral content	35%+	33	18	(38%) †
Other Rorschach Criteria				
10. Color Form responses (CF)	present	31	17	(1) †
11. Texture (FT, TF, T)	present	33	18	no
12. Small details (Dd)	8%+	36	20	no
13. F + %	below 80%	32	43	(82%) †
14. Feminine figure on Card III	present	11	20	no †
Figure Drawing Criterion				
15. Boyish rather than adult male figure	2	24	8	spontaneous drawing of boy†

* Adapted from Table I, Weiner, Thaler, Reiser and Mirsky, "Etiology of Duodenal Ulcer," *Psychosomatic Medicine,* XIX, 1, p. 6.

† Indicates agreement between Takao and ulcer-prone subjects.

Note: Difference between high and low secretors at 5% or above level of significance.

tent. It is noteworthy, however, that the single specific category that best differentiates individuals with ulcers, namely, the depressive anxiety (Thaler, 1957), is represented in Takao's response to Card III. He sees there, "Skeletons scattered about," rather than perceiving the usual humans popularly perceived on Card III. This proneness for depressive moods in ulcer patients is related to frustration in their needs to receive. The scattered skeletons further imply that Takao is concerned with body integrity. On the TAT test given him [8] this was symbolized by seeing the violin on Card I as broken—the only incidence of such a response in his village. In the ulcer-prone individuals the overall percentage of hostile symbolism tends to be lower than for other groups (see criteria 1). In Takao's record there is only one hostile response, that of the quarreling dogs. Direct hostile responses (HH) were found in only 2 of the 36 men tested in his village, so that seeing a quarreling dog suggests that Takao is perhaps somewhat more prone to interpret situations as being hostile in nature or to react aggressively than is true for the villagers generally. Yet, this level is very low. Behavioral evidence supports this picture. This sort of active stance is not necessarily lacking in certain ulcer-prone individuals.

Labile activity is characteristic of ulcer-prone cases. Takao's one color response was a CF response in reaction to "blood" on Card II. Even though limited to one color response, his Rorschach record is consonant with the ulcer-prone group's general tendency toward less controlled color responses (see criteria 10). Lack of body preoccupation material is consonant again with the general findings that ulcer patients, although suffering from physical disability, are not particularly prone to give body content in their responses. Nor does Takao produce content which could be scored oral in nature. This is contrary to some expectations that one would invariably find specific oral content in ulcer records; statistically one cannot separate an ulcer group from others by such criteria (Thaler, 1957).

In summary, the record of the only known individual with an ulcer in a projective survey of Japanese villagers conforms remarkably to findings of research with content symbolism in American clinical groups. In this respect the record offers cogent support for the view that the Rorschach test functions effectively in cross-cultural diagnosis of unresolved personality problems defined in general psychoanalytic terms.

However, the nature of Takao's record is such that one would not automatically assume likelihood of an ulcer. This would be asking for too great an incisiveness on the part of the Rorschach in survey work. Nevertheless, it is interesting to note that the material is directly consonant with the expectations in American ulcer patients, once the fact of the ulcer is known. The point to be made is that the underlying use of symbolism in the Rorschach of this Japanese man appears similar to that of Americans in spite of significant cultural differences.

The Heriots, A Slavey Indian Family

Symbolic content material analyzed cross-culturally is not limited by age, any more than it is in the United States where the test is widely used in child guidance clinics. The following illustrations are summarized from a collaborative study of MacNeish, De Vos, and Carterette,[9] of projective material obtained from a band of Northern Athabascan of the MacKenzie river basin in Canada. The cases considered are those of a Slavey Indian hunter, his wife, daughter, age 13, and son, age 11. The record of the son illustrates the most severe psychological disturbance found in any of the children of the small Indian settlement. The community consists of 56 members, 22 adults over 20. The anthropologists, MacNeish and Carterette, lived with this community over 14 months. During this time they had intimate contact with the children of the community, one of the anthropologists serving as teacher. There is ample observational documentation to substantiate and confirm the interpretations made of the projective material. The particular family we are considering is of special interest because it represents a pattern of maladjustment that is not infrequently found in children referred to American child guidance clinics.

The father, Daniel Heriot, is an extremely passive, ineffectual individual who, without protest, lets his wife assume dominance in their relationship. His extremely placating behavior serves as a device to get others to do things for him. When describing his wife, he says amiably, "People say Liza is just like a man." In fact, he does not like his role of bush hunter and at times will talk on about his envy of the white world where people have, as he puts it, "warehouses full of grub," and don't have to work as the Indians do. In marked contrast to the rather limp, slouching walk of her husband, Liza Heriot displays her vitality in every step. In the presence of strangers Liza acts out the expected Slavey pattern of shy, retiring, soft-voiced womanhood, but in familiar situations her natural exuberance and extroversion emerge. She bellows commands and admonitions to her children, never physically enforcing them, however. She is the only married woman to join the boys of the community in a soccer game. She frequently employs vocal and facial expressions of mock surprise, anger, and indignation, in contrast to the general underplay of expression noted for most Slaveys. She enjoys taking over some of the masculine activities, as well as functioning in her wifely role. Like most Slavey mothers she derives great enjoyment from her youngest baby and will speak with pride and pleasure of the three- and five-year-old boys. But, as is common of most Slavey mothers, she does little tending of them. Her eldest daughter, Beatrice, is assigned this task. Beatrice on occasion cruelly teases her two smallest brothers. In such a case, when the child is crying for its mother, Liza will gaze calmly into space and continue to ignore the scene. Beatrice and Robert, age 13 and 11 respectively, are the two oldest Heriot children. Beatrice, like her mother, is energetic, gregarious, excitable. Although she is quick-tempered, she is also quick to regain her good spirits and to discount failure. In most activities it is she who takes the initiative, always with a great display of confidence. In contrast, Robert is quiet, hyper-sensitive, listless, and given to sulking. He is considered spoiled and his peers described him as a "lazy cry-baby." In a family of five children and an aged, tubercular grandfather, a boy of Robert's age would normally be meeting his share of chores. He flatly refuses to comply with his mother's request for assistance, however. If his mother tries to cajole him into obedience, he either suggests that his sister do it or yells his refusal, going into a sulk. While it is not uncommon for the children of the community to complain of headaches, Robert takes to his bed more readily than anyone else observed. Robert is entering that phase of his life at which by Slavey standards he begins his training for manhood as a hunter. When compared with other men of the village, Robert's father, Daniel, is an unimpressive figure with which to identify. It is probable that Robert's problems are compounded by his elder sister's energetic and dominant personality, which has probably formed a harassment for him from early childhood. Robert apparently wishes to excel at such glamorous or rewarding activities as setting rabbit snares, chopping wood, ice skating, and running on snowshoes. However, he is not capable of withstanding the initial failures concomitant to any new activity. As a result, he quickly becomes hyper-sensitive and moody. The Rorschach protocols of this family are summarized as follows:

The Rorschach record of Daniel Heriot in its affective symbolism reveals a strong dependent quality. Four of his thirteen responses are direct symbols of dependency. Two of them show a concern with authority symbols—Card I an air force officer's cap, and Card VIII the emblem of the Hudson Bay Company with a crown on top. In two others there is a childish tone to the response, Card II, "two bears playing," and Card VII, "two puppies sitting." A second feature of his record is the attitudinal tone of general passivity (passive movement throughout, i.e., holding, sitting). One would infer that his relationship to people does not seem to be particularly strained but rather somewhat immature and playful. The percentage of positive affect in the record is quite high (26 per cent). It is also interesting to note the complete lack of any evidence of hostility symbolism in the Rorschach. Total unpleasant affect is quite low (8 per cent). The Rorschach picture of Liza, the wife, shows some direct contrast to that of her husband. The masculine component of her identification comes out very strongly. The record is replete with masculine striving or aggressive percepts. To cite a few: Card II, two men pulling on a moose; Card V, two fighting buffalo rushing at each other; Card VII, an army soldier's helmet in silhouette; Card IX, a man skinning something. Liza's record shows both hostile aggressive components and cooperative components in the relationships of people with one another. General overall ability is exceedingly high. In her color responses she sees fire, but she is also capable of seeing flowers, giving some pleasant tone to the record. There is also symbolically evidence of underlying orality (Card II, two crows eating; Card X, caterpillars eating). While she shows above-average intelligence, her world is limited to the hunting culture in which she lives, but it is with a masculine rather than a feminine identification that she approaches it. One would infer from the Rorschach, as one sees from the behavioral material, a rather firm, dominating type of ego with some hostile undertones expressed indirectly.

Turning to the children, Beatrice and Robert, we see some of the repercussions of the parental figures. The fourteen responses of Beatrice's Rorschach point to a somewhat more limited intelligence than that of her mother, but one in which again the movement is generally active and the humans are men. On Card III the men are making brew, a standard alcoholic drink, which one may infer as some indication of feelings of cooperativeness between individuals. Responses involving "making brew," "bones with meat," and "men's heads with their tongues sticking out" again give an oral tone to the records, which becomes its outstanding feature. One sees in Beatrice essentially a rather direct identification with the mother as far as personality mechanisms are concerned.

Robert's Rorschach on the other hand is the most disturbed of the entire community. Of his 25 responses, 15 show anatomical preoccupations. These responses include mostly lungs and kidneys. Lungs attest perhaps to hypochondrial concern with tuberculosis, which is a rampant disease among Indians. The kidneys are very often symbolic substitutes for testes. The most characteristic affective symbolism of the record appears in sado-masochistic responses such as "the heart that is cut out" and "the place that they took off the kidneys" or "a body split open." The first response of the entire record, "a nipple," indicates very deep underlying problems. There are, in addition, two responses concerned with food. The two men on Card II, the only human movement response, are two "fat" men. Card III is, in contrast, a "skinny" man. The overall picture of Robert is a boy very sorely beset by fear of castration in classic Freudian terms, more overtly appearing as hypochondriasis but also suggesting strong oral needs underneath.[10] Unlike his sister, who seems to have a ready identification with her mother, Robert, according to both the behavioral and projective evidence, is an evasive, disturbed child who is prey to crippling fears, hypochondrial concerns, and a strong sense of personal inadequacy.

Hypothetically, just as in cases coming to clinics in the United States, a dependent, ineffectual, somewhat devious father, dominated by his wife, offers no solution for a male child through ordinary processes of identification. In spite of being indulged and seeming free of demands or expectations, Robert, growing up in the shadow of his more aggressive mother and sister, seems to have developed childhood disturbances that, within the context of Slavey culture, are strikingly similar to those found in the United States. The Rorschach and TAT material (not cited here) are directly open to modes of analysis used in the American clinical setting. The Rorschach picture of a family configuration, very briefly presented here only in respect to the symbolized expression of affect, sheds light on the interaction of the four members of this family much as would be true for similar material obtained for use within the American culture.

CONCLUSIONS

Man's physiological heredity and his cultural training together determine the specific forms taken by his symbolic communication. Regardless of group, man generally shares the physiological capacity for speech and the consciousness necessary to make use of symbols. The unconscious expression of affective states, whether by gesture, word, or the perception of ambiguous stimuli is less subject to cultural differentiation than the conscious modes of communication, and hence tends toward greater universality.

Similar basic affective states color man's perception of his world, no matter what group he belongs to. He invariably associates these states to certain objects in his experience. The manner in which this association occurs is sufficiently valid and universal regardless of culture to allow the careful observer to use spontaneous percepts given to ambiguous stimuli, dreams and other free associations, even the manner in which supernatural forces are personalized, to come to some cogent conclusions concerning personality configurations prevailing within a specific group.

Differences between groups or cultures occur in the personality mechanisms which are encouraged in the control of affect as well as in the manner in which affects tend to be stimulated or aroused. But no matter how idiosyncratic or uniform the formative experiences seem to be, it is probably impossible to find a cultural group that lacks among its members types of ego integration representing most possible human variations.

Fear, hostility, dependency, positive feelings and the mental mechanisms described by Freud as the basic mechanisms of the human mind in handling the relationship of feeling and cognition are probably represented in the production of Rorschach percepts in surprisingly similar terms from culture to culture.

Regardless of the individualistic nuances possible—big aggressive animals, small weak creatures, beautiful objects may differ in name and variety from region to region—the underlying affect that they represent symbolically has something about it that is broadly human and allows us some footing on a bridge of understanding between cultures.

NOTES

1. A symbol is defined by Webster as "a sign by which one knows or infers a thing. It is that which suggests something else by reason of relationship, association, or convention. It can be a visible sign of something invisible, such as an idea, a quality." In its strict and narrow use in psychoanalysis a symbol is an object, act, or thought representing a repressed desire of which the individual is unconscious.

A representation (a term used by Durkheim, 1933) is defined as "an act or instance of representing, through a likeness, picture, model, image or other reproduction. It can be a dramatic reproduction or performance."

2. The presence of primary affective associations differs also with the respective ego strengths of individuals. It is this differential factor which makes projective tests so useful in clinical psychopathology.

3. The Algerian materials considered in the analysis are selections from a more complete Rorschach analysis presented in a book by Horace Miner and George De Vos, *Oasis and Casbah, Algerian Personality and Culture in Change* (1960).

4. This material is taken from a yet unpublished interdisciplinary research study conducted in three Japanese villages and two cities. The author participated in this study as a Fulbright scholar in 1953–55. Rorschach aspects of the study were done collaboratively with Eiji Murakami, psychologist of Nagoya National University.

5. For a full description of quantitative measures developed by Seymour Fisher see Fisher (1950).

6. Two recent studies with institutionalized Americans in which there was a comparison of content between hostile acting-out and non-acting-out individuals confirms such an interpretation. In Paul Kane's study (1957) with acting-out versus non-acting-out prisoners, he found that those who gave the most hostile content in their records tended to be the prisoners who were seen as hostile by others, although they themselves were not necessarily aware of their own hostility. Some of these men assumed that their behavior was a reaction to a hostile-appearing environment; projection of hostility was a usual defensive maneuver. Irving Wolf (1957) also found in neuropsychiatric cases—including paranoid and other schizophrenic persons as well as individuals classified as psychoneurotic and having character disorders—a significant relationship between acting-out behavior and hostile

content. An attempt directly to relate anatomical material to non-acting-out was not statistically significant. Nevertheless, in examining the relation of hostile and anatomical material in the same records, Wolf concluded that whereas hostility content seemed to be directly related to manifest expression of hostility, "anatomy responses could be viewed as related to a channelizing or controlling activity at work for those individuals concerned with hostile impulses and tensions."

7. The two Arab cases quoted are from Chapter 9 of Miner and De Vos, (1960). The book contains a number of individual analyses of Arabs done by psychological and ethnological methods.

8. The Marui-De Vos Japanese Modification of the Standard Murray Thematic Apperception Test was used. The only modification occurring on Card I was changing the features of the boy to a more Oriental cast.

9. A paper on the results of analysis of three families including sixteen members by means of the TAT and Rorschach as well as ethnographic notes is in preparation for publication under the title, "Variations in Personality and Ego-Identification Within a Slavey Indian Community."

10. Since this chapter is focused on symbolic analysis, no analysis is made of these records on a formal basis. Other personality variables could be demonstrated. For example, the appearance of six space responses in the record of Robert indicates obvious oppositional traits in his character.

BIBLIOGRAPHY

Abel, T. and Hsu, F. 1949. "Some Aspects of Chinese Personality As Revealed by the Rorschach Test," *Rorschach Research Exchange,* and *Journal of Projective Techniques,* 13:285–301.

Alexander, F. 1934. "The Influence of Psychologic Factors Upon Gastro-Intestinal Disturbances: General Principles, Objectives, and Preliminary Results," *Psychoanalytic Quarterly,* 3, 4, pp. 501–39.

Alexander, L., and Ax, A. 1950. "Rorschach Studies in Combat Flying Personnel," *Relation of Psychological Tests to Psychiatry.* New York: Grune and Stratton.

De Vos, G. 1952. "A Quantitative Approach to Affective Symbolism in Rorschach Responses," *Journal of Projective Techniques,* 16:133–50.

———. 1954. "A Comparison of the Personality Differences in Two Generations of Japanese by Means of the Rorschach Test," *Nagoya Journal of Medical Science,* 17:153–265.

———. 1955. "A Quantitative Rorschach Assessment of Maladjustment and Rigidity in Acculturating Japanese Americans," *Genetic Psychology Monographs,* 52:51–87.

Durkheim, E. 1915. *The Elementary Forms of Religious Life.* Glencoe: The Free Press.

———. 1933. *The Rules of Sociological Method.* New York: Macmillan.

Fisher, S. 1950. "Patterns of Personality Rigidity and Some of Their Determinants," *Psychological Monographs,* 64, 1, whole issue.

Frazer, J. 1894. *The Golden Bough*. New York: Macmillan Co., Vols. I and II.

Goldfarb, W. 1951. Chapter 10 in A. Kardiner and L. Ovesey, *The Mark of Oppression*. New York: W. W. Norton.

Kane, P. 1957. "Availability of Hostile Fantasy Related to Overt Behavior," *Illinois Medical Journal*, III, 3, pp. 131–33.

Kapp, F., Rosenbaum, M. and Romano, J. 1947. "Psychological Factors in Men with Peptic Ulcers," *American Journal of Psychiatry*, 103:700–04.

Miner, H., and De Vos, G. 1960. *Oasis and Casbah*. Ann Arbor: University of Michigan Press.

Minsky, L. 1955. "Aspects of Personality in Peptic Ulcer Patients," *British Journal of Medical Psychiatry*, 28:113–34.

Piaget, Jean. 1930. *The Child's Concept of Causality*. London: Kegan Paul.

Radcliffe-Brown, A. 1922. *The Andaman Islanders*. Cambridge: Cambridge-University Press.

Rapaport, D. 1945. *Diagnostic Psychological Testing*. Volume II. Chicago: The Year Book Publishers.

Streitfeld, H. 1954. "Specificity of Peptic Ulcer to Intense Oral Conflict," *Psychosomatic Medicine*, 16:315–26.

Thaler, M., Weiner, H. and Reiser, M. 1957. "Exploration of the Doctor-Patient Relationship Through Projective Techniques," *Psychosomatic Medicine*, 19, 3, pp. 228–39.

Weiner, H., Thaler, M., Reiser, M., and Mirsky, I. 1957. "Etiology of Duodenal Ulcer," *Psychosomatic Medicine*, 19, 1, pp. 1–10.

Wolf, I. 1957. "Hostile Acting Out and Rorschach Test Content," *Journal of Projective Techniques*, 21, 4, pp. 414–19.

About the Chapter

In this case study a series of events in a young man's life, that are concerned particularly with his marriage, are placed in socio-cultural perspective. Relevant personality factors also are analyzed. The authors utilize life history and projective test materials including the sentence completion test and the T.A.T. The case indicates vividly the kind of materials that the culture and personality worker must conceptualize. Drs. Hanks and Phillips use these materials to illustrate some personality trends that are found in many Thai individuals and suggest the way these trends are related to important currents of Thai life.

About the Authors

LUCIEN M. HANKS, JR. teaches both anthropology and psychology at Bennington College. He received his Ph.D. in psychology at Columbia University and then he and his anthropologist bride, Jane Richardson, studied the Blackfeet Indians of Alberta. World War II diverted him to Burma before he and his wife could complete their book on the Blackfeet, *Tribe Under Trust.* Subsequently he joined the Cornell University Thailand Project and became Fulbright Scholar for a year during which some of the following material was gathered.

HERBERT P. PHILLIPS is Assistant Professor in the Department of Sociology and Anthropology at Michigan State University and is continuing his research on Thai peasant personality. As a graduate student at Cornell he spent twenty-two months in Thailand under a Ford Foundation Fellowship. He has contributed articles to professional journals on anthropological method and political anthropology and has served as research assistant at the Harvard Russian Research Center and the Cornell Southeast Asia Program.

Acknowledgments

The data presented in this chapter are portions of a more extensive study of Thai personality, values and world view undertaken during 1956–57. The background information derives from general study of a Thai farming community extending over a decade, sponsored by Cornell University. The writers are indebted to their Thai co-workers, Tatsani Hongladaromp, Tidtaya Suwanacataa, Khamsing Srinawk, and Withun Layraman; to the American Philosophical Society, Ford Foundation, Social Science Research Council, U.S. Educational Foundation and Wenner-Gren Foundation for Anthropological Research for financial support; and to Drs. William W. Lambert, Morris E. Opler, Lauriston Sharp, and Robert B. Textor for their comments. Though the study was made with the support of these people and corporate groups, the conclusions, opinions, and other statements made here are those of the authors and do not necessarily represent those of their supporters.

24

A Young Thai from the Countryside

LUCIEN M. HANKS, JR.

Bennington College

and

HERBERT P. PHILLIPS

Michigan State University

We shall tell of a certain young man from a farming community who moves to Bangkok, marries the niece of his employer, and subsequently chooses to return to the countryside. We selected this sequence of events from the life history of this young man, as told to one of the writers, because it reveals a documentable continuity between social and psychic activity. To demonstrate this continuity the material will be considered under three headings: the geographic, the socio-cultural, and the personal-social settings.

Our story concerns some of the main social and psychological currents of a Thai's life. Perhaps more than any other single event, marriage arouses problems of dependency, loyalty, social status and responsibility which lie deep in the social system. Three years after his marriage these problems appear not only in the young man's account of his life, where

we learn of the events leading to his marriage and the subsequent developments, but also in his attitudes and reactions to these events as
reflected in projective tests.

The informant, Dang, born in 1931 and 26 years old at the time of relating his life history, served as boatman for the research group intermittently over more than six years. He was thus familiar with the general
interests of the research project, knew both writers of this paper, and
was long accustomed to supplying bits of information as he rowed researchers through the canals from one house to another. Dang thus
readily consented to tell his life history.

Outwardly, Dang is the very model of a proper, young Thai villager.
He is personable, helpful, and has a keen sense of social status. The
latter is important because it means that Dang knows how to deal with
people in the approved manner. With inferiors (in his case, simply those
younger than himself), Dang is kind and benevolent; with superiors, he
is polite and unassertive. With superiors he usually restricts himself to an
interesting comment here and there, although often he remains silent.
Unlike some of his compatriots, Dang's social relations run smoothly and
rarely display any uneasiness. He also has a reputation for doing people
favors, be it simply running an errand, or something as time-consuming
as assembling radios for friends free of charge. Most important, perhaps, he appears to be a non-aggressive person. It is a rare occasion when
Dang has a bad word to say about anybody. Like all villagers, he loves to
gossip but he is not critical or backbiting. Rather than say that he dislikes
certain individuals, he calls them "strange." To all outward appear-
ances, therefore, Dang is a pleasant, placid, and in Thai terms, rather
attractive young man. One respected villager said he wished that more
Thai people would behave like Dang.

In all but a few respects, the informant's life history is not untypical of
other villagers of his same age, sex, and economic position. Dang spent
more time in the city than is customary, and his indifference to his future
wife was perhaps more marked than is usually the case. But otherwise,
his major social experiences are quite similar to those of other young
married Thai men.

Altogether, we had nine formal interviews with the informant, totaling
approximately twenty-eight hours. In addition, two hours were spent, at
different times, administering a Sentence Completion Test and a modified Thematic Apperception Test. The TAT was made up of eleven of
the original Murray-Morgan cards with the facial features, clothes, fur-
niture, flora and fauna redrawn to fit Thai conditions. The social situations and artistic effects in the pictures, however, were the same. Both
the TAT and SCT were given to a sample of the village population.
Some of the village test results will be compared with Dang's.

The following is an excerpt from the first interview:

At that time my father's younger brother wanted me to work in Kingphed making cutlery. He was the supervisor at the job. So at the end, I decided to work at Kingphed. (The informant laughs and continues:) Do you want me to tell you about my love affair? (Interviewer replies affirmatively.) The first time I loved a girl was when I was 19 years old. I liked this girl very much; I loved her very much. We got in touch with each other by letter. We didn't have many opportunities to talk with each other because her parents didn't like me. (How do you know they didn't like you?) Every time I went to speak with her, her parents came to sit with us too. And their faces sometimes showed that they were angry and displeased with me, that they didn't like me. (What made you fall in love with her?) Before I fell in love with her, I saw her face and met her every day. And then I wrote her a letter. And then she answered my letter . . . And then I went to work in Bangkok for more than a year. My uncle (father's younger brother) wanted me to marry another girl. She was the niece of my uncle's wife. I didn't listen to their wishes that I marry that girl. He said: when you get married, I'll give you a house. The girl he wanted me to marry is a poor girl but an upstanding person. I pitied her. She used to wash and iron clothes. Then six months later I decided to marry her because I would have a house and an occupation. I didn't love her, but I pitied her. My uncle spent his own money for all the things for the wedding. And after that there was a controversy between my uncle and the person who bought the cutlery. At my uncle's place there was less work; we didn't make as many knives as usual. So I returned to Bang Suaj (a pseudonym) to live with my father. I returned to work in the fields and help my father harvest. The house that my uncle promised me was not given me. Altogether I lived with my uncle for three years.

GEOGRAPHIC SETTING

Three names of localities occur in the narrative. *Bangkok,* the capital city with a population of one million people, holds not only government buildings, a variety of market centers, a few large factories, but a multitude of small household industries manned chiefly by Chinese artisans. *Kingphed* is one of the neighborhoods within the larger city where some of the household industries are located. *Bang Suaj,* the third locality, is a community lying about one and one-half hours by bus from Bangkok on the central plains, where Thailand's bountiful rice crop grows. It is not a compact village, since farmers live in or near the rice land they work, but the Buddhist temple, like a country church in America, provides a center for the nearby people.

Most Bang Suaj residents look enviously, though often with a tinge of rustic apprehension, at the capital city. Every year a few people move from Bang Suaj to Bangkok in search of permanent work, and brief visits by the country people to the city have become an accepted feature of life. Dang expressed fairly typical feelings in the following excerpt from an interview:

I expected that Bangkok would be lots of fun. There is electricity; wherever you go there are cars; it's easy and convenient when you want a good time; there is lots of amusement. I would be able to see things and places I'd never seen before.

Bangkok residents, on the other hand, look down on country folk, and few if any have ever heard of Bang Suaj.

SOCIO-CULTURAL SETTING

Economy

Like 90 per cent of the Bang Suaj household .heads in Bang Suaj, Dang's father operates a farm. Most of these families rent the land they work, though 45 per cent own a portion of the land. While the father began his occupation as a renter, he was able to save enough to buy five acres, an area that is about half the average holding of local residents. His income, however, runs slightly higher than average, for with his maturing children he has been able to rent additional land to work. Some extra income comes from a minor and part-time government office and for acting as overseer of the land of an absentee owner. In over-all wealth he stands slightly above the mean, between the laborer who lacks even the buffaloes and plow to farm and the owner-operator with complete equipment and ten or even fifty acres of land for his use.

We cannot fix the position of Dang's uncle as precisely. Rather than owning the cutlery factory, the uncle is the manager on the premises for some other person who provides the land for the factory, the house, and a portion of the equipment in return for an annual sum. As employer of five or more people in manufacture, he is neither as wealthy as many a manufacturer of jewelry nor as poor as a rough carpenter. He probably stands about average among artisans.

By and large, in countries like Thailand where industrialization is small, demand is great. There is little difficulty in disposing of either rice or cutlery. Buyers ordinarily absorb the entire output of farm or factory minus what the producer retains for his own use. When the buyer no longer took the uncle's wares, the need to produce other articles reflects the probability that the uncle had no alternative liaison to the market. The problem lay in the organization of avenues to the market rather than any substantial reduction in demand.

The major concern in managing either farm or household industry is labor. Production and hence the earnings are both limited by the available labor. On the farm even a renter prospers when his children can provide additional hands for working more land and producing a larger crop. A farmer with much land who can cultivate and reap a crop with his own labor supply earns a better return than a farmer who merely rents the land. But hired workers are expensive in the countryside where cash is scarce; even in Bangkok wage workers are accepted only when necessity demands.

The head of any enterprise prefers a kind of informal "adoption" of the employee. In return for his services the worker receives food, shelter, clothing, and spending money. As this rather intimate employer-employee relationship implies, a liaison through some kinsman or friend sets the condition of employment. Yet once established, it insures stability of labor to the employer and a relatively secure livelihood to the worker. In good seasons the entire group prospers, earns better food, better clothing and even greater leisure, if they choose to turn some of the less desirable work over to a hired worker. In poor times, with the hired workers dismissed, the family members must bend their own backs, work longer hours and enjoy fewer benefits.

In such terms we can understand Dang's uncle's interest in having a young man work with him. The uncle had only one child, a boy who had not even reached school age. Factory production depended on four or five hands; though it cost the uncle more, he was insuring permanent labor with dedication to his interest by having a nephew work for him. Dang described the work in one of the interviews:

> At first when I went to work I was an inexperienced helper. Later I learned to make careful designs and decorations, and I was in charge of the tools, and after that took charge of all the work.
>
> My aunt gave me more money than she gave the others; she gave me 300 baht (approximately $15) a month; all other expenses she paid for. I wanted that job a lot.

We see that Dang was speedily taught the business in order to bring him quickly into a supervisory position and lighten his job. The uncle was doing all he could to lure Dang and hold him.

Family and Social Organization

As one might anticipate from the foregoing considerations, social clusters vary in size largely according to the resources that their members can command. In the country a conjugal family may live in isolation without land or alternative capital. Lacking even plow and buffalo, their children have little economic value and must fend for themselves as quickly as possible. If such a family has relatives of even minor wealth, the children may be absorbed as laborers in the household of better standing, but the isolated family itself must move where wage work draws it and can establish few useful connections. On the other hand, a family with greater resources can join with other kinsmen to improve its standard of living considerably. Though each conjugal unit prefers to occupy its own house, a cluster of households may form to make life easier by tending the fields together, building houses, visiting, and joining to meet the expenses of family celebrations. These clusters, however, are loose and informal rather than binding or strictly defined. They function in the context of the nuclear family, the basic social unit of Thai society.

Dang's father is a member of a cluster of cooperating families with modest resources, yet even the poorest of these households has equipment to work the land it rents. Dang's father with land of his own and nine children, four or five of whom can help in the fields, stands as leader in the cluster, for he is the wealthiest and personally the most sociable in the cluster. Dang's uncle in Bangkok, too, appears to be part of a larger cooperating unit than his own household. He manages the factory for an owner and could scarcely have acquired this position without some kin relationship to the owner or a former worker.

Lest this give a picture of solid kin groups working together and excluding wherever possible non-kinsman, two important qualifications must be mentioned. First, a cluster always presumes status unequals, such as a father giving to his children or an older brother giving to a younger. Second, the arrangement requires continuous validation to furnish permanence. The superior who fails to heed the needs of his inferiors loses them to another group. Sentiment without substance can endure only briefly.

From this it follows that group coherence depends on status inequality. It is difficult for an equal to give anything of value to an equal or to command his "respect." Indeed, he stands as a potential competitor for favors. Group solidarity requires eliminating these points of friction and framing unambiguously the relative rank of each. Within a family, age furnishes the usual rule, even to the point of calling the first-born twin the older though the age difference be reckoned in minutes.

It should be noted, of course, that each family member has both superior and inferior positions. Dang is subordinate to his father but superior to his younger siblings. Even the last born shares these dual roles: he is subordinate to his older brothers and sisters but rules it over the family buffalo.

Group coherence heavily favors kinsmen, for though reciprocation of services with gifts does occur among unrelated people, kinsmen grant greater latitude in awaiting return favors. A wealthy young man can build a following of chance acquaintances, though let there be a single season when his income decreases then his faithful friends of many an evening's sociable drinking vanish. A parent's love expressed in favors need not be reciprocated until a child reaches working age, and an older sibling can count on his younger brother to stand by him through several lean years before turning elsewhere. But counting long on sentiment is hazardous; a wealthy old lady, fearing neglect in her old age, refused to divide her land, saying: "If I give them the land now, they will not care for me. I shall hold it until my death."

Dang, as an unmarried young man of an age to look after himself, was held at his father's home by being given the returns of three acres of rice land to spend as he wished. In return he worked his father's fields. As oldest he was favored more than his younger brothers who received only pocket money besides their clothing and keep. Dang described his father's attitude when the proposal came to move to Bangkok:

> My father did not want me to go to Bangkok. He wanted me to build a house, raise chickens, and expand the project into a good business. And my father wanted me to help him whenever I had spare time. . . . He wanted me to help out my younger brothers and sisters by giving them advice and helping them in farming.

But Dang was a free agent, and ties of sentiment could scarcely hold him before the lure of the city. Moreover, Dang's father himself would have been embarrassed to deny a request by his own younger brother who had no grown children to help him in the factory. So Dang could easily rationalize some benefits even to his father in the move:

> I have lots of younger brothers and sisters. My father wanted me to have a job like the one in the cutlery factory so that I could have a different occupation than being a farmer. Then I could lead some of the younger ones into work other than farming because some of them do not want to work in the fields. And in factory work I could get more money more quickly than if I worked in the fields.

By "giving them advice" and "leading some of the younger ones . . . ," Dang foresaw himself becoming leader of his siblings. But he avoided thoughts of rivaling his father because he would only draw away those of his siblings who did not want to work in the fields. Most would have preferred to live in the city.

Courtship and Marriage

Ideally marriage establishes a working team which holds together through adversity. Of course, young men, meeting girls on visits to neighbors, in work parties, or at celebrations in the Buddhist temple, clearly distinguish between the sex partner of a few minutes and their possible life-long mate. To the latter they express devotion by recurring visits or by love notes. At 19 Dang had a job that took him frequently near the house of his first love. He quickly demonstrated his serious intention by writing the following letter:

> Excuse me, my dear Miss Yupah:
> I hope you will not be angry or tear up this letter inconsiderately without first reading it. Miss Yupah, I really love you, so I am writing this letter to you. Some days, when I haven't been able to see your face, I have felt very

unhappy and depressed. Excuse me, my dear Miss Yupah, do you love me or not? If you love me, would you please write me a letter so that I will know that you love me too. If you do not love me, it is not necessary *at all* for you to write a letter to me. I hope that you will meet only with happiness and be safe from harm and have nice dreams every night.

I love you and miss you

Two days later, Dang received her answer: "If you love me truly, then I want to ask you that we should get to know each other better . . . and I hope that you have nice dreams, and dream of me." Commenting on her response, Dang told us: "She couldn't tell me she loved me, because she was a girl, and girls can't admit their love to a man. But she told me she understood my feelings, and that was enough."

Despite his ardor, Dang's suit was strongly discouraged by the parents of the girl. When asked why her parents objected to him, Dang replied angrily: ". . . it was because (they thought) I was nothing but a damn thing that worked in the fields!" This particular form of rejection was quite painful to Dang. To this day, he suffers a deep sense of inadequacy over his social and economic status.

Dang might have eloped with this girl despite parental opposition. They could have fled to the house of an accomplice. Some days later he could have approached the parents through a go-between to arrange marriage payments which he would offer on bended knees. People say in general that elopement is for the poor or headstrong, but we have no evidence that Dang ever considered this course.

Marriage arranged by the parents requires the consent of the future partners. The older generation values marriage for its contribution to the home labor force or the optimal placement of a child. Negotiations deal primarily with the contribution of each family to the newly formed household. To be sure, traditional rules of matrilocal residence may be applied where the bride's family gives the land, and the groom builds the new house. But few farmers or poor tradesmen in the city can afford to build a house and usually settle for a specified sum of cash or gold. Moreover, the rules apply easily only within a social cluster where few labor shifts are involved. All know that the poorer family bargains at a disadvantage, so that each rejected offer from the other family complicates negotiations with its implication of unworthiness. The parents of a poor girl are likely to have to forego her labor for the benefits of providing well for her, while the parents of a poor boy can bargain with little beyond his reputation for industry.

Dang was neither poor nor headstrong enough to elope with his first love, and thereby he avoided antagonizing potential helpers in establishing his new household. Instead, his marriage was arranged to a poor but dutiful girl. Certain features of the marriage deserve notice. Dang's future bride was also living in his uncle's house prior to marriage. She, the niece of the uncle's wife through a sister, had been brought to Bangkok from the countryside as a helper in the household. Whether or not the uncle and aunt brought the two together for purposes of marriage is uncertain. In any case, the idea was soon put into action, first by sending the two young ones out to amuse themselves together in the city and then by urging the girl to show the young man particular attention. As Dang heeded these gentle pressures but little, the aunt then took to seeking out and destroying half-written letters to his first love in the country, preventing his visiting Bang Suaj, and finally threatening his job in the factory, if he did not consent to marry the niece. In spite of her scheming, Dang never voiced a word of protest to the aunt. The uncle brightened the prospect by promises of a house for the new couple and the offer to Dang of becoming future manager of the factory, despite possible claims of his own son. In addition, the uncle secured the consent of Dang's own parents by offering to underwrite the wedding expenses and thereby paid Dang's father who had lost this son's labor on his farm. These gambits succeeded in retaining and insuring Dang's future services. As Dang said:

> I thought I would try out the marriage and see what it was like because my parents did not have to spend any money on the wedding. And at that time I wanted to be a rich man too because my aunt said she would give me this and that. I thought that although I did not love her very much, the job was more important. I thought more about this job than anything else; so I gave in to the marriage because I thought of the way ahead and of making a living.

So Dang chose the promise of wealth and security over love.

Dang's choice in this matter was not at all unusual. When it comes down to the actual criteria of selecting a mate, most villagers give precedence to practical considerations over reasons of the heart. This is indicated in the results of the Sentence Completion Test (SCT) item, "He (she) wants to get a wife (husband) who . . ." Of sixty respondents, thirty-one said they wanted a mate who "was a good worker," "earned a living," "was rich," or otherwise had high social status. Only two people said they wanted a mate for reasons that could be reasonably defined as sentimental: one man said he wanted to get a wife whom "he loved"; and a woman wanted a husband who "would be a good friend with whom she could discuss things." The other respondents gave completions which were distributed among a variety of categories: eight people wanted mates who were polite, well-mannered, and handsome; six listed abstract personality characteristics such as "good," "strong," and "kind"; and six women wanted husbands who would be faithful. Dang stressed obedience in his reply. The emphasis, however, is clearly on the socio-economic status or productive capacities of the mate.

In line with this pragmatic attitude, most Thai men seem to be much more concerned with the social aspects of marriage—its being a mark of adulthood and adult responsibility—than with its psycho-emotional side. Dang expressed fairly typical feelings when he was asked, "What do you think the purpose of marriage is?"

> The aim of getting married? Is that right? (Interviewer nods "yes.") I think it gives you a stable position in the community. A married man has his own separate occupation, he has his own house. Then, he wants peace—no arguments or quarreling between the husband and wife. That is, they do not have to gallivant here and there after they get married.

Not once in speaking about his marriage did Dang refer to the emotional satisfactions or obligations of matrimony: love, affection, understanding. The closest we get to them is with his reference here to the desirability of marital peace. But this "peace"—cessation of argument and gallivanting—is hardly an emotional satisfaction, unless, of course, he expects not to have it. The strength of practical over emotional considerations was perhaps best summed up by Dang when he said: "If my wife learned how to handle money, then I would probably love her more."

Not even toward his first love, the girl he wanted to marry, did Dang seem to express any deep sense of emotional attachment. Although he said he "loved her and sympathized with her the most," he seemed primarily interested in her physical attributes and the fact that she was socially attractive, "a good catch," as it were. Even his one brief reference to her "character" is highly stereotyped:

> . . . the girl I loved was not ugly or homely; she was a beautiful girl. And normally, there were many people interested in her, because I used to meet them at the store when they used to come to speak to her. But she wasn't interested in them. Men like army officers and schoolteachers . . . (Interviewer: What did that girl have that made you love her?) We saw each other everyday. I don't know what made me love her so much. I loved her and sympathized with her the most. . . . She had a nice figure. The way she spoke and the way she dealt with her neighbors was good too. She had a nice gentle, polite character. I first told my parents and brothers and sisters about her, that I loved her very much. When I saw that they liked her too, my love for her increased and I loved her even more. (Interviewer: Besides her character, were there other things that made you love her?) She never went gallivanting at night.

As might be suspected from these remarks, the first few years of marriage are not particularly easy for many Thai. The emotional poverty of the husband-wife relationship creates numerous psychological strains. Dang suggested one of these when he said, "they do not have to gallivant here and there after they get married." But many do gallivant, and it sometimes contributes to the break-up of the marriage, although a few men who can afford it simply take on minor wives.

Some men are quite cavalier about married life. As Dang said earlier, "I thought I would try out the marriage and see what it was like . . . ," implying that if it were not to his liking he might leave his wife. Actually, Dang seems to have been neither strong enough nor irresponsible enough to withdraw from the marriage, but his remark does reflect a fairly widespread Thai attitude that the obligations of marriage, particularly toward one's mate, are not very binding.

Statistics on the divorce or separation rate in rural Thailand are not reliable. Many marriages are never registered on the government rolls, and people are probably even less inclined to register their divorce or separation. However, marriages seem to be singularly brittle. Their instability is at least suggested by the following figures collected by the authors: *four* months after we had designated a sample of thirty families from which to choose informants, six of those families, or 20 per cent of the sample population, had dissolved. This, of course, does not mean that in twenty months the entire sample would have dissolved, but a year later none of these six families had been reformed; in all but one of the families, the husband and wife were under 30 years of age. Most observers agree that if a marriage can survive either the first five years or until the birth of the first child, it should be able to last a life-time.

Interpersonal Relations

The tensions behind social intercourse usually escape the eye of a foreign visitor who is overwhelmed instead with the ubiquitous affability, politeness, and good humor of Thai social intercourse. However, these happy characteristics are not so much the expressions of any basic light-heartedness as they are techniques for implementing the main precept of social contact: "Avoid face-to-face conflict." The strength of this rule in discouraging expression of negative feelings may be seen in the replies to the SCT item, "People who never show their feelings . . ." Of thirty-seven replies, thirty-four indicate the positive value by such statements as "are good-hearted people who do not want to quarrel" or "think carefully for their own good." Dang agreed with the majority in saying they "are gentle, fine people." The limitation of this rule is evident in the minority reply: "are difficult to get along with; most of them do not like to make friends." In effect, most persons remain at a distance by restricting themselves to jovial, comic, or entertaining conversation.

To achieve greater intimacy requires establishing one's self as a superior or inferior to another through favors in return for services. Depending on the duration and constancy of the exchange, intimacy may increase and one may risk occasional expression of displeasure to an inferior. Dang recited the formula in describing his relationship to his younger brothers:

Now my second and third brothers are grown up, and when I ask them to do some kind of work, they go and do it. They never disobey, and when there is no disobedience, there is no hatred . . . Formerly whenever there was entertainment somewhere I took them with me. My younger siblings loved me a lot.

Between status equals the likelihood of friction is ever present, and decorum reverts to the open means of maintaining distance. Of thirty-eight responses to the SCT item "Friends think of him as . . . ," six converted the item by stating what they thought of friends, e.g., "some people are good to us; some think of getting things from us." Twenty-seven declared friends found favorable qualities, e.g., "a truthful man of his word," but of these, eight gave significant negative phrasings to their answers, e.g., "a good-hearted person who does not speak ill of and bully people."

All through the disquieting prelude and negotiation for marriage, Dang maintained perfectly polite relations with his aunt and uncle. When asked how he felt when his aunt scolded him for writing letters to his first love, he merely replied, "I felt sorry and depressed." He never protested her actions openly. At one point he did say that he felt "anger in his heart," but his word for anger here specifically means "unmanifested anger."

Life Cycle

As compared with an estimated 10 per cent in Bangkok, less than 5 per cent of Bang Suaj's children continue education after the age of 14, the legal age for leaving school. Then the youth enters a formal or informal apprenticeship for a vocation; in Bang Suaj to find an eighteen or twenty-year-old managing a farm is not unusual. At twenty-one men become liable for two years of military or police service and at the same time become formally eligible to enter the Buddhist monkhood. A period of residence and study at the temple is reckoned a desirable preparation for marriage. Dang summarized the sequence of his life as follows:

When my father bought the land, I was 16 years old. When I was 17, I was ordained a novice (at the Buddhist temple) for one Lent. As a novice, I studied religion but failed the exam. So I left the temple. I left and helped my father work the fields for another three years. Then I began to work as boatman. Then I was ordained as a monk when I was 21, and my brother was boatman in my place. I was a monk for one year and then I left. And then I went to study radio in Bangkok for six months. When I finished studying radio, I was called for the army . . . Although I was called, I was not selected. At that time my father's younger brother wanted me to work in Bangkok making cutlery.

Like 90 per cent of his age mates, Dang satisfied government claims for military service before marrying. However, only 30 per cent of his age-group enter monkhood at his age. While Dang does have an acknowledged disability that misfits him for protracted farm labor, the army rejects more than 50 per cent of the farm children on physical grounds. Thus he does not differ markedly from his contemporaries, and though lacking physical stamina, he was still desired as a farm worker. Entering the temple as a novice prior to becoming a monk at twenty-one is unusual and probably represents the initiative of his parents. His uncompleted course in radio repair may be reckoned an effort to find a vocation outside of farming on account of his disability. Otherwise the general features of Dang's life are in no way unique; indeed, as many as an estimated 20–50 per cent of Bang Suaj youth gravitate toward Bangkok for varying periods in the search for an occupation.

PERSONAL-SOCIAL SETTING

To this point we have considered primarily the social setting of the excerpt from Dang's autobiography. Let us now enquire into the subjective side of the social scene. For Dang the move from his father's home to Bangkok proceeded in the approved path toward success. He gained a position as a member of his uncle's family and the advantage of improved social prestige as a city dweller. With increasing control of the factory, he anticipated eventually becoming able to grant favors to his own group of loyal kinsmen. Marriage to the niece moved him nearer the goal. Inevitably certain sacrifices were necessary. He had to forego marriage for love to the country girl with whom he continued to correspond throughout his first year in Bangkok. Even though her parents opposed the match, Dang did not abandon his suit, and many a commentator in Bang Suaj coffee shops affirmed the appropriateness of this proposed local marriage. In one of his few moments of regret Dang recalled a visit to this first love on the very eve of his wedding. Already aware of his engagement to another, she refused to see him, but he caught a glimpse of her face and saw tears in her eyes.

As we have already seen, he also felt he had to submit silently to the transparent machinations of his aunt. Toward his future wife, his feelings were mixed. She had been required by the aunt to serve as accomplice to at least a portion of the scheme, for she read portions of Dang's love letters to her illiterate aunt. Toward her he showed his displeasure and rebuked her for her "bad taste" but then forgave her because "she was just a child at that time." Her spontaneous attentions in washing his clothes or preparing his bed for the night indicated a love for him which he did not reciprocate. More than once, he said: "I didn't love her; I only pitied her." She was perhaps naïve but at the same time had industry, dutifulness, and was eager to please him. Pitted against loss of his job, the advantages outweighed the disadvantages.

We are perplexed, however, to see him abandon his avenue to success. He had been taken into the core of his uncle's family and showered with favors; in principle, he committed himself to his uncle through adversity as well as prosperity. Even his father once told him, "Now you are your uncle's boy." What led him to give this up? Dang's closest attempt to account for this reads simply enough:

> We had to work harder and make less money. I had only enough money to buy food but not enough for anything else.

At no point does he mention any obligation to remain with his uncle, nor are efforts of his uncle to retain him described. This appears to be a plain economic decision. Bang Suaj, where his father welcomed him and his wife and a baby daughter, appeared more advantageous. He could return to the exact spot from which he had departed; he had the income from three acres of land, help in starting the poultry business, and, by arrangement with his younger brother, the job as boatman. Sentiment for his uncle and aunt, if present, was minimal.

The cost of this decision, however, was heavy. We need not consider the possibility of his remaining in Bangkok, for he had neither skills for other kinds of work nor liaisons to other makers of cutlery. He could not afford to become independent at that point in his life. Let us detail some of the costs which become clear in the projective tests.

(1) A sense of failure came from status and standard of living declining to that of countryman. More particularly, as the subsequent evidence shows, he suffered a loss of feeling of independence and achievement in having to reenter the house of his father which he had left to make his own way. On the SCT he responded uniquely to the item, "The most important thing in his life is . . ." with "that work does not turn out as well as expected." Most replied with "earning a living" or "land and home." On the TAT card 3BM his depressive tendency is clear from the following response:

> This is a picture of his being sorry because he is thinking about something that is not successful as he wanted it to be.

Others saw lazy or angry people in the same picture. Then at one point in the interviews Dang observed about himself:

> If we have money, anything we think about we are sure to get. I've never had that experience. I don't have any luck. I have had very little, very little luck.

Dang admits the sense of inadequacy and loss of independence resulting from having to return to his father's house. When asked how he felt about living with his parents, he replied:

Wait a minute, wait a minute . . . it's not good, because it is something that people gossip about in a very critical way. They see that I don't have any ability at all to make my own living by myself. I have to depend on my parents in order to live. That's one thing.

He not only commented on his dependence but the specific obligation he no longer fulfilled to his younger siblings:

I feel ashamed before my younger siblings too. I am embarrassed before my younger siblings in everything. I am afraid that they will criticize me because I have a family already and instead of getting my family established in a place of my own and going out and making a living . . . I must depend upon my father.

This combined sense of personal failure and dependence is perhaps Dang's most obsessive concern. It appears repeatedly in a variety of contexts. When asked about those periods of his life which he would most like to remember and most like to forget, he says:

Ahhh, the time (I would most like to remember) was when I had a lover in Bang Suaj, because at that time I felt content and happy. At that time I had determination to do anything! (Interviewer: And which period of your life would you not want to have?) Right now, at the present time. I have a wife, a child, and I'm beginning not to like it. (Why?) Because I have a family already . . . I have my own child already, and I'm not yet capable of standing up straight on my own two feet.

And when asked about the happiest period of his life, Dang says (with an air of intense frustration):

It's been very difficult for me to find happiness. I haven't had any at all. To find happiness is really difficult. Before I was married, it was fun, but it wasn't happiness! And after I was married, I haven't had *any* happiness. To find happiness is really hard. (Why is that?) Because my home, my palace, has to be where my father and mother live!

(2) We may also infer an increase of hostility among the psychic costs. In the SCT Dang declared, *"I admire nagklengs* [1] *because . . . they have more power,"* a reply given only by two others in this naked form; the majority denied anything admirable or referred to some other quality such as courage. The subsequent item of the SCT reenforces this presumption: *"He wishes he were a nagkleng because . . .* it would make people fear and respect him." While this response was shared with four others, the majority added etiological replies such as "others molest him" or "his family had nothing to eat."

Much of Dang's hostility is directed specifically toward his father and was probably provoked by his having returned to dependence on the father. Thus his response to TAT card 7BM reads:

This is a picture of father and son. The father has continually done good for him by giving him an education and teaching him to do the work and introducing him to good things. After that the father died. The son had many difficulties. He drinks whiskey and is mean. In this picture he is thinking about the goodness of his father, and he will become a good person again. Therefore the picture of the old man that he sees is a picture in his imagination only.

Although the son is the hostile one, it is the father who dies. Dang's struggle with hostility appeared briefly in an interview where he was discussing character:

I think that (if) a person has something happen to him, that makes him bad. For example, we never do anything; we do not even steal little things. And suppose that a (bad) person comes to hurt our father. And maybe we shoot and kill him. Or we know that a thief is going to come and steal from us, and maybe we shoot him dead.

In each case he depicts a justifiable retaliation, though he may also suggest that tragedy enough has happened to turn him bad. However, we clearly note the selection of his father to exemplify an object of violence.

Dang's hostility toward his father is not without realistic foundation. Although our narrative passed over the point, Dang's father was one of the oldest and closest friends of the father of Dang's first love—the very individual who opposed our hero's suit. Further, Dang's father liked the girl. Although a brief word from father to friend would have eased Dang's way considerably, we have no evidence that even a word was said on the son's behalf. Similarly, Dang's father knew that the uncle, his own younger brother, had reneged on his promise of a house for Dang. Yet fearing embarrassment or involvement, or perhaps feeling that he no longer had the responsibility, he again said nothing. Finally, while Dang was still in the monkhood, his father promised him a certain amount of land which he was to receive upon resumption of secular life—"a graduation gift," as it were. Nevertheless, before Dang could leave the temple and secure the land, his father gave it free of charge to two of his own friends (one of whom was the father of Dang's first love). These individuals had wanted the land for many years and saw this as their last opportunity to obtain it. From all available evidence, the father's action here was prompted solely by friendship and an inability to refuse friends a request for a favor.

In each of these instances the father's behavior was, in Thai terms, quite understandable: he wanted to avoid a socially awkward and embarrassing situation with his peers, or in the case of the uncle, his younger brother. However, such behavior hardly makes for a very strong or reliable father figure.

(3) In his distress Dang seeks greater warmth of human contact. Yearning for his first love seems to have reappeared in response to card 6BM of the TAT:

> He is in love with a girl. . . . He wants his mother to ask the girl's parents to permit their daughter to marry him. Mother is not interested because the girl is poor or because something is wrong with her. When the mother was not interested, he was sad because his mother did not love him. But the mother was interested in another girl and will try to ask for the girl for him. (Subsequent questioning reveals that the mother wished her son to marry a rich girl.)

The story reflects many elements of Dang's actual experience, except that some of the characters and their qualities are inverted: here the "mother's" choice is a rich girl, while in real life Dang's wife was poor; in some respects the "mother" is like the aunt, but in her behavior she is more reminiscent of Dang's father who also refused to speak for his son. But whatever the real life referent, Dang feels that the parental figure does not love him. With the added evidence of his reply to card 4 of the TAT, we may also feel reasonably certain that Dang is losing what little affection he may have for his wife. In this story he describes the scene as a household where the husband has just returned from a rendezvous with another woman:

> This is a picture of a man. He is all absorbed in sexual emotion. He has just come home. His wife is telling him not to do like that; it is not good. But her husband does not believe her. He thinks that what he does is good and fun. This picture will end by their not agreeing with each other.

The ending to Dang's story seems to be an almost perfect reflection of his attitude toward his wife. All they do is simply "not agree with each other." There is no emotional bridge here of either hatred or love. They stand as two separate, isolated individuals who are unable or do not want to reach each other. Dang's indifference to his wife goes beyond fantasy. When he was asked point-blank in the interviews whether or not he loved his wife, he said: "At the present time, it's some days: some days I love her, and some days I feel 'choej-choej.' " "Choej-choej" means to feel something, but that something is explicitly nothing.

Dang feels this emotional vacuum in his life and attempts to fill it by continuing to yearn for his first love. As suggested by the TAT, his passion has not yet waned. At one point in the interviews, Dang waxed almost eloquent when he outlined for us his definition of "Perfect Fulfillment"—"a house, enough money, and my first love as my wife." He might have taken his first love into the household as co-wife, a slightly rare but possible practice.

The Psychic Tensions

Moving a step closer to Dang's personality core, we may see two areas of related psychic tensions. The first may be called dependence-independence. The data reveal Dang driven toward independence in the social expectation of his becoming master of his own family and establishment. These independence strivings are supported and reinforced by his early sibling relationships where he had a measure of control over others and by his experience of limited independence in the city. Yet, paradoxically, the only manner of achieving these ends lies in making himself dependent on still another to provide for him. Thus he must continually thank his father for his "goodness," yet make increasing demands on him. The father, however, must husband the home group for himself and grant no more favors than are necessary to maintain his labor force. Dang is expected to develop his own resources, but he feels himself impotent and yearns for power while his past failures flood upon him and undermine his self-confidence.

A second source of tension may be called affiliation-hostility, a conflict between the desire for love and fear of expressing hostility. As we have seen, Dang would have the love of his parents and siblings, though at the same time he is uncertain of his parents' love and his ability to hold his siblings' love. His father's goodness is already suspect, and Dang seems not to realize that his own treatment of his wife exemplifies again the unprovoked withdrawal of love. Under these circumstances hostility arises, as shown by Dang's fantasy of coercing affiliation, but this alternative cannot easily come to the light of day in the face of injunctions to avoid open conflict. Dang is caught in an impasse, neither able to gain the security of affiliation nor vent his spleen through hostility.

Tensions and the Social Order

Let us begin with the working assumption that social systems select and reinforce certain human potentials for reacting and reject others. The Thai system of affiliation with a leader or kinsman who grants favors in return for obedient service encourages dependence and postpones urges of independence. It underscores the benevolent aspects of a superior, his charity, his kindness to his subordinates. The urges for independence are gradually satisfied, in small steps, first as one rules it over one's younger siblings and later as one becomes master of one's own household and leader of many households. Yet every independent position has its counterpart of dependence. Even at the peak of independence both peasant and government official must reckon with other superiors, for there always remain beings higher even than the King.

In this system the only provision for limiting the power of a superior lies in the freedom and risk of changing affiliation. Open expression of hostility threatens reciprocal benefits; fear, if it does not contribute to hostility, merely increases effective submission to the system.

Hostility to an equal or superior is directly expressed only in the most agonizing extremity. In the presence of competitors society takes pains to cultivate tranquil minds. Yet outlets for hostility appear at every turn. One such mode consists in addressing insults to some animal or child within the hearing range of one's adversary. Running away from the trouble is most frequently used, as when Dang left the temple after failing his examination in religion. Suicide is also motivated by the desire to make others feel sorry. Greater spleen may be directly vented by waylaying a person at night when he cannot identify his assailant. Somewhat less daring is required to steal his boat or buffalo and allow him to redeem it at a price negotiated by some intermediary. Indeed, as one grows in legitimate stature within the community, the wise guardian of his group takes increasing precautions to prevent assault and theft.

Thai personality types may then be understood as a variety of adjustments to a social system which maximizes dependence and friendly, though certainly not intimate, relations, while it minimizes the hostile and prematurely independent relationships. Our central character, Dang, may be seen in this perspective as a run-of-the-mill person, affable, generous, and filled with the right impulses but not daring to face the alternatives, not strong enough to assume a risk.

Thai Personality

A social system may be considered a warp through or against which the variety of human adjustments form the woof. To the extent that these warps differ from society to society, we may also speak of group personality. Adding to Benedict's penetrating observations (1946) summarized in Kroeber (1948) we may note finally that the Thai system of organizing life differs from others mainly because of its fluidity. This becomes clear if one thinks of the Chinese family groups where a greater sense of permanence is given (Hsu, 1948). There, authority includes a greater admixture of both justice and mercy than in Thailand, and affiliation presumes an enduring sentiment.

From this vantage point, the Thai personality stands more encapsulated, alone, and isolated than the Chinese. Thai resist strong affiliation as do rejected lovers who fear suffering again. Without strong bonds, they develop no sense of guilt for those they injure and stand ultimately responsible only to themselves, individuals among individuals who differ mainly in the amount of influence they wield. Thus Dang can make demands of others but feel little obligation toward them. As he left his father and uncle with scarcely a second thought, so others can leave him.

Of course, as was indicated by Dang's projective test data, this form of individualism is not entirely without its psychic toll. But on the level of action and conscious decision, the moral for a Thai runs: invest not thy love in a shadow.

NOTE

1. The term "nagkleng" resists precise translation. Robert B. Textor (1956) has probably come closest to defining it with his term "rogue-racketeer." However, there are many "nagklengs" who are community protectors as well as racketeers. Typically a "nagkleng" defies authority, speaks his feelings from his heart, and is manifestly aggressive. He bullies some people (whether they be good, bad or indifferent, and thus he is not a Robin Hood character), and takes care of others. Public attitudes toward "nagklengs" are variously those of fear, awe, dislike, and sometimes admiration.

BIBLIOGRAPHY

Benedict, Ruth. 1946. *Thai Culture and Behavior: An Unpublished War-time Study Dated September 1943.* New York: Institute for Intercultural Studies, Inc. Reprinted as Data Paper Number 4, Southeast Asia Program, Cornell University, Ithaca, New York.

Hsu, Francis L. K. 1948. *Under the Ancestor's Shadow; Chinese Culture and Personality.* New York: Columbia University Press.

Kroeber, Alfred L. 1948. *Anthropology.* New York: Harcourt, Brace & Co. Pp. 589–90.

Textor, Robert B. 1956. "The Northeastern Samlor Driver in Bangkok," in *The Social Implications of Industrialization and Urbanization; Five Studies of Urban Populations of Recent Rural Origin in Cities of Southern Asia.* Calcutta: UNESCO Research Centre on the Social Implications of Industrialization in Southern Asia.

EDITOR'S EPILOGUE

A FINAL WORD

One of the privileges that accrue to the editor of a volume like this one, and perhaps one of the duties as well, is to take a backward look at the completed product and give his impression of what has transpired and its significance. The editor, no matter how clear his original aims, nor how firm his intent to keep the work on its planned course, finds inevitably that a book written by thirty persons in twenty-four chapters, develops a course of its own and a meaning and significance that are almost completely independent of the original direction.

When this volume was conceived, it was intended, with the exception of one or two background chapters, to be focused more or less narrowly on the problem of cross-cultural personality study. We believed then—this was in 1957 before some significant changes occurred in our ideas —that a clear empirical task confronted workers in the culture and personality field, a task that involved certain difficulties but that required only the application of our best talents in a sustained way for its clarification and mastery. This task was simply to find techniques of personality study that would yield rich and representative expressions of personality processes, to develop principles of interpretation that would allow us to understand these expressions no matter how cryptic or exotic, and finally to learn how to combine and organize what had been discovered about individuals into valid and qualified statements about typical group processes. We thought that cross-cultural personality study required that, at each of these stages, the particular cultural processes in the society under study should be taken into account in the solution to these problems; in other words, we believed that the nature of the people being studied and their culture should be allowed to influence study methods, interpretation, and organization. The people who were invited to write for this volume would, it was felt, all be sensitive to this problem, and could make some contribution, direct or indirect, to its solution.

As the chapters accumulated, it became clear that something quite different was occurring. What was to have been the major focus of the book, the problem of finding techniques for cross-cultural personality study, became almost overshadowed by what was originally intended to provide a background and orientation for the uninitiated reader, the discussion of culture and personality theory. Instead of one center of gravity, there are now two, the theoretical and the methodological. This unplanned shift is, however, not completely accidental. It is plain that in the culture and personality field today the greatest interest, and the major excitement, is in theoretical development. There is a general underlying feeling that in a shifting theoretical situation, concern with methods and methodological issues is premature. At a time when workers are still not quite sure *what* they want to describe, preoccupation with the *how* of personality study is uncomfortable and disconcerting. Other disciplines, clinical psychology for example, do not have this problem since workers are generally confident about their basic theories; hence the development of methods is proliferating.

Within the theoretical chapters themselves, there is a remarkable convergence upon one issue. This convergence was completely unplanned and is, therefore, good evidence that an important theoretical change is occurring in the culture and personality field. Since this development in theory constitutes one of the main scientific contributions of the volume, I shall go to some pains to delineate it clearly and point out some of its implications. The relationship of this emerging theory to the image of the empirical task of culture and personality research workers is of special importance and I shall attempt in this final chapter to describe a new view of *what* should be studied.

In focusing on this "new look" in theory, I am aware that I am not considering explicitly the bulk of the methods and methodological chapters. They speak for themselves very clearly and therefore require no explaining or interpreting. There is some danger however that the significance of the earlier chapters will not be immediately apparent. In underlining and spelling out some of the things these chapters have to say, I will be acting much as a literary critic does in pointing out meanings and making interpretations with which the authors themselves may not completely agree. My own involvement with the theoretical issues to be discussed is one of the important bases for the selectivity of the treatment and my perception of the direction of any future development of the culture and personality field undoubtedly colors this discussion. Perhaps I have overemphasized the "newness" of the theme to be described. The theme is almost certainly implied by much of the writing and research of the past decade and may even have been spelled out explicitly by some workers, particularly in sociology. Nevertheless there has not been any general awareness of what has been developing and it seems appropriate to give some public recognition to the "new look."

For a number of years the central and almost official theoretical position of most culture and personality workers has been one that was perhaps best described in Inkeles and Levinson's paper entitled "National Character: The Study of Modal Personality and Sociocultural Systems." This paper stood as a dominant conceptual achievement, clarifying and defining the problem of culture and personality research and mapping out in the most convincing way the task of the research worker. (This position has been described in Singer's chapter in this book and need not be repeated in detail here.) Inkeles and Levinson defined the salient culture and personality problem as having to do with the relevance of personality processes to social system functioning. They were concerned with the congruence, or lack of it, between the personality traits of individuals in the group and the behavioral requirements of the social system. They said:

Insofar as the relevant traits of character are modally present in the population of any society the chances are increased that culturally and structurally important goals will be aspired toward and implemented by the societies' members, thus in significant degree insuring the continued effective functioning of the social system. (p. 1006)

In the present volume, this view is perhaps most systematically stated by Spiro when he is concerned with the way in which personality, or the motivations which mainly comprise it "become crucial variables in the functioning of social systems." In the situation of ideal "congruence," those personality characteristics which are "modally" present or "shared" or "typical" are functionally coherent with the social systems in which they exist. This "fittingness" or "appropriateness" is generally regarded as not being accidental, but as occurring as a result of the systematic socialization of individuals in the group. Through these socialization processes the major value orientations of the culture (see Parsons' chapter) are learned or internalized and are thus transformed into individual motivations. In Parsons' theory the social system is constrained or shaped by the same value orientations in what is referred to as the process of "institutionalization." Thus it "fits" or is isomorphic with the motivational systems of the individual.

Until not too long ago this congruence or isomorphism was assumed to exist. But more recently Inkeles and Levinson and others have recognized the possibility of incongruence, relating it to the situation of social change. Singer, in this volume, has distinguished between those concepts which involve the actual typical or shared characteristics of persons, generally referred to as modal personality, and the socially required personality traits which are now usually known as "social character." Inkeles and Levinson make a strong plea for studies which will describe modal personality and analyze its relationship to socio-cultural systems. The Inkeles, Hanfmann and Beier chapter on Soviet personality and the Soviet social system in this volume is a model for the kind of research-analysis that is needed.

I remember very clearly that in 1956, when I was writing an article on personality and social structure for J. B. Gittler's *Review of Sociology,* the problem seemed to be to discover how to go on from established conceptions which appeared so substantial, so correct, that there seemed to be little else to say. The theoretical chapters in the present volume constitute an answer to this question. I believe that a new conceptual level has been reached, bringing with it a new kind of empirical problem.

One of the reasons why it has seemed so important to search for new concepts is that the old ones provide a particularly culture-bound image of man. As Singer points out, Erich Fromm, himself one of the authors of the concept of social character, sees his formulation as damaging to the conception of man as free and autonomous and be-lieves that it views the possibilities of self-realization and development as restricted. It is indeed incongruous that Fromm, who is perhaps social science's chief spokesman for a "humanistic ethic" of freedom and personal development, is the father of a doctrine which views man as having given up his freedom and spontaneity in favor of being "molded" into a person who is eager to spend his energies for the pur-pose of socially required work. Equally strange is the fact that David Riesman, who like Fromm is one of our main champions of "autonomy," is identified in the minds of most Americans with the idea that persons in our society are rapidly becoming "other-directed" in their motiva-tional orientation, renouncing their freedom and autonomy.

The probable explanation of this incongruity is that the "social character" conceptions of both Riesman and Fromm are in the nature of social criticism. Through them they are calling attention to the renunciation of freedom that is characteristic of modern man. Both look toward the "autonomous" man who will be something other than a bundle of internalized social values. This element of social criticism and of hopefulness about an altered situation in the future is omitted by other workers who use the concept. What is left is an image of man as receiving his motives and being fixed by the socialization process.

What is this new theoretical step which we have been heralding? It lies in the idea that the motivational basis for orderly, appropriate social behavior need not be isomorphic to the role itself. Thus Spiro points out that:

Although cultural goals are parochial, most human drives—because of their rootedness in a common biology and in common conditions of social life—are probably universal. Hence it is generally not too difficult to demonstrate . . . that the quite diverse goals of different societies, as well as the roles which are instrumental for their attainment, are functionally equivalent; they serve to gratify the same drives. (p. 104, above)

In other parts of his discussion Spiro states that the personal goals which lead to certain behavior in individuals may be quite separate from and independent of the meaning which such behavior has for social functioning. However social systems structure the behaviors that are possible within them, so that acts generally have social functions whether they are intended or not.

Here, and in several other chapters, the idea is introduced that social and personality systems need not be symmetrical or isomorphically structured. A small number of different motivations may support a wide variety of different behaviors, or quite diverse motivations in different persons may be the basis for the same role behavior. Since either can be the case, motivations are emancipated from role requirements and we are forced to seek a new conception of the relationship between the two.

Devereux's analysis of the modal personality concept makes very much the same point. He distinguishes between what he calls a "psychologistic" model of modal personality which refers to the actual motives of participants in a social activity, and a "sociologistic" model which refers to the motives which are ascribed to social participation. In the example of the Hungarian freedom fighter which Devereux analyzes in his chapter, he finds that the actual motivations of revolutionary behavior were quite diverse and manifold and that "many highly divergent types of conscious and unconscious subjective motives can impel people to seek gratification through participation in a given social process." The socially ascribed motive, however, is one which from the point of view of the social system makes good sense—for example that the revolutionary behavior was motivated by patriotism, idealism, and heroism—and which becomes a kind of banner under which all sorts of individual motives can be cloaked and expressed. These ascribed motives are therefore considered by Devereux to be instrumental in significance insofar as they stand in a means-end relationship to the more personal motives. One is reminded of Henry Murray's term "subsidiance" in his *Explorations in Personality* when he sought to describe the situation in which one or more needs are activated in the service of another need. His example is amusing and illuminating.

> A politician removes a spot from his suit (n Noxavoidance) because he does not wish to make a bad impression (n Infavoidance), and thus diminish his chances of winning the approval and friendship of Mr. X (n Affiliation) from whom he hopes to obtain some slanderous facts (n Cognizance) relating to the private life of his political rival, Mr. Y, information which he plans to publish (n Exposition) in order to damage the reputation of Mr. Y (n Aggression) and thus assure his own election to office (n Achievement). (p. 87)

In Devereux's paper, as in Spiro's, we are left with the idea that social roles do not require any particular kind of motivational support. But, as Talcott Parsons has stated, "The social problem is to get the patterns (of behavior) whatever their functional significance to the person" (1949, p. 196).

In itself this idea about the relationship between social roles and motivation does not have any revolutionary significance, especially since it has been widely recognized for many years. But what are its implications for a theory of the motivation of social behavior? It seems to require that we throw overboard in its entirety the generally held theory described above and look for some new conception of the motivations of social behavior. If taken seriously, this idea is incompatible with modal personality theory. We believe that the time has now come to take this idea very seriously indeed. It is well known that in science, theories are not discarded when they are proven incorrect; rather, they hang on until a new theory comes along that is better able to explain the known facts. Some elements at least of such a new culture and personality theory are on the scene now and many of them are contained in chapters in this book.

Perhaps the boldest effort at a new theoretical formulation is found in Wallace's chapter in which he seeks to determine the basis of the psychic unity of human groups. He rejects the kind of theory which makes motivational unity the chief requirement for social participation in favor of the idea that shared cognitive capabilities are of much greater importance. Culture means that the members of a group have cognitive maps which Wallace calls "mazeways" which either are the same or "equivalent" in the sense that together they form some kind of meaningful, organized whole. He states that social coordination without uniformity of motive or interest is a higher cultural achievement than cohesion based on motivational uniformity would be, and that diversity, complexity and differentiation are basic to a highly organized system. Wallace is concerned, as I am, with developing a conception of social order which does not require that we abandon the image of man as free and autonomous. His theory suggests, much as the Gestalt psychologists, Kohler and Wertheimer did, that knowing what is required and appropriate tends to produce the appropriate behavior and that a kind of "law of *prägnanz*" operates to elicit from the person the behavior that best "fits" the requirements of the situation. The motivation that is involved in this kind of behavior is apparently the tendency or drive of human beings to increase the quantity of meaningfulness and organization in the cognitive field. Though I may not understand completely Wallace's very rich and complex paper, it seems to me that, even assuming that what he says about the importance for cultural unity of "mazeway" equivalence is correct, we are still left with the need to explain in a more differentiated way than Wallace does, *why* persons lend their energies and actions to social participation. I would grant that one part of the culture and personality problem has to do with the relationship of culture to human cognitive capabilities, and Wallace has done a very important service in pointing this out; but the other part of the problem, that concerned with the nature of the motivation of social action, is no less important. Wallace has dealt with the problem of understanding how people get to know what they should do but not with the question of why they do it.

As said already, the elements of a significant alternative to modal personality theory are found in this volume. Perhaps the most important preliminary step to this alternative theory is the definition of the problem, very clearly stated in Spiro's chapter, as having to do with the motivation not of this or that specific role behavior but of conformative behavior generally. In both Spiro's and Devereux's chapters we find the idea that role behavior is instrumental in relationship to personal needs and motives. But how does it happen that this is so? Why do individual needs get satisfied by appropriate role behavior? And if conformative behavior is instrumental, what is it instrumental to?

Up to now our emerging theory appears to suggest a jungle-like situation in which wholly free and autonomous individuals, in a relatively opportunistic way, make use of the available channels of social participation and the rewards that are attached to them. A great many of these channels or roles have all-purpose rewards, like money, that can be utilized to satisfy quite diverse needs. However, there is much evidence that conformity ordinarily is a generalized and diffuse disposition, not something that occurs only when some desired reward is in sight. One might say that it is the basic way of life of all but a few persons in any society. The essential meaning of most social action is not that the actor wishes to do this or that act, but that he wishes to stand in a conformative relationship to the social demands that exist in the situation. In the great majority of social situations most of us are not concerned with the problem of what to do, but much more with the problem of finding out what is is that would be appropriate. When we know what this is, compliance follows almost automatically. The basic fact is that we are mostly good citizens, persons who want to do what is right, correct, decent, and fitting. The culture and personality issue that we have been working to define in the discussion so far, is not why persons wish to do this or that act, but why they are good citizens. Or, in other terms, what is the motivational basis for the generalized disposition to conformity. Parsons and Shils say:

> In most cases, individuals perform role functions in the division of labor which do not, as such, completely and directly gratify any specific need-disposition or any set of the need-dispositions of their personality system. It is the nature of instrumental action that it should be this way. Conformity with the role-expectations is possible, however, either through a generalized need-disposition to conformity or through instrumental orientations. (1951, p. 152)

David Riesman, in *The Lonely Crowd,* has made one of the few attempts at a culture and personality analysis in these terms. The three kinds of social character he discusses, the tradition-directed, the inner-directed, and the other-directed, are described not simply as character traits of persons, but as modes of conformity, or as different psychological bases for a conformative relationship to social norms. Social character for Riesman consists of the characteristic way of assuring conformity to social requirements. One of these types of character consists of being concerned with and following tradition, another involves being orientated to and following a set of goals internalized early in life, and the third has to do with following the expectations of other people. In slightly different and more psychological terms, the first of the three types involves a respect for and fear of authority, the second a strong superego or conscience, and the third a concern about acceptance and approval in social relationships. It is clear in Riesman's brilliant analysis, which anticipates by many years what I believe will be the future course of the culture and personality field, that these three types of conformity are woven into the fabric of society itself and come as close as anything does to being the central ethos of society and the central meaning of personal experience. The content of the required behavior patterns is external in the sense that it is given by cultural heritage and tradition. But the meaning of action itself, in the present, is indicated not by *what* the person is doing, but by *why* he is doing it, and this is described by his mode of conformity.

Whether the three types described by Riesman are all-inclusive or not is an open issue. I prefer to think that this is an empirical issue that can be settled by the psychological study of individuals. Certainly

Riesman does not claim that his three types are the main ones that will be found in other societies, although it is not easy to conceive of other major types that parallel them. However, it is the task of careful psychological analysis of individuals to describe what the main motivations for conformative behavior are and it is this empirical task that I shall now discuss.

The theoretical transformation noted earlier in this chapter, then, is this: if our general problem is to understand the way in which personality processes are involved in the maintenance of social order, we must no longer think of the motivation of a great variety of diverse behaviors but of a single diffuse disposition or orientation. Instead of positing for each specific behavior of the person—i.e. aggressive behavior, affiliative behavior—its own motivation, we must be concerned with discovering the motivations that underly the generalized mechanism, conformity. The concrete task of the research worker is to clarify the psychology of conformity in the person, in the cultural group, and in human beings generally.

This is a very different task from delineating typical personality patterns. When the modal personality was the crucial variable to be described, the researcher could take that hypothetical and perhaps imaginary structure, the personality, as his object and attempt to describe it. If it turned out to be complicated and illusive, at least the worker knew what his task was and could believe that the technique of personality study might gradually develop and become more adequate to the difficulty of the problem. And he could apply the sophisticated, highly elaborated set of theories and practices that clinical psychologists and others have developed in studying personality in our own society. The study of conformity, *per se,* however, requires a very different kind of methodology. Instead of studying the "whole" person, we are concerned with finding out something quite specific about him. No longer is any personality trend whatever grist for our mill. Most of what we might describe is irrelevant to the particular matter we are trying to clarify, the basis of the subject's conformative orientation. The empirical task is sharply focused and only certain kinds of "hard to come by" information is applicable to it.

Perhaps the most profound change in the situation is that rather than describing the subject, one must focus on his conformative action itself and discover its meaning. In dynamic psychology many of us have been accustomed to thinking of behavior or action as diagnostic of the underlying personality and not very important in itself. In the analysis of conformity we are faced squarely with explaining a particular type of action as the main problem. In doing this, it is possible to differentiate between being concerned with the content of the action, that is with what specifically has been done, and with the relationship with the social situation that is created by the action. As I have stated in Chapter Nine, action always takes place in relation to a setting which, being social, has a normative component defining either appropriate action specifically or the limits and alternatives of appropriate action. The subject's action creates a relationship to this social situation, the main alternative types for such relationships being conformity and deviance. The most important aspect of choice in action is between these two alternatives. The psychologist's problem is first to understand the meaning of the choice—to understand what kind of relationship it creates between person and social situation—and second to unravel the reasons for the choice. Unfortunately we do not have very much that is helpful in relation to this task; it seems to require the kind of prolonged and intensive exploration that goes on in psychoanalysis, in which each newly described motivation is regarded as at least potentially instrumental in relation to other still undiscovered motives.

In a very important sense the study of conformative behavior is closely linked to one of the newest developments in the psychology of personality and personality study—the attempt to understand ego processes and ego functioning. In the last few years the psychoanalytic conception of the ego has expanded considerably. Whereas earlier ego functions were understood mainly as having to do with cognitive functions and with the problem of *how* the organism could best deal with the various problems of living, a newer ego psychology is concerning itself with the way in which the organism establishes goals and values for itself and makes choices and decisions which establish particular kinds of existence and experiencing. It is concerning itself with the relationship of action to situation and the way in which the limits and alternatives of action are influenced and even determined by the scope of the actor's consciousness and orientation. While our understanding of these processes is still very rudimentary, whatever progress is made probably will be directly applicable to our understanding of the kinds of processes that are involved in the resolution of the conformity-deviance problem and the establishment of particular relationships to social situations and social groups.

No detailed description of the technique of such an analysis will be made here, principally because we are not at all clear about how it might be done. For the present it may suffice to point out the nature of the task, with the hope that concentrated research on the problem of conformity analysis will lead to the development of adequate methods in the future. The main point is that a somewhat different orientation to the problem of personality study is not only possible but necessary if data are to be obtained that are relevant to the purposes of investigators of conformative behavior.

In the foregoing discussion I have selected, perhaps rather arbitrarily, one theme from the many that are to be found in this volume, and elaborated and interpreted it. The reasons for this selection will be amply clear to the reader. It constitutes my best guess about the direction of future developments in the culture and personality field. Perhaps it would be more correct to say that this will be one of the directions. It is not necessary to add that guesses often turn out to be wrong and prophecies may come to look very foolish. As this volume testifies, there is a high degree of ferment and diversity in the contemporary scene, and culture and personality problems are defined in many different ways. Some of the differences are terminological, others involve varying theoretical orientations and still others relate to differences in interests. Viewing the whole, one senses a great deal of research and thinking that give promise of breaking out of the molds that we have inherited from the recent past. Theoretically we are becoming much more sophisticated, methodologically more rigorous and substantial, and in developing methods and techniques, more original and ingenious. One hopes that these trends will continue. If they do, we can anticipate a culture and personality field that is potent, beyond any present expectation, in understanding and intervening in human affairs. The one prediction I feel most secure in making is that the field as a whole will gradually encompass more and more of the central issues of man's existence and his efforts at control and transformation and will become, finally, the vital center of a future science of man.

BIBLIOGRAPHY

Inkeles, Alex, and Levinson, D. J. 1954. "National Character: The Study of Modal Personality and Sociocultural Systems." In Lindzey, G. (ed.), *Handbook of Social Psychology,* Vol. II. Cambridge: Addison-Wesley. Pp. 977–1020.

Murray, H. A., *et al.* 1938. *Explorations in Personality.* New York: Oxford University Press.

Parsons, Talcott. 1949. *Essays in Sociological Theory: Pure and Applied.* Glencoe, Ill.: Free Press.

Parsons, Talcott, and Shils, E. A., *et al.* 1951. *Toward a General Theory of Action.* Cambridge: Harvard University Press.

Riesman, David, Denney, Reuel, and Glazer, Nathan. 1950. *The Lonely Crowd: A Study of the Changing American Character.* New Haven: Yale University Press.

INDEX